THE GREAT PLUNDER

www.royalcollins.com

THE GREAT PLUNDER

HOW CHINA LOST ITS TREASURES IN THE 19TH AND 20TH CENTURIES

CHANG QING AND HUANG SHAN
Translated by Daniel McRyan

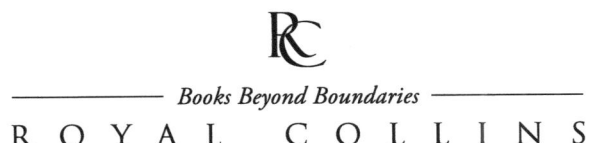

Books Beyond Boundaries

ROYAL COLLINS

The Great Plunder:
How China Lost Its Treasures in the 19th and 20th Centuries

By Chang Qing and Huang Shan
Translated by Daniel McRyan

First published in 2025 by Royal Collins Publishing Group Inc.
Groupe Publication Royal Collins Inc.
550-555 boul. René-Lévesque O Montréal (Québec) H2Z1B1 Canada

10 9 8 7 6 5 4 3 2 1

ISBN: 978-1-4878-1270-6

To find out more about our publications, please visit www.royalcollins.com.

Contents

Preface

IN THE EARLY 19TH CENTURY, a series of interconnected archaeological discoveries and interpretations of ancient literature contributed to a novel academic discipline in Western academia—Orientalism. The year 1840 marked a pivotal moment during the Opium War when the British forcibly opened China's trade doors with artillery fire, prompting Western powers to initiate their involvement and territorial divisions within China. In 1865, Yakub Beg from the Khanate of Kokand in Central Asia launched an invasion of Xinjiang, China, further destabilizing the region. This instability provided an opportunity for Western explorers to venture into Xinjiang.

Within the culturally advanced Western societies, there emerged a craze for delving into the mysteries of the Far East. These nations not only developed a fascination with Eastern cultures, particularly Chinese culture but also believed that the ancient Silk Road, stretching across Europe and Asia, held vast treasures of antiquity. Consequently, Western explorers embarked on journeys along the ancient Silk Road, traversing desolate and uninhabited deserts, exploring the ruins of Buddhist temples, and venturing into uncharted grottoes on cliff faces to uncover the cultural riches of China.

In 1879, the Hungarian geologist Lóczy Lajos (1849–1920, also known as Luo Chuan in Chinese) embarked on an expedition to Gansu in northwest China for geological and geographical research. During his explorations, he serendipitously stumbled upon the breathtaking statues and murals housed within the Mogao Grottoes in Dunhuang. This momentous encounter marked the beginning of the global recognition of the Mogao Grottoes as China's most extensive repository of Buddhist art, achieving widespread fame in the West henceforth.

In December of 1895, the Swedish geographer Sven Anders Hedin (1865–1952) embarked on an expedition to China, undertaking a perilous journey across the formidable Taklimakan Desert in Xinjiang. Though this expedition failed to yield the anticipated results and ultimately ended in disappointment, it nonetheless ignited a profound sense of inspiration among Westerners, subsequently motivating numerous Western scholars to embark on explorations in China. In September 1899, with the generous support of Swedish King Oscar II (1829–1907) and the Nobel family, Hedin ventured into the Taklamakan Desert once more. During this expedition, he made the astounding discovery of the long-abandoned ancient city of Loulan, a revelation that sent shockwaves throughout the West.

Subsequent to these early explorations in China, a succession of prominent figures from various nations—the British, Japanese, Russians, Germans, French, and Americans— entered the historical stage. Among them, Marc Aurel Stein (1862–1943), originally a Hungarian Jew, obtained British citizenship in 1904. Stein held the positions of educational inspector at Punjab University in northern India and principal of Oriental College.

In 1900, Stein, as an archaeologist, conducted excavations at the remains of ancient Buddhist temples located in Miran and Hotan, situated to the south of the Taklimakan Desert in Xinjiang. During these excavations, he made remarkable discoveries, unearthing a wealth of precious Buddhist temple structures, sculptures, and murals. In 1907, during his second expedition to China, Stein achieved a significant breakthrough. He acquired over 9,000 volumes of ancient manuscripts and more than 300 Buddhist paintings from the Tang (AD 618–907) and Five Dynasties (AD 907–960), originating from the newly discovered scripture cave within the Mogao Grottoes in Dunhuang. These invaluable cultural artifacts now reside in the collections of the British Museum and the National Museum in New Delhi, India.

From 1902 to 1905, German archaeologists Albert Grünwedel (1856–1935) and Albert von Le Coq (1860–1930, also known as Li Guke in Chinese), among others, excavated sites in Turpan, Xinjiang, including the ancient city of Gaochang, the Bezeklik Thousand Buddha Caves, and the Kizil Caves. They removed a significant number of Buddhist clay sculptures and exquisite Buddhist murals. Most of these artifacts the Germans took now reside in the Asian Art Museum in Berlin, although many large murals were destroyed during World War II.

In 1903, with the funding of Ōtani Kōzui (1876–1948), the 22nd Abbot of Nishi Hongan-ji and the head of the Honganji-ha sect of True Pure Land Buddhism in Kyoto, Japan, Japanese explorers Watanabe Teshin (1874–1957) and Hori Kenyu (1890–1968) embarked on an expedition in Xinjiang, cutting and removing numerous Buddhist murals from the Bezeklik Thousand Buddha Caves in Turpan. In 1911, Japanese scholars Koichiro Yoshikawa (1885–1978) and Tachibana Zuicho (1890–1968) obtained over 360 ancient Chinese scriptures from the Mogao Grottoes in Dunhuang.

Russians were another active group of explorers in Central Asia. From 1907 to 1909, Russian archaeologist Pyotr Kuzmich Kozlov (1863–1935) excavated the site of the Khara-Khoto, located in the northeast of Ejin Banner, Inner Mongolia, uncovering over 300 Buddhist paintings, numerous sculptures, and ancient documents. Between 1909 and 1915, renowned Russian Orientalist Sergei Fyodorovich Oldenburg (1863–1934) led two expeditions to Xinjiang, where he conducted excavations and research in locations such as Kashgar, Turpan, Kucha, and Dunhuang. Particularly during the exploration of the Mogao Grottoes in Dunhuang, he obtained a significant number of precious artifacts, including ancient colored clay sculptures, murals, literature, and so on. The artifacts collected by these two Russians are now housed in the State Hermitage Museum, Saint Petersburg.

The French Sinologist Paul Eugène Pelliot (1878–1945) embarked on a journey to China in 1908. During his visit, Pelliot secured a remarkable collection of over 6,000 volumes of ancient documents and more than 200 Buddhist paintings from the Mogao Grottoes in Dunhuang. Today, these invaluable treasures find their home in the Guimet Museum in Paris, France.

During this period, Americans also actively participated. Langdon Warner (1881–1955), an American archaeologist and East Asian art historian, organized an expedition to explore the Silk Road in China in 1924 while serving as a professor at Harvard University and curator of East Asian art at the Fogg Museum. Using adhesive tape, Warner removed and damaged 26 Tang Dynasty cave murals, totaling 32,006 square centimeters from the Mogao Grottoes. He also removed a 120-centimeter-tall semi-kneeling colored clay sculpture of a Bodhisattva from Cave 328 at the Mogao Grottoes. Alan Priest (1898–1969), curator of East Asian art at the Metropolitan Museum of Art in New York, developed a deep appreciation for the grand relief titled *Emperor Xiaowen and His Entourage Worshiping the Buddha* on the front wall of Binyang Middle Cave at Longmen Grottoes in Luoyang, Henan. He purchased it for 14,000 silver dollars from the antique dealer Yue Bin (?–1954) of Beijing Colored Glaze Factory and eventually displayed this unrivaled artwork at the Metropolitan Museum of Art.

These Western explorers represented just the initial group of individuals involved in the export of Chinese cultural relics. Their noteworthy expeditions kindled the curiosity of foreign collectors and antique dealers, who formed the second and third categories of individuals contributing to the exodus of Chinese cultural treasures.

The process of "selling" a Chinese cultural relic abroad and integrating it into either public or private collections typically involves several key factors, including the following:

(1) Sellers: These individuals can take various forms. Some may be inheritors of family collections, compelled to part with their heirlooms due to financial difficulties or lavish lifestyles. Others actively seek out antiques with the intent to profit from their sale. Among this latter group, there may be street vendors or even tomb raiders who engage in illegal excavation at archaeological sites.

(2) Antique Dealers: Operating in both Chinese and Western markets, antique dealers play a crucial intermediary role in the dissemination of these relics. They acquire cultural artifacts and subsequently resell them, often realizing a profit from these transactions.

(3) Western Collectors: In Western countries, a significant portion of cultural relics buyers consists of private collectors. These individuals are driven by a deep passion

for ancient art. As they age or upon their passing, they may choose to donate their collections to museums or establish their own museums for public exhibition.

(4) Museum Curators: Supported by various funds and resources, museum curators may directly purchase art pieces from sellers, antique dealers, auction houses, or private collectors for inclusion in museum collections and exhibitions. This circulation channel serves as a substantial source of art collections in museums of various sizes throughout the United States.

Consequently, during the first half of the 20th century, a considerable number of foreign collectors and antique dealers embarked on journeys to China in pursuit of ancient artworks. Concurrently, Chinese antique dealers recognized the burgeoning "business opportunity" and eagerly showcased their own collections to foreign clientele. Additionally, numerous descendants of impoverished Chinese nobility and individuals facing desperate circumstances were compelled to participate in the significant exodus of Chinese cultural relics destined for destinations in the West and Japan. Through these profit-driven endeavors, millions of Chinese artifacts found their way abroad.

Two major antique dealer firms, the Loo-Wu Company and Yamanaka & Co., played pivotal roles in the export of Chinese cultural treasures. Ching Tsai Loo (1880–1957), the founder of the Loo-Wu Company, stood as a prominent figure in the Western antique world during the first half of the 20th century. He established his antique emporium in Paris, France, and extended his reach with branches in the United Kingdom, the United States, and China. Over a span of more than 30 years, the Loo-Wu Company facilitated the exportation of Chinese cultural relics to Western countries, with a particular focus on the United States.

This enterprise played a crucial part in the continual transportation of numerous national treasures to Europe and America, including the renowned national treasures the *Saluzi* and *Quanmaogua* reliefs from the *Six Steeds of Zhao Mausoleum*, which now find their home in the University of Pennsylvania Museum of Archaeology and Anthropology. It is often suggested that during the first half of the 20th century, Ching Tsai Loo was accountable for a significant portion of the Chinese antiques that found their way overseas. While this claim might carry a degree of exaggeration, it underscores Loo's profound impact on the dissemination of Chinese cultural artifacts during that period.

The Yamanaka & Co., established by the Japanese entrepreneur Yamanaka Sadajirō (1866–1936), played a significant role in the trade of Chinese cultural relics. Commencing its operations in 1894, Yamanaka expanded its presence across various cities, including New York, Boston, Chicago, London, Paris, Beijing, and others. Over the course of more than 30 years, the company amassed a vast collection of invaluable artifacts from China. Regrettably, it contributed to the irreplaceable loss of numerous Chinese national treasures to overseas collections. Particularly concerning was its involvement in the illicit excavation of sculptures at the Tianlongshan Grottoes in Taiyuan, Shanxi, starting after 1927. During this period, over 150 exquisitely carved sculptures were stolen from the caves, which traced their origins back to the Eastern Wei (AD 534–550), Northern Qi (AD 550–577), Sui (AD 581–618), and Tang dynasties. This illicit activity resulted in extensive damage to the entire grotto complex.

Nevertheless, the predominant source of artworks in prominent European and American museums is derived from generous donations by private collectors. Charles Lang Freer (1854–1919), an American collector, emerges as a notable exemplar of this philanthropic tradition. He made the remarkable decision to donate his entire collection to the Smithsonian Institution and, in an act of unparalleled generosity, funded the construction of the Freer Gallery of Art in Washington, D.C., to serve as a dedicated space for the display of his amassed artworks. Beyond this extraordinary contribution, Freer also established a fund aimed at supporting the acquisition of Oriental art and fostering research projects focused on Oriental civilization.

This book primarily centers its attention on the first category of individuals responsible for the export of Chinese cultural relics—foreign explorers—and provides a concise introduction to the national treasures they removed from China. Concerning the second category—antique dealers—our focus is directed toward the most prominent figures, namely Ching Tsai Loo and the Yamanaka & Co. As for the third category—foreign collectors—we highlight a singular representative figure, Charles Lang Freer.

The artifacts featured in this book represent a selection of the most significant among the national treasures that have found their way abroad. It's important to note that, due to space constraints, many other national treasures couldn't be included in this narrative. Examples of such exclusions are items like the Gold Double Dancers Double Dragons Jade Set unearthed from the Eastern Zhou Dynasty tomb in Jin Village, Luoyang, as well as the over 20,000 pieces of oracle bones dispersed across 12 countries around the world. Furthermore, it's worth acknowledging that public museums worldwide, including those in Japan, collectively house approximately 1.6 million pieces of ancient Chinese art. This impressive collection, however, represents only around 20% of the total Chinese cultural relics that have been lost to overseas locations. The remaining 80% remain in private hands, often undisclosed to the public. This hidden wealth represents another vast trove of treasures waiting to be explored!

Over a century has elapsed since the first encounters between foreign explorers and China during the late Qing Dynasty (AD 1616–1911) up to the present day. In this passage of time, the loss of national treasures to foreign hands has occurred for a complex interplay of reasons. On one side, Western explorers and colonial powers played a role, but equally significant were the challenging social circumstances prevailing in China during that time. China grappled with issues of weakness, partial loss of sovereignty, frequent conflicts, and widespread suffering among its populace. Within this milieu, national treasures often found themselves undervalued and insufficiently protected. Today, a number of these once-lost national treasures have found a new home in overseas museums, affording us the precious opportunity to catch a fleeting glimpse of their genuine splendor. Nevertheless, some of these treasures remain in private hands, potentially making their reemergence a challenging endeavor.

Following the year 1949, particularly with the advent of China's reform and opening-up policies, numerous scholars embarked on research endeavors regarding the overseas dispersion of cultural relics. Their collective efforts culminated in a broader comprehension of this intricate situation. In the past two decades, due to the concerted actions of the Chinese government and patriotic individuals, a number of national treasures have been successfully repatriated, such as the Buddha head from the north wall of Cave 8 at Tianlongshan Grottoes and the Bronze Min Fanglei. These reclaimed artifacts represent a shared heritage of profound significance for all Chinese people, imbued with rich historical, artistic, and scientific value. As an individual who has conducted extensive research within the three major museums in the United States and has visited most of the pivotal museums in Europe and America, I have often stood in contemplation before the display cases housing Chinese national treasures. In presenting this book, my hope is that readers will not only reflect upon the losses incurred but also come to understand that the safeguarding and preservation of national treasures can only be assured within the framework of a strong nation, global peace, and vigilant protection measures.

Relics are tangible remnants that bear the weight of culture.
Behind them resides an entire framework of civilization.
Their destiny serves as a profound chronicle of a nation's history.

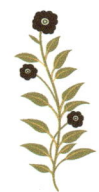

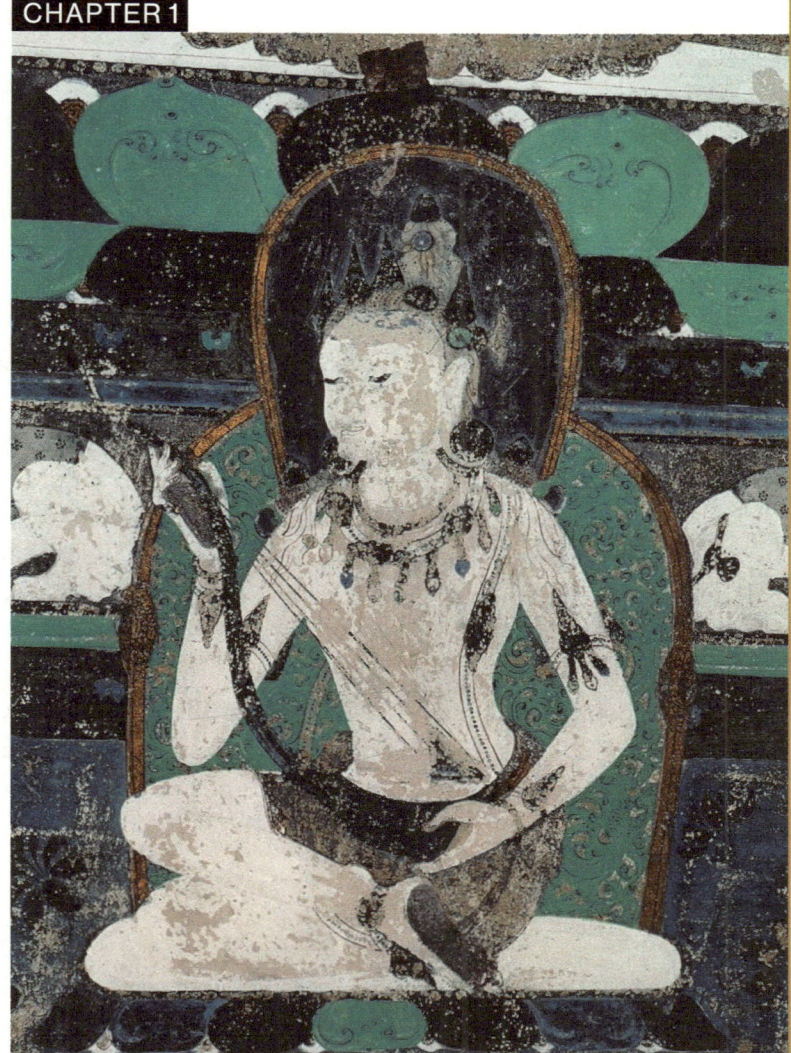

CHAPTER 1

Sven Anders Hedin:
The Trailblazer of
Exploring Western China

— 1886

A brief stay in Iran

— 1888

First time in China with only a brief stay in Xinjiang

— 1890

Iran–Mashhad–Ashgabat–Bukhara–Samarkand–Tashkent–Kashgar

— 1893–1897

First exploration, Stockholm–St. Petersburg–Tashkent–Pamir Mountains–Kashgar–the northern edge of the Tarim Basin–the southern edge of the Taklimakan Desert–Hotan Prefecture Dandan Oilik–Lake Kalajun–Bosten Lake–Hotan Prefecture–northern Xizang–Beijing–Mongolia–Russia–Stockholm

— 1899–1902

Second exploration, Kashmir–Kolkata–Yarkant River, Tarim River, Kaidu River–Lop Nur–ruins of the ancient city of Loulan–northern Xizang–near Lhasa (prohibited to enter)–Leh–Lahore–Delhi–Agra–Lucknow–Varanasi–Kolkata

— 1905–1909

Third exploration, Xizang

— 1927–1933

Fourth expedition, most of Mongolia, Xinjiang, and northern Xizang. Beijing–Baotou–Mongolia–Urumqi–the northern and eastern areas of the Tarim Basin, etc.

1.1 The Geographer Married to China

Unlike now, Central Asia and China remained enigmatic to Europe a century ago. Back then, despite trade exchanges and conflicts between the East and the West, there existed minimal in-depth cultural exchanges among researchers. The fervor for exploration and archaeology that dawned in the 19th century gradually lifted this veil. Among the Western pioneers who ventured into China, Sven Hedin, a geographer, cartographer, explorer, photographer, and travel chronicler, stands as an unequivocally prominent figure. His

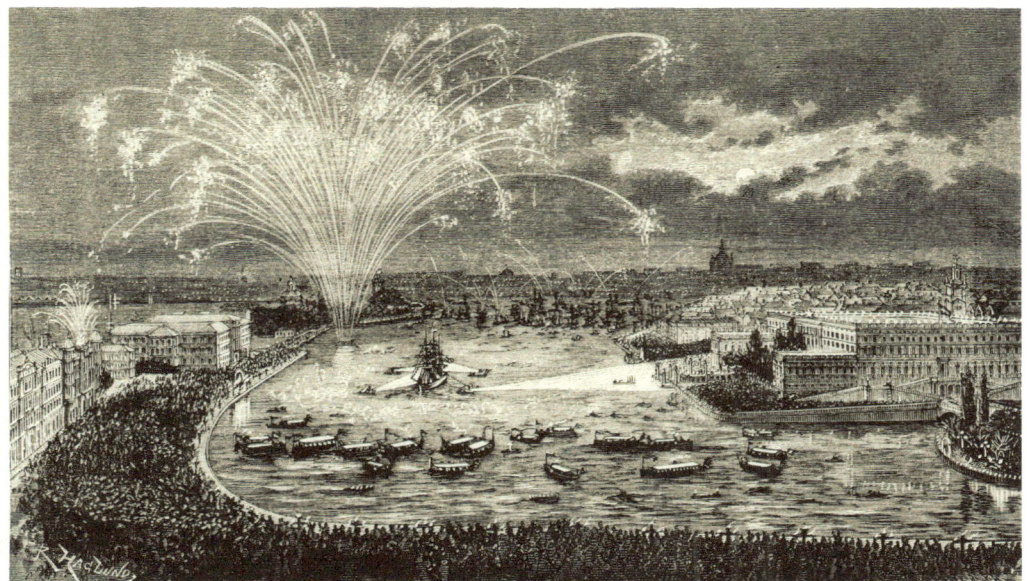

Figure 1-1 *Return of the Vega to Stockholm on April 24, 1880*, engraving by Robert Haglund. The Vega marked the inaugural ship to circumnavigate Eurasia.

trailblazing exploration preceding others, his deep-reaching footprints along the Chinese border, and his exceptional investigative feats have firmly cemented his legacy in the realm of exploration and archaeology.

Sven Hedin was born in Stockholm, Sweden's capital, in 1865. During the 19th century, amid the tidal wave of great geographical discoveries sweeping the globe, explorers and geographers from diverse corners etched their names onto the world map's uncharted territories (Figure 1-1). Spurred by this fervent pursuit, Hedin was drawn to the notion of becoming an explorer. Upon completing high school at 19, he seized the opportunity to work as a tutor in Tsarist Russia, embarking on his inaugural journey across Central Asian nations, commencing in Iran. The vast expanse and distinctive cultural milieu of Central Asia captivated him. Upon his return, Hedin charted his course toward a future as a geographical explorer. In 1886, he enrolled at the University of Berlin, apprenticing under the tutelage of German geographer and sinology specialist Ferdinand von Richthofen (1833–1905). He devoted himself to mastering various Eastern languages, laying the groundwork for his ambition of becoming an explorer.

Richthofen, a renowned geographer, was the first to christen the route linking East and Central Asia to Europe as the "Silk Road." Thanks to him, this historic passageway, facilitating trade, conflicts, and migrations between Asia and Europe for millennia, acquired a romantic and renowned epithet.

Following his tutelage under Richthofen, Hedin unveiled the ancient Loulan civilization, hidden deep beneath the Taklimakan Desert, to the world's explorers and archaeolo-

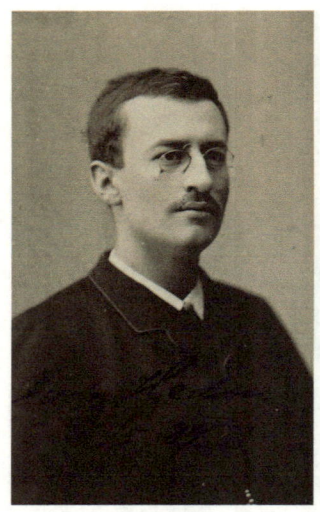

Figure 1-2 24-year-old Sven Hedin (May 31, 1889)

gists in October 1900. This millennia-old city, a jewel on the Silk Road, captivated the international archaeological community's attention, making Hedin the pioneer in significant geographical discoveries across Siberia and Central Asia.

Judging from the preserved images of Hedin, he appeared slender, bespectacled, and exuded an academic vibe (Figure 1-2). Yet, beneath this facade lay an unyielding determination and an unwavering dedication to his cause. Hedin never entered matrimony. When asked about this, his response was, "I am already married to China!" This profound statement underscores his ardor for exploration and his fascination with unraveling China's geography and ancient remnants—a testament to his relentless perseverance.

In his lifetime, Hedin traversed Central Asia on four occasions, meticulously exploring untrodden territories like the Himalayas, the origins of the Yarlung Tsangpo, Indus, and Satluj rivers. He unearthed the ruins of the ancient city of Loulan, the Loulan Cemetery, and its great wall situated in Lop Nur and the Xinjiang desert. From this perspective, it is apt to claim that he, indeed, was married to China.

1.2 The Desert Expedition of Peril

Hedin's inaugural trip to China was rather brief. In 1888, he briefly stayed in Xinjiang, not qualifying as a full-fledged journey but laying the groundwork for his subsequent exploits. An opportunity arose in April 1890 when the diplomatic envoy from the Kingdom of Sweden visited Asia, and Hedin acted as their interpreter. After fulfilling his duties, supported by the king, he initiated his second expedition eastward from Tehran, marking his genuine venture into China.

By December 1890, he had entered Xinjiang, China, from Tsarist Russia, lodging in the renowned local hub of Kashgar until his departure the ensuing year. During these recent months, he discovered that this enigmatic region in Central Asia held untapped treasures, crafting detailed maps around Kashgar, laying a sturdy foundation for future explorations. On October 16, 1893, Hedin set forth on his third journey to Asia. By February of the following year, he ascended the Pamir Mountains, attempting the climb of Muztagh Ata, known as the "Father of Snow Mountains." Failing to reach the summit, Hedin returned to Kashgar on May 1, 1894. It was during this journey that he had his first encounter with the "Sea of Death," the Taklimakan Desert (Figure 1-3).

This desert expedition commenced in Makit, Xinjiang. Sven Hedin made the decision to traverse the Taklimakan Desert from west to east, following the course of the Yarkant River.

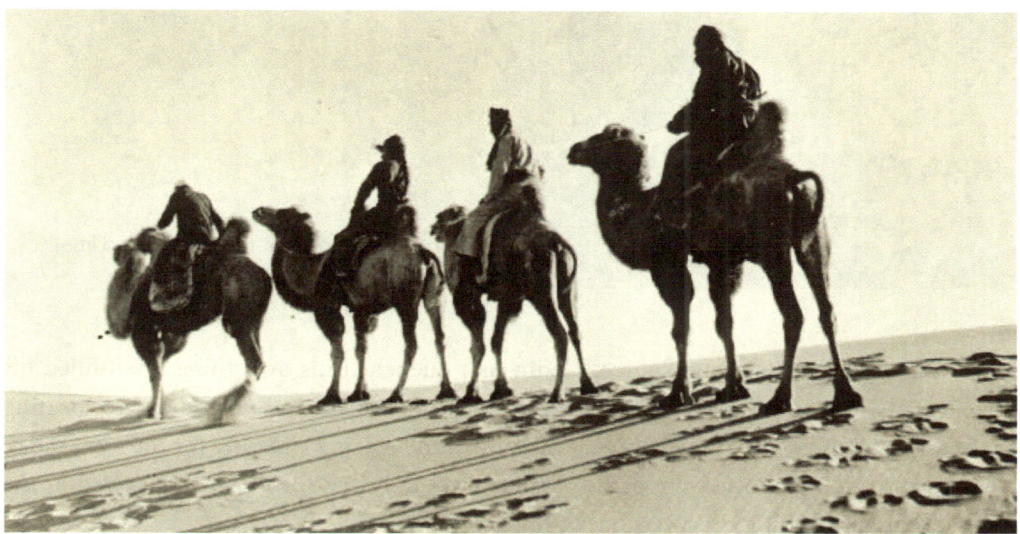

Figure 1-3 Sven Hedin's camel caravan in the desert (early 20th century)

He stood as the first and possibly the sole Western explorer to accomplish this arduous journey across the Taklimakan Desert. While preparing in Makit, he heard numerous tales from local inhabitants about the legend of an "ancient city buried in the sand" near the desert oases. Relying on these rumors and his own instincts, Hedin was convinced that remnants of an ancient city lay nearby. His penchant for adventure often led him to impulsive decisions. On April 10, 1895, his camel caravan set off from the village of Rajlik in Makit. The team comprised eight camels, two dogs, three sheep, one rooster, and ten hens. They carried enough provisions to sustain the team for three to four months and were equipped with a complete set of fur coats, winter clothing, and an array of gear for security measures, including three rifles, six revolvers, and various scientific instruments such as thermometers, altimeters, and compasses. However, due to an oversight, they failed to replenish sufficient drinking water before venturing deeper into the desert.

After more than ten days into their expedition, their water supplies dwindled. The expedition members resorted to consuming human urine, camel urine, and even alcohol stove fuel in an attempt to survive. They contemplated the drastic measure of killing sheep to drink their blood to satiate their thirst. However, they discovered that the sheep's blood had solidified due to the lack of water. In the harsh desert environment, water scarcity meant certain death. The entire expedition faced a grave crisis. Their sole glimmer of hope to survive lay in reaching the distant Hotan River. Yet, upon reaching the river, they found it to be a seasonal river, completely dry during their visit. Confronted with this brutal reality, the morale of the camel team plummeted, losing their determination to press forward. Eventually, only Hedin persevered, and he finally stumbled upon a remaining pond located three miles away from the river valley, later identified as Hedin Pond (Figure 1-4).

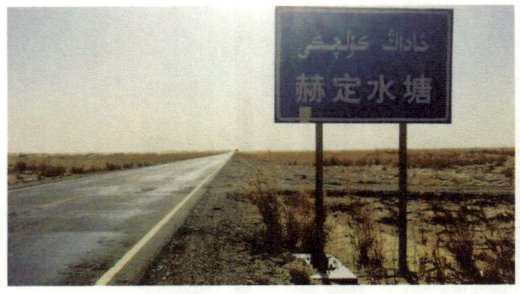

Figure 1-4 Signpost of the Hedin Pond in Xinjiang

With access to this water source, Hedin first quenched his own thirst, then filled his riding boots with water and retraced his steps. He once again crossed the desert, locating his nearly unconscious comrades, saving their lives, and leaving a marker for the lost guides. Subsequently, they followed the paths of shepherds and caravans they encountered in the oases, eventually finding their way out of the desert.

This perilous expedition resulted in the loss of two camel drivers, all eight camels, most of their supplies, two cameras, and 1,800 films, leading to considerable setbacks. Hedin bore witness to the unforgiving nature of the Taklimakan Desert, often termed the Sea of Death. However, the expedition yielded significant information on the geology, biology, and ancient cultural artifacts of the Taklimakan Desert—providing initial historical insights into these aspects. Throughout this expedition, he covered a distance of 26,000 kilometers, mapping 10,498 kilometers on 552 maps and traversing 3,600 kilometers of regions previously untouched by modern civilization. Upon returning to Europe, Hedin recounted his perilous journey in Xinjiang through speeches, leaving his audiences with an acute sense of thirst and a profound respect for his unwavering determination.

Throughout the ages, countless individuals have shown a lack of respect for nature while traversing the east-west passage, ultimately meeting their fateful demise in the perpetual expanse of the Taklimakan Desert. Yet, Hedin's near-death encounter did not deter him; instead, it served as an initial lesson on the geography of the Taklimakan Desert and bestowed upon him invaluable survival skills essential for exploring the most demanding and hostile terrains. This trial became a repository of experiences and teachings. Initially, Hedin grasped the paramount importance of water supply. Consequently, he primarily scheduled his expeditions during winters, ferrying ice cubes into the desert. Second, he forsook bulky equipment and cameras, favoring sketches over photography. This transition also highlighted his talent as a skilled painter, resulting in over 5,000 paintings depicting geographical explorations throughout his lifetime. With these adjustments, the limitless desert submitted to his command, leading him to significant ancient city sites such as Dandan Oilik, Karadong, and Maza-Tageh Castle and culminating in the discovery of the ancient city of Loulan.

In 1896, Hedin embarked once more into the Taklimakan Desert. Building upon the knowledge gathered from the previous expedition, he organized an expedition camel

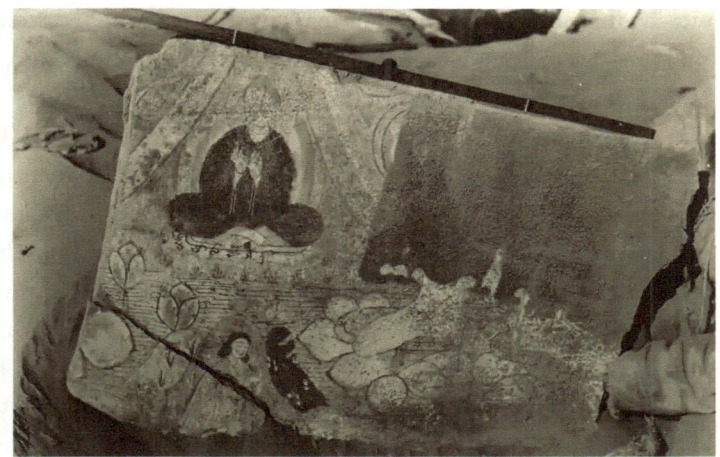

Figure 1-5 Murals unearthed from the Dandan Oilik site (1900–1901, photographed by Stein)

caravan in Tawakule, setting off on an eastward journey across the sands. At dusk on January 23, the camel caravan stumbled upon desolate ruins that had long lost their vitality. This site was Dandan Oilik (meaning Ivory House in Uyghur), later acclaimed along the Silk Road (Figure 1-5). Despite being deeply entrenched within the heart of the Taklimakan Desert and distant from modern rivers, it once stood as a vital town in the ancient Kingdom of Khotan, adorned with myriad Buddhist temple structures. Though most of the ruins lay buried under sand upon Hedin's discovery, with only a few structures peeking out, their majesty deeply moved him. Whether due to limited resources, time constraints, or his preference for geography over archaeology, Hedin refrained from extensively excavating the site, leaving only rudimentary annotations before moving on. Coincidentally, shortly after, British archaeologist Aurel Stein and German geographer and explorer Emil Trinkler (1896–1931), among others, uncovered an array of cultural relics at the same site.

Nevertheless, there remains no dispute that Sven Hedin was the pioneering Western explorer who unearthed the ruins of this ancient citadel in the Tarim River Basin. The revelation of the Dandan Oilik ruins in 1896 marked a significant milestone in the exploration history of Xinjiang. Subsequently, explorers from diverse nations flocked to Xinjiang, gradually revealing thousands of ancient cities hidden within the golden sands.

1.3 The Lucky Shovel and the Ancient City of Loulan

The ancient city of Loulan is nestled in the northwestern expanses of Lop Nur, Xinjiang. Stretching from the vicinity of ancient Yangguan in the east to the western ancient city of Niya and encompassing the Altun Mountains in the south and Hami in the north, Loulan Kingdom once reigned as a celebrated "urban country" along the fabled Western Regions. In the 2nd century AD, it thrived as a bustling hub of commerce, welcoming a myriad of merchants and nurturing vibrant markets. Its well-planned streets bore witness to majestic Buddhist temples and pagodas, forging an indelible link along the illustrious Silk Road. Sima Qian (145–86 BC) wrote in *Records of the Grand Historian · Treatise on the Dayuan* that Loulan and Gushi are cities adjacent to Yanze, and Ban Gu recorded in the *Book of Han · Traditions of the Western Regions*, "The realm of the Shanshan Kingdom, referred to as Loulan, boasts Yuni City as its capital, situated 1,600 *li** distant from Yangguan and 6,100 *li* away from Chang'an. Within its borders, thrive 1,570 households, nurturing a populace of 14,100 vibrant citizens." This is the earliest documentation about Loulan in Chinese historical records, chronicling its location and population back then. Even in contemporary times, its population remains substantial, a testament to its historical significance as a thriving western town of yesteryears.

The *Book of Han* further elucidates Loulan's ecological essence and biodiversity, "The sandy, alkaline soil characterizes the land, limiting arable fields, thereby necessitating reliance on neighboring nations for grains. However, the region boasts jade production and an abundance of reeds, tamarisks, poplars, and Achnatherum splendens. The nomadic locals traverse the terrain in pursuit of water and pasture, tending to a diverse array of animals, including donkeys, horses, and a multitude of camels. Remarkably, their prowess in combat matches that of soldiers hailing from the Ruoqiang Kingdom." In *A Record of Buddhist Kingdoms*, Monk Faxian (AD 337–422) of the Eastern Jin Dynasty (AD 317–420) wrote, "The terrain is rugged and desolate, yet its people, resembling the Han in attire, don distinctive fur garments. The monarch embraces Buddhism fervently, fostering a community of over 4,000 devoted monks initiated into the depths of Hinayana teachings." Xuanzang (AD 602–664), an eminent monk of the Tang Dynasty, also made a simple description of Loulan in *The Great Tang Records on the Western Regions*, "Our journey spanned over a thousand *li* northeastward, unveiling the realm of Nafubo—a land synonymous with the Kingdom of Loulan." These historical records intricately depict the essence of the ancient nomadic city-state of Loulan before the Tang Dynasty, capturing its societal landscape, the religious convictions held by its people, and the intricate tapestry of their daily lives and customs.

From a historical and geographical vantage point, Loulan stands as one among the thirty-six kingdoms dotting the Western Regions—a nomadic city-state situated in close proximity to Han settlement, serving as a pivotal corridor for Han governance over these lands. The annals recount Emperor Wu of the Han Dynasty (r. 140–87 BC) dispatching forces that triumphed in an assault on Loulan, leading to Prince Loulan's dispatch as a hostage to the Han Dynasty (202 BC–AD 220). Seeking equilibrium, the Loulan Kingdom also sent a prince as a hostage to the antagonistic Huns, treading a delicate path between two opposing realms. Merchants found haven while military strategists grappled for dominance. The distinctive geography bestowed Loulan with singular attributes, fostering a milieu

---

* One *li* equals 0.5 km.

adorned with exotic customs, the entrancing dance of exotic beauties, and caravans laden with gold, silver, and spices, amid the tumultuous clashes of gold and iron in brutal conflicts where soldiers converged. During Emperor Zhao's era in the Han Dynasty (r. 86–74 BC), the imperial court stationed troops in Yixun, 2.5 kilometers east of Ruoqiang County in present-day Xinjiang. Loulan underwent a transformation, assuming the name Shanshan, evolving into a strategic linchpin for the Han Dynasty's control over the Western Regions. Henceforth, the Loulan Kingdom weathered wars, trade, and the flux of commerce from the Han Dynasty to the zenith of the Tang Dynasty. Across Chinese historical scrolls, its legacy spans over 800 years.

The great poet Li Bai (AD 701–762) of the Tang Dynasty chanted in "A Frontier Melody," "I wish, with the sharpen'd sword which I'm wearing on the waist, To capture Loulan and put our foes in a fatal plight." The famous border-theme poet Wang Changling (AD 698–757) wrote in "In the Army," "Though the armor torn in constant desert wars, Our men wouldn't return till they beat the Loulans." "Emperor bestows a sword on a starry night; General leads the troop to win the fight (defeating Loulan)." These majestic poems vividly portray the veil of war and the echoes of suffering that shrouded this ancient city-state. Regardless, Loulan remained a crucial border town during the illustrious Tang Dynasty. Yet, puzzlingly, this western enclave vanished without a whisper in historical chronicles. For close to a millennium following the Tang Dynasty, a profound silence enveloped this enigmatic kingdom, its secrets buried beneath shifting sands for reasons unknown. Not until the footsteps of Sven Hedin graced these lands did the erstwhile splendor of Loulan resurface, casting newfound light upon its faded grandeur (Figure 1-6).

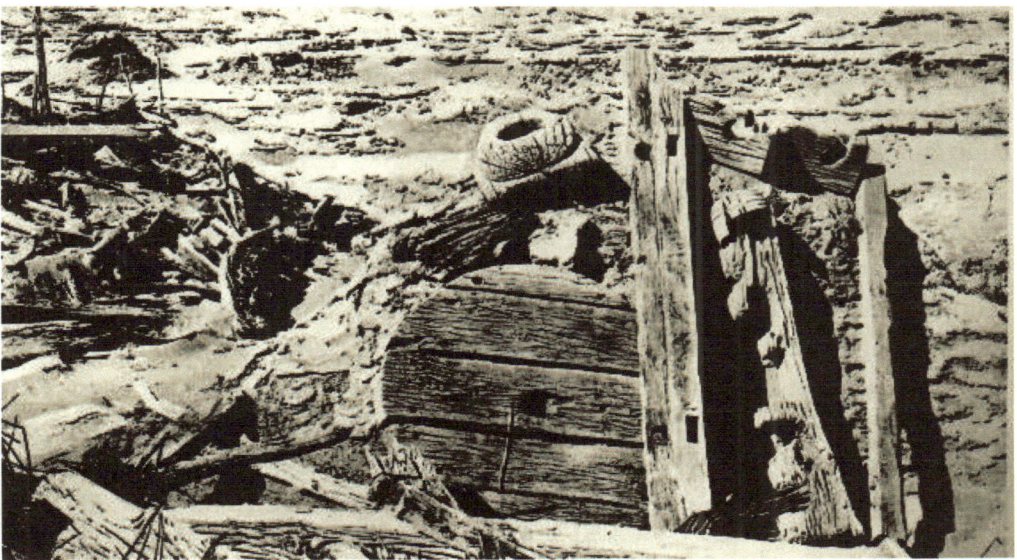

Figure 1-6 The newly discovered ancient city of Loulan, with wheels and inscribed wooden slips scattered on the site (early 20th century)

In September of 1899, aided by the patronage of King Oscar II of Sweden and the Nobel family, Hedin embarked on his second expedition to the Taklimakan. This time, alongside his companions, they navigated the river, spending close to half a year aboard a raft. March of 1900 marked the commencement of their quest for the ancient city of Loulan upon reaching the lower reaches of the Kongque River. Unlike his initial foray into the desert, Hedin was notably more prepared, equipped not only with ice but also ample dry provisions and tents. However, perils persisted throughout the expedition. Menacing black storms and plummeting temperatures scattered his camel team, resulting in the loss of supplies and camel lives. Most critically, the sheepskin bags meant to hold water began to fail. Despite a last resupply at an oasis by March's end, traces of the fabled ruins of Loulan eluded their grasp. Yet, this venture yielded substantial gains, unearthing a trove of cultural relics and invaluable geological insights. Mindful of avoiding past missteps, Hedin swiftly resolved to depart, waiting for the third opportunity to seek for it.

However, fate had an unexpected turn on their return journey when the shovel, instrumental in their well-digging efforts, was inadvertently lost. In an unforeseen twist, the accompanying Lop Nur guide, Ördek, embarked on a quest to recover it, stumbling upon the most momentous discovery of their expedition. In Hedin's recorded account, he recounts Ördek's fortuitous encounter amid a tempest. Amid the swirling sands, Ördek stumbled upon an apparition-like ancient city adorned with towering pagodas and ochre-hued walls—a labyrinth of meandering streets, stacked houses, and a sentinel beacon tower. Hedin's reservoir of knowledge resonated; this was indeed the elusive ancient city of Loulan they sought.

He sensed that the pinnacle of his adventurous journey was on the cusp of unfolding. In his book *My Life as an Explorer*, his sentiments echoed, "How fortunate I was to have forgotten that shovel! Were it not for Ördek's oversight, the opportunity to return and unearth this ancient city—the pivotal discovery of this expedition—would have eluded me. The revelation of this ancient city bestows upon future generations an entirely new understanding of the ancient history nestled in the heart of Asia." Yet, at that juncture, Hedin knew his departure was imminent and resolved to revisit and delve into the ancient city in the coming year.

The subsequent year witnessed Hedin's return to Lop Nur, fully funded and ready to embark on the official exploration of the fabled ancient city of Loulan (Figure 1-7). Intent on unraveling its enigmatic secrets, he extended a reward to local residents for any cultural relics associated with the city's ruins. "A substantial bounty awaits whoever discovers any form of ancient human writing amid these ruins." Responding to this call, local workers unearthed a treasure trove—a small piece of felt, red cloth, intricately braided brown strands, shards of pottery, a multitude of wooden slips inscribed with the Kharosthi texts, 36 Chinese-character paper documents, and several Sogdian manuscripts. Alongside these relics stood an impressive array of coins, grains, pottery vessels, exquisite silk and woolen fabrics, and captivating wood carvings. The sheer number and diversity of these relics aston-

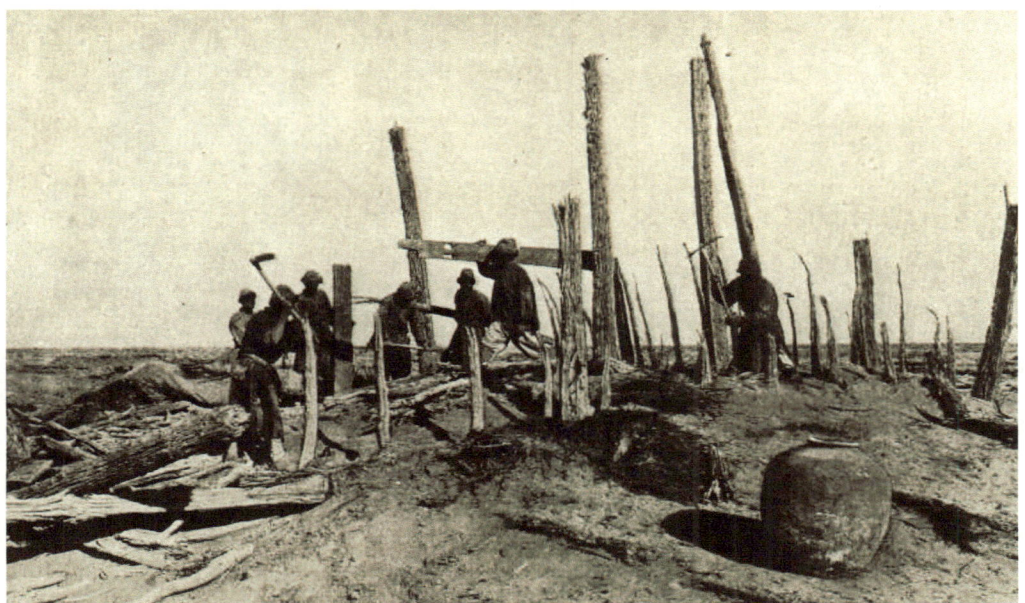

Figure 1-7 Hedin's expedition team excavating houses in the ancient city of Loulan during the early 20th century

ished Hedin; never before had an ancient city yielded such an abundance and diversity of cultural treasures. The aura surrounding the ancient city of Loulan mirrored the mystique of Italy's enigmatic Pompeii—seemingly abandoned overnight, with valuables left untouched.

The fragments unearthed by Hedin's team stand as compelling evidence affirming the site's identity as the ancient city of Loulan. Among these discoveries, a semi-cursive paper fragment from a Chinese document (Figure 1-8) reads, "On March 1, Loulan, Statement, Ji Cheng: Separated and estranged for a long time, my thoughts and longing have accumulated deeply. So I send you this letter for November, telling you things happened these days. The spring is harmonious, and it is appropriate to …" This alludes to Ji Cheng, possibly an official from Loulan during the Western Jin Dynasty (AD 265–317). The fusion of geographical data and archaeological findings culminates in the rediscovery of Loulan—an ancient Central Asian civilization lost for over a millennium.

Subsequent excavations unveiled more discoveries within the ruins of ancient Loulan. The remnant loess city wall,

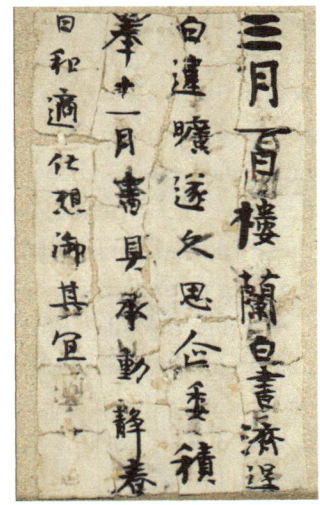

Figure 1-8 *Loulan Ji Cheng Statement on March 1* unearthed by Sven Hedin at the Loulan site in March 1901 (Western Jin Dynasty, 22.5 cm long, 12.5 cm wide, paper, semi-cursive script, now in Museum of Ethnography, Sweden, No. 1903.26.0302)

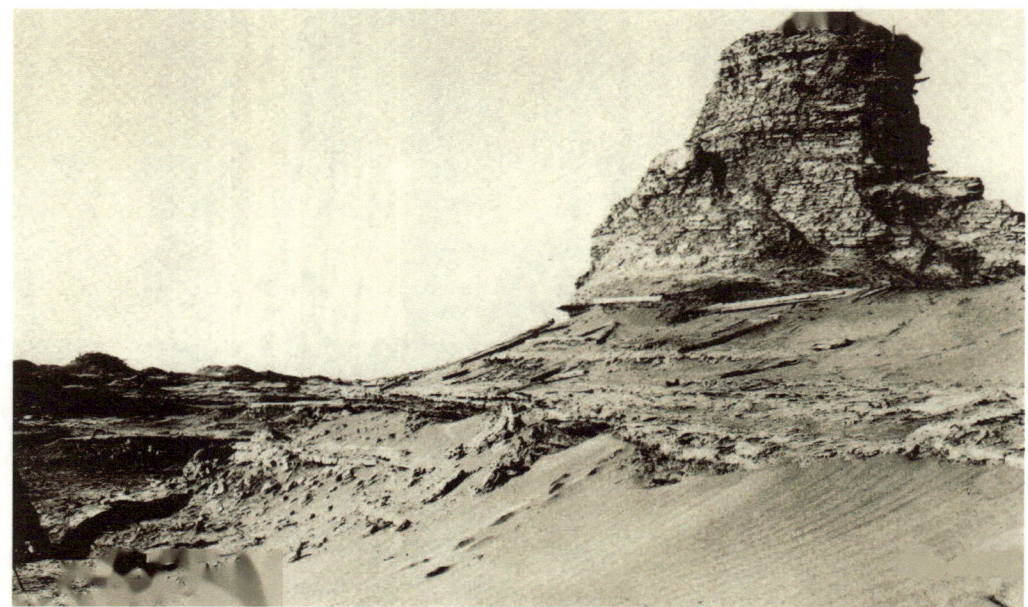

Figure 1-9 Ruins of the pagoda in the ancient city of Loulan built around the Jin Dynasty (photographed by Sven Hedin in March 1901)

measuring 4 meters in height and 8 meters in width, stands as a rarity for a border city of that era. The city's inhabitants ingeniously constructed their homes using abundant desert poplar trees. A south-facing earthen structure at the city's core seemingly served as the abode of the ancient Loulan ruler. Beyond the city's confines, remnants of a beacon tower in the desert were uncovered. The presence of ruined Buddhist temples and pagodas underscores the ancient Loulan people's adherence to Buddhism (Figure 1-9). Collectively, these findings corroborate that the Great Wall once stretched into Xinjiang, while also attesting to the previously underestimated prosperity of this ancient city.

Hedin's pivotal role in the discovery of Loulan catapulted him to fame. As he bid farewell to his guide Ördek, promising a return, he departed for Sweden to commence research on Loulan's culture. His groundbreaking research led to knighthood by the Swedish royal family in 1902, marking the final instance of such an honor bestowed upon a Swede in the nation's history.

Following Hedin's expedition, this highly advanced ancient city became the focal point for numerous explorers in search of treasures. Subsequent expedition teams led by American Ellsworth Huntington (1876–1947) in 1905, by British-Hungarian Aurel Stein in 1906, and by Japanese Ōtani Kōzui in 1908–1909 and 1910–1911, among others, unearthed an astounding array of cultural relics in Loulan and the Lop Nur region. These discoveries included Neolithic stone tools, wooden artifacts, pottery, bronzes, glassware, ancient coins, and a notable manuscript called *Strategies of the Warring States* from the Jin Dynasty (AD 265–420). Remarkably, this manuscript's paper predates Europe's oldest writing paper by six to seven hundred years. Additionally, excavated Han and Tibetan brocades displayed vivid colors and intricate designs, some bearing Chinese inscriptions such as "Han Ren Blesses Our Descendants with Prosperity," "Live Long and Thrive," "Happy and Promising," and "Long Live the Children." These brocades, some from the Central Plains and many from Central Asia, made from the 1st to 2nd centuries AD, confirmed the close cultural exchanges between Central Asia and the Han Dynasty. Amid the fervor for exploration in the Western Regions, these artifacts were among the first cultural relics to travel beyond borders.

Presently, in the northern expanse of Ruoqiang County and west of Lop Nur in the Bayingol Mongolian Autonomous Prefecture in Xinjiang, this ancient city, buried for over 1,600 years by wind and sand, remains silently preserved. It endures as an enduring enigma, still veiled in mysteries, persisting alongside the equally enigmatic Lop Nur.

1.4 The Wandering Lop Nur

In 1933, after a hiatus of 34 years, the 69-year-old Sven Hedin returned to Lop Nur, reuniting with Ördek, the Uyghur guide. Hedin penned a poignant account, describing Ördek's poignant wait spanning more than three decades, rooted in an unwavering belief in Hedin's earnest promise of his imminent return:

> I therefore ordered my rowers to make for the shore. We steered diagonally across the river and landed at the point where the two horsemen had dismounted. The whitebeard slithered down the bank, there hardly 6 feet high, and came on board. He approached me with tears in his eyes and held out his hands to me, hard and horny from time and toil. And it was really Ördek himself. The many years had ravaged him mercilessly. He was thin, shrunken and withered; his forehead was deeply wrinkled, his beard and moustaches hung down to his chest in straggling tufts. He wore on his head a shabby fur cap, and was dressed in a chapan or East Turki coat of the usual kind, bleached and ragged, and secured about the waist by a cloth girdle. His tattered boots had evidently been worn for decades on countless toilsome journeys through desert, steppe and brushwood.

Lop Nur, the wandering lake, held an enduring allure for Hedin. In his book *The Wandering Lake*, he eloquently articulated his profound fascination with this elusive entity. As far back as 1878, the Russian officer explorer Nikolay Mikhaylovich Przhevalsky (1839–1888) had cast doubt on the accuracy of Lop Nur's location marked on Chinese maps. "It is not situated at the southern foothills of Kuruk Tagh Mountain, but rather at the foothills of the Altun Mountains," said Przhevalsky upon his sighting of Lop Nur. "Once a landscape of undulating lakes and teeming wildlife, now lays barren—a desolate expanse of salt marsh."

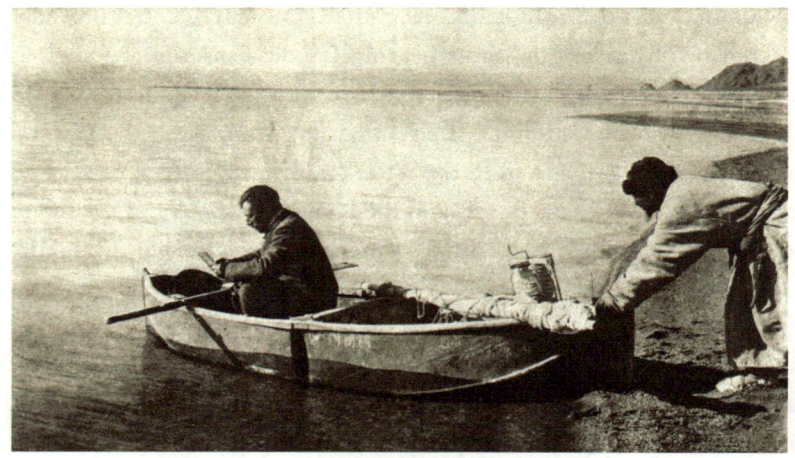

Figure 1-10 Sven Hedin in the Tarim River in the Loulan area (1901)

Astonishingly, when Hedin arrived, Lop Nur's actual location lay two latitudes southward, puzzling the astute geographer. To him, unraveling the enigma of this wandering lake held far greater allure than discovering treasures.

In early January 1891, Hedin's departure from China led him to a small town on Lake Issyk-Kul's eastern bank (now in present-day Kyrgyzstan), where he paid homage at Przhevalsky's grave. This mystery became his lifelong pursuit. Across his three voyages into the Taklimakan Desert in pursuit of Lop Nur, Hedin diligently probed the secrets behind its movements (Figure 1-10). It wasn't until his final entry into Lop Nur that he reached a profound conclusion. In his extensive research, Hedin posited that Lop Nur migrated north-south over a span of approximately 1,500 years. He deduced from local evidence that a European tribe dwelled in the Lop Nur region over 3,000 years ago, vanishing after wandering within Lop Nur's domain. More than 1,500 years ago, Lop Nur's return spurred ecological revival, ushering Loulan into an era of prosperity. The impetus behind Lop Nur's migration lay in sediment accumulation from the Tarim and Kongque Rivers, obstructing Lop Nur's mouth. Centuries of sediment deposition diverted the course of these rivers, compelling Lop Nur's northward drift. Amid scorching temperatures, evaporating lake waters depleted Loulan's resources, desiccating crops, and compelling residents to forsake the city, seeking survival elsewhere—leaving behind a desolate metropolis. Engulfed by the fury of desert storms, Loulan, an ancient Western Regions kingdom within Lop Nur, met its demise, consumed by yellow sands. This unveiled the enigmatic tale behind Lop Nur's movement and the downfall of the ancient city of Loulan (Figure 1-11).

Armed with this revelation, Hedin proposed to the Nanjing government a plan for Lop Nur's revival, "Channel water from the lower reaches of the Tarim and Kongque Rivers into the Lop Desert to resurrect villages near ancient Loulan from 2,000 years ago, transforming those flood plains into arable lands and verdant gardens." This visionary dream sprouted upon Hedin's arrival in Lop Nur in 1900, yet regrettably remained unrealized.

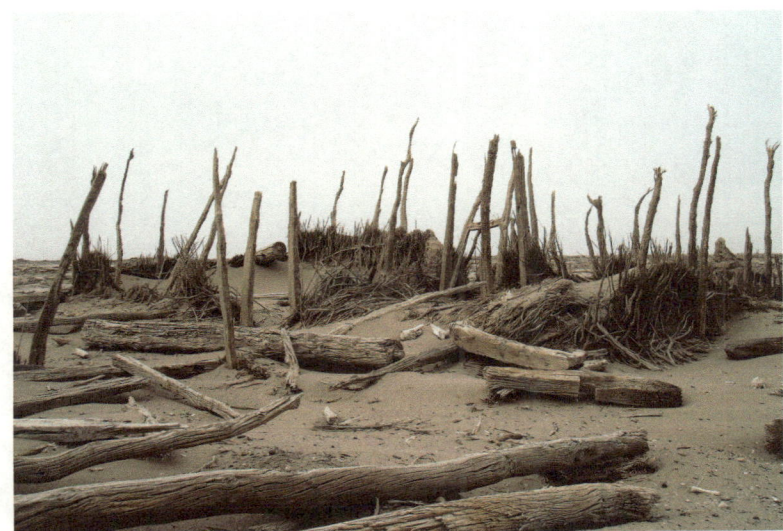

Figure 1-11 A corner of Loulan ruins

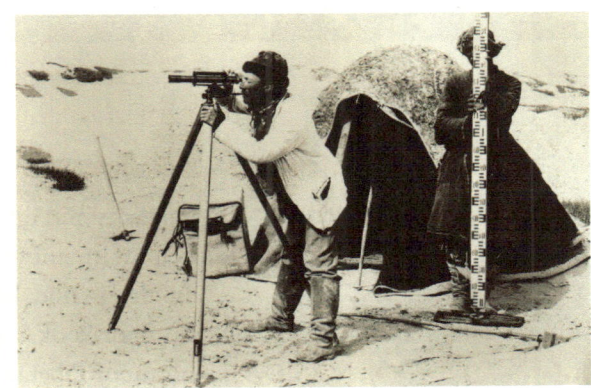

Figure 1-12 Hedin used a level in the Taklimakan Desert to survey the northern shore of Kara-Koschun during his second expedition to Central Asia (1900–1901)

1.5 Sven Hedin's Academic Achievements

Hedin's academic pursuits diverged from the typical motivations of explorers. His primary quest lay in uncovering ancient cities rather than merely treasure hunting. His sense of genuine adventure echoed the sentiment of venturing into uncharted territories—a quest to be the inaugural figure on the map of human exploration (Figure 1-12). This ardor stemmed from his childhood experience of witnessing the triumphant Arctic journey of Swedish polar explorer Nils Adolf Erik Nordenskiöld (1832–1901). The conquest of nature stirred an enduring yearning within him. Throughout his illustrious career, Hedin scaled icebergs and traversed deserts numerous times. While these feats might appear perilous today, he embarked upon them without a moment's hesitation. His extensive explorations often teetered on the brink of calamity, encountering wars and natural disasters that imperiled his life. In moments of jeopardy, he narrowly skirted death multiple times. It is

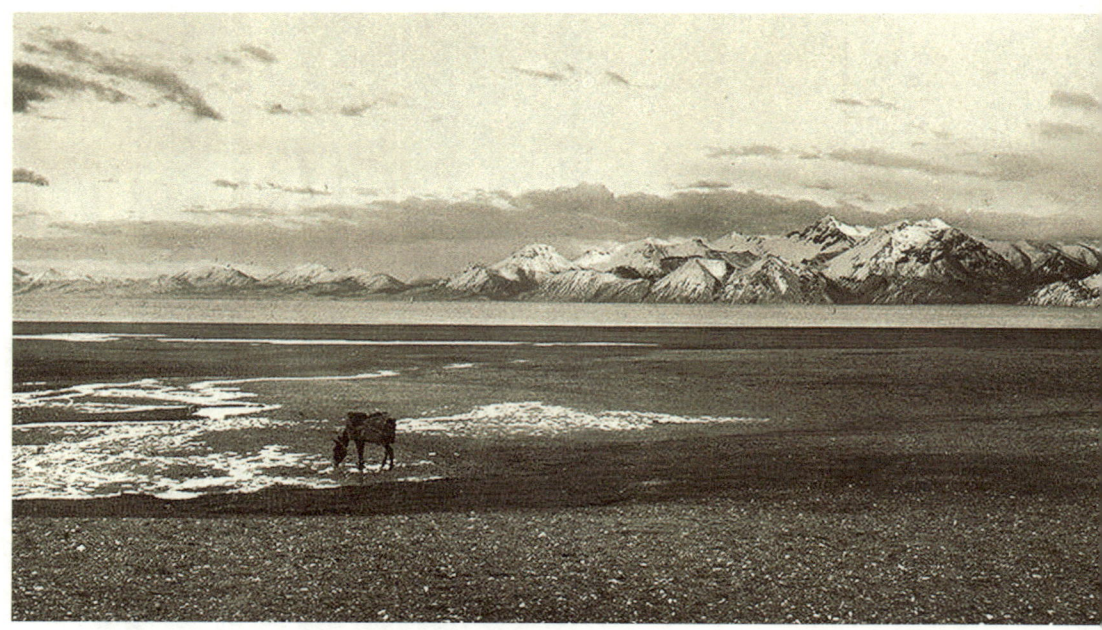

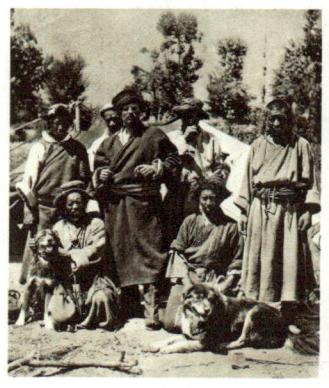

Figure 1-13 Sven Hedin in Xizang (1907–1909)

this audacity and intrepid spirit that sustained his decades-long commitment to archaeology and exploration.

In the period between May and December of 1901, Hedin undertook comprehensive surveys and mapping of the northern Tibetan territories. Encountering obstructions from the local authorities, he redirected his route through India upon his return to his homeland the following year. In 1907, he returned to China, with Xizang still being his primary objective. However, in 1903, British officer Francis Younghusband (1863–1942) led an expedition into Tibet, facing expulsion, and eventually occupied Lhasa with troops from India in the subsequent year. The British incursion led to significant casualties and raised international concerns. Despite this, Hedin's endeavors were more fortuitous compared to prior expeditions by figures such as the French Dutreuil de Rhins (Chinese name Lu Tui, 1846–1894) and Nikolay Przhevalsky. Przhevalsky, during his lifetime, attempted to access Xizang but failed to secure permission. Members of Dutreuil's expedition met tragic ends on the Tibetan Plateau in 1894. In 1906, Hedin succeeded in entering northern Xizang for investigation (Figure 1-13). With a Chinese passport, he fulfilled his aspiration of entering Xizang and became the sole Western explorer received by the Panchen Lama. The Ninth Panchen Thubten Choekyi Nyima (1883–1937)

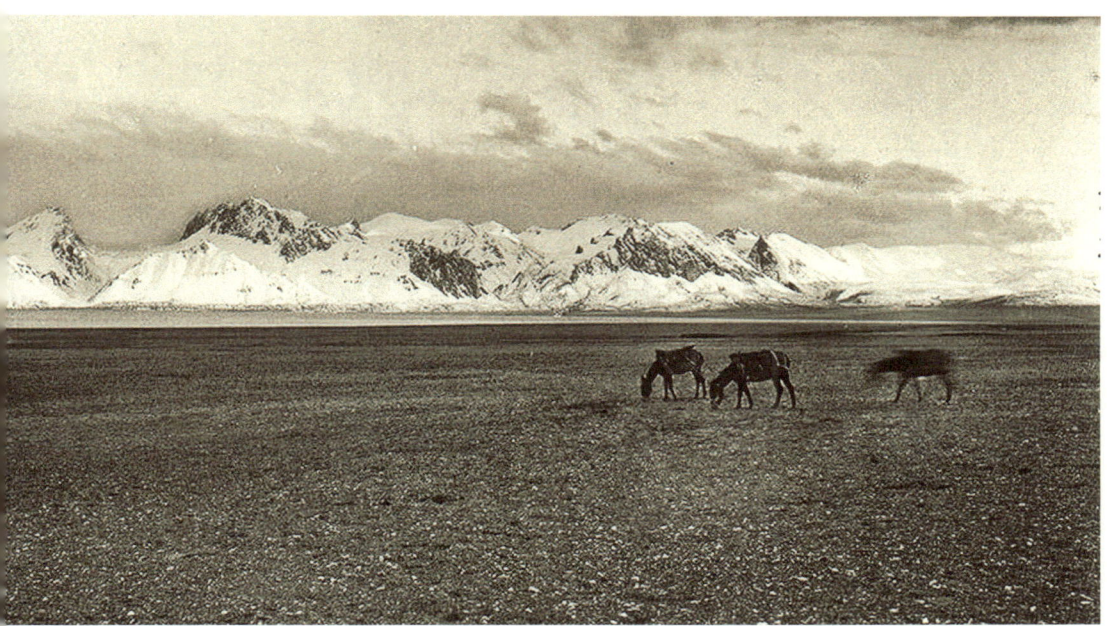

Figure 1-14 Panorama taken by Sven Hedin in Aksai Chin, northwest Xizang (elevation 5,095 meters, September 20, 1906)

consented to Hedin's request in 1907, permitting him to conduct expeditionary research on the Tibetan Plateau (Figure 1-14). Subsequently, Hedin lingered in Xizang extensively, meticulously mapping the topography and waterways of several mountains and rivers.

From a modern perspective, Hedin's academic legacy is unquestionable. His discovery of the ancient city of Loulan and meticulous mapping of Xizang laid a solid groundwork for precise cartography of Central Asia. He was the first European explorer to engage local scientists and research aides during expeditions and to excavate ancient Buddhist sites in Central Asia. Proficient in artistry, his travelogues and scientific documents were adorned with his own watercolor paintings and sketches, lending credibility and allure to his expeditions (Figure 1-15). His lectures on exploration in various countries inspired generations of youth to pursue exploration, earning him recognition even from President Theodore Roosevelt (1858–1919) of the United States. Elected as a member of the Swedish Academy and the Royal Swedish Academy of Sciences, Hedin wielded influence in the selection of Nobel Prizes in science and literature. His research endeavors bridged gaps in the Western knowledge system concerning Xinjiang and Xizang, facilitating China's exploration of Loulan and Tibetan cultures. As an authority on the geography of Xinjiang and Xizang, he enjoyed unrestricted access to monarchs, politicians, geographical organizations, and academic associations across Europe and Asia. He remains one of the few scientists acknowledged by many in China. After departing Xizang in 1909, Hedin immersed himself in the study of Central Asian cultures, returning to Chinese soil 17 years later.

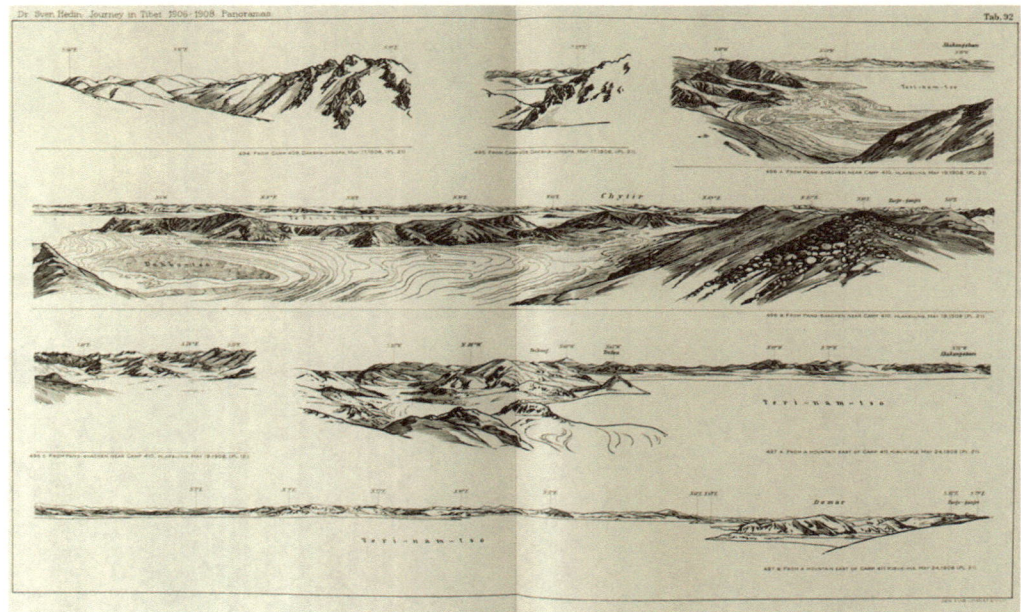

Figure 1-15 Sven Hedin's hand-drawn topographic map of southern Xizang

1.6 Hedin's Expedition College – Northwestern Scientific Expedition

Sven Hedin's fourth expedition stands out as a unique adventure, distinct from its predecessors due to varied sponsors, participants, and objectives. Spanning Inner Mongolia, Xinjiang, and northern Xizang, this expedition was characterized by Hedin as a collaborative effort involving Swedish, German, and Chinese archaeologists, astronomers, botanists, geographers, meteorologists, and zoologists (Figure 1-16).

In 1927, Hedin received a commission from Lufthansa to conduct an inspection journey through the interior of China, aiming to establish a Eurasian route from Shanghai to Berlin. However, due to previous incidents involving the unauthorized removal of cultural relics, the Chinese cultural community had grown distrustful of expeditions led by foreign explorers. Hedin's expedition was met with widespread

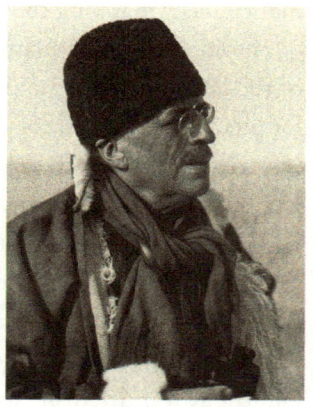

Figure 1-16 Sven Hedin during the fourth expedition to Central Asia (1927–1933)

opposition, seen as an act of cultural relic looting. It was only after Swedish prince and geologist Johan Gunnar Andersson (1874–1960) stepped in with fervent mediation efforts that a resolution was reached. Andersson ensured that all cultural relics inspected during the expedition would be returned to China. Hedin entered into 19 agreements with Chi-

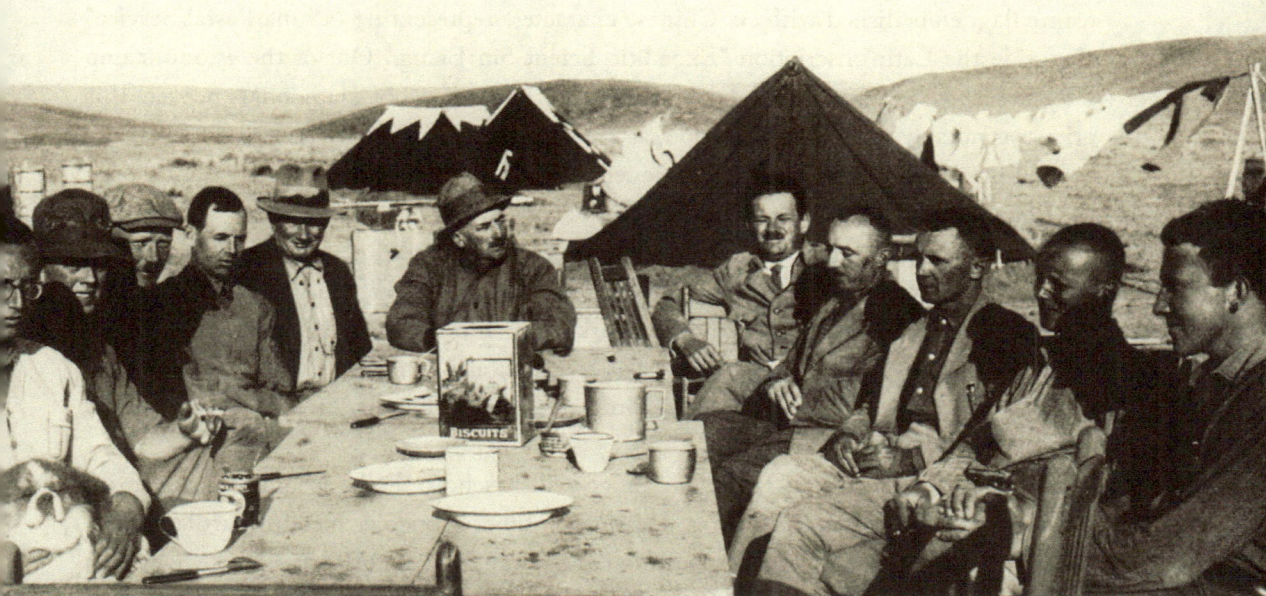

Figure 1-17 Hedin hosted the meeting of the Northwest Scientific Expedition in the Gobi Desert (1927–1933)

nese academic groups titled China Association of Academic Groups Develops Cooperation Measures with Dr. Sven Hedin of Sweden for Organizing a Scientific Expedition to the Northwest, which paved the way for the expedition to gain the necessary qualifications and permissions for the inspection. Originally intended as a meteorological expedition solely under Hedin's supervision, this endeavor transformed into the first multinational and multidisciplinary joint scientific expedition, marked by the involvement of a Chinese expedition team. The majority of cultural relics and specimens collected during this mission remained in China, while only a small portion was brought back to Sweden by Hedin for exhibition and preservation purposes.

The Chinese leader of the Sino-Swedish expedition team was Xu Bingchang (1888–1976), the provost of Peking University and a philosophy professor. The team comprised 15 members, including geologist Yuan Fuli (1893–1987), archaeologist Huang Wenbi (1893–1966), geologist Ding Daoheng (1899–1955), five students from Peking University, and a photographer from the Beijing History Museum. This team consists of scientists from six countries, predominantly Swedes and Chinese, and has 45 members (Figure 1-17). Their investigation spanned geology, geomagnetism, meteorology, astronomy, anthropology, archaeology, and folklore. To ensure safety during the journey, the inspection team members were armed, resembling a protective force. Funds for the entire expedition were raised through Hedin's personal efforts via various channels, including what now seems a commercial approach—issuing the Sino-Swedish Expedition series of stamps by the Republic of China government. The set of four stamps depicted scenes of camels in the camp and the team's flag, embellished with six Chinese characters representing "China Postal Service" alongside the Latin inscription "Expeditio Scient Sin Eiang." Out of the 25,000 stamp sets produced, 21,500 were sold during the expedition at a cost of 5 US dollars per set. This price was notably steep for that period, as Hedin aimed to secure additional funds for the expedition. However, despite their uniqueness, these stamps failed to gain popularity at the time, but they have since become rare collector's items.

Commencing from Beijing on May 29, 1927, the expedition traversed Baotou and Bailing Temple to the Ejin River Basin, reaching Urumqi in February 1928. This historic expedition, equipped with 292 camels, embarked on an international and interdisciplinary scientific investigation in the Gobi Desert of Mongolia and Xinjiang—the largest northwest expedition to date. After eight years, it culminated in a 55-volume *Sino-Swedish Expedition Report*, deemed immensely fruitful.

During the expedition, Yuan Fuli and Swedish scholar Folke Bergman (1902–1946) collected microlithic artifacts from 327 locations in Inner Mongolia; Neolithic artifacts from various places in Xinjiang, such as Chaiwopu of Urumqi, Xinge'er of Turpan, and Miao'ergou of Hami; animal fossils from the Permian and Triassic eras in Fukang; and approximately 10,000 Han Dynasty bamboo slips from the Juyan beacon site in the Ejin River Basin, which were known as Juyan Han slips. Huang Wenbi conducted archaeological surveys and partial excavation in Lop Nur, Turpan, and the Tarim Basin, unearthing numerous pottery and cultural relics.

The team exhibited its findings at the Research Institute of Beijing Women's Normal University on February 6, 1931. Following the completion of the inspection work, the team members diligently crafted individual inspection reports. It was not until May 1933 that all members concluded their inspections. Over the years, participating scholars published numerous research results, contributing significantly to fields like archaeology, botany, geology, geography, and meteorology. The book *History of the Expedition in Asia, 1927–1935*, penned by Hedin during his approximately 6-year stay in China, meticulously captures the rich tapestry of experiences, encompassing joys, sorrows, successes, failures, gains, and losses of those years. Within the preface lies a vivid account of his collaborative journey with the academic circles in China, detailing the process and depth of their cooperation.

I cannot help but emphasize the remarkable nature of our collaboration with our Chinese colleagues—it is nothing short of exceptional. Our partnership operates seamlessly, akin to that of brothers, devoid of envy, strife, or misunderstanding. Nationality or ethnicity holds no significance in our interactions; our sole objective is dedicated to advancing international science. Regrettably, there have been instances in the past where certain Western travelers egregiously offended the sentiments of the Chinese populace. Yet, within our circle, such transgressions are entirely unheard of. In China, the Chinese find themselves in their own abode, while foreigners are esteemed guests who must bear the repercussions of their unfavorable behavior. Personally, the six years I have spent have been immensely rewarding. Working alongside some of the most exceptional scholars in China, both in the field and in Peking, has been an unparalleled privilege. Each of these individuals will forever remain ingrained in my memory with profound appreciation and cherished camaraderie.

After the inspection, Hedin's already illustrious reputation soared higher. However, he found himself burdened with significant debts due to his extensive research endeavors. To repay these debts, he tirelessly delivered numerous lectures. Simultaneously, he dedicated himself to meticulously organizing the vast amount of information gathered during the inspection (Figure 1-18). Commencing in 1937, the comprehensive series of research findings from the expedition, compiled under the title *Reports from the Scientific Expedition to the North-Western Provinces of China under the Leadership of Dr. Sven Hedin*, has stood as a cornerstone document for scholars worldwide in understanding Central Asia to this day. In his pursuit to publish these invaluable inspection reports, Hedin depleted his family fortune. Eventually, he had to resort to pawning his most cherished books to finance the publication of the remaining materials. Huang Wenbi, a Chinese archaeologist who participated in this expedition, authored and published significant works such as *Archaeological Records of Lop Nur*, *Archaeological Records of Turpan*, and *Archaeological Records of the Tarim Basin*. Artifacts excavated during this expedition were sent to Sweden for evaluation, stipulating in the contract their obligatory return to China after three years. Following World War II, the proactive engagement and funding by the US Army Cartography Office for the publication of Sven Hedin's life's work, *Central Asia Atlas*, further underscored his revered status as a godfather in the realm of Central Asian geographical research.

On November 26, 1952, Hedin passed away at the age of 88. His final resting place lies in the cemetery of the Adolf Fredrik Church in Stockholm, Sweden (Figure 1-19). The rights and ownership of all his literary works were entrusted to the Sven Hedin Foundation,

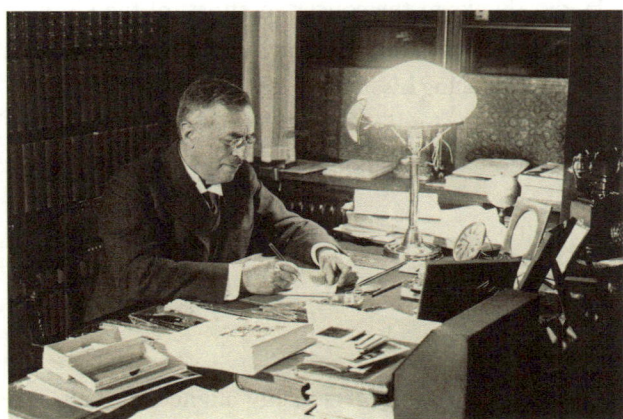

Figure 1-18 Sven Hedin working in his study (1935)

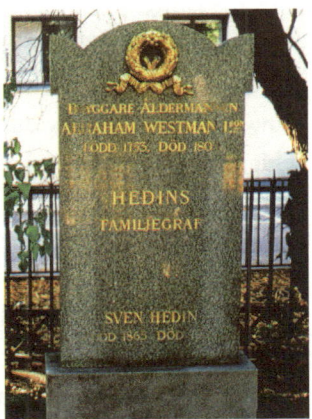

Figure 1-19 Hedin's tombstone in Stockholm, Sweden

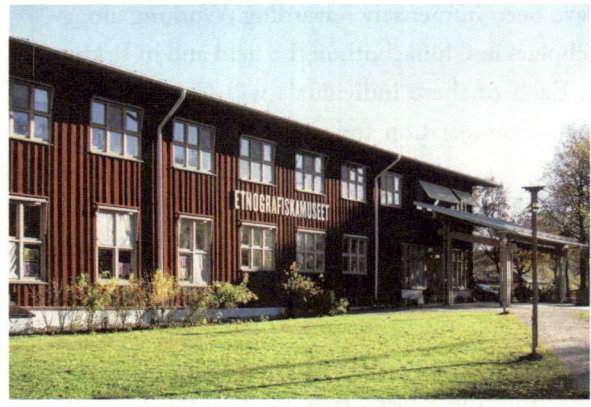

Figure 1-20 Museum of Ethnography, Stockholm, Sweden (2007)

which was established subsequently. This enduring Swedish foundation, still operational today, assumes responsibility for cataloging and preserving Hedin's scientific expedition data. It oversees a vast repository of records from his scientific expeditions and cultural relics brought back to Sweden from China. Their website remains a repository of these valuable records and collections. The majority of the materials procured by Hedin from China are housed and exhibited at the Museum of Ethnography in Stockholm, Sweden, which also serves as the foundation's headquarters (Figure 1-20).

Hedin's research contributions also played a significant role in China's modernization and developmental strides. In 1935, the meticulously drawn route map by Hedin became instrumental for the Republic of China government, aiding in the construction of roads, railways, dams, canals, and irrigation for new pastures across the Tarim Basin and Yanji Basin. Moreover, the Sino-Swedish joint expedition team's discoveries of iron ore, magnetite, petroleum, coal mines, and gold mines sparked subsequent exploitations, contributing to the country's economic resources. The myriad animals, plants, fossils of extinct dinosaurs, and horned animals uncovered during the investigation were acknowledged and named with the suffix "-hedin," a tribute to Hedin thanks to the concerted efforts of the Chinese collaborators. From an academic standpoint, Hedin rightfully earned acclaim as a geologist, explorer, and archaeologist, wholeheartedly embracing his lifelong dedication to exploration. However, like all individuals, he was not without imperfections. Despite his exceptional achievements in academic and professional domains, his political choices have left a stain on his legacy.

1.7 The Scale of Politics

Hedin held distinct and unwavering political beliefs. He staunchly aligned himself as a royalist, harboring opposition toward parliamentary systems while fervently advocating for nationalism and militarism. His convictions rested on the belief that sovereignty superseded

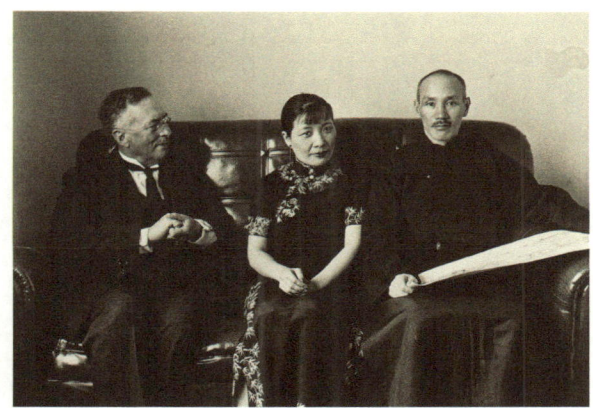

Figure 1-21 Sven Hedin with Chiang Kai-shek and Soong Mei-ling in Hankou (February 1935)

human rights, asserting that a robust nation alone could safeguard itself and, consequently, warrant individual freedoms. At the outset of World War I, he penned articles in support of the German monarchy and its war endeavors, asserting that only a powerful Germany could shield Sweden. However, this political stance resulted in his loss of scientific esteem among Germany's wartime adversaries. Consequently, he faced exclusion from geographical organizations and learned societies and encountered diminished support for future expeditions.

During the era of Nazi Germany, Hedin aligned himself with Hitler, perceiving Germany as a more reliable protector of Sweden compared to the Soviet Union. In 1935, he espoused his unique perspectives on Central Asia to the Swedish, Chinese, and German governments through public speeches. He met with Chiang Kai-shek and Soong Mei-ling in Hankou to engage in political discussions (Figure 1-21). Furthermore, during the 1936 Summer Olympics in Berlin, he held direct discussions with Hitler and his political representatives. Hedin's illusions regarding Germany, his proximity to Nazi officials, and the Nazis' use of his popularity to broadcast messages globally severely tarnished his reputation among the Allies. This led to his isolation within the international and scientific communities.

Throughout his life, Hedin experienced a dichotomy of reputations. He triumphed over numerous adversities, achieving immeasurable glory and fame. Politicians from various nations took pride in associating with him, yet he also weathered periods of hardship and indifference. As a scientist and explorer, he achieved significant success, but his political choices ultimately faltered. His intense nationalism clouded his judgment, blinding him to the true nature of the Nazis. On one hand, his scientific research and expeditions laid the groundwork for geology and geography in Central Asia, Xinjiang, and Xizang in China. On the other hand, his explorations led to the appropriation of cultural relics that originally belonged to other countries. In China's extensive history of cultural dispersion, Hedin was not the first individual to remove cultural relics, but he was the first scholar to leave behind an extensive array of research findings while acquiring cultural relics. He was also the foremost figure who systematically introduced and cataloged them, making noteworthy contributions as an explorer of geography and geology in Xinjiang and Xizang.

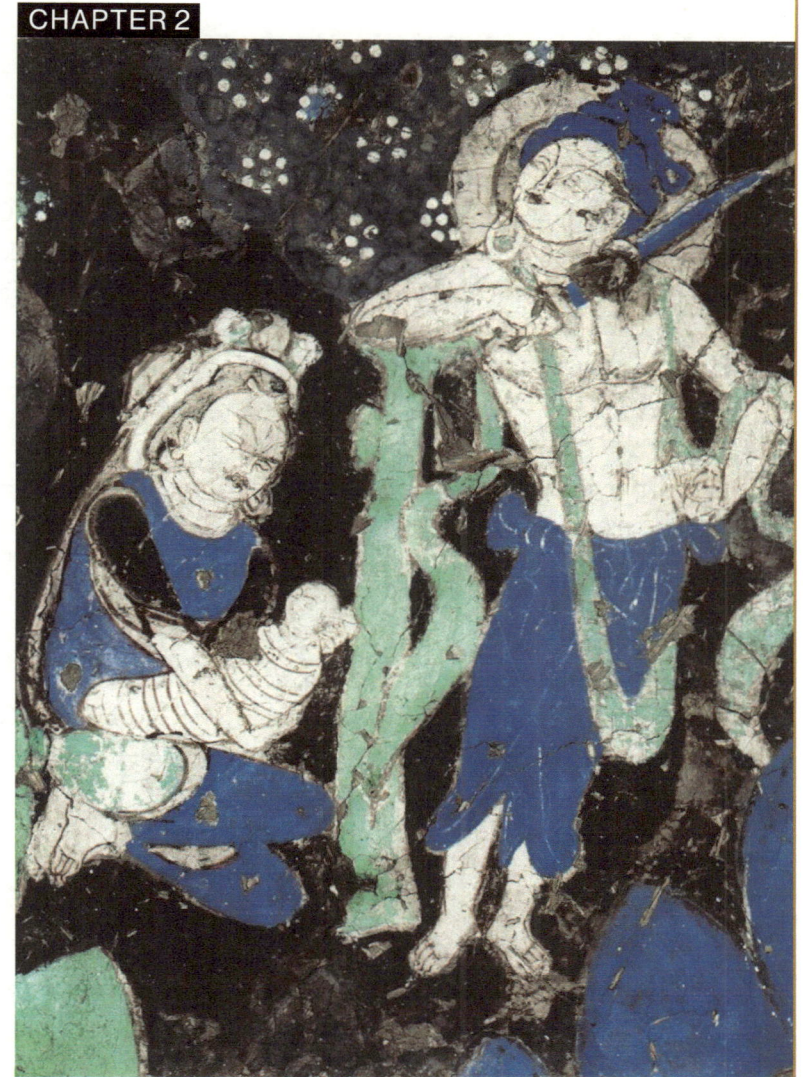

CHAPTER 2

Discoveries of Albert Grünwedel and Albert von Le Coq in Xinjiang

— **December 1902–April 1903**

First expedition

Captain: Grünwedel; members: Le Coq, Huth, Bartus

Route: Ghulja (now Yining, Xinjiang)–Urumqi–Turpan (Ancient City of Gaochang, Bezeklik Caves, Shengjinkou Caves, Toyuk Caves)–Toksun–Karasahr–Kuqa (Kumtura Caves, Kizil Caves)–Aksu–Tumxuk–Maralbexi–Kashgar

— **November 1904–December 1905**

Second expedition

Captain: Le Coq; member: Bartus

Route: Urumqi–Turpan (Ancient City of Gaochang, Jiaohe ruins)–Hami–Turpan–northern edge of Tarim Basin–Kashgar

— **1905–June 1906**

Third expedition

Captain: Grünwedel; members: Le Coq, Pohrt, Bartus

Route: Kashgar–Tumushuk–Kuqa (Kumtura Caves, Kizil Caves, Kerixi Caves)–Korla (temples and Shorchuk Caves)–Turpan–Urumqi–Hami–Toyuk Caves–Shorchuk Caves–Turpan–Urumqi–return

— **June 1913–February 1914**

Fourth expedition

Captain: Le Coq; member: Bartus

Route: Kashgar–Kuqa (Kizil Caves, Kerixi Caves, Senmusaimu Caves, Kumtura Caves)–Tumushuk–Kashgar

2.1 Establishment of the Prussian Royal Turpan Expedition

The Ethnological Museum of Berlin, a precursor to today's esteemed Asian Art Museum in Berlin, stands as an illustrious institution in European Asian art research. Renowned Orientalists Albert Grünwedel and Albert von Le Coq were esteemed contributors to this institution. In the early 20th century, their joint efforts culminated in four transformative expeditions to Xinjiang, resulting in the acquisition of a plethora of cultural relics for Germany's cultural enrichment.

Born in Munich, Germany, in 1856, Grünwedel manifested a profound interest in Asian art from a tender age. His pursuit led him to transition from the Munich Art School to the

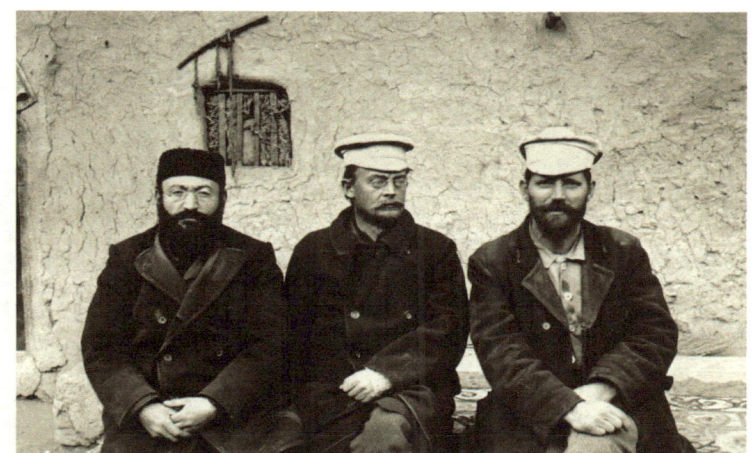

Figure 2-1 Group photo of the German Turpan Expedition's first expedition, taken in the ancient city of Gaochang, Turpan, Xinjiang (left to right: Huth, Grünwedel, Bartus, 1902–1903)

University of Munich at the age of 20, specializing in Oriental studies. By 1883, he assumed the role of curator at the Indian Department of the Ethnological Museum of Berlin. This period coincided with a substantial influx of Gandhara Buddhist art sculptures from north-west India into Europe. Notably, the museum collected 63 Gandhara art treasures excavated from the Swat region in northern Pakistan. Grünwedel conducted extensive research on these artifacts, delving into Buddhist art iconography and Central Asian archaeology. His groundbreaking work culminated in the 1893 publication of *Buddhist Art in India* in Berlin, igniting widespread acclaim and cementing his authoritative stature in Buddhist art research across Europe.

In the evolving landscape of 20th-century Europe, Orientalism emerged as a burgeoning discipline encompassing the exploration of various exotic regions east to Europe, spanning West Asia, Central Asia, and East Asia. Grünwedel aspired to venture into the East, contributing significantly to this field of study. Thus, the Ethnological Museum of Berlin initiated the Prussian Royal Turpan Expedition to Xinjiang on four occasions during this period. The nomenclature of the expedition team, Turpan, derived from the primary destination of the inaugural German expedition led by Grünwedel himself.

In 1902, Grünwedel orchestrated a groundbreaking exploration of the Turpan region, heading a team comprising his assistant, Le Coq, museum technician and administrator Theodor Bartus (1858–1941), Oriental scholar Georg Huth (1867–1906), among others. This marked the inception of the first German Central Asian expedition (Figure 2-1). Upon their arrival in Gaochang, the team meticulously charted the entire layout of the ancient city of Gaochang (Figure 2-2). Their detailed documentation included a comprehensive floor plan and an elaborate description of the ruins of Temple B, situated in the southwest quadrant of the ancient city. Within Temple B, Grünwedel identified a Buddhist temple building he referred to as the "sacred temple," characterized by towering pillars amid the abandoned structure. Its multi-layered small Buddhist niches, adorned with perforations,

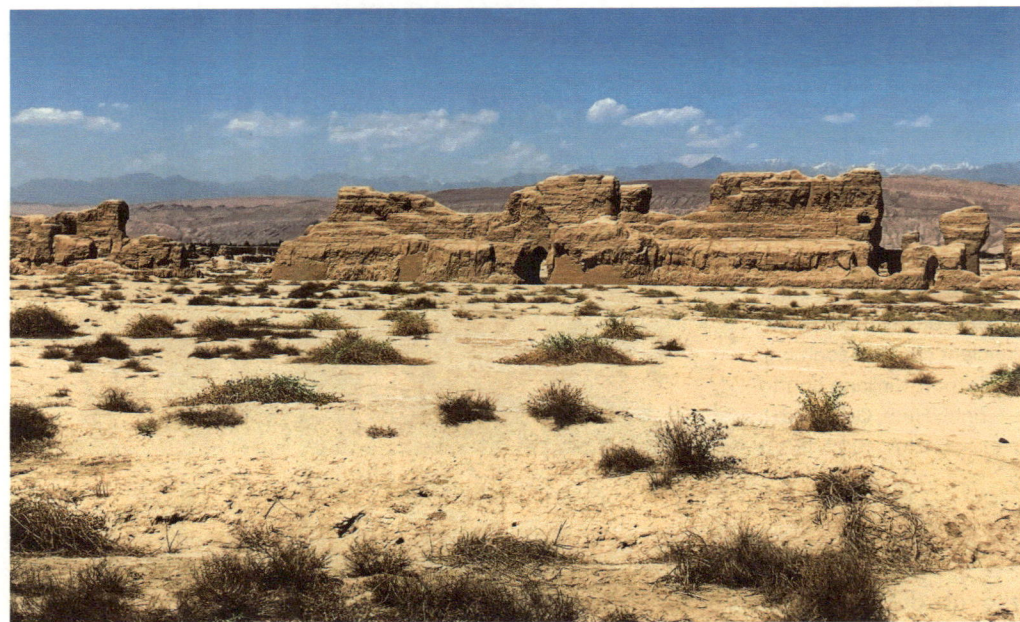

Figure 2-2 Ancient city of Gaochang, Turpan, Xinjiang (photographed by Huang Zhiqing)

and the weathered yet vibrant murals held immense artistic and historical value. The vicinity surrounding this monumental temple exhibited numerous dilapidated architectural remnants believed to be remnants of artisan workshops and commercial establishments from that era. Following a five-month sojourn in the Ancient City of Gaochang, the Grünwedel-led expedition returned to Berlin, laden with 46 boxes containing Buddhist murals, handwritten documents, and sculptures.

This pivotal expedition not only broadened the horizons of German academia regarding Central Asian culture and art but also propelled Grünwedel into the limelight, solidifying his reputation as a revered explorer and Orientalist. Subsequent to this success, the Kaiser and the German government generously funded the following three expeditions, officially naming them the Prussian Royal Expedition. Emperor Wilhelm II von Deutschland (1859–1941), the last monarch of the German Empire, established a dedicated committee for this purpose. The renowned arms manufacturer Alfred Krupp (1812–1887) and Wilhelm II personally contributed substantial funds, envisioning larger-scale explorations. However, Grünwedel's declining health necessitated the search for a new leader. Thus, Le Coq, another passionate researcher deeply immersed in Oriental studies and Grünwedel's assistant on the inaugural expedition, was chosen as his successor.

Albert von Le Coq (Figure 2-3) was born into affluence on September 8, 1860, within a prosperous Berlin family. His privileged background endowed him with both financial resources and ample time to dedicate to exploratory pursuits. Notably, his self-taught mastery of Arabic, Turkic, Persian, and ancient Indian Sanskrit granted him a distinct advantage for venturing into Central Asia. Joining the Indian Department of the Ethnological Museum of Berlin in 1902 at the age of 42, he commenced his journey in the realm of exploration. That same year, he played a pivotal role as Albert Grünwedel's assistant during the expedition to Turpan, Xinjiang, China, laying the foundation for his subsequent leadership in the Prussian Royal Expedition.

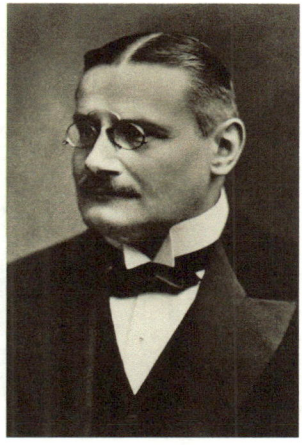

Figure 2-3 Albert von Le Coq

In September 1904, Le Coq spearheaded the Prussian Royal expedition's second journey to the Turpan region from Berlin. Despite his prior collaboration as an assistant to Grünwedel, Le Coq and Grünwedel diverged significantly in their methodologies leading the expedition. A substantial dissimilarity surfaced in their approaches to handling cultural relics, relics found within the monastery, and cave temple ruins that adorned the Silk Road, preserving a rich record of local civilization. Grünwedel, advocating meticulous archaeological excavation, documentation, protection, and comprehensive site-based research, emphasized the integrity of sites without compromising them merely for the acquisition of individual statues or murals. Conversely, Le Coq subscribed to a different ethos, advocating for the removal of all valuable artifacts unearthed during the expedition.

During their first expedition, differences had already emerged between Le Coq and Grünwedel regarding the treatment of cultural relics. However, as Grünwedel held leadership at the time, he firmly rejected Le Coq's proposition to indiscriminately remove all cultural relics, deeming such actions contrary to the spirit of archaeology. In this subsequent expedition, without Grünwedel's restraint, and aiming to acquire more cultural relics to garner greater acclaim than Grünwedel, Le Coq disregarded ethical considerations. He unleashed a campaign of unrestrained pillaging of the cultural heritage within Gaochang, deviating from the principles upheld by Grünwedel and indulging in a spree of looting cultural treasures.

2.2 Catastrophe under the Flaming Mountains

On November 18, 1904, the Prussian Royal Expedition reached Turpan anew. Led by Le Coq and his team, they ventured westward, setting their sights on the ancient city of Gaochang and the Bezeklik Caves, initiating extensive exploration and archaeological endeavors. Situated on the precipitous inclines of the primary peak of the Flaming Mountains, approximately 40 kilometers northeast of present-day Turpan, the Bezeklik Caves (Figures 2-4 and 2-5) have unveiled over 80 grottoes to date. The earliest excavations trace back to the late Southern and Northern Dynasties (AD 420–589), with the majority belonging to the Uyghur Gaochang Kingdom era, while some date as far as the early

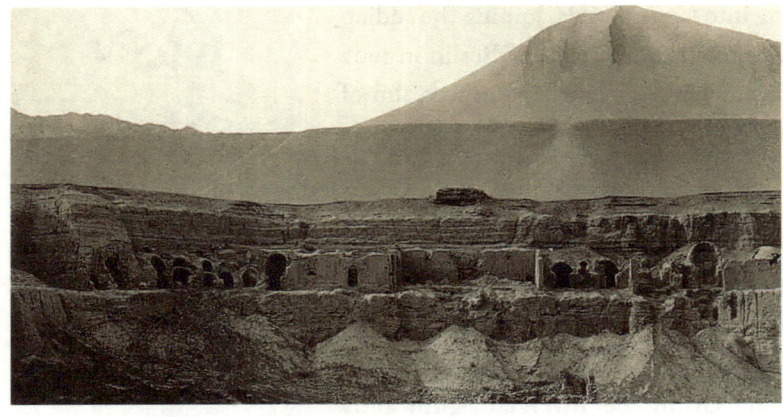

Figure 2-4 Bezeklik Caves in Turpan, Xinjiang (1900s), photographed by the German expedition

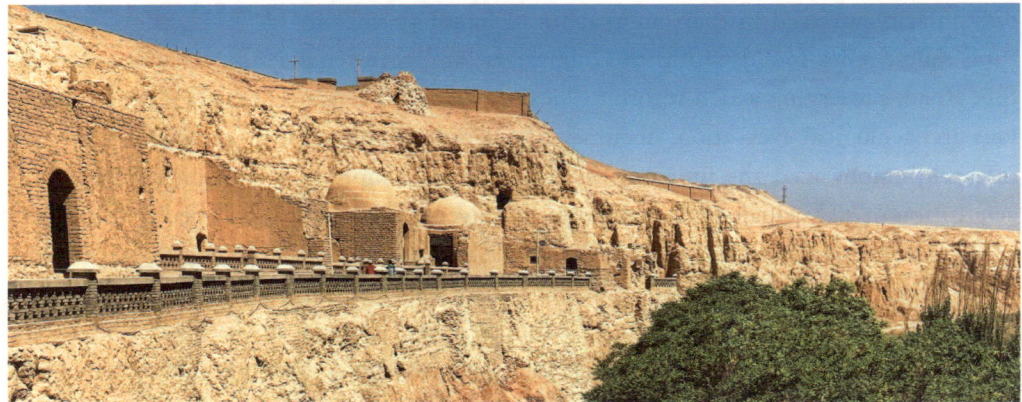

Figure 2-5 The current appearance of the Bezeklik Caves in Turpan, Xinjiang (photographed by Huang Zhiqing)

Yuan Dynasty (AD 1206–1368). Bezeklik, derived from the Uyghur language, signifies somewhere beautifully decorated. Undoubtedly, the vibrant mural art adorning the caves in this region left an indelible impression on foreign explorers like Le Coq. Prior to Le Coq's expedition, this area had remained uninhabited for a century, the grottoes obscured by encroaching quicksand. To facilitate their excavation, the expedition team temporarily lodged in a shepherd's cave positioned at the southern end of the caves.

In his account within the pages of *Buried Treasure of Chinese Turkestan*, Le Coq vividly narrated the moment of discovery:

I got on to these heaps of sand in the left corridor, and as I clambered up the sand slipped down under the weight of my body, so that by constantly lifting my feet high and stamping to get foothold. I dislodged many hundredweights of the heap lying there.

Suddenly, as if by magic, I saw on the walls bared in this way, to my right and left, splendid paintings in colours as fresh as if the artist had only just finished them.

…

If we could secure these pictures the success of the expedition was assured.

The written accounts unequivocally echo Grünwedel's apprehensions—Le Coq's mission appeared directed toward the acquisition of cultural artifacts.

Excitement surged within Le Coq upon his discovery of the cave, prompting an immediate summons to his assistant, urging a hastened pace in excavating the sand. In his notes, Le Coq expressed his elation, "I unearthed three colossal monk statues, larger than life itself" (Figure 2-6). He was, however, unaware at the time that the cave he stumbled

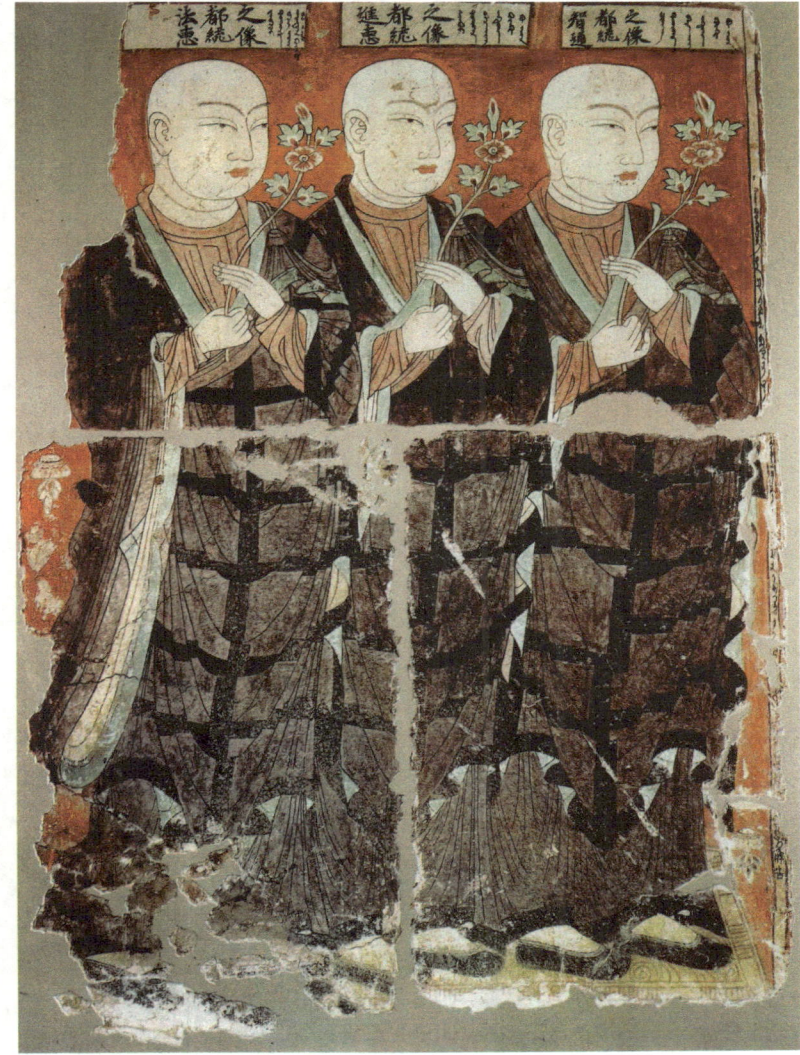

Figure 2-6 The portraits of monks Zhitong, Jinhui, and Fahui from the 9th to 12th centuries from Cave 20 in Bezeklik (now in the Museum of Asian Art, Berlin, Germany)

upon was the largest cave in the Bezeklik Caves. The clearing of the quicksand led to the revelation of extensive mural paintings within the cave. On the towering walls emerged fifteen monumental depictions of Buddha statues, each portraying distinct images, alongside kneeling donor figures bearing offerings, all clad in attire and footwear reminiscent of the ancient Gaochang Kingdom period (Figure 2-7).

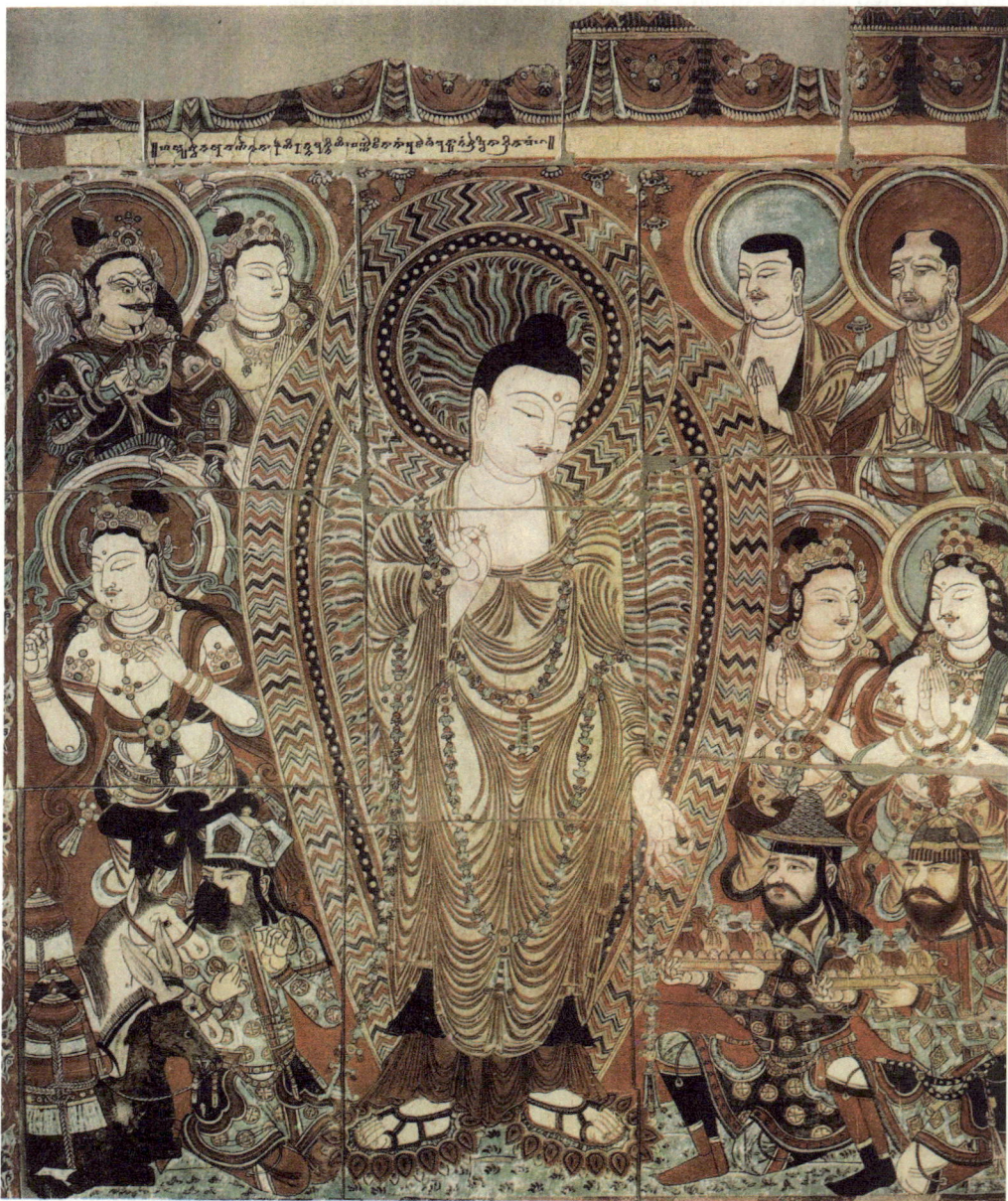

Figure 2-7 Mural of karma story from the 9th to 12th centuries in Cave 20 of Bezeklik (once collected in the Ethnological Museum of Berlin, but destroyed during World War II)

Subsequent investigations unveiled even more astonishing findings. The myriad murals were not standardized creations crafted in an assembly-line fashion. Every character depicted bears unique attire, facial features, and expressions. In essence, each painted figure emerged as a meticulously crafted artistic treasure, embodying diverse identities and images. The portrayals encapsulated the characteristics of multicultural regions, featuring figures such as the bejeweled prince from Indian mythology, the elderly Brahmin adorned with a long beard and dark skin (Figure 2-8), individuals resembling Persians wearing eagle-feathered hats and distinctive hooked noses, as well as red-haired, blue-eyed Sogdians, whom Le Coq mistakenly identified as Europoid. He remarked, "We swiftly associate

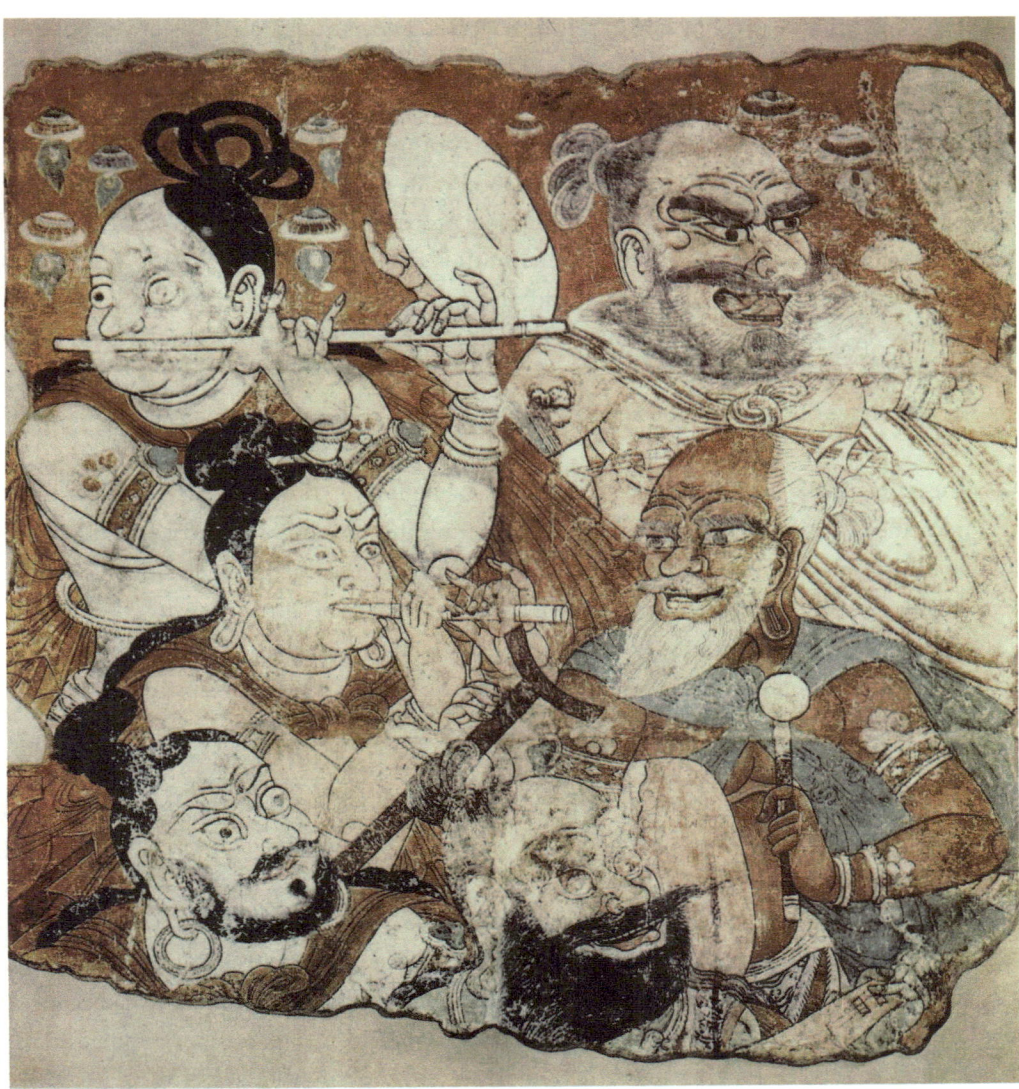

Figure 2-8 Brahmins playing music from the *Nirvana Sutra Transformation Illustration* from the 9th to 12th centuries in Cave 33 of Bezeklik (now in the Museum of Asian Art, Berlin, Germany)

these individuals with Aryans. The attire of these redheads, with their characteristic suspenders and high boots, signifies the diversity of races." Throughout his observations, Le Coq documented numerous murals and statues that depicted the amalgamation of various peoples.

Similar to Sven Hedin, Le Coq swiftly appraised the worth of these artifacts. These artworks, representing a tapestry of multi-ethnic, multinational, and multicultural expressions, stand unparalleled globally and shine as the most radiant jewels within the entire Silk Road culture. Without hesitation, Le Coq resolved to transport these cultural treasures back to Germany, yearning to cement his status as the most renowned and celebrated explorer in his homeland.

The expedition team continued their discoveries, unearthing a plethora of vibrant murals and numerous colorful Buddha statues. Le Coq's approach to handling these artifacts was characterized by a stark simplicity and lack of finesse. Utilizing then-advanced foxtail saws, he and his assistants began the process of meticulously cutting out each mural individually. They enlisted the aid of local laborers to wrap these invaluable relics in hay for transportation. Their purportedly advanced processing methods involved the use of wooden boards to bolster and stabilize the murals before employing saws to sever parts of the murals together with layers of mud and soil from the caves. However, due to the limitations of the cutting range, murals towering two to three meters high were crudely sectioned into several pieces.

In subsequent notes, Le Coq reflected:

> The sole path to safeguard these exquisite exemplars of Buddhist art rested in a meticulous and systematic relocation. Entrusting this arduous and intricate task to my adept, well-trained assistants, we embarked on the formidable endeavor …
>
> By dint of long and arduous work we succeeded in cutting away all these pictures. After twenty months of travelling they arrived safely at Berlin, where they fill an entire room of the museum. This is one of the few temples whose sum-total of paintings has been brought to Berlin.

In reference to the Buddhist temple, specifically Cave 20 within the Bezeklik Caves, all 15 majestic murals were meticulously severed and carefully packaged, the largest among them towering at a height of 3.5 meters.

Driven by an insatiable fervor for cultural relics, Le Coq obstinately disregarded Grünwedel's persistent objections, leading to a grievous pillaging of cultural treasures across the entirety of the Bezeklik site. This precedent set by Le Coq influenced subsequent explorers like Stein and Tachibana Zuicho (1890–1968) from Japan, who adopted similar methodologies, employing tools that, contrary to modern practices, inflicted damage upon the murals. The use of foxtail saws resulted in inherent harm to the murals themselves, causing wear and tear along the joints when reassembled. Stein was shocked by

Le Coq's methods upon inspecting the work site at Bezeklik Caves. In a letter to a friend, Stein expressed his astonishment, remarking on the crude methods employed by Le Coq as "not reflective of genuine archaeology but more aligned with treasure hunting." Yet, he succumbed to utilizing a similar approach for his own acquisitions.

In 1904, Le Coq extended his explorations to the Toyuk Caves in Turpan (Figure 2-9), unveiling yet another trove of invaluable and precious murals.

2.3 Exquisite Murals from Bezeklik Caves

The most striking murals within the Bezeklik Caves are the karma story murals, often found adorning the side walls of cave chambers or corridors. These paintings illustrate the con-

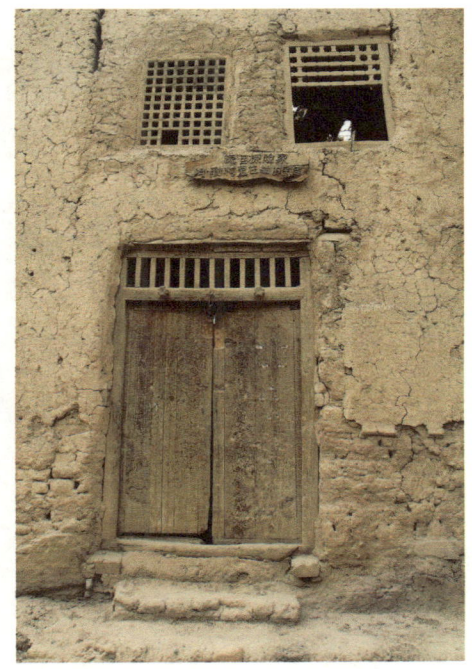

Figure 2-9 Le Coq's residence when he investigated the Toyuk Caves in Xinjiang in 1904 (photographed by Li Xiao)

cept of karma, depicting the factors contributing to the formation of phenomena such as awareness, divine retribution, and the genesis of things. Buddhism posits that all living beings endure suffering, attributing various hardships encountered in society to specific principal and secondary causes. It emphasizes that a devout belief in Buddhism allows a correct understanding of the essence behind these phenomena.

The karma-themed murals portray scenes where the Buddha expounds on karma to all sentient beings during his teachings. Suffering, anxiety, anger, and delusion are linked to karma spanning past and present lives. Whether passers-by, disciples, gods, or bodhisattvas inquire, the Buddha elucidates the nature of suffering and its origins. Similar murals are found not only in the Bezeklik Caves but also in the Dunhuang and Kizil Caves. However, the karma story murals in the Bezeklik Caves stand out as the most spectacular. With their rectangular compositions and central focus, these murals exhibit exceptional craftsmanship and comprehensive narratives, ranking among the finest in karma-themed artwork.

One notable mural, once housed in the Museum of Asian Art in Berlin (sadly destroyed during World War II), is a representative karma story mural among all such artworks in Cave 20 of Bezeklik (Figure 2-10). Dominating the central space of the mural is a towering standing Buddha, flanked by disciples, Bodhisattvas, deities, Dharma protectors, and various secular figures filling the gaps around the Buddha. With 3.6 meters in height and 2.3 meters in width, this artwork includes an inscription in Central Asian Brahmi letters

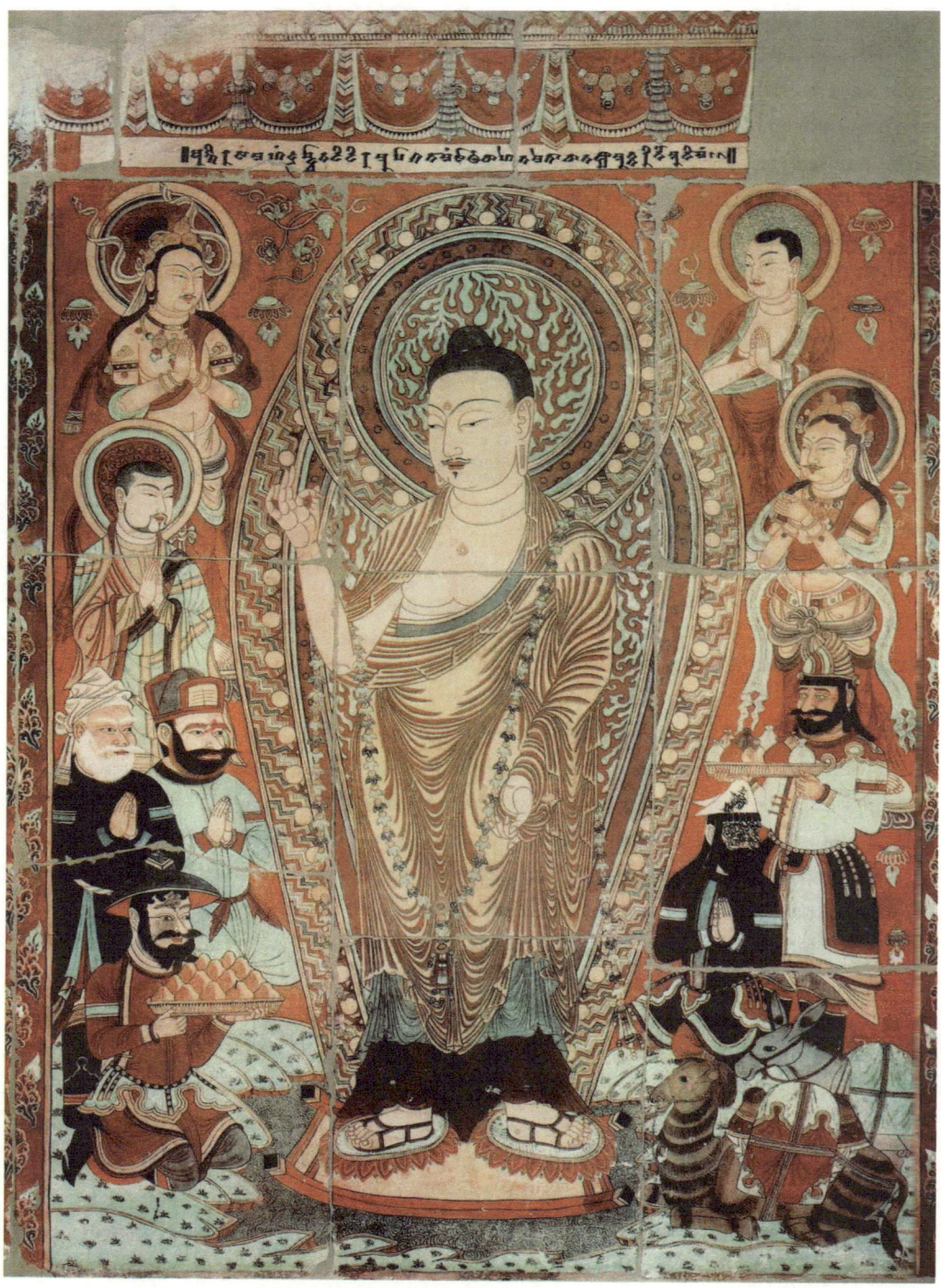

Figure 2-10 Part of the mural of karma story from the 9th to 12th centuries, taken from the inner wall of the north corridor of Cave 20 in Bezeklik (once collected in the Ethnological Museum of Berlin, but destroyed during World War II)

and Sanskrit at the top, recounting a merchant's encounter with a powerful deity from the Heavenly Palace, swiftly ferrying the deity across the river upon sighting it. In the depiction, the standing Buddha appears to preach while standing on a flat-bottomed wooden boat amid undulating water waves. Nine figures in veneration adorn both sides of the Buddha, including two disciples and two Bodhisattvas atop, following the conventional Buddhist composition. At the bottom, five earthly figures are depicted kneeling by the water's edge: one characterized by a black beard, black hair, red eyebrows, and striking green eyes; another adorned with a brown beard, red eyebrows, and deep black eyes; an elderly figure distinguished by white hair and a matching beard; and further, a figure featuring black hair, a gray beard, black eyebrows, distinctive pointed eyes, and an elongated nose. These figures seem intricately interwoven into the mural's narrative. Their attire, hats, and distinct clothing styles are emblematic of Central Asian and Persian origins. Notably, on the mural's lower right side, the depiction of camels and gray donkeys carrying a domed treasure chest portrays the quintessential imagery of Persian merchants intertwined with their concurrent Buddhist beliefs vividly (Figure 2-11).

In addition to the karma murals, sutra murals also hold significance among the murals in the Bezeklik Caves. Typically found on the side walls and ceilings of the caves, these include depictions such as the *Nirvana Sutra Transformation Illustration*, *Pure Land Transformation Illustration*, *Lotus Sutra Transformation Illustration*, and *Medicine Buddhas Sutra Transformation Illustration*. Remarkably akin in composition to the Tang Dynasty sutra transformation illustrations in Mogao Grottoes of Dunhuang, these murals signify the profound influence of the Central Plains region on Uyghur Buddhism. Furthermore, the prevalent portrayal of Thousand Buddhas here, some adorned with hanging flags and pagodas on their backs or inscribed with Buddha names in Chinese, has earned the Bezeklik Caves the moniker the Bezeklik Thousand Buddha Caves. These murals faithfully reflect the artistic influences prevalent during the Tang Dynasty.

Among the treasures of Cave 32, entirely relocated by Le Coq, numerous donor portraits stand out. Particularly noteworthy are the murals *Uyghur Donors* on both sides of the cave door's front walls. The male donors in these murals wear robes with coiled collars, belts around their waists, high peach-shaped crowns atop their heads, and sport beards—a clear testament to the influence of Tang Dynasty aristocratic attire on Uyghur nobility. Le Coq also removed notable murals such as the *Portraits of the Uyghur Noble Family* from the front wall in the main chamber of Cave 25, the *Portraits of the Sali Family* in Cave 20, and the *Portrait of the Uyghur King* in Cave 31. These masterpieces among male donor murals (Figure 2-12) showcase the distinct characteristics of the era and the nation.

Moreover, the Museum of Asian Art in Berlin housed a portrait of female donors from Cave 20, portraying two Uyghur girls holding flowers. These figures, with fair complexions and devout expressions, bear a Uyghur text inscription on the right, identifying them as *Portrait of Her Royal Highness Princess Joy*. This depiction offers a glimpse into the authentic image of a Uyghur noblewoman (Figure 2-13). These donor images and inscriptions serve

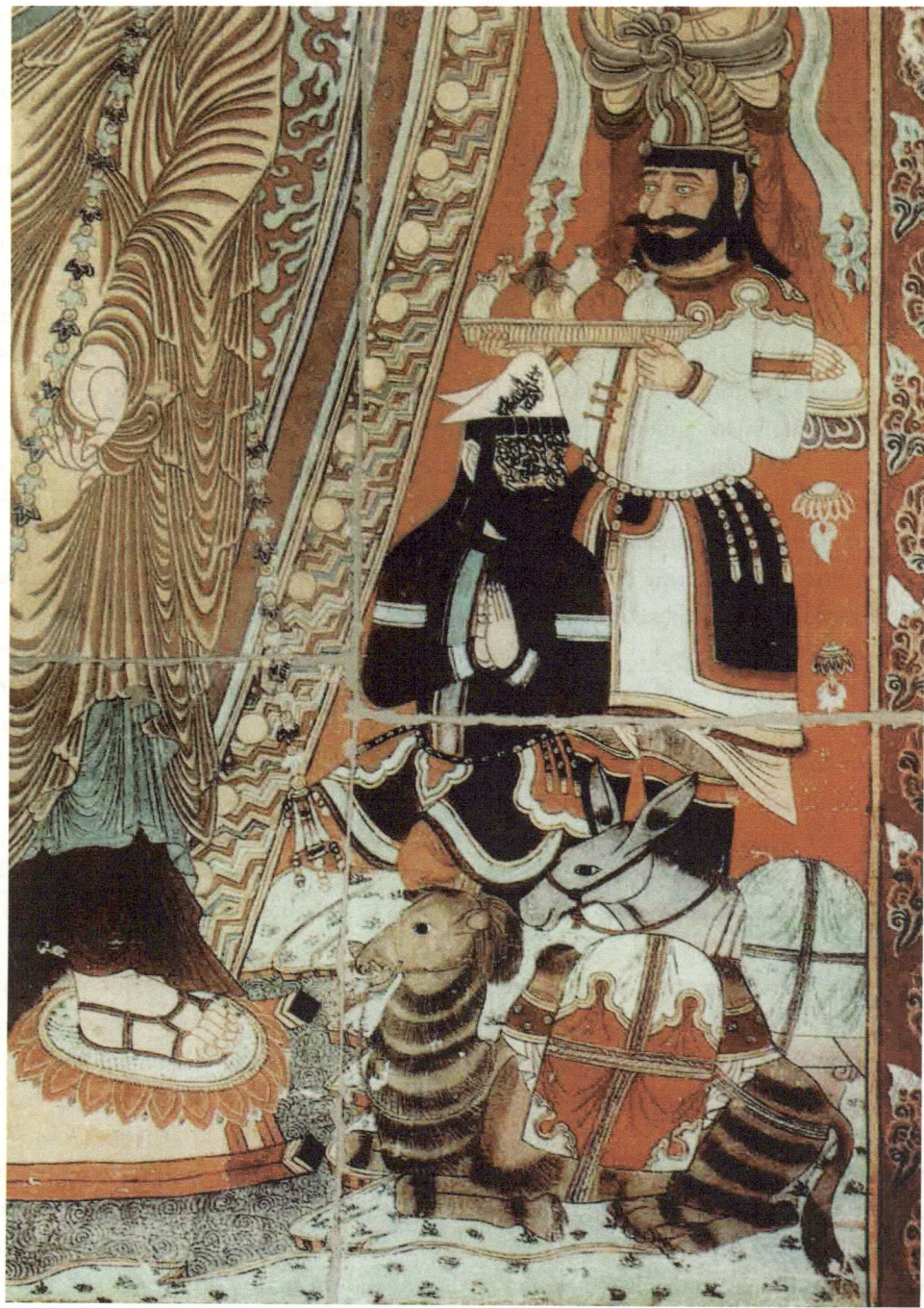

Figure 2-11 Part of the mural of karma story from the 9th to 12th centuries, taken from the inner wall of the north corridor of Cave 20 in Bezeklik (once collected in the Ethnological Museum of Berlin, but destroyed during World War II)

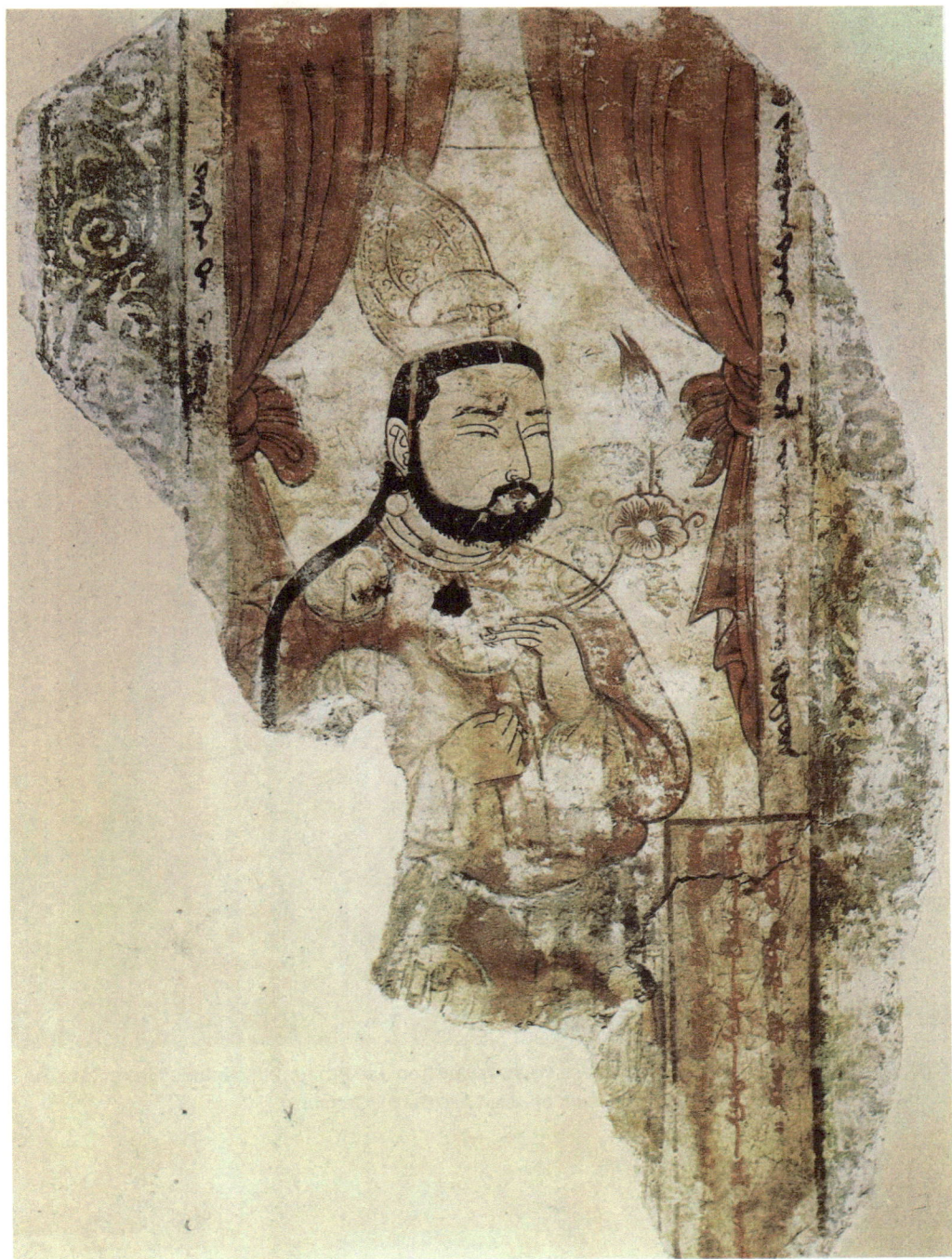

Figure 2-12 *Portrait of the Uyghur King* from the 9th to 12th centuries in Cave 31 of the Bezeklik Caves (now in the Museum of Asian Art, Berlin, Germany)

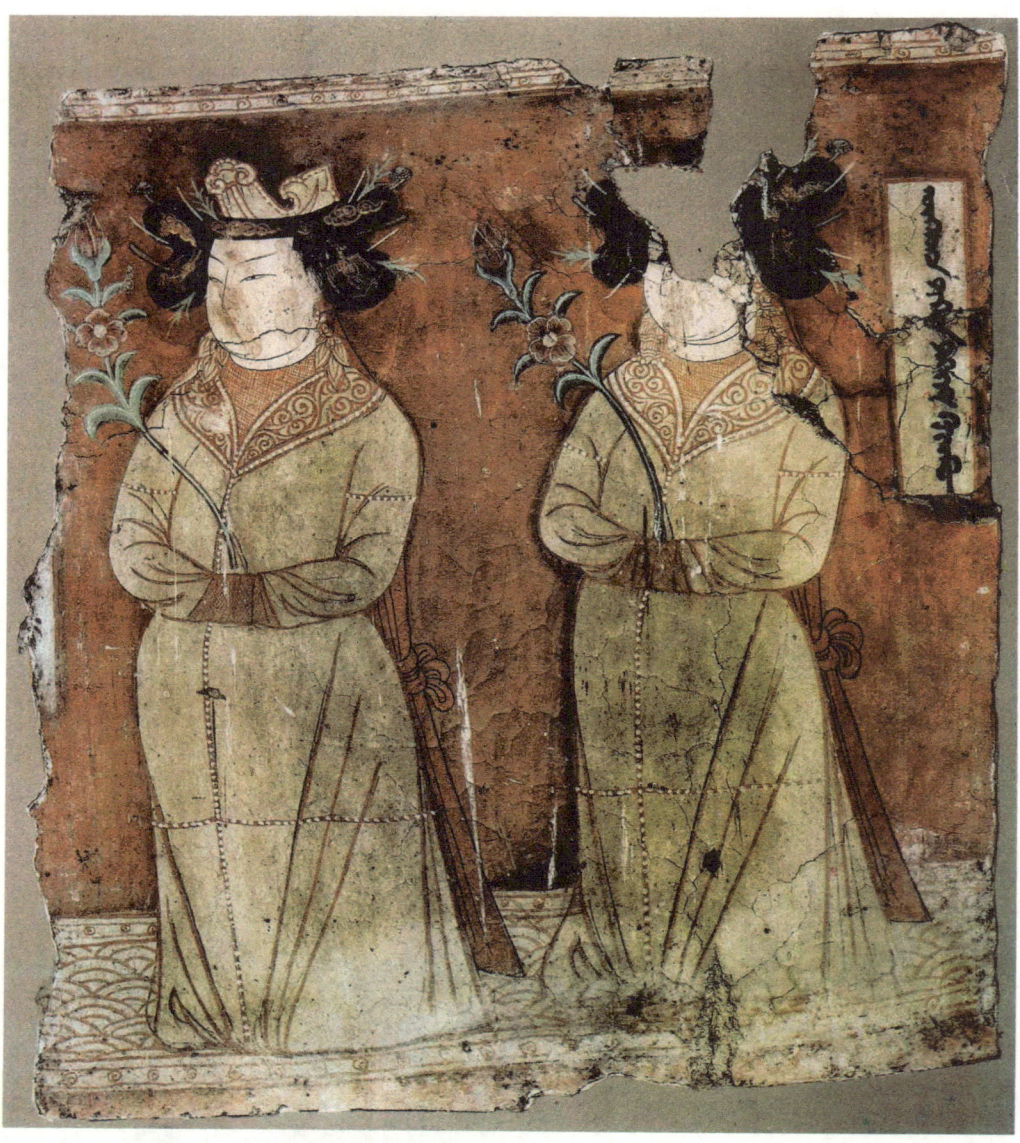

Figure 2-13 *Portrait of Her Royal Highness Princess Joy* from the 9th to 12th centuries from Cave 20 of the Bezeklik Caves (now in the Museum of Asian Art, Berlin, Germany)

as invaluable resources for researching Uyghur-era costumes and crowns and contribute significantly to our understanding of the culture and art of the ancient Uyghur Gaochang Kingdom.

2.4 National Treasures Destroyed during War

In the Bezeklik Caves, the echoes of Buddhist art from the Central Plains resonate alongside the unique artistic tapestry woven by the Uyghurs and the cultural nuances inherited from Kucha and Persia. These revelations substantiate the vibrant tapestry of cultural exchanges between the Turpan Basin, the Central Plains, and the Hexi Corridor. The confluence of Eastern and Western cultures, seamlessly interwoven with the artistic expressions of diverse ethnic groups, gave birth to the unparalleled Turpan art culture.

Yet, in the poignant reality of today, we are left only with the wistful remembrance of the Bezeklik Caves' erstwhile grandeur. The legacy of Le Coq's pillage casts a somber shadow, as a plethora of once-exquisite murals suffered the heartless fate of being mercilessly severed into fragments and transported to Berlin.

In the throes of his plunder, Le Coq rationalized, "Rather than leaving these murals to the erosive whims of nature, let us send them to Berlin for superior protection." Little did he anticipate the cruel twist of fate awaiting these treasures. In the tumultuous year of 1945, as the curtains fell on World War II, the British and American coalition's strategic bombing raids on Germany engulfed Berlin in an inferno. The very city that was meant to safeguard these treasures was reduced to rubble, and the murals Le Coq sought to protect succumbed to the relentless flames of war. Anticipating the impending destruction, the Ethnological Museum of Berlin initiated an ambitious relocation effort to shield cultural relics. However, the monumental challenge of dislodging and relocating the large murals fixed on the exhibition hall walls proved insurmountable (Figure 2-14). The museum staff took a calculated risk, leaving the larger murals in situ, under the assumption that Allied bombs might spare them. Tragically, their gamble failed, and the ruthless bombs obliterated

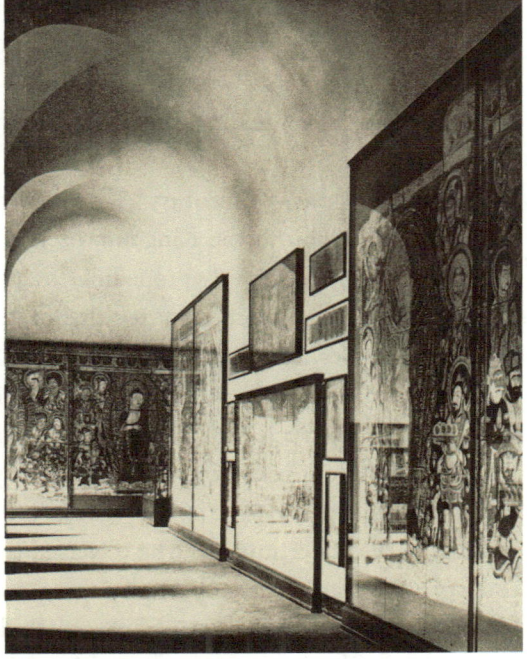

Figure 2-14 Murals from the Bezeklik Caves in the exhibition hall of the Ethnological Museum of Berlin (before 1945)

the museum, along with these irreplaceable murals. Today, only the illustrations preserved in Le Coq's 1913 book echo the original splendor of these lost masterpieces. In addition, the Soviet army engaged in a systematic looting of Berlin, dispersing Chinese cultural relics across museums in Russia, further distancing these treasures from their origins.

The enduring murals of the Bezeklik Caves, standing resilient for over a millennium, were on the cusp of becoming timeless witnesses to history. Alas, destiny had other plans. At the site of the Bezeklik Caves today, Cave 20 stands as a poignant, empty testament to what it once was. The once-looted murals, now reduced to ashes, leave only photographs and written accounts to chronicle this tragic chapter—a history etched in sorrow.

2.5 Explore the Ancient Ruins of Kucha

The final two endeavors of the Prussian Royal Expedition unfolded in 1906 and 1913, marking expeditions that set their sights on Kuqa and Baicheng, nestled along the northern fringes of the Taklimakan Desert. Over several months in each location, the expedition meticulously conducted their "investigations." These regions once formed the heartland of the ancient Kucha Kingdom, a bastion where Buddhism flourished. Particularly, the Kizil Caves stand as an unparalleled repository of Buddhist art, constituting a focal point for the German expedition's endeavors (Figure 2-15).

The Kucha Kingdom, an expansive realm along the Silk Road's northern trajectory in Xinjiang, emerged as a pivotal player. Around the mid-2nd century AD, monks from the Kushan Empire in northwest India traversed into Xinjiang, actively translating Buddhist scriptures and disseminating Buddhism. The people of Kucha gradually embraced Buddhism.

During the mid-3rd century AD, renowned monks from the Kucha Kingdom embarked on a mission to the Kingdom of Wei (AD 220–265) during the Three Kingdoms era (AD 220–280), zealously propelling the cause of Buddhism. By the 4th century, Buddhism in Kucha had reached its zenith, boasting more than 10,000 monks and over 1,000 Buddhist temples and pagodas in the capital area. Palaces adorned with Buddha statues exemplified the pervasive influence of Buddhism. Some temples, adorned with opulence, stood as colossal structures. The 5th and 6th centuries AD emerged as the apogee of Kucha Buddhism's evolution. During this era, an array of cave temples materialized, reflecting the vibrant spiritual and artistic efflorescence. As Xuanzang embarked on his westward journey to India in the 7th century AD, he traversed the Kucha Kingdom. Notably, he observed the country's proficiency in orchestral singing and dancing, surpassing neighboring nations. Here, practitioners delved into Hinayana Buddhism, directly embracing Indian teachings and precepts. The stone caves, nestled in secluded mountains and forests, resonated with the contemplative needs of monks, embodying the Kucha Kingdom's inclination to employ caves as pivotal Buddhist sanctuaries.

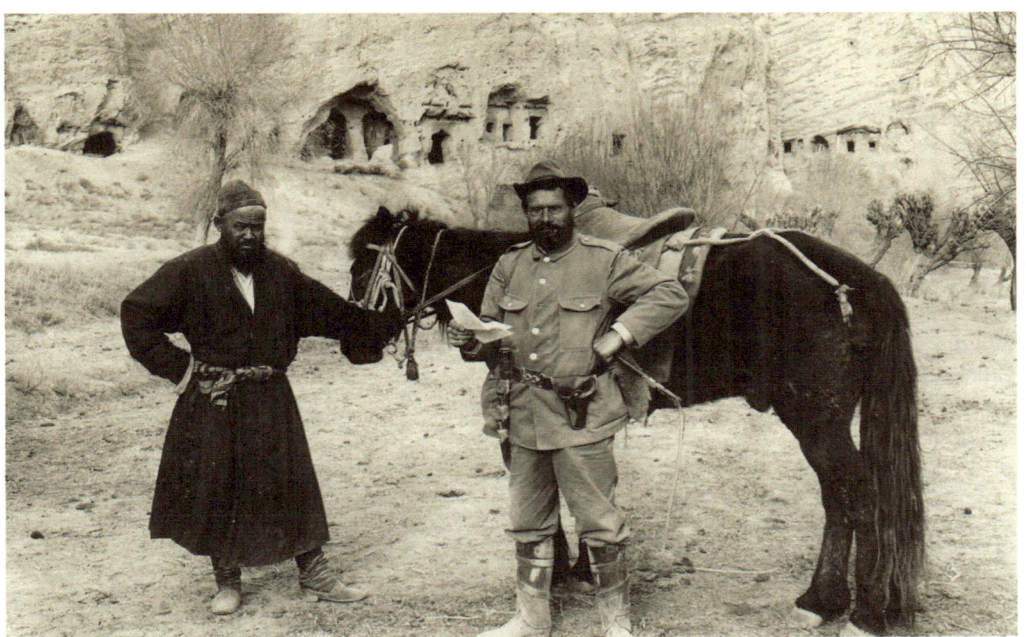

Figure 2-15 Le Coq in front of the Kizil Caves in Baicheng, Xinjiang (1906)

There is an expanse of caves adorning the narrow east-west corridor of the Kucha Kingdom. Kuqa and Baicheng emerge as focal points. In Kuqa, marvels like Kumutura, Kizilgaha, Mazabaha, and Senmusaimu Caves beckon, while Baicheng proudly hosts Kizil, Taitaier, and Wenbashi Grottoes. Xinhe County, on the other hand, boasts Tuohulakeaiken. And the Kizil Caves reign supreme, standing as the largest and most enduring in the Kucha expanse.

Perched on the cliff along the north bank of the Muzati Valley in the southeast of Kizil Town, Baicheng County, this treasure trove encompasses 236 caves, over 70 of which house mesmerizing murals (Figure 2-16). Originating from the late 3rd century AD to the early 8th century AD, these caves initially served as sanctuaries, housing Buddhist halls, lecture halls, sermon halls, monks' quarters, and various living spaces. Now, the intricate layout includes central pillar caves and statue caves for worship (Figure 2-17), square caves for preaching, as well as contemplative spaces like monks' quarters and zen caves. Together, they harmoniously constitute a comprehensive temple system.

In the annals of exploration, the Kizil Caves attracted attention as early as 1903 when Japanese scholars Watanabe Teshin and Horiuchi Kenyu extracted murals and excavated cultural relics. On February 26, 1906, the third German expedition team arrived. Led by Grünwedel, the team comprised luminaries such as Le Coq, Bartus, and H. Pohrt (Figure 2-18). Upon reaching the Kizil area, situated approximately 60 kilometers southeast of Baicheng County, the expedition was greeted with a revelation from a local guide. This informant shared that a cluster of concealed caves lay nestled near the mountains, a locale

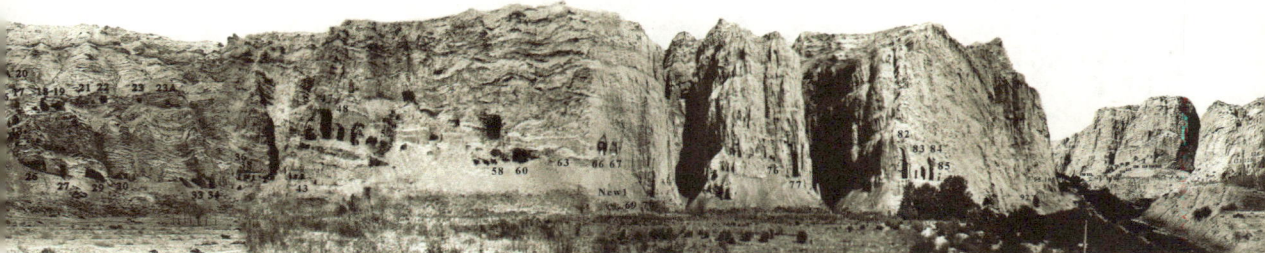

Figure 2-16 Appearance of the Kizil Caves in Baicheng, Xinjiang, 1906–1907 (photographed by Grünwedel)

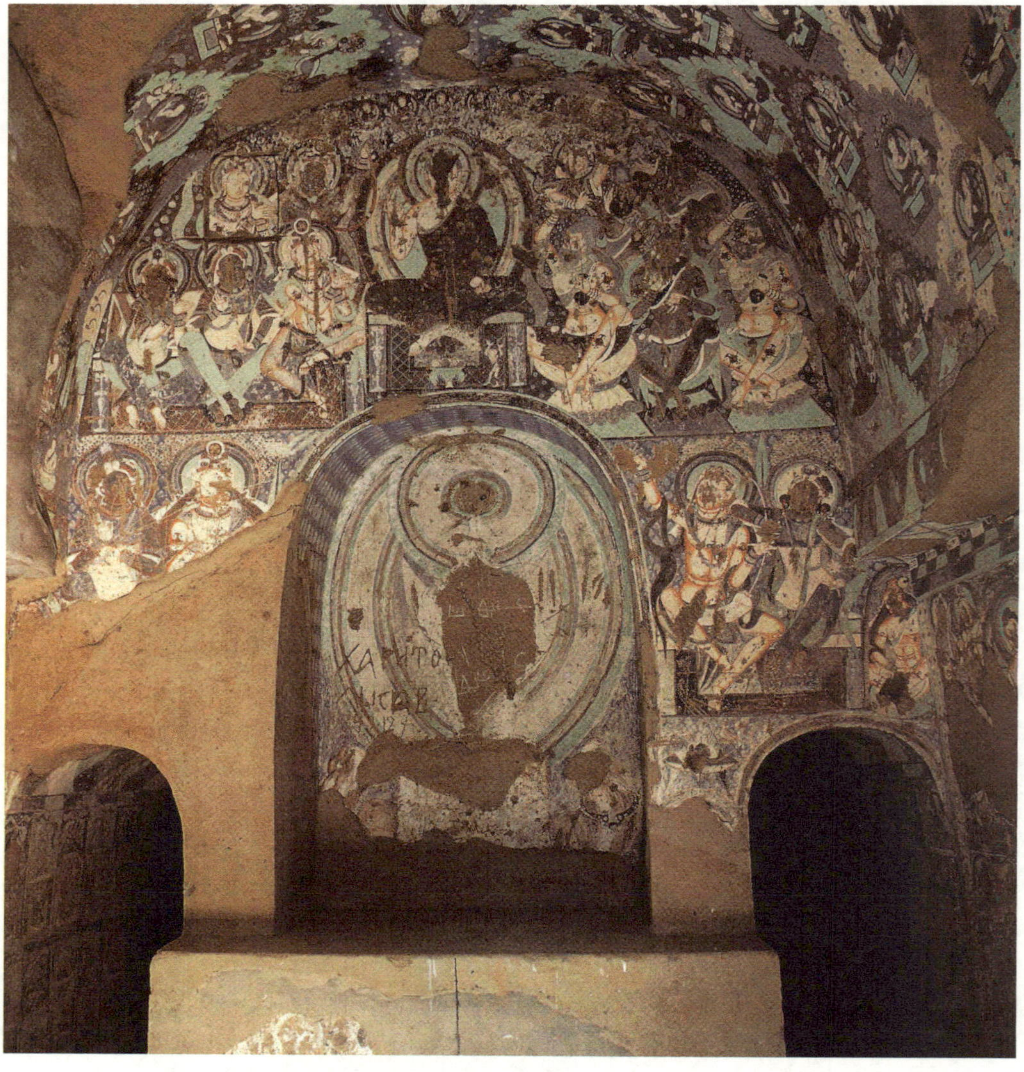

Figure 2-17 A panoramic view of the main wall of Cave 80 of Kizil Caves in Baicheng, Xinjiang

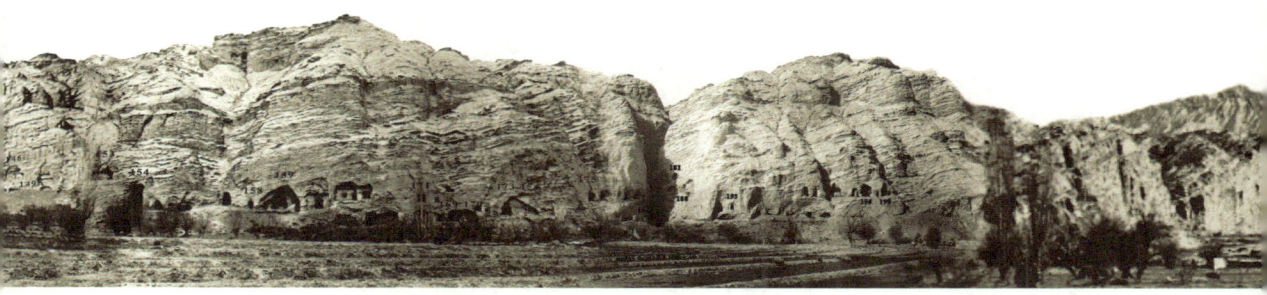

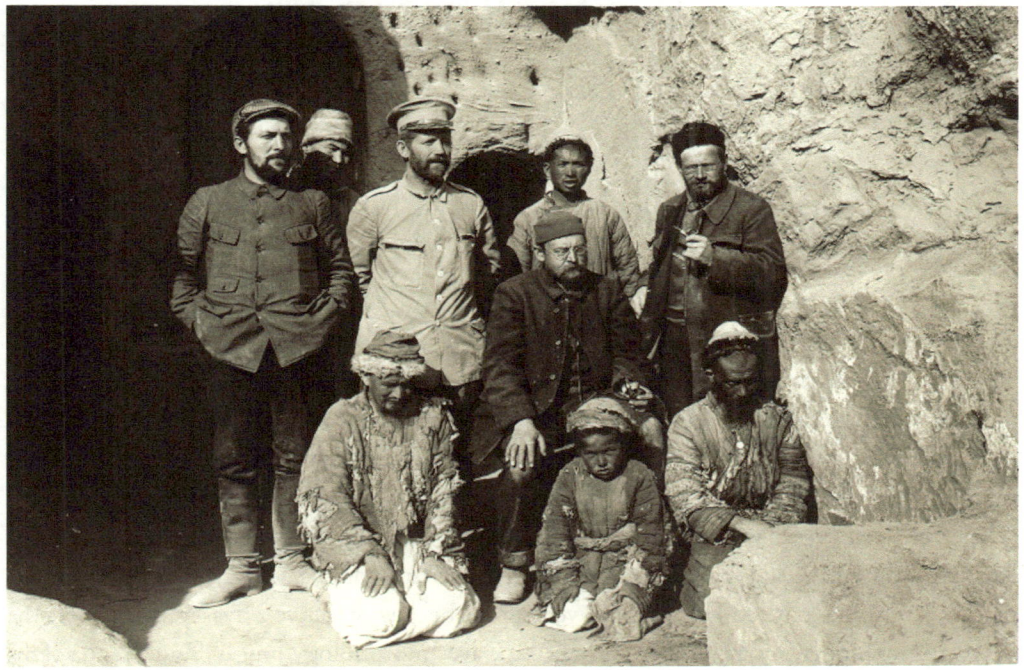

Figure 2-18 The third German Turpan Expedition took a group photo in Cave 4 of the Kizil Caves in Baicheng, Xinjiang (Grünwedel sits in the middle, Le Coq is first from the right in the back row, Bartus is wearing a military uniform in the middle of the back row, and the first from the left in the back row is Pohrt, 1906)

where previous Japanese explorers had toiled for an extensive three-month span. Promptly, Le Coq and Bartus embarked on horseback to investigate. Their journey led them to a remarkable find—an enigmatic village adorned with hundreds of caves, perched on the cliff of a mountain overlooking the river. Le Coq and his companions secured two modest huts from a local farmer, establishing a base for a meticulous exploration and excavation initiative. In this captivating landscape, Grünwedel, with a primary focus on archaeological

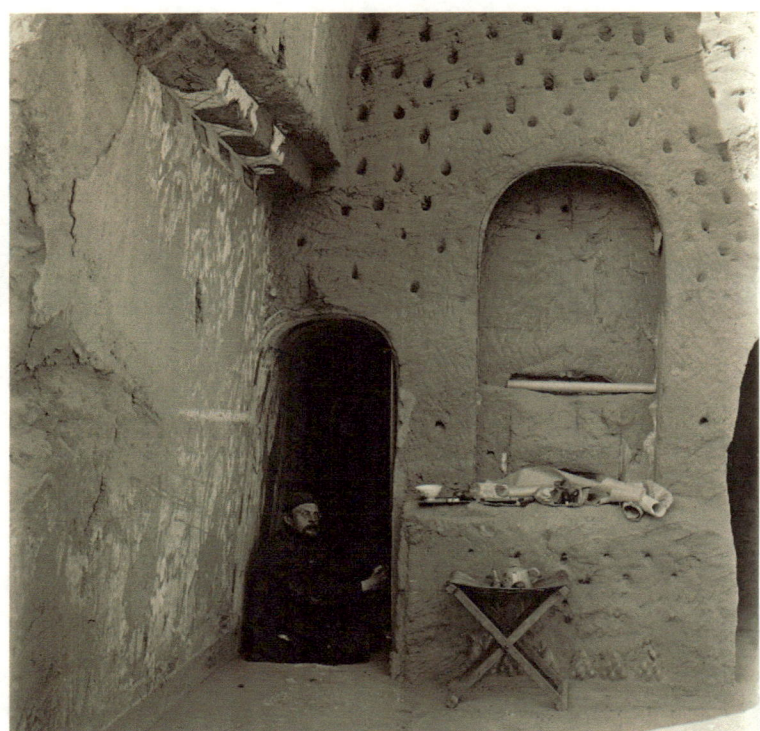

Figure 2-19 Grünwedel recorded the murals in Cave 4 of the Kizil Caves (1906)

scrutiny and documentation, meticulously chronicled the cave shapes, mural content, layouts, and decorative intricacies (Figure 2-19). Concurrently, Le Coq and Bartus, with a spirit of intrepid discovery, uncovered a trove of treasures within some caves—precious ancient manuscripts, wood panel paintings, statues, and fragments of murals and other cultural relics. Pohrt, entrusted with the task of photography, skillfully captured the external allure of the caves, their intricate structures, and the mesmerizing murals, undertook measurements of the caves, and created comprehensive maps. This investigative odyssey completed the surveying, mapping, and recording of the Kizil Caves' morphology, mural themes, and spatial distribution. Amid this thorough examination, each cave was meticulously numbered and bestowed with a name.

In this notable expedition, the team meticulously extracted a segment of cave murals, unveiling a treasure trove of ancient manuscripts. The culmination of the second expedition resulted in the repatriation of an impressive collection of 224 crates brimming with cultural relics to Germany. The credit for the delicate task of excising the Kizil Caves' murals primarily rests with Le Coq. In his vivid portrayal of the cave's murals, Le Coq remarked, "The artworks found in this sanctuary stand as the most exquisite we have encountered in Xinjiang. They depict the myriad forms of the legendary Buddha and the diverse scenes in which he is portrayed, bearing distinct traces of pure ancient Greek characteristics." Le Coq was referring to the captivating paintings illustrating Buddhist karma stories and Jataka stories adorning the side walls and summit of the front chamber's central pillar in Kizil. Le Coq fervently championed the removal of everything from the caves, with a particular emphasis on the murals. His ambitious plan even included transporting the entire dome of a small Buddhist temple laden with murals back to Berlin. However, Grünwedel dissented, advocating for a comprehensive approach that involved measuring, mapping, and studying the site as a whole. He foresaw that moving the artifacts would compromise the integrity of the site. Although Le Coq reluctantly compromised on this occasion, a subsequent expedition led by him resulted in the removal of the frescoed dome (Figure 2-20).

The fourth German Turpan Expedition, spearheaded by Le Coq and accompanied solely by Bartus, embarked on its journey, arriving at the mesmerizing Kizil Caves on

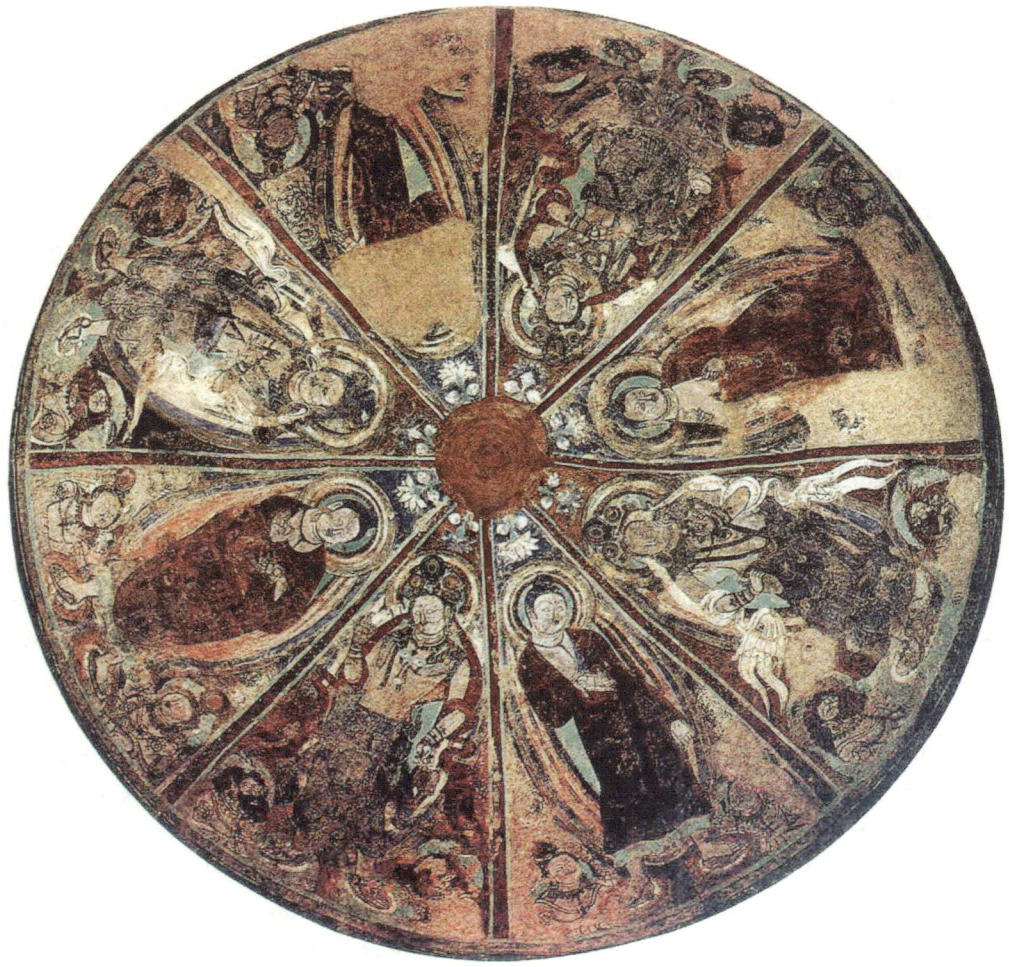

Figure 2-20 Taken from the dome of the main chamber of Cave 123 of the Kizil Caves (now in the Museum of Asian Art, Berlin, Germany)

July 1, 1913. Commencing their endeavor the very next day, unencumbered by Grünwedel's influence, Le Coq forged ahead with confidence and audacity. The primary mission of this expedition was crystal clear: to delicately sever the captivating murals, meticulously package them into crates, and transport these cultural treasures back to Berlin. The tally of this endeavor surpassed that of its predecessors, with a staggering 156 crates laden with cultural relics being carefully extracted from Xinjiang.

2.6 The Murals Taken from the Kizil Caves

When Le Coq and his companions delicately selected murals for extraction in Kizil, their discerning eye sought out pieces boasting superior preservation and profound expressive content—what they deemed exquisite masterpieces. Within the Kizil Caves, the central pillar cave and the statue cave emerged as the focal points of the cavernous ensemble, serving as sacred spaces where devout monks paid homage to the Buddha. Notably, the central pillar cave, in this context, did not adhere to the typical design featuring a tower pillar at the center of the cave chamber. Unlike the Indian Chaitya Caves encircling pagodas for reciprocal worship, a concept that transcended to Kucha and garnered the favor of believers, the sandstone texture of the Kizil Caves proved too fragile to mimic the lofty and expansive caves of India. Consequently, skilled craftsmen, guided by the visions of the monks, transformed the Indian Chitaya Cave into a grand rectangular cavern with a soaring ceiling. They intricately carved a Buddhist niche into the central point of the main wall, housing a statue of Sakyamuni—an homage to the cave's primary purpose of idol worship. Adjacent to the main niche on the main wall, a semicircular corridor was hewn inward, facilitating worship around the corridor. The substantial mass retained in the center, coupled with the Buddhist niche on the front wall, symbolized the pagoda in the Indian Chaitya Cave. This metamorphosis gave rise to the original central pillar cave of the Kucha Kingdom (Figure 2-17). The statue cave served a parallel function, with the key distinction lying in the absence of a niche on the main cave wall. Instead, a commanding standing Buddha statue, towering over 10 meters, took center stage. Flanking the colossal Buddha, the lower portions faced the same direction, while a corridor was later excavated to accommodate the devout believers' acts of worship.

Contemporary visits to the Kizil Caves may not reveal the vibrant hues of the sculptures that once adorned its interiors. Nevertheless, thanks to the diligent efforts of Le Coq and his contemporaries, a substantial collection of painted heads and busts has been unearthed from the Kizil Caves, standing as invaluable artifacts for the scholarly exploration of Kizil's painted sculptures. These figures, with distinctly European-style countenances, stand bare from the waist up, adorned with intricately crafted necklaces and ornaments. Facial features are meticulously captured, with some sporting mustaches on their lips. Their voluminous hair is artfully fashioned into intricate buns atop their heads, and in some instances, regal crowns grace their figures. The sculptures, characterized by their remarkable realism, portray either Bodhisattvas or celestial beings (Figure 2-21).

The narrative woven into the murals of the central pillar cave revolves around the theme of Sakyamuni. Above the cave door on the front wall of the front chamber, one typically encounters a mural of Maitreya Bodhisattva preaching, destined to become a Buddha in the future world. The central ridge of the cave roof is adorned with celestial phenomena such as

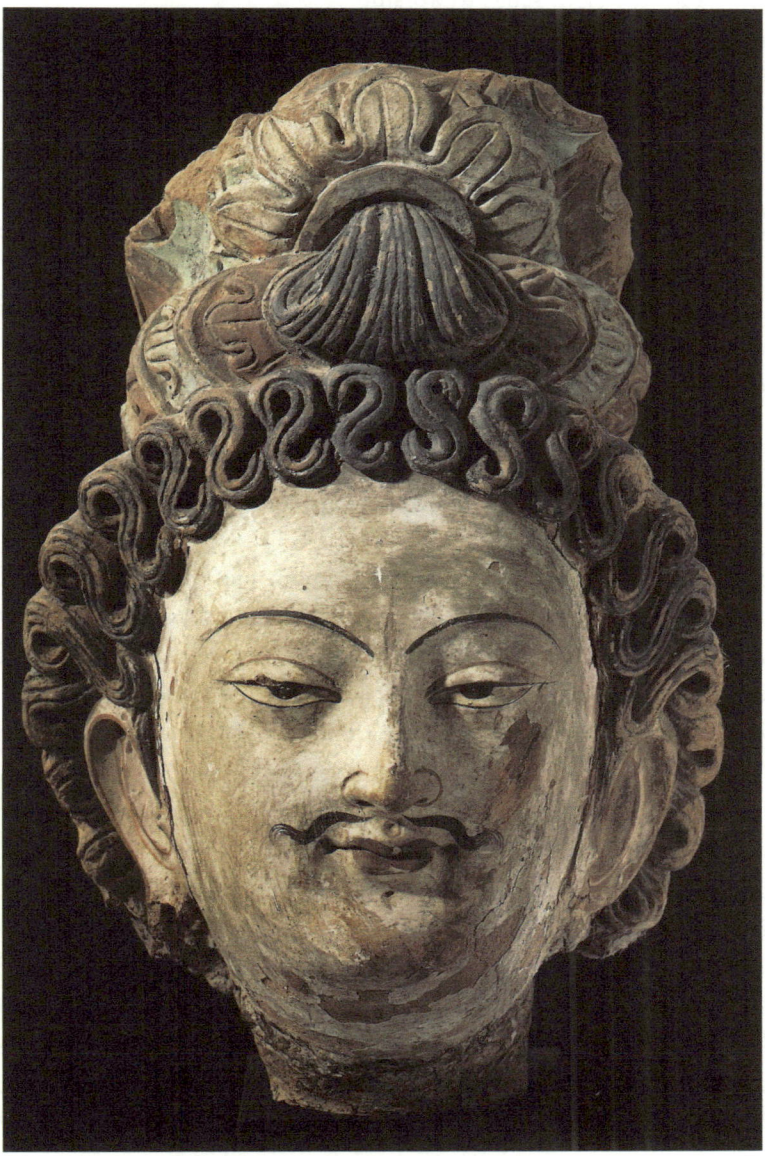

Figure 2-21 A clay sculpture of a Bodhisattva or a celestial being head from the 5th to 6th centuries in Cave 77 of the Kizil Caves (38 cm high, now in the Museum of Asian Art, Berlin, Germany)

the sun, moon, and wind gods, alongside standing Buddha statues holding alms bowls. The curved surface at the apex of the cave reveals intricately drawn interlaced diamond-shaped grids illustrating karma and Jataka stories; the left and right walls are divided into upper and lower layers of squares, each hosting murals portraying Buddhist stories centered around Buddha within the grid. In the back chamber, composed of corridors, murals unfold around the narrative of Sakyamuni's Nirvana. This encompassing storyline includes depictions of Sakyamuni's birth, entering Nirvana, mourning with disciples, burning coffins, and the division of Śarīra for the eight kings to worship.

Why is there an abundance of stories related to Sakyamuni in the worship cave? The answer lies in the profound emphasis Hinayana believers place on personal practice and liberation. The distinctive feature of Kucha Hinayana Buddhism lies in its emphasis on meditation practice. The term "zen," originating from the Sanskrit word for "quiet meditation" and "thinking cultivation," underscores the imperative for Buddhists to concentrate on one situation, eliminate distracting thoughts, and attain complete liberation. Embracing Sakyamuni as a guiding light in the art of zen, Buddhists find profound inspiration in the invaluable tapestry of the Buddha's successful journey through numerous lifetimes of dedicated practice. Therefore, they must see it first: as one enters the central pillar cave, the focal point is the Buddha statue in the main niche. Subsequently, attention is directed to the side walls and cave top, adorned with Buddhist biographies and karma and Jataka paintings. Navigating the space, practitioners encounter scenes of Buddha's birth, Nirvana, and murals depicting the eight kings dividing Śarīra and constructing pagodas for worshipping.

Among the murals excised by Le Coq, a standout piece is the exquisite semicircular portrait of cross-legged Maitreya Bodhisattva and attendants, originating from the front chamber of a central pillar cave above the cave door (Figure 2-22). Maitreya Bodhisattva is portrayed with a bare upper body, a lower-body skirt, and a silk cloth draped behind the shoulders. Holding the Dharma seal with the right hand, Maitreya sits with legs crossed at the ankles, signifying his residence in the Tusita Celestial Palace, preaching the Dharma—a manifestation of the future Buddha. Flanking Maitreya are four celestial beings, attired similarly and sitting with crossed feet and hands in front of their chests, looking devout, some engaged in dialogue, creating a warm and engaging atmosphere.

A captivating artifact known as the *Coffin Burning Illustration*, housed in the Museum of Asian Art, Berlin, originates from the inner wall of a corridor within a central pillar cave in the Kizil Caves (Figure 2-23). At its heart, the mural portrays a wooden coffin cradling the revered remains of Sakyamuni, adorned with delicate lacquer artwork. It shows flames gracefully ascending from the coffin lid, signifying the poignant act of cremation. Positioned to the left, a disciple tenderly opens the coffin, revealing Sakyamuni's reclined form. His gaze is fixed upon a woman in the lower left corner, her outstretched arms reaching toward him. The sides of the coffin are adorned with depictions of celestial beings presenting treasures and disciples solemnly joining hands in mourning. The overall composition

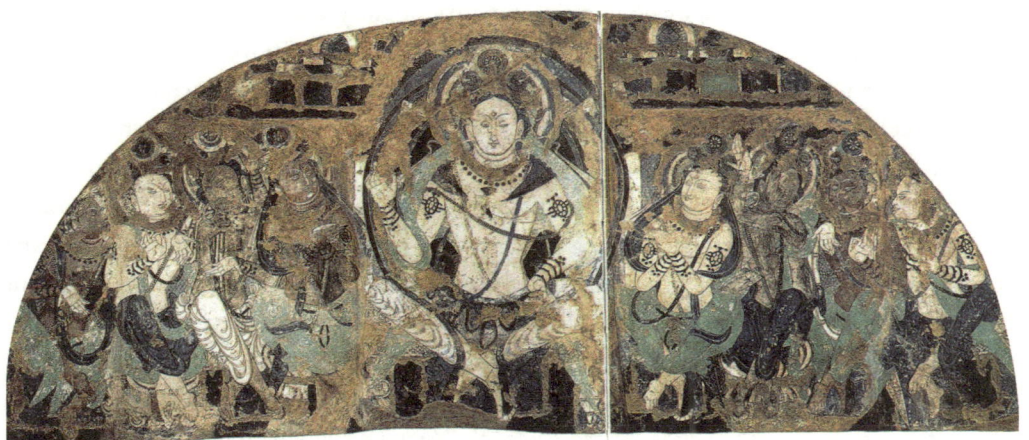

Figure 2-22 The mural of cross-legged Maitreya Bodhisattva and attendants on the front wall of Cave 224 of Kizil Caves above the cave door (now in the Museum of Asian Art, Berlin, Germany)

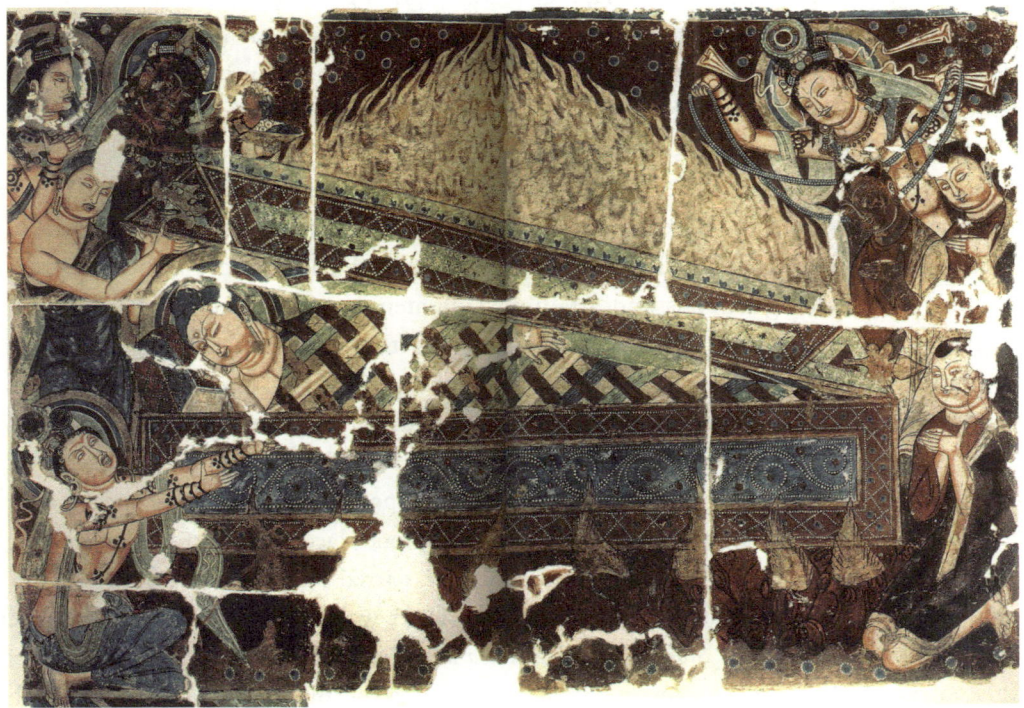

Figure 2-23 *Coffin Burning Illustration* from the back chamber corridor of Cave 205 of Kizil Caves from the 4th to 6th centuries (now in the Museum of Asian Art, Berlin, Germany)

radiates a solemn ambiance, weaving a rich tapestry of storytelling. The backstory unfolds with Lady Maya, Sakyamuni's mother, who, having passed away shortly after his birth, resided in heaven. Upon learning of Sakyamuni's imminent entry into Nirvana, she descended from the celestial realms, yearning for a final glimpse of her son. Tragically, by the time she arrived, Sakyamuni had already transitioned into Nirvana, and his funeral pyre blazed. Yet, employing his supernatural prowess, he miraculously opened the burning coffin, allowing for a poignant reunion with his grieving mother. While depictions of Sakyamuni's Nirvana abound in Buddhist art throughout China, the rarity of artworks capturing the poignant meeting of mother and son amid the backdrop of a burning coffin renders this particular piece exceptionally precious.

Among the murals taken by Le Coq, one that stands out in its exquisite detail is the *Story of King Ajatasaratu Knowing the Buddha's Nirvana*, which graced the inner wall of the left corridor within Cave 205 (Figure 2-24). Delving into its narrative roots, the *Sarvastivada Vinaya Miscellany*, as translated by the venerable Tang Dynasty monk Yijing (AD 635–713), recounts the tale of Ajatasaratu, the monarch of Rajagaha in ancient India, who embraced Buddhism and became a devoted lay disciple of the Buddha. Following the Buddha's transcendence into Nirvana, the Buddha's principal disciple, Kāśyapa, harbored concerns that the news might shatter King Ajatasaratu. Fearing the monarch's potential demise from shock, Kāśyapa summoned Varshakara, a trusted minister, and readied various emergency remedies. The bath jar brimmed with freshly curdled butter and the alluring fragrance of sandalwood perfume. The stage was set as they beckoned the king to the tranquil confines of the garden. Within the serene confines of the garden, King Ajatasaratu beheld a transcendent *Four Phases Diagram* gracefully unveiled by Varshakara. This intricate tableau unfolded the profound chapters of Sakyamuni's existence: from his birth to subduing demons and attaining enlightenment, followed by the poignant moment of delivering his inaugural sermon (turning the wheel of Dharma for the first time in Sarnath) and culminating in the serene bliss of Nirvana. These visual vignettes subtly hinted at the trajectory that the Buddha would traverse in his earthly sojourn. In a sudden realization, King Ajatasaratu knew the truth that the Buddha had entered Nirvana. Overwhelmed by this revelation, he uttered poignant wails before succumbing to a momentary unconsciousness. Hastily, his ministers placed him amid the aromatic allure of butter and perfume, where, gradually, he stirred back to consciousness. This poignant episode finds artistic expression on the inner wall of the left corridor of Cave 205, immortalized as the *Story of King Ajatasaratu Knowing the Buddha's Nirvana*. In this portrayal, the intricate narrative indirectly unfolds the Buddha's life to the faithful, using the poignant scene of King Ajatasaratu learning about the Buddha's Nirvana as a narrative device. What sets this masterpiece apart is the unique canvas held by Varshakara, which depicts four distinct storylines: the divine descent of Sakyamuni at his birth, the transformative sermon in Sarnath, subduing demons and attaining enlightenment, and the serene culmination of Nirvana under the sāla. The composition is harmoniously complete,

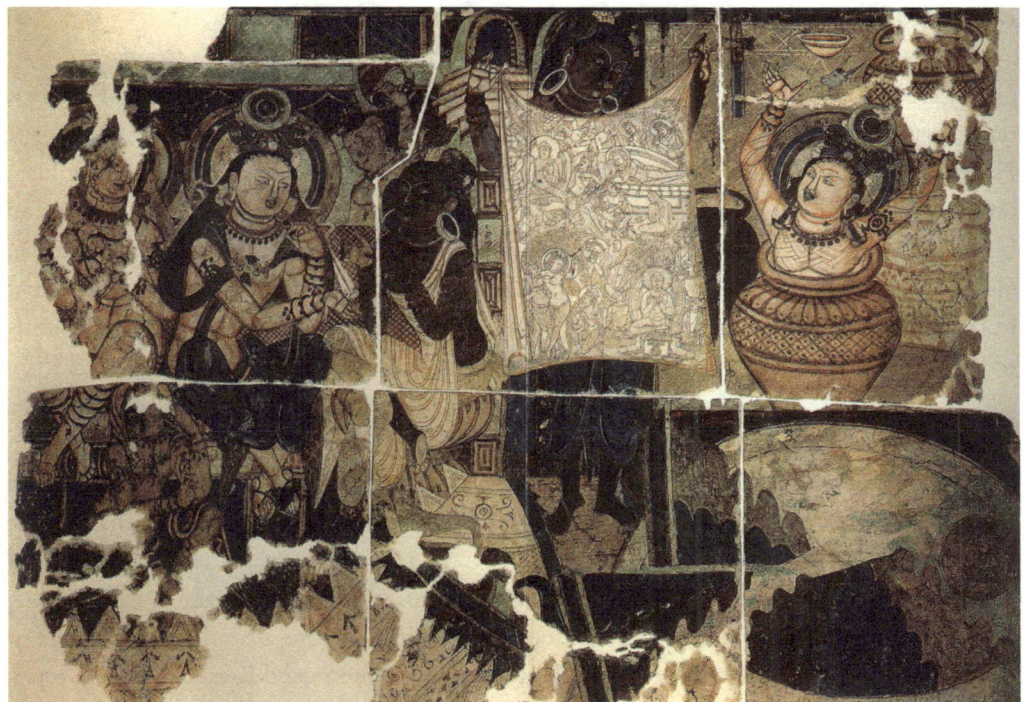

Figure 2-24 The *Story of King Ajatasaratu Knowing the Buddha's Nirvana* in the 4th to 6th century, from the inner wall of the left corridor of Cave 205 of the Kizil Caves (once in Ethnological Museum of Berlin, but destroyed during World War II)

and the meticulous line work renders it a standalone masterpiece, earning it the moniker of a "painting of paintings" (Figure 2-25). Regrettably, the ravages of World War II erased this beautiful mural from the annals of time.

The mesmerizing mural art of the Kizil Caves not only embodies the distinctive and robust stylistic traits of the Kucha Kingdom but also bears the indelible imprint of influence from the rich tapestry of Indian and Central Asian Persian cultures. These artistic marvels serve as living testaments to the profound interweaving of the Kucha region's cultural tapestry with the vast expanse west of Congling. In our contemporary exploration of Kizil murals, it is imperative to cast our gaze not only upon the well-preserved murals within the caves but also to immerse ourselves in the curated collection housed at the Museum of Asian Art in Berlin, Germany.

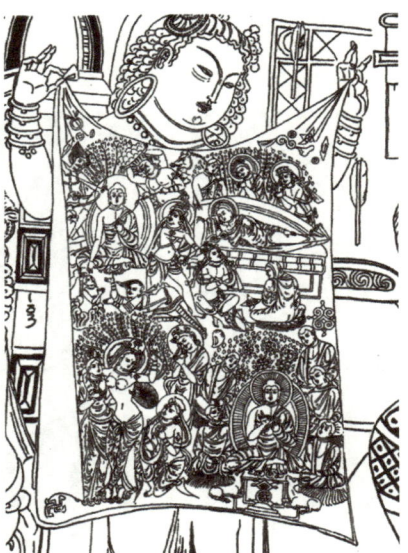

Figure 2-25 Partial survey drawing of the *Story of King Ajatasaratu Knowing the Buddha's Nirvana*, painted by Grünwedel

2.7 The Shorchuk Temple Statues Taken Overseas

Today's Yanqi Hui Autonomous County in Xinjiang, nestled in the embrace of history, once served as the regal seat of the Yanqi Kingdom, a lineage that flourished from the Han to the Tang Dynasty. A mere 30 kilometers northwest of Yanqi County unfolds a tapestry of antiquity called the Shorchuk Temple, a Uyghur term translating to "thousand houses." It comprises of two temple ruins, one to the south and the other to the north, along with a quaint grotto group. The grandeur of the south and north temples is evident in their substantial size, featuring main halls, monks' quarters, pagodas, and other architectural relics. The construction of these edifices, characterized by walls fashioned from adobes interspersed with reeds and grass, is believed to date back to the Tang Dynasty, extending through the Yuan Dynasty. However, a closer inspection reveals whispers from the Northern and Southern Dynasties period, as evidenced by the broken Buddha and Bodhisattva statues and scattered remnants of bricks found behind the main hall of the South Temple.

On the southern slope of the northwest mountain adjacent to the north temple, approximately ten grottoes were meticulously excavated (Figure 2-26). Notably, some of these grottoes share a cave structure similar to that of the renowned Kizil Caves. However, the distinctiveness of Caves 1, 2, and 3 sets them apart: within these caves, a rectangular low altar graces the cave floor. Positioned behind this altar is a sizable back screen that seamlessly ascends to the cave's ceiling, enveloping both the altar and the back screen itself. This architectural feature serves a dual purpose, emulating the function and visual impact of a central pillar cave—an innovative Buddhist altar cave, mirroring the structures

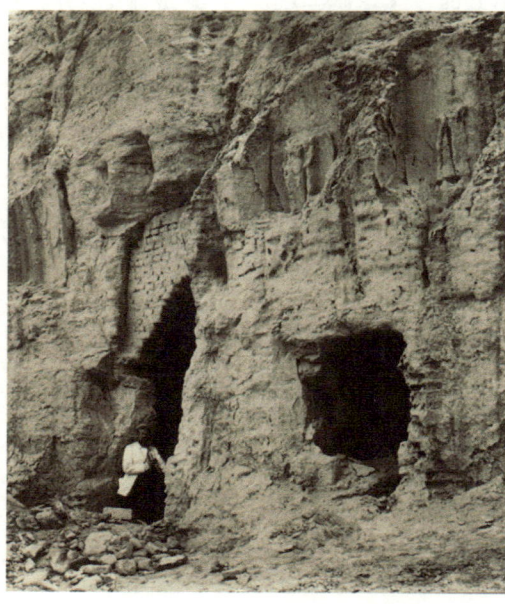

Figure 2-26 The appearance of the Shorchuk Temple photographed by the German expedition team (1900s)

of terrestrial temples and halls. What makes these caves truly exceptional is the absence of counterparts elsewhere in Xinjiang. Yet, intriguing parallels can be drawn with the Dunhuang Mogao Grottoes to the east of Yanqi, where large Buddhist altars gained popularity during the late Tang and Five Dynasties periods, exhibiting a similar basic structure. Moreover, the Yanqi Buddhist Altar Cave reveals captivating artistic details, including cloud patterns and intertwining branches painted on its ceiling. Cave 4's main chamber showcases an elaborate composition of wavy branches and vines, adorned with depictions of Bodhisattvas or Lotus Children, featuring embellishments of cloud heads, camellias, and curled leaves—each element exuding a distinct Han nationality artistic flair. In AD 692, Wu Zetian (AD 624–705) designated Yanqi as one of the four towns under the Anxi Protectorate, marking it as a hub of frequent activities for the Han people. The distinct cave shapes and mural styles with Han characteristics observed in the Shorchuk Temple suggest that these artistic elements might have been introduced by Han monks post the 8th century. A closer examination of the murals in Caves 7 and 8 of the Shorchuk Temple reveals the presence of a rhombus checkered pattern typical of the Kucha style, a technique originating from the Kuqa and Baicheng regions. These artistic phenomena vividly illustrate the profound cultural impact left by Buddhist monks traversing from east to west, imprinting Yanqi as a significant town in the expansive northern desert landscape.

During multiple expeditions in the early 20th century, Le Coq and his team explored and excavated Buddhist artifacts in Yanqi, extracting a significant number of exquisite Buddhist sculptures from China. The majority of these sculptures were crafted during the 7th and 8th centuries AD, corresponding to the zenith of the Tang Dynasty and the peak era of Buddhism's development in the Yanqi Kingdom.

One notable artifact is a clay sculpture of a seated Buddha (Figure 2-27), now housed in the Museum of Asian Art in Berlin, which was acquired by Le Coq from the Shorchuk Temple. This statue stands at 66 centimeters, featuring water ripples on the surface of the ushnisha and bun. The Buddha's countenance is akin to a melon seed, with downward-looking eyes emanating compassion. The distinctive shaping of eyebrows and nose aligns with the characteristic style of Gandhara Buddha statues, presenting an overall appearance that uniquely reflects European influences. Clad in a cassock with the right shoulder exposed, the attire adheres closely to the body, accentuating the Buddha's aesthetically pleasing features such as a tall chest, slender waist, and trim abdomen. This sculpture, rooted in Gandhara style, illustrates the enduring influence of Gandhara on the countries along the northern desert route even during the 7th and 8th centuries AD. It is noteworthy, however, that the influence of the Gandhara style during this period was not as dominant as it was in earlier times. While inheriting the traditional artistry of Gandhara, the Yanqi Kingdom concurrently absorbed the cultural nuances of the Tang Empire. For instance, within the Shorchuk Temple caves, numerous standing Buddha statues bear a resemblance to those from the Tang Dynasty.

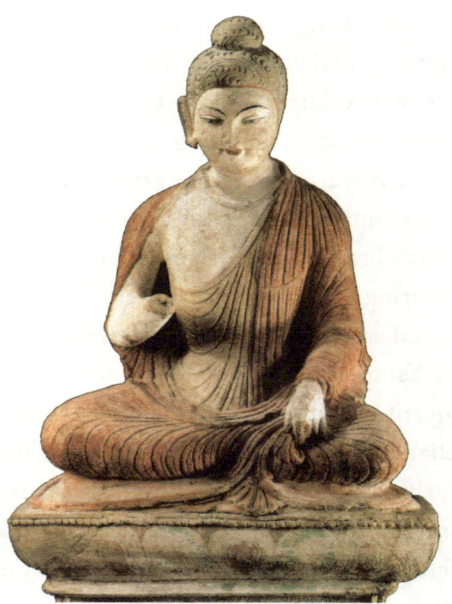

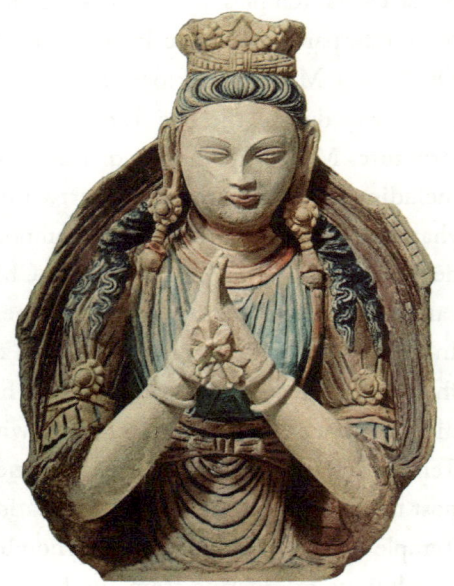

Figure 2-27 Seated Buddha statue from the Shorchuk Temple (now in the Museum of Asian Art, Berlin, Germany)

Figure 2-28 Deity statues from the Shorchuk Temple (now in the Museum of Asian Art, Berlin, Germany)

The celestial beings statues within the confines of the Shorchuk Temple possess round faces with delicately pointed lower jaws. Their eyebrows and noses pay homage to the enduring traditions of Greek and Roman sculptures. Yet, the harmonious synthesis of these features finds its distinctive expression in the cultural tapestry of the Kucha region. Adorned in celestial grandeur, these deities don flower crowns upon their heads, their cascading hair gracefully draping over bare shoulders. Bedecked with necklaces, armlets, *yingluo*,* and bracelets, they have their lower bodies clad in long skirts. The statues' physique resonates with plumpness and health. The figures often don silk cloth, elegantly draped around their shoulders, forming expansive half circles (Figure 2-28). These features collectively constitute the defining characteristics of the celestial being statues lining the Silk Road in North Xinjiang. This artistic legacy finds echoes in the ancient Kucha Kingdom, with analogous statues discovered in Baicheng and Bachu. Evidently, the statues of celestial beings in the Yanqi Kingdom perpetuate and cherish the artistic traditions of Kucha, underscoring its central role in their developmental narrative.

The concept of celestial beings, denoting sentient beings inhabiting the heavens of the desired realm, and those in the form realm, traces its roots to ancient Indian folk beliefs. This belief system seamlessly integrated into Hinayana Buddhism, evolving into a pervasive element of Buddhist worship. Master Xuanzang's records reveal the prevalence of

* A ring-shaped neck ornament or fashion jewellery.

Hinayana Buddhism in the Yanqi Kingdom during that era. In alignment with Hinayana doctrines, which acknowledge only Sakyamuni as the current Buddha, the ultimate goal for believers is to attain liberation from the cycle of reincarnation and achieve the status of Arhat. Consequently, the prospect of ascending to heavenly realms in the afterlife became a cherished aspiration for ordinary believers. In the eyes of these devotees, the celestial realms offered a sublime beauty far surpassing that of the mortal world. Thus, the abundance of statues depicting celestial beings was made within the temples and grottoes of Hinayana Buddhism in the Yanqi Kingdom.

Within the Shorchuk Temple, a multitude of clay statues, christened as Brahmin by Western explorers, have emerged, unveiling distinctive features that resonate with the essence of Central Asian aesthetics: their hair elegantly coiled into buns adorned with cloth, eyes exuding profound depth, and prominent high noses, all set against an aura of contemplation. Their countenance is marked by stern eyebrows, figure-eight mustaches, and curly beards, evoking an expression of solemn intensity. Well-preserved full-length statues depict these Brahmin as being bare-chested, adorned solely in shorts. Their upper bodies, however, are bedecked with necklaces, *yingluo*, armlets, and bracelets—mirroring the regal embellishments adorning the Bodhisattva statues. The silk draping gracefully behind their shoulders forms elegant half circles (Figure 2-29). Historically, Brahmins occupied the pinnacle of ancient Indian society as the highest caste. In the Buddhist narrative, they were deemed heretical and subject to salvation by Sakyamuni. Numerous disciples of Sakyamuni, prior followers of Brahmanism, underwent

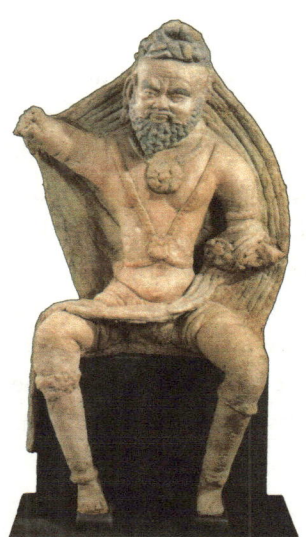

Figure 2-29 Brahmin statue from the Shorchuk Temple (now in the Museum of Asian Art, Berlin, Germany)

a transformative journey under the Buddha's teachings. Contrary to the typical portrayal of emaciated, fig-leaf clad figures in Buddhist art, the Brahmin statues discovered in the Shorchuk Temple defy convention. They present a robust, powerful physique, shattering the stereotype of the frail Brahmin. Adorning themselves with the same resplendent decorations as the divine statues, these Brahmin figures come in big numbers. The profusion of Brahmin statues within the Shorchuk Temple is a deliberate artistic endeavor. It seeks to underscore the Buddha's profound compassion and universal salvation, showcasing his benevolent reach to all sentient beings. In concert with the statues of gods and humans, these Brahmins play a pivotal role in framing the grandeur of the Buddha's image.

Furthermore, an array of statues portraying armored warriors, depictions of majestic animals like horses and elephants, and celestial beings crafted with meticulous detail using molds have been unearthed. Each of these artifacts seems to convey a nuanced Buddhist narrative. Additionally, a wooden statue narrates the story of Buddha Sakyamuni's tireless efforts in spreading the teachings of Buddhism. These sculptures, discovered by Le Coq and fellow explorers, shed light on the multifaceted grandeur of the Shorchuk Temple in Yanqi. Beyond its grand and expansive temple buildings, the temple's caves are adorned with an exquisite array of sculptures.

Between 1902 and 1914, German expeditions under the leadership of Grünwedel and Le Coq embarked on four journeys along the northern Silk Road route in Xinjiang, China. Over the course of these 12 years, an astounding 423 boxes of rare cultural relics were transported to Germany. The final shipment, which arrived in Berlin in April 1914, coincided with the outbreak of World War I, marking the end of the Germans' extensive exploration of Asia. Many of these cultural relics found a home in the Ethnological Museum of Berlin, constituting the renowned Turpan Collection (Figure 2-30). This collection included Buddhist murals, painted sculptures, artifacts from archaeological excavations, fragments of ancient buildings, and delicate paper and silk paintings. In addition to the Ethnological Museum of Berlin, the German National Library and the Turpan Research Laboratory of Berlin-Brandenburg Academy of Sciences and Humanities also received portions of scriptures, manuscripts, and textiles. Notably, the collection, although labeled as the Turpan Collection, largely originated from the distant Kuqa and Baicheng areas, where the ancient Kucha Kingdom thrived. The invaluable Kizil Caves murals, among the most significant in the collection, are now housed in the Museum of Asian Art in the western suburbs of Berlin.

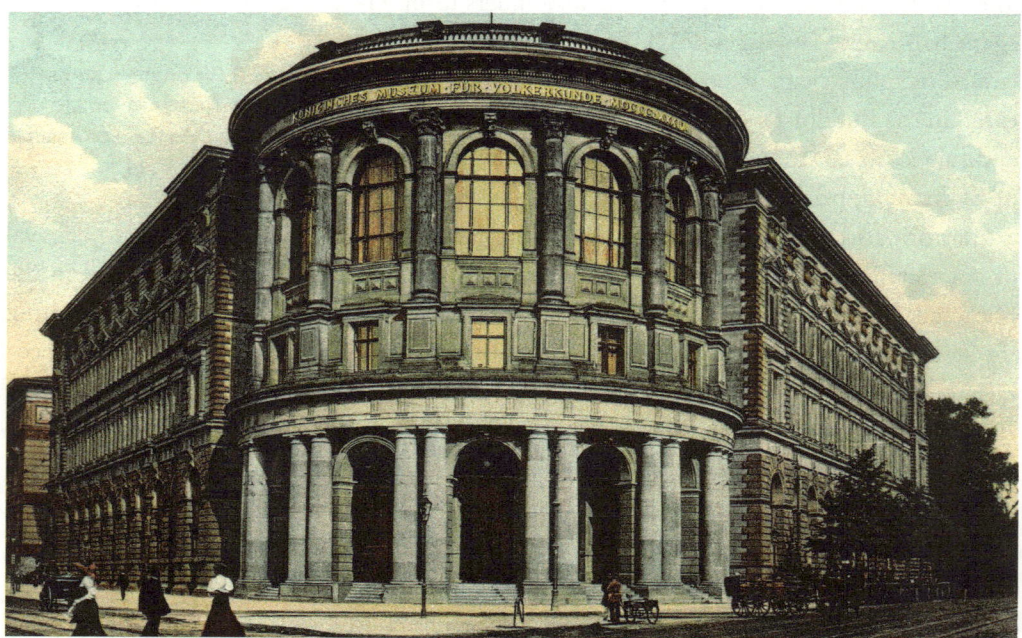

Figure 2-30 Ethnological Museum of Berlin (1905)

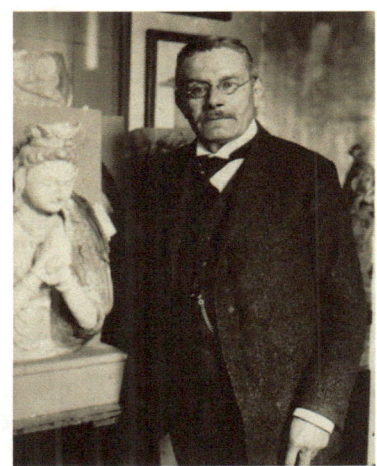

Figure 2-31 Photo of Le Coq and a statue of celestial beings taken from the Shorchuk Temple (taken approximately at the opening ceremony of the exhibition in 1928)

In a letter to Stein, Le Coq poetically reminisced about his Xinjiang expedition, "I often think with joy of the ten months I spent in that remote place. My time there will always be one of the happiest times of my life." The Xinjiang cultural relics acquired by Le Coq and his peers brought them luck and satisfaction and earned them respect. However, it's essential to acknowledge that their actions took a toll on the integrity of Chinese culture, particularly the loss of large murals during World War II. This historical misfortune remains a somber chapter for Chinese culture, eternally remembered by the Chinese people.

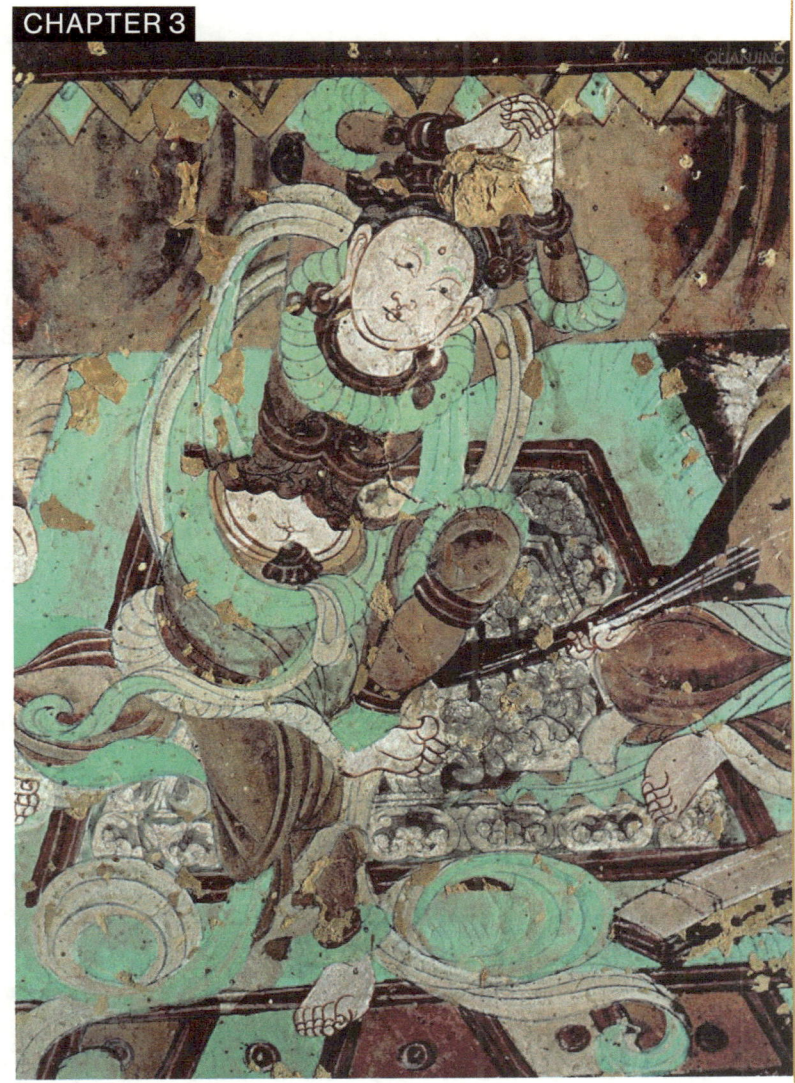

CHAPTER 3

Dunhuang Made Stein Famous

— 1900–1901

First expedition, the southern edge of the Tarim Basin–Hotan–Niya ruins–Miran ruins–Loulan ruins

— 1906–1908

Second expedition, the southern edge of the Tarim Basin–Rawak ruins of Hotan–Niya ruins–Miran ruins–Dunhuang–northern edge of the Tarim Basin–Turpan–Taklimakan Desert–Hotan–Kunlun Mountains

— 1913–1916

Third expedition, the southern edge of the Tarim Basin–Miran ruins–Dunhuang–Khara-Khoto ruins on the Ejin River in Inner Mongolia–Turpan (Astana, Bezeklik Caves)–Kuqa (Kizil Caves)–Kashgar–Pamir Plateau (Afghanistan border)–Sistan region in western Iran

— 1930–1931

Fourth expedition, the southern edge of the Tarim Basin–Dunhuang and the east area–Turpan (Astana, Bezeklik Caves)–Kashgar

3.1 The Linguistic Genius that Doesn't Speak Chinese

In the annals of Chinese cultural diffusion, a notable figure demands recognition–none other than Marc Aurel Stein (1862–1943), a distinguished British polymath hailing from Hungary (Figure 3-1). His impactful legacy spans across the realms of archaeology, art history, linguistics, geography, and exploration. His four expeditions, spanning from 1900 to 1901, from 1906 to 1908, from 1913 to 1916, and later from 1930 to 1931, traversed the landscapes of Central Asia and China, with a specific focus on Xinjiang and Gansu regions. The cultural treasures unearthed during these ventures remain invaluable resources for global Dunhuang studies.

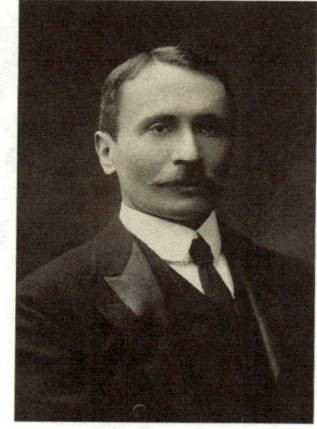

Figure 3-1 Stein in 1909

Beyond his professional prowess, Stein exhibited exceptional personal qualities. Proficient in an array of languages, including Hungarian, German, English, French, Greek, Latin, Persian, and Sanskrit, he further delved into Kashmiri and Turkic languages. Undeterred by adversity, Stein fearlessly braved mountainous terrains and desert landscapes. He is a meticulous planner with a keen sense of opportunity, and many of his works endure as primary references for Dunhuang and Turpan studies. It is astonishing to note that this intrepid explorer, responsible for transporting a wealth of cultural artifacts from China and an indispensable figure for the world Dunhuang research societies, initially lacked proficiency in Chinese upon his entry into China.

Born into a Jewish family in Budapest, Hungary, in 1862, Stein faced the prevalent discrimination against Jews in Europe. To counter this discrimination, his family arranged for his baptism into Christianity, allowing him to assimilate into society more seamlessly. Consequently, Stein, raised in a Jewish household, became a Christian, affording him the opportunity to learn Hungarian and German. His initial exposure to Oriental studies occurred during his tenure at the Hungarian Lutheran (Martin Lutheran) High School after graduating from elementary school in 1877.

Lajos Lóczy, director of the Hungarian Institute of Geology, played a pivotal role as Marc Aurel Stein's inaugural mentor in Orientalism and archaeology. Lóczy, having visited the Mogao Grottoes from 1877 to 1880, was the first scholar to introduce Dunhuang art to Europe; Stein, captivated by Lóczy's speeches and reports, developed a keen interest in Asia. Post high school, Stein embarked on a scholarly journey at the University of Vienna in Austria, the University of Leipzig, and the University of Tübingen in Germany, specializing in Oriental studies. Under the tutelage of Rudolph von Roth (1821–1895), a professor of Indo-European languages and religious history at the University of Tübingen and the most authoritative professor of Sanskrit manuscript research, and Georg Bühler (1837–1898), a professor of Indian philosophy and antiquities at the University of Vienna, Stein solidified his foundation in Orientalism. From them, Stein learned Sanskrit and Persian, and during that time, he meticulously studied the experiences of his idol, Alexander the Great (356–323 BC), and delved into exploration literature, particularly *The Travels of Marco Polo* and *The Great Tang Records on the Western Regions*. Inspired by these works, Stein resolved to explore the East and see for himself the geographic and human tapestry they depicted.

In 1883, at the age of 21, Stein earned a doctorate in philosophy from the University of Tübingen. Subsequently, he engaged in postdoctoral research at the University of London, the University of Oxford, and the University of Cambridge, focusing on Oriental linguistics and archaeology. So far, his linguistic prowess encompassed Hungarian, German, Greek, Latin, French, English, Sanskrit, and Persian. However, a conspicuous absence in his linguistic repertoire was Chinese, a deficiency that would later pose a significant challenge in his adventurous career. Returning to Budapest for military service in 1885, Stein acquired state-of-the-art military topographic surveying skills. His scholarly pursuits continued in England in 1886, where he researched ancient coins and published his maiden academic paper, "Zoroastrian Deities On Indo-Scythian Coins." Thus, the initial phase of the legendary explorer's academic journey concluded.

In 1887, at the age of 25, Stein's postdoctoral studies culminated, leading to his simultaneous appointments as Inspector of the University of the Punjab in British India and Director of the Oriental College in Lahore. Eagerly anticipating his Asian and Chinese exploration, from 1888 to 1899, Stein conducted administrative duties while delving into the ancient culture and geography of Kashmir. His studies extended to the exploration of Gandhara Buddhist art in Lahore, laying the intellectual groundwork for his later quest for Gandhara-style artworks in Xinjiang and Gansu.

During his career, Stein undertook a series of archaeological and geographical expeditions in the northwest frontier provinces of British India, with two notable projects capturing special attention. One venture involved scrutinizing the route of Alexander the Great's eastward expedition, aiming to uncover remnants of the legendary conqueror's army. The other focused on investigating the eastward paths taken by Xuanzang and Marco Polo, seeking the Buddhist holy places and ancient cultural cities mentioned in *The Great Tang Records on the Western Regions* and *The Travels of Marco Polo*. If he came to India to have the opportunity to fulfill his dream, then after 1893, he finally began to make it happen step by step.

Stein's ambitious dreams of exploration found fertile ground in the continuous discovery of ancient documents in Central Asia. In 1889, a pivotal moment transpired when Hamilton Bower (1858–1940), a British intelligence officer, embarked on a mission to apprehend the Afghan criminal Dad Mahomed, who was responsible for the murder of the esteemed British Central Asian explorer Andrew Dalgleish. Operating undercover as an organizer of hunting activities, Bower established an intelligence network spanning Afghanistan, China, and Russian Central Asia. In order to hunt down the murderer and collect intelligence, he came to Kuqa, an ancient city on the northern edge of Tarim, where he serendipitously acquired a manuscript on birch bark from Guran Kediaj, setting in motion a remarkable sequence of events. The manuscript, later known as the Bower Manuscript, consisted of 56 pages bound in wood. A year later, he brought this manuscript with texts that nobody understood back to India and handed it to Professor Augustus Frederic Rudolf Hoernlé (1841–1918), a German Indologist and philologist. The scholar quickly identified it as a manuscript written in Brahmi letter. Though incomplete, it contains seven distinct texts dating back to the 5th century AD, making it one of the oldest surviving books globally (Figure 3-2). This ancient manuscript on witchcraft and medicine was named Bower Manuscript by the Royal Society of Asia. As a result, the young Lieutenant Bower's fame soared globally. Hoernlé also published his research results under the name Bower Manuscript, which immediately sparked a sensation in British India and European academic circles.

From 1893 to 1898, under the advice of Hoernlé, who was Director General of the Bengal Asiatic Society, British India, the Indian government tasked British and Indian diplomatic missions in Central Asia with acquiring cultural relics. This endeavor resulted in Kolkata's collection of a substantial number of artifacts from the Taklimakan Desert in

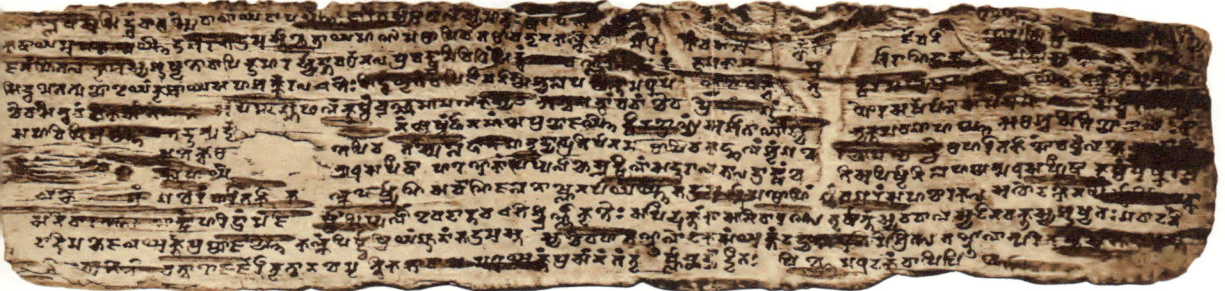

Figure 3-2 A page from the 5th–6th century Bower Manuscript discovered in Kuqa, Xinjiang, now housed in the Bodleian Library of the University of Oxford

Xinjiang, including ancient manuscripts. However, there is no exact location or date for these cultural relics. Therefore, skepticism emanated from both British Indian scholars and European academic circles regarding the authenticity of the enigmatic manuscripts with "unknown texts" and prints. However, it was the unveiling of Professor Hoernlé's findings on these newly discovered ancient documents in Xinjiang that kindled a fervent enthusiasm within Stein for his own exploration. Driven by the need to substantiate various hypotheses and suspicions surrounding these artifacts, Stein drew inspiration from the early Prakrit and Kharosthi Buddhist texts uncovered by the French explorer Jules-Léon Dutreuil de Rhins (1846–1894) during the period spanning 1891 to 1893. The intricate clues led him to set Hotan as the destination for his first investigation.

After Sven Hedin unveiled the enchanting secrets of the Dandan Oilik ruins, Xinjiang has transformed into a revered haven in the hearts of global explorers. Countries such as Sweden, Russia, the United Kingdom, and Japan eagerly orchestrated expeditions to this trove of treasures. Recognizing the urgency of unearthing primary sources, Stein swiftly formulated his action plan. On September 10, 1898, he presented his proposal to the Punjab government in a meticulously crafted submission. In his eloquent appeal, Stein articulated, "The endeavor I seek approval for necessitates the endorsement and backing of local and highest authorities for an archaeological expedition to the Hotan region and surrounding ancient sites in Xinjiang, China." As the year 1899 dawned, on New Year's Eve, the British Ministry of Home Affairs and the Indian government's Ministry of Finance preliminarily sanctioned Stein's application for the Xinjiang expedition. Embarking on his journey, Stein arrived in Kolkata, the bustling capital of British India, on May 6. Here, he assumed the role of the principal of a Muslim school, becoming a "civil servant" of the Bengal government. Simultaneously, the Xinjiang expedition plan transitioned from the Punjab government to the Bengal government.

The plan was then laid before the discerning eyes of the Governor of Bengal, Sir John Woodburn (1843–1902), for approval. With sagacity, Woodburn granted Stein a year to delve into the mysteries of Xinjiang, endowing him with an archaeological fund of 14,000 rupees, generously contributed by the central government, the Bangladesh government, and the Punjab government, with personal salaries graciously provided by the Bangladesh government. At this pivotal juncture, Stein, seized the long-awaited opportunity to set foot in China—an alluring land that had captivated his imagination for so long.

3.2 Dandan Oilik, Overlooked by Sven Hedin

The Tarim Basin in Xinjiang, nestled in the heart of Asia, is cradled by Tian Shan (Mountain of Heaven) to the north, the Kunlun Mountains to the south, the Congling Range (Pamir Plateau) to the west, and the Nan Shan (Southern Mountain) formed by the Kunlun Mountains to the east. Stein, with a keen sense of imagery, christened it Asia's Heartland. At its core lies the Taklamakan Desert, flanked to the north and south by elongated oases known as the famed southern and northern routes of the ancient Silk Road in Xinjiang. Since the inception of the Silk Road, this region has been a crucible for extensive cultural exchanges between East and West, resulting in the harmonious fusion of Persian civilization from the Tigris and Euphrates valleys, the classical legacies of Greece and Rome, the Buddhist ethos of India, and the ancient traditional culture of China. For Stein, embarking on his maiden Chinese exploration, this extraordinary region became his inaugural destination (Figure 3-3).

In October 1899, Stein embarked on a preliminary exploration of Bihar in western Kolkata, setting the stage for his Xinjiang expedition. Commencing with a pilgrimage to the sacred sites of Magadha, he retraced the footsteps of Xuanzang, advancing along

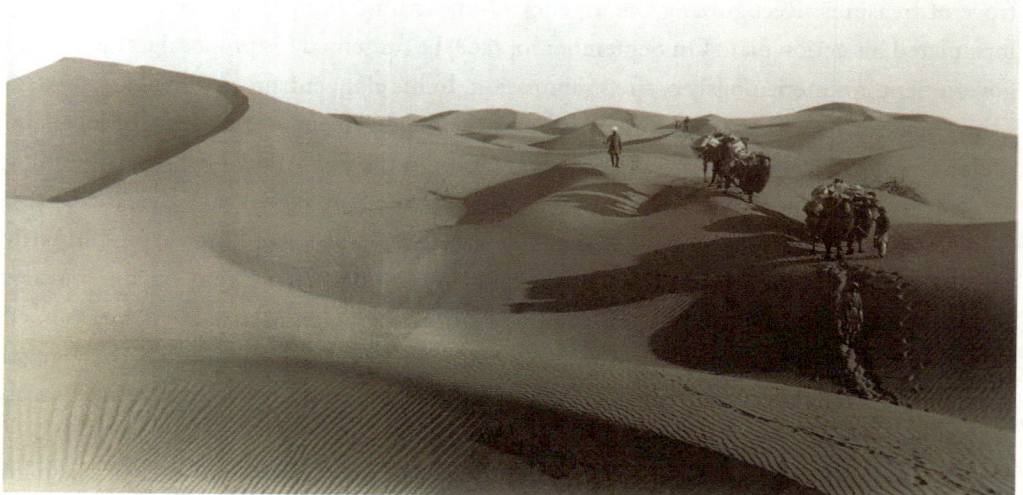

Figure 3-3 Stein Expedition advancing from the Taklamakan Desert to the Keriya River in Xinjiang (1900s)

the foothills of the Palasnath Hills, meticulously inspecting various Buddhist landmarks. Relying on the rich narratives of *The Great Tang Records on the Western Regions*, Stein unearthed forgotten ancient pathways, ultimately returning to Kolkata from Kayi. In March 1900, he headed northwest to the Rawalpindi region in Punjab, assuming the role of Inspector of Schools. Swiftly thereafter, he secured a passport and a Chinese name card for use in Xinjiang. On May 31, Stein officially embarked on his Xinjiang expedition, selecting a route that led him from the enchanting Srinagar in Kashmir to the storied towns of Gilgit and Leh, culminating in his arrival at the vibrant Kashgar in Xinjiang.

Accompanied by an entourage, Stein initially traversed the ancient Gilgit route, crossing the Pamir Plateau into the realm of China on June 29, exploring the antiquities near Kashgar with keen interest. On September 11, he departed Kashgar for an extensive survey of Hotan. On the 17th, in Yarkand, Yarkant County, Stein acquired a captivating collection of artifacts. By October 13, his expedition reached Hotan, greeted warmly by the affluent local merchants under the organization of Pan Zhen (1851–1926), the Qing Dynasty's governor of Hotan. In historical records, the governor is often referred to as Hotan Anban, a fusion of Chinese and Manchu. Anban represents the Manchu transliteration of *angbang*, signifying a minister. Pan Zhen pledged unwavering support to Stein's explorations around Hotan. Subsequently, Stein conducted meticulous geological and geographical surveys of the southern mountains of Hotan (a part of the Kunlun Mountains) and delved into the ancient sites within the Hotan oasis. On November 25, he and his team advanced to the historic capital site of Yurturgan, commencing his first extensive excavation and ultimately yielding an impressive collection of nearly a hundred artifacts.

Hotan, known as Khotan in ancient times, boasts a legendary founding tale. As chronicled by Xuanzang in *The Great Tang Records on the Western Regions*, the Kingdom of Jusadanna spanned over 4,000 *li*, with more than half of its territory covered in sandy land. Within its borders, there were over 100 Buddhist temples and over 5,000 monks, predominantly devoted to the study of Mahayana Buddhism. Legend has it that the prince of Ashoka the Great of India (r. 268–232 BC) had his eyes gouged out. In a fit of rage, Ashoka the Great expelled numerous ministers and wealthy families. Forced to migrate, these exiles settled in the western reaches of the Kingdom of Jusadanna, establishing their own realm. Subsequently, a prince from the East faced conviction and was exiled to the eastern border of the Kingdom of Jusadanna, where he declared himself king. A conflict ensued between the two nations, and the prince from the East emerged victorious. In his later years, with no heirs, he visited the abode of Vaiśravaṇa to seek divine intervention. A boy was miraculously carved from the god's forehead during prayer. However, the child refused human milk. Fearing for the boy's short life, the king sought the gods' assistance in fostering the child. Suddenly, the land in front of the temple swelled with breasts. The baby found nourishment here, ultimately growing up to inherit the throne. Henceforth, the people of this land claimed descent from Vaiśravaṇa, and Jusadanna came to signify "earth milk." The Kingdom of Jusadanna, mentioned by Xuanzang, refers to the ancient Kingdom of Khotan.

The revelation of the Kingdom of Khotan marked Stein's initial triumph, an unforeseen bounty when he first petitioned the Indian government. In that initial application, he meticulously cataloged a plethora of ancient documents, coins, sculptures, paintings, and various cultural relics unearthed by the local populace. Stein articulated, "Hotan today was once the epicenter of ancient Buddhist culture, a culture that unmistakably originated in India and bears distinct Indian characteristics. Systematic excavation of these ancient ruins, I believe, will yield immensely significant discoveries for the exploration of ancient Indian culture." Little did he anticipate that this discovery, beyond its immense importance for unraveling ancient Indian culture, would serve as a pivotal moment in unveiling Xinjiang Buddhist art to the global stage, ushering in a new era of research into Xinjiang's cultural tapestry.

Contrary to Sven Hedin, Stein held the conviction that the crux of archaeology lay in the excavation and study of cultural relics. The means of acquisition, whether through personal excavation or substantial financial transactions, mattered little to him. During his inaugural expedition to China, among the cadre of treasure hunters employed by Stein was an elderly seeker from Yulong Kashgar Village (Figure 3-4). The cultural artifacts this seasoned treasure hunter brought back from the Dandan Oilik site successfully captivated Stein's attention. Consequently, he orchestrated an extensive excavation of this seldom-explored ancient desert site from December 19, 1900, to January 3, 1901. The outcome was nothing short of remarkable—Stein unearthed a total of 15 temple structures and around 180 cultural relics.

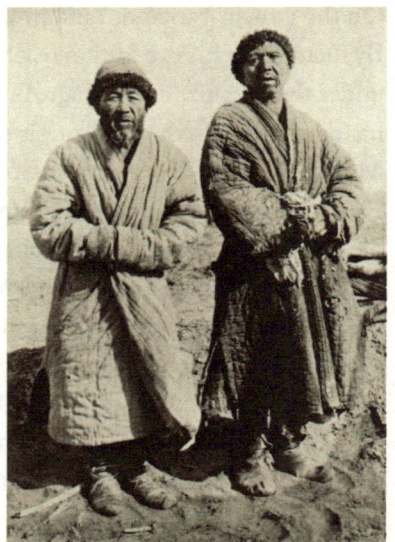

Figure 3-4 Local treasure hunters Pratt and Ibrahim in Hotan (1900–1901, photographed by Stein)

The architectural design of these temple houses comprises a quaint square courtyard enclosed by walls crafted from wood and mud. At the heart of this space, a pagoda or Buddha statue, mounted on a square base, stands tall, creating a harmonious worship corridor that follows the right-handed tradition. Some of these temples boast meticulously arranged paintings adorning their outer walls. The small seated Buddha portraits, collectively known as the Thousand Buddhas (Figure 3-5), are estimated to trace their origins back to the 5th century. The construction methods employed in these temples align seamlessly with the prevailing traditions of the early Kucha Kingdom, underscoring that the introduction of Buddhism to Khotan brought forth the Indian concept of circumambulating pagodas and venerating Buddha.

Stein later penned:

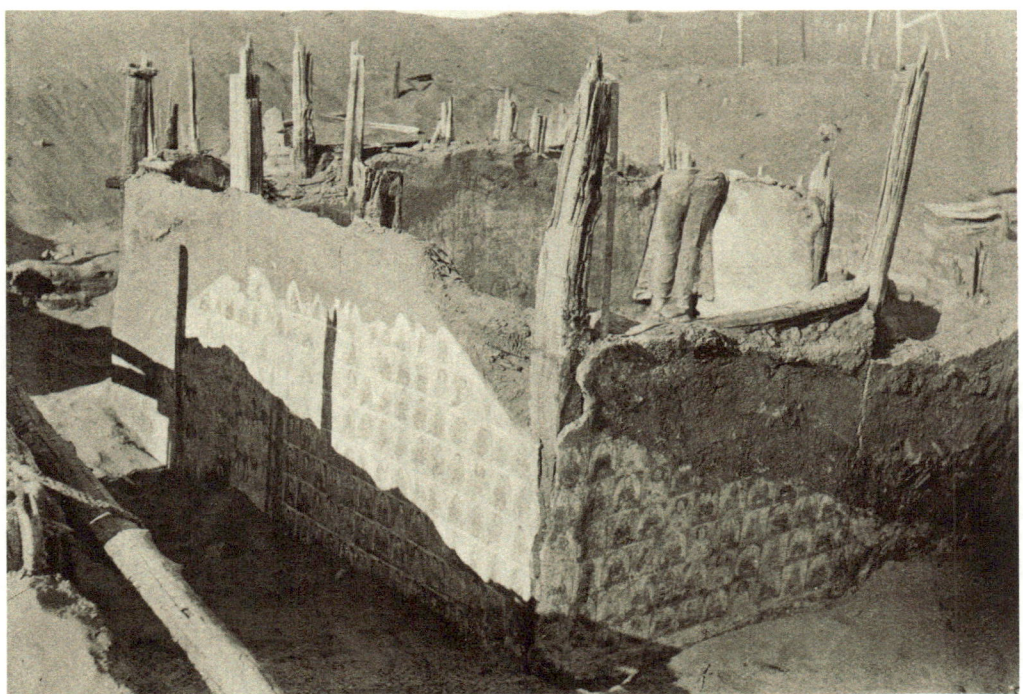

Figure 3-5 The southeast corner of temple site No. 2 from around the 5th century and the mural of Thousand Buddhas excavated by Stein in Dandan Oilik (photographed by Stein in 1900–1901)

In that expansive plain, it felt as if I were gazing upon the luminous sprawl of an immense subterranean city. Could this be the formidable desert, seemingly devoid of life and human presence? I realized that the enchanting and grandiose panorama before me was a sight I might never have the privilege of witnessing again.

Remarkably, a few years earlier, Sven Hedin found himself in the same position. Yet, the two explorers opted for divergent paths. The Dandan Oilik ruins, overlooked by Sven Hedin, emerged as the genesis of Stein's acclaim. Indeed, history unfolded in such a captivating and dramatic manner.

3.3 Tale of the Dragon Goddess

While meticulously restoring the Dandan Oilik Temple ruins, Stein uncovered a treasure trove of murals and wooden panels, each narrating captivating legends and tales. Among these artworks, some were depictions of the legends of Khotan.

One particularly captivating mural, found in the Dandan Oilik temple site No. 2, stands out for its delicate line drawings and light hues. The artwork portrays a half-naked woman

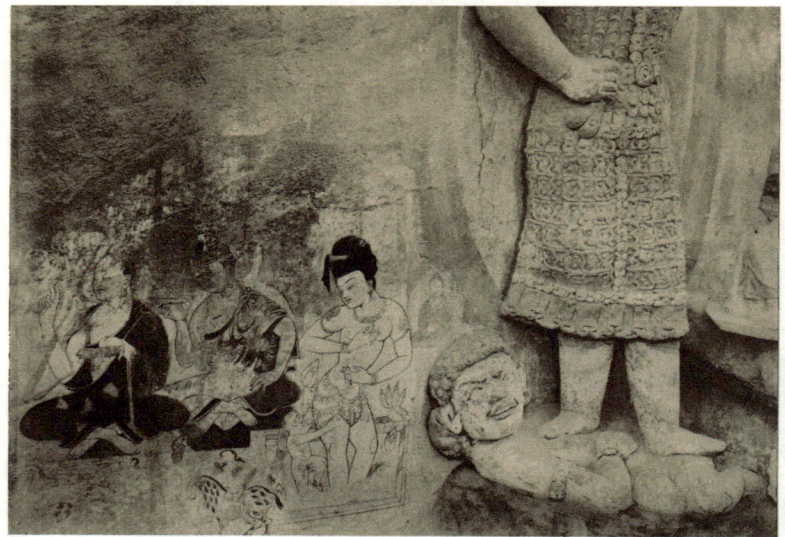

Figure 3-6 The statue of the Heavenly King and the mural of the *Dragon Goddess Seeks a Husband* from temple site No. 2 of about the 5th century AD excavated by Stein in Dandan Oilik (photographed by Stein in 1900–1901)

standing in a lotus pond, a boy holding her right leg with both hands while gazing upward. Adjacent to the lotus pond is a figure elegantly mounted on a horse (Figure 3-6).

This mural draws inspiration from the legend of a courtship of the Dragon Goddess of the ancient Kingdom of Khotan, as chronicled in *The Great Tang Records on the Western Regions*. The tale recounts a large river southeast of the royal city of Khotan, which dried after the Dragon Goddess Lingbo's husband passed away. The Dragon Goddess, claiming that a husband was necessary for her to control the river, requested the king to select a noble minister for her to restore the water's flow. In a symbolic gesture, the chosen minister rode a white horse into the water with only the horse returning to the land, and the river resumed its course. The mural captures the essence of this courtship story, exhibiting a distinct Dunhuang mural style. What adds intrigue is the composition's resemblance to sculptures of Venus and Cupid from ancient Greece and Rome in the 1st century BC. This mural serves as compelling evidence that the Hotan region had already begun integrating Chinese and Western cultures and arts, underscoring the Silk Road's pivotal role in East-West cultural exchanges.

Numerous similar paintings depicting ancient Khotan legends and stories were discovered in the Dandan Oilik ruins. Notably, the wood-panel painting titled *Silk Princess*, unearthed from temple site No. 10, stands out as one of the best-preserved and clearest wood-panel paintings (Figure 3-7). This tale, also documented in *The Great Tang Records on the Western Regions* by Xuanzang of the Tang Dynasty:

> In times of old, our land knew not the delicate thread spun by silkworms. Upon hearing of these silken marvels flourishing in the Eastern Kingdom, The king dispatched envoys to request this precious bounty. The sovereign of the Eastern

Kingdom, however, guarded the silkworms as a cherished national secret and was hesitant to share. Stringent security measures were imposed, forbidding silkworms from leaving the realm without explicit orders. Undeterred, the king of Jusadanna devised a clever plan. He propsed marriage to the princess of the Eastern Kingdom, artfully entreating her, "Our realm has yet to grace itself with the touch of silk and mulberry seeds. Could you, noble princess, bring forth some to weave garments for your adornment?" Inspired by this request, the princess covertly sought out the coveted treasures. Silkworm cocoons were cunningly concealed within the recesses of her hat. As the wedding procession approached the border control, every soul underwent scrutiny—every soul, that is, except the princess and her hat. None dared to inspect. Thus, the artistry of mulberry silkworms gracefully flowed into the land of Jusadanna.

Capturing this enchanting tale in a wood panel painting, the princess of the Eastern Kingdom assumes center stage, her headdress and crown accentuated. To enhance clarity, a bowl of silkworm cocoons is placed between them. The messenger on the princess's right subtly gestures to the crown, hinting at the hidden silkworm cocoons. Adjacent, another figure stands beside a loom brimming with warp threads, further illuminating the narrative's thematic richness.

Within the confines of another wooden panel discovered at the Dandan Oilik temple site No. 10, a deity with a rat's head takes center stage, while at the left end, a man offers flowers in homage. According to *The Great Tang Records on the Western Regions*, this rat-headed deity once aided the king of Khotan in repelling the invasion of the Huns. To convey their profound veneration, Buddhist artists in Khotan purposefully adorned the sacred Buddhist temples with depictions of myths and legends, narratives that diverged from traditional Buddhist themes. Despite the narratives having no direct connection to Buddhist philosophy, the artists believed that the figures portrayed in these paintings bestowed joy and tranquility upon the people of Khotan. In a poignant sense, the roles

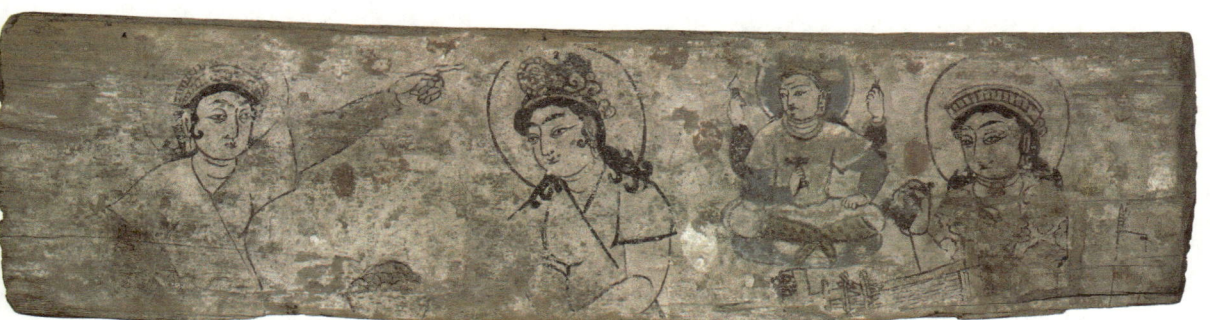

Figure 3-7 The wood-panel painting of *Silk Princess*, Stein discovered at the ruins of Dandan Oilik temple site No. 10 (12 cm × 46 cm × 2.2 cm, now in the British Museum)

played by these depicted personalities mirrored the impact of Buddhism itself—bringing happiness and peace to the community.

Among the wood panel paintings at temple site No. 10, a noteworthy find is a double-sided single-person seated portrait. One side portrays the image of a four-armed warrior god with a substantial beard. Because of its distinct resemblance to ancient Persians, its presence in Buddhist temples, and its adoption of the common Bodhisattva posture, Stein referred to it as the Persian Bodhisattva (Figure 3-8). This serves as another compelling instance of the fusion between Eastern and Western cultures and religions. On the reverse side of this wooden painting is a portrait of a god with three heads and four arms (Figure 3-9). This deity, adorned with tiger skin around the waist and accompanied by two reclining cows, features a main head with an indigo face, bearing unmistakable male characteristics consistent with Indian mural art. The dual faces of this panel potentially represent a celestial deity in Buddhism and a local patron saint of Khotan. Stylistically, it predominantly aligns with the Greek classical art style prevalent in India. Through these paintings, the profound influence of artistic styles from Persia and India on Buddhist art in Khotan becomes apparent, showcasing their interdependence and coevolution.

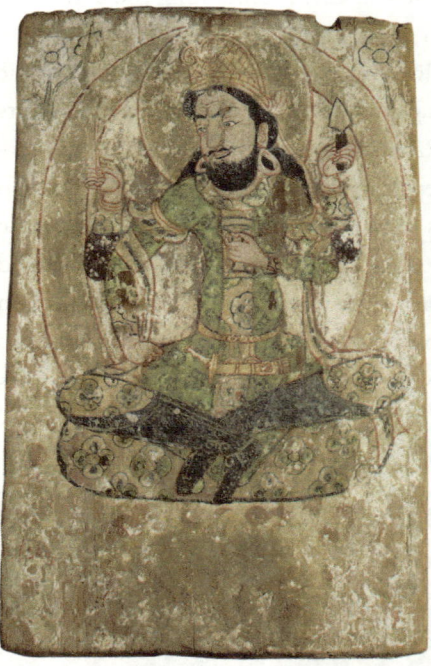

Figure 3-8 The wood-panel painting of *Persian Bodhisattva*, Stein discovered at the ruins of Dandan Oilik temple site No. 10 (33.5 cm × 21 cm × 2.5 cm, now in the British Museum)

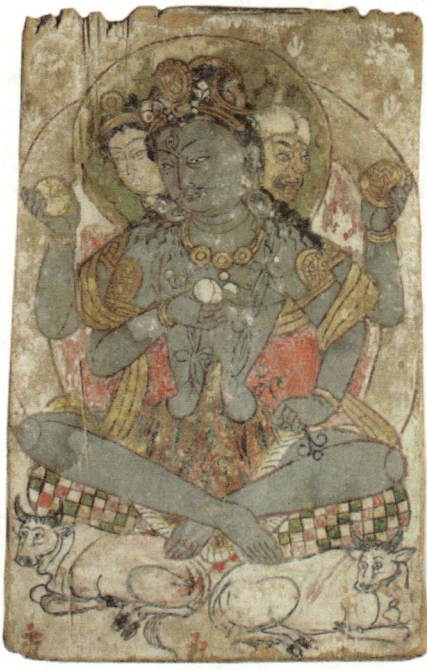

Figure 3-9 The wood panel painting of *The Three-Headed and Four-Armed God Portrait*, Stein discovered at the ruins of Dandan Oilik temple site No. 10 (33.5 cm × 21 cm × 2.5 cm, now in the British Museum)

These invaluable paintings exhibit an exceptional blend of artistic prowess and historical significance, serving as crucial historical artifacts for delving into the rich tapestry of Central Asian culture, Silk Road history, and the cultural legacy of Dunhuang. In Stein's own words, "While these depictions emerged several centuries after the flourishing of Gandhara art in India, the unmistakable influence of the Greek style remains vividly apparent."

3.4 Kharosthi Script and Han Dynasty Bamboo Slips from the Niya Ruins

In January 1901, Stein unearthed the hidden remnants of an ancient urban civilization buried beneath the sands of Niya in present-day Minfeng County, Hotan (Figure 3-10). Within a mere two weeks, spanning from January 28 to February 13, Stein embarked on an extensive excavation expedition around the Niya River Channel. In a house named *yamen* (the workplace of local government in ancient China), he unearthed a plethora of wooden slips adorned with inscriptions that presented a challenge to decipher due to their numerous unreadable words. Immersed in the thrill of this archaeological triumph, Stein's enthusiasm led him to dedicate an entire night to decrypting several lines of text on the wooden slips, all while braving the chilling temperatures within his tent. Following rigorous research, he ascertained that these inscriptions belonged to the Kharosthi

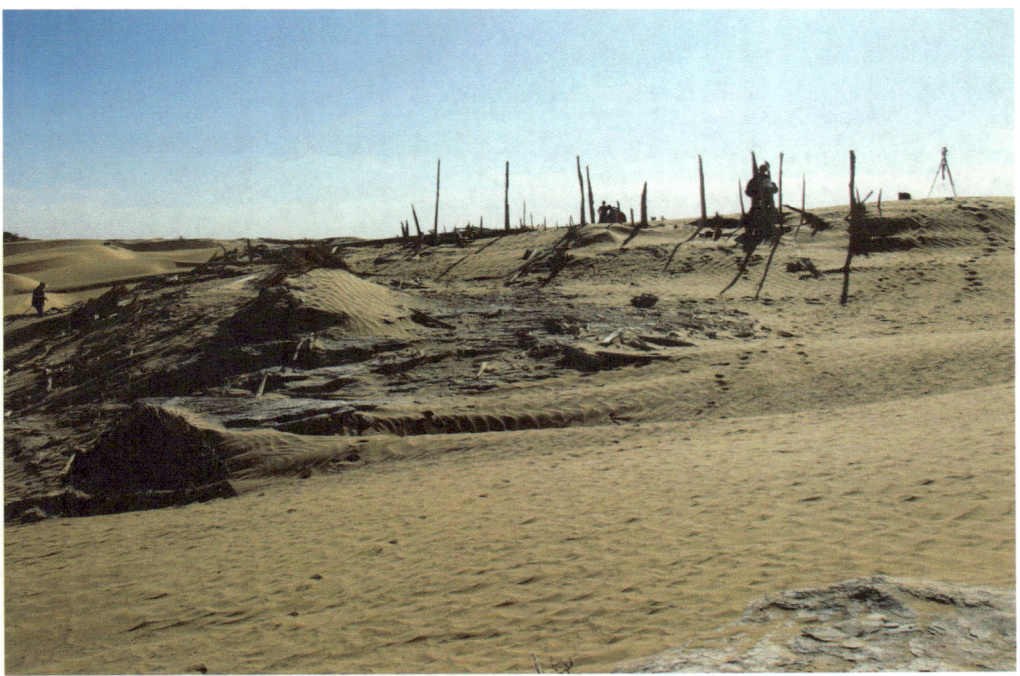

Figure 3-10 Niya ruins in Minfeng County, Hotan, Xinjiang

script, emerging concurrently with the Brahmi script around the 3rd century BC during the Asoka period of the Mauryan Dynasty in India (Figure 3-11). Originating in ancient Gandhara, this script gained prominence across Central Asia, serving as a crucial language for trade and Buddhism along the Silk Road. However, the Kharosthi script faced an abrupt and unforeseen decline in the 5th century AD. Its usage dwindled, with no nation continuing its adoption, ultimately fading into obscurity throughout the annals of history. The collection of Kharosthi script slips, spanning over 200 years, discovered by Stein, emerges as a treasure trove of cultural relics. These artifacts not only offer valuable insights into the evolution and demise of the Kharosthi script but also serve as pivotal historical materials for understanding the amalgamation of diverse ethnic groups along the ancient Silk Road.

Later, Stein made a remarkable discovery in Niya, uncovering numerous Chinese slips dating back to the Wei and Jin dynasties. These artifacts hold immense documentary and historical significance. An illustrative example is the one with an elucidating annotation on N.xv.No.326, "20th day of October of the lunar calendar in the fifth year of Taishi,

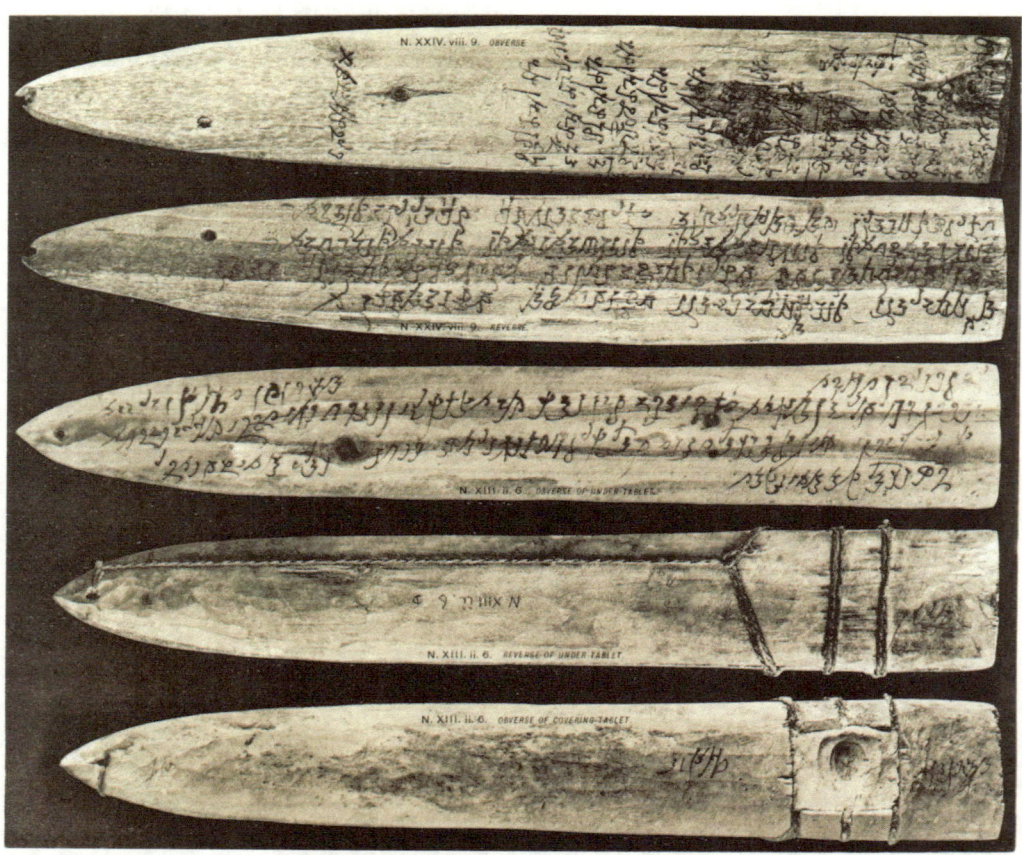

Figure 3-11 The Kharosthi script wooden slips discovered by Stein at the Niya ruins (1921, from *Serindia: Detailed Report of Explorations in Central Asia and Westernmost China*, Plate XXIV)

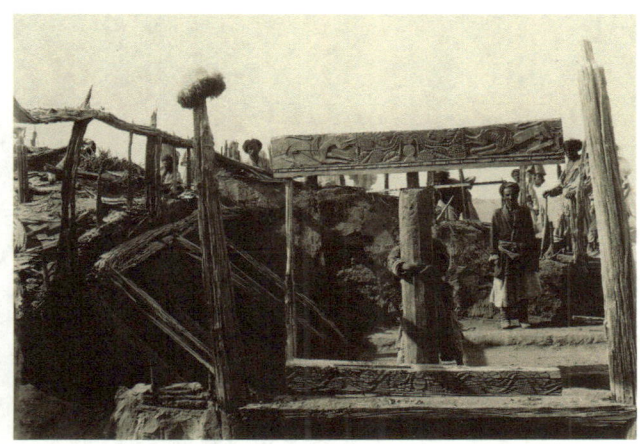

Figure 3-12 Scene of Stein's excavation at the Niya ruins (October 1906)

the governor of Dunhuang." This information, such as the fifth year of the Taishi period corresponding to AD 269, aligns with the dating of Kharosthi script wooden slips contemporaneously unearthed. Concurrently, the coherence of these bamboo slips with discoveries in other Central Asian regions facilitates a more precise reconstruction of the societal norms in Niya during that era. This extends to a nuanced understanding of the region's political, economic, and cultural evolution. The arid desert climate of Niya played a pivotal role in the preservation of various artifacts, including paintings, slips, wooden chairs, tables, and intricately carved door frames reflecting the distinctive artistry of the Kushan Empire. Stein transported these objects, now housed in the British Museum (Figure 3-12), back to England.

Notably, the Kushan Empire, a formidable state spanning Central Asia from the 1st to the 3rd century AD, held strategic prominence along the Central Asian Silk Road. Positioned at the crossroads of this vital trade route, it emerged as a pivotal hub for the production and exchange of Chinese silk, lacquerware, Southeast Asian spices, ancient Roman glassware, and linen fabrics. Furthermore, it served as a significant nexus for the dissemination of Mahayana Buddhism to mainland China. Despite its historical significance, the enigmatic nature of the Kushan Empire persists due to the convolution of historical data from diverse sources and an unclear chronology.

Stein's inaugural archaeological expedition was characterized by a tight schedule. In a concerted effort to maximize excavation coverage, Stein allocated merely two weeks to each site before moving on. Upon completing the archaeological endeavors in Niya, he redirected his focus to the ruins of the Rawak Stupa, situated approximately 40 kilometers northeast of Hotan County, on the opposite bank of the Yurungkash River, from April 11 to 18, 1901. The Rawak Stupa, featuring a pagoda as its centerpiece, manifested a near-square architectural layout. At its core stood a three-story circular pagoda, boasting a diameter of around 9 meters. The temple's surrounding area extended approximately 50 meters in length and 43 meters in width, enclosed by sturdy walls. Adorning both sides of

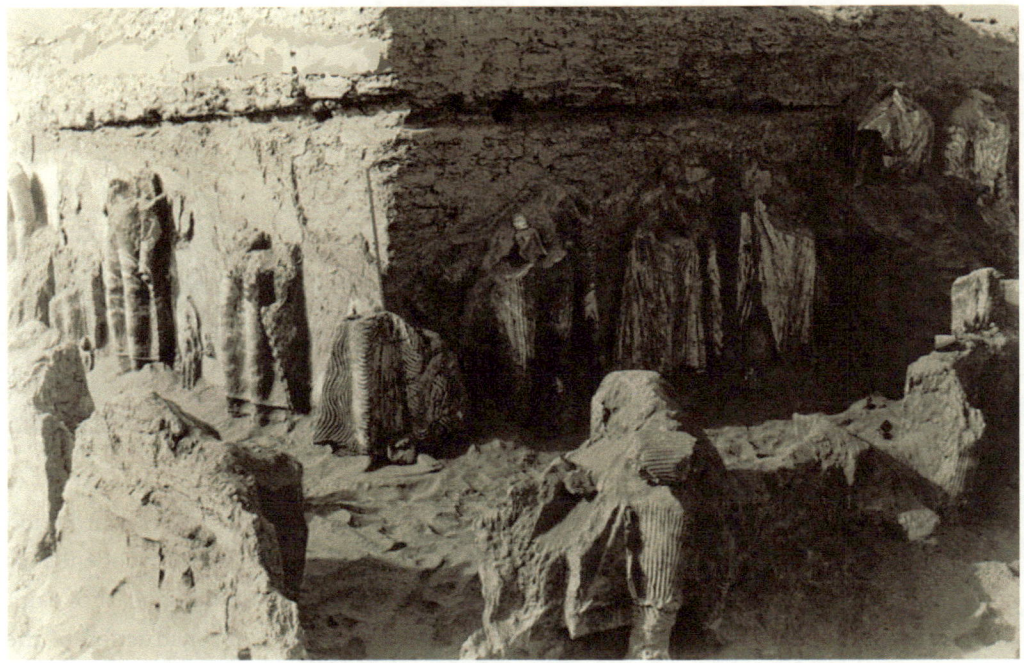

Figure 3-13 The ruins of the Rawak Stupa and its clay Buddha statues discovered by Stein in Hotan, Xinjiang (1901)

these walls were towering statues, depicting Buddha and Bodhisattva figures, surpassing life-size in scale. Stein unearthed a rare collection of art relics in the history of Central Asian archaeology. Particularly concentrating on the intersection of the south wall with the west wall, over 90 relief statues of standing Buddha (Figure 3-13), dating back to the 5th to 6th centuries AD, were revealed, showcasing a fusion of Indian Gandhara and Gupta artistic styles. This rich artistic heritage underscored the profound cultural ties between Khotanese culture and the broader tapestry of Indian and Central Asian cultures during that era.

Stein, recognizing the cultural significance of the Rawak Stupa, meticulously transported smaller Buddha statues while carefully mapping and photographing those that couldn't be moved. Tragically, upon his return for a second expedition to Hotan, he found that the locals had inflicted irreparable damage on these statues, driven by a curiosity to uncover potential treasures concealed within the artifacts that this foreigner was crazy about. Consequently, the specimens and photographs Stein brought back to the British Museum stand as the sole surviving records of the Rawak Stupa, preserving the splendor of ancient Hotan clay sculpture art on foreign soil.

On May 12, 1901, Stein concluded his expedition, returning to Kashgar before embarking on a journey that spanned Fergana, Samarkand, Merv, and Baku. Carrying approximately

1,500 excavated cultural relics, he reached London on July 2, officially concluding the first Central Asian expedition. These cultural relics find their present home primarily in the Department of Oriental Antiquities at the British Museum and the Oriental Department of the British Library.

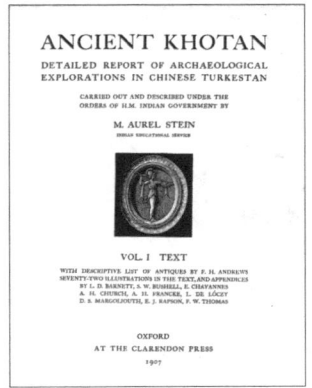

Following the initial Central Asian exploration, Stein authored a *Preliminary Report on a Journey of Archaeological and Topographical Exploration in Chinese Turkestan*, presented at the 12th International Congress of Orientalists in Hamburg, Germany, in 1902. This report generated considerable academic interest, directly contributing to the establishment of the International Central Asia and Far East Exploration Association. Building upon the Preliminary Report, Stein penned *Sand-Buried Ruins of Khotan: Personal Narrative of a Journey of Archaeological and Geographical Exploration in Chinese Turkestan*, along with a comprehensive academic monograph titled *Ancient Khotan*. Published by Clarendon Press, Oxford, in 1907, the latter stands as an indispensable resource for Chinese and international scholars delving into the study of Central Asian cultural relics (Figure 3-14).

Figure 3-14 Title page of Stein's *Ancient Khotan* (published in 1907)

3.5 Winged Angels at Miran Ruins

Stein's second expedition surpasses the first in terms of notoriety, particularly due to its significant contributions to the collection of Dunhuang documents now housed in the UK. In 1904, Stein, having become a British citizen, formulated an ambitious plan for another archaeological exploration in China. Embarking on this venture in April 1906, he secured funding through a collaboration between the British Indian government and the British Museum. Prior to the expedition, discussions arose concerning the distribution of the cultural relics Stein would bring back. An agreement was reached to allocate a portion to the British Indian government and the remainder to the British Museum. This period marked a pinnacle of audacity in Stein's pursuit of Chinese cultural relics. During his stay in Kashgar, Stein enlisted the services of a remarkable individual, Jiang Xiaowan (1858–1922), as a "master" and translator. Proficient in linguistics and highly studious, Jiang played a crucial role in Stein's second expedition. Notably, he assumed the responsibility of instructing Stein in the Chinese language throughout the course of the expedition (Figure 3-15).

During the course of the second expedition, in addition to revisiting the Hotan and Niya ruins, Stein and his expedition team embarked on a decision to excavate the ancient Loulan ruins and conduct a thorough exploration of the Hexi Corridor. On October 8,

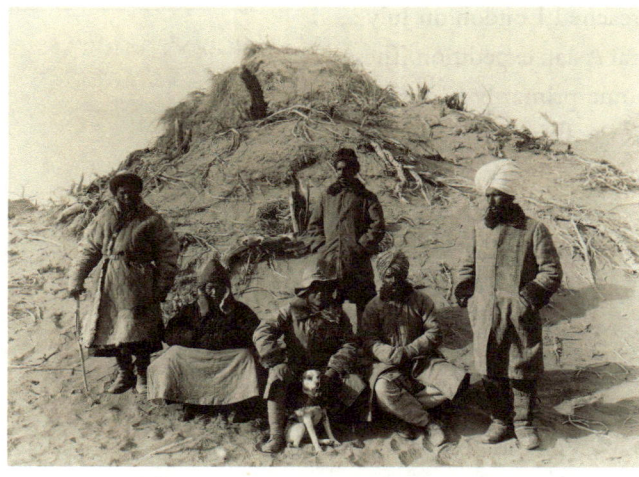

Figure 3-15 Stein's second expedition to China taken in Xinjiang (seated from left: Jiang Xiaowan, Stein, Rai Bahadur Lal Singh; standing from left: Ibrahim Beg, Jaswant Singh, Naik Ram Singh)

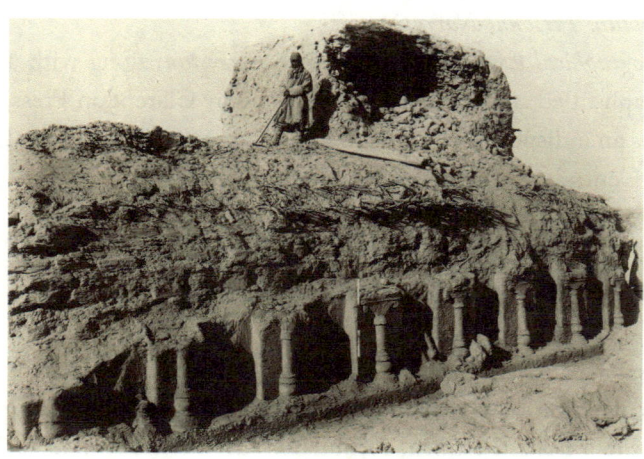

Figure 3-16 Stein excavated the pagoda at site No. 2 in Miran, Ruoqiang, Xinjiang (December 1906)

Stein commenced the second excavation in Hotan Rawak, followed by a return to the Niya ruins for further investigations later in October. Subsequently, in November, the expedition set its sights on the Loulan ruins in Lop Nur. Upon reaching the Lop Desert, the team initiated excavations at the Ruoqiang Miran ruins located to the south of Lop Nur.

Miran site No. 2 emerged as a pagoda structure resembling the Rawak Stupa, featuring a central pagoda (Figure 3-16). Surrounding the pagoda were six towering seated Buddha statues, positioned in unison along the outer wall facing the colonnade. The Buddha statues exhibited distinctive Gandhara artistic style in terms of body shape and clothing patterns. Notably, the unique aspect of the Han area influenced the stylistic representation of the Buddha's head, setting it apart from the conventional Gandhara art.

Miran site No. 3 unfolds as a structure characterized by an outer square and an inner circle. At its heart stands a circular adobe pagoda, surrounded by square walls, each side measuring approximately 9 meters, forming a spacious corridor about 1.2 meters wide around the pagoda. What astonished Stein was that at this desolate and remote site on the shores of Lop Nur in the heart of Asia, amid the solitude, there were seven depictions of European classical "angels" adorning the corridor of site No. 3. Positioned in the middle of the corridor, these "angels" captivated attention with their gaze fixed on a focal point, boasting large, expressive eyes and slightly pursed lips—a reminiscent echo of the captivating heads found in ancient Greek girl portraits (Figure 3-17). Remarkably, these figures were not Western angels but rather Gandharvas and Kinnara—celestial beings renowned for their musical, singing, and dancing prowess among the eight Buddhist guardians. Also found in the murals of the Dunhuang Caves, these charming deities utilized music and dance to disseminate the subtle teachings of Buddhism throughout the Buddhist realm. While not originating from Western angelic traditions, their prototypes can be traced back to images in Greek and Roman classical art. The influence of Alexander the Great, who introduced European classical art to the Gandhara region, paved the way for these angelic depictions. With the flourishing cultural exchanges between the Shanshan Kingdom and the Kushan Empire, these Western-inspired angelic images found a purpose as guardians and promoters of Buddhism in the Buddhist temples at the southern edge of the desert.

In the Miran site No. 3, a captivating fragment of a mural comes to life, portraying Sakyamuni Buddha alongside his six disciples. These figures, with their wide-open eyes, exude distinctive Central Asian features, hinting at a narrative intertwined with the life of Buddha. Meanwhile, in the adjacent corridor of site No. 5, a mural unfolds, illustrating the Jataka story of Prince Sudana—a prior incarnation of Sakyamuni. Known for his philanthropy and compassion toward the less fortunate, Prince Sudana mistakenly bestowed the

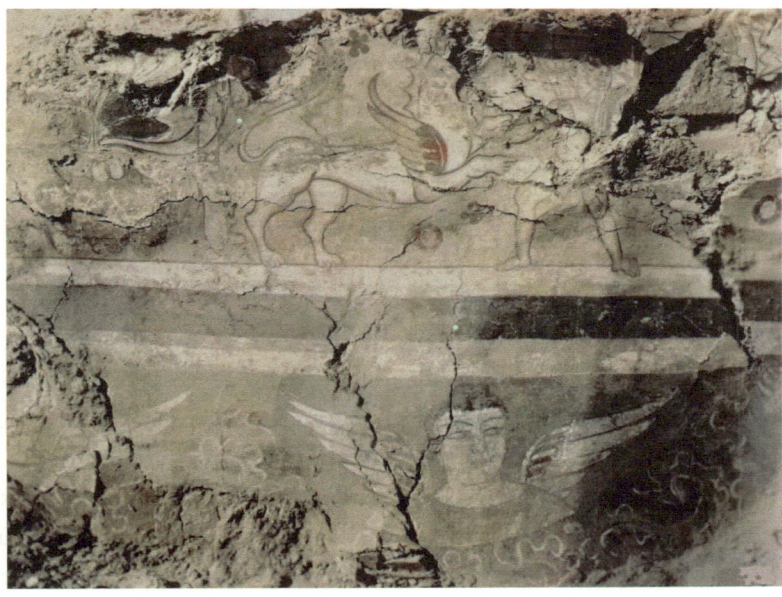

Figure 3-17 The *Winged Angels* mural Stein discovered at the Ruoqiang Miran site No. 3 in Xinjiang (December 1906)

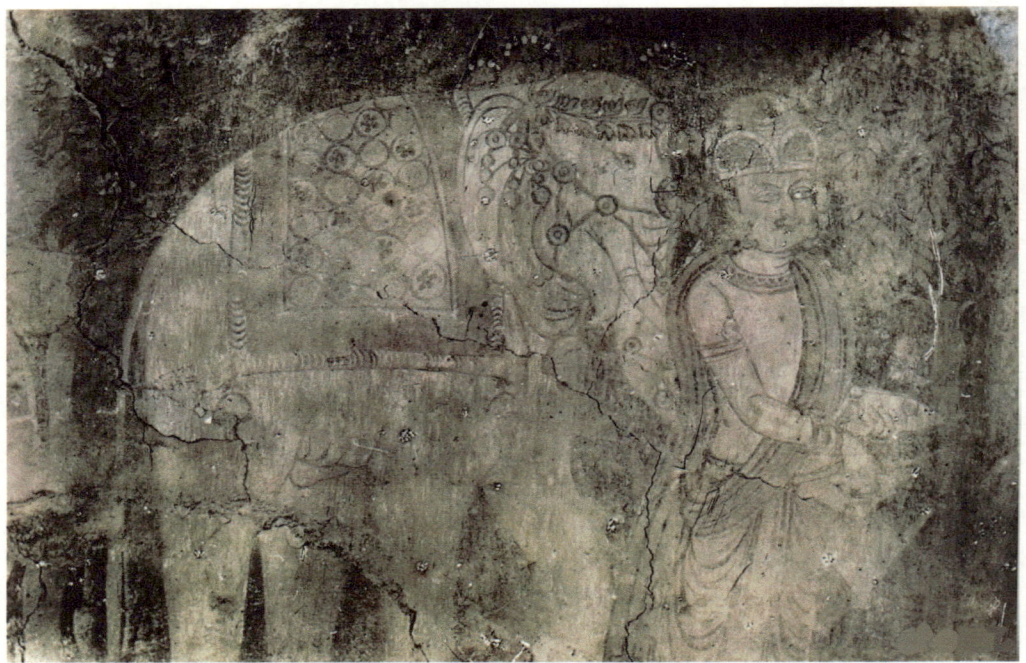

Figure 3-18 The *Jataka Story of Prince Sudana Giving away the White Elephant* mural Stein discovered at Ruoqiang Miran site No. 5 in Xinjiang (1906–1907)

sacred white elephant belonging to his father upon the Brahmins of an adversary nation. The depiction of Sudana in the mural reflects typical Central Asian male characteristics (Figure 3-18). Below this portrayal, young men and women carry corrugated flower cables, all with wide-open eyes, a recurring theme also found in the Śarīra container of King Kanishaka of the Kushan Empire unearthed in Cakra of Pakistan, as well as in the surface reliefs of sarcophagi from the ancient Roman Empire. This motif serves as a celebration of the accomplishments of revered figures.

In the extensive excavations led by Stein in Lop Nur, encompassing 14 ruins, the renowned Tibetan Fort (Figure 3-19) among them, over 500 precious cultural relics were unearthed. From the aforementioned Miran temple ruins, they also took away the murals and expressive clay sculptures reflecting the Buddhist art of the Gandhara culture in Xinjiang. Dating back to the 3rd to 4th centuries AD, when Kharosthi script was prevalent in the Shanshan Kingdom, the murals in the Buddhist temples of Miran showcase a potent blend of Gandhara art style, incorporating influences from Western art. These Buddha statues and murals stand as faithful chronicles, offering a vivid account of the millennia-old history of cultural exchanges between the East and the West.

In Lop Nur, beyond the excavation of ruins, Stein undertook another significant endeavor. In his work *Ancient Loulan*, he masterfully detailed his deduction that Loulan in China corresponds to the Kroraina area in the Kharosthi script. The wooden slips unearthed

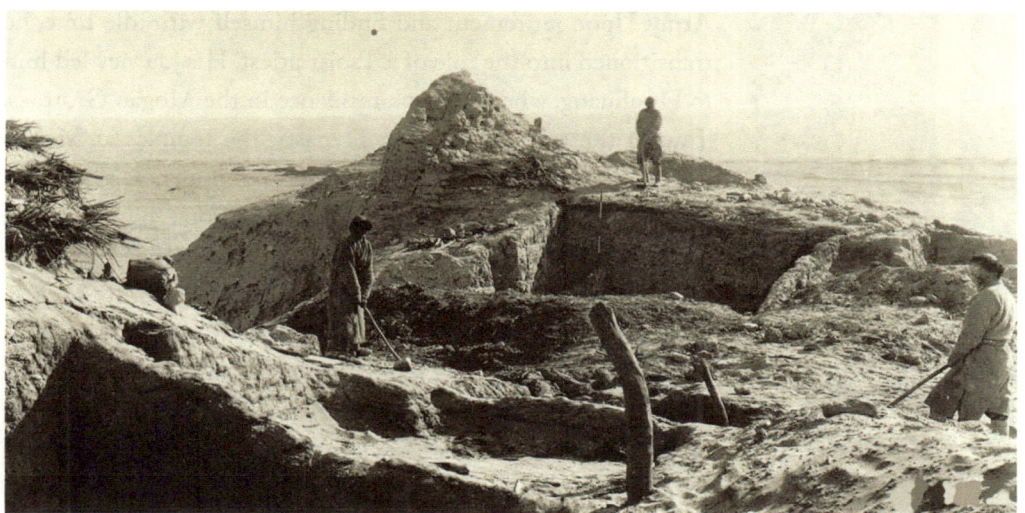

Figure 3-19 Stein excavated ancient city ruins south of Lop Nur, Xinjiang (1906–1907)

by Stein in Niya were inscribed in the Kharosthi script, also known as Gandhara, a variant of the ancient common language prevalent in ancient northwest India, particularly in the present-day Peshawar region of Pakistan. Stein's deductive prowess unfolded through an intricate analysis of the accounts presented by Zhang Qian (c. 164–114 BC), the Western Han Dynasty explorer, who paved the way for the exploration of the Western Regions. Stein proposed that "Loulan" is the Chinese transliteration of an indigenous toponym. Drawing a parallel between "Loulan" and "Kroraina" in the Kharosthi script, he surmised that the name originated from "Kroraina" or "Krorayina" in the Kharosthi script. After a meticulous examination of numerous documents and scrolls, Stein conclusively established that Loulan corresponds to Kroraina in the Kharosthi script.

Even when viewed through a contemporary linguistic lens, Stein's analytical approach is striking. Given the absence of a corresponding pronunciation for the semivowel "r" in the Chinese phonetic system, the challenge of transliterating foreign names into Chinese, and the absence of established rules for such transliterations before the Tang Dynasty, Stein's reliance on "lou" as a close approximation to replace "kro" is noteworthy. Similarly, the resonance between the pronunciation of "lan" and "raina" or "rayina" further adds to the linguistic intrigue of his deductions.

3.6 Wang Yuanlu's Unexpected Gains in Dunhuang

Before delving into Stein's whereabouts, it is imperative to shed light on another notable figure—Dunhuang Taoist priest Wang Yuanlu (1849–1931) (Figure 3-20). Hailing from Macheng, Hubei Province, Wang initially served as a soldier in the Suzhou (Jiuquan) Patrol

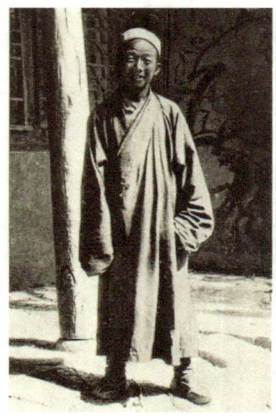

Figure 3-20 Taoist priest Wang Yuanlu (photographed by Stein in 1907)

Army. Upon retirement and finding himself with idle time, he transitioned into the role of a Taoist priest. His journey led him to Dunhuang, where he took residence in the Mogao Grottoes. Toward the end of the Qing Dynasty, the temples at Mogao Grottoes were strategically divided into upper, middle, and lower sections based on the terrain's elevation—higher in the south and lower in the north. The upper and middle temples accommodated lamas from the Red Sect of Tibetan Buddhism, engaging in the teachings and recitation of Buddhist scriptures in Tibetan. On the other hand, the lower temple, known as the Taiqing Palace, became the abode of Taoist priests. Drawing on his knowledge of Chinese and proficiency in reciting Taoist scriptures, Wang became a sought-after figure for conducting Taoist ceremonies, gradually improving his livelihood.

On June 26, 1900, Taoist priest Wang, fueled by his determination to restore the Mogao Grottoes, stumbled upon a concealed small cave within the corridor of Cave 16 (Figure 3-21). Upon entering this modest cavern, he discovered an astonishing sight—neatly arranged cloth bags occupying a space of only 19 cubic meters. Each bag cradled over a dozen volumes of ancient documents, accompanied by spread-out

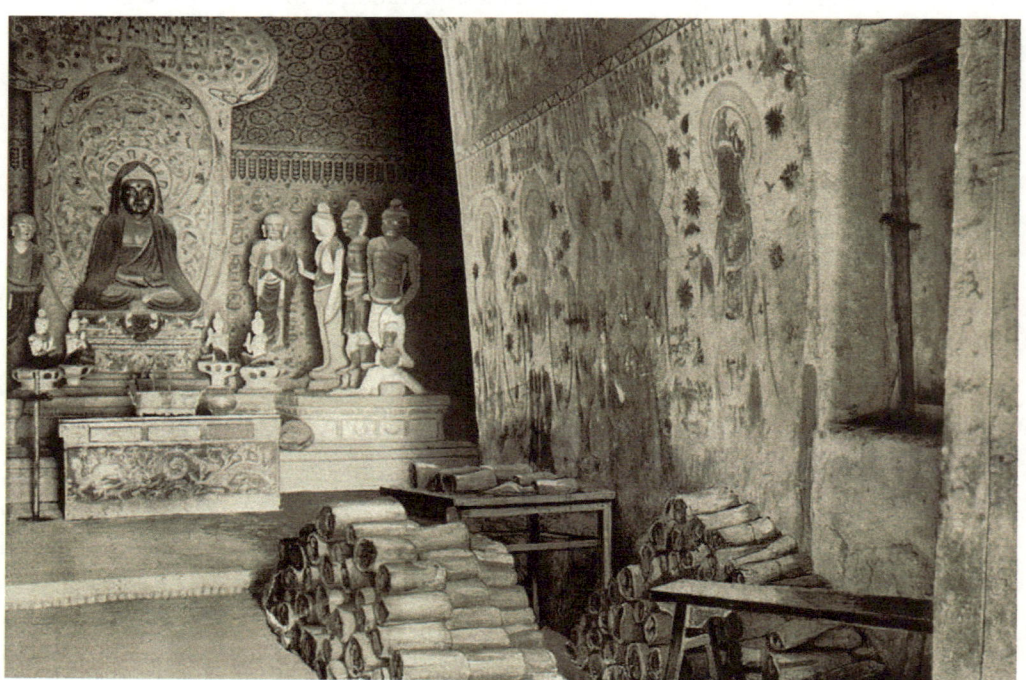

Figure 3-21 The Library Cave (Cave 17) and some ancient documents found on the side wall of the corridor in Cave 16 of the Mogao Grottoes (photographed by Stein in 1907)

books, Buddhist paintings on silk streamers, ancient woodblock prints, as well as copper and wooden Buddhist ritual instruments. Noteworthy murals adorned the north side of the cave, depicting trees and maids, while the west wall's niche housed a stone tablet—the Stele of Hong Bian's Edict from the fifth year of Dazhong in the Tang Dynasty (AD 851).

Hong Bian was a renowned monk in Dunhuang during the late Tang Dynasty. In the midst of Tibetan rule over Dunhuang in the 8th–9th century, Hong held the esteemed position of law professor at Shimen of Shazhou. His dedication and valor during Zhang Yichao's (AD 799–872) campaign to reclaim Dunhuang in AD 851 earned him the title Head Monk of Hexi, leader of monk's politics, law, and regulations, in Shimen from the Tang Dynasty. He received the rare honor of wearing purple—a distinctive tribute reserved for eminent monks, and was bestowed with the name "the great virtue worshiped at the altar inside and outside the capital." The Library Cave was later excavated as a testament to the influential monk Hong, also known as the "portrait hall" and "statue hall," earning it the alternative designation of Hong Bian Statue Cave (Figure 3-22).

Upon Taoist priest Wang's revelation of the enigmatic portrait cave, it was apparent that the statue of Hong Bian, containing his ashes bag, had been relocated, and the cave repurposed for the storage of scriptures. The origins of the multitude of documents stacked within the Library Cave and the reason for its closure remained a persistent mystery. Wang Yuanlu, in his unsuspecting discovery of Cave 17 in the Mogao Grottoes, unwittingly unearthed a site that would achieve global renown in the future.

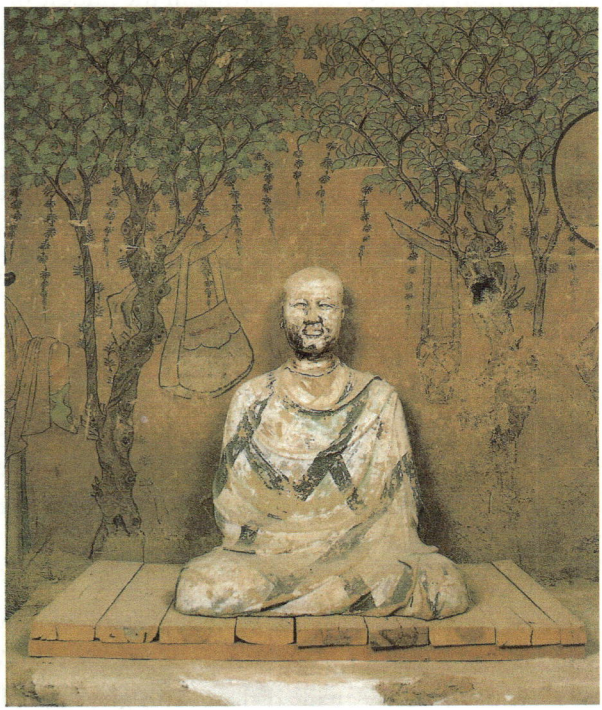

Figure 3-22 Interior view of Hong Bian Statue Cave in Cave 17 of Mogao Grottoes

Despite Wang Yuanlu's immediate report of the Library Cave's treasures to the Dunhuang County Magistrate, his efforts went unnoticed. The Qing government, regrettably, failed to implement protective measures, permitting him only the cave's sealing for preservation.

While the Dunhuang gentry overlooked the significance of these treasures, Wang held a divergent perspective. He once presented a box of scriptures to the Ansu Daotai (a rank of reginal governor), a Manchurian named Tingdong (1866–1918). Tingdong, unimpressed by the calligraphy, deemed it inferior to his own handwriting. However, an encounter with a departing Belgian at Jiayuguan's tax department marked a turning point. Tingdong gifted a portion of the scriptures to the Belgian, who later shared the tale with General Changgeng and a Daotai local surnamed Pan in Xinjiang. This revelation stirred interest among foreigners in Xinjiang, with the intrepid explorer Stein emerging as the first to set out for Dunhuang in pursuit of its fabled treasures upon hearing the news.

On February 11, 1907, Stein concluded a comprehensive excavation at the Miran site, meticulously packing and dispatching the unearthed cultural relics to Kashgar. Embarking on a journey to Dunhuang, Gansu, on February 21, Stein's arrival in March coincided with the news of the discovery of a Buddhist Library Cave in the Mogao Grottoes, relayed to him by a Uyghur businessman from Urumqi.

Stein's exploration of the Mogao Grottoes unfolded across five distinct visits—four in 1907 and one in 1914. The initial survey in March 1907 left him thrilled by the rich artistic value emanating from the cave murals (Figure 3-23). May emerged as his primary period of activity, with the first visit occurring in the middle of the month, aligning with the bustling temple fair commemorating Buddha's birthday at Mogao Grottoes. Stein chronicled this experience in his work, *Serindia: Detailed Report of Explorations in Central Asia and Westernmost China*:

> Although abundant opportunities and numerous relics beckon for the study of Buddhist art, it is prudent to initially confine activities to archaeology. This approach minimizes the risk of provoking public discontent and averts potential hazards.

On his second visit, on May 21, Stein returned to Mogao Grottoes after the dispersal of the temple fair. Setting up his tent, he prepared for an extended period of hard work aimed at uncovering the treasures concealed in the secret chambers. However, an unexpected turn of events occurred when Taoist priest Wang ventured out to seek alms. With the sealed treasure residing in the stone chamber, Stein redirected his efforts to investigate the nearby area temporarily.

By the end of May 1907, marking Stein's fourth visit to Mogao Grottoes, Wang had returned. Stein was ready for some long-term work with the assistance of Jiang Xiaowan, a Hunanese translator enlisted from Shule. Despite Wang's lack of comprehension of the documents' value, he guarded them with great care. Perhaps out of fear of displeasing the

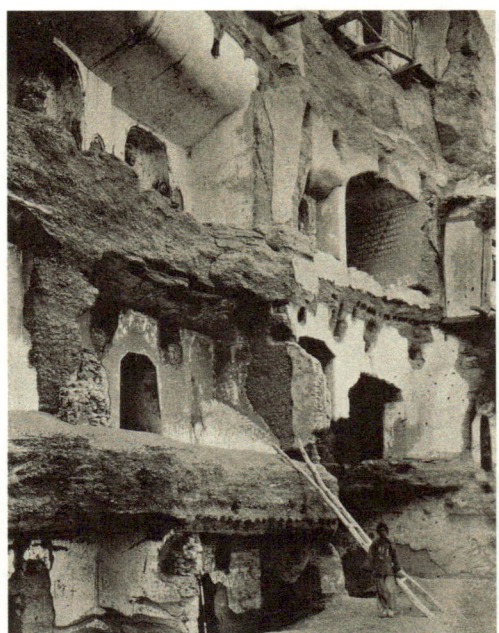

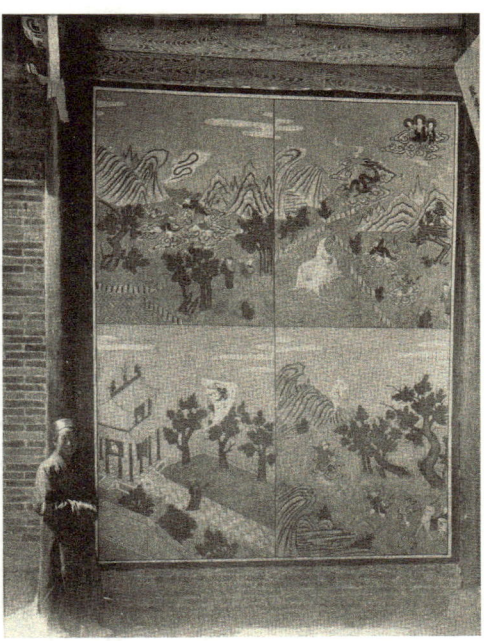

Figure 3-23 The cave group near Cave 432 of Dunhuang Mogao Grottoes (photographed by Stein on May 31, 1907)

Figure 3-24 Wang Yuanlu in front of the newly painted *Journey to the West* mural in Cave 16 of the three-story Mogao Grottoes (photographed by Stein in 1907)

gods or triggering public outrage, he unveiled them to little, which made Stein's pursuit difficult, as even "(all his money) used to lure him and his monastery was not sufficient to overcome his religious sentiments or the fear of public disapproval." However, Stein found inspiration in the murals of the lower temple, depicting the *Journey to the West*, executed by a less skilled painter commissioned by Wang (Figure 3-24). Though ignorant of Buddhism, Wang displayed deep reverence for the eminent monk Xuanzang of the Tang Dynasty, providing a potential breakthrough for Stein.

Stein utilized his limited proficiency in Chinese to conveyed to Wang his admiration for Xuanzang and narrated his own journey, following in Xuanzang's footsteps from India through treacherous mountains and deserts to the Mogao Grottoes. Clearly moved by Stein's words, Wang, that night, clandestinely revealed several manuscripts hidden in the secret chamber. A fortuitous coincidence came to Stein's aid when he learned that the initial volumes taken by Wang were the Buddhist scriptures translated by Xuanzang. Stein and Jiang took advantage of this revelation and depicted it in an almost superstitious tone that the spirit of Tang Monk Xuanzang in heaven entrusted these secret chambers to Wang Yuanlu, anticipating Stein's return to take the scriptures back to India. Energized by this belief, Wang's courage soared, and the following morning, he ushered Stein into the coveted secret chamber.

As Stein vividly recounted the scene within the secret chamber:

Heaped up in closely packed layers, but without any order, there appeared in the dim light of the priest's flickering lamp a solid mass of manuscript bundles rising to a height of nearly 10 feet. They filled, as subsequent measurement showed, close on 500 cubic feet, the size of the small room of chapel being about 9 feet square and the area left clear within just sufficient for two people to stand in.

With newfound enlightenment, the Taoist priest eagerly began to unveil the papers, one bundle after another.

Among the manuscripts (Figure 3-25), there lay "a sizable parcel swathed in colorless and resilient canvas. Upon unwrapping it, a treasure trove of ancient paintings emerged, boasting harmonious colors that remained as vibrant as new."

Stein discreetly observed Wang's apparent nonchalance toward these precious papers and works of art. A profound sense of surprise and relief washed over him. However, he reasoned, "It's prudent not to display excessive enthusiasm at this point." Indeed, this restraint swiftly took effect, as Wang's indifference to the relics appeared even more res-olute. To dispel Wang's lingering apprehensions toward public opinion, Stein suggested a donation of merit money to the temple, subsequently settling the price. They mutually agreed that, until Stein departed China, the origins of these discoveries would remain known to no one except the three of them. "Thereafter, Jiang bore the responsibility of transporting them alone, which took seven nights. The load grew increasingly weighty, necessitating transportation by vehicles."

In the end, Stein acquired twenty-four boxes brimming with manuscripts, along with five more meticulously filled with relics—paintings, embroideries, and other exquisite artworks. All these cultural treasures made their way to the British Museum in London. Astonishingly, Stein secured this extraordinary collection for a mere 40 pieces of horseshoe

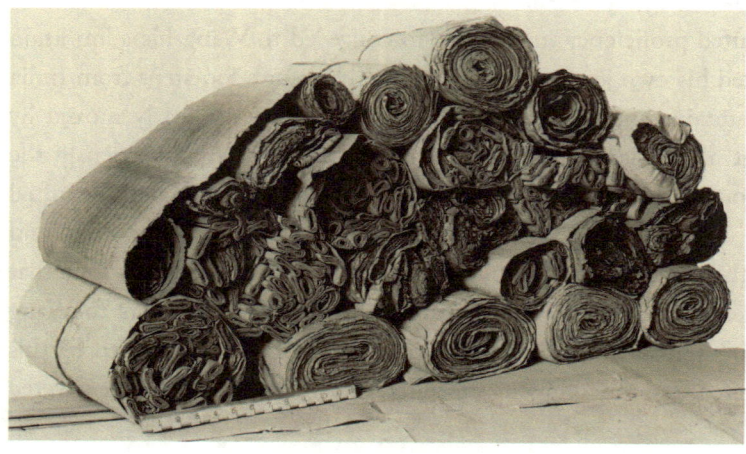

Figure 3-25 Bundles of ancient documents just moved out of the Dunhuang Library Cave (photographed by Stein in 1907)

silver, equivalent to 500 rupees. For Stein, this transaction represented an unparalleled deal. These manuscripts formed the cornerstone of the future 7,000 Dunhuang documents housed in the British Library (Figure 3-26).

3.7 Dunhuang Paintings Collected in the British Museum

The Dunhuang paintings, restored after years of meticulous effort, finally emerged in their resplendent glory. These exquisite artworks, having slumbered in obscurity for nearly a millennium, embarked on a transoceanic journey to find a new home in foreign lands, where they continue to captivate hearts with their timeless allure.

Hailing from the Library Cave, over 300 paintings on paper, silk, and linen from the

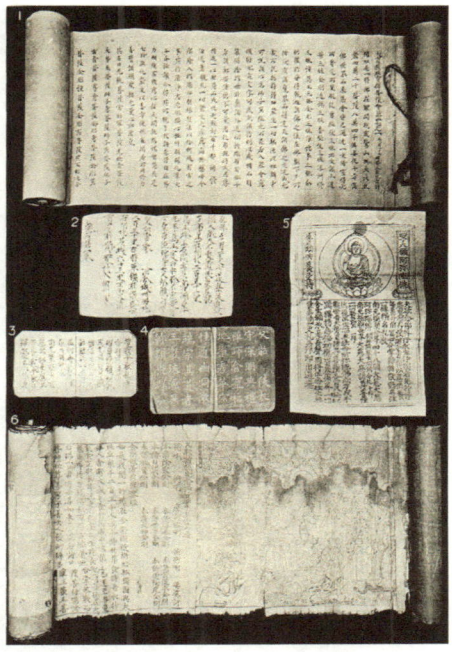

Figure 3-26 Part of the Chinese documents from the Dunhuang Library Cave (now in the British Library)

Tang and Song dynasties represent invaluable treasures in the annals of Dunhuang's artistic history and, by extension, China's cultural legacy. While only a limited number of paintings from the Tang, Five Dynasties, and Song dynasties have endured the ages, their scarcity has only heightened their appeal to art historians, who have studied them carefully and published numerous papers on them. These treasures, discovered within the Library Cave, are rightfully acknowledged as rare national treasures. Stein carried away more than 200 pieces of the collection, which is now housed in the British Museum in London, while Paul Pelliot transported over 100 pieces to the Guimet Museum in Paris.

Stein's acquisitions span a diverse array of themes, ranging from depictions of specific Bodhisattvas making wishes to sublime Pure Land paintings portraying the Western Paradise. Some are ingeniously presented as flags, slender and elongated, adorned with triangular flagheads and billowing rectangular streamers embellished with dangling weights. Adorning these streamers are vivid portrayals of Jataka stories, single images of Buddhas, Bodhisattvas, and protectors (Figure 3-27), with the image of Avalokitesvara being particularly prevalent, embodying the compassionate Bodhisattva revered for saving all living beings. Some are hanging scroll paintings, and the biggest of them reveal grand depictions of the Buddhist Paradise, with a focus on the ethereal beauty of the Western Paradise housing Medicine Buddha and Amitabha. The depicted subject matter aligns seamlessly with Buddhist scriptures. The primary Buddhist figures within the artworks exude grace, solemnity, and magnificence, indicative of the stylistic influence of renowned artists from

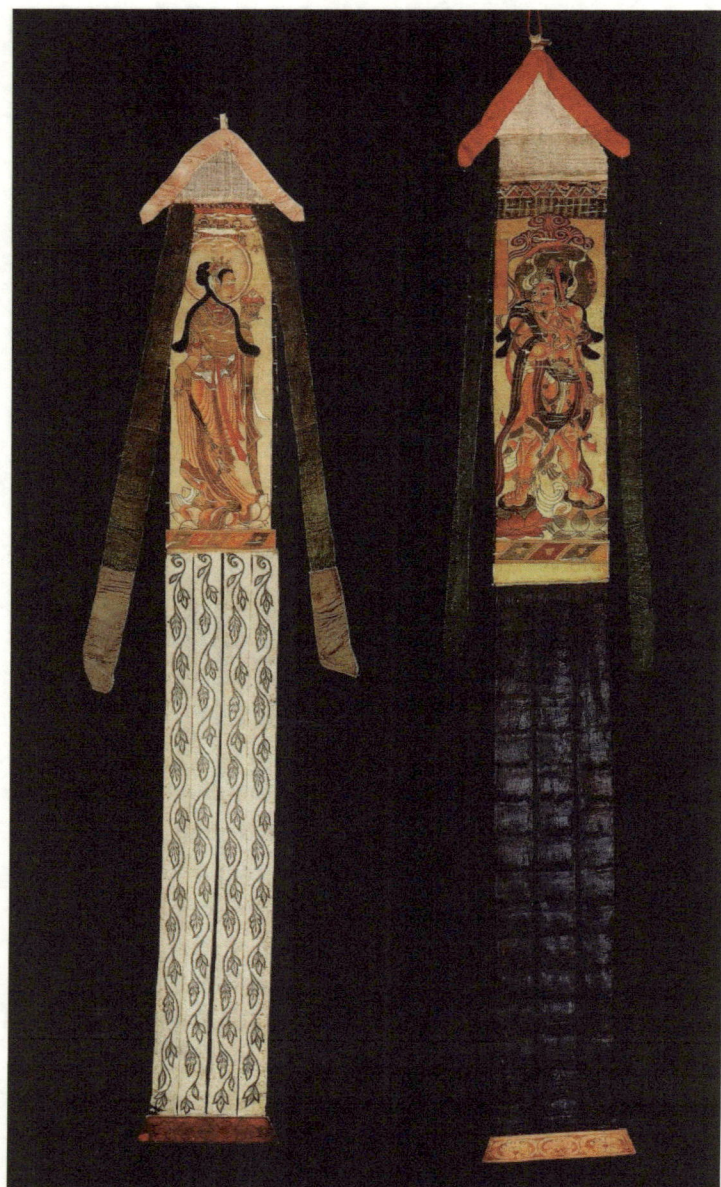

Figure 3-27 Silk-colored Bodhisattva flags (left, 172.5 cm long, 18 cm wide) and Vajra warrior flags (right, 187.5 cm long, 18.6 cm wide) from the Dunhuang Library Cave in the late 9th century of the Tang Dynasty (now housed in the British Museum)

that era. Intricately detailed hand-scroll paintings unravel narrative-rich content, vividly portraying scenes such as the sequential judgment of ghosts by the kings of hell. Below, we delve into a selection of examples.

Tejaprabhā Buddha and the Five Planets, an exquisite Tang Dynasty masterpiece held by the British Museum, measuring 80.4 cm × 55.4 cm, with the museum number 1919.0101.0.31 (Figure 3-28), unfolds a celestial tableau featuring the Tejaprabhā Buddha and five planets adorned with embellishments on top. There are notes on the painting that

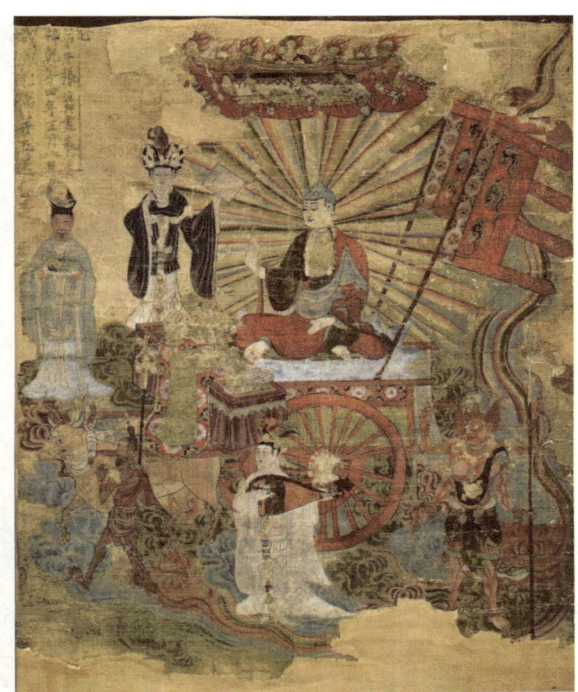

Figure 3-28 The hanging scroll painting *Tejaprabhā Buddha and the Five Planets* from the Dunhuang Library Cave, dated to the fourth year (AD 897) of Tang Emperor Qianning's reign (now housed in the British Museum)

read: "To Tejaprabhā Buddha and the gods of five planets, on January 8 of the fourth year of Qianning (AD 897), presented by disciple Zhang Huaixing." The Tejaprabhā Buddha is a divine figure with the power to subdue the Sun, the Moon, and stars, quelling disasters and dispelling difficulties. Ancient Chinese believed that celestial bodies influence atmospheric changes, thus giving rise to earthly calamities. The veneration of Tejaprabhā Buddha dawned during the Tang Dynasty, blossomed into full magnificence amid the Song and Yuan dynasties, and gracefully persisted until the Ming Dynasty (AD 1368–1644) graced the historical stage. In the depiction, the Tejaprabhā Buddha and the gods of the five planets gracefully ride upon vibrant clouds, with the Buddha emanating an immense glow, signifying his awe-inspiring power. The chariot, driven by the Tejaprabhā Buddha, is drawn by a majestic bull and faces leftward. Positioned in a counterclockwise arrangement around the chariot, the gods of five planets each embody distinct characteristics. Jupiter, portrayed as a woman with an ape crown, holds paper and pen; Mercury, as an official in black attire with a pig crown, gracefully wields flowers and fruits; Saturn, a Brahmin figure, wears a cow crown and clutches a tin staff; Venus, depicted as a woman with a bird crown, dons white training attire while playing the *pipa*; Mars, a formidable four-armed warrior with a donkey and horse crown, brandishes weapons in each hand.

At the altar before the bullock cart stands a set of meticulously crafted sacrificial vessels. The radiant golden hues that once adorned the face and body of the Tejaprabhā Buddha

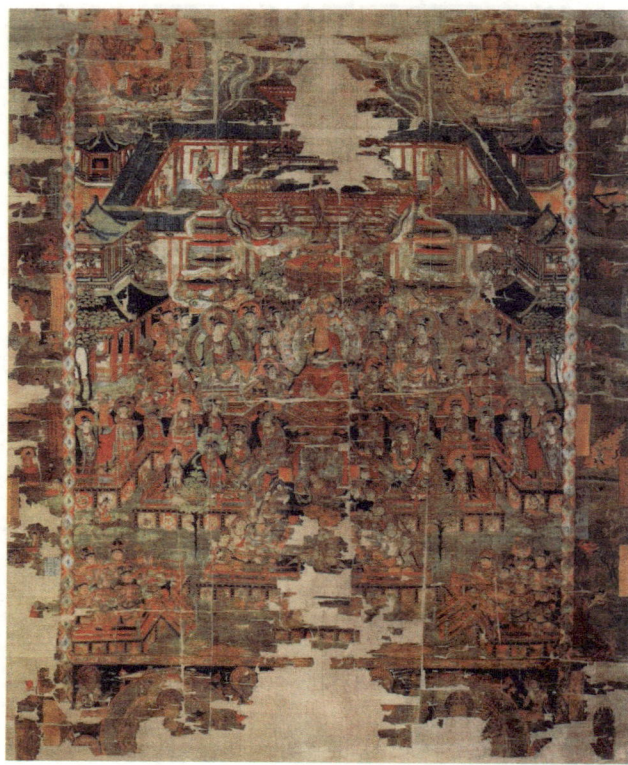

Figure 3-29 Hanging scroll of the silk *Medicine Buddhas Transformation Illustration* of about the 9th century AD, from the Dunhuang Library Cave (206 cm long, 167 cm wide, now housed in the British Museum)

have been expertly restored. Remnants of wide purple silk at the mural's summit suggest its former use as a hanging streamer, although regrettably, only an 11.5 centimeters high ribbon of the upper silk remains, with the lower frame lost to time's passage.

Another captivating silk painting from the Tang Dynasty, *Medicine Buddhas Transformation Illustration*, graces the collection with its larger-than-life presence, measuring 206 cm × 167 cm and bearing the number 1919.0101.0.36 (Figure 3-29). Transformation illustrations usually depict the contents of Buddhist scriptures and stories derived from the Buddhist legends. In *Medicine Buddhas Transformation Illustration*, the Pure Land for the Medicine Buddha is the Eastern Glazed Paradise (Vaidūryanirbhāsā), so Medicine Buddha is also called Medicine Glazed Buddha (Bhaiṣajya-guru-vaiḍūrya-prabha-rāja). This painting may be the largest surviving Dunhuang silk painting, and its composition is comparable to the most complex Pure Land illustrations in the Dunhuang Caves murals.

This painting can be divided into three sections. On the leftmost expanse, an eloquent long streamer unveils the entire saga of "The Medicine Buddha's Twelve Vows," portraying his altruistic aspirations to alleviate the suffering of all sentient beings. These vows embody the noble pursuit of peace, happiness, and freedom from maladies, encapsulating the essence of the Medicine Buddha's religious mission. From top down, the rightmost streamer unveils the "Nine Brutal Deaths," enumerating various distressing pathways such as illness, starvation, drowning, burning, murdering, and suicide, among others. The Medicine Buddha is endowed with the power to transcend these tragic demises, saving beings away from such untimely fates. At the heart of the scroll lies Medicine Buddha's Pure Land, intricately structured into six floors. The first floor introduces Sahasrabhuja and Thousand-Bowl Manjushri; the second floor depicts the majestic Pure Land of the Medicine Buddha; the third floor showcases the grand assembly of the Medicine Buddha Triad and their entourages; the fourth floor portrays the scene of various Buddhas and Bodhisattvas guiding believers to be reborn in the Pure Land of the Medicine Buddha; the fifth floor presents a joyous scene of song and dance welcoming the reborn into the Pure Land, along with the imagery of the lotus pond. The sixth floor reveals the celestial presence of Cintāmaṇicakra and Amoghapāśa, accompanied by their devoted entourage, embodying the prevalent Avalokitesvara belief of the era.

The central figure, the Medicine Buddha, sits serenely in the lotus position, his right hand in the Dharma mudra on his chest, his left hand cradling a medicine bowl. Flanked by two attendant Bodhisattvas, Sūryaprabha and Candraprabha, a triad is formed. Sūryaprabha and Candraprabha also have entourages comprising heavenly kings and demons. In the bustling tableau below the triad, the depiction of the Pure Land world unfolds, depicting the jubilant reception of departed souls through song and dance, complemented by scenes of sentient beings passing away in the lotus pond. On the central stage depicted in the painting, a jubilant ensemble of singers and dancers extends a warm welcome to all living beings. At the heart of this lively scene, a graceful dancer stands, elegantly waving streamers, spinning silk, and dancing with enchanting poise. Flanking her on either side are two dancing children, with the leftmost one rhythmically beating a drum suspended from his chest. Adorning the periphery of a serene lotus pond are twelve divine generals, six on each side, standing as vigilant guardians of the resplendent Pure Land. The altar hosts a golden incense burner delicately poised on a three-legged tray. Positioned on either side of the altar, four musicians each engage in a symphony of melodic harmony. The left side resonates with the sounds of the *pipa*, lyre, *konghou*, and other instruments, while the right side offers the melodic notes of the *xiao*, *sheng*, flute, clapper, and more. A dancer takes center stage, accompanied by a human-head bird-body Kalaviṅka skillfully playing a cymbal. There should have been a bird in front of it, which is now mutilated. (Figure 3-30). Remarkably, the painting seamlessly fuses elements of both Chinese and Western cultures within its musical ensemble. The *qin*, a revered instrument in Chinese tradition, harmoniously coexists with the *pipa*, which finds its roots in Western origins. Together, they produce a symphony of Buddhist melodies, infusing the surroundings with a warm and joyous atmosphere.

Some scholars believe that the presence of Manjushri assumes a pivotal role in *Medicine Buddha Sutra*, for which significance the *Medicine Buddhas Transformation Illustration* adds the portrayal of the Thousand-Bowl Manjushri. Certain scholars postulate compelling

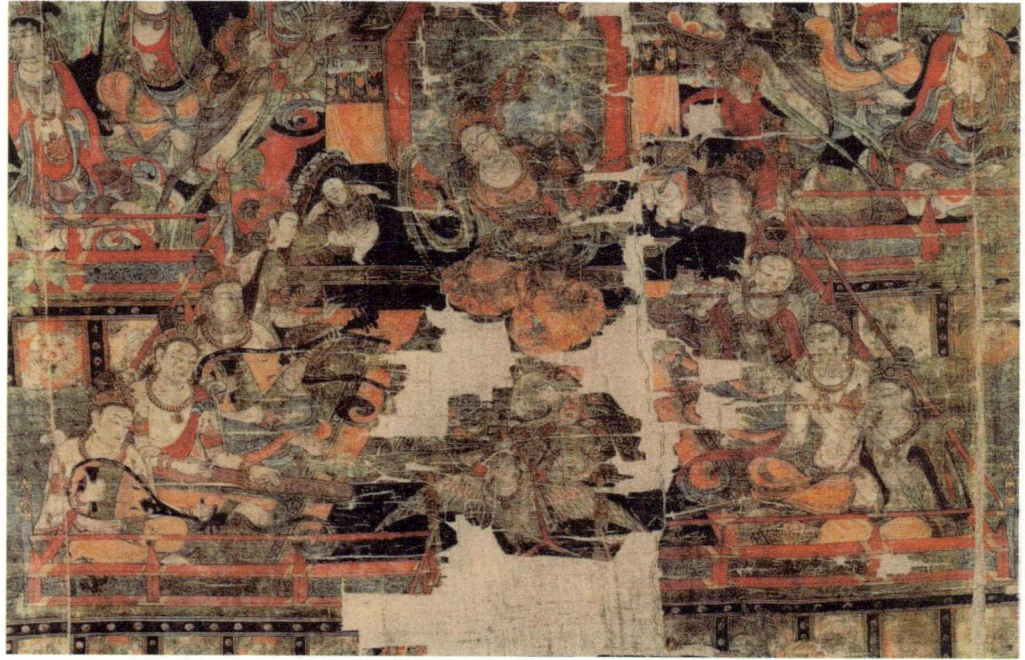

Figure 3-30 Dancers, musicians, and the Kalaviṅka bird in *Medicine Buddhas Transformation Illustration*

parallels between revered Bodhisattvas such as Sahasrabhuja, Cintāmaṇicakra, Thousand-Bowl Manjushri, and Amoghapāśa, suggesting a profound connection with the Medicine Buddha's spiritual realm. Some think this convergence of esoteric Bodhisattvas manifests within the realms of the *Medicine Buddhas Transformation Illustration.*

The meticulously preserved large silk painting, *Guiding Bodhisattva* (Figure 3-31), was also transported to London by Stein. As a testament to the enduring legacy of Dunhuang paintings beyond geographical boundaries, it captures the essence of Avalokitesvara Bodhisattva guiding the departed soul of an aristocratic woman toward the Western Paradise. The Guiding Bodhisattva is a Bodhisattva that guides the souls of the deceased to the Pure Land. Though not explicitly named in traditional Buddhist scriptures, it finds its visual manifestation in this exquisite piece discovered within the Dunhuang Library Cave. According to the confirmation of relevant classics, Avalokitesvara shares the function of Guiding Bodhisattva.

The Bodhisattva depicted in the painting adorns himself with *yingluo* and a dignified heavenly garment. His right hand gracefully holds a long-handled incense burner, from which a delicate wisp of incense gently rises. Within the ethereal smoke, vibrant clouds form, revealing the sacred Pure Land treasure pavilion. In his left hand, the Bodhisattva cradles a lotus, and beneath it hangs a guide flag, symbolizing his role in leading the souls of the departed. Trailing behind the Bodhisattva is a woman embodying the departed soul. Positioned in the upper right corner of the painting are three Chinese characters, "Yin

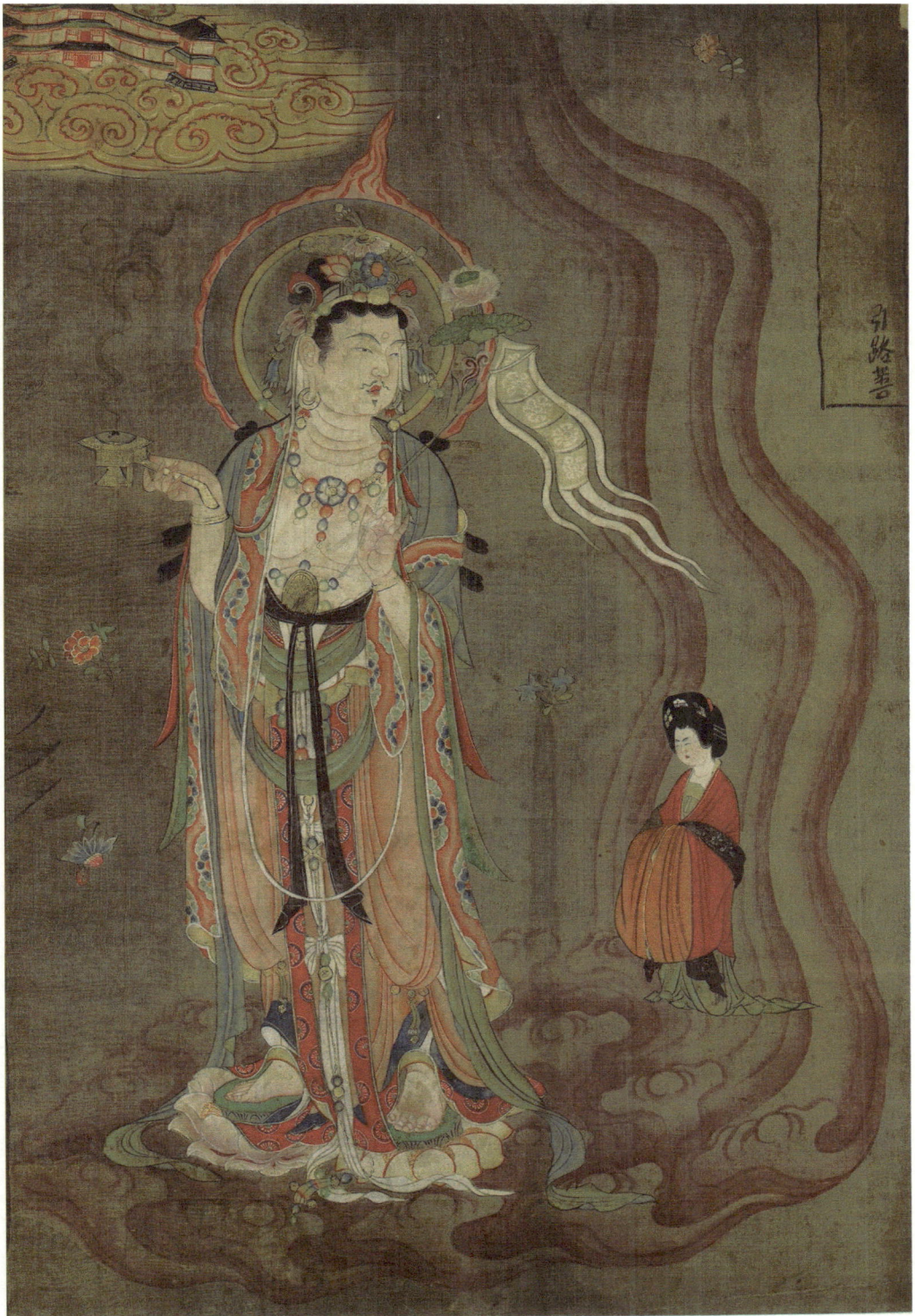

Figure 3-31 Hanging scroll of *Guiding Bodhisattva* from the Dunhuang Library Cave in the 8th century of the Tang Dynasty (80.5 cm long, 53.8 cm wide, now housed in the British Museum)

Lu Pu" (Guiding Bodhisattva), serving as the title. The artwork portrays the monumental Bodhisattva and the diminutive soul standing atop auspicious clouds descending from above, embarking on a journey toward the Western Paradise. The woman following the Bodhisattva mirrors the image of the deceased in life, donning a traditional Tang Dynasty hairstyle. Her attire, coiffure, and even her plump visage mirror the characteristics depicted in *Court Ladies Adorning Their Hair with Flowers* by Zhou Fang, an artist from the flourishing Tang Dynasty. This confirmation underscores her esteemed status within the narrative of the painting.

The paintings that Stein carried away are not only masterpieces of exquisite craftsmanship but also radiate vivid colors, showcasing the pinnacle of Buddhist artistry during the Tang Dynasty. These artworks eloquently convey the timeless beauty of ancient allure, providing invaluable insights for the scholarly exploration of Chinese painting.

Within the collection of Buddhist paintings from the Dunhuang Library Cave that Stein acquired, a multitude of engraved and printed works stand out. Predominantly illustrations extracted from Buddhist scriptures, these pieces boast a wealth of content. Beyond their significance in unraveling the history of book publishing, these Buddhist prints prove to be invaluable aids in the study of Buddhist iconography. One noteworthy example among Stein's acquisitions is the *Diamond Sutra*, printed in the ninth year of Xiantong during the Tang Dynasty (AD 868). This particular sutra stands unparalleled, as no older or more complete printed book has been unearthed worldwide. The volume features an arresting depiction of the Buddha delivering a sermon, situated at the forefront (Figure 3-32). A detailed inscription above the illustration reveals that the scene portrays the Buddha expounding the *Diamond Sutra* in Jetavana of Shravasti. The artwork portrays the Buddha beneath an umbrella cover, flanked by a flying apsara on either side. His retinue includes disciples, Bodhisattvas, two Dharma protectors, and an individual resembling a lay official. An offering table adorned with offerings graces the foreground, while an elderly monk, identified as Subhuti, kneels before the altar table, engaging the Buddha in questioning—a prologue to the *Diamond Sutra*. The monastery's floor is meticulously paved with square tiles bearing floral and plant patterns. The fine and powerful lines in this painting attest to the artist's exceptional stereotyping techniques. Transported to England by Stein in 1907, this particular copy is now treasured within the esteemed collection of the British Library.

3.8 More Gains for the UK

In the span of 31 years, from 1900 to 1931, Stein conducted four comprehensive inspections of Xinjiang, during which he amassed a remarkable collection of cultural relics totaling over 10,000 items. His meticulous inspection reports and diaries eloquently document these acquisitions, providing a vivid account of his endeavors. The second and third expeditions

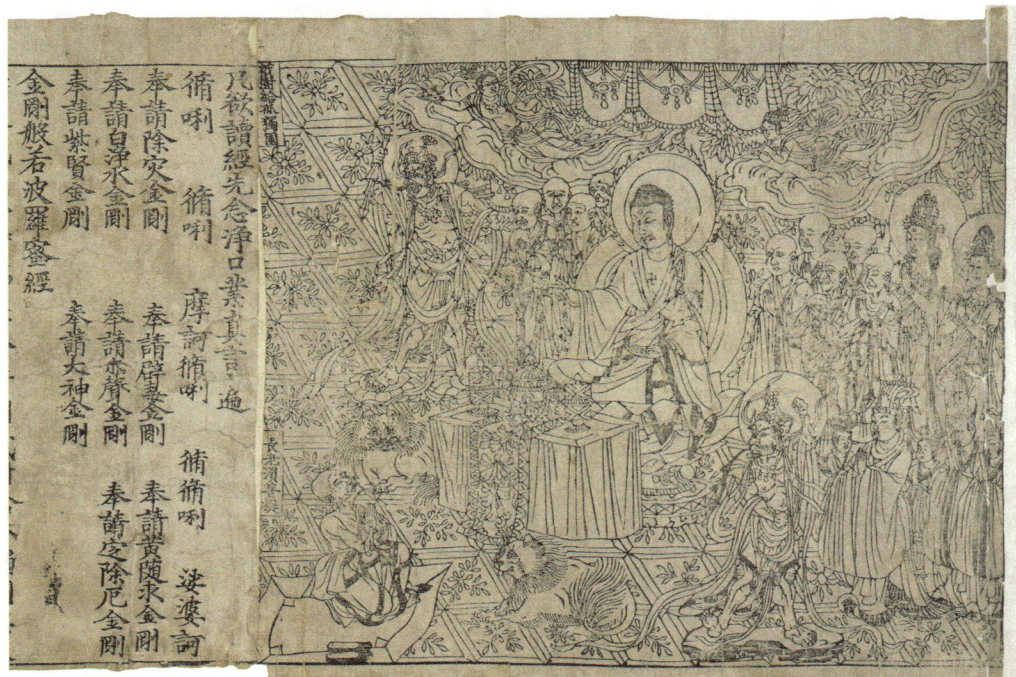

Figure 3-32 *Buddha Preaching Illustration* on the frontpage of Block-printed edition of *Diamond Sutra* unearthed from in the Dunhuang Library Cave in the 9th year of Xiantong (AD 868) in the Tang Dynasty (paper print, 27.8 cm high, 240 cm long, now housed in British Library)

yielded more than 7,000 documents, currently safeguarded in the British Library. These documents encompass a diverse range of languages, including Chinese, Tibetan, Sogdian, Turkic, Uighur, Kharosthi, and Sanskrit, with additional materials from Hotan and Turpan (Figure 3-33). The published *Dunhuang Documents in the British Collection* and the ongoing *Dunhuang Legacies in the British Library* serve as a meticulous presentation of the Dunhuang documents meticulously housed at the British Library. While Stein's collection was extensive, it is essential to note that his limited understanding of sinology and Chinese led him to predominantly select well-preserved scriptures. Consequently, the academic value of his manuscripts falls below that of later French sinologists, notably Pelliot, who arrived at Dunhuang subsequent to Stein.

Upon his return to England after the second expedition, Stein received widespread acclaim for his obtaining the cultural relics from Dunhuang. Everyone wanted to befriend him, calling him the first British explorer of the East. Over the ensuing three years, Stein remained an active figure in Europe, participating in British investiture ceremonies, delivering lectures at universities, and completing the publication of archaeological work reports. Despite the acclaim, Stein harbored an unwavering desire—to revisit Dunhuang and retrieve the remaining artifacts.

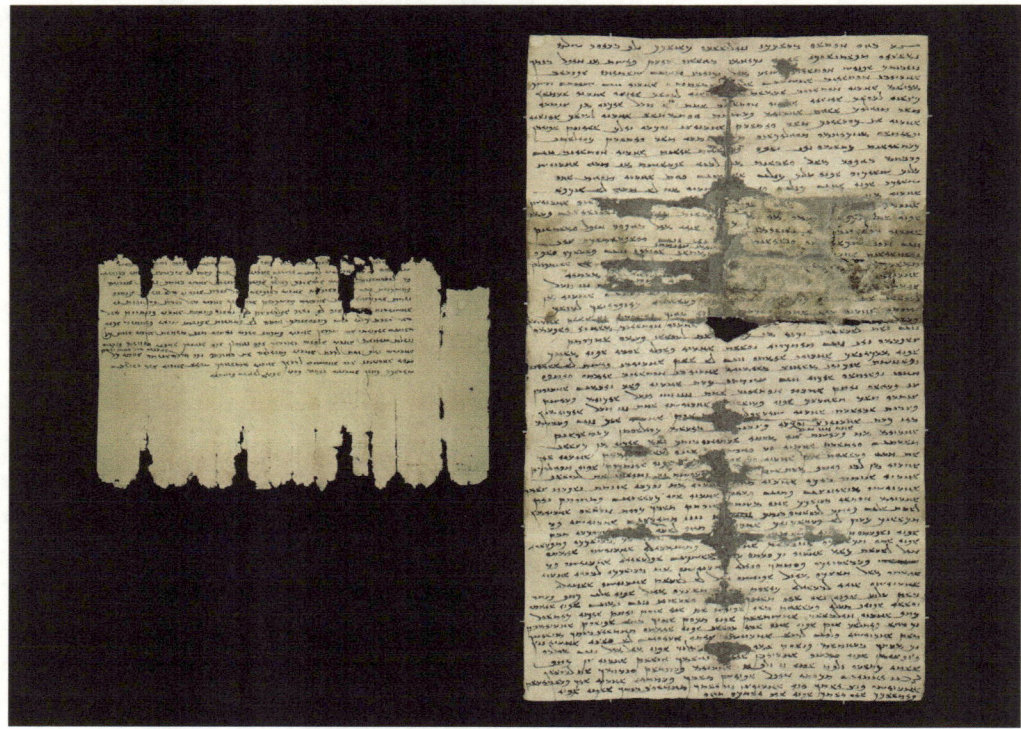

Figure 3-33 Two Sogdian documents (c. AD 313) from the Dunhuang Library Cave (ink on paper, the right one is 42 cm high and 24.3 cm wide, now in the British Library)

In early 1914, Stein, accompanied by his expedition team, arrived in Ruoqiang, Xinjiang, commencing his third expedition. At the Miran ruins, he meticulously removed exquisite murals that had eluded him during the second expedition. Prior to extraction, Stein employed careful techniques, partially chiseling the wall behind the mural and sawing off the brick and wood structure. This method aimed to preserve the integrity of the mural as much as possible. Through this destructive grab, Stein successfully obtained 11 pieces of murals, placing them on backing pads and securing them in six large boxes for transportation (Figure 3-34).

In March 1914, Stein made a triumphant return to Dunhuang. At the renowned Mogao Grottoes, he received a warm welcome from Wang Yuanlu, who greeted him with the familiarity of old friends. Wang candidly recounted the events of 1909 when, under various pressures, the Qing government decided to nationalize the Dunhuang documents. He expressed sorrow over the uncouth handling of the artifacts of the government and regretted not entrusting all the documents to Stein. However, Wang Yuanlu's honesty was not absolute; before the remaining documents were taken to Beijing, he clandestinely concealed over 1,000 volumes. Most of these documents were acquired by Stein, who had paid a mere 500 taels of silver for them.

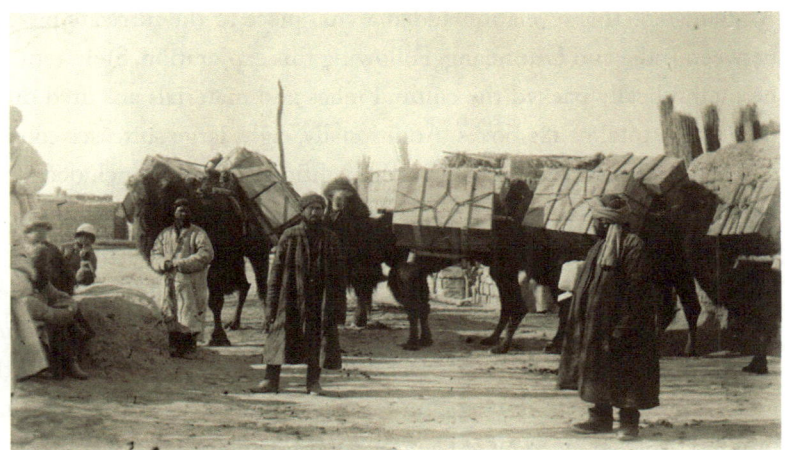

Figure 3-34 Stein packed and shipped away the cultural relics obtained at the Miran ruins (February 1, 1914)

Having secured the last treasures from Dunhuang, Stein proceeded northward along Jiuquan to the Ejin River, arriving in May 1914 to inspect the ruins of Khara-Khoto. Officials warmly welcomed him along the way. Khara-Khoto, a significant town in the northern part of the Western Xia Kingdom (AD 1038–1227), had been the residence of the Yan Army Division, and Ejin City in the Yuan Dynasty. Situated on the edge of the Badain Jaran Desert east of the Nalin River in present-day Inner Mongolia, it succumbed to the encroachment of quicksand in the early Ming Dynasty, disrupting the vital post road from the Hexi Corridor to the Mobei area. From 1907 to 1909, during a Central Asian expedition, Russian explorer Pyotr Kozlov discovered this captivating ancient city and its more than 300 Buddhist paintings, including a considerable number of tantric thangka paintings with a distinct Tibetan Buddhist style. Inspired, Stein would like to try his luck there as well.

In June 1914, Stein's explorations in Khara-Khoto yielded an abundance of documents written in Han, Tangut, Turpan, and Uighur languages, discovered amid garbage dumps and ruined towers. Notably, he uncovered a well-preserved document in Persian.

By October 1914, Stein had reached Turpan, Xinjiang, commencing the extraction of murals from the Bezeklik Caves. His efforts resulted in approximately 90 boxes of murals. Throughout this period, officials of varying ranks in Xinjiang extended their hospitality to Stein, entertaining him in succession. To these officials, the ancient caves appeared as abandoned relics, and they showed no remorse for the murals being taken away by foreigners. Their primary aim was to foster friendships with outsiders. Despite their well-intentioned gestures, Stein found their hospitality burdensome, expressing his discontent in his diary and lamenting the hindrance it posed to his inspection and research endeavors. By February 1915, Stein had amassed a staggering 141 boxes of cultural relics around Turpan.

In May 1915, Stein revisited Kuqa, examining the Kizil Caves. Capturing the essence of these remarkable murals through photography, Stein recognized their significance as a crucial link connecting the Mogao Grottoes in Dunhuang with the Bamiyan Caves in

Afghanistan. This revelation added a vital piece to the intricate puzzle of cultural heritage between India and Dunhuang. Following this exploration, Stein returned to Kashgar, where he methodically packed the cultural relics and materials acquired during his third expedition into a total of 182 boxes. Additionally, eight large suitcases contained films, negatives, and other items. Thus, Stein's third expedition officially concluded after a span of two years and eight months.

Rather than immediately penning a travel note upon concluding his third expedition, Stein continued his writing efforts for the subsequent decade. His dedicated focus culminated in a comprehensive research report titled *Innermost Asia: Detailed Report of Explorations in Central Asia, Kan-su and Eastern Iran*. He also delved into the identification and understanding of Dunhuang cultural relics. In 1923, Stein also published a separate volume of maps, *Memoir on Maps of Chinese Turkistan and Kansu from the Surveys Made during Sir Aurel Stein's Explorations, 1900–1, 1906–8, 1913–5*. This atlas meticulously documented Stein's routes and findings in multiple archaeological endeavors, serving as an invaluable reference for scholars engaged in Dunhuang studies.

Stein's prolific research career persisted until 1925. At this juncture, Harvard University expressed interest in employing the nearing-retirement-age Stein to collect cultural relics from western China. In the twilight of 1929, Harvard University extended a prestigious invitation to Stein, beckoning him to deliver a series of 10 reports on his Central Asia expeditions at the esteemed Lowell Institute. And the university further honored him by appointing him as an honorary fellow at the Fogg Museum, and embarked on a mission to secure 100,000 US dollars in support for Stein. Amid these enticements, Stein found himself tempted by the prospect of aiding the United States in acquiring cultural relics. However, his commitment came with a stipulation: the British Museum must contribute £3,000 and actively participate in the distribution of the cultural relics. Remarkably, the three parties swiftly reached a harmonious consensus. In 1930, Stein, representing Britain and the United States, organized a new expedition to delve into the southern edge of the Tarim Basin, Dunhuang and east area to it, Turpan, and other locations (Figure 3-35). Unfortunately, this venture faced challenges due to cultural relics protection laws issued by the Republic of China government, among other factors, leading to its premature termination. Cultural relics obtained through improper means were temporarily housed in the British Consulate in Kashgar and later transferred to the Peking Antiquities Preservation Committee after negotiations with the Xinjiang Provincial Government.

Prior to departing the Chinese border, Stein photographed the antiquities acquired during his final expedition. These photographic records found a home in the Department of Oriental and Indian Collections of the British Library (Figure 3-36). These images remain invaluable resources for consultation and scholarly study. Remarkably, this expedition stands as a singular anomaly in Stein's illustrious exploration career—it lacks any written records. Notably, Stein refrained from discussing the details of this fourth expedition in public. The academic community remains in the dark about the specifics of this endeavor, and it

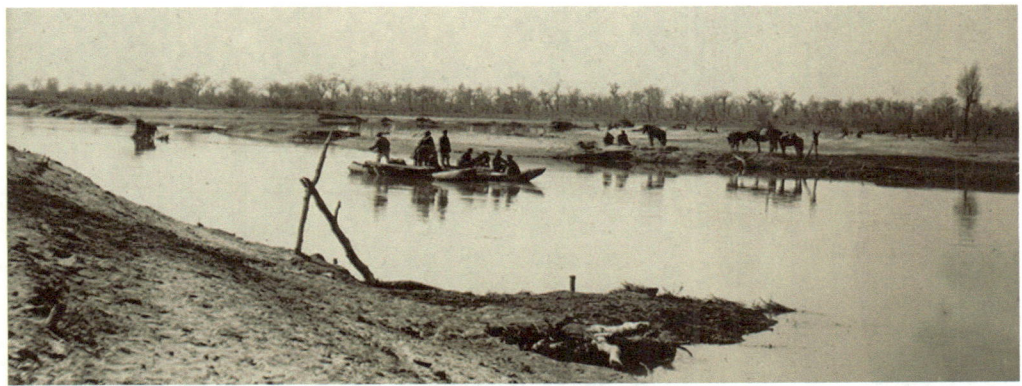

Figure 3-35 Stein's fourth expedition at the Kongque River on the southern edge of the Tarim Basin (March 1931)

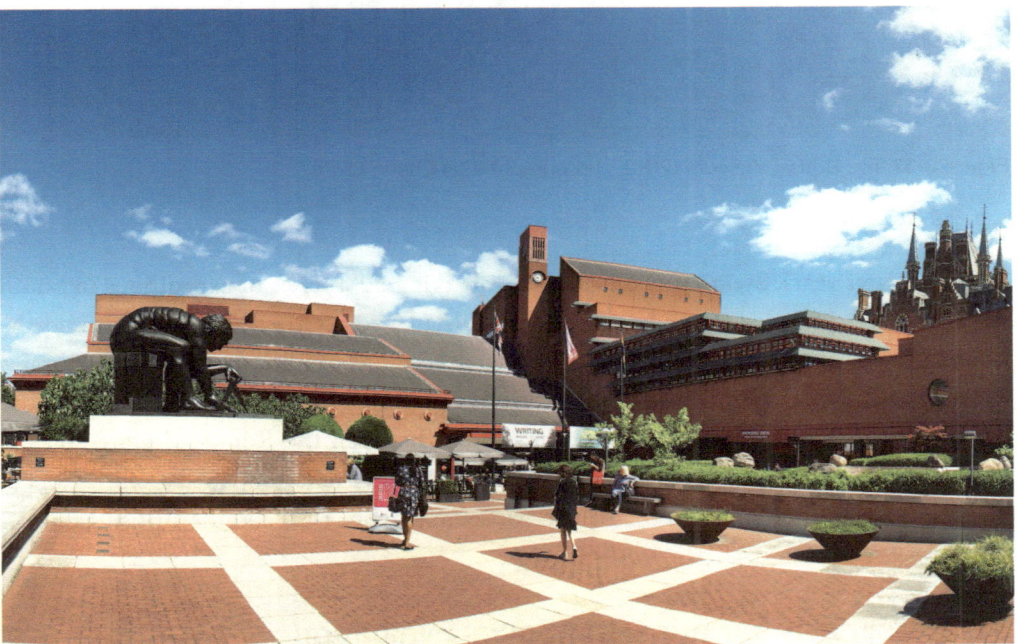

Figure 3-36 The British Library (2019, photographed by Chang Qing)

stands as an enigma in Stein's exploratory legacy. It is conceivable that Stein regarded this expedition, which regrettably failed to bring back Chinese cultural relics, as exceptionally unsuccessful. He was merely ashamed of the failure. Adding to the intrigue, another curious twist emerges: the cultural relics relinquished by Stein mysteriously vanished in China just a few years later. Regrettably, these secrets concealed deep in history remain shrouded in uncertainty, with no one possessing the knowledge to unravel the mystery except for the individuals directly involved, who are nowhere to be found.

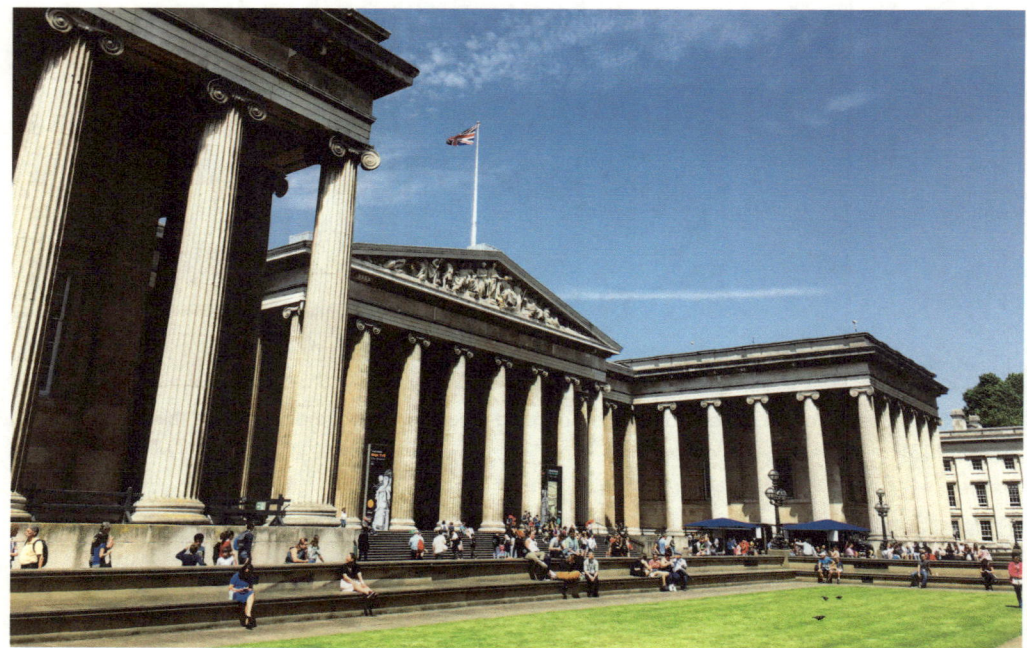

Figure 3-37 The British Museum (2019, photographed by Chang Qing)

In his later years, Stein resided in India, embarking on a series of expeditions to South Asia. His focus included the Indus Valley, Baluchistan, and Greco-Buddhist sites in northwestern India. He also explored Western Asia, delving into topics such as the Euphrates River Civilization, Alexander the Great's battlefields and marching routes from the Battle of Erbil to his return to Babylon, and the borders between the Roman Empire and the ancient Parthian Empire in present-day Iraq. All cultural relics obtained from these explorations found their home in the British Museum (Figure 3-37) and the British Library.

3.9 Personal Reputation and Social Evaluation

Contemporary American historian Owen Lattimore (1900–1989) esteemed Stein as the preeminent figure of his generation, seamlessly blending the roles of scholar, explorer, archaeologist, and geographer (Figure 3-38). Recognized as one of the paramount explorers of the 20th century, Stein dedicated his entire life to the pursuit of exploration, displaying remarkable resilience in the face of challenges and adversity. Even when a few toes froze off during an expedition, he refrained from complaint. Living a frugal existence, Stein possessed neither a house nor a private asset. It's astonishing to consider that a man who amassed such an impressive collection of cultural relics left behind only books and carefully labeled boxes, bearing labels such as Personal Letters, Work Records, Map Information, etc.

Stein's boundless energy fueled his prolific writing endeavors, with numerous books and countless letters to his name. This relentless commitment left him with little time to establish a family. In the West, he received numerous accolades, including the Founder's Medal from the Royal Geographical Society in 1909. The British King bestowed upon him the title of Companion of the Order of the Indian Empire in 1910, later naming him the Knight Commander of the Order of the Indian Empire in 1912. Harvard University honored him with an appointment as an Honorary Fellow of the Fogg Museum in 1929. The list of distinctions continued, with the Gold Medal of the Royal Asiatic Society of Great Britain and Ireland in 1932 and the Gold Medal of the Society of Antiquaries of London in 1935.

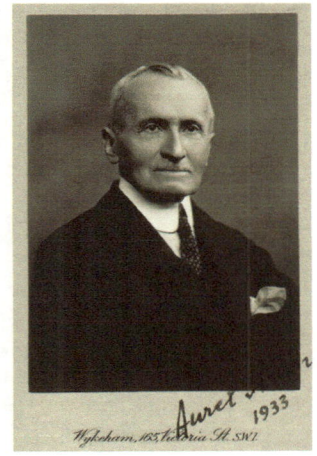

Figure 3-38 Stein's signed photo in 1933

Stein's achievements extended beyond his native Hungary, as he received the Campbell Memorial Gold Medal, the Huxley Medal, and various honorary medals from geographical and antiquarian societies worldwide, including France, Sweden, and the United States. His homeland recognized him with the Cross of Merit and a special Medal of Honor. Additionally, Stein held positions as a researcher at the French Institute and an honorary academician of the Belgian Academy of Sciences. Numerous universities, including Oxford and Cambridge, conferred upon him various honorary degrees. The National Portrait Gallery in London and the Manchester Art Gallery proudly preserve his portraits in their collections.

From an academic standpoint, Stein is widely esteemed within the international exploration, archaeological, and historical communities. His groundbreaking discoveries in Xinjiang and Gansu, coupled with his initial research on the cultural relics unearthed, attest to the profound and far-reaching influence of Chinese culture in Central Asia. Notably, Stein's work has helped restore the narrative of exchange between Eastern and Western civilizations facilitated by the Silk Road. Consequently, Western academic circles rightfully recognize him as a key figure in the establishment of international Dunhuang studies. In the realm of Chinese Dunhuang studies, Chinese scholars also acknowledge the significance of Stein's inspection reports and research papers, considering them indispensable for contemporary research in the field. However, it is essential to address a critical issue: Stein's legacy is marred by the irreversible damage inflicted upon numerous heritage sites in Xinjiang, Gansu, and other regions of China. An archaeologist's primary responsibility is to investigate, document, and safeguard archaeological sites. Regrettably, Stein deviated from this ethical mandate by transporting acquired cultural relics to his home country and conducting expeditions with this objective in mind.

Among Western explorers in the East, Stein, though not the earliest, gained unparalleled renown due to his substantial contributions to Western countries. Unfortunately, his legacy is tainted by accusations of extensive looting of Chinese cultural relics. In the

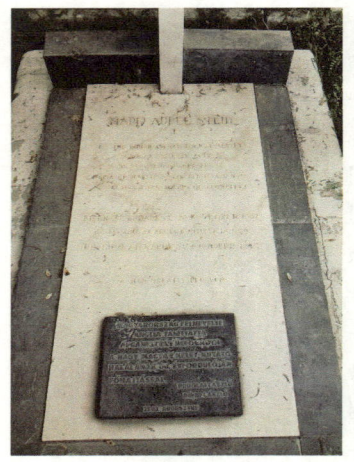

Figure 3-39 Stein's tomb in the British Military garrison (Sherpur Cantonment) in Kabul, Afghanistan

radiant splendor that surrounds him, an equal number of scattered records embellish the tapestry of Chinese culture. While Stein's academic achievements should not be outrightly dismissed, it is equally imperative not to use these accomplishments as a veil to conceal the questionable aspects of his behavior.

In October 1943, during an archaeological expedition in Afghanistan, the 81-year-old Stein succumbed to illness, passing away from a stroke after contracting bronchitis from a cold. His final resting place is situated near the British military garrison in Sherpur, Kabul (Figure 3-39).

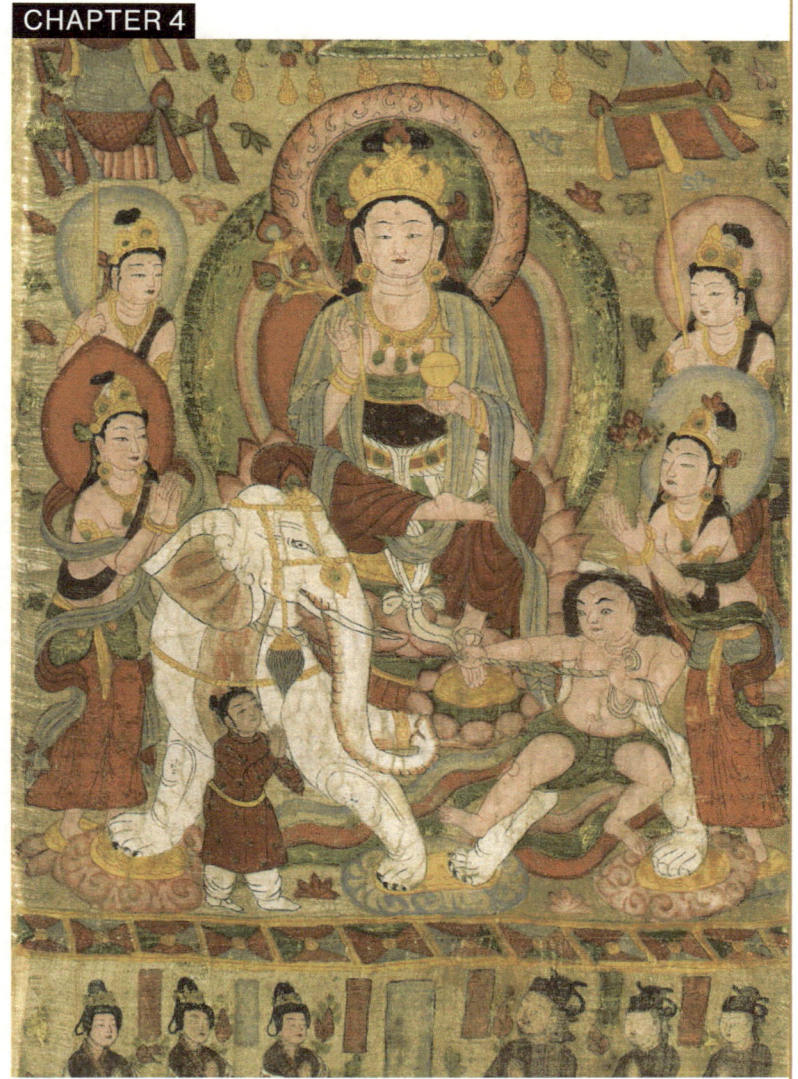

CHAPTER 4

Pelliot, the Latecomer

— 1906–1909

Paris–Moscow–Tashkent–Kashgar–Tumxuk–Kuqa (Kumtura Caves, Subashi Buddhist Temple ruins)–Urumqi–Turpan–Hami–Dunhuang–Xi'an–Beijing

4.1 An Orientalist and Polyglot

Born in Paris, France, in 1878, Paul Eugène Pelliot (1878–1945) (Figure 4-1) dedicated his life to Sinology. In contrast to his Western counterparts, Pelliot wasn't primarily focused on exploration. He was more than an Orientalist or archaeologist; he was a linguist, fluent in English, German, Russian, Chinese, Persian, Tibetan, Arabic, Vietnamese, Mongolian, Turkish, and Tocharian, among various other languages. His mastery of numerous Eastern languages stemmed from the prevailing circumstances of his time.

Upon completing high school, Pelliot pursued English studies at the University of Paris. Subsequently, he delved into Chinese studies at École des Langues Orientales Vivantes (School of Living Oriental Languages) and further specialized in Eastern language history at the French National School of Oriental Languages. After graduation, he apprenticed under the renowned French sinologist Émmanuel-Édouard Chavannes (1865–1918) (Figure 4-2) and the Indology and Buddhist scholar Sylvain Levi (1863–1935), immersing himself in Sinology.

During the early 20th century, Western scholars undertook extensive academic research across Asia, encompassing China, the Middle East, India, Southeast Asia, and beyond. Prominent linguists from Western Europe ventured to the enigmatic East, exploring colonial culture, literature, history, and philology. These endeavors thrived, giving rise to the 20th-century craze for Oriental studies. Philosopher Jacques Derrida (1930–2004) posited that this Oriental fever harbored a concealed agenda. Derived from Michel Foucault's (1926–1984) power and knowledge theory, the concept of Orientalism justified pan-colonial policies, idealizing and romanticizing Asian colonies, thereby facilitating colonial rule in the East.

Amid this backdrop, in 1899, Pelliot, esteemed for his linguistic expertise, was selected as a sponsored student for the Indochina Antiquities Survey. Established in 1898, this association was renamed the École Française d'Extrême-Orient (French School of the Far East) in Hanoi in the next year. It is part of a network of research institutions set up by France in Southeast Asian colonies, and these centers conducted not just archaeological and geographical surveys but also extensive linguistic studies. Upon arriving in Vietnam in 1900, Pelliot made three expeditions to China, amassing antiquities and ancient books and collaborating with collectors, including descendants of Zuo Zongtang (1812–1885), a prominent late Qing Dynasty official.

In Beijing in 1900, Pelliot found himself trapped in the French Embassy during the Boxer Rebellion. After several months, he managed to escape. During the siege, Pelliot conducted two daring forays against Qing troops and Boxers, capturing a Boxer flag. This action allowed the besieged French in the embassy to have fresh fruit. He also aided non-Chinese-speaking embassy staff. Fluent in Beijing dialect, Pelliot even ventured out of the embassy during a ceasefire, engaging in an affable conversation with Qing army generals, and was escorted back by the Qing army. His bravery earned him the French Legion of Honor. Although this could have led him into an official diplomatic career, his mentors, Chavannes and Levi, both influential figures in Sanskrit studies at the Collège de France, intervened to steer this linguistic prodigy away from the path of diplomacy and deeper into Oriental studies.

In 1901, at the young age of 23, Pelliot returned to Hanoi and assumed the role of a young Sinology professor at École Française d'Extrême-Orient. While deeply engrossed in studying the historical geography of Indochina and extending his focus to Southeast Asia, he diligently reviewed various versions of cataloged Chinese books. He showed keen interest in foreign religions and pagan sects in China, exploring the intricate relationship between the origins of Chinese Buddhism and Taoism. This enabled him to discern local connections between China and India, garnering attention from prominent sinologists. In 1901, he embarked on his second visit to China, bringing back a wealth of Chinese, Mongolian, and Tibetan literature and artistic pieces for École Française d'Extrême-Orient. Continuing his explorations, in 1902, Pelliot ventured to China for the third time, amassing a substantial collection of books and sculptures. His notable contribution came in 1903 when he translated the *Customs of Cambodia*, penned by Zhou

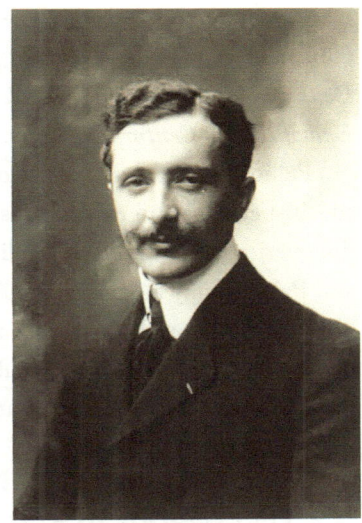

Figure 4-1 Pelliot

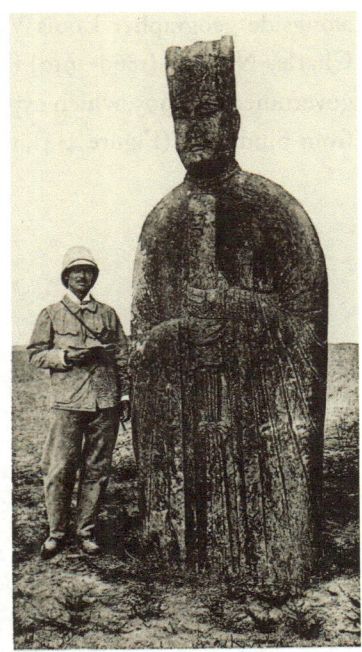

Figure 4-2 The famous French sinologist Émmanuel-Édouard Chavannes inspected the Yongzhao Mausoleum of Zhao Zhen, Emperor Renzong of Song Dynasty, in Gongxian County, Henan (1907)

Daguan (1266–1346) during the Yuan Dynasty, into French with detailed annotations and published it in Paris. Returning to France from Vietnam in 1904, he promptly published *Deux itinéraires de Chine en Inde à la fin du VIIIe siècle* (*Two Routes from China to India at the End of the 8th Century*) in Paris.

Pelliot's significant reputation in China began to flourish after 1906, owing to his extensive inspections and expeditions. In 1905, upon learning of Aurel Stein's new archaeological discoveries in Central Asia, Pelliot was commissioned by the French Academy of Epigraphy and Paleography alongside the Asiatic Society to orchestrate an expedition to Central Asia. The findings from his expeditions in Xinjiang and Gansu, coupled with his subsequent in-depth research into Chinese culture, solidified his position as the foremost scholar within the European Sinology community.

4.2 Discoveries in Kuqa, Xinjiang

In pursuit of his investigation into China, Pelliot formed a three-person expedition team alongside geographer Louis Vaillant (1834–1914) and natural historian and photographer Charles Nouette (1869–1910) (Figure 4-3). Securing a permit and passport from the Qing government in 1905, which explicitly requested officials along their route to aid and refrain from hindrance (Figure 4-4), they commenced their journey from Paris to China on June

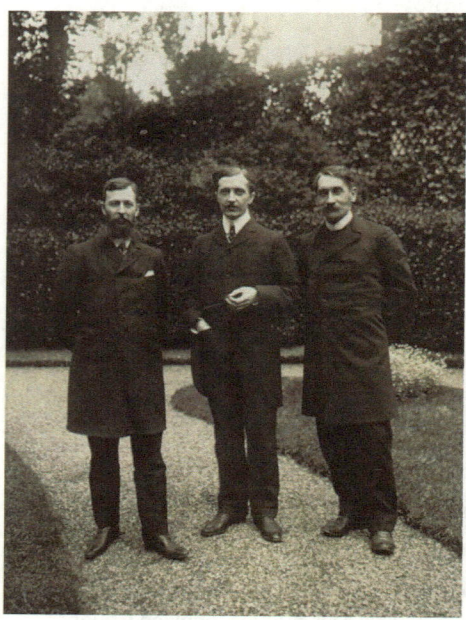

Figure 4-3 Pelliot's expedition team's photo before departure (from left: Vaillant, Pelliot, and Nouette, 1906)

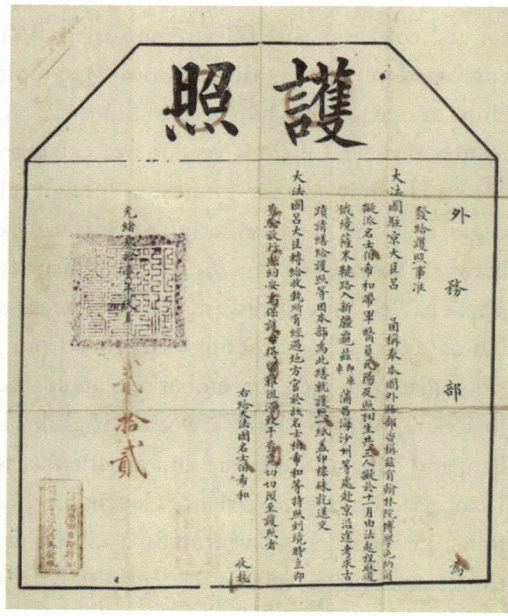

Figure 4-4 Passport issued to Pelliot by the Qing government (1905)

15, 1906. Traveling via Moscow and Tashkent, they entered Xinjiang, China, by train. Initially knowing nothing about Russian on the train from Moscow to Tashkent, Pelliot astounded fellow passengers by conversing fluently in Russian by the time they reached Kashgar, prompting admiration for his extraordinary brain and impeccable memory. Upon their arrival in late August, they stayed at the Russian Consulate General in Kashgar. Pelliot's linguistic prowess impressed local Qing officials, swiftly fostering friendship. These officials promised various facilitations for their expedition. Pelliot initiated inspections and excavations of three pre-Islamic monuments in the Kashgar Oasis, followed by a month-long exploration of numerous Buddhist sites in the region.

Xinjiang, an expansive region, was highly competitive for Western scholars exploring its territories. Knowing that early arrivals reaped plentiful rewards while latecomers risked finding nothing, Pelliot chose a northern route to Kuqa and Baicheng rather than following Stein's path to the southern edge of the Taklimakan Desert.

The surroundings of the Taklimakan Desert once hosted flourishing oasis nations along the Silk Road, including Kucha in the north, Khotan in the south, Shanshan in the east, and Gaochang in the Turpan region. The ruins of these ancient civilizations preserved the invaluable heritage of the Western Regions, encompassing their diverse linguistic systems. During his inspections, Pelliot learned and familiarized himself with the languages of various ancient nations as he traversed the land. His fluent communication in Chinese allowed him to freely interact with local Qing officials and residents without the need for interpreters, facilitating their expeditions (Figure 4-5).

The expedition arrived at the village of Tumxuk, situated between Kashgar and Kuqa, on October 29, 1906, and remained in the area until December 15 of the same year. It was here that Pelliot discovered the sole extensive group of Buddhist sites on the western

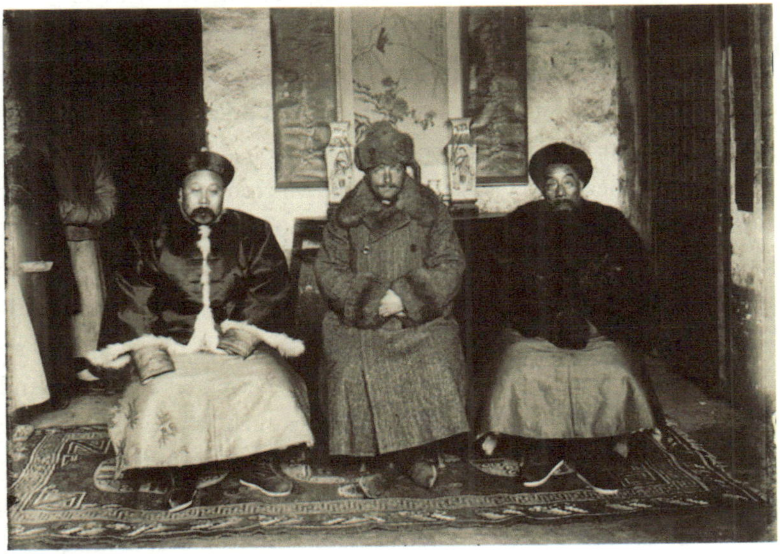

Figure 4-5 Photo of Pelliot with the Kuqa County Magistrate and the Aksu Daotai during his inspection in Kuqa (photographed by Nouette in 1907, now in the Guimet Museum, Paris, France)

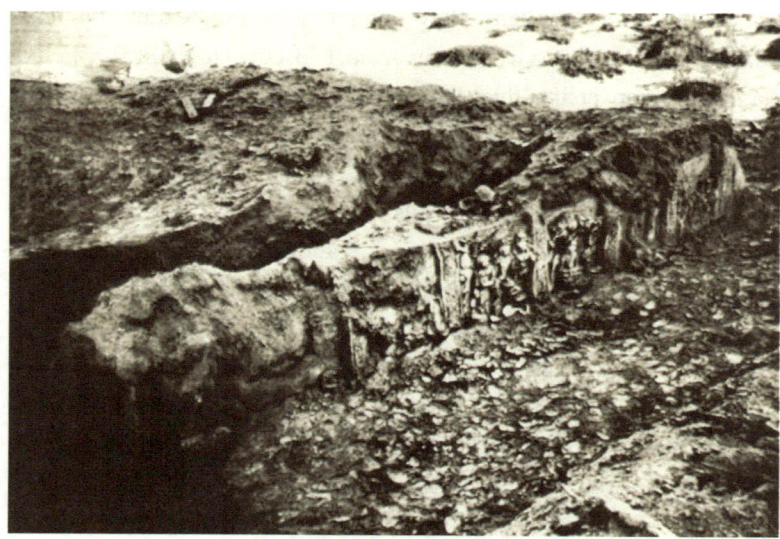

Figure 4-6 Part of the Buddhist ruins excavated by Pelliot's expedition in Tumxuk, Xinjiang (1906)

fringes of the Kucha Oasis (Figure 4-6). Excavations unearthed Buddhist clay statues, murals, pottery, sundries, sculptures, prints, etc. The ruins encompass a Buddhist temple structure dating back to the 6th and 7th centuries AD. Within these ruins lies a wall adorned with a series of exquisite relief sculptures depicting various figures, including Buddhist Bodhisattvas, flying apsaras, believers, and potentially Jakata stories and legends of the Buddha. These sculptures served to convey the tales of the Buddha's virtuous acts and miracles. Pelliot's photographs of these sculptures revealed remarkable details: the Bodhisattvas and flying apsaras, featured prominent top knots, full Western-like faces, robust muscular physiques, and natural, relaxed postures. Notably, the depictions of Buddhist devotees portrayed slender figures imbued with inner strength, characterized by prominent high noses, deep-set eyes, and thick beards. These representations likely drew inspiration from real-life ascetics dwelling in the Western Regions. The arrangement of these vividly colorful sculptures exhibited precision and seamless integration with the temple's architectural design (Figure 4-7).

Among these reliefs was one narrative from the Jataka tales; it is recounted that in a past life, the Buddha, while engaged in meditation and spiritual practice, maintained complete stillness to safeguard a bird nesting on his head until the newborn fledgling emerged from its shell and took flight unharmed. Over numerous lifetimes, the Buddha, known as Sakyamuni, diligently pursued spiritual enlightenment and ultimately attained Buddhahood. Within Buddhist scriptures, these Jataka tales abound with accounts of the Buddha's altruistic acts, embodying virtues such as patience, compassion, generosity, and rescue. Among the hundreds of Jakata tales, this is merely one of them.

After meticulously recording these archaeological findings, Pelliot unceremoniously disassembled three large colored statues, unfortunately damaging them during removal,

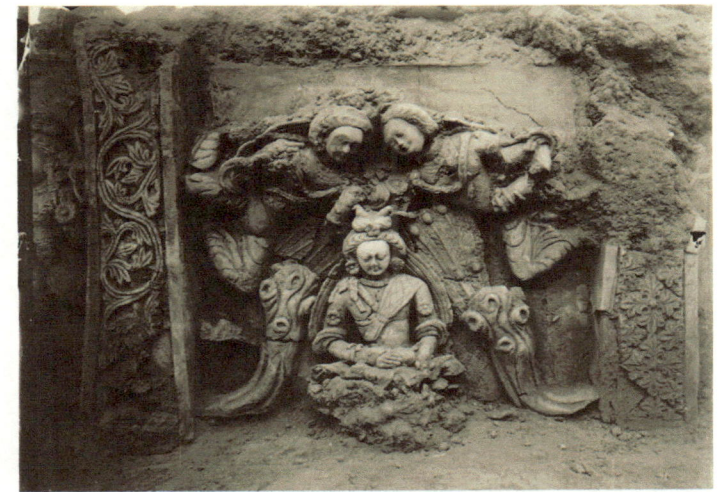

Figure 4-7 Three Buddhist relief sculptures excavated by Pelliot's expedition in Tumxuk, Xinjiang (photographed in 1906, now in the Guimet Museum, Paris, France), top of which showing the Jataka story of Buddha from the 6th to 7th centuries AD

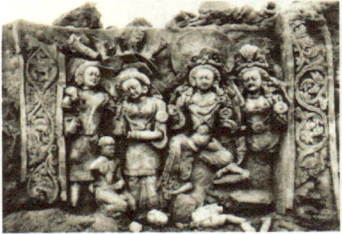

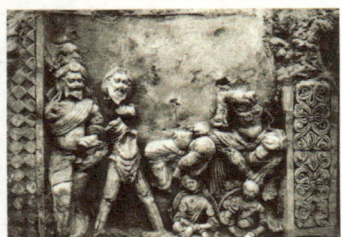

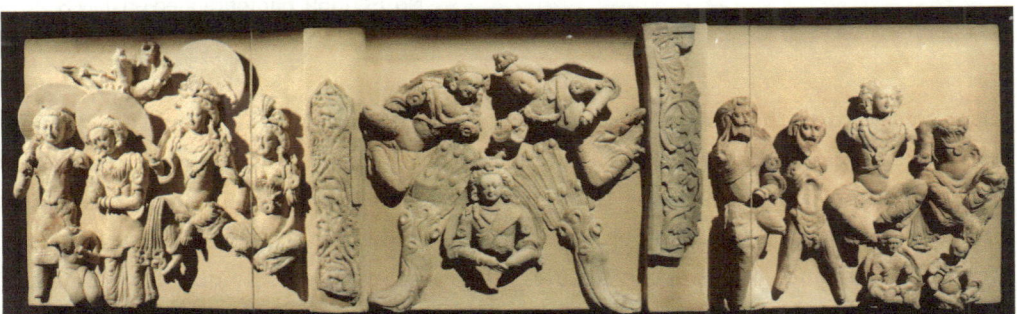

Figure 4-8 Three relief sculptures from the 6th to 7th centuries AD from Tumxuk, Xinjiang (now in the Guimet Museum, Paris, France, No. EO1055, EO1056, EO1057, photographed by Chang Qing on July 3, 2019)

when compared with the photos taken at excavation. Long transportation has made it worse by impairing part of their details, especially the honeysuckle pattern decoration next to each group of colored sculptures. Presently exhibited at the Guimet Museum in Paris, these sculptures have lost their original essence, appearing cramped and rigid (Figure 4-8).

At Tumxuk, Pelliot also acquired numerous well-preserved Bodhisattva heads (Figure 4-9). It remains uncertain whether these were deliberately detached from complete sculptures or unearthed fragments. This particular Bodhisattva head represents a later

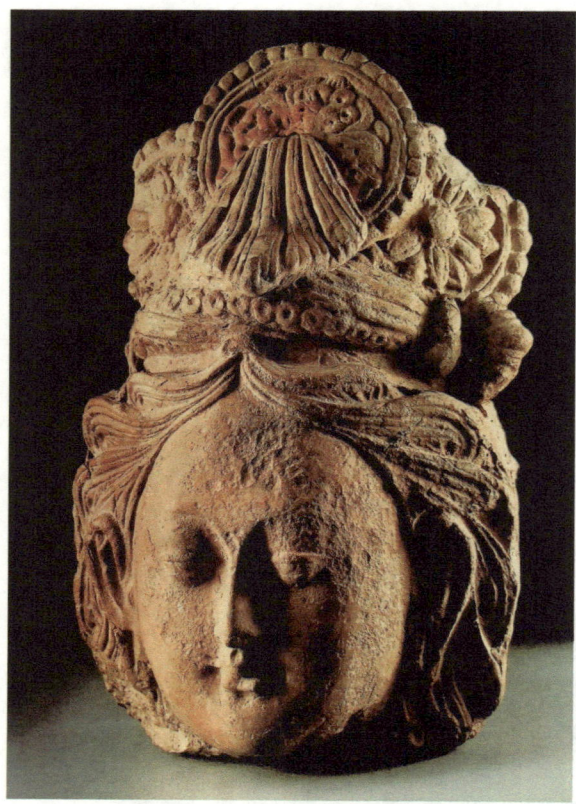

Figure 4-9 Clay Buddha head from the 6th to 7th centuries AD in Tumxuk, Xinjiang (now in the Guimet Museum, Paris, France, No. EO1059, photographed on July 3, 2019)

phase compared to the aforementioned three vibrant statue groups. It stands as a quintessential example of artistry from the late period at Tumxuk, showcasing the remarkable craftsmanship of ancient Xinjiang sculptures. The countenance of this Bodhisattva bears a resemblance to a full, round moon, characterized by sharply defined eyebrows and nose, evoking a semblance to European features. The eyes are set slightly deeper within their sockets, complemented by a petite mouth with a faint, gentle smile. This sculpture harmoniously retains the artistic influences of the Gandhara style, which is evident in its execution. Notably, the Bodhisattva adorns three floral-shaped ornaments crafted from circular beads upon their head, a motif commonly found embellishing Bodhisattva statues in both Gandhara and Gupta art traditions.

In 1907, the expedition reached Kuqa, where Pelliot conducted surveys and excavations for eight months. He excavated the remains of Buddhist temples in Duldur and Subashi near Kuqa, unearthing numerous invaluable cultural artifacts. Notably, he discovered an ancient document inscribed in an unknown language, later deciphered by his mentor Levi as Tocharian B (Kuchean), an extinct Indo-European language dating back to the 6th to 7th centuries. Its linguistic characteristics, defying geographical confines, displayed more resemblances to present-day Western European languages. This revelation challenged the

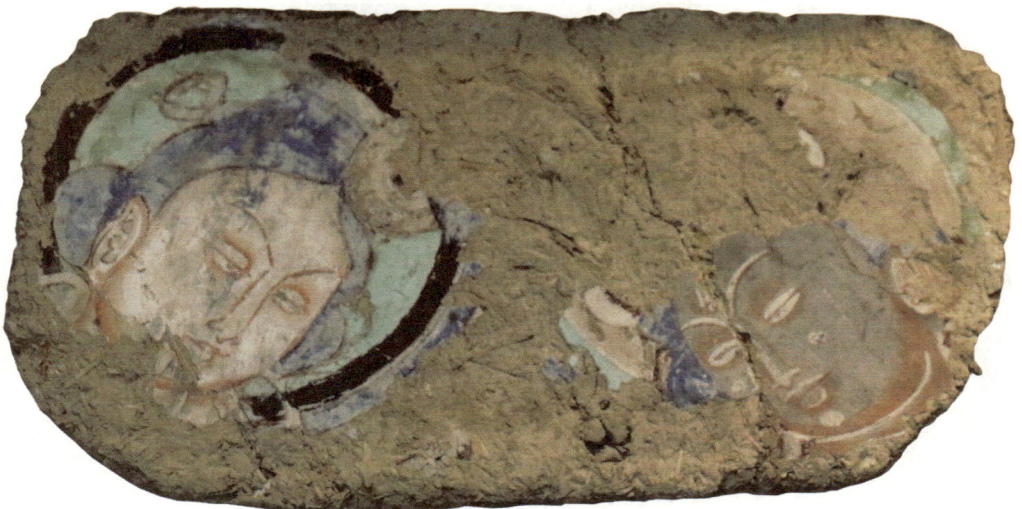

Figure 4-10 A mural of Buddhist teachings from the 6th to 7th centuries AD removed by Pelliot in Kizilgaha, Kuqa, Xinjiang in 1907 (now in the Guimet Museum, Paris, France, photographed by Chang Qing on July 3, 2019)

traditional understanding of language development based on regional centers. Additionally, Pelliot inspected caves such as Kumtura and Kizilgaha in Kuqa, removing some murals (Figure 4-10).

Their journey led them to Urumqi in October of the same year, where Pelliot met the Duke of Lan, Zailan (1856–1916), also known as his courtesy name Dingfu, a member of the House of Aisin-Gioro. As the third son of Yizong, Prince Dun (1831–1889) and the cousin of Emperor Guangxu (r. 1875–1908), he was once named General and Duke. In the turbulent events of 1900, Zailan and his associates were involved in instigating Empress Dowager Cixi (1835–1908) to align with the Boxers, fostering an attack against foreigners. Amid the chaos of the Boxer Rebellion, he seized the opportunity to engage in looting and extortion, using religion as a pretext to perpetrate violence against innocent individuals, even sparing neither the clan ministers. Following the capture of Beijing by the Eight-Power Allied Forces in July 1900, Cixi, Guangxu, Zailan, and others fled westward. Subsequently, in a bid to reconcile with the great powers, the Qing court identified Zailan as a pivotal figure among the "primary culprits." Consequently, Zailan was stripped of his title, convicted, and initially sentenced to death, which was later commuted to imprisonment in Xinjiang in 1901. Thereafter, Zailan resided in Dihua (now Urumqi, Xinjiang) and Suilai (presently Manas Town, Manas County, Xinjiang). Given his status as a member of the imperial family, Rao Yingqi (1837–1903), the then governor of Xinjiang, afforded Zailan preferential treatment, refraining from strict control. As a result, Zailan enjoyed a life of opulence and prominence in Xinjiang for a period, exerting dominance in the region (Figure 4-11).

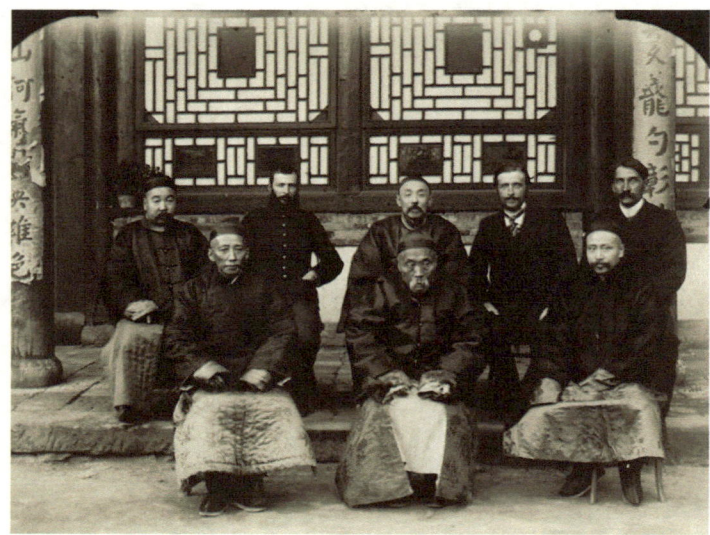

Figure 4-11 Group photo of Pelliot (second from right in back), Zailan (first from right in front), and other Qing officials taken in Urumqi (photographed by Nouette in 1907)

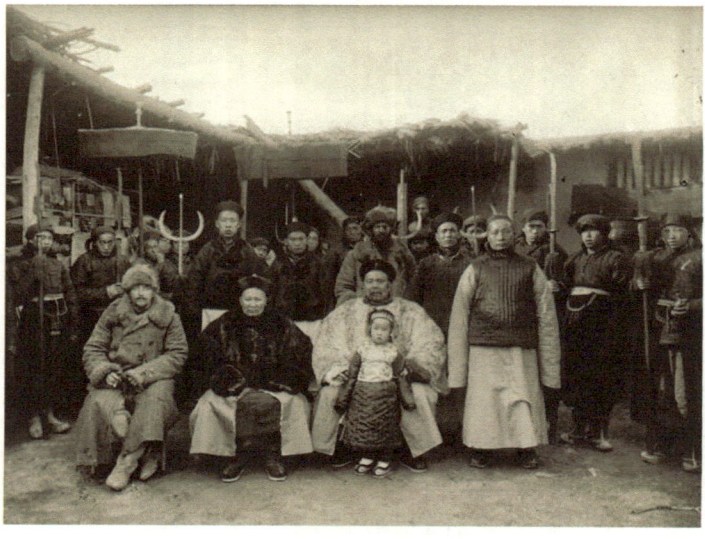

Figure 4-12 Group photo of Pelliot with the local generals, family, and soldiers of the Qing Dynasty when he went to Dunhuang via Hami (photographed by Nouette at the end of 1907 or early 1908)

Earlier, Wang Yuanlu, credited with the discovery of the Library Cave, had entrusted a collection of ancient documents to local government officials. Seizing the opportunity, Zailan, residing in Xinjiang, acquired some of these documents through different channels.

Upon their encounter, Zailan gifted Pelliot a volume of the *Lotus Sutra*, originally discovered in the Library Cave at Dunhuang. This generous gift deeply intrigued Pelliot, prompting an immediate decision to embark on an eastern expedition. Pelliot set forth, journeying through Turpan and Hami (Figure 4-12), driven by the desire to explore the treasures concealed within Dunhuang.

4.3 Treasure Hunt and Investigation in Dunhuang

In February 1908, Pelliot's expedition team reached the
Mogao Grottoes in Dunhuang and made acquaintance
with Wang Yuanlu (Figure 4-13), the guardian of the
caves. To negotiate access to the Library Cave, Pelliot
adopted Stein's established approach entirely. Leveraging
his fluent Chinese and profound knowledge of Sinology,
Pelliot swiftly developed a rapport with Wang, earning his trust. The Han Taoist priest, genial and astute,
claimed that divine intervention in a dream revealed the
location of the Library Cave to him. He also disclosed
to Pelliot that his British counterparts had provided him
with a substantial sum of money. Initially concerned by
reports of Stein retrieving thousands of volumes from the
cave, Pelliot harbored fears of scarce remaining scriptures. However, upon Wang Yuanlu granting access and
unlocking the cave door, Pelliot was astonished. Inside,
he discovered scriptures stacked in tiers, towering as tall
as a person, cramming the cave to its limits.

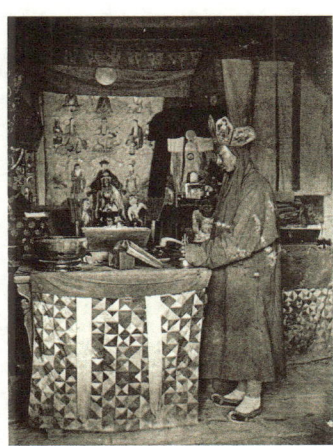

Figure 4-13 The Taoist
priest Wang guarding the
Mogao Grottoes in Dunhuang
(Photographed by Pelliot's
expedition in 1908)

Pelliot chronicled this striking moment in his diary:

> At last, the key was in my possession. On Shrove Tuesday, March 3, I entered the
> sanctum. I was dumbfounded! Eight years ago, there was a leakage of volumes
> from the Library Cave, leading me to believe that the collection had significantly
> dwindled. But can you fathom what I saw? Upon entering the 2.5-meter-square
> aperture, the three walls were adorned with scrolls, each wall laden with stacks as
> high as a person, two to three layers deep. A multitude of Tibetan manuscripts were
> wedged amid two wooden boards, bound with ropes, resting in a corner. Vague traces
> of Chinese and Tibetan characters were discernible in other bundles ... Bodhisattva
> statues were arranged all the way to the entrance of the Library Cave.

Pelliot's diary unraveled a mystery among Dunhuang scholars regarding Stein's absence
of photographs of the cave, despite his three-day stay in the Library Cave and his habit
of taking photos. Pelliot elucidated this quandary—the cave was so densely packed with
scriptures that maneuvering within was impossible. Cameras at the time were not portable,
and the confined space couldn't accommodate the cumbersome apparatus needed for photography. Only after Stein and Pelliot relocated numerous scriptures, creating space, was
it feasible to capture images. Nouette took the solitary photo of the Library Cave during
Pelliot's examination of the scriptures in candlelight (Figure 4-14).

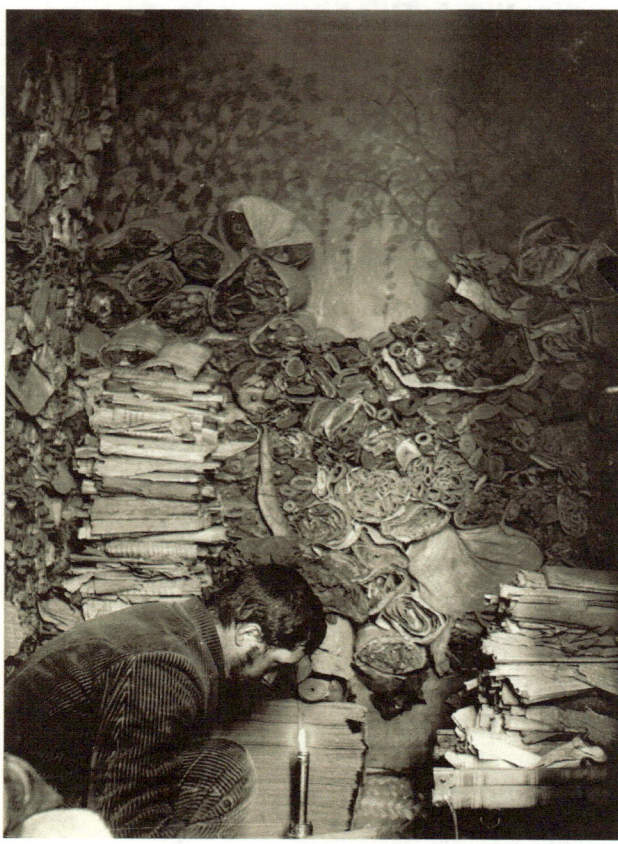

Figure 4-14 Pelliot reading ancient documents in the Library Cave (photographed by Nouette in 1908)

Pelliot discerned that Wang Yuanlu wouldn't surrender all the documents, prompting him to set an ambitious objective: to swiftly scan through the scriptures and extract the most invaluable parts. Amid the lingering smoke of candles and the millennia-old dust, he persevered, reading under dim candlelight, often perusing through a hundred volumes of documents in a single hour. His diary bore witness to these relentless efforts:

> I swiftly decided to conduct at least a superficial examination of the Library Cave, a compass for my exploration. I must unravel the 15,000 to 20,000 volumes nestled within the Library Cave one by one. There's no luxury of pondering too long; otherwise, I won't complete them within six months. But I must unfurl each scroll at least once … The next step is to categorize the scrolls: one, the essential content, must be obtained at all costs; the other, demanding diligent effort … Despite my tireless labor, this task consumed over three weeks … Subsequently, I commenced negotiations with Wang Yuanlu, eager to expedite discussions to avoid squandering more time …

Since Stein lacked proficiency in Chinese, the documents he seized, though in excellent condition and complete, predominantly consisted of Buddhist scriptures, many devoid of significant research value. Unlike Stein, Pelliot scrutinized all the remaining documents. He meticulously set criteria: only non-Chinese scrolls with inscriptions on both sides of the cave being considered, exclusively acquiring the scarce secular documents housed in the cave, while refraining from obtaining the commonplace Chinese and Tibetan scrolls already in his possession, because they held immense archaeological significance, comprising social and economic records (account documents and contracts), along with historical and geographical manuscripts. This meticulous selection process facilitated Pelliot's acquisition of all the artistic treasures and the crux of the documents within the library that Stein had overlooked. Consequently, the collection housed in Paris was greatly elevated in value compared to its counterpart in London.

In this manner, Pelliot devoted three intense weeks, day and night, sifting through the copious remaining documents, cherry-picking some Chinese manuscripts, particularly focusing on linguistics, archaeology, or other facets he deemed valuable, neglected by Stein. To broker this deal with Wang, he secured over 6,000 volumes of manuscripts for the price of a silver ingot weighing approximately 50 taels for a bundle of manuscripts. Additionally, he acquired more than a hundred Tang and Song Dynasty paintings, streamers, fabrics, wooden ritual items, movable type printing molds, and other ceremonial paraphernalia. Proficient in 13 languages, Pelliot meticulously chose high-quality documents, including the newly discovered *Wang ocheonchukguk jeon* (*An Account of Travel to the Five Indian Kingdoms*) by Hyecho (704–783), a Tang Dynasty Silla monk, and the Nestorian *Éloge de la Sainte Trinité* (*Hymn of Perfection of the Three Majesties*), among others. In that same year, Pelliot authored "A Medieval Library Rediscovered in Gansu," published in the *Bulletin de l'École Française d'Extrême-Orient*, Volume 8, No. 314, 1908. This article excerpted from a letter penned by Pelliot to his superior Sinai on March 26, 1908, vividly portrayed his experiences at the Mogao Grottoes and stands as the earliest European documentation of Dunhuang's manuscripts.

Judging from Nouette's photos captured within the Library Cave, the scrolls on the wall behind Pelliot remain unopened, arranged in packages and bundles categorized by their content (these packages, each encompassing approximately ten rolls, were segregated according to the nature of the scriptures). Evidently, during the time of photography, many scrolls within the Library Cave remained unopened. Subsequently, all these packages were unraveled, and following Pelliot's criteria, he selected valuable documents and all remaining paintings. Afterward, the documents not chosen were haphazardly piled, resulting in an upheaval among the ancient documents stored within the cave. This random arrangement has made it impossible to entirely reconstruct the systematic structure of Chinese Buddhist scriptures. Concerning the current state of the Library Cave, some scholars have proposed the "refuge theory," suggesting that local inhabitants, monks, and elites accumulated various documents, scriptures, paintings, and utensils within the cave as a sanctuary during the invasion of foreign adversaries. The invasion that the Dunhuang people sought refuge from was attributed to the Western Xia, who invaded Dunhuang in 1035. They deduce this conclusion from the situation that no Western Xia documents were discovered within the cave during the scrutiny, and the Chinese and Tibetan documents, silk paintings, and Buddhist statues, among other items, were found "in a very messy state due to abandonment in the cave" since there was a hurried closure of the Library Cave. Nevertheless, the disarray within the cave was not entirely the result of closure, but rather ensued due to the rummaging carried out by Stein, Wang Yuanlu, Pelliot, and others. Initially, the scriptures were meticulously arranged in order within the cave, challenging the establishment of the "refuge theory."

In addition to obtaining relics from the Library Cave, Pelliot became the first foreigner to remove murals from Dunhuang. This action was recorded by Stein, who revisited the Mogao Grottoes in Dunhuang in 1914 and discovered someone had damaged a mural, slicing off a section depicting a monster from a procession of Bodhisattvas in Cave No. 8. Wang Yuanlu directly attributed this act to Pelliot. Stein's recorded observation stated, "From the mural depicting the procession of Bodhisattvas, a long strip of the picture was cut away, exposing the inscription column on the mural pictured below. These alterations must have been executed by Pelliot." Paradoxically, it was the sight of these destructive marks that convinced Stein of the viability of removing murals, prompting him to adopt a similar course of action. Consequently, in April 1914, he also removed several murals from the Mogao Grottoes.

During their time at the Mogao Grottoes, Pelliot and Nouette conducted extensive investigations of the caves (Figure 4-15), capturing photographs of statues and murals, coding the caves, and meticulously documenting them, including unreadable inscriptions on numerous murals. Over a century later, many murals in the Mogao Grottoes have faded, making the ink lines and inscriptions indistinct, and certain cave settings have also been altered. Pelliot's meticulous records serve as valuable historical information for the study of the Mogao Grottoes (Figure 4-16). The outcomes of these field investigations were later published as the *Les grottes de Touen-houang* (*The Dunhuang Caves*) and *Grottes de Touen-houang : Carnet de Notes de Paul Pelliot* (*Pelliot's Notes on Dunhuang Caves*).

The Dunhuang Mogao Grottoes, established in the second year of Jianyuan (AD 366) during the pre-Qin Dynasty, has traversed the history of ten dynasties spanning from Northern Liang (AD 397–439), Northern Wei (AD 386–535), Western Wei (AD 535–557), Northern Zhou (AD 557–581), Sui, Tang, Five Dynasties, Song, Western Xia, to the Yuan era. This expansive complex encompasses architectural structures, painted sculptures, and murals, signifying a repository of exquisite Buddhist art. Within its west section, there are 492 caves adorned with painted sculptures and murals, along with an assortment of monk caves, zen caves, auxiliary rooms, and grottoes situated in the north section. It stands as the most extensive existing treasury of Buddhist art globally. Pelliot once expressed, "The Thousand Buddhas Caves (Mogao Grottoes) is one of the most crucial elements of ancient

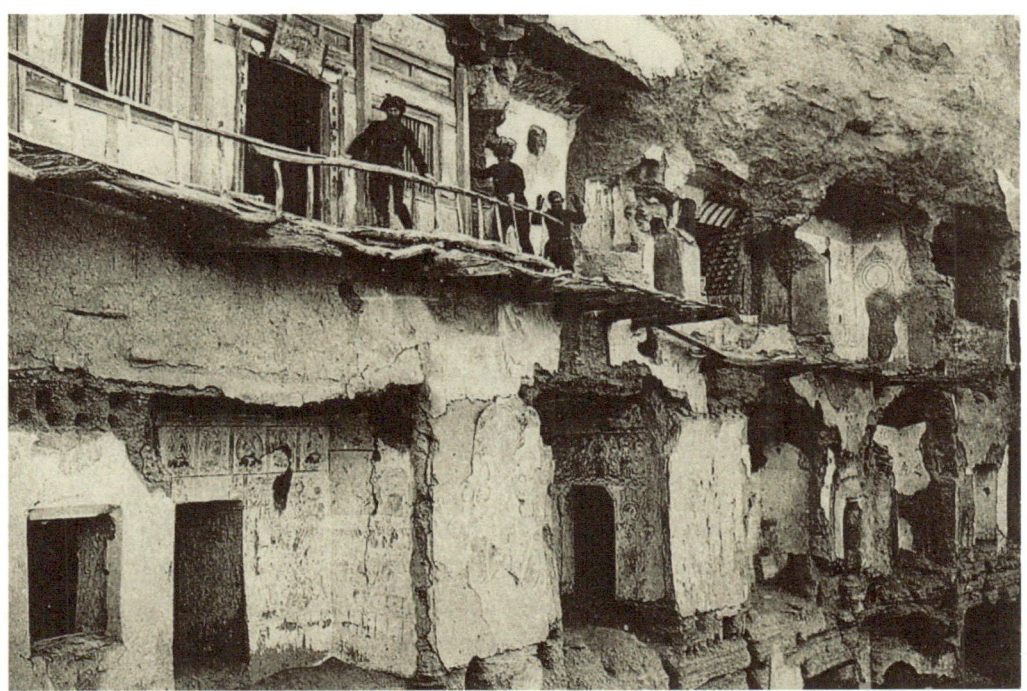

Figure 4-15 French expedition team inspecting the Mogao Grottoes (photographed by Nouette in 1908)

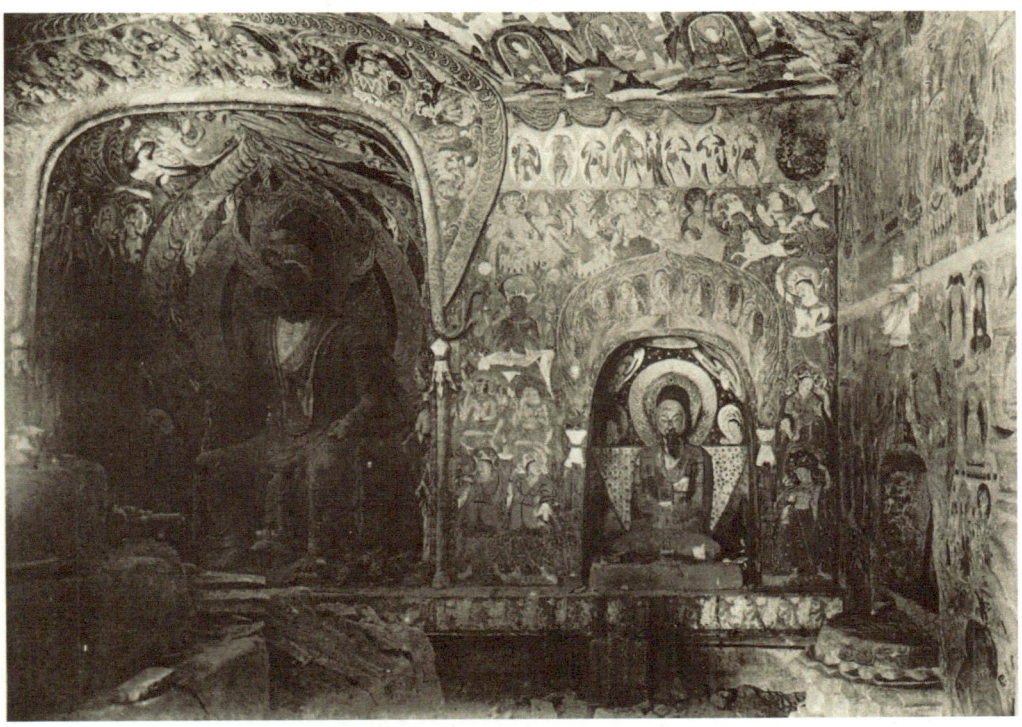

Figure 4-16 A partial photo of Cave 285 of the Mogao Grottoes in the Western Wei Dynasty published in Pelliot's *Les grottes de Touen-houang* (1908)

culture in Central Asia and East Asia. Dunhuang serves as a bridge between Chinese culture and the Western world, thus connecting ancient Asian civilizations to the Far East. This oasis acted as the pathway for the greatest travelers of the past, journeying between the East and West." His assessment of the Mogao Grottoes could not have been more apt.

4.4 Dunhuang Paintings Housed in the Guimet Museum

In a manner reminiscent of Stein, Pelliot's collection of cultural artifacts was predominantly arranged based on historical classifications of Western art. Among the more than 6,000 ancient manuscripts retrieved from the Library Cave, all are housed within the National Library of France, while over 100 paintings, over 20 wood carvings, alongside a substantial assortment of silk flags, sutras, and various silk fabrics were initially stored in the Louvre but were later relocated to the Guimet Museum in 1947. It's regrettable that certain scriptures containing both illustrations and texts were artificially separated, hindering the effective study of the original documents and their illustrations. Although Pelliot procured fewer paintings from the Library Cave than Stein, researchers believe that both collections complement each other. The paintings preserved by the Guimet Museum date back to the 8th to 11th centuries AD, spanning from the Tang Dynasty to the Northern Song Dynasty (AD 960–1127). These artworks encompass numerous portraits of significant figures such as Maitreya, Sahasrabhuja, Water-Moon Avalokitesvara, Compassion-Mercy Avalokitesvara, Amoghapāśa, Samantabhadra Bodhisattva, Vaiśravaṇa, among others. Additionally, the collection comprises paintings illustrating various Buddhist narratives, sutra transformations, Ksitigarbha Bodhisattva, and the Yama of Hell. Most of these paintings are crafted on silk, while some are rendered on linen or paper. Notably, there is a substantial number of offering flags portraying Bodhisattvas, roughly around 50, primarily crafted from linen.

Cataloged as P.4518-39 in the Guimet Museum, the painting unveils a narrative of a wandering monk traversing distant lands, escorted by a majestic tiger. This slender-faced monk, trekking a long way, dons a bamboo hat atop his head, carries a weighty burden upon his back, wears hemp shoes upon his feet, and grasps a fly-whisk in his hand. His pilgrimage appears bound for India, a sacred quest to procure invaluable scriptures. However, beneath his feet, auspicious clouds cradle him. He transcends mere mortal steps, arriving amid billowing clouds and veils of mist. Notably, a cloud materializes ahead, hosting a serene Buddha in repose. Beneath this divine being lies the notes reverently honoring the "Namo Ratnasambhava" (Figure 4-17). The Ratnasambhava, also known as the Baosheng Buddha, as elucidated in Buddhist scriptures, dwells in the Western realm. It is one of the Five Dhyani Buddhas. In Vajrayāna School, he assumes the role of the Southern Buddha, accumulating boundless merits through the blessings of the Cintamani Stone. His benevolent essence fulfills the aspirations of all sentient

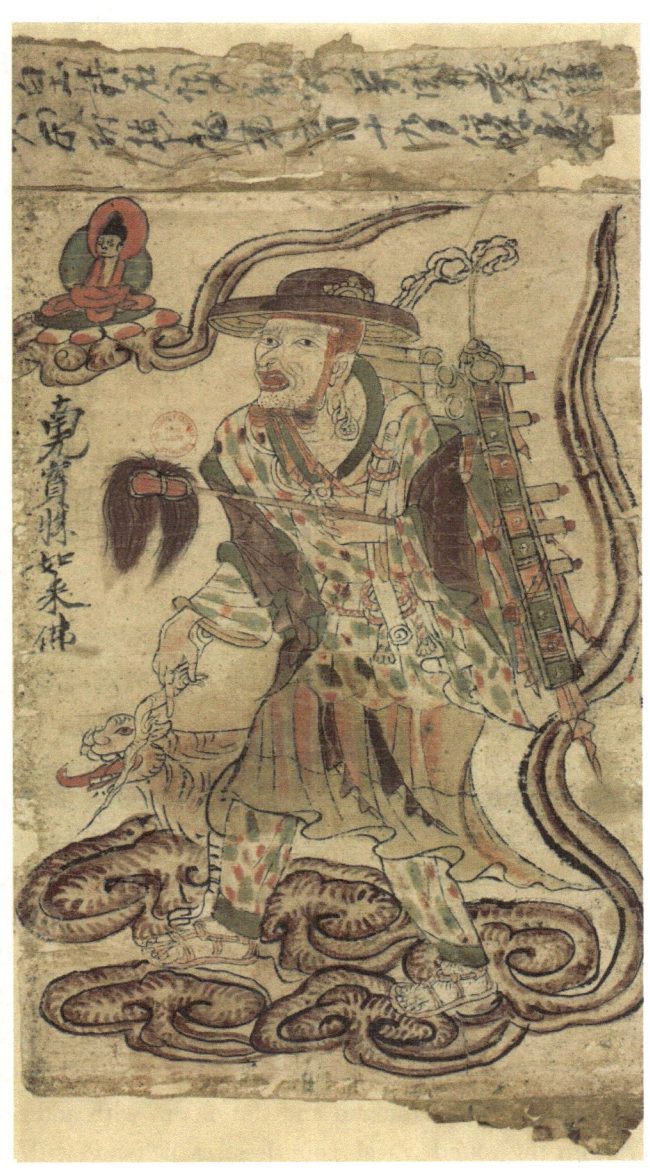

Figure 4-17 *A Walking Monk*, a 9th-century Tang Dynasty painting from the Library Cave (color on paper, 55 cm × 31.8 cm, now in the Guimet Museum, Paris, France, No. P.4518-39)

beings. Evidently, the seated Buddha soaring ahead of the wandering monk symbolizes the revered Ratnasambhava referred to in the notes. Throughout the Tang Dynasty, among the venerable masters who undertook the noble task of retrieving scriptures from India, there was one named Baosheng. Ratnasambhava also assumes the sacred duty of safeguarding the West, thus establishing a reasonable link between monks embarking on scriptural journeys and their reverence for Ratnasambhava. This exquisite artwork traces its origins to Chang'an, the capital of the Tang Dynasty. Historical documents from this era attest to renowned painters in Chang'an adorning temple walls with murals depicting

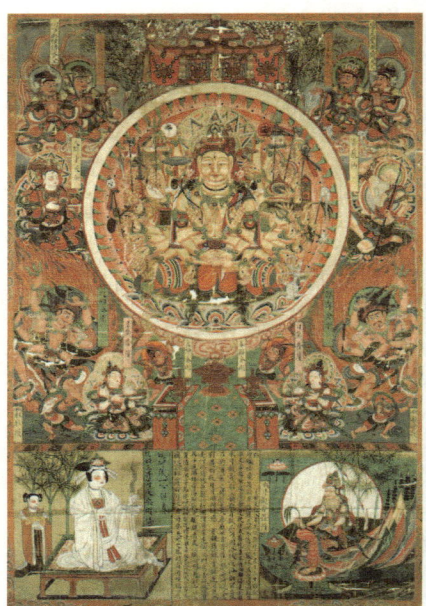

Figure 4-18 The hanging scroll painting *Sahasrabhuja* from the Library Cave in the 8th year of Tianfu of the Later Jin Dynasty (AD 943) (color on silk, 123.5 cm × 84.5 cm, now in the Guimet Museum, Paris, France, No. MG17775)

wandering monks. Over time, amid the late Tang Dynasty, Five Dynasties, and the Northern Song Dynasty, an evolution transpired, where the very walking monk himself evolved into the revered figure known as Ratnasambhava. The enigmatic inclusion of a tiger as the monk's companion unfolds through a prism of cultural symbolism. In Han Chinese tradition, the white tiger stands as one of the four celestial guardians positioned in the west. Therefore, it is customary for traveling monks venturing to and from the Western Regions to be accompanied by these revered white tigers.

The Library Cave paintings brought to France by Pelliot include a remarkable hanging scroll painting portraying *Sahasrabhuja* on silk (Figure 4-18). The notes attribute this masterpiece to Ma Qianjin, a distinguished figure holding the third highest official rank in imperial China. He painted it to expiate the sins of his dead mother two days before the ullambana, specifically on July 13, 8th year of Tianfu, Later Jin Dynasty (AD 943). The composition of the painting is intricate, featuring a prominent theme, a well-defined arrangement of primary and secondary characters, and vibrant, fresh colors. This artwork serves as a valuable resource for studying Buddhist art in Dunhuang during the Five Dynasties period. At the center of the top part of the painting is the Sahasrabhuja, seated in a lotus position atop a grand lotus seat within a round wheel. This deity's forty-two large hands hold various mystical instruments and treasures, including two raised big hands holding the sun and the moon, with additional hands clasped on the chest. Within the round wheel, countless small hands with eyes in their palms are depicted. The subordinates of Avalokitesvara are symmetrically painted, surrounding the outside of the round wheel. The titles alongside these figures denote their identities: the Four Heavenly Kings occupy both sides at the top, followed by Saraswati and Vasu in the lower part, with an incense burner placed on the offering table below them. Flanking the table are Sun Bodhisattva and Moon Bodhisattva holding offering plates, while Ucchuṣma, Vajra of Dispelling Poison, Great God Vajra, Guhyapada, and others stand on both sides. Additionally, the two small statues at the bottom sides of Vajra represent the elephant-headed Vinayaka and the pig-headed Vinayaka.

The lower segment of the painting depicts the donors, and there is a lengthy vow in the middle of the painting. The vow elucidates that the primary deity in the upper portion is the Great Compassionate Avalokitesvara Bodhisattva, and the purpose of creating this artwork is to "save the country and protect the people, rescuing individuals from peril." On the right side, a depiction of Water-Moon Avalokitesvara is portrayed, seated on five-color mountain rocks in a half-lotus posture, with a lotus on the left foot, a willow branch in hand, and a backdrop of a purple bamboo forest. The head is slightly lowered, and the eyes are looking at the lotus pond in front, as if thinking. This portrayal of Water-Moon Avalokitesvara is a rare early painting with distinct notes. On the left side of the vow, a female donor is depicted seated on a couch, accompanied by a standing maid. The donor, attired in white clothing and a headdress, holds a long-handled incense burner in her right hand while holding an incense in her left. The accompanying green ink book's title beside her reads, "Presented by my deceased mother, A Zhang of the Trailokya Temple Mahayana Enlightenment Upāsikā." This is interpreted as a symbolic representation of Ma Qianjin's deceased mother, Azhang, utilizing the religious significance of the painting to perform meritorious acts on her behalf (Figure 4-19). The ullambana is a religious ceremony aimed at saving departed souls. That he painted it two days prior to the ceremony added significance to seeking salvation for his mother.

The *Sutra of Ten Kings of Hell*, whose full name is the *Sutra of Buddha Telling that King Yama Received the Seven Rebirths in the Pure Land of the Four Preliminary Rebirths*, is a significant local Chinese scripture. This scripture is considered an apocryphal text in traditional Buddhist views, believed to have been compiled by monk Zangchuan between AD 720 and AD 908. In ancient times, Chinese monks created many similar "apocryphal texts" based on Indian Buddhist thought. Despite being dismissed by the orthodox Buddhist community, categorized as "suspicious records," and excluded from The Chinese Buddhist canon, such apocryphal works contributed significantly to the cultural assimilation process in China. The *Sutra of Ten Kings of Hell* combines the Taoist principle that human actions

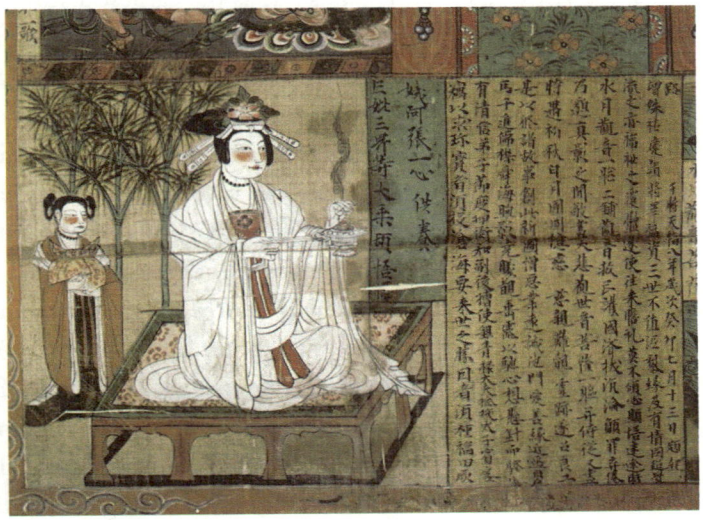

Figure 4-19 Donor in the hanging scroll painting *Sahasrabhuja*

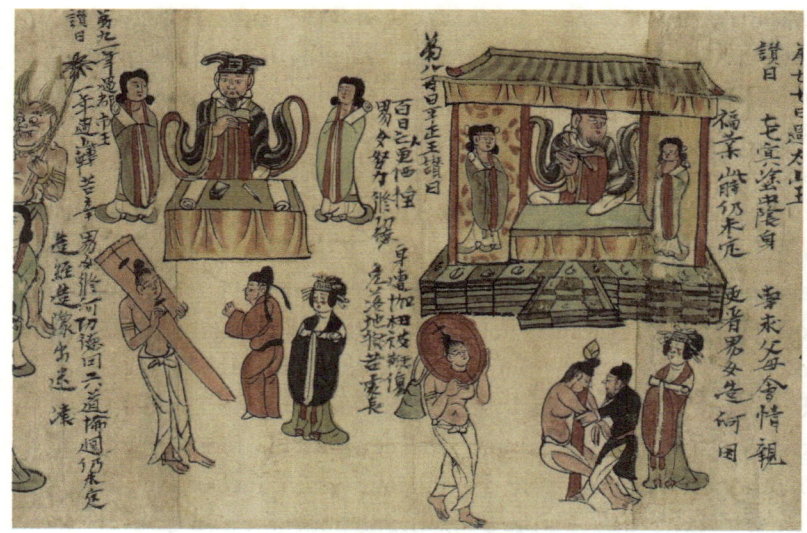

Figure 4-20 Part of *Transformation of the Ten Kings of Hell* hand scroll from the Five Dynasties in the 10th century AD from the Library Cave (color on paper, 30.7 cm × 615.2 cm, housed in the National Library of France, No. Pelliot chinois 2870)

are recorded and have an impact on individual destinies. Inspired by the figure of the Hell King Yama from Hinduism, it formulates the concept of the Ten Kings of Hell, responsible for judging spirits in the afterlife. Some of the depicted kings, such as King of Taishan, are not present in Indian canonical texts. Instead, they originate from Chinese Taoist beliefs and local folk traditions.

The painting, known as the *Transformation of the Ten Kings of Hell*, visually represents the core themes found in the *Sutra of Ten Kings of Hell*. It illustrates the scenario where the departed are judged by the Ten Kings of Hell three years following their demise, along with the various agonizing tortures and suffering they endure. Among the artworks housed in the Library Cave and subsequently taken by Pelliot, the hand scroll portraying the *Transformation of the Ten Kings of Hell* stands out as the earliest discovered painting that conveys the essence of the *Sutra of Ten Kings of Hell* (Figure 4-20). Within the Library Cave, a total of 46 distinct copies of the *Sutra of Ten Kings of Hell* were crafted and inscribed in as many as 13 languages, including Uighur, Chinese, Tangut, and Tibetan. This specific portrayal, *Transformation of the Ten Kings of Hell*, is presumed to be an illustrative representation of one of these 46 sutras. However, regrettably, its accompanying text has been lost over time. Aside from this particular scripture, there were five other sacred texts adorned with illustrations, of which Pelliot obtained three volumes, while Stein acquired two.

Apart from the *Transformation of the Ten Kings of Hell*, another artwork related to the Ten Kings of Hell was found in the Library Cave—*Ksitigarbha and the Ten Kings* hanging scroll painting. Ksitigarbha, also recognized as Ksitigarbha Bodhisattva, holds a significant place in Buddhism as a Bodhisattva dedicated to rescuing sentient beings across the six realms. The veneration for Ksitigarbha originated in the Tang Dynasty. According to *Daśacakra Ksitigarbha Sutra*, translated by Xuanzang during the Tang Dynasty, the name

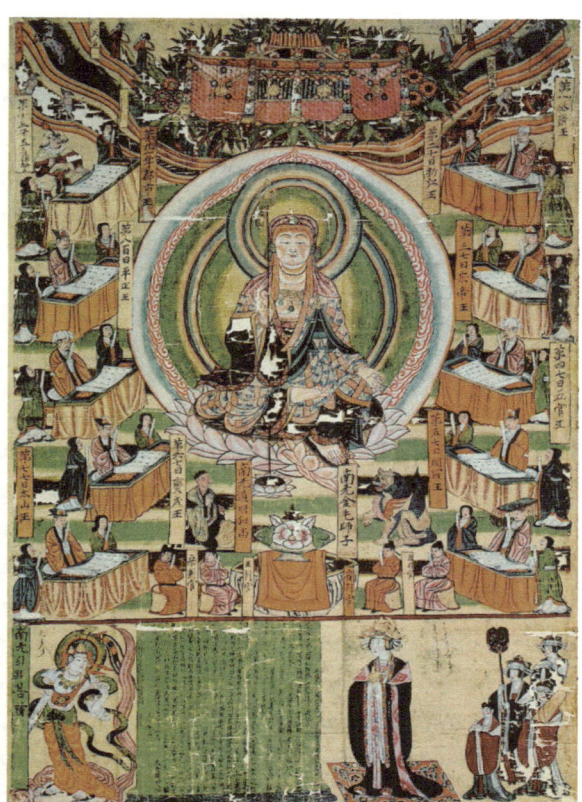

Figure 4-21 The hanging scroll painting *Ksitigarbha and the Ten Kings* from the Library Cave in the 8th year of the Taiping Xingguo period in the Northern Song Dynasty (AD 983) (color on silk, now in the Guimet Museum, Paris, France)

signifies being "steadfast in suffering like the earth while meditating profoundly and discreetly like a hidden treasure." This revered Bodhisattva harbored a fervent wish to alleviate the suffering of all sentient beings in hell, earning the epithet Lord of the Netherworld. Throughout the 10th century, as Buddhism underwent further assimilation into Chinese culture, Ksitigarbha gradually emerged as a central figure associated with relieving the anguish of the six paths of reincarnation. The Bodhisattva became intertwined with the ten kings of hell, an adaptation from Chinese beliefs. Ksitigarbha Bodhisattva frequently manifests as a monk to aid all sentient beings. The *Ksitigarbha and the Ten Kings* hanging scroll painting, crafted during the eighth year of the Taiping Xingguo period (AD 983) in the Northern Song Dynasty, is housed at the Guimet Museum. The focal point is Ksitigarbha Bodhisattva, resembling a monk seated in a lotus position atop a lotus flower. In the depiction, the Bodhisattva holds a tin staff in the right hand, capable of unlocking the gates of hell, and a pearl in the left, symbolizing salvation for all beings, with an adorned canopy hovering above. Flanking Ksitigarbha are the King Yama rājā and their attendants on either side, with two lions and four Hell Judges in front. The lower section of the painting portrays the female donor who financed the artwork, attended by her retinue, along with a note of the vow written in ink (Figure 4-21).

Numerous Dunhuang paintings are presently housed in esteemed collections at the British Museum in London and the Guimet Museum in Paris, France. These paintings stand as the quintessence of cultural relics from the Library Cave, showcasing the remarkable artistic prowess of the Chinese civilization during medieval times. Recognized as one of the most significant archaeological finds of the 20th century worldwide, the loss of cultural artifacts from the Library Cave remains a sorrowful chapter in Chinese history, an irreplaceable loss for the nation.

4.5 Fate of Dunhuang Manuscripts

In 1909, after Pelliot safely transported the Dunhuang cultural artifacts he had acquired, he departed Dunhuang and headed toward Beijing. Unlike many other Western scholars, Pelliot's profound proficiency in the Chinese language was not only reflected in his scholarly endeavors but also significantly aided his social interactions. Pelliot nurtured strong relationships with several Chinese scholars in Beijing, engaging in frequent exchanges. He brought only a small number of ancient Chinese manuscripts from Dunhuang to Beijing and presented them to Duanfang (1861–1911), viceroy of Zhili and an avid collector, along with esteemed scholars like Luo Zhenyu (1866–1940) and Wang Guowei (1877–1927). This pivotal moment marked the awakening of the Qing government and literati to the true value of these cultural relics. Pelliot advocated within the Chinese academic community, emphasizing that over 10,000 volumes of important manuscripts resided in the Dunhuang stone chambers. He urged immediate measures to protect these treasures from potential seizure by others. Recognizing the essence of Chinese culture, Pelliot, perhaps out of internal remorse, cautioned himself: never venture back to northwest China in search of treasures. True to his word, Pelliot refrained from returning to northwest China and devoted his focus solely to studying Chinese culture.

Upon persistent urging from Chinese scholars and Pelliot, the remnants from Dunhuang garnered serious attention from the Qing government. In 1910, the Qing Dynasty's Ministry of Education dispatched a telegram to Mao Qingfan (1849–1927), governor of Shaanxi and Gansu, stating that everything housed in the caves would be gathered and safeguarded within the provincial confines. Consequently, the Ministry of Education allocated 6,000 taels of silver and instructed Chen Ze, magistrate of Dunhuang County, to collaborate in this endeavor. Post Pelliot's departure, Taoist priest Wang, foreseeing the situation, prepacked two wooden barrels with what he considered valuable scriptures, labeled "scripture transfer barrels." The remaining manuscripts were left piled in the cave. However, when Qing officials arrived to collect and transport these documents, a distressing scene occured. The manuscripts were hastily wrapped in mats and loaded onto large carts. Unfortunately, many were pilfered while en route to Dunhuang County's *yamen*, resulting in the loss of numerous scriptures. After various officials and handlers along the transportation route stole numerous manuscripts, only over 8,600 scrolls made it to Beijing. Subsequently, a man named Li Shengduo (1858–1937) made a move on them. Li Shengduo, with a courtesy name of Yiqiao, was from Dehua, Jiangxi (now Jiujiang), a bureaucrat, avid book collector, and advocate for constitutionalism during the late Qing Dynasty. He once traveled to Europe and the United States to study constitutional government. Li obtained access to these manuscripts through the escort responsible for their transportation to Beijing. He meticulously handpicked several ancient manuscripts with significant meaning and fresh insights, including a Tang Dynasty Nestorian manuscript called *Zhi Xuan An Le Jing*. This likely constituted the last batch of exquisite manuscripts from the Library Cave. Most of these were cataloged in the *Catalogue of Dunhuang Manuscripts Collection by Li Muzhai*, authored by his son Li Pang. Li Shengduo left behind Buddhist manuscripts deemed less valuable, which were assigned to the Qing Ministry of Education. Longer scrolls were divided to maintain the original count of over 8,600 rolls. According to *Records of the Remaining Dunhuang Manuscripts* by historian Chen Yuan (1880–1971), several volumes' fragments, when combined, bear evidence of theft by Li Shengduo, who tore and pilfered the scrolls at that time. Today, more than 8,600 scrolls of ancient Buddhist manuscript fragments are housed in the National Library of China in Beijing. With only a few volumes of ancient lost scriptures remaining, it appears that the essence of the collection has been lost.

Most of the manuscripts taken by Li Shengduo eventually found their way to Japan. His descendants primarily sold them to a Japanese entrepreneur. In 1936, this entrepreneur gifted the collection of Dunhuang scrolls to Japanese Orientalist Haneda Toru (1882–1955) for research. After assuming the presidency of Kyoto University in 1938, Haneda stored these ancient scrolls in the university president's office for cataloging and research. To safeguard them from air raids in the summer of 1945, the entrepreneur requested Haneda to transfer these Dunhuang documents in two batches on July 13 and 15 to the Osaka Takeda Pharmaceutical factory for storage. By August 1, the documents were relocated to the warehouse of the Nishio Shinpei family's house in Oyama Village, Taki County, Hyogo Prefecture. This collection included over 300 other manuscripts, alongside the 432 ancient scrolls purchased from Li Shengduo, stored in Japan. Haneda compiled the *Catalog* (the Dunhuang section titled the *Dunhuang Secret Scrolls Catalog*) and photographed them. After Haneda's passing, the photographs were exhibited in the Haneda Memorial Hall, while the Dunhuang documents stolen by Li Shengduo were concealed within the Kyo-U Library of Takeda Pharmaceutical. Since 2009, Kyo-U Library has begun releasing its Dunhuang volumes collection, titled *Dunhuang Secrets Scrolls*, comprising a catalog and a video album.

In summary, the Qing government's rushed transfer of the Library Cave documents from Dunhuang to Beijing failed to uncover Wang Yuanlu's concealed scriptures, resulting in the scattering of numerous Chinese and Tibetan documents and palm-leaf manuscripts among the populace. Expeditions led by Japanese Ōtani Kōzui in 1911–1912, Stein's revisit to Dunhuang in 1914, and the Russian Oldenburg's expedition to the Mogao Grottoes in 1914–1915 procured hundreds of Dunhuang Manuscripts, scrolls, silk paintings, and fragments from the area from Taoist priest Wang. This man-made catastrophe in the early 20th century dispersed these treasures globally, with no hope of full restoration. However, this dispersion of Dunhuang documents facilitated the global dissemination of Chinese culture. As scholars worldwide delve into the Library Cave's cultural relics, Dunhuang studies have evolved into an international discipline, still showcasing its unparalleled allure today.

Throughout their explorations, Pelliot and Stein saw each other as significant rivals. Pelliot, troubled by the fact that Stein often achieved victories within a short timeframe during several expeditions, was unaware that Stein received support from British Indian authorities, leveraging an intelligence network in China to gather information and even receive telegrams about his next destination. This led to Stein's persistent concern that wherever Pelliot went, crucial documents and materials would be looted. Stein's diary reflected this worry, as he rushed through various sites, spending minimal time excavating, driven by the desire to surpass Pelliot and uncover treasures first. This mutual apprehension persisted until Pelliot returned to France, finally allowing Stein's journey in China to become less fraught and exhausting.

Pelliot concluded his expedition and returned to Paris in October 1909. However, he faced harsh criticism from colleagues at the École Française d'Extrême-Orient, who believed the expedition wasted public funds and brought back forged documents. These colleagues mistakenly assumed that the British explorer Stein had taken all the documents from the Library Cave. It was not until Stein published his adventure notes in 1912, revealing that numerous ancient documents remained in Dunhuang, that these suspicions about Pelliot were assuaged.

4.6 Pioneer of Western Sinologists

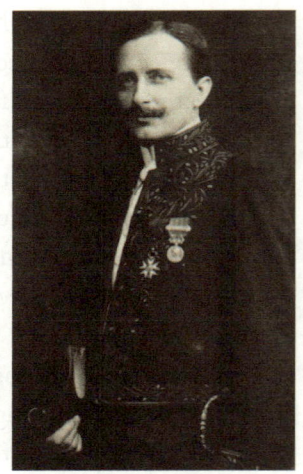

Pelliot's deep expertise in Sinology and his Chinese adventure experiences propelled him to fame, garnered honors, and solidified his crucial standing in the global sinology community. In 1911, the Collège de France entrusted Pelliot to deliver a special lecture on Central Asian history and archaeology. Amid World War I, he enlisted in the army and served as Undersecretary of the Army Attaché at the French Embassy in Beijing from 1916. His pinnacle in Sinology arrived in May 1921 when he was elected as an academician of the French Academy of Epigraphy and Literature, marking a high point in his Sinology career (Figure 4-22). Over the next two decades, alongside research and lectures, he took charge of editing the prominent

Figure 4-22 Academician Pelliot in Paris (1921)

European sinology magazine *T'oung Pao*. Additionally, in December 1935, he assumed the presidency of the French Asia Society.

From 1909 onward, Pelliot meticulously documented his investigations and penned numerous books. His Sinology research, spanning catalog editions, philology, archaeological art, religious culture, transcontinental commerce, and frontier history and geography, was mainly published in journals such as the *Bulletin of the French School of Asian Studies*, *T'oung Pao*, and *Journal Asiatique*. Notably, works like his "Dunhuang Thousand Buddha Caves" and various papers significantly influenced the Sinology community. Pelliot's accomplishments stemmed from his proficiency in diverse Asian languages, his meticulous attention to edition revision, and his pursuit and utilization of new historical materials. Collaborating with Chavannes in 1911, he co-authored the paper "Un traité manichéen retrouvé en Chine" (A Manichaean Treaty Found in China). Furthermore, in 1933, his extensive paper "The Great Voyage of the Chinese in the Early Fifteenth Century" made a substantial impact. Many of his works, such as *Pelliot's Adventures in the Western Regions*, have been translated into Chinese.

Pelliot encapsulated his inspection of the Mogao Grottoes in Dunhuang within four extensive volumes (actually bound into six volumes) known as the *Les grottes de Touen-houang* (*The Dunhuang Caves*), complemented by 1,530 photographs. Though fewer in number compared to Stein's over 5,000 photos, Pelliot's distinct achievement lay in translating and researching the collected documents. His studies encompassed Buddhist scriptures like the Sanskrit *Mahaprajnaparamita Sutra*, the Khotanese *Vajra Prajnaparamita Sutra*, the Khotanese *Buddhist Collection*, and the 15-foot-long *Uighur Manichean Hymns*. He published numerous books, quoting from various sources and exhibiting expertise in multiple languages. Pelliot not only translated *The Travels of Marco Polo* but also annotated Mongolian and Turkic terms within it, resolving chronology issues concerning Genghis Khan that perplexed many scholars. Pelliot passed away in 1945. Over the subsequent 50 years until 2000, his disciples and other scholars published ten volumes of his posthumous works. One commentator remarked that "Pelliot was not just a top-notch sinologist in France but also the forefather of all Western sinology experts." "Without Pelliot, Sinology would have lacked a guiding light."

Pelliot was dedicated to academia and guarded the ancient documents he collected as cherished treasures, rarely allowing others access, let alone publication. Consequently, until his passing in 1945, he personally safeguarded these documents, sharing them sparingly. Even *Notes from the Journeys: 1906–1908*, Pelliot's pivotal work on Western Regions archaeology, remained unpublished for an extended period after his death. It wasn't until 2008, on the centennial anniversary of Pelliot's Western Region expedition, that *Pelliot's Adventures in the Western Regions* was finally published. This publication, jointly spearheaded by the French Far East Museum and the Guimet Museum and under the direction of Jean-Francois Jarrige, an academician of the French Academy of Sciences, offered a comprehensive overview of Pelliot's academic achievements.

Pelliot never underestimated contemporary Chinese academic circles; he wholeheartedly comprehended and recognized the development and accomplishments of Chinese academics from the early Qing Dynasty. Fu Sinian (1896–1950), a renowned scholar and historian in modern China, held a close personal relationship with Pelliot. He aptly summarized Pelliot's academic traits: "There are several aspects of Mr. Pelliot's approach to Chinese studies that starkly differentiate him from most Western scholars engaged in China: first, Mr. Pelliot's bibliographic knowledge is astounding, including everything from old to new; second, his adeptness in employing new materials is unparalleled—when such materials surfaced, he never remains indifferent; third, his superior ability to comprehend and embrace the achievements of Chinese scholars sets him apart, unlike many Western sinologists who confine themselves solely to Western Sinology."

Pelliot's appreciation for the accomplishments of Chinese scholars was evident in his active engagement with the academic community. During his lecture on Chinese drama in Frankfurt on October 26, 1926, Pelliot emphasized the three key facets essential for effective "China Studies": (1) bibliography and book collection, (2) physical object curation, and (3) fostering relationships with Chinese scholars. He also critiqued the state of Chinese studies in Germany as far from the others. His interactions with numerous eminent Chinese scholars over several generations highlighted the mutual engagement between the global sinology community and the Chinese academic sphere in the early 20th century. This interaction not only enhanced European and American understanding of Chinese academia but also facilitated insights into China's local academic circles. Pelliot contributed to this exchange by publishing the article "New Perspectives on Chinese Art and Archaeology," introducing Europe to the research findings of Luo Zhenyu and Wang Guowei. He also placed considerable importance on contemporary archaeological discoveries in China, maintaining close ties with Chinese archaeologists (Figure 4-23).

Simultaneously, during the Republic of China era, Chinese academic circles highly esteemed and admired Pelliot. In late 1932, Pelliot revisited China, aiming to study the contemporary development of Chinese literature and history and acquire practical books for the China Institute of the University of Paris. His arrival in Peking via Hong Kong and Shanghai was warmly welcomed by various esteemed institutions such as the Institute of History and Philology of Academia Sinica, Yenching University, Fu Jen Catholic University, and the Society for Research in Chinese Architecture. The Peking Morning News Office and local scholars and dignitaries hosted welcome banquets and invited him to deliver lectures. In 1939, he was elected as a researcher at the Institute of History and Philology, Academia Sinica, China.

Pelliot was committed to fostering Sino-French cultural exchanges. In the early 1920s, he played a pivotal role in establishing the Chinese Studies Department of the Institute of Liberal Arts at Peking University, fostering collaboration between the institution and the international academic community.

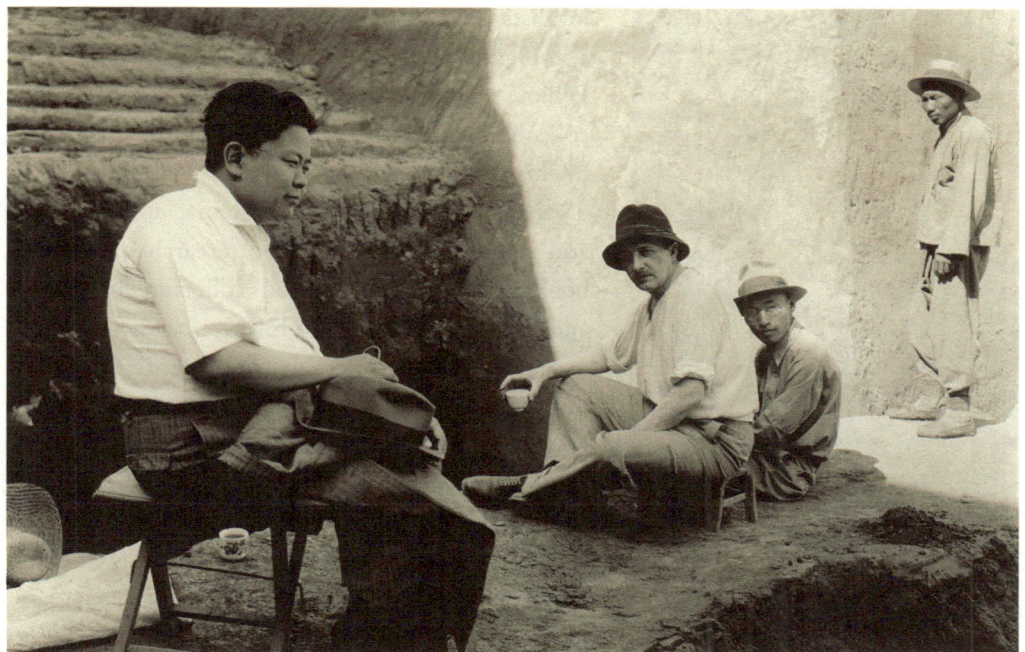

Figure 4-23 Pelliot inspected the archaeological excavation site of Yin ruins in Anyang (from left: Fu Sinian, Pelliot, Liang Siyong, spring 1935)

Pelliot succumbed to cancer in Paris on October 26, 1945. The Guimet Museum in Paris pays homage to him with one of its galleries named after Pelliot, showcasing ancient cultural relics and artworks from Xinjiang and Dunhuang that he had collected and acquired (Figure 4-24). The ancient documents Pelliot collected from China are preserved at the National Library of France. Some lists of 60 influential foreigners in China over the past century have ranked Pelliot as second among the Seven Best Sinol-

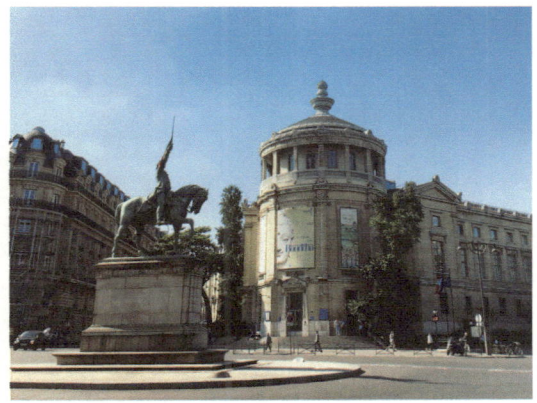

Figure 4-24 Guimet Museum, Paris, France (photographed by Chang Qing on July 3, 2019)

ogists. However, regarding academic achievements, Pelliot undoubtedly holds the foremost position.

Lastly, let's delve into the intriguing personality of Pelliot's wife—Marianne Skoupenska-Karvoskij (1890–?) (Figure 4-25). A Russian by nationality, Marianne met Pelliot in Vladivostok, eastern Siberia, after the October Revolution, where many Russian

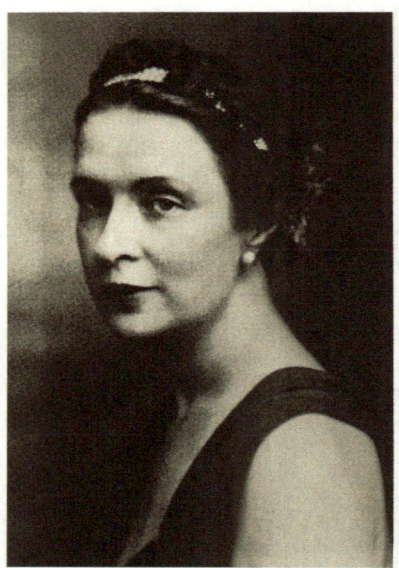

Figure 4-25 Pelliot's wife Marianne Skoupenska-Karvoskij

loyalists sought refuge. They married on October 2, 1918, and subsequently returned to France. After Pelliot's passing, Marianne was left with a substantial collection of his books and manuscripts, treasured by his students and colleagues. Marianne, aware of the significance of these items, donated some and sold batches to scientific research institutions, book vendors, scholars, and collectors in Europe and the United States. However, with intentions to fetch higher prices, she diligently erased a multitude of notes Pelliot had penciled in many books during his lifetime. Scholarly and collector communities regarded these annotations as valuable, encapsulating Pelliot's thoughts and research on these texts—regrettably, they were erased by his wife. Marianne bequeathed some of Pelliot's manuscripts to his students and donated other belongings to the Guimet Museum.

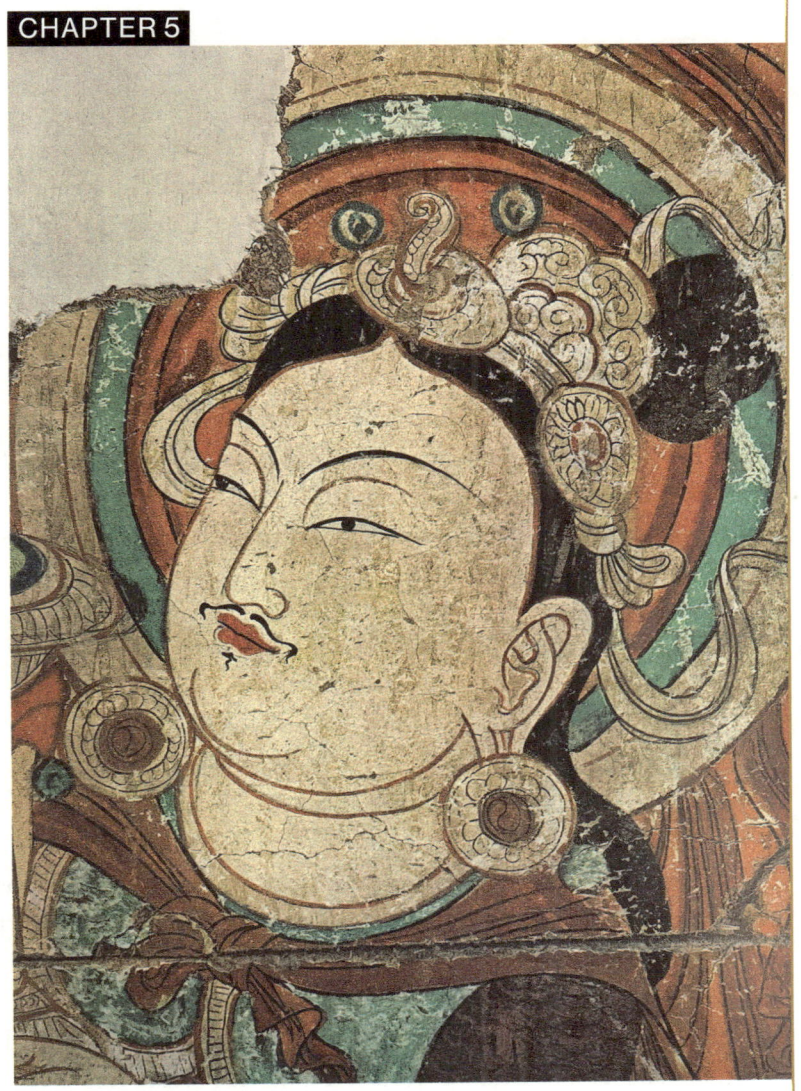

CHAPTER 5

The Western Expedition of Ōtani Kōzui and His Buddhist Team

1902–1904

First expedition

Members: Watanabe Tesshin, Hori Kenyu, Honda Eryu, Inoue Koen

Route: London–Russia–Kashgar–Hotan–Kuqa, Baicheng (Kizil Caves)–Xi'an–Japan

1908–1909

Second expedition

Members: Tachibana Zuicho, Nomura Eizaburo

Tachibana Zuicho and Nomura Eizaburo's route: Beijing–Mongolia–Junggar Basin–Turpan (Bezeklik Caves)–Korla

Tachibana Zuicho's route: Korla–Loulan ruins–Ruoqiang–Hotan–Kashgar–Over the Karakoram Pass–Leh City

Eizaburo Nomura's route: Korla–Kuqa (Kizil Grottoes)–Aksu–Kashgar–Over the Karakoram Pass–Leh

1910–1912, 1911–1914

Third expedition

Members: Tachibana Zuicho, Yoshikawa Koichiro

Tachibana Zuicho's route (1910–1912): London–Russia–Tacheng–Urumqi–Turpan–Loulan ruins–Qiemo–Across the Taklamakan Desert–Kuqa–Kashgar–Hotan–northern Xizang–Qiemo–Ruoqiang–Dunhuang–Anxi–Hami–Turpan–Urumqi–Siberia–Japan

Yoshikawa Koichiro's route (1911–1914): Japan–Shanghai–Wuhan–Lanzhou–Dunhuang–Hami–Urumqi–Turpan–Yanqi–Kuqa (Kumtura Caves, Subashi Buddhist Temple ruins, Kizil Caves)–Kashgar–Hotan–Ili–Urumqi–Turpan–Hami–Dunhuang–Jiuquan–Beijing–Japan

5.1 A True Pure Land Buddhism Expedition Team

When Western explorers embarked on journeys to Xinjiang, Gansu, and other regions for the excavation of cultural relics, a distinctive group of Japanese explorers also made their way onto Chinese soil. What set them apart from their Western counterparts was not only their role as explorers but also their identity as monks belonging to Japan's Jodo Shinshu sect (The True Pure Land Buddhism).

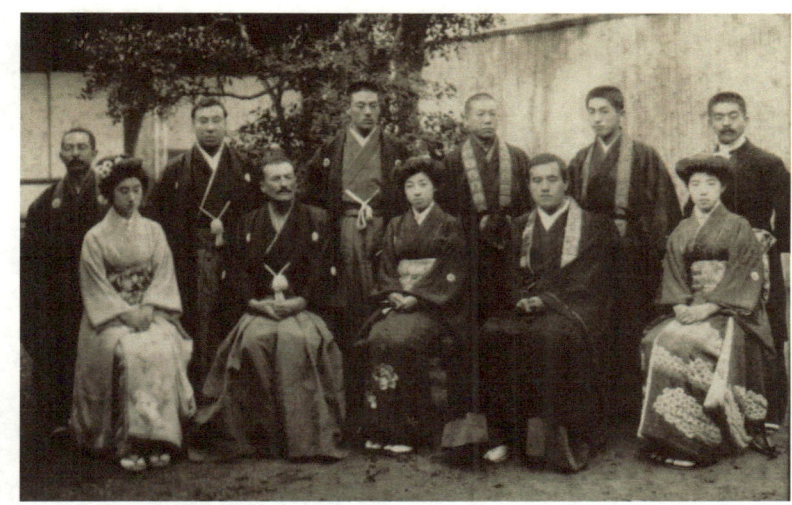

Figure 5-1 Ōtani Kōzui (front row, second from right) and his family

The structure of Buddhism in Japan deviates from that of other Asian countries, characterized by family temples inherited and managed within family units. Ōtani Kōzui (1876–1948), known by his Buddhist name Kyōnyo, hailed from a Buddhist family (Figure 5-1). His father, Ōtani Kōson, served as the 21st abbot of Nishi Hongan-ji (Figure 5-2) in Kyoto, representing the Jodo Shinshu sect. As the eldest son, Ōtani Kōzui underwent training to become the 22nd successor of Nishi Hongan-ji from a young age. Initiated into monastic life at the age of 9, he furthered his education at the academy. In 1898, at the age of 22, Ōtani Kōzui married Kujō Kazuko, the sister of Empress Teimei (Emperor Taisho's wife). This matrimonial connection made Ōtani Kōzui and Emperor Taisho, who reigned from 1912 to 1926, brothers-in-law, establishing the Ōtani family as relatives of the emperor. Feeling the influence of Western culture on Japanese Buddhism, Ōtani Kōson, one year after Kōzui's marriage, funded his study in London. During his three-year sojourn in Europe, Kōzui developed a profound interest in the abundant Buddhist relics collected by European scholars in Central Asia and beyond. His exposure to the outcomes of Sven Hedin, Stein, and others' Central Asian expeditions left an indelible impression. Visiting museums across various countries, he marveled at the vast array of cultural relics and treasures sourced from China by expedition teams worldwide. Stein's Central Asian expeditions, in particular, left him deeply awestruck. This experience prompted him to decide to explore Central Asia on his return trip, marking the beginning of Japan's exploration of northwest China.

In stark contrast to European Christian expeditions, predominantly led by scholars, Ōtani Kōzui's team comprised solely of Buddhist monks. Since 1902, he has organized three expeditions to Central Asia, Xinjiang, Kashmir, Gandhara, India, and other locations under the banner of exploring Buddhist relics. Funding for these endeavors primarily came from the contributions of nearly 10 million Japanese believers. Consequently, the

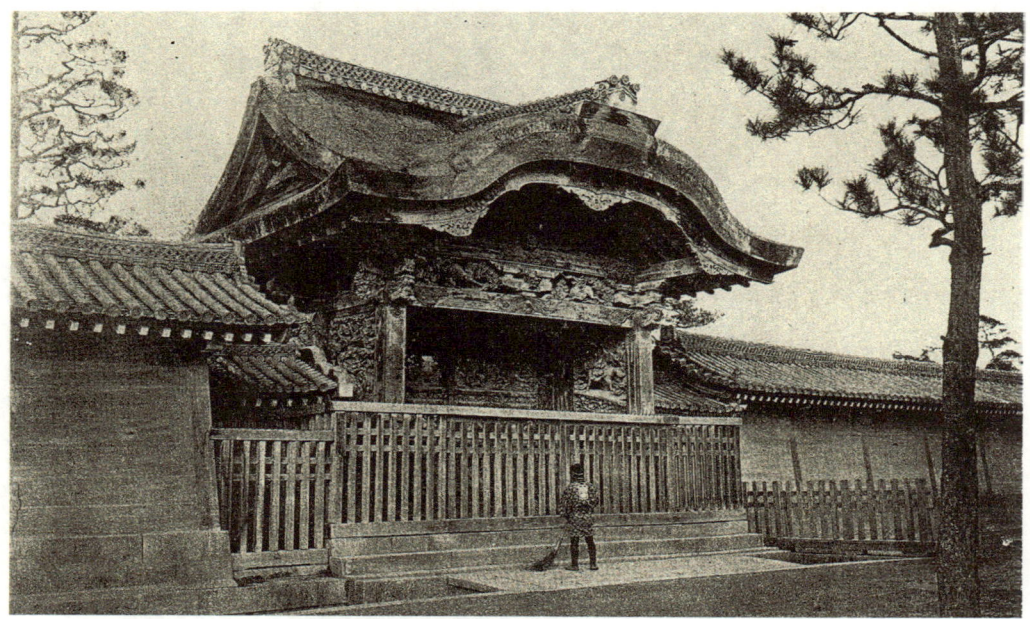

Figure 5-2 Nishi Hongan-ji in Kyoto (1901)

Ōtani Expedition operated as a private venture, distinct from Western explorers funded by government agencies with close ties to museums. Notably, the monk explorers received little formal training in archaeology or art history, possessed no excavation experience, and lacked awareness of cultural relic protection. They ventured into remote and uninhabited deserts, haphazardly digging at various ruins, seeking treasures indiscriminately, changing locations frequently, and maintaining unpredictable trajectories. As a result, they left behind no systematic investigation records of ancient ruins. The information that has come down to us consists only of personal notes and diaries, presenting a plethora of challenges for later scholars attempting to study the cultural relics they brought back. Undoubtedly, their purported exploration and excavation activities inflicted considerable damage on ancient Chinese ruins, rendering the prospect of their restoration nearly unimaginable.

The inaugural Central Asian expedition led by Ōtani Kōzui unfolded from 1902 to 1904. The team, composed of five monks—Ōtani Kōzui, Watanabe Tesshin (1874–1957), Hori Kenyu, Honda Eryu, and Inoue Koen—ventured into China. Fueled by Kōzui's passion for Buddhism in the Western Regions, the expedition commenced in August 1902 from London, traversing Russia, passing through Samarkand, and finally arriving in Kashgar, Xinjiang, China. The team split into two groups in Taxkorgan, with Ōtani Kōzui leading Honda Eryu and Inoue Koen to cross the Mintaka Pass, reaching present-day Gilgit, Pakistan, and Srinagar, India. Unfortunately, Kōzui lost the chance to personally explore Central Asia due to his obligations. In January 1903, Kōzui received news of his father's demise, prompting a hasty return from Kashgar to Kyoto, Japan. He inherited the position of the 22nd abbot of Nishi Hongan-ji and the title of Count (Figure 5-3). The remaining four team members were divided into two teams and entered Xinjiang, where their East Asian appearance ensured minimal local suspicion. This advantage made their excavations smoother and less encumbered than those of European expeditions.

Watanabe Tesshin and Hori Kenyu followed the South Silk Road into Hotan in Xinjiang, exploring the Kuqa and Baicheng areas for four months (Figure 5-4). In April 1903, they reached Baicheng and, guided by villagers, discovered the Kizil Caves. The team investigated various cave areas, capturing murals and cave exteriors in photographs. However, they also initiated the unfortunate practice of cutting murals in some caves (Figure 5-5), marking the commencement of the Kizil Caves disaster. Subsequent expeditions from different countries viewed the Kizil Caves' murals as coveted trophies, subjecting the site to widespread devastation. Nomura Eizaburo of Ōtani Kōzui's second expedition further contributed to the tragedy in March 1909, cutting more murals at the Kizil Caves. In 1912, Yoshikawa Koichiro (1885–1978) from the third expedition followed suit, copying and cutting murals. Their *Archaeological Atlas of the Western Regions* documented 11 Kizil Caves murals. Most of these severed artworks were scattered globally, some finding their way into private collections. The bulk of the remaining murals in the caves fell victim to German expeditions and were later housed in the Ethnological Museum of Berlin.

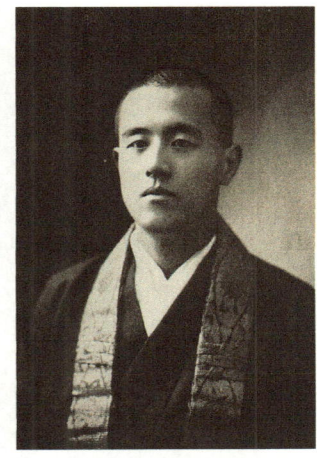

Figure 5-3 Young Ōtani Kōzui in monk attire

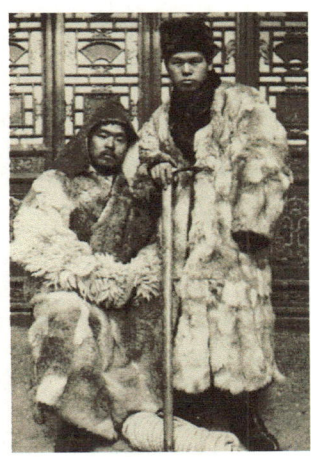

Figure 5-4 Watanabe Tesshin (right) and Hori Kenyu during their expedition (1902–1904) to Xinjiang

For the Japanese expedition team, the acquisition of murals marked just one facet of their overall expedition bounty. As they meticulously cleaned the caves, their findings extended beyond artworks to encompass a treasure trove of documents and wooden slips. Among these discoveries was the renowned *Kongmusi Documents in the Fifth Year of Jianzhong of the Tang Dynasty*. Kongmusi, an administrative office established in the Tang Dynasty, presided over matters such as prison litigation, deportation, and accounts. This official document shed light on travel and public inspection in Xinjiang during the Tang Dynasty, offering insights into governance, corveé labor, and taxation in the region. Additionally, the expedition yielded documents like the Tang Dynasty temple account books in Kuchean (Ōtani Document No. 541, MS00541). Even today, these documents remain crucial materials for studying the Silk Road.

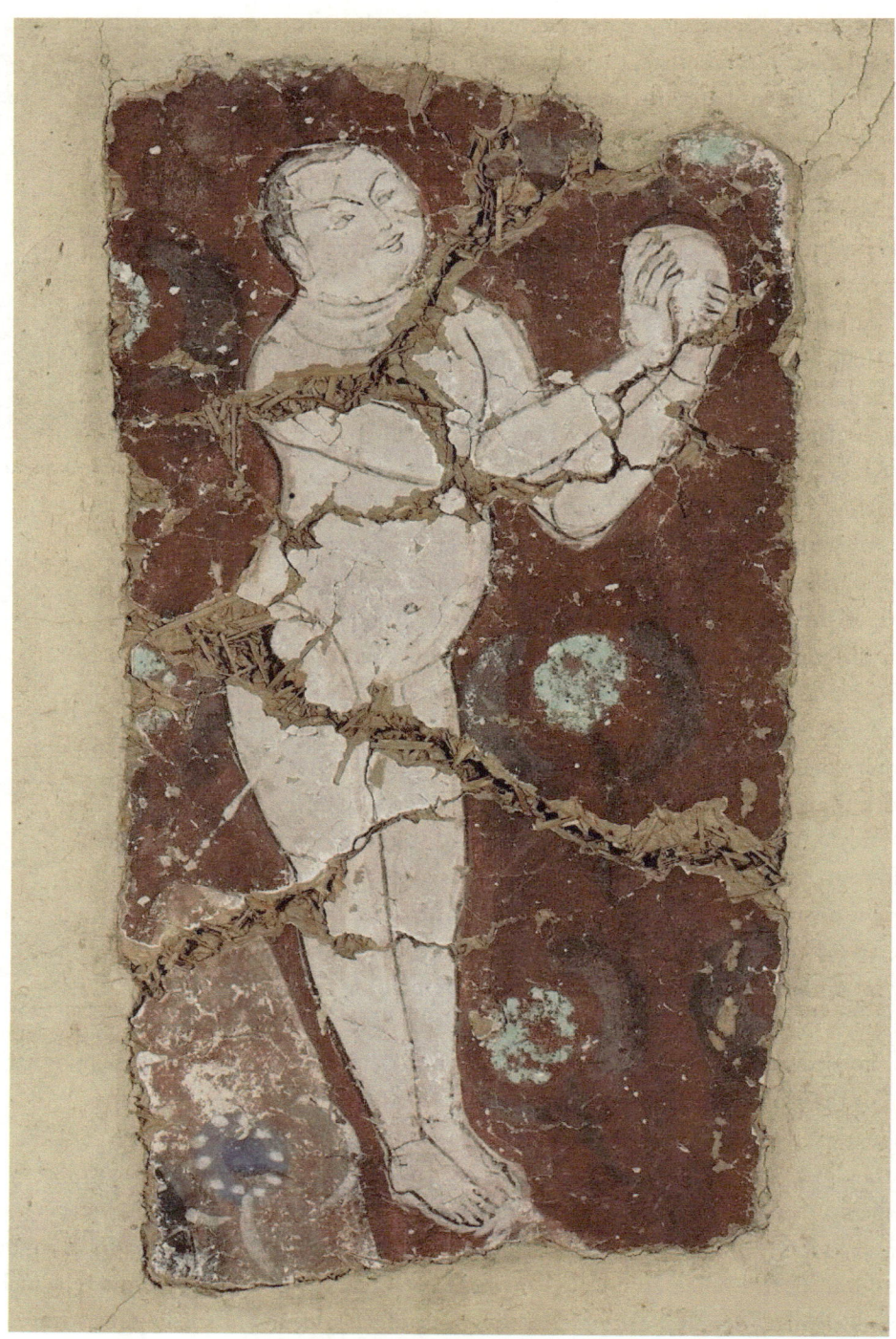

Figure 5-5 Part of the mural of the karma story taken from the outer wall of the right corridor of Cave 206 of the Kizil Caves in Baicheng, Xinjiang, by the Ōtani Expedition (now in the National Museum of Korea in Seoul)

The Ōtani expedition also delved into numerous tombs, unearthing documents with a distinctive purpose. Rather than serving as records, these documents underwent a curious transformation—repurposed as waste paper. This waste paper, derived from old documents, was fashioned into paper clothing, paper coffins, and paper boots to enshroud the deceased. Scholars have yet to unravel the mystery behind this peculiar practice, conjecturing it to be a specific custom of the time. This custom, however, inadvertently played a role in preserving these documents in Xinjiang's arid climate. Currently stored at Ryukoku University in Kyoto, these written historical materials provide a glimpse into the social conditions of Xinjiang during that era, collectively known as the Ōtani Documents.

With each expedition to ancient ruins, the Ōtani team engaged in indiscriminate digging and plundering. Watanabe Tesshin succinctly captured their approach in *On the Ancient Road to Central Asia*, stating, "Every place that needs to be excavated has been excavated." In May 1904, Watanabe and Kenyu Hori concluded the first Central Asian expedition, returning home via Xi'an laden with a substantial haul of Chinese cultural relics acquired during their transformative journey.

5.2 Li Bo Documents Unearthed in Loulan

Following the success of the initial expedition, Ōtani Kōzui orchestrated a second expedition in 1908–1909, entrusting the exploration primarily to Tachibana Zuicho (1890–1968) and Nomura Eizaburo. Their primary focus laid on uncovering the secrets of Turpan, Loulan, and Kuqa, among various other ancient ruins. Tachibana Zuicho, a native of Nagoya, emerged as a prominent figure—a monk of the Jodo Shinshu Hongan-ji sect and a renowned explorer of Buddhist relics in Japan (Figure 5-6). His early education at Shinshu Middle School in Kyoto proved influential, and the favor of Ōtani Kōzui, the abbot of Nishi Hongan-ji, secured his invitation to partake in Ōtani's second expedition to the Western Regions.

Of all the expeditions orchestrated by Ōtani Kōzui, the second expedition stands out as the most prolific, yielding

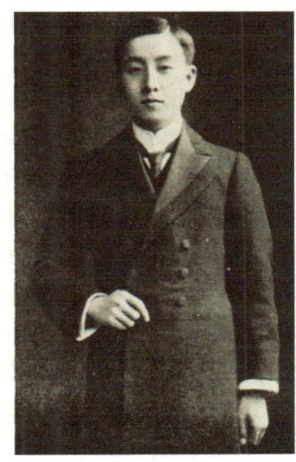

Figure 5-6 Young Tachibana Zuicho

significant discoveries in Turpan and Loulan, meticulously documented in his book, *New Records of Western Regions*. Commencing their exploration in June 1908, Nomura Eizaburo and Tachibana Zuicho embarked from Beijing, traversed Mongolia, and entered the Junggar Basin to delve into the ruins surrounding Turpan. Their initial stop led them to the Bezeklik Caves, where they were met with a disheartening sight—numerous murals in the caves had suffered extensive damage. Locals attested that European excavators had taken away the finest murals while intentionally vandalizing the remainder. Indignantly, the two Japanese explorers declared, "If this is true, the purportedly civilized European scholars' intention to monopolize the world's treasures can be deemed more despicable than that of thieves." Undeterred, Nomura and Tachibana pressed on, discovering a cave adorned with "colorful murals." The depictions featured Buddhas and Bodhisattvas in various poses—some folding their hands, others scattering flowers, and some engaged in musical pursuits. The celestial beings' graceful dance postures and the menacing expressions of devils were lauded for being "highly accomplished in color and brushwork." Intriguingly, they also encountered clay Buddha statues described as "full of life, extremely wonderful, gorgeous, and spectacular." Despite their earlier expressions of anger toward the Europeans' mural theft, the Japanese explorers, motivated by their quest for cultural relics, employed a specialized foxtail saw to "cut seven pieces of the murals that were enough to appreciate, and obtained seven pieces of clay Buddha statues." After all, that was the main purpose of their journey.

In February 1909, Nomura Eizaburo and Tachibana Zuicho split up in Korla. Nomura conducted excavations and surveys around Kuqa before proceeding to Kashgar via Aksu. Between March 18 and 20, 1909, he embarked on significant excavations in the Kizil Caves, cutting away portions of the rhombus Jataka and Karma Story murals on the side wall of Cave 206, and the mural of Brahmin Drona, the presiding officer of the division of sarira among the eight kings, within the *Picture of the Eight Kings Dividing the Sarira* on the inner wall of the left corridor of Cave 224 (Figure 5-7). Meanwhile, Tachibana Zuicho ventured into the Lop Nur Desert to explore Loulan, about to make a pivotal discovery at the age of 19.

Tachibana's expedition was facilitated by the assistance of another explorer, Sven Hedin. Ōtani, during his European study tour, had met Sven Hedin through various channels and extended a strong invitation for him to visit Kyoto. Hedin arrived in Nagasaki in November 1908 and left Japan in December. During his stay in Kyoto, he resided in Hongan-ji. Under Ōtani Kōzui's warm hospitality, Hedin eventually shared the precise coordinates of the ancient city of Loulan before departing. Ōtani, washed over by elation, urgently transmitted the coordinates to Tachibana and Nomura in Turpan via telegram. At the beginning of that telegram wrote, "2588 ninety degrees 2590 forty-one degrees." This code was the coordinates of the ancient city of Loulan—90 degrees east longitude and 41 degrees west longitude. Only Hedin, as a geographer and the discoverer of the ancient city of Loulan, could provide such accurate geographical coordinates. The numbers "2588" and "2590" were likely passwords established by Ōtani and his disciples. Employed to secure the telegram information, this encrypted code was a measure to prevent unauthorized access. Ōtani, often regarded as not just a sponsor for the expedition but also a senior spy, was therefore proved by this telegram his dual roles.

With the insights from the experienced Hedin, the Japanese expedition team, once trailing behind archaeological teams from various countries, emerged as the frontrunner. Leading the third group of foreigners to access the ancient city of Loulan after Hedin and Stein, Tachibana uncovered the renowned Li Bo Documents of the Sixteen Kingdoms in

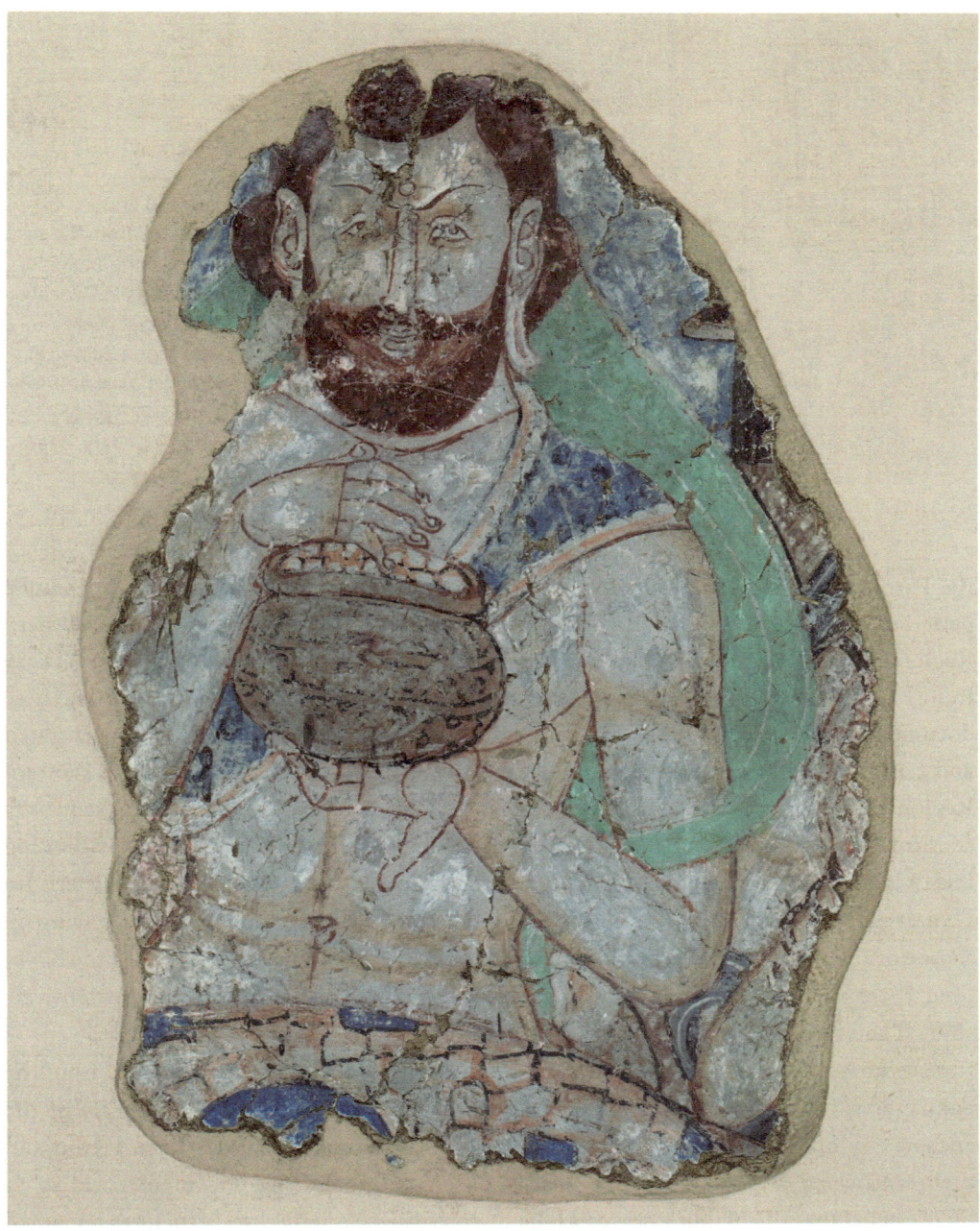

Figure 5-7 Mural of the 7th-century Buddhist disciple Drona dividing the Sakyamuni sarira for the Eight Kings taken from the Kizil Caves in Baicheng, Xinjiang (40.5 cm long, 28 cm wide, now in the Tokyo National Museum, No. TA-168)

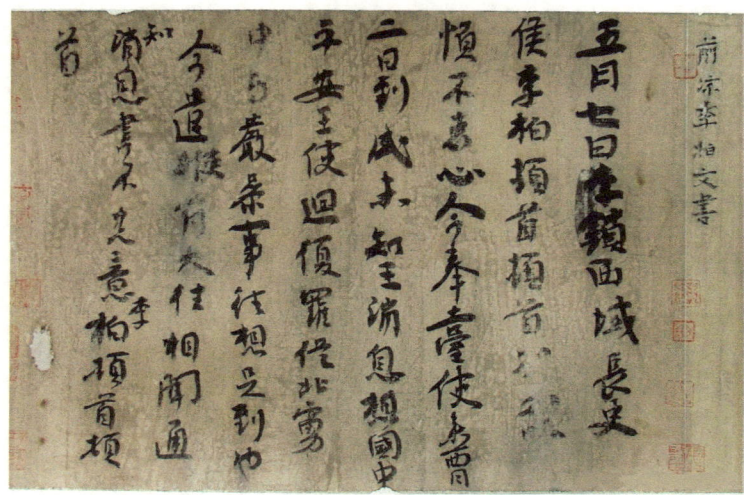

Figure 5-8 Li Bo Documents from the third year of Xianhe's reign of the Eastern Jin Dynasty (AD 328) discovered by Tachibana Zuicho at the Loulan ruins in 1909 (currently in Ryukoku University Library, Kyoto, Japan)

the Former Liang Period (AD 324–376) (Figure 5-8). Li Bo, an official during the Xianhe period of the Eastern Jin Dynasty (AD 326–334), served as the chief official of the Western Regions. The discovered documents comprised drafts of letters written by Li Bo in AD 328 from Haitou, the bank of Lop Nur Lake, to King of Yanqi and several other kings. These documents, found among the Former Liang bamboo slips, stood as the most concentrated and rich material from that era, offering evidence of Former Liang's rule in the Western Regions. As Li Bo was documented in the *Book of Jin*, these documents consequently confirm the authenticity of history. The calligraphy within these documents, exhibiting the style of official script alongside traces of the running script popular in the Eastern Jin Dynasty, is a rare calligraphy work from the Sixteen Kingdoms period. Scholars, relying on these documents, successfully confirmed numerous ruins of the ancient city of Haitou. Over time, these documents and antiquities evolved into crucial historical materials extensively studied and discussed by Orientalists globally.

Tachibana Zuicho's records indicate that the Li Bo Documents were sourced from the Sanjianfang (three houses) ruins, denoting the large adobe building at the heart of the ancient city of Loulan discovered by Sven Hedin. During excavations there, Hedin and Stein uncovered numerous wooden boards, paper scraps, and silk documents, leading to Stein's belief that the building served as the town's *yamen*. As only three structures remained on the site, it became known as the "Sanjianfang." Tachibana accidentally unearthed the Li Bo Documents, though the details of how and where he obtained them, as well as information about other unearthed cultural relics, remain undocumented. Unfortunately, Tachibana's diary, which may have provided additional insights, was lost in a fire. Also, he contradicted himself on several occasions while discussing this excavation, sparking continuous debates among historians concerning matters related to the Li Bo Documents. Furthermore, his lack of basic archaeological skills and the absence of scientific records during his haphazard excavations not only resulted in the destruction of the archaeological site but also significantly diminished the research value of the obtained items.

Subsequently, Tachibana proceeded to Kashgar along the south road of the desert via Ruoqiang and Hotan, reuniting with Nomura. Together, they traversed the Karakoram Pass and entered Leh. Regardless of the journey's intricacies, they concluded their second 18-month expedition with an abundance of murals and Buddhist statues obtained from the Bezeklik Caves and Kizil Caves, along with the treasures uncovered in the ancient city of Loulan.

5.3 Dunhuang Bounty Transported by 100 Camels

Ōtani Kōzui's third expedition to Central Asia unfolded from 1910 to 1912 and 1911 to 1914, spearheaded by two individuals.

Prior to this expedition, Ōtani Kōzui took Tachibana Zuicho to Europe in preparation. There, they not only surveyed the archaeological achievements of renowned explorers like Hedin, Stein, Pelliot, and Le Coq, but also gathered the latest insights about Central Asia's Western Regions, along with coordinates of crucial archaeological sites. These preparations laid the groundwork for their forthcoming investigative activities.

In August 1910, Tachibana embarked on the journey from London, traversing China via Russia and reaching Tacheng in Xinjiang. The route included Urumqi, Turpan, and a return to the Loulan region for inspection. Proceeding north from Qiemo, the expedition crossed the formidable Taklimakan Desert to Kuqa in northern Xinjiang. The journey continued west from Kuqa to Kashgar, south from Hotan into northern Xizang, and then back to the Qiemo and Ruoqiang areas for further inspection. The circuit around the Taklimakan Desert resembled more of a quest for antiquities than an archaeological exploration. Despite conducting some excavations in Turpan, Loulan, Hotan, and other regions, the team's movements were swift, and they neglected timely reporting to Ōtani Kōzui in Japan.

By 1911, Ōtani Kōzui, growing anxious due to the prolonged silence from Tachibana Zuicho, dispatched his protege Yoshikawa Koichiro to China in search of him. Yoshikawa's journey took him through Shanghai, Wuhan, and Lanzhou, arriving at Dunhuang on October 5, 1911. He documented caves (Figure 5-10) and telegraphed various parts of Xinjiang, seeking Tachibana. Simultaneously, Yoshikawa engaged in treasure-hunting activities in Dunhuang. Meanwhile, Tachibana, dressed as a Uyghur, was heading from Ruoqiang to Dunhuang. Meeting a Uyghur who informed him of a Japanese seeking another Japanese in Dunhuang, Tachibana learned in a letter that Ōtani Kōzui had sent Yoshikawa Koichiro. Rushing to Dunhuang on January 26, 1912, Tachibana (Figure 5-9) joined Yoshikawa, and the two departed Dunhuang in February 1912, heading to Urumqi via Hami.

Tachibana and Yoshikawa achieved substantial gains (Figure 5-11) in Dunhuang. During the prolonged wait for Tachibana Zuichao, spanning four months, Yoshikawa carried out an

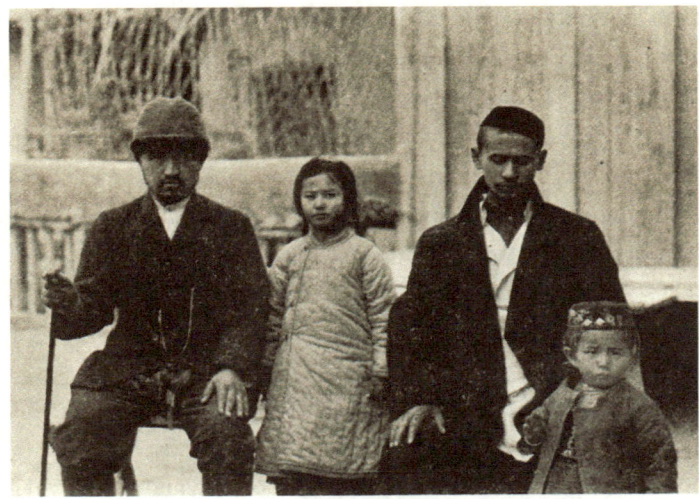

Figure 5-9 Tachibana Zuicho (first from left) with his landlord's family in Dunhuang (1912)

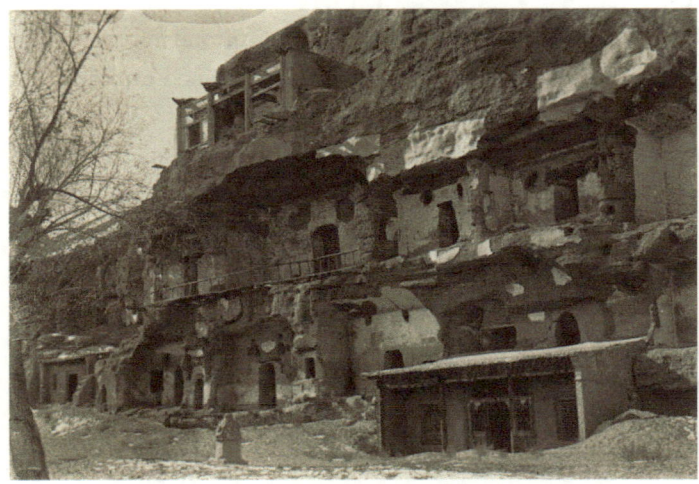

Figure 5-10 The appearance of Dunhuang Mogao Grottoes photographed by the Ōtani Expedition Team (1911–1912)

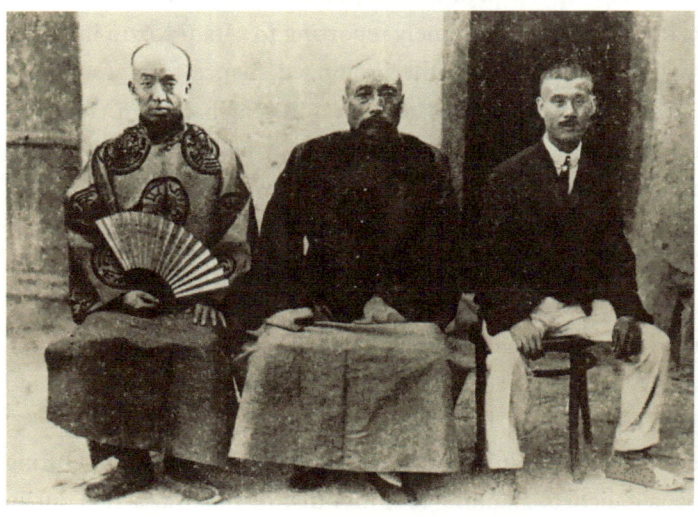

Figure 5-11 Yoshikawa Koichiro (first from right) with the telegraph director and county magistrate of Anxi County (September 13, 1911)

intricate operation within the Mogao Grottoes. Using specialized chemical tape, he meticulously detached 26 square meters of exquisite murals, along with "two exquisitely crafted and well-preserved Buddha statues" from one of the caves. Through negotiations with the monks, Yoshikawa successfully purchased these artifacts and discreetly stowed them away in his luggage. Prior to departing, he bestowed 11 taels of silver upon Taoist Wang, accompanied by a deceitful acquisition of a batch of Tang Dynasty scriptures. By this juncture, the Library Cave within the Dunhuang Mogao Grottoes had been emptied, as most of the remaining scriptures were transported to Beijing following the Qing government's orders issued by the Dunhuang magistrate. As previously detailed, the astute Taoist Wang Yuanlu had concealed certain valuable scriptures in the "scripture transfer barrels" and subsequently sold them to various foreign expedition members who frequented Dunhuang. Wang, by now accustomed to interactions with foreigners, displayed no surprise upon the arrival of the Japanese expedition and harbored no guilt in providing them with documents. Upon Tachibana's arrival in Dunhuang, both he and Yoshikawa engaged in repeated communication with Wang, resulting in the acquisition of a substantial number of scriptures. According to Yoshikawa's recollection, Wang's demeanor while delivering the documents resembled that of "a thief transporting stolen goods."

During their stay in Dunhuang, Yoshikawa obtained over 100 volumes of written scriptures, while Tachibana acquired an impressive 260 volumes (Figure 5-12). Yoshikawa also amassed rubbings of inscriptions and numerous cave photographs. In February 1912, they organized a caravan of over 100 camels laden with 86 pieces of luggage, totaling more than 6,000 kilograms, to transport their newfound treasures out of Dunhuang (Figure 5-13).

As their stay prolonged, the anxious Ōtani Kōzui repeatedly urged Tachibana and Yoshikawa to return home promptly. Due to their contrasting work habits and personalities,

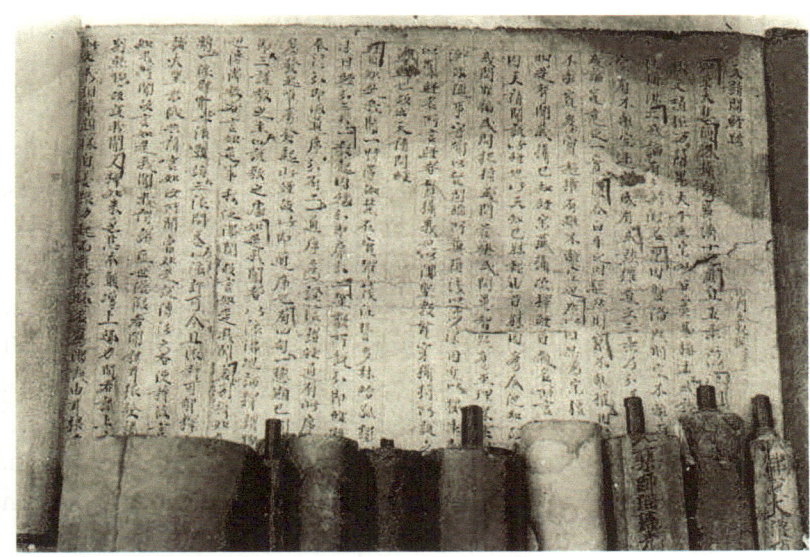

Figure 5-12
Ancient documents obtained by the Ōtani expedition team in Dunhuang in 1911–1912

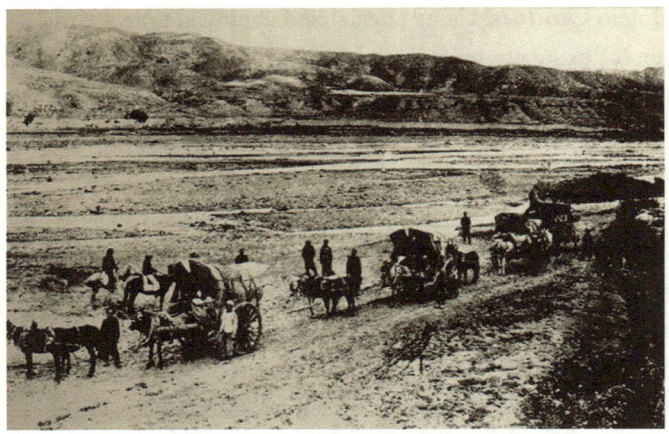

Figure 5-13 Japanese Ōtani expedition team leaving Dunhuang loaded with cultural relics (1912)

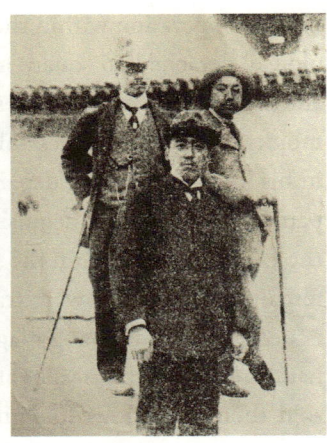

Figure 5-14 Tachibana Zuicho, Yoshikawa Koichiro, and Li from Anxi (1912)

the two explorers decided to embark on separate journeys (Figure 5-14). Yoshikawa set his course westward toward Turpan, while Tachibana headed east to Anxi. In Anxi, Tachibana received another urgent telegram from Japan. Ōtani demanded Tachibana to return home without delay. Thus, he had no choice but to retrace his steps, heading westward to catch up with Yoshikawa, traversing Hami, and ultimately reaching Turpan. From Turpan, Tachibana continued his journey to Urumqi before finally making his way home via Siberia.

Following his departure from Dunhuang, Yoshikawa continued his archaeological pursuits near Turpan. During the sweltering weather when excavation proved challenging, he ventured across the Tianshan Mountains, sojourned near Jimusar, and explored the Bogda Mountains. As temperatures cooled, he returned to Turpan. This cyclical pattern persisted until February 1913. His itinerary then led him through Yanqi to Kuqa, where he investigated sites such as the Kumtura Caves and Subashi Buddhist Temple. Subsequently, Yoshikawa moved on to the Kizil Caves, where he spent a few days cutting out murals, capturing photographs, and copying selected artworks. Continuing his journey, he headed west to Kashgar, south to Hotan, and north to Aksu, Yining, and other locations, conducting investigations into Buddhist relics. His travels were also an aimless circuit around the Taklimakan Desert.

Lacking formal archaeological training, Yoshikawa demonstrated astuteness by choosing areas previously explored by others for comprehensive and detailed excavation and investigation. Although this method may not have yielded the most exceptional cultural relics, the sheer number of sites visited resulted in a substantial harvest. Yoshikawa eventually retraced his steps, returning eastward to Urumqi. His route took him through Turpan, Hami, Dunhuang, Jiuquan, and other locales before reaching Beijing in May 1914. Finally, he returned to Japan with the collected cultural relics, which were meticulously packed into nearly a hundred pieces of luggage.

5.4 Treasures of the Ōtani Family

Yoshikawa Koichiro's return marked the official conclusion of Ōtani Kōzui's ambitious three expeditions to northwest China, a remarkable 12-year odyssey. The fruits of these expeditions, brimming with cultural relics, found their way to Japan. Some adorned the halls of Ōtani Kōzui's villa, Nirakusō, nestled on the outskirts of Kobe (Figure 5-15), while others found a home in the Imperial Museum of Kyoto, now recognized as the Kyoto National Museum. Hailing from the Six Dynasties period (AD 220–589), these relics hold profound significance in Dunhuang studies, though the exact count remains elusive. Historical snippets suggest a staggering total, approximating 40,000 items, spanning a diverse array—Buddhist scriptures, classics, historical documents, Western language manuscripts, paintings, sculptures, dyeing and weaving, embroidery, ancient coins, printings, etc. Dominating Ōtani's collection are Chinese books and tablet rubbings, with whispers of thousands of unique and rare copies.

In a grand showcase in November 1912, Ōtani Kōzui exhibited his curated collection at Nirakusō. These treasures, sourced from the Xinjiang region, had been meticulously chosen by experts in 1910. The crowning achievement of this venture was the publication of the *Archaeological Atlas of the Western Regions* in 1915, featuring 11 murals from Kizil and 6 Buddhist scripture manuscripts. This seminal work endures as the cornerstone for Japanese Dunhuang scholars, providing invaluable insights into Japan's exploration of Central Asia. *The Complete Works of Ōtani Kōzui* stands as a comprehensive repository, encapsulating the outcomes of Ōtani Kōzui's three expansive inspection endeavors.

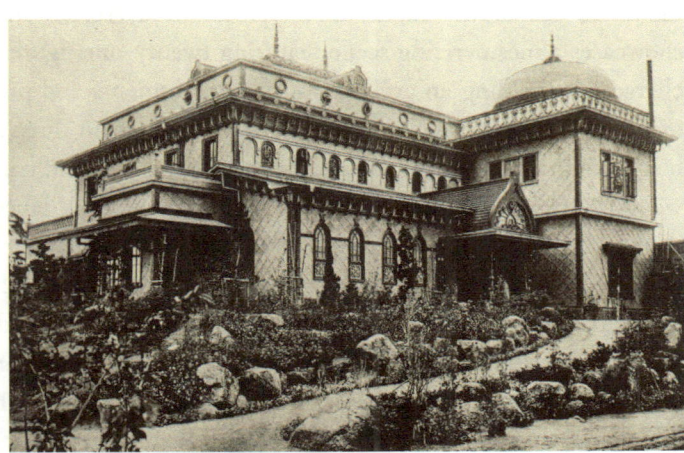

Figure 5-15 Ōtani Kōzui's villa Nirakusō located outside Kobe (first half of the 20th century)

A profound distinction characterizes the three Ōtani expeditions when compared to their Western counterparts. Unlike the scholarly compositions of Western teams, his expedition members lacked a scholarly background and possessed no knowledge of archaeology. Their fieldwork, marked by a lack of meticulousness, extended across an excessively broad scope. The cultural relics they procured did not stem from scientific excavations, and the absence of comprehensive original records complicated later efforts to organize their findings. Notably, the acquired relics lacked a systematic numbering system, contributing to confusion during post-expedition analysis. Illustrative of this difference is Zuicho, whose research proficiency remained modest, confined to the compilation of works like the *Directory of Dunhuang Buddhist Scriptures*. Consequently, no official archaeological report was ever published regarding their inspections. The team's work diaries, however, assumed the role of written materials, offering insights into their investigations and the cultural relics unearthed. A transformative moment occurred in 1937 when these diaries were found to be expressed in the two volumes of *New Records of the Western Regions*. This publication, a compilation of the team's diaries, revealed murals, exterior photographs of the Kizil Caves, cave configurations, and mural schematics. Compounding the disparity with Western expeditions was the primary focus of Ōtani's endeavors—treasure hunting. The materials and cultural relics they acquired, while extensive, bore diminished value compared to those secured by Western explorers. Tragically, this pursuit for treasures resulted in severe damage to historical sites and antiquities.

Within the rich tapestry of cultural relics amassed by Ōtani Kōzui, a singular wooden lacquered sarira box emerges as a captivating highlight (Figure 5-16). Unearthed by the keen eyes of Watanabe Tesshin and Hori Kenyu in 1903 at the West Temple of the Subashi Temple in the ancient Kucha Kingdom of Xinjiang, this unique artifact stands at 32.3 centimeters tall and presently resides in the esteemed collection of the Tokyo National Museum. Distinguished by its round shape and a pointed lid adorned with intricate lacquer paintings, the sarira box stands apart from the square counterparts and saira coffins typical in mainland China. Instead, it exudes a pronounced Western influence. The surface of the box showcases a mesmerizing scene featuring twenty-one figures clad in Western attire. These characters, wielding an array of musical instruments and props, engage in a lively display of singing and dancing. The visual narrative unfolds in three distinct parts. The front of the box, constituting the first part, portrays six hand-in-hand dancers and two solo performers wielding sticks. Bedecked in various masks and vibrant dance costumes resembling armor, they set the stage for a vivid spectacle. The second part, from the vantage point of the dancers, introduces musicians brandishing diverse musical instruments, including two children carrying a sizable drum and bronze trumpeters. In addition, within the captivating scene, there are also figures skillfully playing upright and phoenix-headed *konghou*, panpipes, drums, and brass horns. The artist's meticulous craftsmanship extends to the expressive interactions among these characters, with some immersed in music and dance, casting glances backward, and dancing children serving as the audience. This masterful depiction

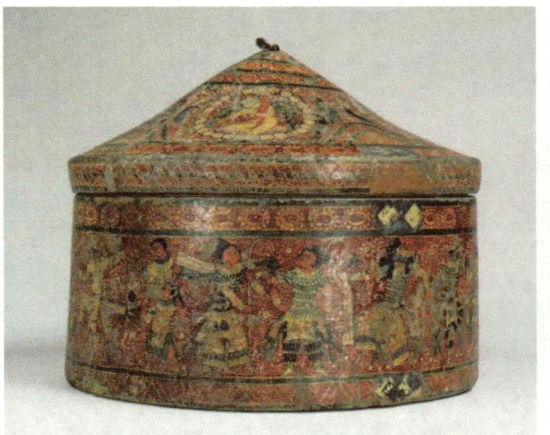
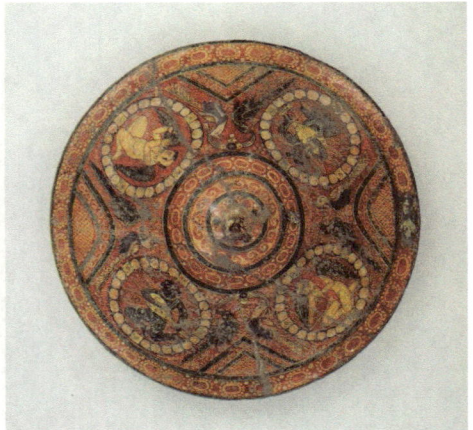

Figure 5-16 A wooden lacquered sarira box from the 6th to 7th centuries AD found in the Western Temple of the Subashi Temple (32.3 cm high, now in the Tokyo National Museum, No. TC-557)

fosters a joyous and lively atmosphere. The final part unveils a man and a woman bearing long streamers. Drawing a connection to ancient funerals, where such streamers guided the souls of the departed to the Western Paradise, scholars posit a correlation between this musical and dance composition and funeral rites. The portrayal of local funeral customs on the container of Sakyamuni's sarira aligns seamlessly with the artifact's religious function.

Adorning the lid of the pointed hat-shaped box are four distinct units, each intricately crafted with beads and featuring painted depictions of naked boys. These ethereal figures, adorned with either bird wings or cicada wings, engage in the enchanting act of playing instruments such as the *bili*, *konghou*, crooked-neck *pipa*, *pipa*, etc. Some scholars posit that these naked boys may represent Kalaviṅka, a bird in Buddhism renowned for its melodious tunes. In the Buddhist tradition, Kalaviṅka embodies a fusion of bird and human, often appearing with a human upper body and a bird's lower body, capable of producing harmonious music. Although the depicted children differ in their lower body structure—possessing wings rather than bird-like attributes—they bear a striking resemblance to the winged angel murals discovered by Stein in the ruins of Miran. This suggests a potential influence from traditional European art, with their religious identity likely akin to the Chinese flying apsaras.

Beyond the Ōtani expedition, similar sarira boxes were discovered by Pelliot and the German expedition team, all originating from the ruins of the Subashi Temple, located 20 kilometers north of Kuqa County. This temple, known as the Queli Temple or Zhaoguli Temple (Figure 5-17) during the Tang Dynasty, encompasses pagodas, caves, halls, and monks' chambers across a sprawling 180,000 square meters—making it the largest Buddhist temple ruin uncovered in Xinjiang to date. Standing atop a vantage point, one can still sense the grandeur of the Buddhist scene that once unfolded within the structure. The Subashi Temple, constructed during the Wei and Jin dynasties, holds a significant place in history

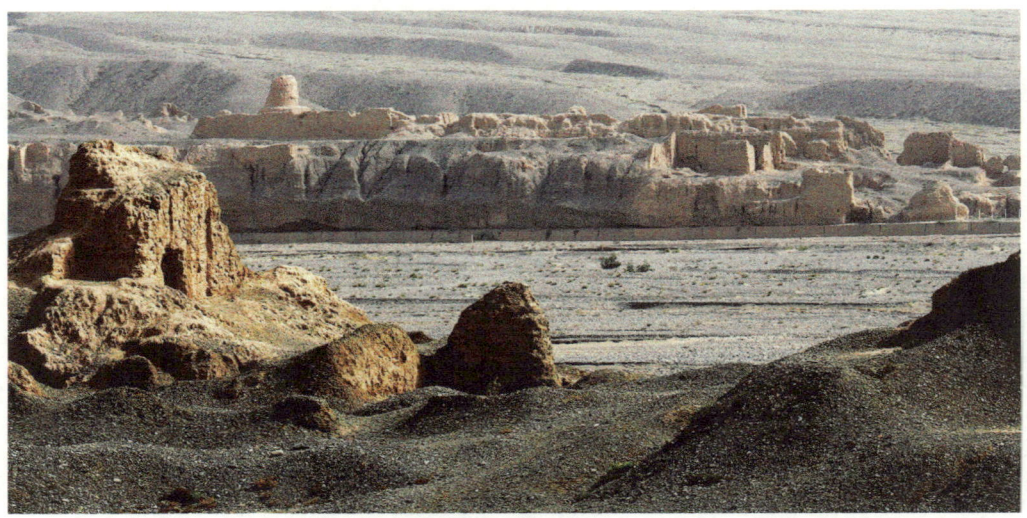

Figure 5-17 The ruins of the Subash Temple in Kuqa, Xinjiang (photographed by Xiyuyuanfang of Toutiao)

as the venue where Kumarajiva (AD 344–413), a revered monk from Kucha and one of ancient China's three great translators of Buddhist scriptures, delivered his inaugural lecture. Attaining its zenith during the flourishing Sui and Tang dynasties, the temple boasted a thriving community of tens of thousands of resident monks, drawing worshippers from all corners. Notably, Xuanzang, the distinguished Tang Dynasty monk renowned for his pilgrimage to India to obtain Buddhist scriptures, lingered at the Subashi Temple for over two months during his journey. In the mid-7th century AD, following the establishment of Kucha Town by the Anxi Protectorate of the Tang Dynasty, the temple became a hub for lectures by eminent mainland monks. This cultural exchange significantly contributed to the widespread dissemination of Tang Dynasty culture in Xinjiang. Regrettably, the temple met its demise in the 9th century due to the ravages of war. Subsequently, influenced by the advent of Islam, this once-magnificent Buddhist sanctuary fell into complete abandonment after the 14th century. The temple's existence remained hidden until the 19th century when foreign explorers unveiled its historical splendor.

The cultural treasures acquired by the Ōtani expedition, now housed in the Tokyo National Museum, encompass a remarkable Tang Dynasty sarira and various Buddhist sculptures, among which the gilt-bronze Buddha head holds a place of prominence (Figure 5-18). This relic, a product of the Ōtani expedition team's inaugural venture, is exceptionally rare as very few Buddhist-themed sculptures in Xinjiang have been preserved fully. In the wake of the Islamic forces' incursion in the 14th century, all Buddhist sculptures in Xinjiang were systematically eradicated, rendering gilt-surfaced copper artifacts even scarcer. This bronze statue, exhibiting the characteristic style of Gandhara in Central Asia, features a

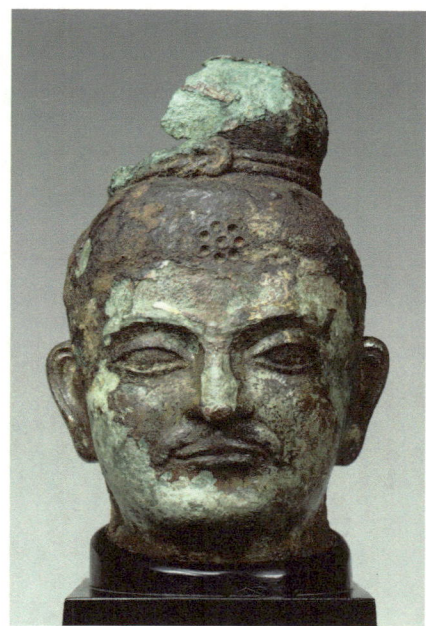

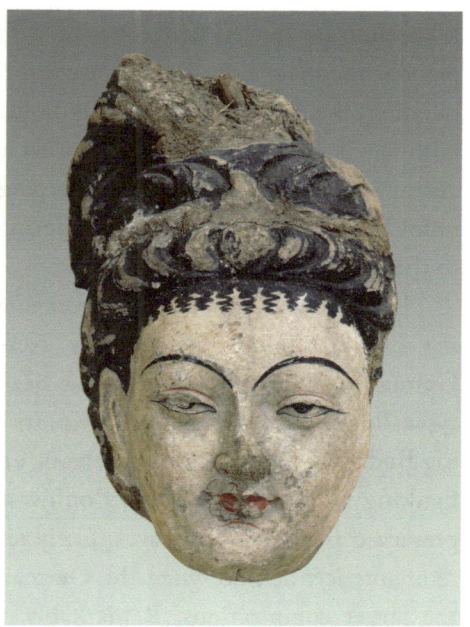

Figure 5-18 A gilt-bronze Buddha head from the 3rd to 4th century AD discovered by the Ōtani expedition in Hotan in 1902–1904 (17 cm high, now in the Tokyo National Museum, No. TC-456)

Figure 5-19 A clay Bodhisattva head from the 7th to 8th century, Tang Dynasty, acquired by Nomura Eizaburo from the Kumtura Caves in Kuqa, Xinjiang in 1908–1909 (28 cm high, now in the Tokyo National Museum, No. TC-648)

distinctive high nose, wide eyes, European facial features, and a bun atop the head. It serves as a valuable artifact offering insights into the relationship between ancient Buddhist art in Xinjiang, the Kushan Empire, and the concurrent Chinese and Indian Buddhism.

Another notable piece within the Tokyo National Museum's collection is the painted head of a Tang Dynasty Bodhisattva (Figure 5-19), discovered during the Ōtani expedition's examination of the Kumtura Caves. Kumtura is the transliteration of Uighur and means beacon tower in the desert. These caves, located about 30 kilometers southwest of Kuqa County, Xinjiang, were dug slightly later than the Kizil Caves. It is the second largest group of caves in the area of Kucha and Baicheng, once being the center of the ancient Kucha Kingdom. Standing at 28 centimeters in height, the Bodhisattva head exhibits slender eyebrows and a round face, exemplifying a fusion of Han, Tang, and Kucha styles.

The museum also boasts murals from the Bezeklik Caves, obtained by the Ōtani expedition. These murals, representing the typical Tang Dynasty style, showcase Uighur paintings of post the 10th century. Among them is a striking mural featuring a standing Bodhisattva holding an umbrella (Figure 5-20). Clad in armor-like clothing, this Bodhisattva's style closely resembles certain Bodhisattva costumes from the Song Dynasty in the Central Plains. Another striking mural (Figure 5-21) depicts a statue of a Bodhisattva in a kneeling posture. Gazing upward with profound piety at the main Buddha portrayed in the original painting, the Bodhisattva tenderly holds a plate in both hands, featuring an incense burner at its center. As the smoke delicately ascends, this poignant scene unfolds, symbolizing the reverent offering of incense to the main Buddha.

As previously mentioned, the expansive standing Buddha murals meticulously excised by the German expedition team within the Bezeklik Caves typically featured complementary pairs of supporting Bodhisattvas, Dharma protectors, and disciples flanking both sides. The two Bodhisattva murals, preserved from different caves, likely represent the remnants left behind when the Germans removed the larger compositions. Remarkably, these fragments were salvaged and acquired by the Ōtani expedition. Both murals employ a sophisticated light concave and convex blending painting technique. In this method, the initial outline is meticulously traced with an ink pen, followed by a gradual blending of the outline, layer by layer, from thick to light, originating at the edge of the outline. This meticulous process imparts a profound three-dimensional quality to the human body, particularly accentuating the bridge of the nose, forehead, eyebrows, and eyes, creating a striking effect that elevates the face from the two-dimensional plane. This painting technique, initially introduced to Central Asia from Europe and subsequently transmitted from Central Asia to mainland China, is documented in Chinese history books as the Concave Painting Method or the Tianzhu Method. Additionally, both murals prominently feature the distinct Kucha painting style, characterized by slender eyebrows, full and round faces, and well-defined cheeks—traits reminiscent of mural characters from the Kucha region. It is evident that these murals, adorned with vibrant

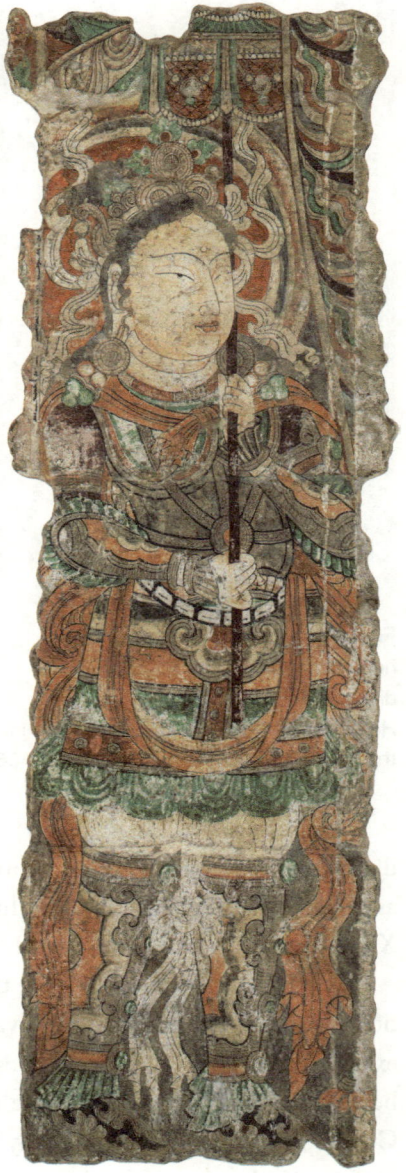

Figure 5-20 The mural of a standing Bodhisattva holding an umbrella from the 10th to 11th century AD in the Bezeklik Caves in Xinjiang, acquired by the Ōtani Expedition in 1908–1909 from the Gaochang Uighur period (now in the Tokyo National Museum, No. TC-552)

colors and fluid lines, stand as quintessential products born from the fusion of Eastern and Western painting techniques.

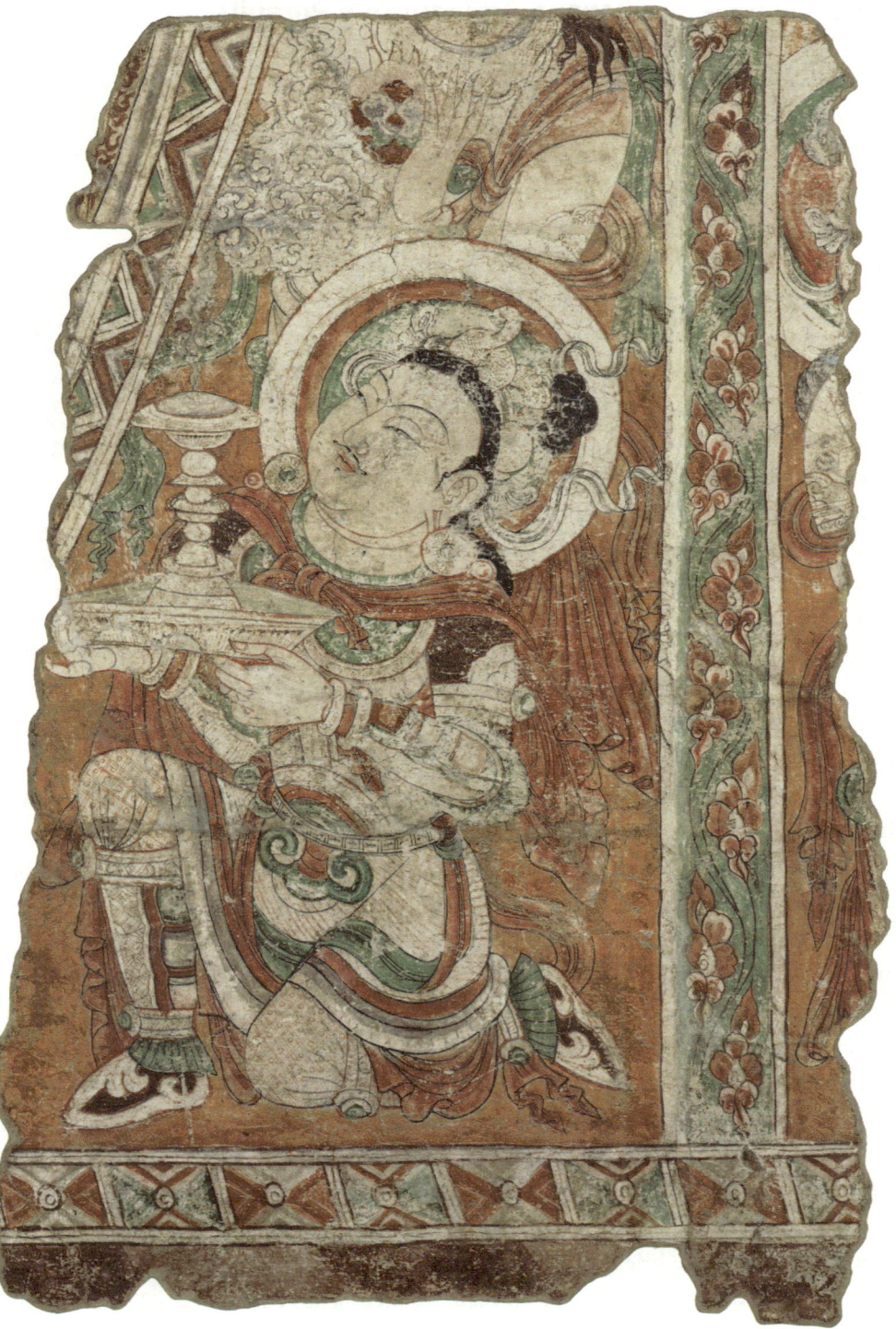

Figure 5-21 The mural of the Bodhisattva statue from the Gaochang Uighur period from the 10th to 11th century AD in the Bezeklik Caves in Xinjiang, acquired by the Ōtani expedition in 1908–1909 (now in the Tokyo National Museum, No. TC-553)

5.5 A Diverse Life beyond Adventurous Pursuits

Ōtani Kōzui, as a relative of the emperor, held the esteemed title of count and served as the abbot of a renowned temple with a sizable following. Given such a distinguished background, one would anticipate a life of prosperity. However, the trajectory of his career as a temple abbot and the circumstances of his later years unfolded in an unpredictable and regrettable manner. Despite the worldly success of the three Central Asian expeditions he generously funded, these endeavors came under scrutiny for their substantial costs. As early as the third expedition, allegations of corruption among the monks surfaced, further compounded by Ōtani Kōzui's inadequate management of the temple. Notably, he directed a considerable amount of funds donated by believers toward sponsoring expeditions, resulting in substantial debts burdening the Nishi Hongan-ji family temple. In 1914, amid a financial crisis and scandal, Ōtani Kōzui found himself condemned and accused by various segments of society. Faced with these challenges, he was compelled to relinquish

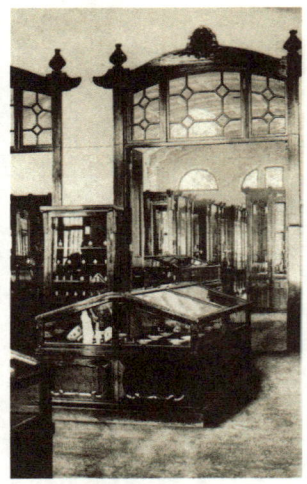

Figure 5-22 The exhibition hall of Ōtani Kōzui's deposits in the Lüshun Museum during the Japanese occupation (photographed before 1946)

his title of abbot and count. His eldest son, Ōtani Kōshō (1911–2002), succeeded him in the role. Following this tumultuous period, Kōzui chose a life of seclusion.

The dispersion of cultural relics acquired through three Otani expeditions marked a significant chapter in their journey. Ōtani Kōzui, expressing a desire to reside in Northeast China during Japan's occupation, carried with him a diverse collection as he left Kobe for China. This included ten mummies from Xinjiang, over 700 ancient Chinese manuscripts, sculptures, and numerous other cultural relics, alongside a library of 20,000 books. Facing financial challenges and debts, he opted to sell a portion of the remaining cultural relics and Nirakusō to Kuhara Fusanosuke (1869–1965). Kuhara subsequently dispatched this collection to the Korean Governor-General Museum, now housed in the National Museum of Korea in Seoul. Another portion was presented to the Kyoto Museum in Japan, which now resides in the Tokyo National Museum. Certain relics found their way to antique dealers. Cultural relics repatriated to China were stored in the Ōtani Library in Dalian and Lüshun. The artifacts left in Lüshun eventually found a home in the Kanto Hall Museum (later renamed Lüshun Museum) (Figure 5-22). These relics, accompanied by selected expedition members' diaries, were briefly cataloged and published in the *New Records of Western Regions*. Before Ōtani Kōzui's passing in 1948, wooden boxes containing relics from Dalian were discovered at Nishi Hongan-ji and generously donated to the Ryukoku University Library. The majority of the relics left in Lüshun remain preserved in the Lüshun Museum (Figure 5-23). Among these, over 600 Dunhuang manuscripts were transferred to the

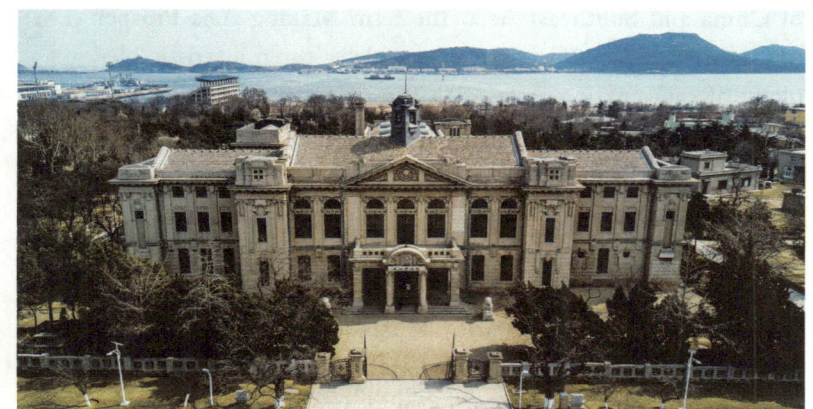

Figure 5-23
Appearance of
Lüshun Museum

Beijing Library for safekeeping in 1954. This collection has stood the test of half a century, witnessing a poignant twist of fate as a considerable number of these relics ultimately returned to the embrace of the motherland, evoking emotions of reflection and appreciation.

In addition to his explorations and role as an abbot, Ōtani Kōzui actively participated in political activities, establishing close ties with numerous heads of state. In 1913, Ōtani met Sun Yat-sen (1866–1925) and, on Sun Yat-sen's recommendation, served as an advisor to the government of the Republic of China. In 1914, grappling with the substantial debt issues of Nishi Hongan-ji, he resigned as its abbot. Subsequently, he immersed himself in agricultural pursuits across China, Southeast Asia, Turkey, and other regions, maintaining an extended stay in China. During this period, he actively collaborated with the Japanese government, constructing the Wuyou (worry-free) Garden in the outskirts of Shanghai and establishing a radio station for espionage activities. Leveraging his status and influence in the Buddhist community, he fervently supported the Japanese government's assertive expansionist and aggressive initiatives against China. In 1933, he relocated to Dalian from Shanghai and established a facility for manufacturing steel helmets to meet the military requirements of the Japanese army. He held successive roles as a cabinet counselor and cabinet adviser under the leadership of figures such as Fumimaro Konoe (1891–1945) and Koiso Kuniaki (1880–1950). Additionally, he played a pivotal role as a member of the Greater East Asia Construction Review Council, while assuming other important positions. In these capacities, he fervently advocated for robust and stringent measures against China.

From 1939 to 1941, Ōtani Kōzui took charge of editing and publishing the *Ōtani Kōzui Making Asia Prosper Collected Essays*, *Ōtani Kōzui's Asia Plan*, *China's Future and the Mission of the Japanese Empire*, and so on. In these publications, he advocated for the Southern Advance theory on behalf of the Japanese government. During this period, Japan contemplated two invasion routes: a northern route involving an invasion of the Soviet Union, where it was to join forces with the German army, and a southern route, encompassing the invasion of China and Southeast Asia. The term Making Asia Prosper in Ōtani Kōzui's publications encapsulates the militaristic ideology of rejuvenating Asia, with the objective of establishing a Greater East Asia Co-Prosperity Circle. It becomes evident that his political views were strongly aligned with Japan's radical militarism prevailing during that era.

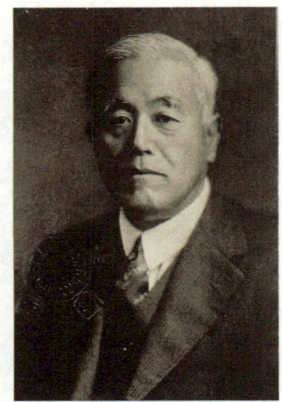

Japan faced defeat in 1945, and Ōtani Kōzui, a prominent figure who ardently supported Japan's militaristic aggression, was detained by the Soviet army. He underwent house arrest in the Dahe Hotel (now Dalian Hotel). In 1947, he was permitted by the Soviet Union to return to Japan after he was diagnosed with bladder cancer. Kōzui passed away the following year in Beppu City, Oita Prefecture.

Figure 5-24 Ōtani Kōzui

Throughout his life, his multifaceted identities as a monk, explorer, politician, and geographer interwove, forming a complex and three-dimensional narrative (Figure 5-24). As an explorer, he authored prolifically, with his works encompassed in *The Complete Works of Ōtani Kōzui*. In his role as a monk, he engaged in the translation and discussion of Buddhist scriptures, producing notable works such as *The Great Infinite Life Sutra*, *The First Meaning and Truth*, *The Solemnity of Bliss*, The General Principles of Buddhism, Speeches on the Vimalakirti Sutra, Taliki Shinshū, Hundred Jottings, etc. In the field of geography, he studied under Sven Hedin and authored *Geographical Records of India*, among other books. In politics, he notably leaned toward militarism.

As the abbot of Nishi Hongan-ji, Ōtani Kōzui faced challenges, notably accumulating substantial debts and ultimately being compelled to resign. While achieving commendable feats in Buddhist studies as a monk, he fell short in embodying the compassion advocated by Buddhism, becoming excessively entangled in external and malevolent thoughts. In his political and royal roles, he actively supported Japan's aggressive actions and expansion in Asian countries, seemingly oblivious to the devastating impact of war on the people of other nations. As an explorer, the expeditions he organized were viewed as endeavors primarily aimed at plundering cultural relics for treasure hunting. Not only did these expeditions fail to yield scientific survey data, but they also displaced numerous cultural relics.

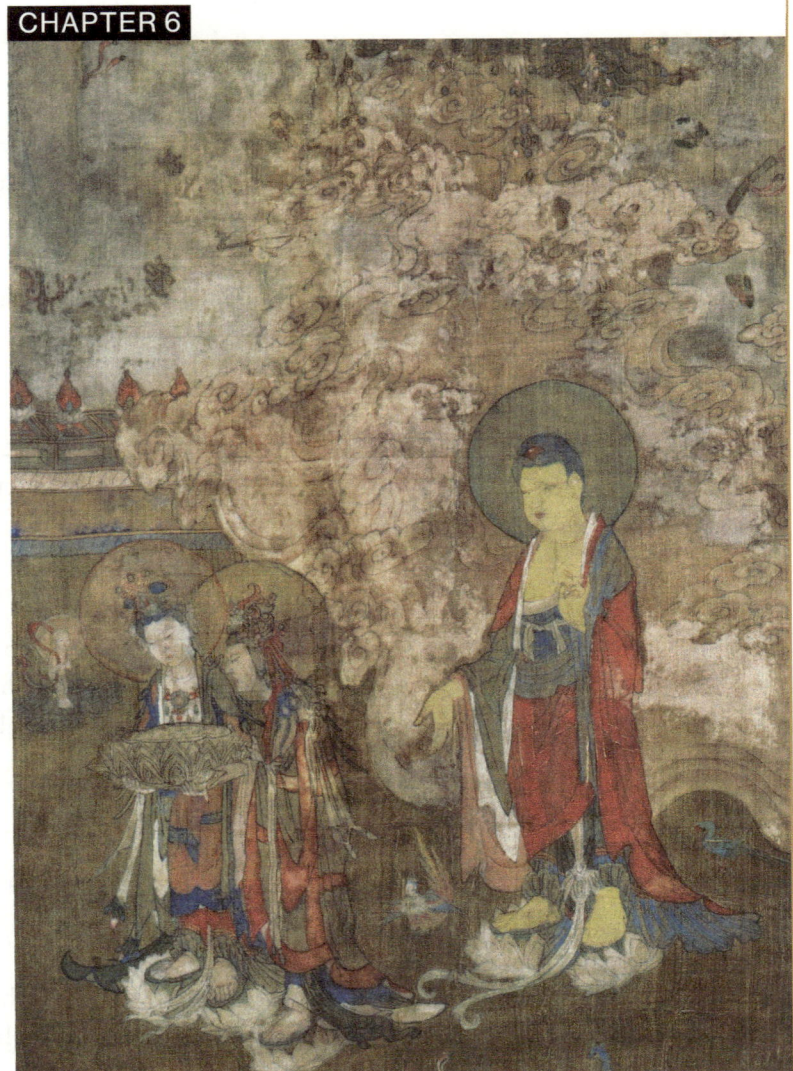

CHAPTER 6

Pyotr Kuzmich Kozlov and the Khara-Khoto Treasures

— 1884

First expedition, Kyakhta–Gobi Desert–Origin of the Yellow River–Tanggula Mountain–northern Xizang–Xinjiang (Lop Nur, Tarim River)–Karakul

— 1889–1890

Second expedition, Karakul–Issyk-Kul–Tian Shan–Southern Xinjiang–Yarkant–Kashgar–Niya Ancient City–Lop Nur–Lake Zaysan–Russia

— 1893–1895

Third expedition, Karakul–Tian Shan–Turpan–Hami–Dunhuang–Qilian Mountains–Amne Machin–Qinghai–Origin of the Yellow River–Turpan–Lake Zaysan–Russia

— 1899–1901

Fourth expedition, Kyakhta–Khovd–Altai Mountains–Central Gobi–Tengger Desert–Hexi Corridor–Xi'ning–Qinghai Lake–Qaidam Basin–Chamdo–Source of the Yangtze and Yellow Rivers–Lanzhou–Küriye (today's Ulaanbaatar, Mongolia)–Kyakhta–Russia

— 1904

Fifth expedition, Russia–Küriye (visiting the Dalai Lama Thubten Gyatso)

— 1907–1909

Sixth expedition, Moscow–Irkutsk–Kyakhta–Küriye–Tüshiyetu Khan Aimag, Sain Noyon Khan Aimag–Khara-Khoto ruins–Northern edge of Ala Shan Desert–Dingyuan Camp, the capital of Ala Shan Banner–Amdo Tibetan area–Qinghai Lake–Lanzhou–Khara-Khoto ruins–Khalkha Mongolia–Küriye–Russia

— 1923–1926

Seventh expedition, Küriye–Noin-Ula Mountain (excavation of Xiongnu tombs)–Khentii Mountains–Khara-Khoto

6.1 The Never-Ending Russian Expedition

Nikita Yakovlevich Bichurin (archimandrite monastic name Hyacinth, 1777–1853) was a Russian sinologist credited as the founder of Russian Sinology and Oriental studies. He was a former corresponding academician of the Russian Academy of Sciences (Figure 6-1). Ordained in 1800, he became a priest. In 1807, he arrived in Beijing as part of the Orthodox Beijing Mission and served there for 15 years. After returning to China in 1822, he dedicated himself to translating and researching Chinese classics at Valaam Monastery. He translated key Chinese texts such as the Four Books (*The Great Learning, The Doctrine of the Mean, The Analects*, and *Mencius*), *Three Character Classic*, and *Tongjian Gangmu* (Outline and Details of the Comprehensive Mirror in Aid of Government). He authored dictionaries and grammar books like *Elements of Chinese Grammar* and comprehensive works about Chinese folk customs and geography, such as *Detailed Chronicles of China,*

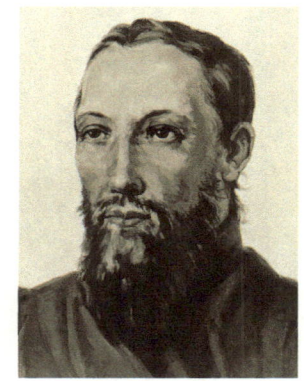

Figure 6-1 Portrait of Bichurin by Nikolay Bestuzhev (1791–1855)

Chinese Folk Customs, and *Ethnic Groups of Ancient Central Asia*. The Chinese school founded by Bichurin in Kyakhta laid the groundwork for Chinese teaching in Russia. This marked the establishment of Oriental studies in Russia, providing a foundation for future Russian explorers visiting China.

By the late 19th and early 20th centuries, as expedition members from various Western countries were still competing for access to China, Tsarist Russia, owing to its border proximity, had already commenced expeditions in northwest China. These Tsarist Russian expedition teams, with a focus on geography, climatology, botany, zoology, ethnology, and archaeology, aimed to meticulously compile a comprehensive topographic and humanistic archive of East Asia. In a collaborative effort, Russia's spy agencies partnered with official organizations, orchestrating numerous expeditions across the expansive territories from East Asia to West Asia during the second half of the 19th century and the early 20th century.

Pyotr Petrovich Semyonov (1827–1914) stood as a prominent Russian geologist, statistician, and entomologist, leading the Russian Geographical Society for over four decades. He vowed to explore the unknown Tian Shan. In 1856, he initiated his inaugural expedition from Barnaul to the Altai Mountains, venturing as far as Lake Issyk-Kul. The following year, he delved into the heart of the Tian Shan, ultimately publishing the pioneering treatise *Travel Notes on the Tian Shan* in 1858. Semyonov's most notable discovery pertained to the origin of the Tian Shan, and in recognition of this monograph, Tsar Nicholas II (r. 1894–1917), half a century later, bestowed upon him the honorary title Tian-Shansky (meaning "of Tian Shan").

Nikolay Przhevalsky (Figure 6-2) emerged as one of the trailblazing Tsarist Russian explorers. Having served in the Tsarist Russian army since his youth, he rose to the rank of lieutenant and regimental staff officer in 1863. His military reconnaissance efforts commenced in 1867, focusing on the Ussuri border against Russians, Manchus, and Koreans. Not only did he successfully fulfill military and intelligence objectives, but he also amassed a substantial collection of natural history specimens encompassing geology, flora, and

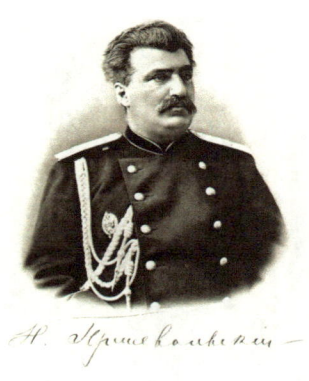

Figure 6-2 Photo and signature of Russian explorer Przhevalsky

fauna. Recognized by the Russian Academy of Sciences and the Royal Geographical Society, Przhevalsky garnered official political and financial support for border activities in China. Commencing in 1870, he led four expeditions to western China, covering diverse regions such as Beijing, the Taklimakan Desert in Xinjiang, the Inner Mongolia Plateau, the Qinghai-Tibet Plateau, and even Kekexili area in Qinghai. During his second expedition from 1876 to 1877, he made the groundbreaking discovery of Lop Nur in Xinjiang, causing a sensation in the geography community. This discovery laid the groundwork for Sven Hedin's later identification of the ancient city of Loulan adjacent to Lop Nur.

In 1879, during his third expedition to Central Asia, Przhevalsky reached Dunhuang with a fervent desire to explore the Tibetan region, a territory forbidden to foreigners at the time. As a result, his exploration route circumvented nearly all the regions surrounding Xizang. Despite his relentless efforts, the challenging plateau geography of Xizang, surrounded by natural obstacles, rendered access to key areas impossible without local government authorization. Despite Przhevalsky's determination, entry into the Tibetan region remained elusive. Faced with these geographical constraints, he redirected his route toward the foothills of the Tian Shan, with the hope of eventually crossing it to reach Xizang. Tragically, at the age of 49, he succumbed to illness after accidentally consuming contaminated water at the edge of Issyk-Kul. This intrepid explorer, much like Sven Hedin, chose a life of adventure over domestic stability and never married. In his own words, "I want to run to the desert again, where I will have absolute freedom and the career I love. I will be a hundred times happier there than getting married and living in a splendid palace."

Following in Przhevalsky's footsteps was Grigory Nikolaevich Potanin (1835–1920), a Russian ethnographer, natural historian, and Central Asian explorer. Leading an expedition from 1876 to 1877, Potanin collected biological specimens and conducted ethnographic research in Khovd, Mongolia. His travels took him to Hami in eastern Xinjiang in mid-March 1877. Later, from 1884 to 1886, Potanin, along with Augustus Ivonovitch Skassi, explored northern China, venturing from Inner Mongolia through the Ordos Desert and the Qinghai-Tibet Plateau. Their journey included documenting local vegetation in Gansu and Qinghai and marking the desert locations of ancient ruins.

Johann Albert von Regel (1845–1909) was a Russian doctor, botanist, Central Asian researcher, and archeologist who focused on plant investigations in Central Asia. His 1879–1880 visit to Turpan resulted in a comprehensive report on the abandoned Buddhist temples and relics scattered across the Turpan area.

Gombojab Tsybikov (1873–1930), a Buryat Mongolian, distinguished himself as a Russian Orientalist, geographer, and explorer (Figure 6-3). Sent by the Russian Geographical

Society on November 25, 1899, Tsybikov embarked on a mission to enter Xizang. During this period, the Qing government restricted access to foreign scholars, prompting him to assume the guise of a Buryat pilgrim embarking on a spiritual journey to Xizang. He successfully reached Lhasa in August 1900 and spent over a year traversing various regions in Xizang and Qinghai. Concluding his expedition on April 4, 1902, Tsybikov returned home. Proficient in Tibetan and equipped with advanced scientific education from Russia, he achieved notable success in Tibetan studies. His renowned work, *Buddhist Pilgrims in the Holy Land of Xizang*, published in 1919 and translated into Chinese, delves into Xizang's religious system, offering insights into customs, monastery establishments, monk life, sect branches, etc.

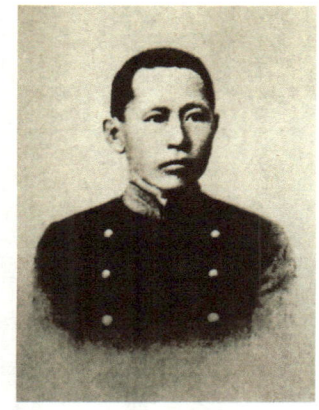

Figure 6-3 Russian Orientalist, geographer, and explorer Tsybikov (1900)

Tsybikov's contribution extended further as he brought back approximately 300 volumes of Tibetan classics from Xizang, providing invaluable resources to the Russian Tibetan scholar community of his time.

In the latter half of the 19th century, Tsarist Russian expeditions predominantly focused on gathering information about geographical maps, plants, animals, and local residents, rather than engaging in archaeological excavations. This emphasis was influenced by the political considerations of the Russian state at the time. For these individual explorers, the pursuit lay in a sense of mission and fulfillment derived from exploring uncharted territories, traversing mountains, and navigating deserts. Notable figures in Russian exploration with a focus on archaeology, such as Kozlov and Oldenburg, will be discussed below.

6.2 Discovery of the Important Frontier Town of Western Xia

Pyotr Kuzmich Kozlov, a participant in Przhevalsky's final two expeditions, explored Xinjiang and Qinghai. Born into an artisan family in Dukhovshchina, Smolensk, Kozlov's life took a transformative turn when, in 1884, Przhevalsky convinced him to join the military. Despite graduating from the St. Petersburg Military School (Figure 6-4) in 1887, Kozlov's true passions lay in zoology and archaeology. Inspired by Przhevalsky, he aspired to become an outstanding explorer. Over the course of 40 years, from 1884 to 1926, Kozlov undertook seven expeditions to Xinjiang, Mongolia, Xizang, Qinghai, Gansu, Sichuan, and other regions in China, becoming one of the explorers who made the most expeditions to China. His fifth and sixth expeditions, conducted between 1899 and 1901, yielded particularly significant results. In 1893, Kozlov, along with two teammates, embarked on a Central Asian expedition. By 1895, he led independent expeditions in the region. From 1899–1901, he explored the basins of the Yellow River, Yangtze River, and Mekong River. During this

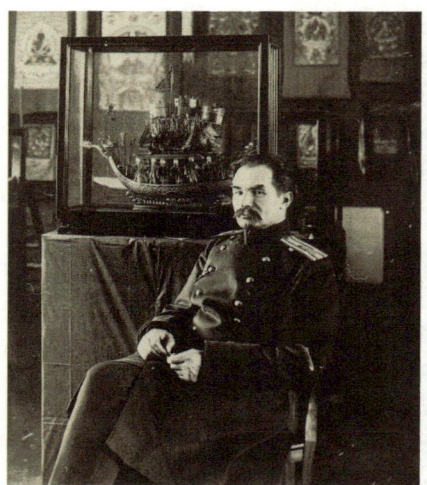

Figure 6-4 Kozlov in military uniform and what he obtained (1910)

time, he collected Bactrian textile samples dating back 2,000 years. In recognition of his outstanding achievements, he was awarded the Constantine Medal in 1902. Subsequently, Kozlov diverged from his mentor's path, focusing on archaeological excavations. His groundbreaking work included two notable excavations at the Khara-Khoto and Noin-Ula Mountains, catapulting him into the ranks of world-class explorers and Central Asian scholars alongside Hedin and Stein.

A pinnacle in Kozlov's career was the discovery and excavation of the ruins of Khara-Khoto ruin. From 1907 to 1909, leading the sixth Russian expedition team, Kozlov uncovered the ancient Western Xia city's ruins on the edge of the Badain Jaran Desert on the east bank of the Nalin River in Ejin Banner of Ala Shan League, Mongolia.

Khara-Khoto, also known as Black City, was constructed during the Western Xia Dynasty. In 1908, inspired by records in Potanin's book, Kozlov explored Inner Mongolia and unearthed the ruins (Figure 6-5) of this city, a pivotal moment marking the inception of modern Western Xia studies.

In the year 1038, Li Yuanhao (1003–1048), the leader of the Tangut tribe, established the Great Xia regime, designating Xingqing as its capital in present-day Yinchuan, Ningxia. This realm later became the Western Xia Dynasty. The nomadic Tangut tribe progressively asserted control over Gansu, Ningxia, Qinghai, and parts of northern Shaanxi and Inner

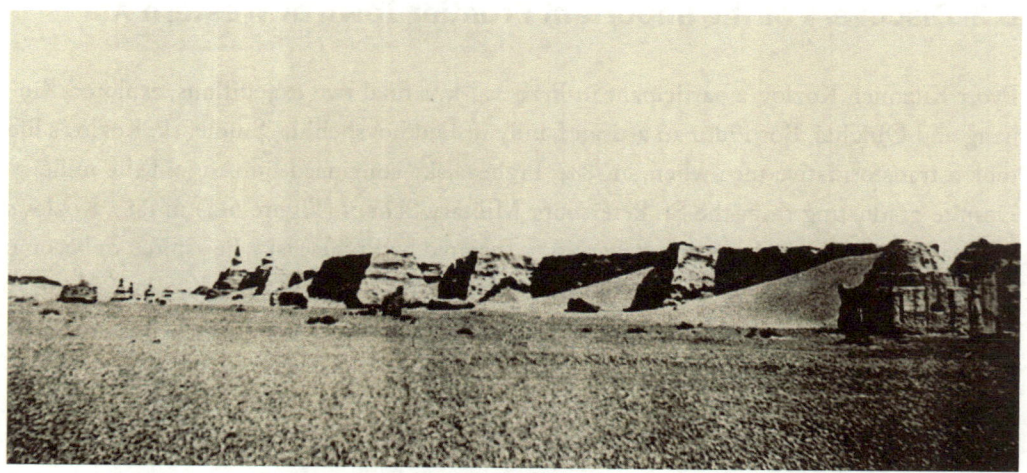

Figure 6-5 The ruins of the southwest section of the Khara-Khoto city wall in Western Xia (photographed by Kozlov in 1908)

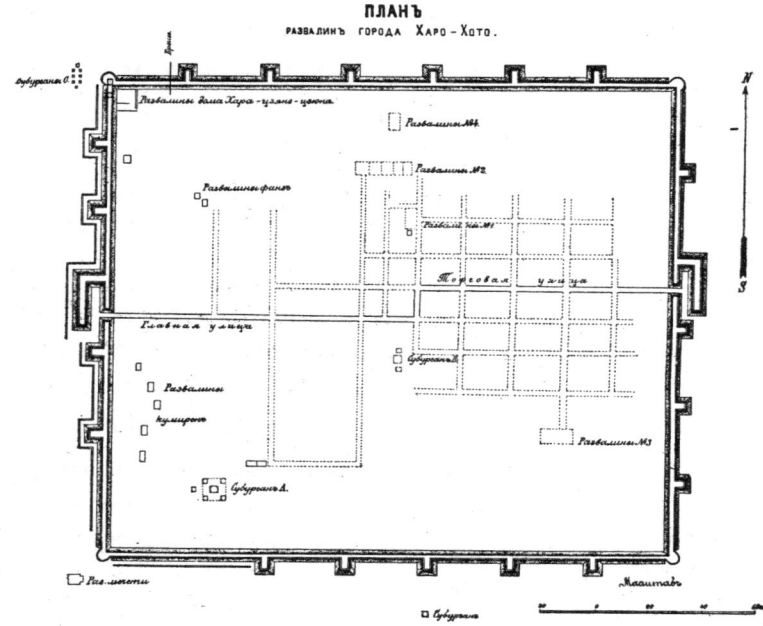

Figure 6-6 The floor plan of Khara-Khoto drawn by Kozlov in 1908–1909 (adopted from Kozlov's book *Mongolia and Amdo and the Dead City of Khara-Khoto*

Mongolia until Genghis Khan's (1162–1227) conquest in 1226. Khara-Khoto held strategic significance as a crucial frontier town of Western Xia and a pivotal transportation fortress along the Silk Road (Figure 6-6). Marco Polo documented the city, referring to it as "Ejin" in his travel notes, depicting a vibrant community in the north of the desert, as part of Western Xia, with residents devoted to the worship of religious idols, substantial livestock farming, and skilled falconry. Agriculture and animal husbandry sustained the populace, while trade activities were relatively sparse.

Li Yuanhao, the visionary founder of Western Xia, possessing a profound understanding of Tubo and Chinese languages, recognized the importance of cultural development. Drawing inspiration from diverse sources, he assimilated elements from various ethnic groups, resulting in the creation of the intricate Western Xia script. Buddhism flourished under his reign, with this deeply devout Western Xia emperor inviting monks and craftsmen from the Central Plains, Xizang, and the Uighurs. Their collective efforts led to the construction of pagodas and temples, fostering a vibrant Western Xia Buddhist culture and art. The Tangut nomads, initially devoid of written records, displayed a multicultural and prosperous societal tapestry under the influences of surrounding Uighur, Central Plains, and Tubo cultures.

Dge Shes Gtsang Soba, a disciple of Düsum Khyenpa (1110–1193), 1st Gyalwa Karmapa, head of the Karma Kagyu school of Tibetan Buddhism, was graciously invited by the fifth Western Xia Emperor Li Renxiao (1124–1193) to impart the Dharma in Western Xia and held in high regard as a guru. *A Scholar's Feast* documents Emperor Taihu of the Western

Xia Dynasty expressing his desire for Düsum Khyenpa to visit Tsurphu Monastery. When Düsum Khyenpa couldn't come, his envoy, Dge Shes Gtsang Soba, a new disciple, took up the role. Thus, Dge Shes Gtsang Soba journeyed to Western Xia and became the guru to its emperor. While the exact timeline of his visit to Western Xia is unclear, the Tibetan document *lHo rong chos 'byung*, written in 1446, estimates his stay from 1189 to 1218, with his passing in Western Xia's Xiliangfu (Liangzhou, now Wuwei, Gansu).

Notably, not only the Kagyu school but also Jueben Master of Jiongbawa, a disciple of the third-generation head of the Sakya school, Drakpa Gyaltsen (1147–1216), was regarded as a guru by Western Xia. This underscores strong evidence that Tibetan Buddhism took root in Western Xia and became a mainstream religious belief. Kozlov's discovery of Tibetan Buddhist sites and cultural relics in Khara-Khoto further supports this historical fact.

The profound significance of the Khara-Khoto findings lies in their contribution to the study of the development history of Tibetan Buddhism. Tibetan Buddhism underwent an early propagation period followed by a later propagation period. In the middle of the 9th century, Langdarma (AD 799?–842), the last king of the Tibetan Empire, initiated an anti-Buddhist movement, marking the end of the early propagation period. It wasn't until a century later that Tibetan Buddhism entered the later-propagation period. Due to the continuous renovation of monasteries by successive lamas and the destruction of Buddhist sites during the anti-Buddhist movement, finding relics from the Tubo period in Xizang is challenging. However, in the ruins of the Western Xia, particularly in Khara-Khoto, Tibetan Buddhist artworks are remarkably well-preserved. The abandonment of the city, coupled with minimal disturbances, ensured the intact preservation of Western Xia culture and early Tibetan Buddhist art. The ruins of Khara-Khoto hold immense value for preserving this cultural and religious heritage.

Kozlov's earlier attempts to locate the ruins of Khara-Khoto proved unsuccessful (Figure 6-7), mirroring the challenges faced by his preceding expedition team. The

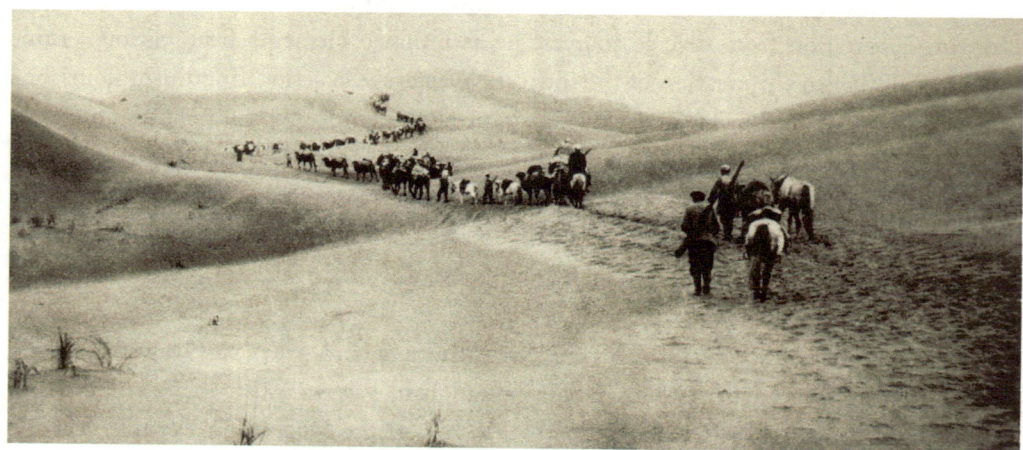

Figure 6-7 Kozlov's expedition to the ruins of Khara-Khoto (1907)

local Torghut tribe, residing in the area, refrained from divulging the precise location of the ruins and instead led them away from Khara-Khoto. However, in 1907, a turning point occurred when Kozlov encountered the welcoming Barkin Jasagh family during an inspection. These Mongolian nobles granted by the Qing Dynasty lived a modest nomadic lifestyle, whose hospitality extended to the Russian guests. Recognizing the nomads' fascination with his novel weapons, Kozlov presented prepared guns as gifts to them and local Torghut leaders, thereby earning their trust. This gesture allowed Kozlov to proceed under the guidance of local hosts and eventually reach the elusive ruins of Khara-Khoto.

Kozlov recorded:

At last, we laid eyes on the city, sprawling across the rugged sandstone terraces. In the northwest corner, a conical pagoda with a spire graced the city wall, diminishing in size as it ascended, reminiscent of an external fortress. Approaching the city, our path was strewn with fragments of broken pottery, and the silhouette of the fortress blurred amid rising sand dunes. Finally, atop the mesa, the ancient city unveiled her enchanting exterior.

The square-shaped ruins of Khara-Khoto rested on robust and coarse sandstone. Functioning as a transportation fortress during its time, the city boasted tall and formidable walls, reaching a thickness of up to three meters in some sections. The well-preserved city walls delineated neat streets paved with small patterned stones. Architecturally pleasing structures adorned the city, featuring rows of pagodas of varying sizes. Notably, the tallest pagoda stood in the northwest corner, as mentioned in Kozlov's account (Figure 6-8).

Subsequently, the expedition team made significant discoveries within the architectural ruins. They uncovered large-sized thangkas (Tibetan Buddhist scroll paintings) and various cultural relics, including manuscripts inscribed with characters unfamiliar to them. Further research revealed that this script, sharing similarities with Chinese characters and characterized by intricate strokes, was the renowned Western Xia script. Due to limited water and supplies, the team spent only a week in Khara-Khoto, meticulously documenting their findings, and then packed various cultural relics such as Buddhist statues, paintings, documents, and copper coins. These artifacts were sent back to the Royal Geographical Society of Tsarist Russia.

The Royal Geographical Society of Tsarist Russia received these exquisite cultural relics with profound astonishment. Sergey Fyodorovich Oldenburg, possessing familiarity with Buddhist scrolls, swiftly discerned the unique and highly valuable nature of the treasures within this ancient city. Recognizing the significance, Oldenburg and the Tsarist Russian government promptly directed Kozlov, who had relocated camps, to swiftly return to Khara-Khoto and resume excavation work. The objective was to secure as many cultural relics as possible before other expeditions could lay claim. Upon Kozlov's return, the sight

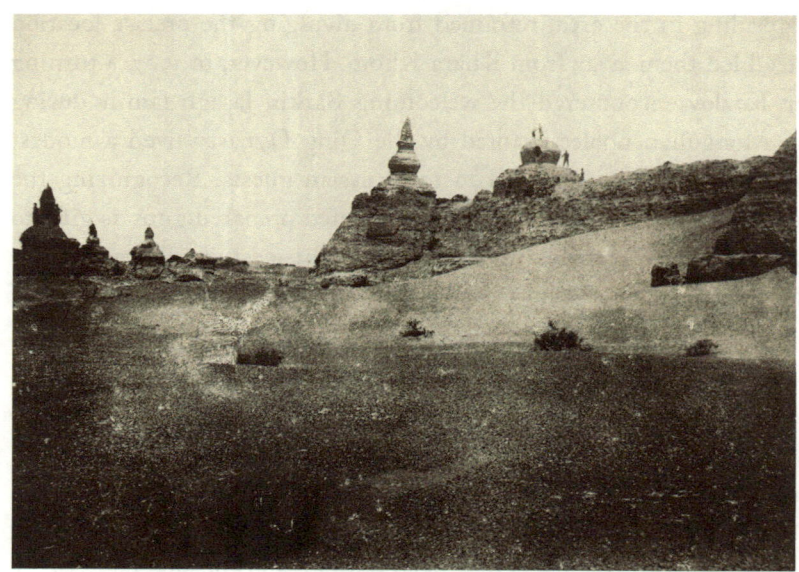

Figure 6-8 The pagoda at the northwest corner of the Khara-Khoto city wall (1908)

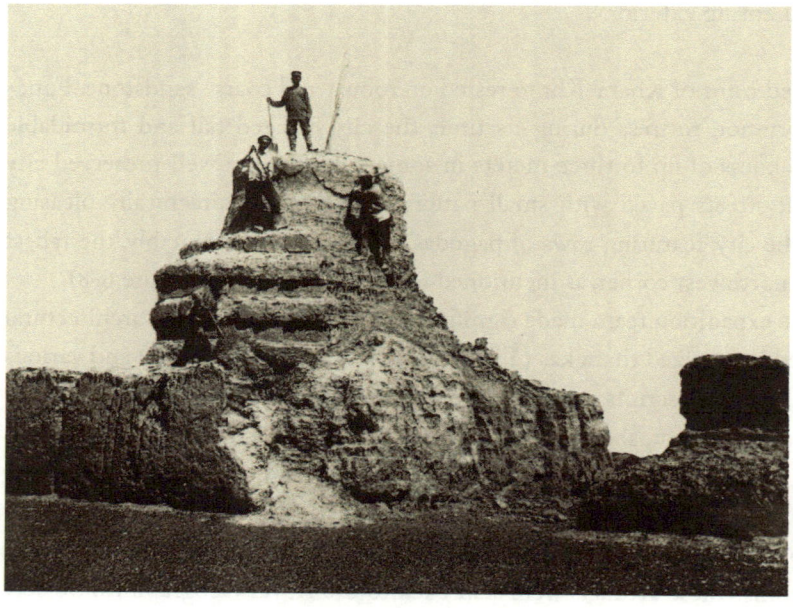

Figure 6-9 Kozlov's excavation of the pagoda in Khara-Khoto (1909)

that greeted him filled him with delight—Khara-Khoto remained untouched by other expedition teams, preserving its untouched state since their departure. The clay Buddha statues he had unearthed but lacked time to transport still sat there, seemingly awaiting his return. With the endorsement of the Royal Geographical Society, Kozlov initiated a comprehensive excavation effort. This went beyond retrieving surface cultural relics; he also delved into opening pagodas in search of potential treasures within (Figure 6-9).

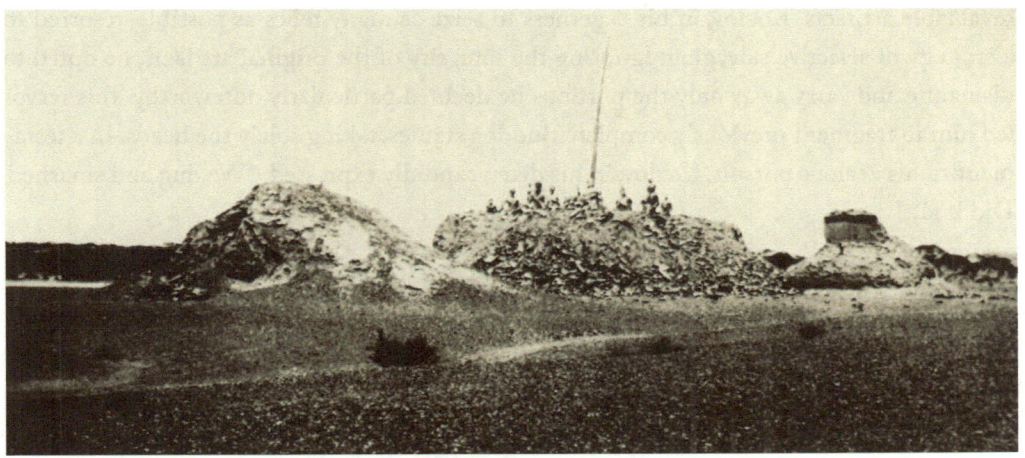

Figure 6-10 The ruins of the Glorious Sarira Pagoda excavated by Kozlov in Khara-Khoto (June 1909)

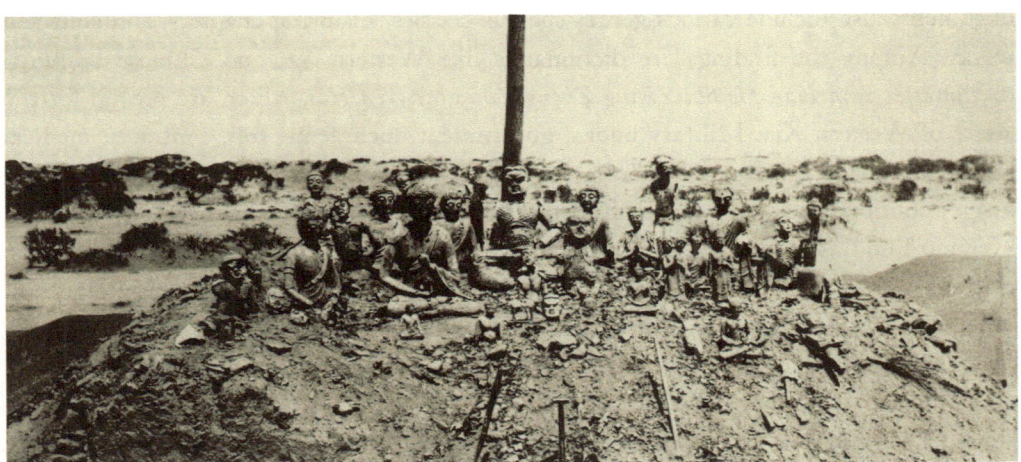

Figure 6-11 A group of clay Buddha statues on the ruins of the Glorious Sarira Pagoda (June 1909)

In June 1909, Kozlov successfully excavated the ruins of a pagoda known as the Glorious Sarira Pagoda (Figures 6-10, 6-11). The 13-square-meter underground palace at the base of the pagoda revealed over 20 life-size Buddha statues and a plethora of books, along with numerous scripture manuscripts in Chinese, Mongolian, Tibetan, and Western Xia languages. Additionally, more than 300 Han-style Buddhist paintings and Tibetan-style thangkas were discovered. This remarkable find profoundly energized Kozlov, propelling him to excavate additional pagoda ruins during the subsequent archaeological process and yielding a bountiful harvest of cultural relics.

Overwhelmed by the sheer abundance of cultural relics, the challenge arose of transporting this extensive trove of items, a task too immense for hundreds of horses to accommodate. Driven by exhilaration and perhaps overlooking the imperative to preserve these invaluable artifacts, Kozlov, in his eagerness to seize as many relics as possible, resorted to a strategy of selective salvaging. Ignoring the integrity of the original artifacts, he opted to dismantle and carry away only the portions he deemed particularly noteworthy. This fervor led him to fragment previously complete Buddha statues, taking solely the heads. In a testament to his zealous pursuit, Kozlov, in his diary, candidly expressed, "We dug and smashed. Did it all."

6.3 Han-Tibetan Treasures

The array and abundance of cultural relics unearthed by Kozlov from the ruins of Khara-Khoto are truly remarkable. Beyond the globally renowned Western Xia prints and manuscripts, the collection encompasses Chinese, Tibetan, Uighur, Turkic, Jurchen, and Mongolian, among other classics. Predominantly consisting of Buddhist scriptures, these documents also include various genres such as classics, histories, chapters, and collected works. Among the findings are dictionaries like Western Xia and Chinese bilingual dictionaries *Fan Han He Shi Zhang Zhong Zhu* and *Wen Hai*, which are pivotal for the study of Western Xia. Military books, government documents, folk contracts, medical books, almanacs, oracles, and more provide precious insights into the Western Xia language, politics, economy, culture, history, religion, law, and social customs. Additionally, over 300 Buddhist paintings, more than 20 woodblock prints, and over 70 wood carvings, clay statues, copper and gold-plated casts, silk and linen fabrics, coins, banknotes, and other artifacts were excavated, offering a vivid portrayal of the brilliance and grandeur of Western Xia. This treasure trove opens up new avenues for the study of Buddhist art and related history.

In the autumn of 1909, this proud collection of ancient cultural relics arrived in St. Petersburg and found residence in the new building of the Royal Geographical Society of Russia. It made its public debut in early 1910 (Figure 6-12). Subsequently, artifacts related to art and archaeology were sent to the Ethnology Department of the Russian Museum of His Imperial Majesty Alexander III, while books and manuscripts were preserved at the Russian Academy of Sciences, now the Institute of Oriental Studies. In 1933, the cultural relics were transferred to the Eastern Department of the State Hermitage Museum, making it the largest collection of Western Xia cultural relics in the world, totaling more than 3,500 pieces.

This represents only a preliminary catalog of these artifacts. Russian scholars dedicated half a century to meticulously categorizing and understanding the cultural relics, underscoring their vast number (Figure 6-13). It wasn't until 1996, following the collapse of the Soviet Union, that Russia gradually completed the initial compilation of documents—a process spanning nearly a century. Even in the 21st century, these documents continue to be compiled.

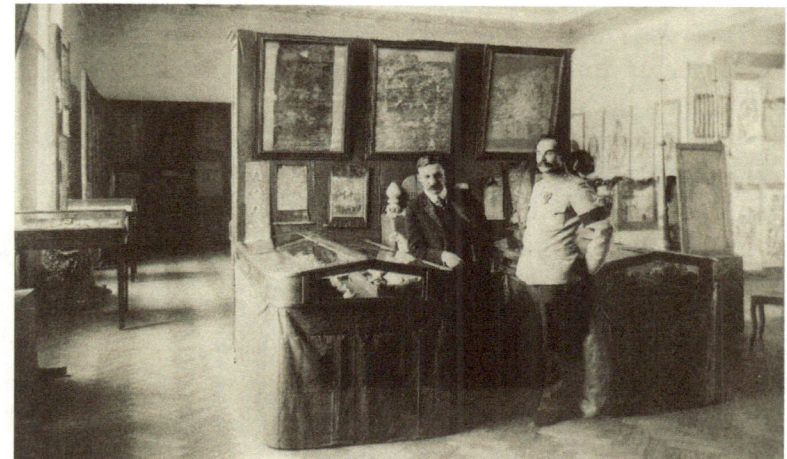

Figure 6-12
Kozlov and the
Secretary of the
Royal Geographical
Society of Russia
in the Exhibition
Hall of Khara-Khoto
Discoveries (1910)

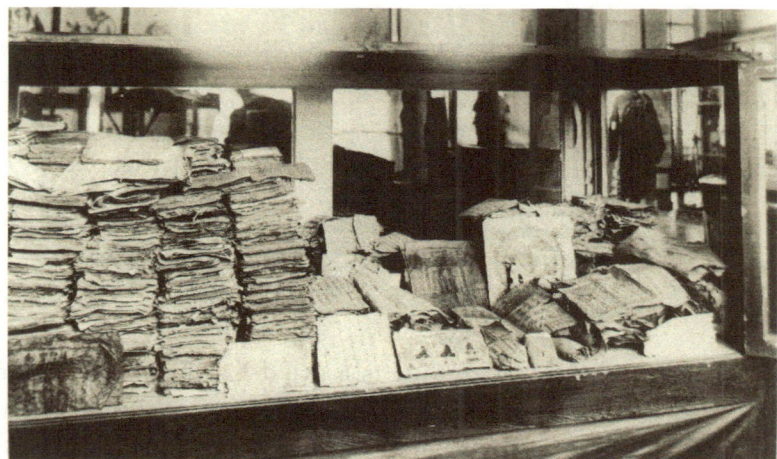

Figure 6-13 Part of
the Khara-Khoto
manuscripts (1910)
exhibited by the Royal
Geographical Society
of Russia

The paintings retrieved by Kozlov from the Khara-Khoto ruins can be categorized into three distinct styles: one reflecting Han style influenced by the Song Dynasty, another reflecting Tibetan influence, and a third showcasing a fusion of Han and Tibetan styles.

Many of these paintings, presented in the Tibetan Buddhist thangka style, feature a unique trapezoidal frame, different from the rectangular format seen in Han Chinese paintings. The themes predominantly center around Tibetan Buddhist figures, such as Bodhisattva Tara (Green), Dakini, Uṣṇīṣa Vijaya, Vaiśravaṇa, and Tibetan-style Buddhas and Bodhisattvas. Notably, a thangka depicting a Tibetan guru (Figure 6-14) stands out, using a realistic approach to portray this revered lama. This depiction underscores the Tibetan Buddhist practice of venerating gurus as incarnations of Buddha and Bodhisattva. The inclusion of male and female donors from Western Xia in the lower corners of the painting highlights the widespread influence of Tibetan guru worship in Western Xia.

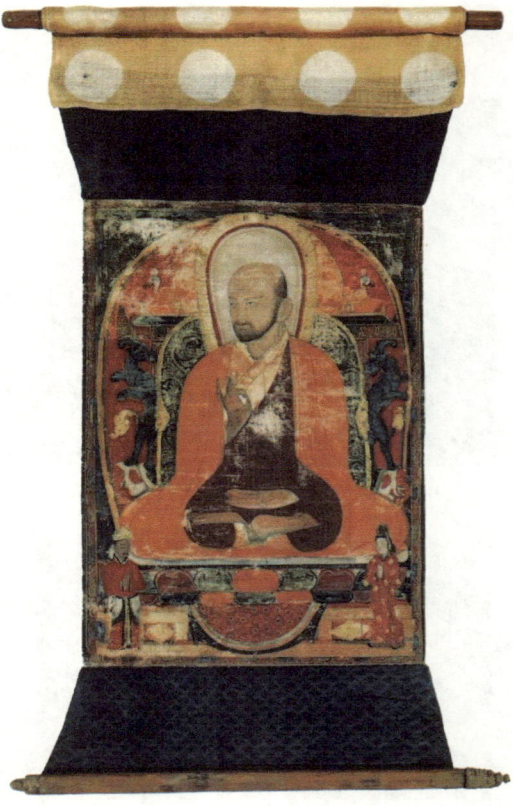

Figure 6-14 *Portrait of the Guru* thangka from the 12th century AD of the Western Xia Dynasty (cotton coloring, 64 cm high, 33.5 cm wide, now in the State Hermitage Museum, Russia, No. X-2400)

Amitabha Raigō (Figure 6-15) is a grand hanging scroll painting influenced by the artistic style of the Song Dynasty. The focal point of the painting is Amitabha Buddha, the principal Buddha of the Western Paradise. The name Amitabha is derived from the Sanskrit term Amitabha, signifying infinite light, portraying the Buddha as the embodiment of infinite light. The Buddha's countenance is full, with a red bead visible in front of a low bun—a distinctive feature reminiscent of Song Dynasty Buddhist statues. Song Dynasty Buddha statues often featured more exposed chests, exuding a graceful demeanor, and this portrayal aligns with that characteristic. Accompanying Amitabha on the left side of the painting are Avalokitesvara and Mahasthamaprapta Bodhisattva, both serving as attendants to Amitabha. Avalokitesvara is distinguished by the nirmāna-buddha atop his crown, while Mahasthamaprapta bears a treasure vase on his. In the lower-left corner, a mustached figure in brown robes represents the departed, guided by the Three Bodhisattvas of the West. Clasping his hands in prayer for Buddha and Bodhisattva's salvation, this figure exhibits the distinct attire and hairstyle of Western Xia men. A wispy green smoke, symbolizing the soul, rises from the figure's head, transforming into a charming naked boy poised to descend into the lotus held by the two Bodhisattvas. The boy will be led to the Western Paradise for rebirth (Figure 6-16). A white light emanates from the Buddha's white hair,

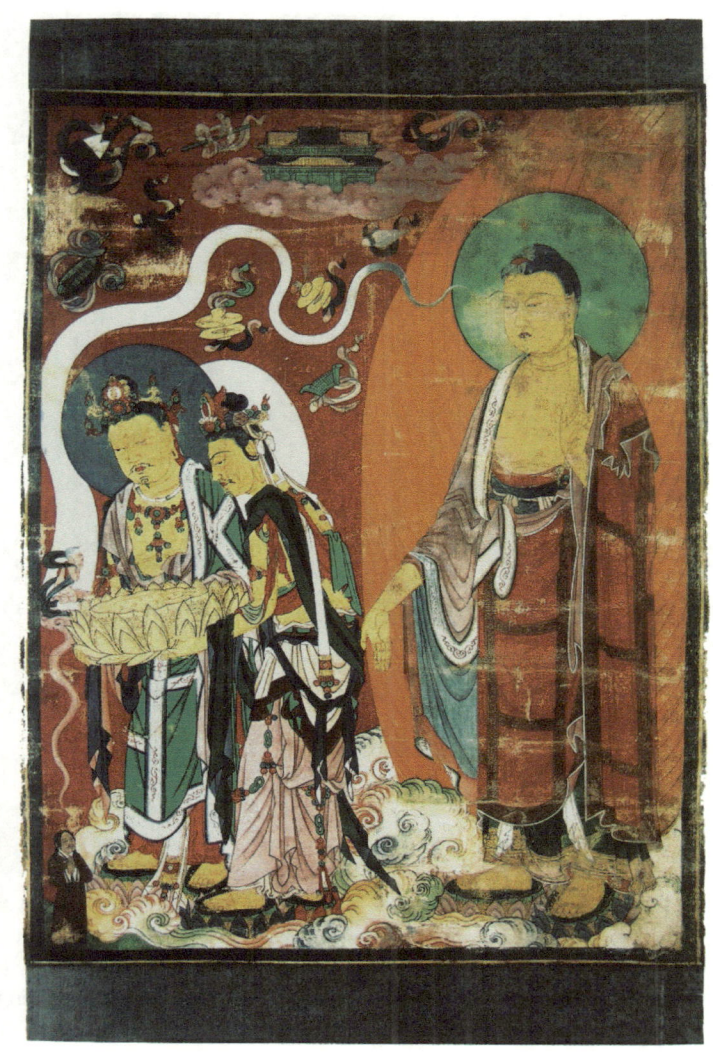

Figure 6-15 Hanging scroll painting of *Amitabha Raigō* from the 12th century AD of the Western Xia Dynasty (linen coloring, 99 cm high, 63.8 cm wide, now in the State Hermitage Museum, Russia, No. X-2411)

casting radiance on the boy. The depiction includes a palace floating on clouds at the top, representing the Pure Land of the West. Musical instruments like *pipa*, flute, and cymbals hover above, seemingly playing the enchanting music of Buddhism. Stylistically, the work exhibits compositional traits of the Song Dynasty in the Central Plains, but its vibrant colors—such as the pronounced contrast of blue, green, gold, and red—reflect the palette characteristic of Tibetan traditional paintings. Hence, it embodies a fusion of Han and Tibetan artistic styles.

Conversely, paintings featuring light and subtle colors draw inspiration from the Central Plains style and are abundant in Khara-Khoto. The hanging scroll painting *Water-Moon Avalokitesvara* showcases low color contrast, creating a tone that is soft and elegant (Figure 6-17). This style, combining Bodhisattva figures with everyday landscapes, is said

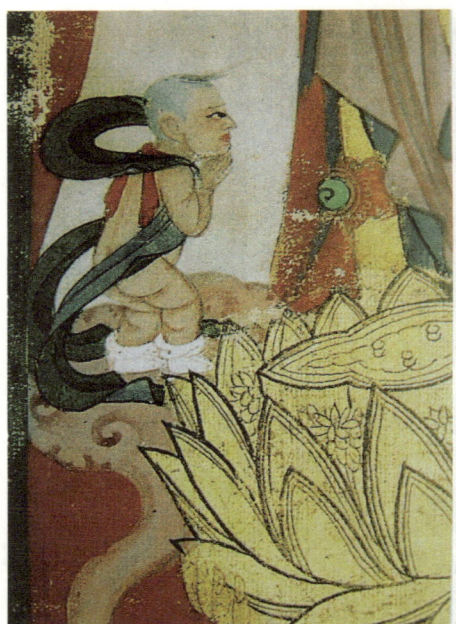

Figure 6-16 The naked boy in the hanging scroll painting *Amitabha Raigō*

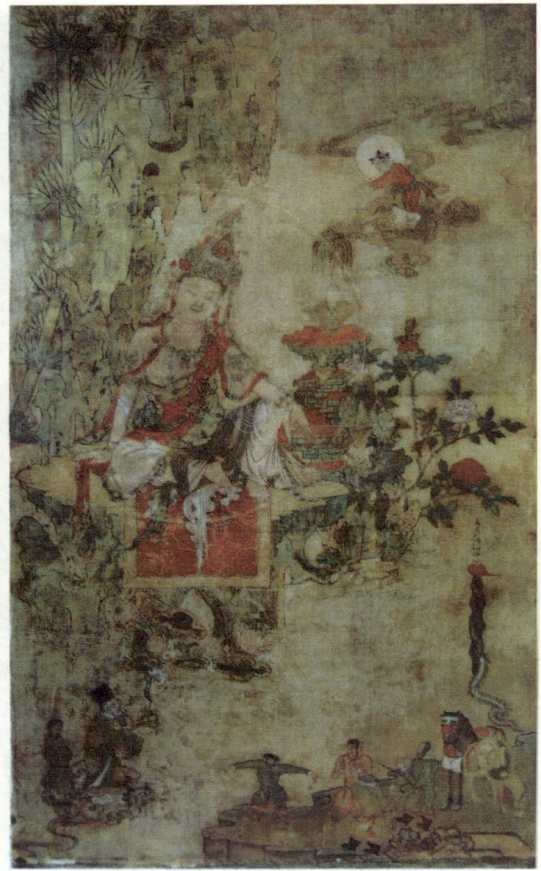

Figure 6-17 Hanging scroll painting *Water-Moon Avalokitesvara* from the 12th century AD of the Western Xia Dynasty (color on silk, 101.5 cm high, 59.5 cm wide), now in the State Hermitage Museum, Russia. No. X-2439)

to have originated from the works of Zhou Fang, a painter during the prosperous period of Tang Dynasty, but gained popularity only after the Five Dynasties. In this painting, Avalokitesvara sits on a rock in a relaxed posture, set against a backdrop of rocks, bamboo forests, and peonies. A clear spring flows beneath, adorned with lotus leaves, embodying the theme of Water-Moon Avalokitesvara. Adjacent to Avalokitesvara, a stone platform supports a water purification bottle with willow branches inserted, while Sudhanakumāra on a cloud in the upper right pays homage to the deity. The artist incorporated secular figures at the funder's request, featuring an old man burning incense in the lower left corner, accompanied by a boy, and several individuals with shaved heads in the lower right—all attired as Western Xia people. Some play musical instruments, others sing and dance with animated gestures, and horses bear flagpoles leading souls. This painting likely portrays the scene of the departed elder being escorted to the Western Pure Land by Avalokitesvara during a funeral conducted by relatives. It represents the Western Xia people expressing their religious sentiments through the art form of the Central Plains.

The hanging scroll painting *Tejaprabhā Buddha and the Eleven Lumins* (Figure 6-18) also adopts an intriguing Central Plains style, illustrating the Western Xia people's astronomical perspective on the universe. Similar to the Tang Dynasty silk painting *Tejaprabhā Buddha and the Five Planets* (Figure 3-28), obtained by Stein from the Dunhuang Library Cave, this work features the Tejaprabhā Buddha seated on a lotus throne in the center, holding a golden ring in both hands, surrounded by 11 anthropomorphic depictions of classical planets. Its theme may originate from the *Buddha Speaks of Tejaprabhā Buddha Eliminating Disasters and Auspicious Dharani Sutra*, translated by the eminent monk Amoghavajra (AD 705–774) of the Tang Dynasty, known for its astrological significance. Among the eleven figures, the Sun and the Moon are depicted in regal attire, resembling emperors and empresses. Saturn is characterized by a red-bearded figure with a bull's head, while Venus is represented by an aristocratic woman wearing a phoenix-stepping crown and holding a *pipa*. The figure with

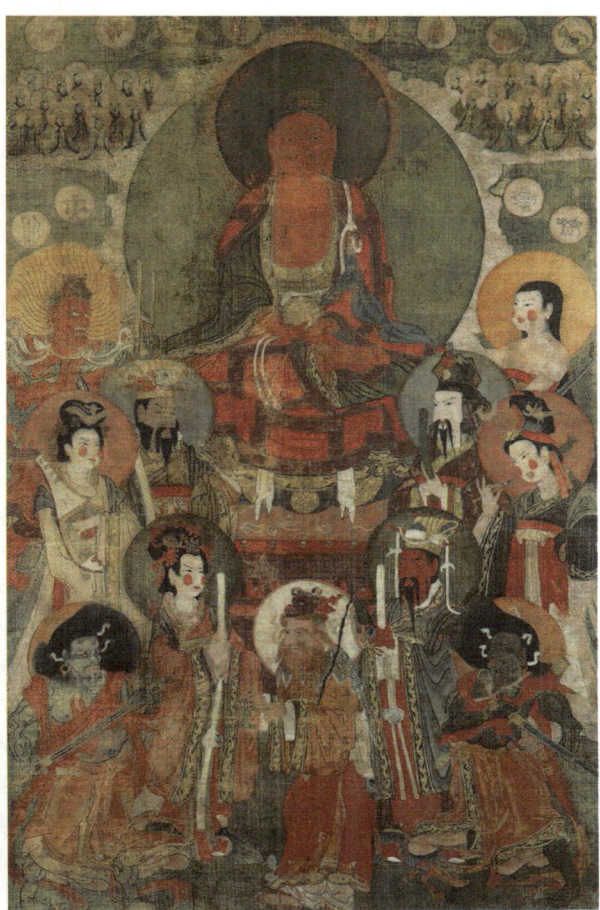

Figure 6-18 Hanging scroll painting *Tejaprabhā Buddha and the Eleven Lumins* from the 11th century AD of the Western Xia Dynasty (color on silk, 102 cm high, 66 cm wide, now in the State Hermitage Museum, Russia, No. X-2424)

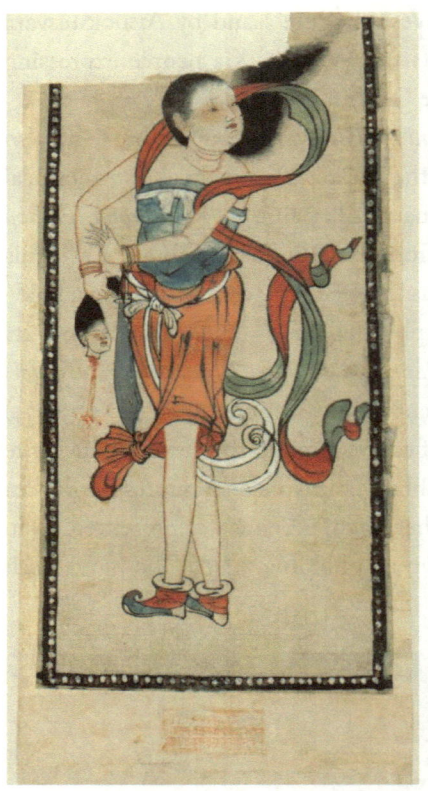

Figure 6-19 *Constellation Yuebei* from the 11th century AD of the Western Xia Dynasty (color on paper, now in the State Hermitage Museum, Russia)

a boar's head on their hat symbolizes Jupiter, and a female scholar holding a brush and scroll with a monkey atop her head personifies Mercury. A bureaucrat wearing an official hat represents the constellation Ziqi. Positioned to the left of the Buddha is a formidable four-armed Mars brandishing a trident, while a topless, exposed figure representing the constellation Yuebei, with loose hair at the back, mirrors Mars symmetrically. At the bottom of the group are the wrathful protectors Rahu and Ketu from India. Remarkably, the painting not only features the twelve ancient Greek constellations arranged around the Buddha statue but also includes the twenty-eight Indian constellations represented by two groups of officials in the upper part of the composition.

In another Western Xia painting, a sole depiction of the constellation Yuebei is presented (Figure 6-19). Manifesting as a disheveled woman with a bare chest, she holds a human head in her right hand. Scholars from the West contend that this portrayal bears similarities to the Greek mythological figure Medusa, suggesting a combination of Buddhist and Western mythological themes. Consequently, it may represent a novel thematic creation arising from the synthesis of Indian, Greek, and Chinese astrological elements, showcasing the remarkable harmony in Western Xia's cultural integration.

The paintings unearthed from Khara-Khoto in Western Xia also include rare Taoist paintings, representing traditional themes of the Han people. Taoism, stemming from the philosophical teachings of Laozi and evolving into China's traditional religion after absorbing elements of ancient folk worship and primitive beliefs, was established around the same period as the introduction of Buddhism to China during the late Eastern Han Dynasty. The Western Xia Dynasty, flourishing between the 10th and 13th centuries, experienced the influence of this traditional Chinese religious thought. A hanging scroll painting of *Zhenwu the Great Emperor* (Figure 6-20) serves as a clear testament to this influence. Zhenwu the Great Emperor, or Xuanwu the Great Emperor, is centrally depicted in the artwork. Adorning his hair without a crown, he is known as the "ancestral master without a crown." According to ancient Chinese cosmology, the sky is divided into five "palaces," and Xuanwu is recognized as the Lord of the Northern Palace, the God of the North. The turtle and snake at Zhenwu the Great Emperor's feet originally represented the northern Xuanwu in ancient folk beliefs. Only during the Song Dynasty did Xuanwu begin to be depicted as a military general. He has a serious and handsome countenance, bare feet, and hair and is garbed in a black robe with gold armor beneath. It is believed that he possesses the power to attract good fortune and ward off evil. Four attendants with distinct images stand behind him, symbolizing constellations in the northern sky: the woman and flag-bearer on the left represent the Big Dipper and Ursa Major, which hold the ability to conquer death in Taoism; on the right is the guardian deity of another constellation, holding an urn that signifies cremation, a prevalent funeral ritual among the Western Xia people. This painting stands as one of the few Taoist cultural relics discovered in the Western Regions, bearing significant importance in studying the dissemination of Taoism in Western Xia.

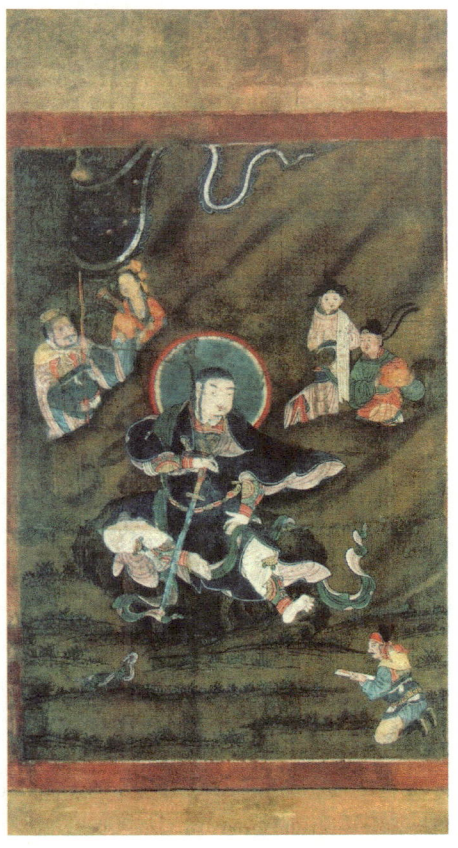

Figure 6-20 Hanging scroll painting *Zhenwu the Great Emperor* from the 12th century AD of the Western Xia Dynasty (color on silk, 91.5 cm high, 47 cm wide, now in the State Hermitage Museum, Russia, No. X-2465)

6.4 The Mysterious Double-Headed Buddha Statue

Numerous Western Xia Buddhist statues were unearthed in Khara-Khoto, particularly in the underground palace of the Glorious Sarira Pagoda excavated in Khara-Khoto. Kozlov, facing a plethora of scriptures and treasures, employed 40 camels to transport the extensive collection. However, the sheer size of the life-size Buddha statue prevented its simultaneous transportation. Consequently, Kozlov buried the remaining items, including the large Buddha statues, in a concealed location. He marked the site with the intention of retrieving the artifacts later. Unfortunately, upon Kozlov's return to Khara-Khoto a few years later, the markings had vanished without a trace. Despite an exhaustive search, he could not locate the hidden treasures. Nonetheless, among the statues that he had successfully transported, a remarkable double-headed clay Buddha statue emerged as a masterpiece.

In comparison with sculptures from the same period, the clay double-headed Buddha statue (Figure 6-21) stands out for its distinctiveness. Featuring two heads and four arms,

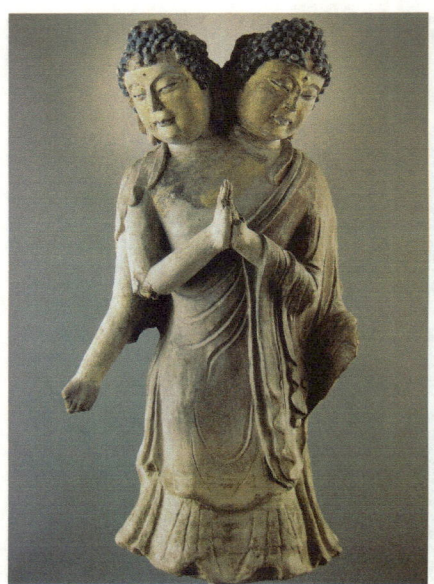

Figure 6-21 A 13th-century painted double-headed Buddha statue from the Western Xia Dynasty (62 cm high, now in the State Hermitage Museum, Russia, No. X-2296)

the statue adheres to the stylistic conventions of the Song Dynasty. The hands are clasped together in front of the chest, with the head proportionately larger than the body. The body's patterns are abstract and lack realism. Although the theme of a double-headed Buddha appeared in Tang Dynasty murals at the Mogao Grottoes and in the Sichuan Grottoes, this particular statue is a unique standalone sculpture. The story behind the double-headed Buddha is documented in *The Great Tang Records on the Western Regions* by the Tang monk Xuanzang. In ancient Gandhara, India, a humble man dedicated to Buddhism toiled for years, finally saving the money of a gold coin. He entrusted the gold coin to a painter, requesting the creation of a colored Buddha statue in the temple as an expression of reverence for the Buddha. Although the money was insufficient for the work, the compassionate painter, touched by the man's devotion, ceased discussing the price and pledged to complete the painting. Shortly after the first man departed, another impoverished individual arrived, also seeking to use a single gold coin to commission a Buddha painting. The painter, combining the money from both patrons, engaged a master to jointly paint a Buddha portrait. A few days later, the two patrons returned to the temple for worship. The painter pointed to the newly painted Buddha portrait, proclaiming, "This is the Buddha portrait you both asked me to paint." Confused, the patrons questioned how a single Buddha portrait could represent the wishes of two individuals. The painter clarified, assuring them that he had not pocketed any funds, and the entirety of their contributions had been invested in this Buddha portrait. However, due to practical constraints, it could only be painted as a single entity. He vowed that the Buddha portrait would manifest auspicious changes if he was not lying. Upon the completion of his explanation, the Buddha portrait exhibited supernatural power, gradually transforming into a magnificent depiction of two Buddha heads coexisting in a single body, radiating a dazzling light. Witnessing this miraculous event, the two humble patrons were convinced, and their belief in Buddhism deepened and strengthened by the extraordinary display of divine intervention.

As for whether this image embodies the unique aesthetics of the Western Xia people, further research by scholars is necessary to provide a comprehensive answer.

6.5 A Fruitful Explorer

In the autumn of 1909, the treasures from Khara-Khoto were transported to St. Petersburg, marking a turning point for Kozlov, bringing him both acclaim and wealth. The cultural relics discovered immediately ignited the interest of expedition teams from various nations. Stein, drawn by the news, led a British expedition in 1914, followed by an American team in 1923, and a Swedish expedition led by Bergman in 1927–1928. Unfortunately, Kozlov's earlier excavations had significantly depleted the treasures, leaving these subsequent expeditions with meager findings, and they essentially returned empty-handed.

Prior to his sixth expedition to China, Kozlov wrote to his close friends, "I am more determined than ever to delve into excavations. If lucky, I hope that the ancient treasures unearthed would comfort the Royal Geographical Society." This resolve persisted until the downfall of Tsarist Russia in 1917.

After the downfall of Tsarist Russia in 1917, Kozlov continued his archaeological endeavors. From 1924–1925, he discovered numerous Xiongnu tombs dating from the Han Dynasty in the Noin-Ula Mountains in Mongolia. Noin-Ula Mountains stands 100 kilometers north of Ulaanbaatar, its slopes adorned with a scattering of tombs nestled in the low valleys. From west to east, there are prominent sites such as Suzhukete Cemetery, Zhulumute Cemetery, Gudejierte Cemetery, etc. Expert research has revealed that these tombs, dating from the 1st century BC to the 1st century AD, surpass 200 in number. Kozlov meticulously excavated six large tombs and four smaller ones, unearthing the earliest tombs of Xiongnu nobles discovered up to that point. Within these ancient resting places, he uncovered a trove of Han Dynasty and Xiongnu cultural relics. This invaluable collection of artifacts offers a glimpse into the social history of the Xiongnu and sheds light on the intricate history of cultural exchanges between the East and the West. Noin-Ula Mountain's excavations serve as a rich tapestry, weaving together insights into the Xiongnu culture, daily life, and the social structure prevalent in the region during the 1st century AD. As the nomadic communities of yesteryear thrived on the sustenance of water and grass, and with urban ruins absent, these tombs stand as crucial datasets, unraveling the intricate social fabric of these nomadic peoples from two millennia ago. Kozlov's dedicated efforts in this endeavor underscore his indispensable contribution to our understanding of the Xiongnu legacy.

Regrettably, Kozlov did not finalize the archaeological report on the excavation data from the Xiongnu tombs. This task was ultimately undertaken by Umehara Sueji (1893–1983), a Japanese Oriental archaeologist enrolled in European studies and an honorary professor at Kyoto University. Collaborating with Soviet scholars, Umehara Sueharu completed the report. Tragically, many of the scholars who contributed to this research met their demise during the subsequent Great Purge, a dark period in history. The unfortunate consequences included the suppression of academic publications, and the archaeological

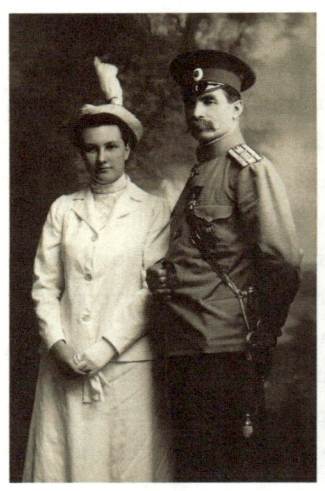

Figure 6-22 Kozlov and Elizabeth in 1912

report remained unpublished. It was not until 1960 that Sueji Umehara managed to see the report through to publication.

In contrast to certain explorers who remained unmarried, Kozlov took a different path and married Elizabeth Kozlova, who was 29 years his junior (Figure 6-22). Their family life was marked by happiness and lacked the typical conflicts between career pursuits and personal relationships. Elizabeth, an ornithologist herself, actively joined her husband in the final expedition to Central Asia. During this expedition, she focused on observing birds in the Central Asian region. Subsequently, Elizabeth authored numerous books and academic papers dedicated to the avian world. Their unique story unfolds as a couple exploring together, delving into diverse areas of investigation within the same geographical domain, a rare narrative in the annals of human exploration.

Throughout his life, Kozlov dedicated himself to exploration, investigation, and research, earning several honors along the way. His journey spanned the tumultuous period

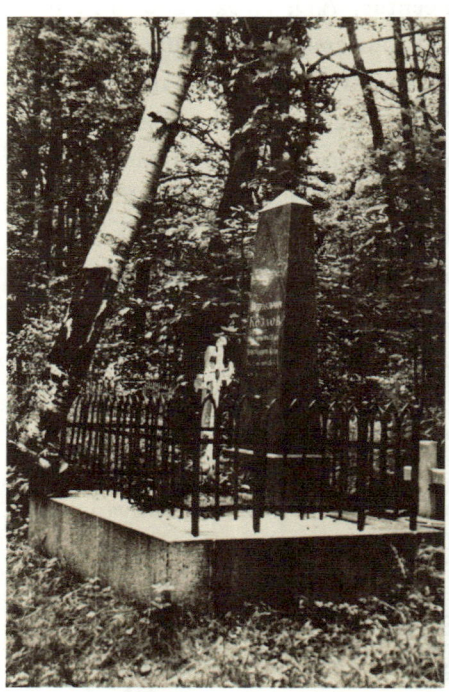

Figure 6-23 Kozlov's tomb in St. Petersburg, Russia (first half of the 20th century)

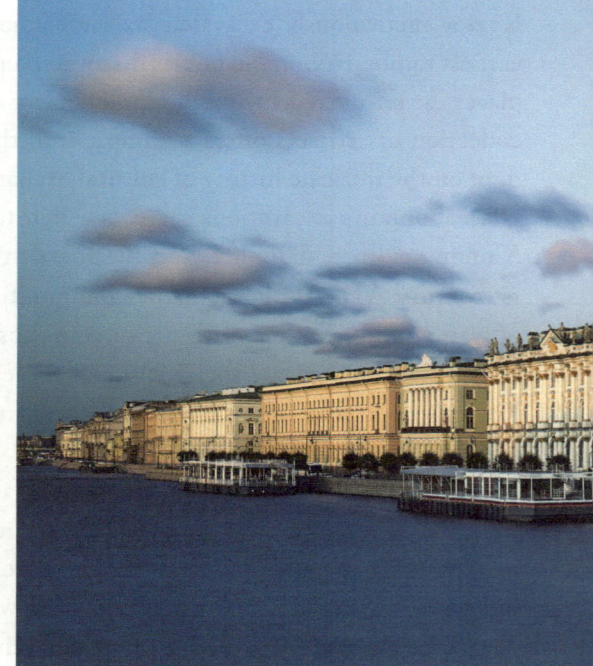

of late Tsarist Russia, World War I, the February Revolution, the October Revolution, and the nascent days of the Soviet Union—a time of unprecedented upheaval in Russian history. Notably, he achieved honorary membership in the Dutch, Russian, and Hungarian geographical societies in 1896, 1910, and 1911, respectively. Additionally, Kozlov received the Medal of the Royal Geographical Society of Russia in 1902 and the Medal of the Italian and British Geographical Societies in 1911. After concluding his exploration career in 1926, he settled in Novgorod, located in northwest Russia. In 1928, Kozlov was honored with election to the Ukrainian Academy of Sciences. He passed away on September 26, 1935, in Petergof, St. Petersburg (Figure 6-23).

Kozlov was a prolific writer, producing a total of 62 monographs from 1895 to 1941. His most renowned work is *Mongolia and Amdo and the Dead City of Khara-Khoto* (1923), which has been translated into English, German, Japanese, and other languages. This masterpiece is followed by *Mongolia and Kham* (1905–1906), *Three-Year Travel Notes on Mongolia and Xizang (1899–1901)* (1913), among others. These publications offer valuable insights into the history, religion, economy, customs, and ethnic relations of various local ethnic groups. Two notable books, *The Dalai Lama in Xizang* (1907) and *Xizang and the Dalai Lama* (1920), document his encounter with the 13th Dalai Lama Thubten Gyatso (1876–1933) in Küriye (now Ulaanbaatar, Mongolia) in 1905. The British War Department grew uneasy during

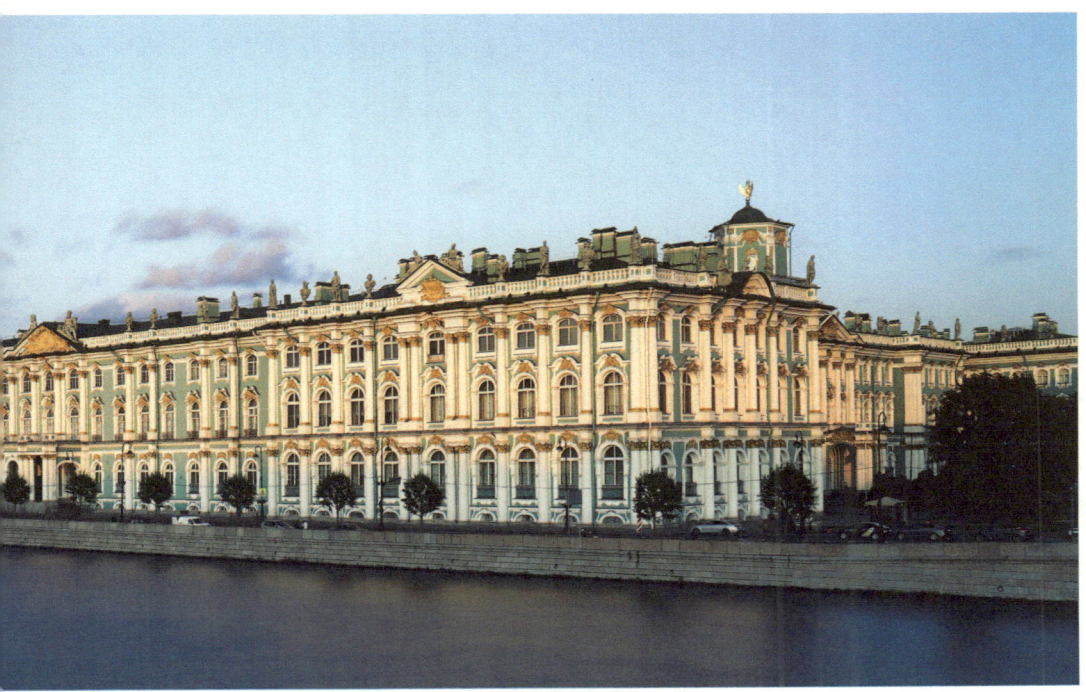

Figure 6-24 State Hermitage Museum, St. Petersburg, Russia (photographed by Pedro Szekely)

this encounter, suspecting Kozlov of potential military espionage due to their monitoring of his expedition. However, his interactions were purely academic, maintaining amicable relations with fellow Western explorers. The majority of the cultural relics he acquired in China are housed in the State Hermitage Museum in St. Petersburg (Figure 6-24), drawing increasing attention from Chinese scholars.

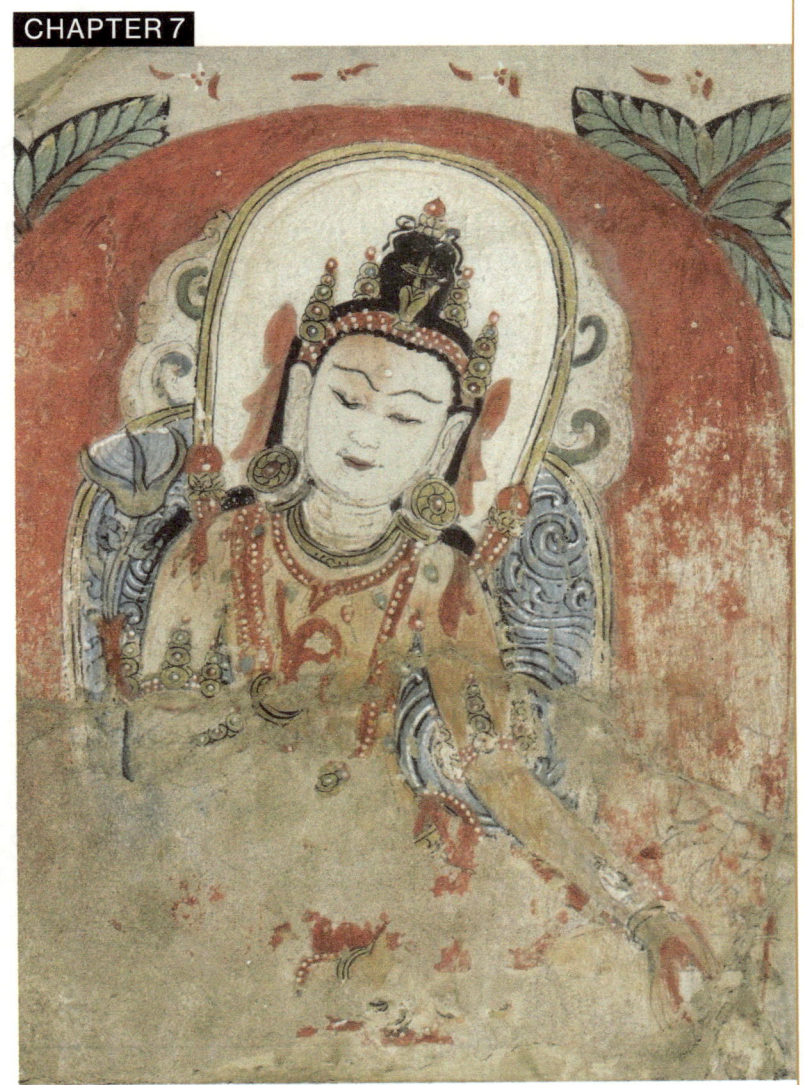

CHAPTER 7

The Discerning Oldenburg

— 1909–1910

First expedition, St. Petersburg–Omsk–Tacheng–Urumqi–Yanqi (Shorchuk Temple)–Turpan (Jiaohe Ancient City, Turpan Ancient City, Gaochang Ancient City, Astana, Shengjinkou Caves, Bezeklik Caves, Mutougou, Tuyugou Caves), Kuqa (Subash Temple ruins, Senmusaimu Grottoes, Kerixi Grottoes, Kizil Caves, Kumtura Caves)

— 1914–1915

Second expedition, St. Petersburg–Tacheng–Urumqi–Turpan–Hami–Dunhuang

7.1 A Strong Successor

Sergey Fyodorovich Oldenburg (1863–1934) stands as a towering figure in the realm of Oriental studies, being one of the founders of Indology and the history of Buddhist art. Born in Byankino, Russia, he hailed from a lineage steeped in military valor, with his grandfather having served as a general in the Russian Royal Army. Before he turned 10, Oldenburg lived with his father in Germany, Switzerland, and France, as his father was a brigade commander in the Cossack host. Embarking on his academic journey in 1881, Oldenburg entered the Department of Oriental Languages at St. Petersburg University. Specializing in Sanskrit and Persian, he delved into the intricate realms of Buddhism. His scholarly prowess made him the favored student of the esteemed

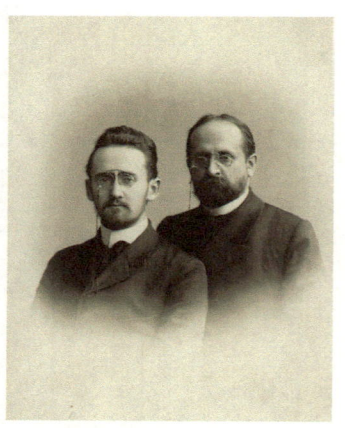

Figure 7-1 Young Oldenburg (left) with his older brother

Tsarist Russian sinologist Vasily Pavlovich Vasilyev (1818–1900) (Figure 7-1). Driven by an insatiable passion for Oriental studies, Oldenburg expanded his linguistic repertoire to include Arabic, Iranian, Chinese, and Tibetan. A two-year sojourn in England and France deepened his insights, where he crossed paths with Levi, a renowned Sanskrit scholar and Pelliot's mentor. In 1889, Oldenburg returned to his alma mater as a visiting lecturer, eventually ascending to the position of professor in 1897. In 1900, he was elected as a researcher at the prestigious Russian Academy of Sciences (Figure 7-2). In 1908, Oldenburg became a full-fledged member of the Russian Academy of Sciences. In 1916, he assumed the directorship of the Asian Museum, an institution under the aegis of the

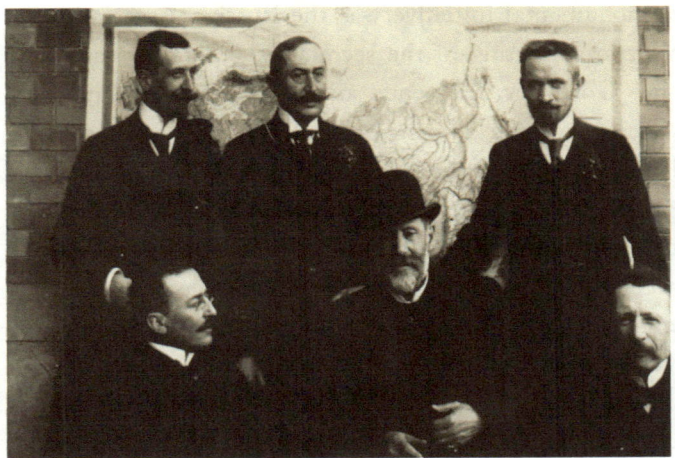

Figure 7-2 Oldenburg (first from right in the back row with Russian scholars

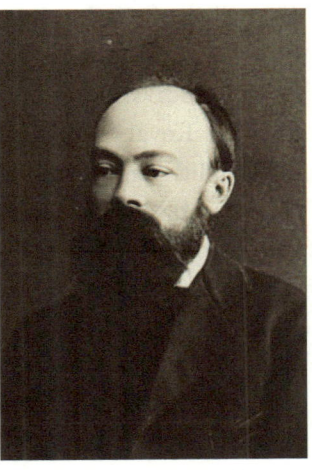

Figure 7-3 Russian archaeologist Klementz

Russian Academy of Sciences. After the February Revolution of 1917, Oldenburg found himself serving as the Minister of Education in the Provisional Government of Alexander Kerensky (1881–1970). Simultaneously, from 1904 to 1929, he held the esteemed position of Permanent Secretary of the Russian Academy of Sciences. Oldenburg's enduring commitment to Mahayana Buddhist texts manifested in his extensive studies, a dedication that spanned many years. His scholarly pursuits took him to the heart of northwest China, where, between 1909–1910 and 1914–1915, he led the Russian archaeological team on two groundbreaking expeditions. The Mogao Grottoes in Dunhuang, Gansu, became a focal point of exploration during his second expedition.

In 1898, the Russian Academy of Sciences entrusted D. A. Klementz (1847–1914) (Figure 7-3) with the leadership of an expedition to explore Turpan. The team examined the ancient city of Gaochang, excavated the Astana Cemetery, and surveyed and mapped the mesmerizing Bezeklik Caves, where their efforts revealed a trove of artistic treasures, adorned with murals featuring inscriptions in Central Asian Brahmi and Uighur scripts. The team returned triumphant, bearing several printed Buddhist scriptures in both Sanskrit and Uighur scripts, akin to the early engravings of Hinayana Buddhist scriptures later uncovered by the German Turpan expedition. Klementz encapsulated the expedition's findings in a German report titled *Report on the Turpan Expedition of the Russian Academy of Sciences of St. Petersburg* in 1898, sparking a newfound fascination with scientific research endeavors in Central Asia within the Russian academic community.

In 1900, the Russian Archaeological Society made the decision to embark on a comprehensive three-year investigation of the Tarim Basin. Their ambitious plan encompassed explorations in Turpan, Hotan, Kuqa, and other regions nestled in the southern

Tian Shan. Spearheading this monumental initiative was the Russian Association for East Asian Studies, a dynamic trio consisting of the secretaries-general of the Royal Geographical Society of Russia—Golgoriev, Klementz, and Oldenburg. On January 1, 1903, the Royal Geographical Society and the Association for East Asian Studies, under the insightful guidance of Oldenburg, endorsed the archaeological surveys of Turpan and Kuqa led by Klementz. Recognizing the significance of this mission, Tsar Nicholas II (1868–1918) extended his approval on February 28, allocating a substantial sum of 5,000 rubles from the state treasury to facilitate the association's comprehensive exploration.

On March 22, 1904, Klementz presented a detailed expedition plan to the Association for East Asian Studies. However, he declined the role of captain, citing the need to raise funds for the venture. Consequently, he recommended the artist and photographer Samuil Martynovich Dudin for Turpan and dispatched Berezovsky to Kuqa. Dudin later became one of the two key members of the 1909 Turpan expedition led by Oldenburg.

Between 1906 and 1907, A. I. Kokhanovsky headed an expedition to revisit Turpan. The team acquired 20 documents, including one Sanskrit manuscript, nine Chinese manuscripts, two Tibetan manuscripts and prints, one Mongolian print, three Uighur manuscripts, two bilingual Uighur and Chinese documents, and numerous Manichaean documents in Sogdian. These materials were initially handed over to the Royal Geographical Society of Russia and later transferred to the Asiatic Museum. Oldenburg compiled the *Concise Catalog of Antiquities Collected by Dr. Kokhanovsky* from Turpan based on them.

Following successful expeditions, an exhibition showcasing the cultural relics and materials obtained by Russia's archaeological expeditions in Xinjiang was held in the Winter Palace in 1908. This exhibition played a crucial role in the Tsar's decision to allocate special funds for further investigations in Xinjiang. It also officially confirmed Oldenburg's trip to China in June 1909. Consequently, the Russian Central and East Asia Association devised a comprehensive investigation plan, entrusting Oldenburg with the task. The Tsar approved a budget of 85,000 rubles for an eight-month inspection tour in Xinjiang by Oldenburg and Dudin for the following two years. The approved project funding this time significantly exceeded that given to Klementz, indicating the emperor's trust in Oldenburg. In addition to financial support, Oldenburg put together an "all-star" expedition team, with himself, Permanent Secretary and Associate Academician of the Russian Academy of Sciences, serving as the team leader. The team included Dudin, responsible for copying and photography; mining engineer Smirnov, overseeing surveying and mapping; and archaeologists Kamensky and Petrenko, responsible for archaeological excavations. Kamensky fell ill on the way to Urumqi and returned to Russia early. Despite this setback, the expedition team was notably stronger than the previous solo expedition. The focus of this expedition was on excavating ancient ruins in Kashgar, Turpan, and Kuqa, among other locations, serving as a precursor to the second exploration of Dunhuang.

7.2 Harvest in Turpan and Kuqa

In June 1909, Oldenburg (Figure 7-4) organized his inaugural Russian expedition to Xinjiang, building upon the groundwork laid by the Klementz expedition. The team commenced excavations and inquiries in Kashgar, Turpan, and Kucha, among other locations, culminating in the acquisition of a substantial number of artifacts by the close of 1910.

Oldenburg's approach and investigative style are best encapsulated by the adage "patience yields precision." In his notes, he censured other expedition teams for their hasty and destructive handling of cultural relics, contending that their "excavation work lacked system and was solely driven by the pursuit of various artifacts and artworks." He criticized their emphasis on "conducting extensive excavations primarily to unearth treasures, especially various manuscripts." Essentially, Oldenburg disapproved of the previous foreign expedition teams in Xinjiang, highlighting their focus on treasure hunting rather than engaging in scientific archaeological endeavors.

In contrast to his predecessors Stein, Le Coq, and Ōtani Kōzui, Oldenburg, as a latecomer, harbored no aspirations of being the fastest. Instead, he sought to conduct scientific, logical, and comprehensive inspections, advocating for a methodical examination of monuments while considering both the whole and each constituent part. Oldenburg condemned the practice of collecting museum exhibits based solely on the researcher's preferences, as he believed it often compromised the integrity of the monuments. He vehemently opposed the invasive actions of prying off details from buildings, stripping murals from walls, and other forms of vandalism committed by certain expeditions. Instead, he adopted scientifically sound archaeological recording methods—such as photography, surveying, sketching, copying, and detailed documentation—to preserve the record of ancient ruins. Undoubtedly, this meticulous approach epitomizes the correct methodology for archaeological investigation.

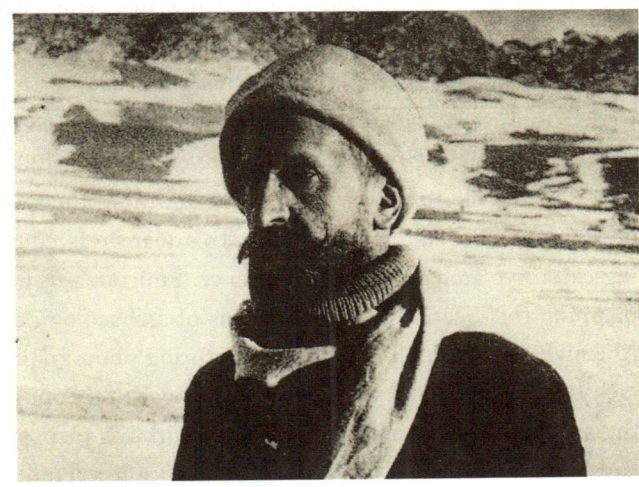

Figure 7-4 Oldenburg during his expedition in Xinjiang (early 20th century)

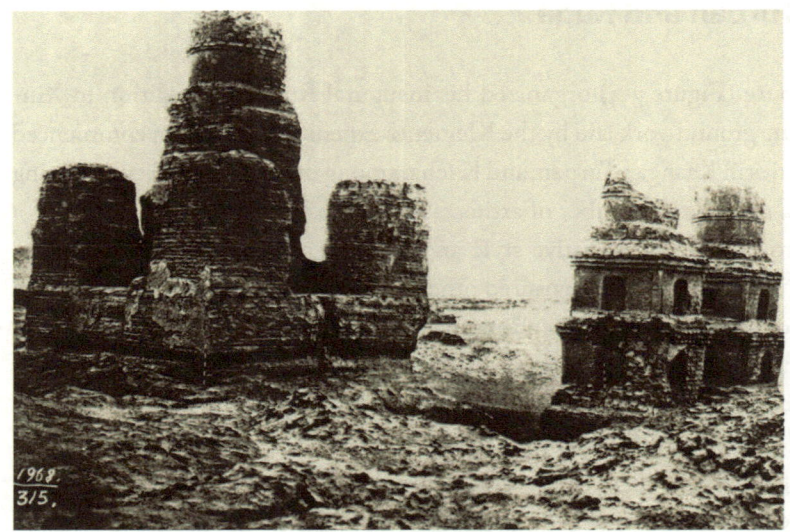

Figure 7-5 Ruins of pagodas in the Jiaohe Ancient City, Turpan (photographed by Dudin of Oldenburg's first expedition team in 1909–1910)

Oldenburg's expedition team displayed unparalleled meticulousness during their exploration of Turpan. On September 29, 1909, the team made their arrival in Turpan, initiating a comprehensive inspection that spanned from October 3 to November 12 of the same year, encompassing almost a month and a half. Their journey closely followed the footsteps of Klementz and Germany's Grünwedel, marking ancient sites of interest. Commencing with the examination of the Jiaohe Ancient City (Figure 7-5), Turpan Ancient City, and Gaochang Ancient City, all in close proximity to Turpan, the team meticulously proceeded with their investigations. Subsequently, they explored numerous cave temple ruins situated near Astana Village, the northern Turpan Canyon, Shengjinkou, Bezeklik, Mutougou Village, and Tuyugou.

A considerable amount of time was dedicated to referencing and comparing the cave and temple ruins numbered by Klementz and Grünwedel. On-site mapping and photography were integral components of their methodology. Oldenburg took the initiative to renumber the caves, temples, and other sites previously cataloged by Klementz and Grünwedel. For instance, he reassigned numbers to Temple Z, Building H, and the grand temple within the ancient city of Gaochang. Even the Ya'er Lake Caves underwent a renumbering process, now aligned with Cave 8. In addition, the team dedicated significant efforts to on-site mapping and photography. This team was equipped with two members possessing extensive archaeological experience. Smirnov's responsibilities included surveying and mapping the locations and floor plans of archaeological structures and caves (Figure 7-6). Meanwhile, Dudin, in addition to capturing photographs, contributed by drawing relevant architectural plans and creating line drawings of the murals on transparent paper. Noteworthy are the subtle variations between Smirnov's planographic map of the Bezeklik Caves and Grünwedel's rendition, offering significant reference value for subsequent researchers.

Their works serve as invaluable resources for contemporary scholars seeking to comprehend the state of ruins across various locations.

In the realm of the Oldenburg expedition team's exploration data in Turpan, a portion has seen the light of publication, yet a substantial part remains unpublished and, in some cases, uncompiled. This treasure trove of information is currently housed within the esteemed walls of the State Hermitage Museum in St. Petersburg. While Oldenburg initially stood firm against the removal of murals, criticizing Klementz's methodology, the allure of hidden treasures proved challenging to resist during the actual investigation. Despite his principled stance, Oldenburg found himself advocating for the extraction of a significant number of murals, surpassing even the previous Russian expedition's endeavors.

Following the Turpan investigation, the team set its sights on the Kuqa area, with the Kizil Caves as the primary focus. Oldenburg oversaw the extraction of numerous murals, exemplified by the *Buddha Preaches Dharma* mural (Figure 7-7) on the inner wall of the right corridor of Cave 198. The Buddha statue at the center, adorned in a robe with the right shoulder exposed, embodies a Kucha smudged painting style. The countenance is rounded and replete, accentuated by a circular halo casting both a frontal and rear glow. Encircling the Buddha are flying apsaras, guardians, disciples, and Bodhisattvas, each bearing distinct expressions that resonate with the distinctive features of individuals hailing from the Central Asian and Western Regions. The murals also feature delicate light-colored flowers on dark backgrounds, a hallmark of Kucha mural artistry. Another remarkable example resides in the side wall of the main chamber of Cave 198A, adorned with murals of naked gods boasting

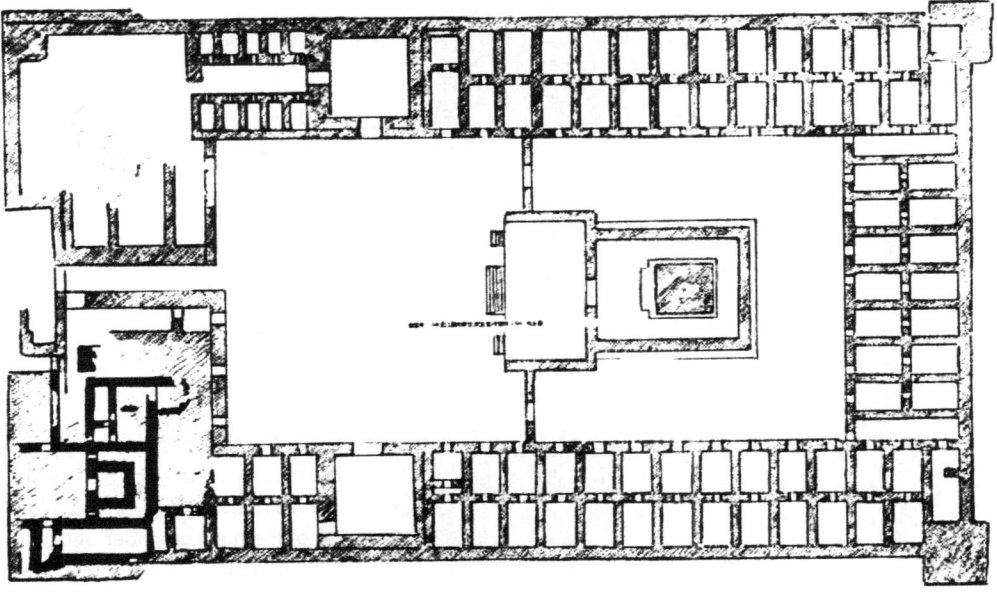

Figure 7-6 Plan of Temple B in Gaochang Ancient City mapped by Smirnov (1909–1910)

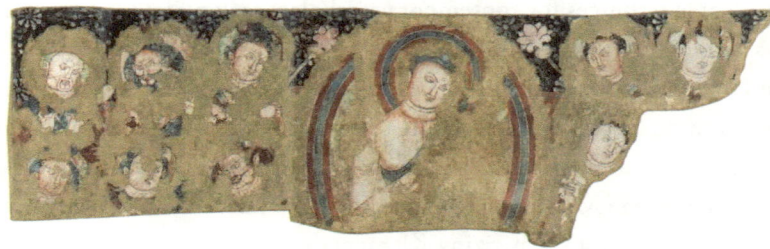

Figure 7-7 The *Buddha Preaches Dharma* mural from Cave 198 of the Kizil Caves (now in the State Hermitage Museum, St. Petersburg, Russia)

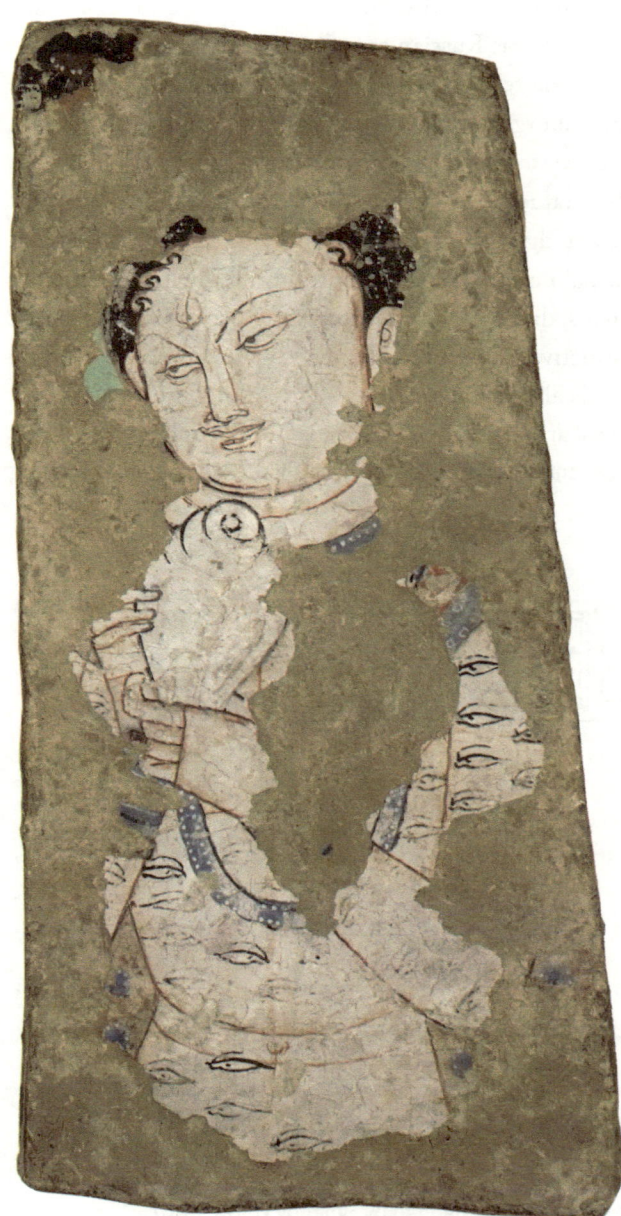

Figure 7-8 Mural of a celestial being with thousands of eyes painted all over his body taken from the side wall of the main chamber of Cave 198A of the Kizil Caves (now in the State Hermitage Museum, St. Petersburg, Russia)

thousands of eyes (Figure 7-8). The celestial figure gracefully clasps a conch shell with both hands, positioned before his chest—an exquisite rarity in itself. Though incomparable to the German-removed murals, Oldenburg, driven by academic discernment, refrained from taking artworks he deemed lacking in scholarly value. Consequently, the Kizil Caves still house a substantial collection of exquisite murals.

Oldenburg's initial inspection yielded over 30 boxes filled with murals, wood carvings, various artworks, nearly a hundred manuscript fragments, and more than 1,500 expedition photos. Among the manuscript fragments are secular documents in diverse languages such as Chinese, Uighur, Sogdian, and Sanskrit, offering a glimpse into property contracts, marriage agreements, and legal documents—a valuable resource for understanding the ancient social customs of Turpan. Preserved in the State Hermitage Museum, these Chinese artifacts, alongside other documents, have been digitized for global scholarly study.

This monumental expedition stands as Russia's most extensive endeavor in the Turpan region. Subsequently, Oldenburg delved into research based on the acquired information, publishing a series of noteworthy results, thus earning him the highest accolade from the Russian Archaeological Association—the prestigious Grand Gold Medal.

7.3 Lucky Surprise

Oldenburg had long harbored an interest in Dunhuang, but due to constraints such as time, funding, and personnel, his initial foray was delayed. Nevertheless, as a neighboring nation sharing borders with China, Tsarist Russia held high regard for intelligence collection in Xinjiang. The early 20th century witnessed keen attention from Tsarist Russia on the archaeological landscape in Xinjiang, particularly monitoring the progress of rival expeditions from countries like the United Kingdom, France, and Japan. In 1914, in a bid to keep pace with other national endeavors, Oldenburg's proposal for a Dunhuang expedition swiftly gained approval from the Archaeological Association. With financial backing secured, Oldenburg promptly organized a second expedition, embarking from St. Petersburg in May 1914.

The composition of the second expedition team featured photographer and painter Dudin, painter Binkenberg, mining engineer and topographic surveyor Smirnov, and ethnologist Romberg, alongside translators and assistants. The division of labor was distinct, and resource allocation was more judicious. Correspondence preserved by Dudin reveals that during Oldenburg's earlier Turpan expedition, Dudin served not only as the team's photographer but also as Oldenburg's assistant, overseeing the management of funds, supplies, and document logistics. Dudin liaised with trading stations and consulates, coordinated document transportation across various departments, and even hired seven Cossack guards for added security (Figure 7-9), as well as translators and pastry chefs. This strategic move addressed the shortcomings encountered in the first Xinjiang expedition, ensuring that all

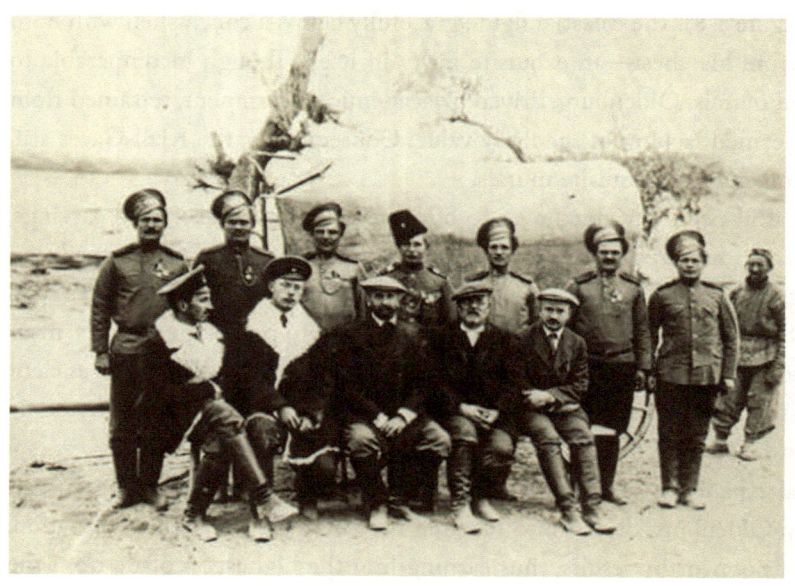

Figure 7-9 Oldenburg (middle in the front row) with the second expedition team (1914–1915)

supplies were safeguarded and transported under Cossack escort—a reflection of Oldenburg's childhood experiences and profound trust in his Cossack guards.

The primary objective of this expedition was to establish a reliable foundation for dating Buddhist relics in northwest China. The team meticulously prepared and crafted a detailed work plan and aspired to conduct a comprehensive inspection of the Dunhuang caves with the intent of publishing their findings in the form of an archaeological report.

In 1914, Oldenburg led the expedition through Tacheng, traversing Urumqi, Turpan, and Hami in Xinjiang. After an 80-day journey, they reached the Dunhuang Mogao Grottoes on August 20 of that year. Although there is no recorded interaction between Oldenburg and Taoist Wang, it is conceivable that, following "pleasant" collaborations with Stein, Pelliot, and others, Taoist Wang would have welcomed Oldenburg's arrival with keen interest. In the Mogao Grottoes, Oldenburg spent three days and subsequently redefined the overall work plan.

In his diary, Oldenburg wrote, "At 2:45, I arrived at the Thousand Buddha Caves with Dudin and took a look at the caves. At 4 o'clock, the two-wheeled vehicle came. I visited them all and was very impressed." This visceral impression left an indelible mark on his subsequent work arrangements. Instead of renumbering the numerous caves, as he had done in the past, Oldenburg opted to adopt Pelliot's numbering system while supplementing the caves overlooked by Pelliot. They meticulously documented the Mogao Grottoes, embarking on an intricate journey of research that involved surveying and mapping floor plans and cross-sections of the caves from the ground up, as well as keeping written records of the shape and content of the caves. In a collaborative effort, Smirnov and Binkenberg ingeniously crafted detailed cross-sections and plans. Simultaneously, Dudin and Romberg tirelessly captured thousands of photographs both inside and outside the south and north caves. Pioneering a novel approach, they seamlessly connected select photographs with corresponding plans, culminating in the creation of a comprehensive 10-meter-long and approximately 2-meter-high general plan and elevation. This masterful rendition authentically mirrors the captivating appearance of the north and south caves. Employing rigorous scientific archaeological methods, the team meticulously documented the statues, eaves, tops, four walls, bottoms, and more of the Mogao Grottoes. Photography, painting, sketching, surveying, and meticulous text recording were all dedicated to capturing the intricate details of the cave murals and sculptures (Figures 7-10). Furthermore, they undertook the less explored task of archaeological cleaning in the northern section of the Mogao Grottoes, an aspect often overlooked by scholars. Oldenburg methodically organized and compiled the acquired information, offering detailed descriptions and comprehensive analyses of each cave. The photos and cross-sections meticulously arranged by Oldenburg stand as unparalleled records, providing the most direct and authentic insights into the visual splendor of the Dunhuang Mogao Grottoes during the early 20th century. These records hold not only an exceptionally precious historical significance but also immense value for research endeavors.

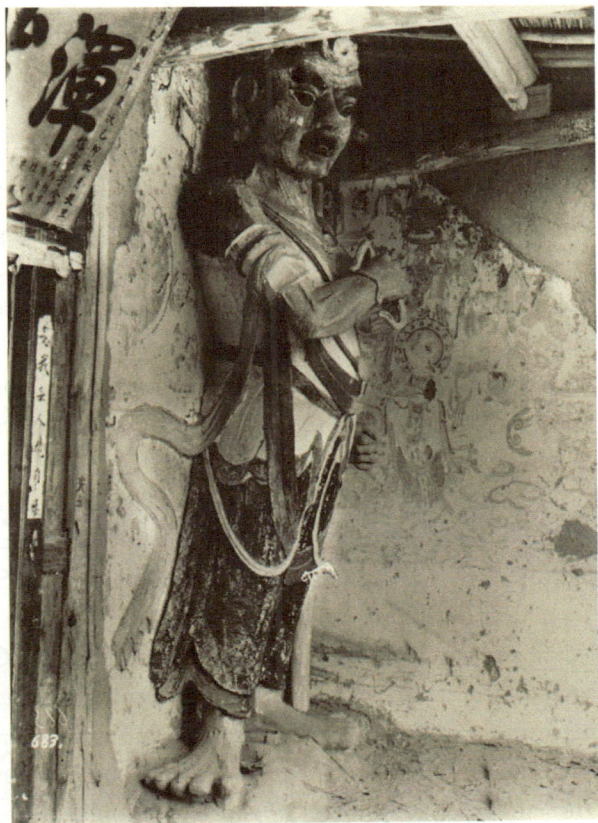

Figure 7-10 The colorful statue of the Heavenly King of the Sui Dynasty in Cave 292 of the Mogao Grottoes in Dunhuang photographed by the Oldenburg's second expedition team (1914–1915)

Oldenburg meticulously mapped a total of 443 caves, a task fraught with challenges as most of these caves were laden with yellow sand from the Gobi Desert, accumulated over thousands of years. Drawing floor plans and capturing the murals necessitated the laborious task of cleaning the sand. Oldenburg's patience and unwavering dedication were rewarded with the discovery of cultural relics within the Dunhuang caves. These relics included murals that had detached from the walls and broken into pieces, fragments of Buddha sculptures strewn on the ground, or silk paintings trampled into hardened clumps of mud. Remarkably, Oldenburg's efforts brought to light treasures ignored by the expedition teams led by Stein, Pelliot, and Ōtani. While traversing the yellow sand in the caves to observe statues and murals, these earlier teams had overlooked the hidden gems within. Oldenburg's meticulous work not only yielded archaeological data such as survey maps, copy drawings, and photographs in Dunhuang but also unearthed a plethora of artworks. These included residual sculptures, murals, silk paintings, linen paintings, paper paintings, and prints—all of immense historical value. The invaluable information uncovered by Oldenburg serves as a rich resource for archaeology, contributes to the protection of the Dunhuang Caves, and significantly enhances the study of mural art.

After an extensive series of investigations and studies, Oldenburg tentatively established that the Mogao Grottoes were excavated over 1,500 years ago. The preservation of the murals to this day is attributed to the arid climate of Dunhuang. The expedition's diligent work persisted until early 1915, but unfortunately, it was abruptly interrupted due to the outbreak of World War I, compelling an early return.

Throughout the entire expedition, Oldenburg, while committed to the principle of cultural relic protection, selectively extracted certain murals and cultural artifacts, such as the vibrant Buddha seat back screen in Cave B77 in the northern area of the Mogao Grottoes. Notably, Oldenburg took a distinctive approach to the treatment of murals. Personally selecting a group of them, he organized the documentation process, leading the initiative to photograph, copy, and record these artworks. In a rather unique move, he pioneered the method of cutting out entire pieces, resulting in the removal of 16 complete murals. This approach, relatively speaking, proved more secure and convenient compared to future practices, such as those employed by the American Warner, involving the use of tape to adhere and peel off murals.

While engaged in the cleaning of Cave D464, Oldenburg and his Cossack guards serendipitously stumbled upon 130 invaluable pieces of ancient Uyghur wooden movable type. Despite arriving in Dunhuang after explorers like Stein, Pelliot, Tachibana Zuicho, and Yoshikawa Koichiro, and with cultural relics in the Library Cave already sold by Taoist Wang and confiscated by the Qing government, the Oldenburg expedition team still managed to acquire documents through searching and purchasing. A significant discovery was made in a cave, yielding more than 10,000 manuscript fragments covered in mud, distinct from the complete documents obtained by other Western explorers from the Library Cave. These fragments, although in poor condition, date back to the late Northern Liang period

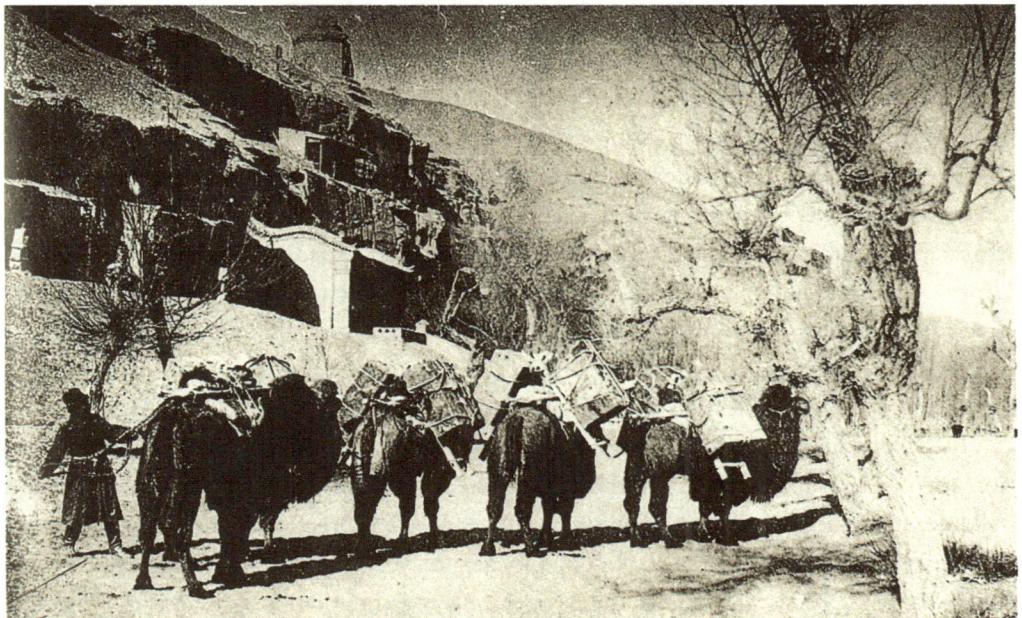

Figure 7-11 Oldenburg's second expedition team carrying cultural relics ready to leave Dunhuang Mogao Grottoes (January 26, 1915)

of AD 434, with the latest one dating to AD 1002, the fifth year of Xianping in the Song Dynasty. Spanning a considerable time frame, these fragments offer a valuable and comprehensive insight into various aspects of history, providing a substantial supplement to the Library Cave documents.

On January 26, 1915, the Oldenburg expedition team commenced their return to China, carrying with them an extensive collection of photos from the Dunhuang Caves, along with plan and section drawings of 443 caves, hundreds of copied paintings, and detailed transcripts. Additionally, they transported removed murals, various cultural relics, painted sculptures, and mural fragments unearthed from the caves, as well as locally acquired artifacts such as documents, scriptures, paper paintings, silk fabrics, etc. Notably, they also departed with several complete and exquisite painted sculptures—a departure from the practices of previous Western explorers in Dunhuang, perhaps a result of negotiation with Taoist Wang Yuanlu. This move marked a significant achievement, as they filled several large carts with the entirety of their cultural relics, declaring their triumphant success (Figure 7-11).

7.4 Treasures in the State Hermitage Museum

Oldenburg, with his knowledge of Sanskrit and Buddhism, stands out for the unique cultural relics he obtained in Dunhuang. According to records, he meticulously collected 66 streamer paintings, 137 silk paintings, 43 paper paintings, and 58 fabric pieces. Additionally, Oldenburg cut out 14 murals and transported 28 large and small painted statues. The collection also includes a wealth of scattered cultural relics, notably comprising 11,014 Dunhuang documents. Among these, 364 manuscripts were relatively complete, including scrolls in Chinese and Uighur procured from Taoist Wang. Oldenburg's manuscript documents are a remarkable trove, featuring lost Sanskrit Buddhist manuscripts from India, with 10,650 fragments, including the manuscripts left by the previous expedition teams in the Mogao Grottoes, the fragments abandoned by the Qing government during the removal of the Library Cave documents, and Tibetan documents overlooked by the others due to lack of interest. His collections add to the cultural wealth preserved in the Mogao Grottoes, boasting exceedingly high collection and research value.

The Oldenburg expedition team amassed a substantial volume of invaluable investigation and research materials in Dunhuang. As the Mogao Grottoes faced ongoing natural and human-induced threats, Oldenburg's data emerged as precious historical information for the restoration of the caves' original appearance. This treasure trove of materials includes six written descriptions of the Mogao Grottoes, meticulously detailing 177 caves, around 2,000 black and white photographs, as well as actual measurements, plans, copy drawings, line drawings of murals, Oldenburg's diaries and notes, and those of other investigators, such as Dudin's notes about Dunhuang murals. Upon his return, Oldenburg deposited the manuscripts he obtained in the Asian Museum, now housed in the St. Petersburg branch of the Institute of Oriental Studies of the Russian Academy of Sciences, amounting to more than 10,000 pieces. The various artworks, surveying and mapping materials, expedition diaries, and more found their places in the Russian Ethnology Museum and other locations, eventually being consolidated in the Eastern Department of the State Hermitage Museum. The quantity and significance of Dunhuang cultural relics collected in Russia stand on par with those in London and Paris, establishing a formidable legacy of cultural preservation.

The State Hermitage Museum houses the most exquisite Dunhuang artwork acquired by Oldenburg. Among the cultural relics obtained are streamers, crafted from silk and paper, with linen varieties being the most prevalent. This preference arises from the simplicity of the plant fiber production process and the cost-effectiveness of materials. Linen, a common textile material for over 1,000 years, is known for its durable preservation compared to silk. One notable piece is a painted Bodhisattva streamer dating from the Five Dynasties (Figure 7-12), crafted from linen. Typically employed in rituals and suitable for year-round display in halls, these triangular pointed streamers hold significance in guiding the soul, according to some scholars. The depicted standing Bodhisattva serves as a leader guiding souls to the Western Paradise, with a painted canopy beneath the triangular streamer head symbolizing the Bodhisattva's dignity. The artwork distinctly captures the Tang and Five Dynasties' Bodhisattva style, featuring a round and serene face, a high bun, a crown atop the head, hands clasped together, and silk drapery adorning the arms. Regrettably, the original

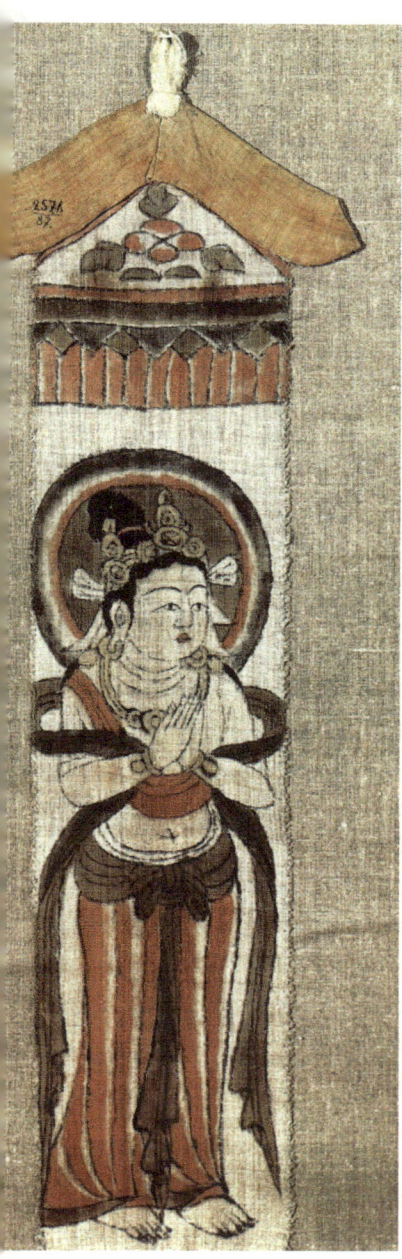

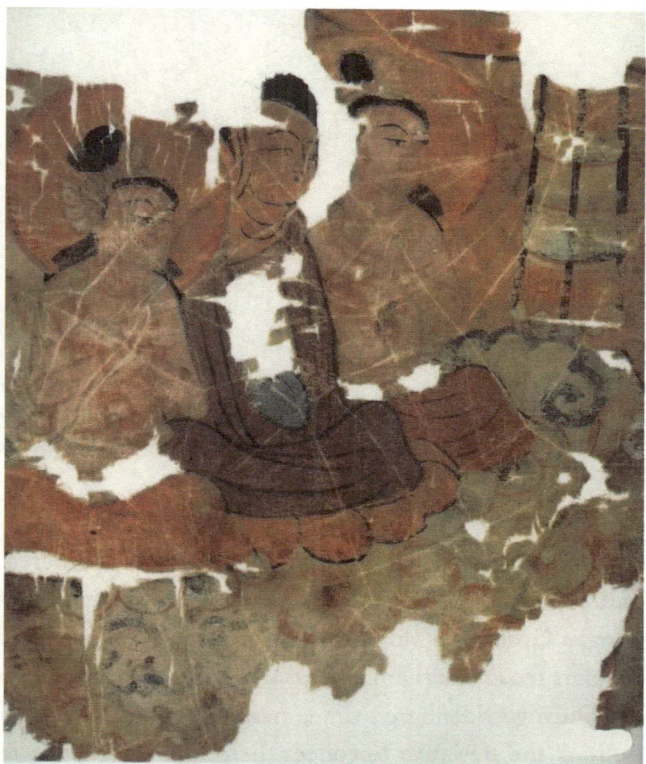

Figure 7-13 Fragments of silk painting of Amitabha and assisting Bodhisattvas (Three Bodhisattvas of the West) in the late Tang Dynasty taken from the Mogao Grottoes in Dunhuang (now in the State Hermitage Museum in St. Petersburg, Russia)

Figure 7-12 A painted Bodhisattva streamer dating from the Five Dynasties taken from the Dunhuang Mogao Grottoes (now in the State Hermitage Museum, St. Petersburg, Russia)

streamers and ribbons have been lost. Comparable linen streamers are also present in the Stein Collection at the British Museum.

Oldenburg's collection extends to numerous fragments of silk paintings, among which is a small yet exquisite remnant (Figure 7-13). These fragments portray the Three Bodhisattvas of the West—Amitabha, Avalokiteśvara, and Mahasthamaprapta—seated side by side on a lotus platform amid clouds. The silk painting depicts the religious scene of the Three Bodhisattvas descending from the sky to guide virtuous individuals to the Western Paradise. Such images with religious significance did not appear alone but likely constituted a small part of larger paintings like the *Amitabha Sutra Transformation Illustration* or *Amitayurdhyana Sutra Transformation Illustration*.

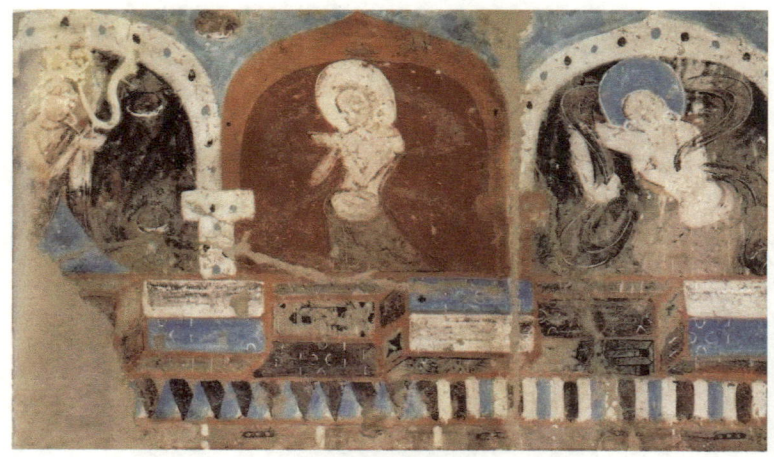

Figure 7-14 Fragment of the *Heavenly Palace Music Mural* of the Northern Wei Dynasty from Cave 263 of the Mogao Grottoes in Dunhuang (now in the State Hermitage Museum in St. Petersburg, Russia)

Like many broken paintings originating from a different source than what Pelliot, Stein, and others obtained, these fragments were salvaged by Oldenburg from the sand in the Mogao Grottoes. While Taoist Wang may have perceived them as mere debris, discerning scholars recognize them as treasures with substantial research and historical value.

During Oldenburg's time, many murals in the Mogao Grottoes were peeling off, and he took the initiative to collect them. For instance, a *Heavenly Palace Music* mural from Cave 263 of the Northern Wei Dynasty (Figure 7-14) showcases the distinctive characteristic of "*xiugu qingxiang*" of the musicians, which refers to the Northern Wei's representative art style of "delicate figure with a lean body." The mural presumably peeled off from the upper part of the side wall, a common location for murals of this theme during the Northern Dynasties. Other fragments, including those of a standing Bodhisattva, depict the concave and convex halo-dye painting method from the Western Regions. Additionally, there are murals featuring a thousand Buddhas, donors, gods, and male donor figures in Cave 263, repainted during the Five Dynasties, and various broken murals of warriors, plants, and decorative patterns with uncertain origins. All peeled off from Mogao Grottoes, worth collecting and preserving.

Notably, Oldenburg took the initiative to cut off the horizontal mural *Jataka Story of Śyāmaka* from Cave 124 of the Sui Dynasty in the Mogao Grottoes (Figure 7-15). This mural, measuring 17 centimeters in height and 144 centimeters in width, follows the format of Buddhist story paintings popular in the Northern Dynasties. Depicting eight scenes of the story in a long-scroll style, the mural narrates various episodes, including the king embarking on a hunting expedition; inadvertently injured Śyāmaka wailing at the prospect of leaving his blind parents without care; the remorseful king conveying the tragic news Śyāmaka's parents; their heart-wrenching cries resonating so loudly that the heavens and earth are moved; the miraculous intervention of Emperor Śakra, bringing Śyāmaka back to life. This remarkable mural, narrating the story of Śyāmaka Jataka, draws its inspiration

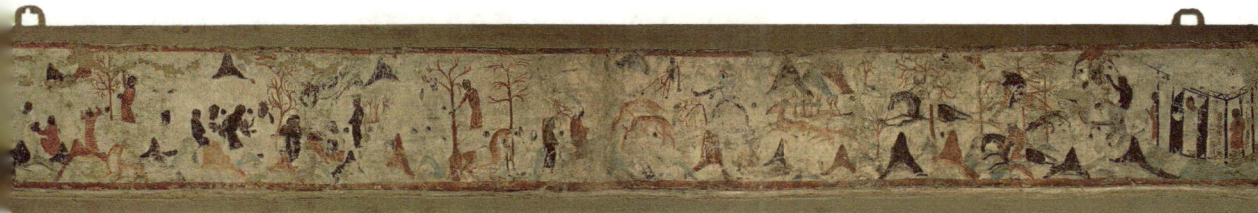

Figure 7-15 The horizontal mural *Jataka Story of Śyāmaka* taken from Cave 124 of the Sui Dynasty Mogao Grottoes in Dunhuang (now in the State Hermitage Museum in St. Petersburg, Russia)

from the *Six Paramita Sutra* translated by Kang Senghui, a revered monk during the Three Kingdoms period in the Wu State (AD 222–280), spanning the years from the first year of Taiyuan to the fourth year of Tianji (AD 251–280). The mural's visual storytelling technique exhibits a clear influence from the multi-scene comic strip format that originated during the Han Dynasty. Comparable stylistic influences are discernible in works such as the long scroll *Admonitions of the Court Instructress* by Gu Kaizhi (c. AD 345–409), an eminent painter from the Eastern Jin Dynasty, presently housed in the British Museum. While the *Jataka Story of Śyāmaka* originates from India, it did not gain popularity in its country of origin. Instead, it found resonance in the cultural and philosophical milieu of the Northern Zhou and Sui Dynasties in China, characterized by the promotion of Confucian ideals and governance centered around the principles of filial piety. The German explorer Le Coq made a noteworthy discovery of the *Jataka Story of Śyāmaka* murals in Caves 114, 178, and 186 within the Kizil Caves.

Oldenburg's discreet acquisition of 28 vibrant statues from the Mogao Grottoes in Dunhuang, a record unmatched by Western archaeologists, remains a lesser-known aspect of his remarkable discoveries. In contrast to his counterparts, Oldenburg opted for a low profile, choosing not to publish photos of these statues, keeping them shrouded in secrecy for many years. Consequently, this extensive collection remained relatively unknown, a stark contrast to the scrutiny faced by American professor Warner, who acquired only one Dunhuang-painted sculpture. Among Oldenburg's acquisitions, a notable emphasis is placed on heads, exemplified by the heads of two ascetic Sakyamuni statues crafted around the Northern Wei Dynasty (Figure 7-16), as well as the heads of disciples and Bodhisattva statues from the Sui Dynasty, and Bodhisattva statues from the Tang Dynasty, among others. These detached heads likely originated from ancient, deteriorated, colorful statues, subsequently

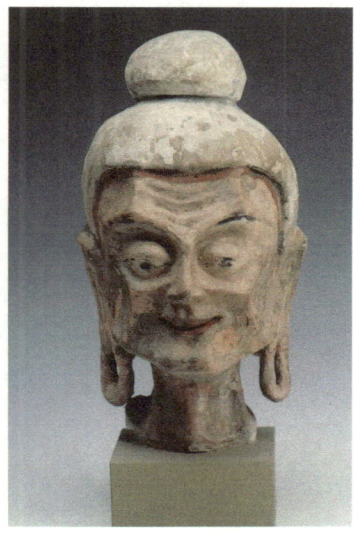

Figure 7-16 Head of Sakyamuni from the Northern Wei Dynasty from Mogao Grottoes in Dunhuang (now in the State Hermitage Museum, St. Petersburg, Russia)

dislodged and buried in the cave by shifting sands before being unearthed by Oldenburg. These artifacts may have been deemed of little value in Taoist Wang's eyes.

In stark contrast, the most invaluable treasures lie in the vibrant statues that Oldenburg carefully removed from the depths of the Mogao Grottoes. Within the central pillar caves of the Northern Wei Dynasty, molded relief sculptures were frequently affixed to the central pillar's surface, often secured with stakes. Over the passage of time, numerous sculptures detached, leaving behind a multitude of voids on the central pillar. Transporting us back to the early years of the Republic of China, within the disused caves of the Northern Wei Dynasty in the Mogao Grottoes, accumulated quicksand covered the ground, concealing the fallen sculptures. In his meticulous exploration, Oldenburg uncovered these hidden treasures, diligently clearing away the quicksand and revealing an astonishing array of discoveries (Figure 7-17).

Among his findings were several intact statues, an even more precious revelation. Oldenburg not only identified the origin of these painted sculptures but also meticulously

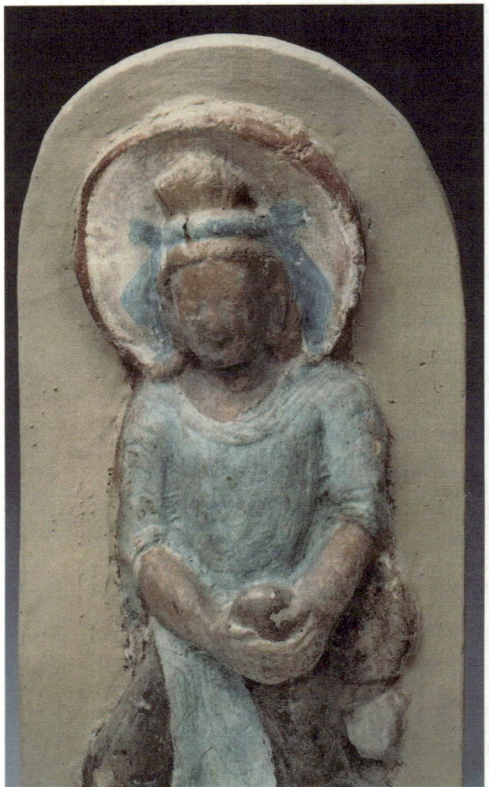

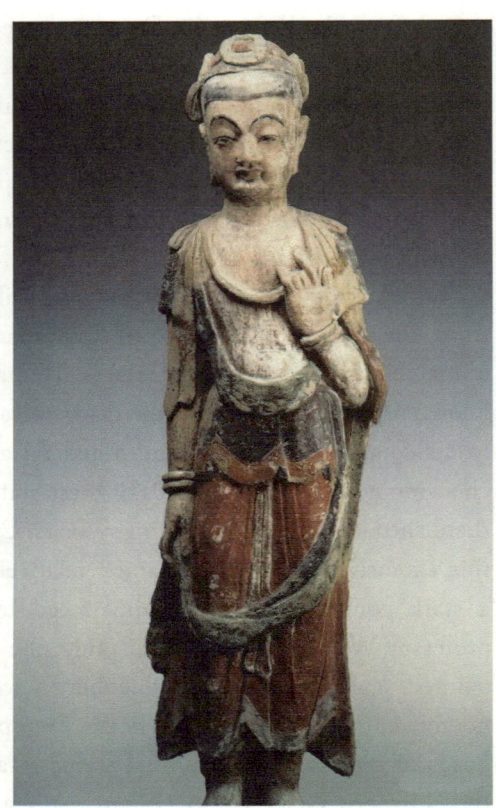

Figure 7-17 Molded relief sculpture of Bodhisattva from the Northern Wei Dynasty from Mogao Grottoes in Dunhuang (now in the State Hermitage Museum, St. Petersburg, Russia)

Figure 7-18 A painted standing statue of Bodhisattva from the Sui Dynasty from Cave 253 of the Mogao Grottoes in Dunhuang (now in the State Hermitage Museum, St. Petersburg, Russia)

recorded the caves from which they originated. An Ananda statue from Cave 128 of the Northern Zhou Dynasty exudes a childlike charm with a delightful smile, capturing the distinctive slender form characteristic of the disciple statues from Northern Zhou Dynasty. A standing Bodhisattva statue from the same Cave 128 showcases the tubular body commonly observed in Bodhisattva statues from the Northern Zhou Dynasty. Additionally, a standing Bodhisattva statue relocated from Cave 253 of the Sui Dynasty (Figure 7-18) unveils the unique feminine and slender figure, particularly emphasizing the slight "S" shaped twist of the body and a gently protruding lower abdomen—a testament to the artist's exceptional skill in capturing nuanced details. Furthermore, a pair of crouching lions from Cave 321 of the Tang Dynasty once served as guardians within the cave, representing rare statues within the Mogao Grottoes.

Oldenburg also relocated a set of statues from Cave 111 in the Song Dynasty, including an Ananda statue, a Mahākāśyapa statue, and a Bodhisattva statue (Figure 7-19). Ananda and Mahākāśyapa, both close disciples of Sakyamuni, frequently appear together in Buddhist art, symbolizing the dual images of one young and one elderly monk. Originally,

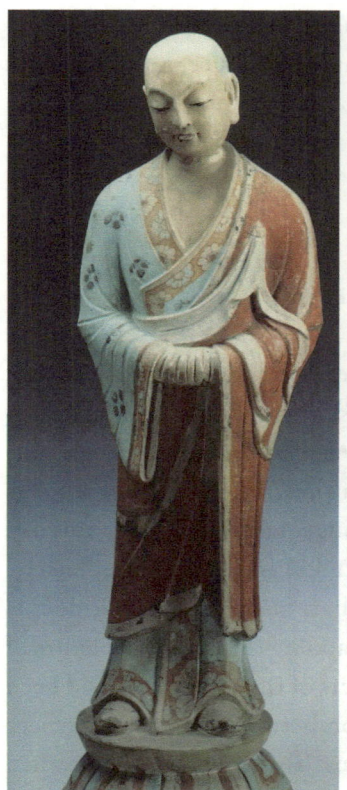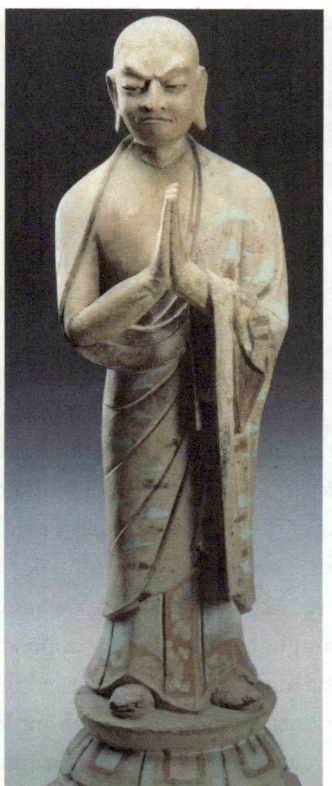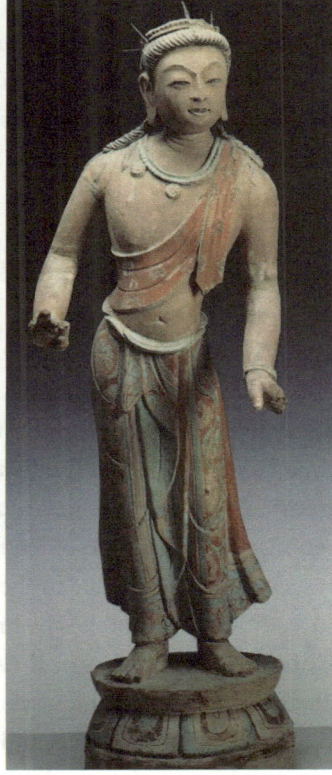

Figure 7-19 (left to right) painted standing statues of Ananda, Mahākāśyapa, and Bodhisattva from the Northern Song Dynasty from Cave 111 of the Mogao Grottoes in Dunhuang (now in the State Hermitage Museum, St. Petersburg, Russia)

Cave III likely housed colorful statues depicting one Buddha, two disciples, and two Bodhisattvas, but Oldenburg moved three of them. These statues exhibit exceptional sculptural craftsmanship, innovatively blending the robust yet slender style of the Tang Dynasty. The extant painted sculptures from the Song Dynasty (Northern Song Dynasty and Western Xia Dynasty) in the Mogao Grottoes are exceedingly scarce, and Russia's collection of Song Dynasty painted sculptures helps fill this void.

Originally displayed for public veneration within the caves, these intact painted statues were visible to all. However, in the eyes of Taoist Wang, they were aged statues lacking the divine aura they once possessed. Faded and weathered, these statues were deemed unworthy of worship, and discarding them seemed no great loss. Taoist Wang's true appreciation lay in newly crafted Buddha statues, commissioned with funds raised through charity. For the old painted statues, he aspired to restoration, involving fresh paint to revive their brilliance—a sentiment shared by many ordinary Buddhists toward aging statues. Many of the garishly repainted statues found in the Mogao Grottoes today were "creations" from the time of Wang, where he had unskilled artisans reapply vibrant colors. Taoist Wang's attitude toward the ancient painted sculptures of the Mogao Grottoes created an opportunity for foreign expedition teams. In Oldenburg's eyes, Taoist Wang's contemporary statues were considered with no value at all. The exchange of cultural relics with Taoist Wang involved donating incense money to assist Wang in building new statues or restoring old ones. While Oldenburg's publications may not detail the transaction process with Wang, one can envision the negotiations that took place. History, it seems, played a curious jest on the Chinese nation.

7.5 A Checkered Political and Academic Career

As early as 1897, during his tenure as a professor at St. Petersburg University, Oldenburg founded the academic journal *Buddhist Library*. The Buddhist manuscripts acquired during his expeditions in 1909 and 1914 gained exposure in the academic community through continuous publication in the *Buddhist Library*. This facilitated manuscript research by scholars from various countries in China at the time. The journal continues its publication to this day, serving as a guiding resource for researchers in Dunhuang studies and Indian Buddhism.

For many years, due to the secrecy of Oldenburg's work diary and limited public disclosure of the cultural relics he brought back to Russia, understanding the complete picture of Chinese cultural relics in Russia and clarifying historical facts of the inspections had been challenging. Recent improvements include the collaboration between Shanghai Ancient Books Publishing House and relevant Russian organizations. This collaboration resulted in the publication of 17 volumes of *Dunhuang Documents Collected in Russia* and six volumes of *Dunhuang Artworks Collected in Russia* in 1997. These volumes encompass all Dunhuang cultural relics obtained by the expedition. Additionally, translations of Oldenburg's diaries and related materials are underway, providing valuable insights into the Dunhuang Caves and the activities of the Oldenburg expedition team.

Oldenburg, highly esteemed in Russian and international Oriental academic circles, faced political challenges within his country. The political turmoil and frequent power changes in Russia made it difficult for him to align with a specific faction (Figure 7-20). After the February Revolution in 1917, he initially supported the bourgeois Provisional Government, serving as Minister of Education. However, the October Revolution led by the Russian Communist Party shifted the political landscape, and Oldenburg found himself under the proletarian regime. Despite these political shifts, he remained active in both

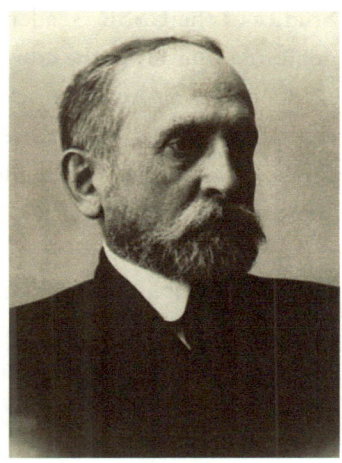

Figure 7-20 The old Oldenburg

political and academic spheres after the Sovietization of Russia. He even had two interviews with Lenin (1870–1924) in 1918 and 1921. Through his association with Lenin, Oldenburg successfully forged an alliance between the Bolsheviks and ethnographers, a group dedicated to the study of Asian races. Despite being arrested by the Cheka (All-Russian Extraordinary [or Emergency] Commission for Combating Counter-Revolution and Sabotage) in 1919, Oldenburg continued to operate the Academy of Sciences under Stalin's (1878–1953) government until his dismissal in 1929.

Oldenburg maintained his academic engagement throughout his life. From 1916 to 1930, he served as the director of the Asian Museum (Figure 7-21), and in 1930, the Institute of Oriental Studies of the USSR Academy of Sciences was established, incorporating the Asian Museum. Oldenburg served as the first director of the Institute of Oriental

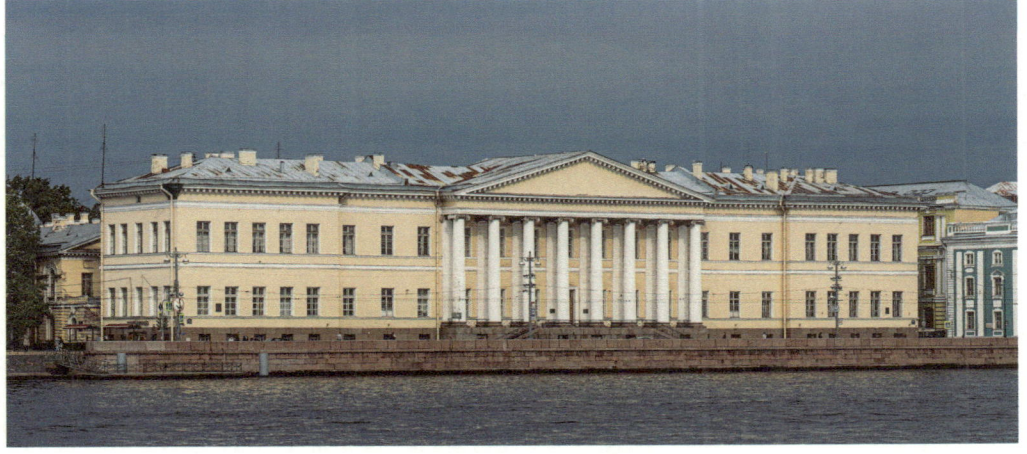

Figure 7-21 The former location of the Asian Museum in St. Petersburg, Russia (Photography by A. Savin)

Studies of the USSR Academy of Sciences from 1930 to 1934. Until his death in 1934, he dedicated himself to the administration of the institute in St. Petersburg.

Considering his life of exploration and academic accomplishments, Oldenburg was a central figure in Russian Oriental scholarship from the late 19th century to the early 20th century. His influence extended internationally, with a broad range of academic research, approximately 300 published works, and a focus on ancient and medieval Indian culture and religion. He also played a pivotal role in the development of Tibetan studies in Russia. Notable contributions to Dunhuang studies include his articles "Thousand Buddha Caves," published in 1922, and "Art in the Desert," published in 1925. His posthumous manuscript, *Dunhuang Caves*, remains a valuable masterpiece.

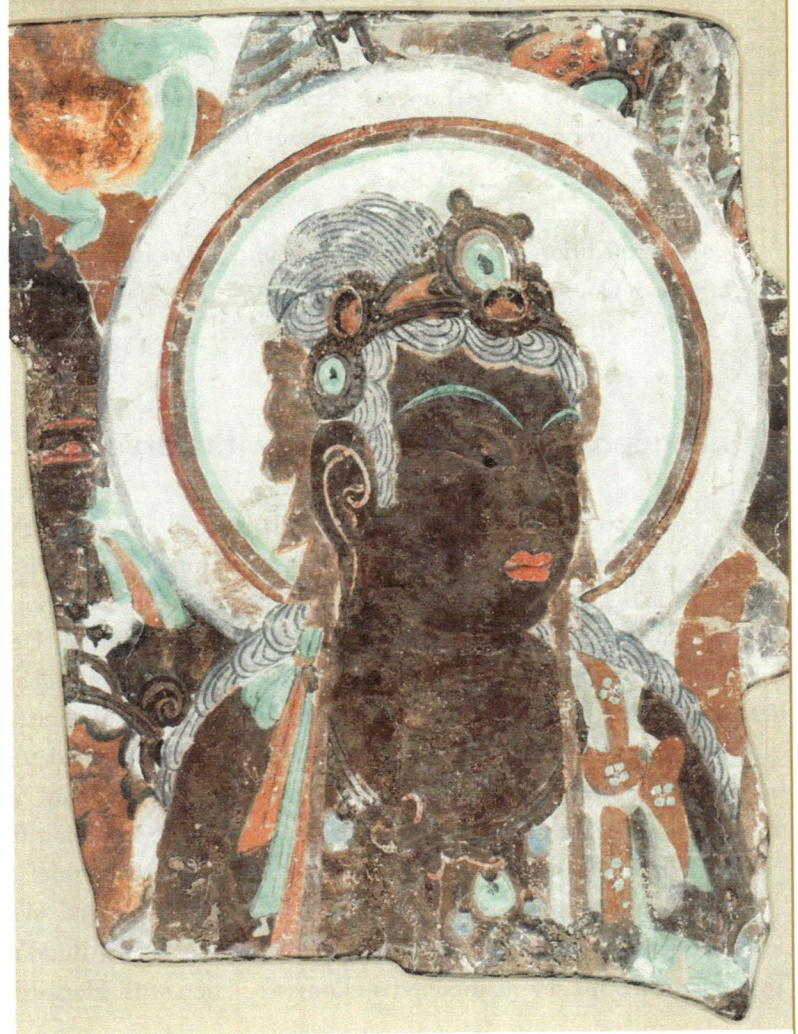

Langdon Warner,
the Ambitious American

8.1 Langdon Warner, Intertwined with Harvard

As European countries, Tsarist Russia, and Japan had already marked their presence on the exploration routes in Xinjiang and Gansu, the United States, determined not to be left behind, soon dispatched a distinctive explorer to partake in the opportunities. This explorer was Langdon Warner (1881–1955), the nephew-in-law of former US President Theodore Roosevelt (1858–1919) (Figure 8-1). Warner, characterized by his tall and handsome stature, held dual reputations in both China and the West: he was celebrated as one of the finest explorers and archaeologists in the United States, often likened to the iconic character Indiana Jones from the movie *Raiders of the Lost Ark*. In Japan, he earned acclaim for protecting Kyoto and the ancient city of Nara from US bombing during World War II. However, in China, he became notorious as an alleged treasure thief.

Born into a family of lawyers in Massachusetts, USA, in 1881, Warner commenced his academic journey at Harvard University in 1899, focusing on Buddhism and archaeology. Throughout his life, he maintained a close association with Harvard. After graduating in

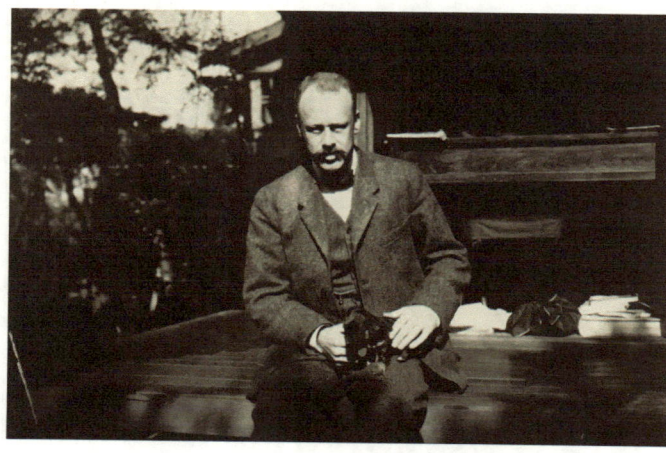

Figure 8-1 Warner in Japan (1908)

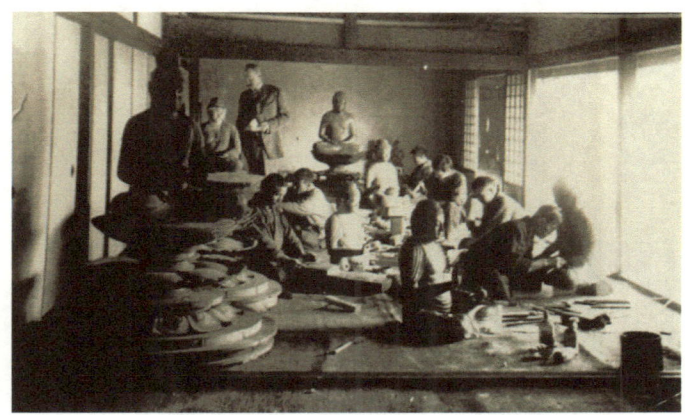

Figure 8-2 Warner (standing behind) at the Buddha statue carving workshop at Hōryū-ji in Nara, Japan (1907)

1903, Warner joined the geological and archaeological expedition led by geologist Raphael Pumpelly (1837–1923) to explore Russian Central Asia, sparking a lifelong passion for archaeological exploration. Returning to Harvard in 1905 for a year of archaeological studies, he then ventured to Japan in 1906 to specialize in Buddhist art (Figure 8-2). Embracing the Japanese apprenticeship method, Warner studied under the guidance of Okakura Kakuzō (1863–1913), a preeminent art educator and philosopher in Japan during the Meiji period (1868–1912). As a key figure in the enlightenment era of modern Japanese civilization, he became a representative icon of Japanese Oriental aesthetics and commanded high respect in the United States. Okakura's profound aesthetic philosophy left a lasting impact on Warner's life.

In 1909, Warner returned to the United States, and the following year, he entered a new chapter in his life by marrying Roland Roosevelt, niece of the former president. Despite his personal life taking unexpected turns, his professional journey continued with diverse experiences. In 1910, he embarked on investigations of Buddhist art in Korea and Japan, leveraging his knowledge and expertise in Asian art. In 1913, Warner introduced the first Oriental Art course at Harvard University, focusing on the history of Chinese and Japanese art (Figure 8-3). Simultaneously, the Smithsonian Institution in Washington funded his Asian expedition for a year or so, which was unfortunately interrupted by the outbreak of World War I. In 1916, Warner arrived in China with the purpose of collecting Chinese cultural relics for the newly established Cleveland Museum of Art in Ohio. During this time, Warner received an invitation from the renowned American industrialist and art collector Charles Lang Freer (1854–1919) to travel to Beijing. In this role, he took on the responsibility of negotiating with the newly established government of the Republic of China to establish the American School of Archaeology in Peking. However, due to concerns about the potential outflow of cultural relics, the Chinese government approached Warner's proposal cautiously. While not rejecting it outright, they politely indicated that the matter would be revisited for further discussion. With the prospects of establishing a school in China

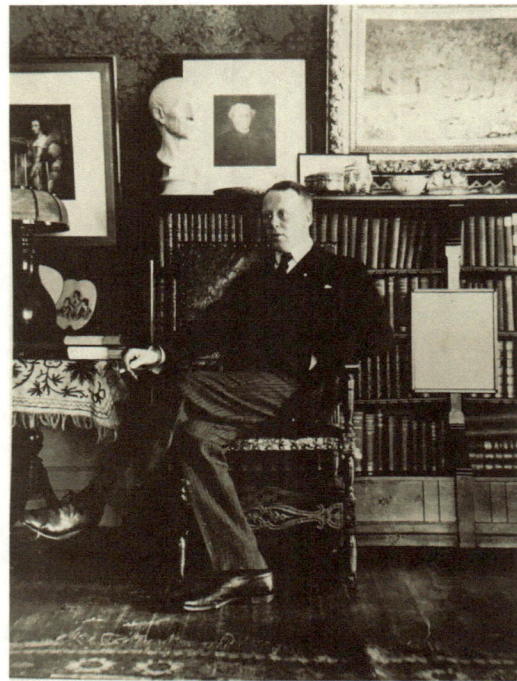

Figure 8-3 Warner teaching at Harvard University (1913–1916)

appearing uncertain, Warner returned to the United States. He continued his contributions to institutions such as the Cleveland Museum of Art, the Pennsylvania Museum, and the Fogg Museum, among others. Despite the challenges, Warner's experiences in China significantly enriched his understanding of Chinese culture and art history.

Warner has seen cultural relics brought from northwest China by individuals such as Stein, Pelliot, Le Coq, and Kozlov in London, Paris, Berlin, and St. Petersburg, among other places. He has also engaged with renowned experts and sinologists in Western Regions' art and read their works, thus developing a keen interest in northwest China and fostering a desire to conduct field investigations. In 1922, the Fogg Museum at Harvard University sought an individual to embark on an expedition to northwest China for an antiquity collection, making Warner the ideal candidate. He was subsequently appointed a professor at Harvard University and the curator of Oriental art at the Fogg Museum. In 1923, he organized his inaugural archaeological expedition to inspect the Silk Road.

Arriving in Beijing in July 1923 with his team member Horace Jayne and translator Wang Jinren, Warner received substantial support from warlord Wu Peifu (1874–1939) for their expeditions in China. En route to Dunhuang, he visited the Longmen Grottoes in Luoyang, Henan, a site he had long anticipated.

Having expressed admiration for the reliefs of *Emperor Xiaowen and Empress Wenzhao of the Northern Wei Dynasty Worshiping the Buddha* to Okakura Kakuzō in the United States, Warner was delighted to witness them in person. Freer took photos of these two reliefs of worshiping the Buddha at the door, and he must have described them to Warner (Figure 8-4). At that time, the book *Mission archéologique dans la Chine septentrionale* (*Archaeological Mission to Northern China*) by French sinologist Chavannes, after conducting archaeological surveys in China, was already well-known in the world, and it featured these two photos of worshiping Buddha. Upon reaching Longmen Grottoes, Warner sent a letter to his wife in Kaifeng, expressing his enthusiasm:

> At Longmen Grottoes, you can see what ancient Chinese sculptures looked like in their heyday. Please note the figures worshiping Buddha—their composition is as good as the decorative carvings of the Pantheon in Rome, and as for the lines of the reliefs, I think they are no less impressive … Sensei (Okakura) thinks they are of great importance. The West should be able to access the treasure trove of top-notch Chinese sculptures. It is a pantheon that has not yet been opened. It can be as grand as the entire Acropolis, waiting for people to study and study. (Figure 8-5)

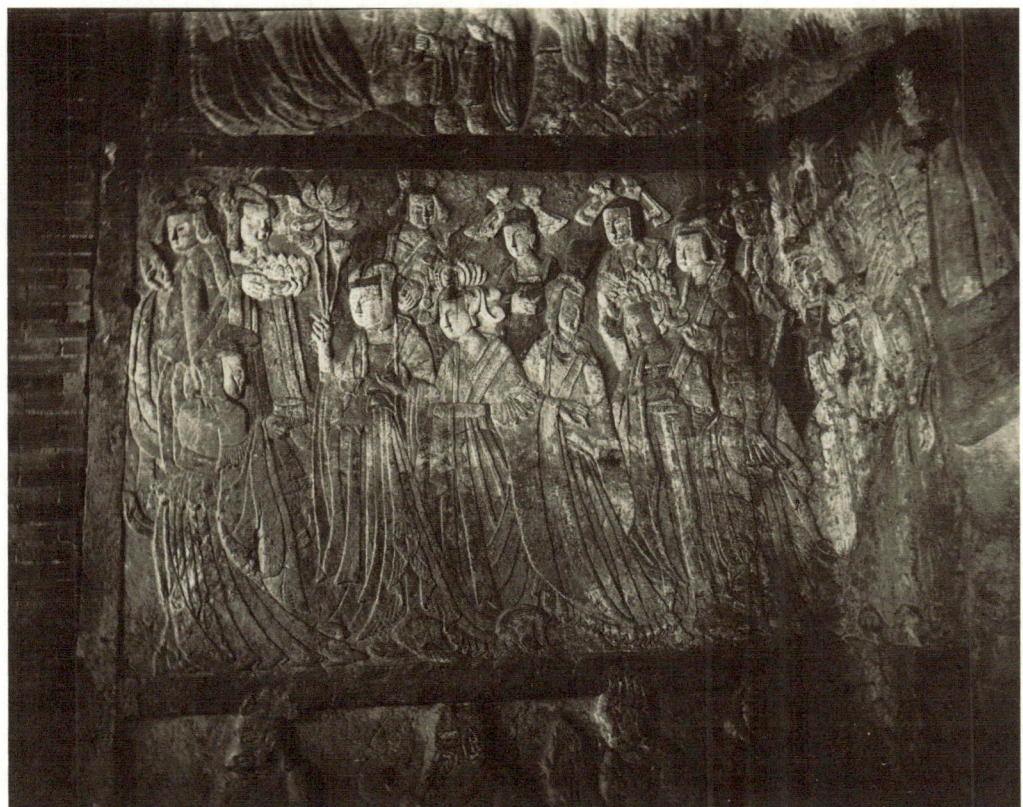

Figure 8-4 *Empress Wenzhao Attending Buddhist Rituals with Her Court* and the statues of gods and kings on the south side of the front wall of the Binyang Middle Cave of Longmen Grottoes in Luoyang, Henan in the early 6th century of the Northern Wei Dynasty (photographed by Freer and Zhou Yutai in 1910)

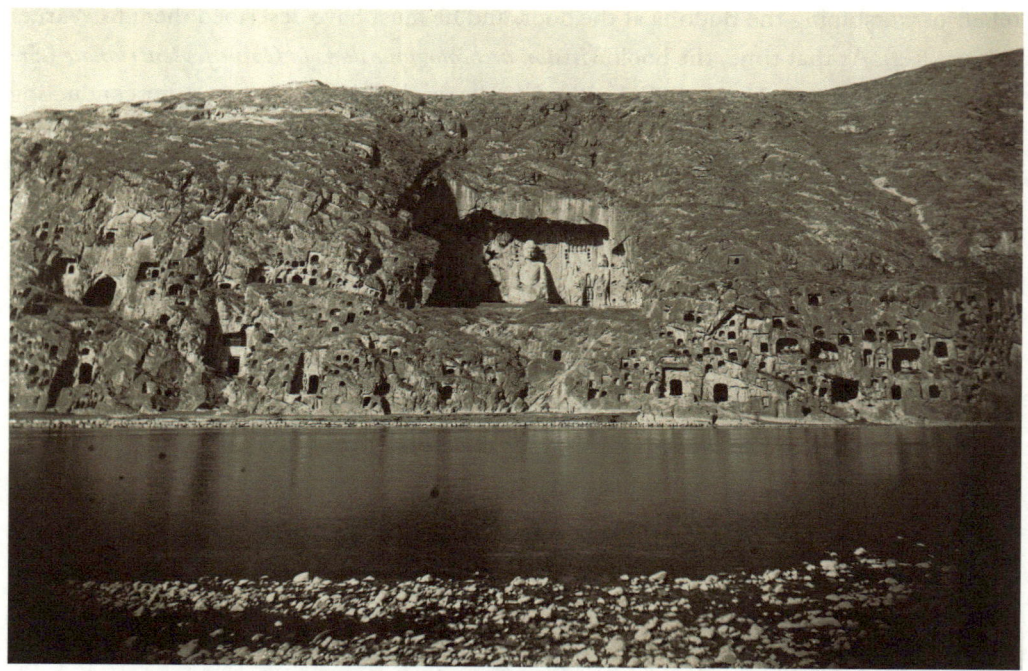

Figure 8-5 The area from Putai Cave to Huoshao Cave in the West Mountain of Longmen Grottoes in Luoyang, Henan (centered on Fengxian Temple, photographed by Freer and Zhou Yutai in 1910)

Despite its historical significance, the Longmen Grottoes, excavated in the late Northern Wei Dynasty and flourishing in the Tang Dynasty, had suffered extensive damage over centuries due to wars and occupation. Locals sold statues from the Longmen Grottoes, both large and small, to foreigners for profit. Consequently, Longmen Grottoes, one of the three largest caves in China, suffered devastation as early as the early years of the Republic of China. Warner documented both the magnificence and brutal destruction of the Longmen Grottoes in his notes:

> In general, the sheer quantity and exquisite craftsmanship of the cultural relics at the Longmen Grottoes are truly incredible. From my perspective, the renowned relief figures of *Empress Wenzhao Attending Buddhist Rituals with Her Court* are already considered among the finest works of Chinese art. However, when compared to what I witnessed at the Longmen Grottoes, they pale in significance. The Seated Buddha and his eight attendants—needless to say, it stands as one of the greatest sacred sites in the world ... The recent damage to the Longmen Grottoes is as severe as we've heard, with sculptures having their heads knocked off and newly broken ones exposed everywhere. Deliberate excavation of some statues and random toppling by soldiers have resulted in a scene so horrific that it almost induces a feeling of sickness.

Warner saw more than a dozen sculptures from Chinese caves at the Cernuschi Museum in Paris. Upon inquiry, he discovered that Westerners were using images to pilfer sculptures from the Longmen Grottoes. It became evident that the photos published by Chavannes had become a buying guide for Westerners seeking to acquire Longmen statues from China. Rushing to Longmen, they scoured the site based on catalog-like photos, placed orders with Chinese dealers, and commissioned local craftsmen to steal the statues. Fearing that his own research publication might lead to similar consequences, Warner expressed concern in his diary, stating, "That kind of thing will hurt my conscience extremely." It appears he initially had an instinct to protect Chinese cultural relics. However, upon reaching Dunhuang, this instinct seemed to be overridden by desire.

After departing Longmen in Luoyang, the expedition team reached Xi'an and officially commenced their investigation. Approaching Dunhuang, they initially visited the ruins of Ejin Banner Khara-Khoto in Inner Mongolia, spending

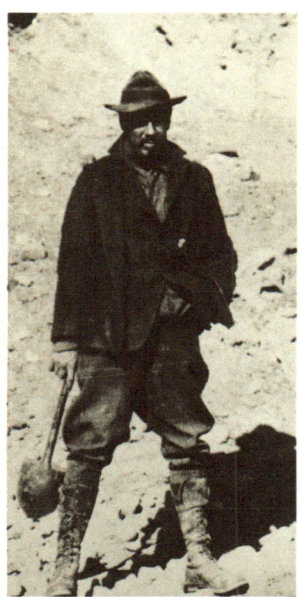

Figure 8-6 Warner at Ejin Banner Khara-Khoto ruins, Inner Mongolia (1923)

about two weeks on the inspection (Figure 8-6). Warner observed that this site had already been excavated by earlier expeditions, including Kozlov, thus yielding nothing of substantial value. Driven by the goal of acquiring relics for the Fogg Museum, Warner swiftly abandoned the site and proceeded to Dunhuang. During the journey, Jayne returned to Beijing due to health reasons.

8.2 Purchased Dunhuang Statues and Murals

In January 1924, Warner reached the Mogao Grottoes in Dunhuang, initially targeting the ancient manuscripts and paintings in the Library Cave. However, finding it empty with no more documents to collect, he shifted his focus to the statues and murals in the caves.

Dunhuang at that time had undergone changes from a few years earlier. In 1917, following the victory of the October Revolution led by Lenin in Russia, the remnants of the original Russian Imperial Army, led by Major Boris Annenkov (1889–1927), faced defeat by the Red Army. Over 1,400 of them fled into the Yili region of Xinjiang in 1919. According to Chinese law, Xinjiang authorities confiscated their weapons and decided to send them to Gansu to disperse their power. In November 1920, over 900 of Annenkov's army remnants were deported to Dunhuang by the Xinjiang government. However, the Dunhuang authorities, concerned about the county's safety, refused to allow them to station in the city. Instead, they believed it would be safer to place them more than 20 kilometers away in the

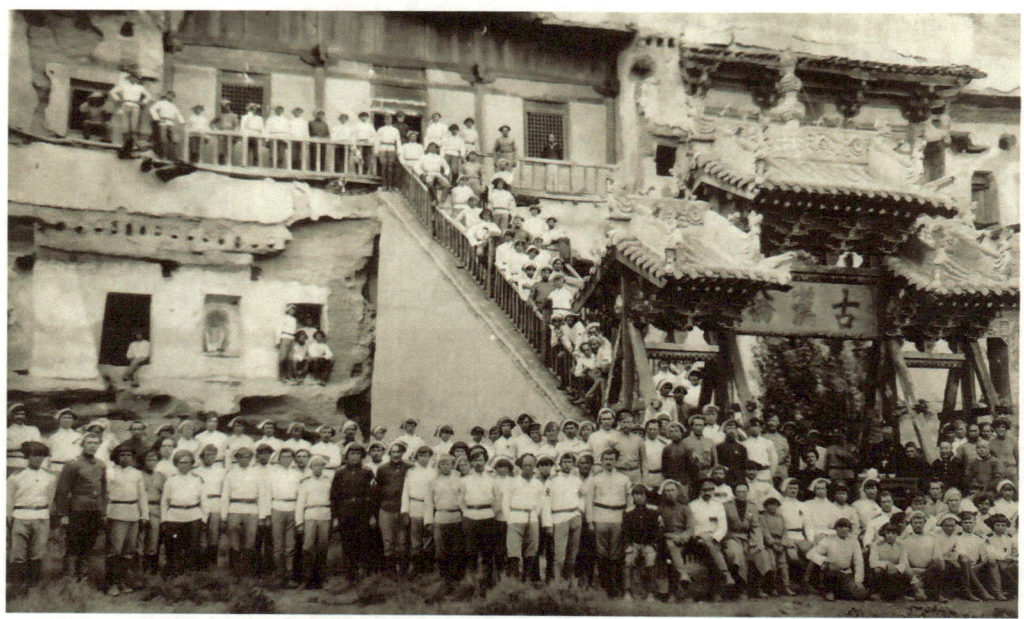

Figure 8-7 Tsarist Russian soldiers in Mogao Grottoes (1921)

Mogao Grottoes. So, these more than 900 people resided in the Mogao Grottoes for eight months (Figure 8-7). They dismantled doors, windows, and plaques in the caves and temples for firewood, using pots to light fires for cooking in the caves. Many exquisite murals were blackened by smoke and became unrecognizable. Furthermore, some individuals carved random scrawls on the murals, cutting off hands, gouging out the eyes of painted Buddha statues, and even digging into their bodies to check for hidden treasures. Their actions caused severe damage to the Buddhist artworks in the Mogao Grottoes. In August 1921, these remnants of Tsarist Russia were deported out of Dunhuang and sent to Shanghai, Tianjin, and other locations.

While Warner was dismayed by the destruction of some caves, he remained determined to extract painted sculptures and murals from the Mogao Grottoes. To facilitate his work, Warner offered gifts to Taoist Wang, the guardian of the Mogao Grottoes at the time. Wang generously agreed to allow him to take the murals, considering ancient murals to be of little value compared to those painted by the artist he hired. Warner's primary focus was on Cave 323, which dates back to the Tang Dynasty.

In the Tang Dynasty Mogao Grottoes, Buddhist history became a popular theme, drawing inspiration from legends originating in India and China. These legends narrate stories with a magical touch, recorded by monks or believers throughout Buddhism's long history. Compiled by monks and disseminated as true histories, these stories often feature protagonists who existed in history, yet the narratives are clearly shaped and embellished by editors. As the believers in Buddhism considered these stories to be true, monks painted them on cave walls to provide a visual representation for additional worshippers. Cave 323 at the Dunhuang Mogao Grottoes is known for its depictions of such stories, possessing exceptional artistic and historical value.

On the south wall of Cave 323, a mural depicts the story of Gao Kui in Yangdu during the Eastern Jin Dynasty obtaining a golden statue. The eminent monk Daoxuan (AD 596–667) of the Tang Dynasty recorded this story in his work *Ji Shen Zhou San Bao Gan Tong Lu* (Collected Records of Miracles Relating to the Three Jewels in China), written in the first year of Linde (AD 664). During the Xianhe period of the Eastern Jin Dynasty (AD 326–334), Gao Kui, a local official in Danyang, acquired a golden Buddha statue under the Zhanghou Bridge. This statue lacked a backlight or a Buddha seat. According to the Sanskrit inscription on the back, it was carved by the fourth daughter of King Ashoka of India. When Gao Kui arrived at the entrance of Changgan Alley with the golden Buddha statue, the oxen pulling the cart refused to move forward. As a last resort, a Changgan Temple was built there to house the golden statue, which is believed to be the present-day Changgan Temple in Nanjing. A year later, a fisherman discovered a golden lotus seat, and a pearl diver found a gold backlight on the seabed. Both items were remarkably consistent with the golden statue enshrined in Changgan Temple. These events are depicted in the murals. In the mural, the upper part depicts a radiant Buddha statue, lotus seat, and backlights painted respectively on the left, middle, and right, illustrating the acquisition of the golden statue, statue base, and backlights separately. In the middle of the mural, beneath the Buddha statue and the lotus seat, a small boat sails on the sea with several monks, boatmen, and a welcoming Buddha statue (Figure 8-8). In the lower part, there was originally a larger boat mooring against the shore, carrying seven monks and laymen, along with two boat trackers. They have just welcomed a standing Buddha statue under the treasure tent, adorned with four streamers flying in front and behind. Six monks on the shore hold streamers to greet him (Figure 8-9). This mural, taped off by Warner in 1924, is now housed in the Harvard Art Museums, with traces of the removed mural still visible on the south wall of Cave 323, including two boat trackers and monks and laymen welcoming the Buddha at the lower edge of the mural.

However, the current condition of this looted mural is concerning, as the facial features of the depicted characters appear blurred. This is attributed partly to the oxidation of the lead-based paint in the air and partly to the damage incurred when Warner taped it down. Mineral pigments possess a certain thickness, and although the glue adheres to the pigments on the surface of the mural, the remaining color that hasn't been removed is still visible on the wall inside the cave. The mural he took away naturally lacks some original facial details. Therefore, his act of pasting the mural undoubtedly resulted in serious damage. According to statistics from the Dunhuang Academy, Warner used his special adhesive tape on the murals, peeling off sections from Cave 320, Cave 321, Cave 323, Cave 328, Cave 329, Cave 331, Cave 335, and Cave 372, totaling 26 square meters of exquisite Tang Dynasty murals, equivalent to 32,006 square centimeters.

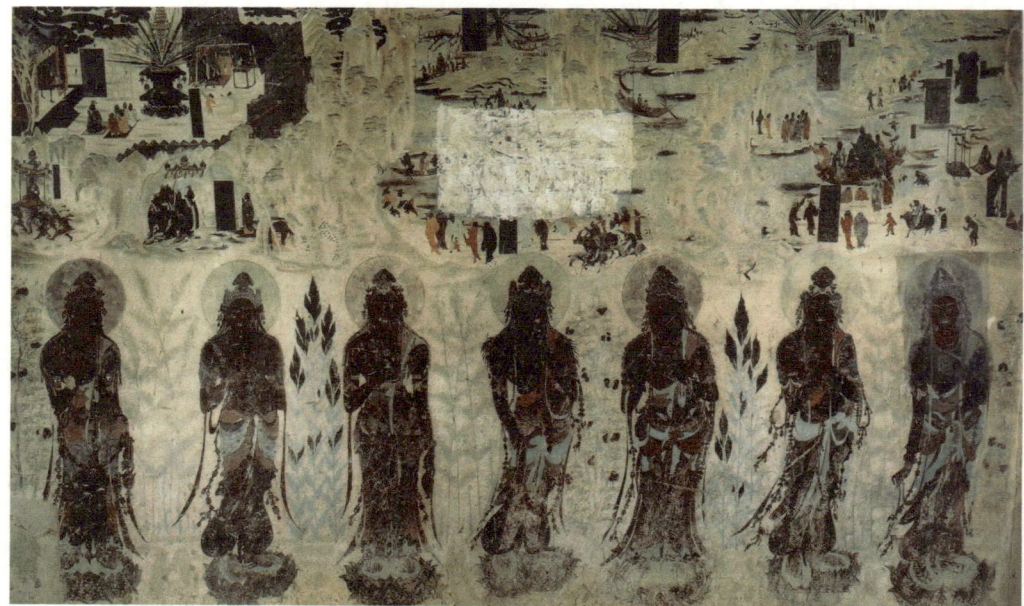

Figure 8-8 *The Story Mural of Gao Kui in Yangdu of the Eastern Jin Dynasty Obtaining the Golden Statue* from the 7th century AD in the early Tang Dynasty on the south wall of Cave 323 of the Mogao Grottoes and the traces of the murals glued away by Warner

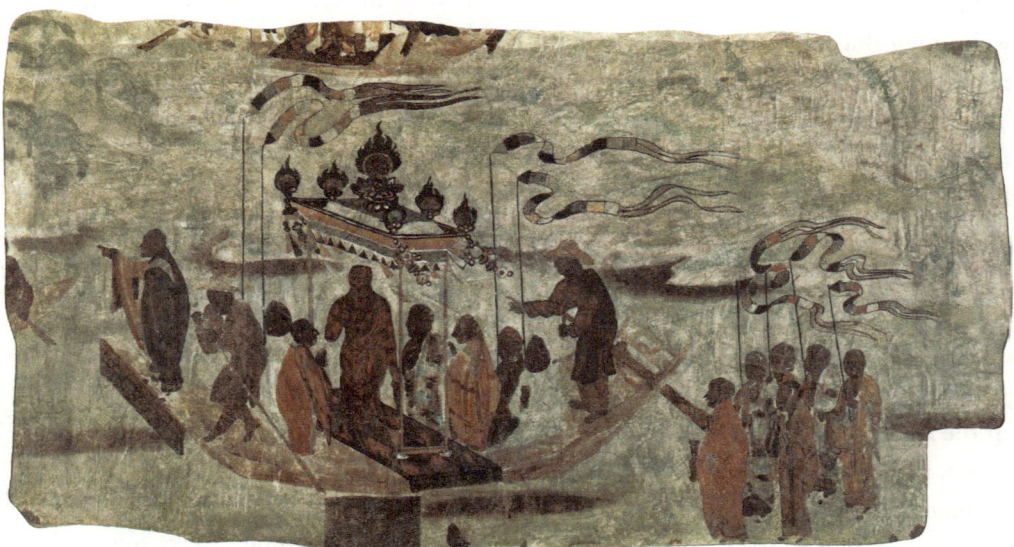

Figure 8-9 Part of *The Story Mural of Gao Kui in Yangdu of the Eastern Jin Dynasty Obtaining the Golden Statue* on the south wall of Cave 323 of the Mogao Grottoes (currently in the Harvard Art Museums, No. 1924.41)

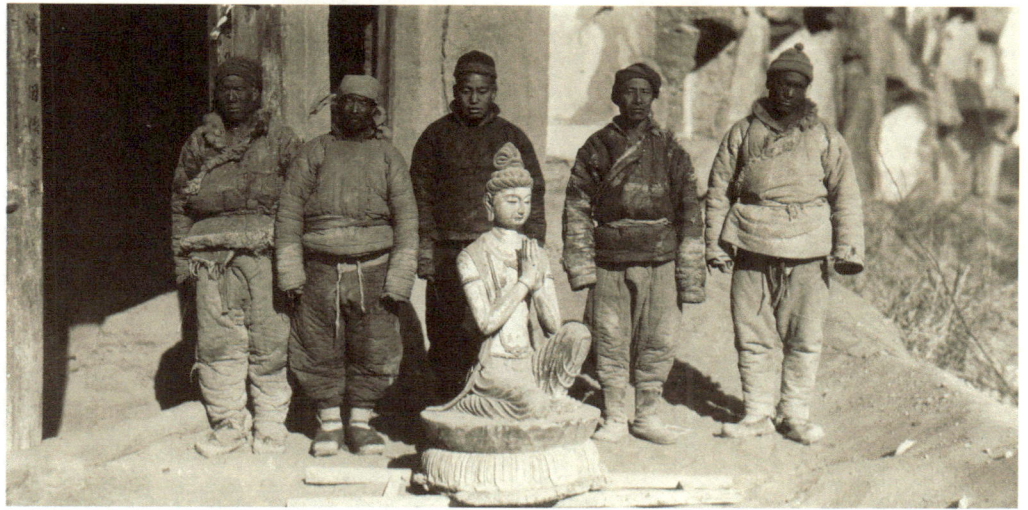

Figure 8-10 Warner removed the half-kneeling painted Bodhisattva statue from Cave 328 of the Tang Dynasty Mogao Grottoes in Dunhuang (1924)

Simultaneously, Warner secured a 120-centimeter-high Tang Dynasty exquisite painted sculpture—a Bodhisattva statue (Figure 8-10)—from Cave 328, striking a deal with Taoist Wang for 70 taels of silver. Warner meticulously documented the transaction details with Wang, who displayed a remarkably "open-minded" attitude toward Warner's use of strong glue to detach the murals, and he didn't hold the ancient colorful statues in the cave in high regard. His focus was on restoring the old statues and crafting new ones, which he considered a testament to his skill and a source of pride. Should Warner take away these new creations, it would equate to erasing Wang's accomplishments. When Warner expressed his desire to take a painted statue from the Mogao Grottoes, Wang assumed he meant a new statue and promptly declined. This left Warner baffled, and he hastily clarified that he merely intended to take an old one. Relieved, Wang agreed. Warner, overjoyed at securing Wang's approval, realized that Wang didn't comprehend the value of these ancient statues and regarded them as mere discarded and flawed items. Once again, Warner, like other members of foreign expeditions, took advantage of Wang's ignorance.

The statue of the kneeling Bodhisattva from the flourishing Tang Dynasty that Warner relocated was originally positioned on the right edge of the main niche in Cave 328, as one of the eight statues of Buddha on both sides of Sakyamuni Buddha (Figure 8-11). This Buddhist niche featured Ananda and Mahākāśyapa standing beside Sakyamuni, with two seated and two kneeling Bodhisattvas on each side of the niche, along with squatting Bodhisattvas. These eight statues surrounded the central Buddha, naturally guiding visitors' gazes to the majestic Buddha figure. These sculptures, distinct from stone statues, were crafted from a mixture of soil, straw, paper, and other fibers wrapped around a wooden framework to create an embryo. Shaping was done using a bamboo scraper, and

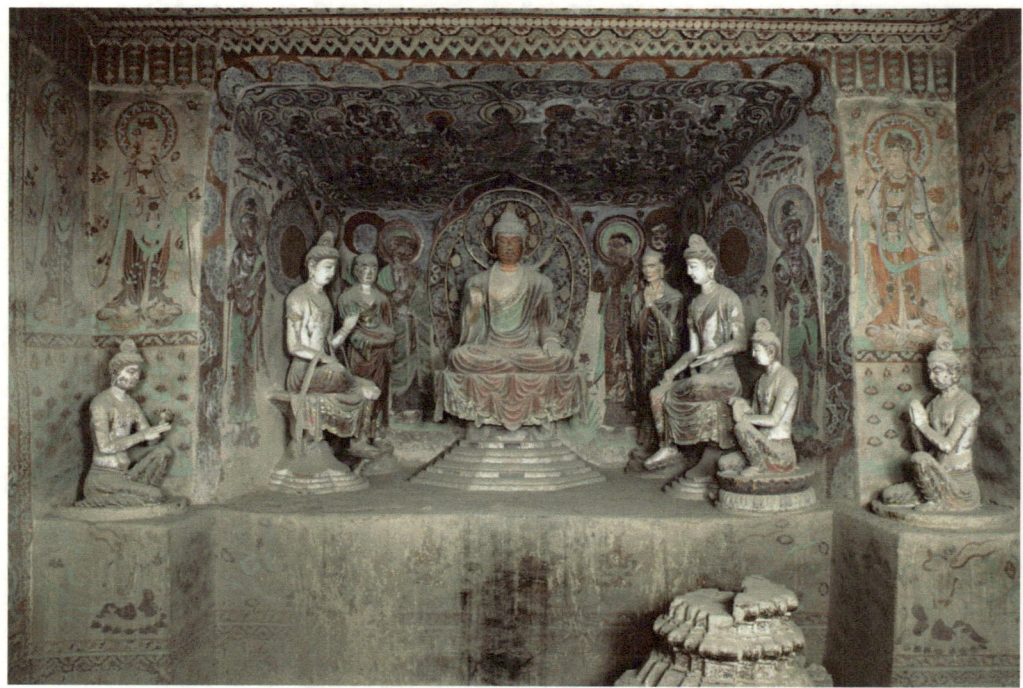

Figure 8-11 The main wall of Cave 328 of the Tang Dynasty Mogao Grottoes in Dunhuang

after the soil dried, they were painted white and adorned with intricate details such as color painting, piling, and gold tracing. The Bodhisattva statue, characterized by its slender and graceful form with a plump face, stands as a quintessential representation of Dunhuang Buddhist art.

In Warner's pursuit of removing the Bodhisattva statue, he irreversibly damaged its base, preserving only the part connected to the lotus base. This action resulted in severe harm to the statue. Additionally, three statues in the same cave, exhibiting nearly identical poses, differ significantly from the state of the one preserved at Harvard University. Despite careful cleaning and repair efforts within the cave, these statues remain extensively damaged, with colors appearing less vibrant compared to the restored ones at Harvard. The latter has undergone a restoration process, with mud and dust eliminated and many original colors shining as before. The smooth and ivory-like luster emanating from the Bodhisattva's arms is evident (Figure 8-12). Notably, this reflects different cultural relic restoration philosophies: some museums aim to showcase relics in their original appearance, utilizing processes like polishing or coloring on parts with known original features. In contrast, many other museums prioritize avoiding damage, refraining from processes like polishing or coloring. This diverse approach is evident in the varied presentation of artifacts, such as gold and silverware, which appear darkened due to oxidation in some museums, while appearing bright and reflective in others, as if recently used.

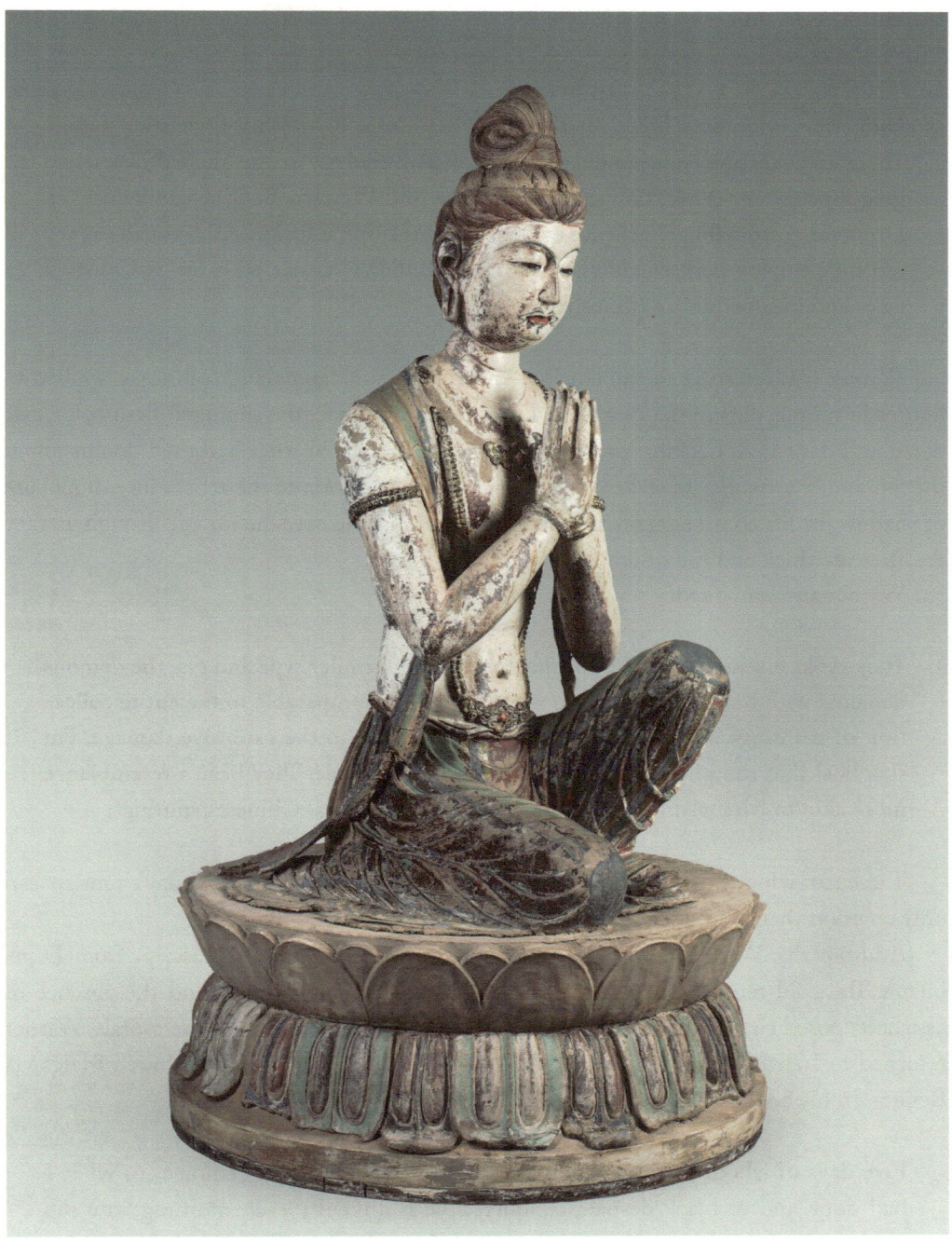

Figure 8-12 A painted statue of a kneeling Bodhisattva from Cave 328 of the Tang Dynasty Mogao Grottoes in Dunhuang (122 cm high, now in the Harvard Art Museums, No. 1924.70)

Warner's records encompass detailed descriptions of various murals and sculptures within the cave:

Numerous sculptures found in the caves date back to the Six Dynasties period. These caves feature central pillars, cross-footed Buddhas, wedge-shaped noses, and long tapered necks—a confluence of Eastern and Western Buddhist influences in Dunhuang, providing conclusive evidence of this cultural fusion. Additionally, many grottoes employ dark shadows, resulting in Buddha statues with fat and bloated faces and indiscernible outlines.

Warner was referring to the concave and convex smudge dyeing technique applied to figures in murals during the Northern Dynasties. Over time, the smudged flesh color oxidized and darkened. Lacking an understanding of murals, Warner harbored doubts about the remaining artworks, mistakenly attributing the oxidization to the artist's intentional use of shadow. In his comments on the Buddha statues in the cave, he noted, "Rough as they are, they are thick and full of power."

Warner also remarked:

They evoke a sense of Turpan for me. In caves of a similar type and era, the demons depicted with bold brushstrokes possess a strength comparable to the entire collection of paintings and sculptures here. However, due to the extensive damage, I'm skeptical that the photos can truly capture their essence. They bear a resemblance more akin to Michelangelo's sculptures than conventional Chinese paintings.

These surviving texts document the Mogao Grottoes in the 1920s. Today's tourists can only envision them through old photos and written accounts.

Additionally, Warner acquired a fragment of the *Lotus Sutra* manuscript from Dunhuang. The cold temperatures at that time hindered the use of glue, and the absence of assistants posed challenges. After completing the process of peeling off the murals, Warner returned to Lanzhou in April 1924 and then proceeded to return to the United States via Beijing. In his book *The Long Old Road in China* (Figure 8-13), he described:

Five days of labour from morning till dark and five nights of remorse for what I had done and of black despair, conquered with difficulty each morning, saw the fragments of paintings securely packed in felts and lashed tightly between flat boards, ready for the eighteen-weeks' trip by springless jolting cart, railroad, and ship to the Fogg Museum at Harvard (Figure 8-14).

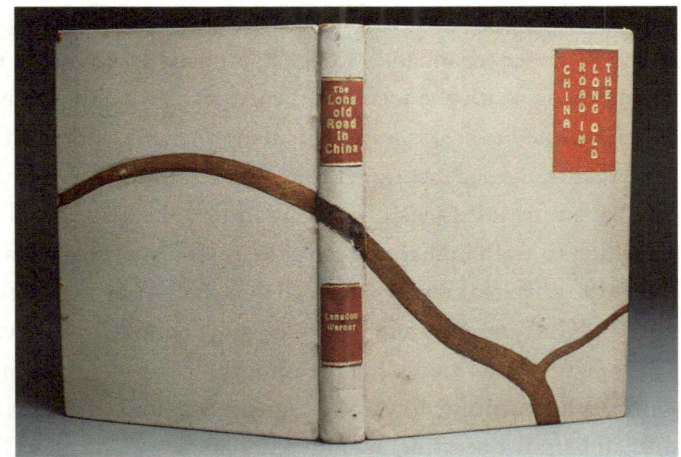

Figure 8-13 *The Long Old Road in China* by Warner, published in 1926

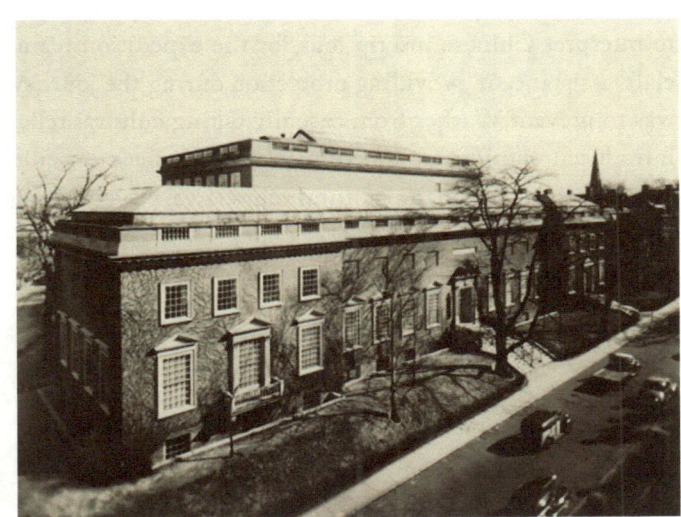

Figure 8-14 Harvard University's Fogg Museum in 1927

8.3 Failed Second Expedition

Following his initial journey to China, Warner returned to Harvard with cultural relics, garnering unprecedented commendation and support from the patrons of the Fogg Museum. Buoyed by this success, he swiftly decided to organize a more extensive expedition, with Dunhuang as the primary destination, aiming to unveil additional high-quality murals and transport painted sculptures. Thus, he embarked on assembling a second expedition team. Intent on carrying out this expedition more thoroughly and efficiently, he rigorously tested glue formulas in the United States, meticulously preparing for his return to the Mogao Grottoes. Warner put together a highly skilled team, appointing Jayne as deputy leader, enlisting Richard Starr for photography, and bringing on Daniel

Thompson for glue formulation and mural extraction. Alan Priest (1898–1969) took charge of mural preservation, and Horace P. Stimson assumed the roles of surveyor, recorder, and team doctor. With the focus on the exquisitely detailed Cave 285 in the Mogao Grottoes, Warner aimed to relocate its contents to the United States (Figure 8-15).

During his second expedition, Warner harbored another aspiration. As mentioned earlier, on his initial visit to China in 1916, he was tasked by Freer to establish a school in China to train archaeological talents. Despite Freer's passing, Warner remained committed to this goal and sought collaboration with a Chinese institution to delve into the study of Chinese culture. His choice was Peking University. However, during this period, Chinese scholars recognized the importance of safeguarding cultural relics, resulting in a shift in their attitude toward foreign archaeological teams. Combined with the prevalent anti-imperialist sentiments and xenophobia among the Chinese populace, his plans to cooperate with Peking University had to be set aside. Nevertheless, Chen Wanli (1892–1969) from Peking University volunteered to accompany him. Officially, Chen's role was to interpret Chinese inscriptions for the expedition team, and he also sought local officials' assistance in providing protection during the journey. In reality, his covert objective was to prevent Warner from casually taking cultural relics. Consequently, his colleagues introduced significant impediments to Warner's expedition activities while effectively safeguarding Dunhuang cultural relics. Every event along the way found its place in his personal diary, *Westward Journey Diary*.

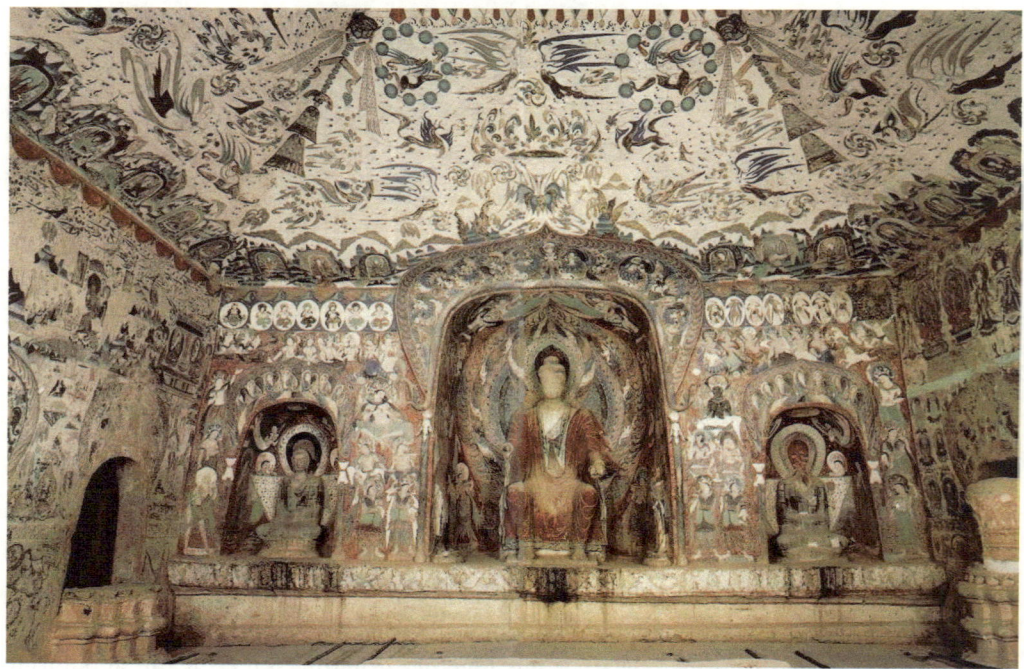

Figure 8-15 Interior of Cave 285 of the Western Wei Dynasty Dunhuang Mogao Grottoes

On February 16, 1925, the expedition team departed from Beijing, commencing their inspection. By May 19, they had reached Dunhuang. However, their request to inspect the Thousand Buddha Caves was initially rejected by the local authorities. Warner's prior destructive actions had left the local population resentful, and their inquiries made to Taoist Wang embarrassed Wang greatly. After deliberations, the Dunhuang County Government imposed a set of restrictions and regulations on the team. These included not staying at the Mogao Grottoes overnight, being accompanied and monitored by locals during cave visits, returning to the county on the same day, and strictly prohibiting any damage to murals or other cultural relics.

Moreover, the locals organized a monitoring team to keep a close eye on the expedition team's activities, with the looming possibility of armed conflict. Under such stringent surveillance, Warner and his team managed to purchase a local Dunhuang manuscript, the *Mahaprajna Sutra*, and took some photographs of the caves. Their inspection had to be concluded hastily, and they spent a total of only three days in Dunhuang before departing on May 23. Subsequently, they visited the Anxi Yulin Caves, where they took some photos. In 1938, Warner published the monograph *Buddhist Wall-Paintings: A Study of a Ninth-Century Grotto at Wan Fo Hsia*, which was the first to introduce this group of caves, making a significant academic contribution. The team also visited and photographed the Xiangdong Caves (the Queen Mother Palace Caves) in Jingchuan County in the Longdong region of Gansu Province.

On May 30, 1925, the May 30 Movement erupted across China. Peking University decided not to cooperate with Harvard University, sending a telegram to Chen Wanli to sever ties with the expedition team and return to school early. Taking into account the domestic situation in China, the United States also sent a telegram instructing Warner and his team to conclude their activities and return home. After Warner returned to Beijing, he continued to collect significant works of art for American museums. Together with his student Laurence Sickman (1907–1988), he visited the residence of Puyi, the last emperor of the Qing Dynasty, in Tianjin, as well as antique shops and markets in Liulichang, searching for various cultural relics that met the museum's selection criteria. In August 1925, Warner returned to Harvard University, while Sickman stayed in Beijing to continue the collection of cultural relics (Figure 8-16). In 1927, Warner was hired as a visiting scholar by the American Academy of Arts and Sciences.

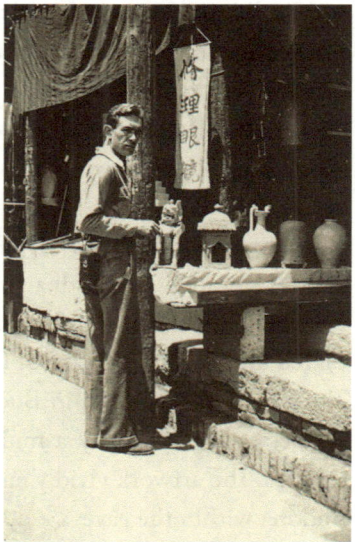

Figure 8-16 Lawrence Sickman at Luoyang Antique Market (1932)

8.4 A Contradictory "Protector of Cultural Relics"

Warner viewed his art inspection activities as "heroic," believing that his inspections and collection of cultural relics were crucial for protecting Chinese cultural heritage from destruction. He pointed to his observations at the Longmen Grottoes as evidence of the necessity of such actions.

Adorning the front wall of the Binyang Middle Cave, excavated during the Northern Wei Dynasty by Emperor Xuanwu in the Longmen Grottoes, are depictions of Emperor Xiaowen and Empress Wenzhao in the act of worshiping Buddha. In the early 1930s, the carved depiction of *Empress Wenzhao Attending Buddhist Rituals with Her Court* was stolen, and pieces of the sculpture were seen in the antique markets. When Sickman visited Longmen Grottoes in 1931, the vast portrayal of emperors and empresses worshiping Buddha, covering over ten square meters, was still intact. However, by late 1932, Sickman noticed fragments such as "a broken hand, a broken Buddha head, fragments of relief niche decoration and inscriptions" at a Beijing antique dealer. Immediately, with deep art appreciation, Sickman recognized that these fragments originated from the reliefs of *Emperor Xiaowen and Empress Wenzhao of the Northern Wei Dynasty Worshiping the Buddha* in the Binyang Middle Cave of Longmen Grottoes.

The Binyang Middle Cave features a horseshoe-shaped plan and contains a group of three Buddhas representing the past, present, and future, along with accompanying disciples and Bodhisattva statues. The depictions of emperors and empresses worshiping Buddha are situated on the lower layers of the north and south sides of the front wall doors, while the upper layer includes scenes of Vimalakīrti and Manjushri Bodhisattva preaching, as well as reliefs of Jataka stories of Mahāsattva prince sacrificing his life to feed the tiger, and Vessantara, a prince who gives away everything he owns. There are also relief sculptures of the Ten God Kings in the lower layer. The portrayal of *Emperor Xiaowen and Empress Wenzhao of the Northern Wei Dynasty Worshiping the Buddha* (Figure 8-17) captures the grand ceremony of Buddha worship within the Northern Wei Dynasty's imperial court. Featuring a multitude of figures and intricate composition, this depiction was meticulously carved under the patronage of Emperor Xuanwu, dedicated to earning merit for his parents. The two teams engaged in Buddha worship, one led by the emperor and the other by the empress, surrounded by a multitude of attendants bearing flowers, incense burners, and tributes. The artwork vividly encapsulates the ceremonial procession as they pay homage to Buddha within the cave.

Upon observing the fragments of the Buddha worshipping relief, Sickman became aware of potential damage to the Binyang Middle Cave within the Longmen Grottoes. He approached Yuan Tongli (1895–1965), director of the Peking National Library and a member of the Central Antiquities Preservation Commission of the Republic of China, seeking his protection for the Longmen Grottoes. However, Yuan rejected the proposal. When Sickman revisited Longmen in 1933, most of the *Empress Wenzhao Attending*

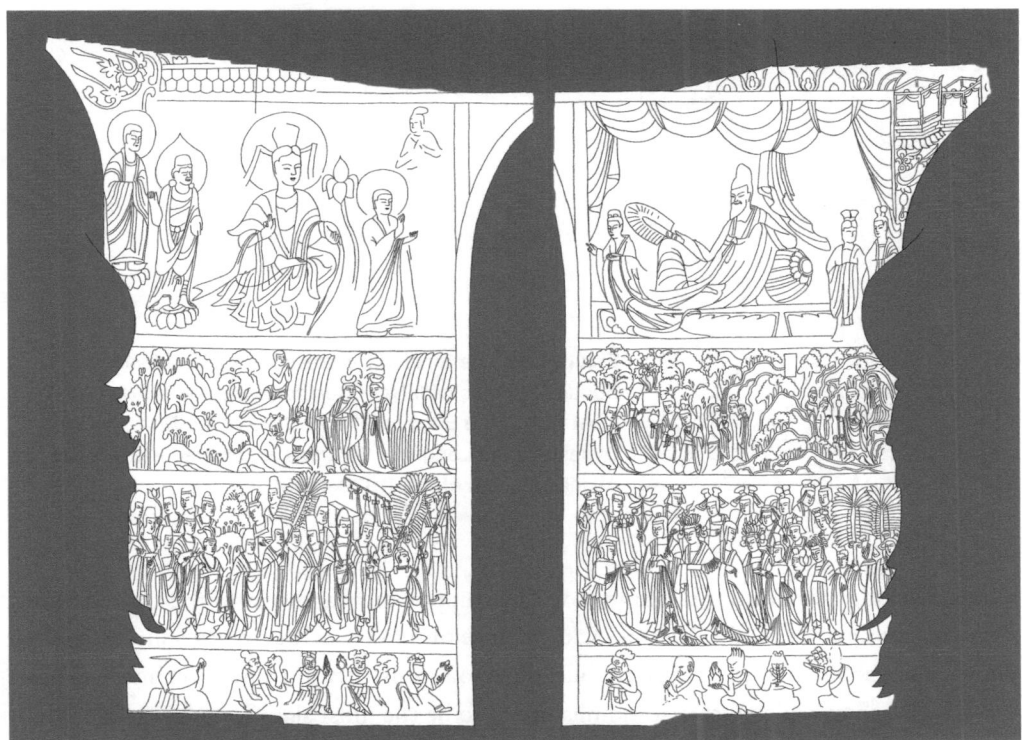

Figure 8-17 Actual measurement of the four-story reliefs on both sides of the front wall doors of the Binyang Middle Cave in the Northern Wei Dynasty at the Longmen Grottoes in Luoyang, Henan (from *Research on the Longmen Grottoes* by Mizuno Seiichi and Nagahiro Toshio)

Buddhist Rituals with Her Court had vanished. During Sickman's final visit to Longmen in 1934, he observed that the *Empress Wenzhao Attending Buddhist Rituals with Her Court* had been extensively stolen. Subsequently, he discovered that this significant relief sculpture had been acquired by numerous collectors, with most located in Beijing, Zhengzhou, Kaifeng, Shanghai, and even Germany. Due to the Longmen Grottoes' composition of Cambrian limestone, characterized by its hardness and fine texture, thieves attempting to steal these stone sculptures typically worked at night, chiseling randomly without regard for the integrity of the cultural relics. Consequently, these large stone statues were reduced to indistinguishable fragments in the hands of the thieves. Therefore, Sickman proposed the idea of collecting these fragments to Warner. After considering the proposal, Warner reached out to patrons of the Fogg Museum and the Nelson-Atkins Museum of Art, and the two institutions ultimately decided to collaborate in acquiring the fragments.

The collection of these fragments spanned over a year. In 1935, Sickman returned to the United States and assumed the role of curator for the Eastern Department at the Nelson-Atkins Museum of Art. Over the subsequent years, he diligently gathered both large and small fragments of the *Empress Wenzhao Attending Buddhist Rituals with Her Court* from

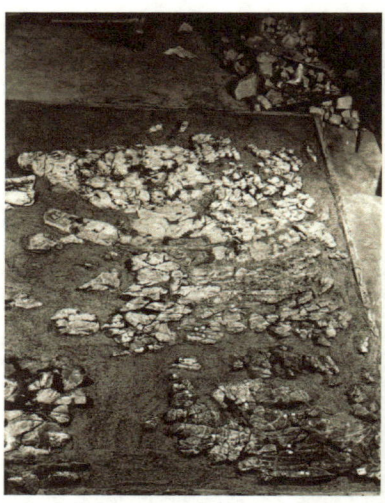

Figure 8-18 The relief of *Empress Wenzhao Attending Buddhist Rituals with Her Court* from the south side of the front wall of the Binyang Middle Cave of the Northern Wei Dynasty in the Longmen Grottoes assembled in the Nelson-Atkins Museum of Art. (1939–1940)

China. Packing them into three large boxes, he shipped the fragments to the United States. Between 1939 and 1940, the Nelson-Atkins Museum of Art meticulously spliced together photos and rubbings from previous publications to reconstruct this Buddhist image (Figure 8-18). Sickman considered this accomplishment to be the most significant in his life. Many years later, he reflected on the situation and wrote:

> Back then, I was a content and simple young man. Today, my temples have grayed, my body is bent, and my mind is not as sharp. Nevertheless, I successfully assembled the complete relief of *Empress Wenzhao Attending Buddhist Rituals with Her Court* (Figure 8-19). Journeying from place to place, spanning from Kaifeng to Zhengzhou, and even reaching Shanghai, I painstakingly collected each piece bit by bit—half a head here, a sleeve there, and a hand from Mr. Xia. Hundreds of tiny fragments … However, in the end, we meticulously pieced together the most significant single relief of early Chinese sculpture. I believe we have made a meaningful contribution to Chinese art and the world, and its true value can only be assessed by future generations. It took us three months of careful assembly, akin to a group of children sitting around all day, experimenting with this piece and that. Which piece should be placed where? Does it fit properly? Is it an eye or a fragment of dress lace?

Fate, in a whimsical twist, played a trick on him. Three months after completing this "jigsaw puzzle," Sickman went to China, only to discover that more fragments of the Buddha statues were still in China. He began to suspect that he had purchased some fake fragments. Despite collecting the fragments of Longmen stone carvings with the intention of saving the scattered ceremonial Buddha relief from antique dealers across China, they continued to be sold wherever he bought them. Did his desperate collection and purchasing

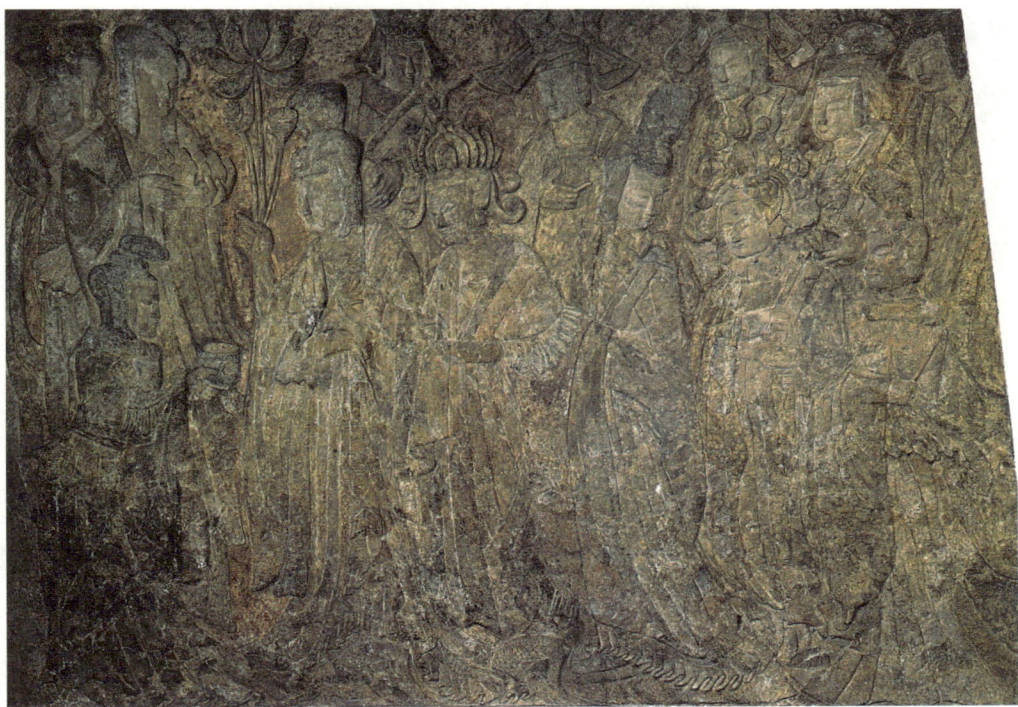

Figure 8-19 *Empress Wenzhao Attending Buddhist Rituals with Her Court* around AD 522 in the Northern Wei Dynasty, taken from the south side of the front wall of Binyang Middle Cave in Longmen Grottoes (203.2 cm × 278.13 cm, now in the Nelson-Atkins Museum of Art, Kansas City, USA, No. 40-38)

behavior unintentionally intensify the theft of Longmen Grottoes? Did good intentions lead to evil consequences? This conflicting question plagued him with self-doubt, casting a shadow over his entire life.

Another source of lifelong guilt for Sickman was the complete chiseling out of *Emperor Xiaowen Attending Buddhist Rituals with His Entourage* (Figure 8-20) by Alan Priest, the curator of Oriental Art at the Metropolitan Museum of Art in the United States. Alan Priest, a student of Warner who went to China with Warner's second expedition, considered Sickman a competitor. Upon learning that Sickman had obtained the fragments of *Empress Wenzhao Attending Buddhist Rituals with Her Court*, Priest promptly went to Beijing in the capacity of the Metropolitan Museum of Art's curator. In October 1934, he signed a contract with Yue Bin (1896–1954), an antique dealer in Liulichang, Beijing, to purchase *Emperor Xiaowen Attending Buddhist Rituals with His Entourage*. In 1935, Yue Bin successfully acquired this Buddha relief with the cooperation of bandits, security chiefs, and stonemasons in the Luoyang area, and it was subsequently collected by the Metropolitan Museum of Art that same year.

Whether it is *Empress Wenzhao Attending Buddhist Rituals with Her Court* or *Emperor Xiaowen Attending Buddhist Rituals with His Entourage*, these two rare treasures arrived in

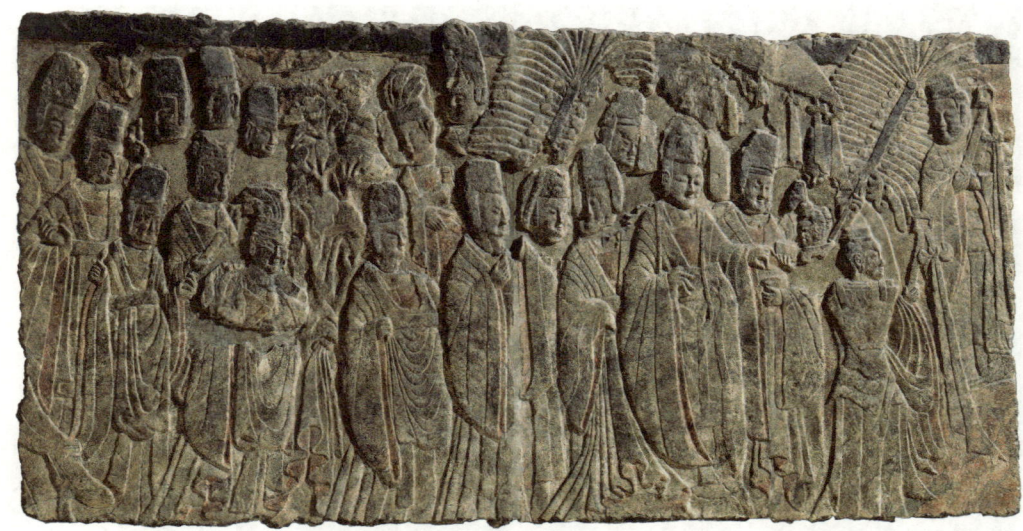

Figure 8-20 *Emperor Xiaowen and His Entourage Worshiping the Buddha* around 522 AD in the Northern Wei Dynasty, taken from the north side of the front wall of Binyang Middle Cave in Longmen Grottoes (208.3 cm × 393.7 cm, now in the Metropolitan Museum of Art, New York, USA, No. 35.146)

the United States as a pile of fragments, making identification challenging. Thanks to the persistent efforts of researchers, these two large reliefs were pieced back together and found their place in the Nelson-Atkins Museum of Art in Kansas City and the Metropolitan Museum of Art in New York, respectively. However, issues persist as some relief fragments may be fake, and the piecing together process is marred by numerous omissions and errors. Visible to the naked eye are incoherent lines between the relief characters and their bodies, as well as unrecoverable details like ribbon skirts, crowns, and necklaces. Facial expressions and other features, such as Emperor Xiaowen's stiff and disproportionate face, are evident, casting doubt on the authenticity of these reliefs. Moreover, in the present-day US antique market, head portraits of individuals from Buddhist ritual reliefs occasionally surface (Figure 8-21). Regardless of the ongoing authenticity debate, these two reliefs will not be returned to China, and the front wall of the Binyang Middle Cave in Longmen Grottoes remains forever unrestored.

Beyond these two reliefs of worshiping the Buddha, numerous museums in Europe and the United States possess Longmen Grottoes stone statues with challenging authenticity (Figure 8-22), documenting the tragic history of Longmen's century-old destruction. Whether it is the Fogg Museum, the Nelson-Atkins Museum of Art Museum of Art, the Metropolitan Museum of Art, or other museums that acquired the reliefs from Longmen Grottoes, they are all implicated in this history. Whether it was Sickman, who painstakingly pieced together *Empress Wenzhao Attending Buddhist Rituals with Her Court*, Alan Priest, who directed the forced removal of *Emperor Xiaowen Attending Buddhist Rituals with His*

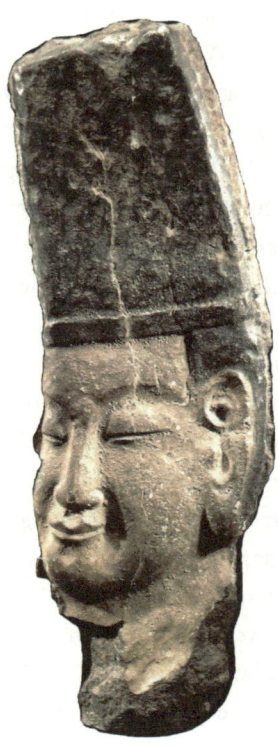

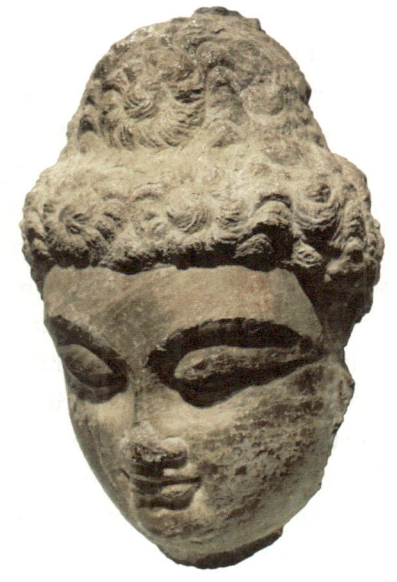

Figure 8-21 The head of Emperor Xiaowen's attendants from *Emperor Xiaowen and His Entourage Worshiping the Buddha* from the Binyang Middle Cave of Longmen Grottoes around AD 522 in the Northern Wei Dynasty appeared at the New York antique market in March 2017 (photographed by Chang Qing)

Figure 8-22 The head of the cave master Buddha in the Dongshan Drum Tower of Longmen Grottoes during Wu Zetian's reign (AD 684–704) (currently in the Asian Art Museum, San Francisco, USA, No. B60S38+, photographed by Chang Qing)

Entourage, or Yuan Tongli, who refused to protect the caves according to Sickman's notes, the stonemasons who carved out the Buddha statues in the cave, and even Warner, who was indirectly involved, will forever be intertwined with the Longmen Grottoes in the century-old history of cultural relic dispersion in China.

Driven by different motivations, Alan Priest and Sickman received contrasting evaluations from the Chinese. Alan Priest, who actively collaborated with Chinese profiteers to take *Emperor Xiaowen Attending Buddhist Rituals with His Entourage* to the United States, is criticized by the Chinese as an "imperialist cultural relic thief." On the other hand, Sickman, who played a pivotal role in collecting and integrating *Empress Wenzhao Attending Buddhist Rituals with Her Court*, is appreciated for saving this artistic masterpiece. Consequently, his actions have earned him respect in China, and he has maintained positive relations with the Chinese government.

Warner also commended Sickman's approach, even collaborating with him in saving *Empress Wenzhao Attending Buddhist Rituals with Her Court*. Warner staunchly defended their actions, stating, "If we are criticized for buying those fragments, then the love, labor, and money we spent in assembling these fragments should make all the accusations disappear. This work is a great contribution to China, and China has done nothing greater in this matter. It is worth noting that much of the destruction was done to satisfy orders from Western collectors using images supplied by buyers." Therefore, in his opinion, blame should first be directed toward the Chinese themselves for the loss of the artwork. According to Warner, neither he nor Sickman, along with other American museums, bear any responsibility; rather, their actions were driven by a genuine passion for preservation.

Examining remaining documents and diaries, it becomes evident that each person and museum involved sought to evade responsibility for the loss of cultural relics at Longmen Grottoes, engaging in finger-pointing and blame-shifting. The Metropolitan Museum of Art has maintained secrecy regarding the process of *Emperor Xiaowen Attending Buddhist Rituals with His Entourage* entering the museum, with all participants having passed away, leaving the assessment of merits and demerits to future generations.

Warner's looted cultural relics from Dunhuang are currently housed in the Harvard Art Museums. Calls from many Chinese individuals urge Harvard to return these painted sculptures and mural fragments. However, the museum contends that the purchase bill provided by Warner proves legal acquisition in Dunhuang, making their return unnecessary. This issue extends beyond Harvard, involving almost all Western museums holding Chinese cultural relics.

Such a response appears reasonable, considering that during that period, China lacked cultural relics protection laws, and there were no restrictions on allowing precious cultural relics to leave the country, as is the case today. Certain procedures, such as sales contracts, official cooperation approval, or permission from cultural relic custodians like Taoist Wang, were required for foreigners to acquire cultural relics in China. However, the undeniable reality is that Chinese cultural relics suffered significant damage in the process of their loss, emphasizing the importance of repatriating Chinese cultural relics to their place of origin.

8.5 Protectors of Nara and Kyoto

A few years ago, a documentary on World War II aired on China Central Television, recounting a remarkable episode. In 1945, sensing the fervor of the Japanese to engage in the war, the US military decided not to conduct targeted bombings against Japan, not limiting their attacks to military targets, but regardless of military and civilian buildings, bomb until the entire city turned into scorched earth. Tokyo was the focal point of the bombings, ultimately becoming a desolate landscape. However, the Americans, aware of Japan's rich history and culture, aimed to spare cities abundant in cultural relics. They sought the assistance of the renowned Chinese ancient architect Liang Sicheng (1901–1972), who was invited to the US warship in the Pacific engaged in attacking Japan. Liang marked two circles on a map of Japan, designating Nara and Kyoto. Consequently, the US military refrained from bombing these two cities, preserving countless ancient buildings and cultural relics.

Indeed, Nara and Kyoto are the two Japanese cities that preserve an abundance of ancient cultural relics. The Nara region holds historical significance, being the initial site where the capital was established in unified Japan. In AD 592, Asuka-kyo, Japan's earliest capital, emerged in the present-day Asuka region in Nara Prefecture. (This region, now Asuka Village, lies at the foothills of the southern end of the Nara Basin.) Subsequently, Fujiwara-kyo was constructed in the northwest (present-day Kashihara region of Nara Prefecture) of Heijo-kyo in AD 690, followed by Empress Genmei's (r. 707–715) relocation of the capital to Heijo-kyo in AD 710. Heijo-kyo (the contemporary urban area of Nara City) mirrored the layout of Tang Chang'an City, marking the political center of Japan for over 70 years during the Nara period. The Nara period, recognized for Japan's comprehensive adoption of Chinese influence, saw the imperial court dispatching envoys to the Tang Dynasty multiple times. These envoys returned with various artifacts, shaping a distinctive Japanese culture while faithfully preserving elements nearly obscured in China. In AD 784, the capital of Japan was moved to Nagaoka-kyo (now the junction of Muko City, Nagaoka-kyo City and Kyoto in Kyoto Prefecture). The Nara area, encompassing temples like Todai-ji, Yakushi-ji, and Kofuku-ji, witnessed the pinnacle of Buddhism during this period, maintaining prosperity and earning Nara the moniker of the "Southern Capital."

Kyoto, historically known as Heian-kyo, holds a pivotal position in Japanese history and culture. Designated as the capital of Japan in AD 794, it served as the political and cultural center throughout medieval and modern times until the capital was relocated to Tokyo in 1869. During the construction of Heian-kyo, the city was meticulously planned, drawing inspiration from the layout design of Luoyang City, the eastern capital of the Tang Dynasty. Heian-kyo's layout featured a palace city situated in the northwest corner, with the south and east sections forming Waiguo City. This city was divided into two parts: the west side, known as Chang'an (Ukyo), and the east side, named Luoyang (Sakyo). However, sakyo, representing Chang'an, experienced a rapid decline due to its low-lying and swampy terrain. In contrast, Sakyo, synonymous with Luoyang, thrived in terms of population and development. Over thousands of years, Kyoto has meticulously preserved numerous official offices, residences, Buddhist temples, and shrines. Together with Nara, Kyoto stands as the most representative showcase for observing Japanese traditional culture.

At the end of World War II, the US military did indeed take measures to protect certain Japanese cultural heritage. Despite bombing numerous cities, including Tokyo, and dropping atomic bombs on Hiroshima and Nagasaki, Nara and Kyoto were spared from destruction. However, the credit for this protection cannot be attributed to Liang Sicheng, as he was far away in Yunnan, China, avoiding the war and had no opportunity to influence decisions made on US warships in the Pacific.

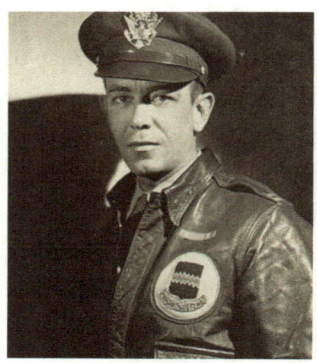

Figure 8-23 Sickman who enlisted in the army during World War II

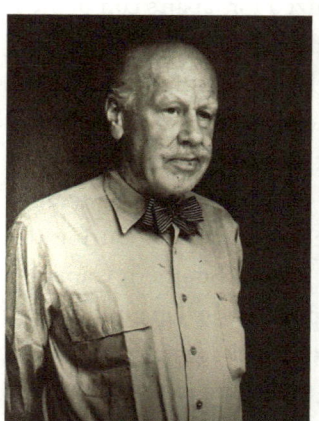

Figure 8-24 Warner as MFAA branch consultant in Japan (1946)

This protective measure was tied to a special agency of the US military. In 1943, as the United States entered World War II, the Allied forces established the Monuments, Fine Arts, and Archives (MFAA) Program. This program was affiliated with the Civil Affairs and Military Government Sections of the Allied Armies, and the primary goal of the MFAA Program was to assist and protect historical and cultural monuments in war zones during and after World War II, preventing war-related damage. The department consisted of approximately 400 military and civilian experts, collaborating to locate and return art and other culturally significant items that had been stolen or hidden by the Nazi government. Sickman, a student of Warner (Figure 8-23), enlisted in the army during World War II and served in this department.

In 1945, as the war with Japan approached its end, George Stout and Major Sickman, members of the MFAA, proposed establishing an MFAA chapter for Japan. Consequently, the Arts and Monuments Division of the Civil Information and Education Section was established under the General Headquarters of the Supreme Command of the Allied Powers in Tokyo.

From August 1945 to mid-1946, Stout served as the head of the department. During World War II, Langdon Warner, an archaeologist and director of the Oriental Department at Harvard University's Fogg Museum, held the position of the nation's top expert on Chinese and Japanese art history. From April to September 1946, he was engaged as a consultant to Japan's MFAA branch, providing advice on safeguarding Japan's cultural heritage (Figure 8-24). Notable members of this department also included the renowned Asian art historian Sherman Lee (1918–2008).

The suggestion to protect Nara and Kyoto, Japan, from US bombing during World War II has varying opinions. First, Sickman and Sherman Lee, working in the MFAA branch in Japan from the beginning, are likely to have proposed this measure. Second, as students of Warner, they probably discussed the idea with him before making suggestions. Therefore, it's plausible that the recommendation originated from Warner. In 1955, Emperor Showa of Japan awarded Warner the Order of the Sacred Treasure, recognizing his contribution to the study of Japanese art and culture (Figure 8-25). The Order of the Sacred Treasure, established in 1888, is awarded to individuals who have rendered meritorious service in public affairs and have been engaged in public service for many years. In the

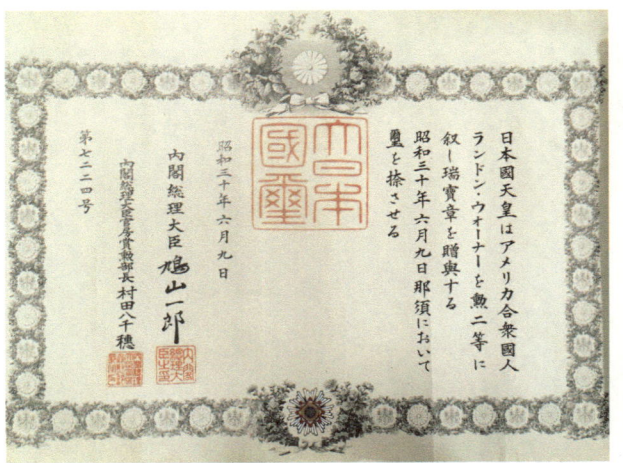

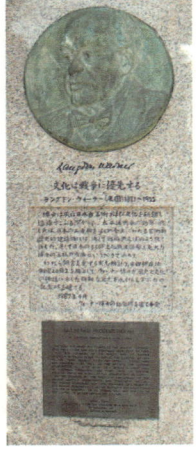

Figure 8-25 The Order of the Sacred Treasure awarded to
Warner by Emperor Showa of Japan on June 9, 1955

late stages of World War II, not only Nara and Kyoto but also Kamakura was spared from
Allied bombing. Kamakura served as the political center of the Kamakura shogunate from
1192 to 1333 and was the actual capital of Japan during that period, preserving numerous
historical and cultural relics. In April 1987, Japanese cultural groups established a monu-
ment to Warner in Kamakura to commemorate his role in protecting Japan's three ancient
capitals (Nara, Kyoto, and Kamakura) in the late World War II. The protective measures
taken by the US military are believed to have been rooted in Warner's recommendations
(Figure 8-26).

Thirdly, some individuals suggest that the idea to protect Nara and Kyoto, Japan, from
US bombing during World War II came from Henry Lewis Stimson (1867–1950), the US
Secretary of War. However, Stimson was not an expert on Japanese art history. Even if he
made such suggestions, it is likely that he consulted experts like Warner, Sickman, Sherman
Lee, and others. In summary, during the late stages of World War II, when the US military
was conducting strategic bombing in Japan, especially in preparation for using atomic
bombs, deliberate efforts were made to avoid targeting Kyoto and Nara, ancient cities rich in
historical relics. This strategic decision effectively protected Japan's cultural heritage, which
is considered an integral part of the cultural heritage of all mankind, and the contribution
of those involved, including Americans, cannot be overlooked.

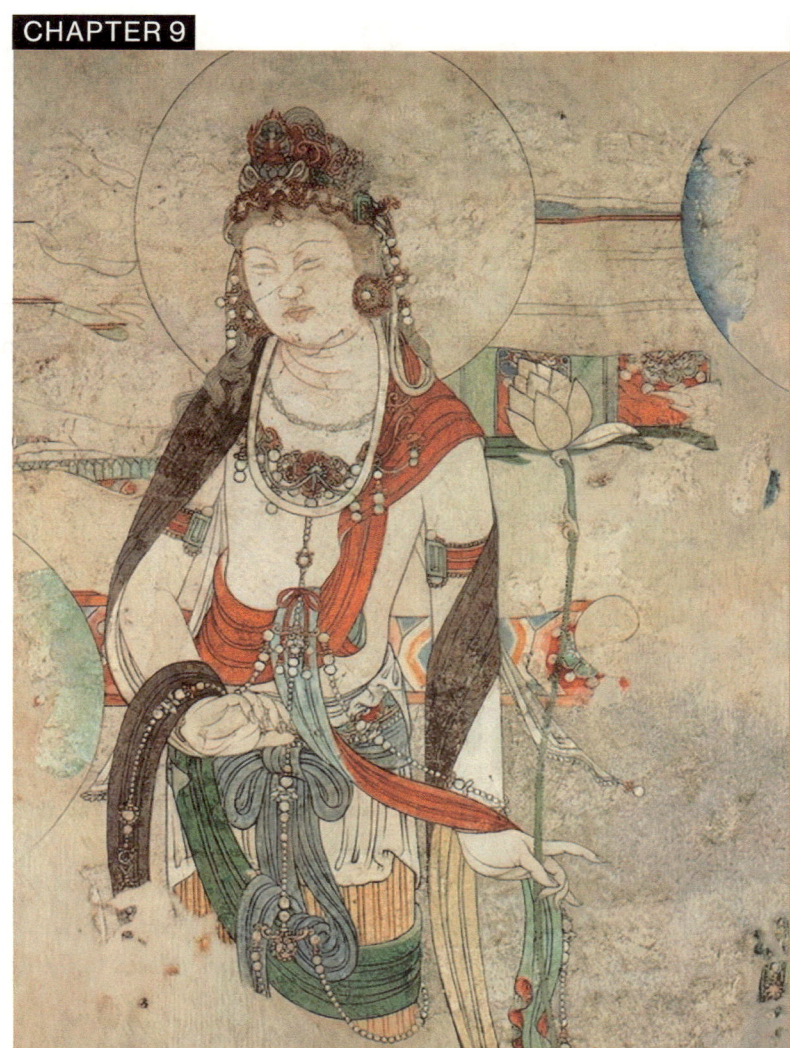

Antique Dealer:
Ching Tsai Loo

— 1908

Ching Tsai Loo opened Laiyuan & Co. in Paris, with branches soon opened in Beijing and Shanghai, thus starting his own antique business.

— 1915

Loo and Shanghai native Wu Qizhou opened the largest antique shop in the United States, Loo-Wu Company, on the corner of Madison Avenue and 57th Avenue in New York. Among the *Six Steeds of Zhao Mausoleum* of the Tang Dynasty, *Saluzi* and *Quanmaogua* were smuggled out of Xi'an and transported to the United States by Loo.

— 1928

The royal tombs of the Eastern Zhou Dynasty and noble cemeteries were discovered in Jincun, Luoyang, Henan. Many of the cultural relics were sold to the United States by Loo.

— 1935

London held the China Art World Expo, and Loo donated a 5.78-meter-high white stone standing Buddha statue from the Sui Dynasty to the British Museum.

— 1948

At Chen Mengjia's instigation, Loo donated the Warring States bronze Linghu Sizi kettle unearthed in Jincun, Luoyang, Henan, in 1928 to the exhibition hall of cultural relics in Tsinghua University.

9.1 From Paris to New York

When a cultural relic is sold from China to overseas countries, it undergoes a series of steps involving various entities. This process includes Chinese cultural relic sellers, both individual and familial, Chinese and Western antique dealers, and Western archaeologists and collectors, including museum curators. Western archaeologists excavate and acquire cultural relics from ancient sites, subsequently transporting them to museums in their respective countries. Some relics may be handed over to relic dealers or kept in the archaeologists' personal collections. Cultural relic sellers, often heirs or intentional seekers, play a crucial role in overseas sales by offering relics to antique dealers who act as intermediaries between sellers and buyers.

Antique dealers play a pivotal role in deciding which countries to export cultural relics to and identifying potential buyers, based on market dynamics. Transactions can occur privately or through large public auctions organized by these dealers. Throughout history, substantial sums of money have been involved in grand auctions featuring Chinese cultural relics, orchestrated by cultural relic dealers.

The final link in this transaction chain is the Western buyers of cultural relics, who can be categorized into private collectors and museum curators. Private collectors acquire relics out of passion and interest, while museum curators use public funds to directly purchase cultural relics, contributing to the enhancement of museum collections. Museums then publicly display these artifacts. Therefore, compared with private collectors, curators are often more generous and with more substantial demands. Antique dealers often value the opportunity to collaborate with museum curators, taking pride in the fact that their acquired artifacts may be purchased and showcased in renowned museums.

Among the numerous antique dealers in the West specializing in trading Chinese cultural relics, Loo-Wu Company and Yamanaka & Co. stand out as the most renowned. In the first half of the 20th century, these entities virtually monopolized the trade of selling Chinese cultural relics to major museums in the United States. Their straightforward business model involved transporting valuable ancient Chinese cultural relics abroad and selling them to affluent and influential foreign collectors or museums.

Ching Tsai Loo (1880–1957), the founder of the Loo-Wu Company, played a pivotal role in the Western antique circle (Figure 9-1). Born in Lujiadu, Huzhou, Zhejiang, in 1880, he originally bore the name Huanwen before later adopting the name Ching Tsai (Figure 9-2). Born into poverty and orphaned at a young age, Loo was initially fostered in the family of a distant cousin. Subsequently, he joined the affluent Zhang family in Nanxun, where he worked as a servant for Zhang Jingjiang (1877–1950), the eldest son of the Zhang

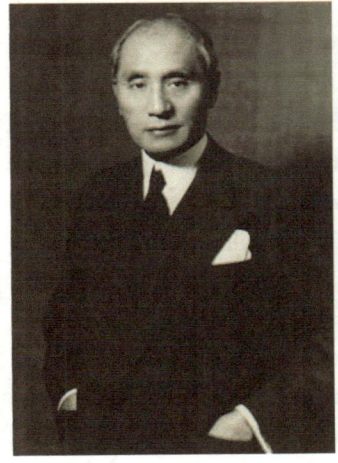

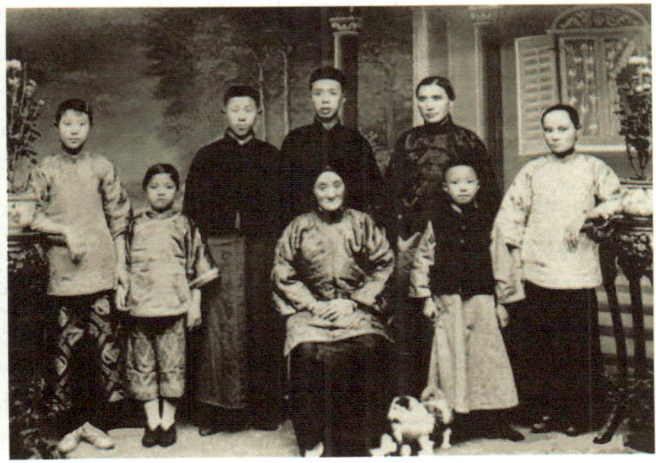

Figure 9-1 Ching Tsai Loo

Figure 9-2 Ching Tsai Loo (second from right) with his family (taken around 1900)

family. Zhang Jingjiang, a native of Huzhou, Zhejiang, hailed from a prosperous family of silk merchants in the south of the Yangtze River. Despite being physically disabled, he earned a reputation as a hero and a close friend of Sun Yat-sen. Later, he became sworn brothers with Chiang Kai-shek and held a prominent position as one of the four elders of the Kuomintang, serving as the Chairman of the Standing Committee of the Central Executive Committee. In 1902, Zhang Jingjiang assumed the role of commercial counselor of the Qing court in France. Due to limited mobility, he brought Loo with him to Paris.

Once in Paris, the astute Zhang family swiftly assisted Zhang Jingjiang in establishing the Ton-ying trading company, which primarily dealt in tea, silk, and antiques, enjoying considerable prosperity. The late Qing Dynasty's political turmoil resulted in the loss of many Chinese antiques, sparking a craze for collecting Chinese artifacts abroad. For instance, a small white porcelain bowl from the Song Dynasty, purchased for ten silver dollars in Shanxi, could fetch 10,000 US dollars in Paris. Similarly, a 300 silver dollars ceramic Avalokitesvara acquired from a temple was sold to the Metropolitan Museum of Art in New York for 500,000 US dollars. The value of antiques surged rapidly, contributing to the substantial profits of Zhang Jingjiang's trading company, whose earnings were dedicated to supporting Sun Yat-sen's revolutionary cause.

During this period, Loo, originating from humble beginnings and initially unfamiliar with the language, embarked on his journey as an errand boy, doorman, and apprentice in an antique shop. Diligently immersing himself in the intricacies of the antique business, he gradually acquired proficiency in English and French. Bolstered by Zhang Jingjiang's support, Loo swiftly ascended to the position of shopkeeper at the antique store of the Ton-ying Company. In 1908, as Zhang Jingjiang returned to China to aid Sun Yat-sen in the revolution, the 28-year-old Loo chose to reinvent himself. Renaming himself Ching Tsai Loo, he officially founded his own enterprise, Laiyuan & Co., in Paris. Expanding his footprint, he established branches in Beijing and Shanghai, initiating his foray into the world of antiques. C. T. Loo, an English abbreviation for his new name, now adorns labels and documents accompanying cultural relics in major museums across the United States, Britain, France, and beyond.

Even during his employment at Ton-ying Company in Paris, Loo foresaw the United States emerging as the epicenter of the global antique market. Zhang Jingjiang, known for his kindness and generosity, did not harbor resentment toward Loo for parting ways. On the contrary, he granted permission for Loo to retain his company's clientele. Capitalizing on the customer base cultivated over the years, Loo, fueled by ambition, joined forces with Shanghai native Wu Qizhou in 1915. Together, they inaugurated Loo-Wu Company, the largest antique shop in the United States, strategically located on the corner of Madison Avenue and 57th Avenue in New York. Specializing in the sale of Chinese cultural relics to the United States, Loo-Wu Company already exhibited a well-defined division of labor. Loo managed overseas customer communication, while partners Zhu Xuzhai and Miu Xihua in Beijing handled procurement and shipment to Wu Qizhou in Shanghai. From

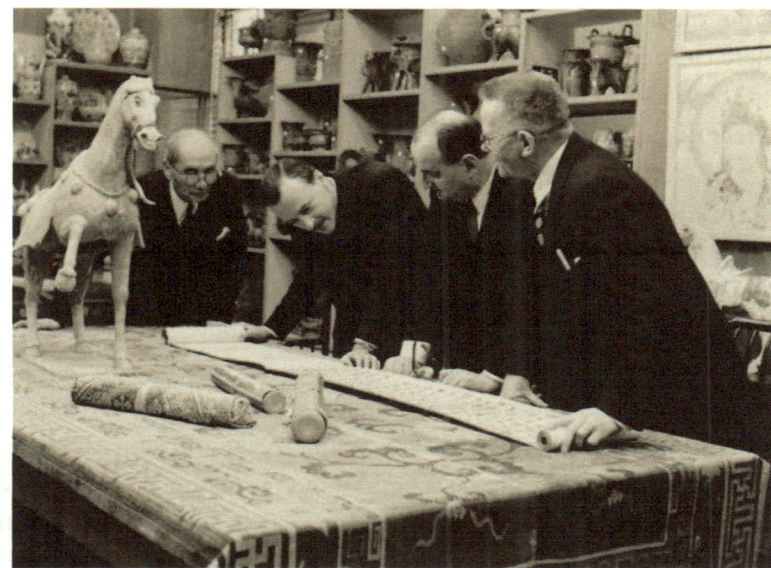

Figure 9-3 Loo receiving important customers to view ancient Chinese calligraphy works in his antique shop (first half of the 20th century)

there, the relics were transported to Paris or New York. Thus, Loo-Wu Company emerged as the earliest, largest, and most enduring Chinese cultural relics export enterprise.

Before Loo started business in New York, several East Asian cultural relics dealers had already gained prominence in the United States, selling Chinese cultural relics to Western audiences. During this time, while Loo was still engaged in his work in Paris, the New York branch of the Japanese Yamanaka & Co. had been operating since 1899, more than a decade lead than the Loo-Wu Company. However, Loo strategically charted the course for his company's operations, leveraging domestic resources and relationships to transform Loo-Wu Company into the most professional Chinese cultural relics export enterprise.

Eager to swiftly penetrate the market, Loo drew inspiration from the opulent store decorations of his competitors. He adorned his establishment with an array of antiques and cultural relics, creating an all-encompassing ambiance designed to allure antique enthusiasts into his store (Figure 9-3). In a bid to expand his clientele further, he composed a letter to the oil tycoon John Davison Rockefeller, Jr. (1874–1960), introducing himself and attaching an extensive list of clients he had amassed during his work at Tong-yin. His adept English skills and impressive calligraphy, coupled with the endorsement of his clients, contributed to his success in the United States.

Soon, renowned figures in the American collecting realm became his patrons. In addition to John Rockefeller Jr., notable names included bankers such as J. P. Morgan (John Pierpont Morgan Sr., 1837–1913), Benjamin Altman (1840–1913), and Richard Eugene Fuller (1897–1976), among others. Another crucial client was Charles Lang Freer (1854–1919), whom Loo encountered at the Panama-Pacific International Exposition in San Francisco. As the foremost collector of Chinese cultural relics in the United States from the late 19th to the early 20th century, Freer acquired a substantial number of Chinese cultural relics from Loo. Before his passing, Freer bequeathed his entire collection to the US federal government, funding the establishment of his museum, the renowned Freer Gallery of Art.

9.2 Flowing Money and Cultural Relics

In addition to ceaselessly captivating individual buyers, Loo dedicated substantial efforts to captivating museums with substantial financial resources, formidable purchasing capabilities, and discerning demands. Distinguished institutions such as the Metropolitan Museum of Art in New York, the Museum of Fine Arts in Boston, the Fogg Museum at Harvard University, and the Freer Gallery of Art in Washington, D.C., were high-priority targets for his endeavors. Loo actively nurtured connections with the heads of the Asian departments at these prestigious museums, proactively engaging in the donation of ancient works of art to foster and strengthen positive relationships. During his stay in Beijing in 1917, he proactively reached out to the director of the University of Pennsylvania Museum, expressing his intention to provide information about collections suitable for their museum.

His strategic efforts yielded extensive connections and substantial profits. In 1921, Loo proposed selling a Tang Dynasty bronze Avalokitesvara head to Rockefeller for 40,000 US dollars, but Rockefeller negotiated it down to 25,000 US dollars. The two engaged in persistent negotiations, with neither party yielding. Eventually, Loo opted not to proceed with the deal with Rockefeller and successfully sold the statue to the Museum of Archaeology and Anthropology at the University of Pennsylvania for 40,000 US dollars. Despite this particular deal not materializing, Loo continued working diligently to maintain a positive relationship with Rockefeller and successfully concluded other deals subsequently. Over the 30 years following Freer's passing, the Freer Gallery of Art invested 860,000 US dollars to acquire 124 pieces from Loo, significantly enhancing the gallery's exhibition area featuring bronzes, jades, and Buddhist statues. This underscores the importance of the connections that Loo held in high regard.

To ensure a steady supply of cultural relics for sale, Loo proactively enlisted people to search for precious artifacts, sparing no expense (Figure 9-4). In 1914, he organized an expansive antique exhibition in Paris, showcasing, among other items, six fully carved Buddha statues from the Xiangtangshan Grottoes. Located in Handan, Hebei Province, near Yecheng (present-day Linzhang of Hebei, where Hebei and Henan meet), the capital of the Northern Qi Dynasty, the Xiangtangshan Grottoes, built in Gushan Mountains, boast three areas: North Xiangtangshan, South Xiangtangshan, and Little Xiangtangshan (Shuiyu Temple). The North Xiangtangshan Grottoes were funded by the Northern Qi royal family, and legends suggest that its north grotto was the actual burial site of Gao Huan (AD 496–547), a powerful minister of the Eastern Wei Dynasty. The construction of South

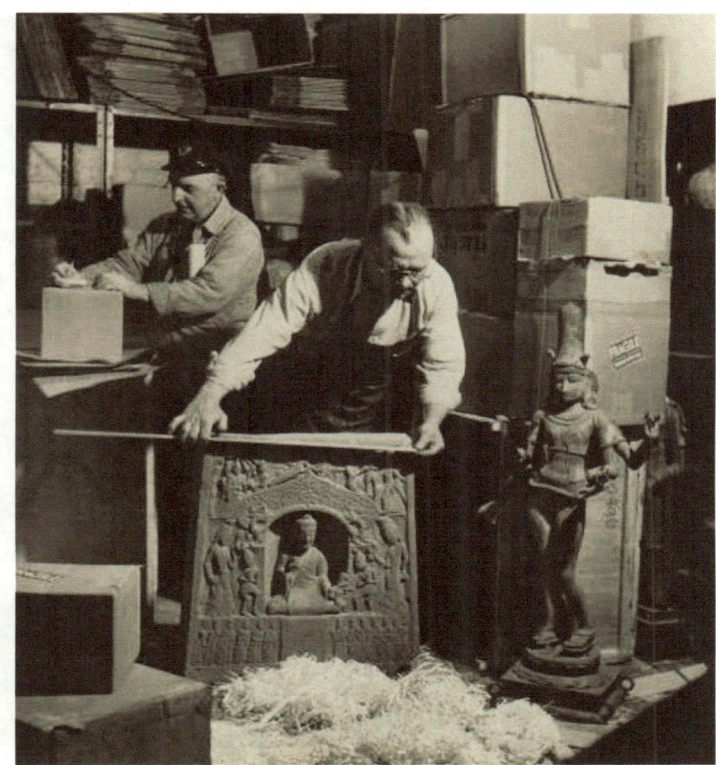

Figure 9-4 Loo unpacking and registering the Northern Wei Dynasty Buddhist statue stele shipped from China (first half of the 20th century)

Xiangtangshan and Little Xiangtangshan was funded by nobles at that time. The statues in the Xiangtangshan Grottoes exhibit a unique artistic style, extending from the graceful lines and clear statues of the late Northern Wei Dynasty, influenced by the Southern Dynasties (AD 420–589) and the Western Regions, distinct from the robust and majestic style of the Yungang Grottoes in Datong, Shanxi during the mid-Northern Wei Dynasty.

Regrettably, such significant Northern Qi grottoes have endured a state of disrepair for an extended period, largely attributed to the plundering by cultural relic dealers during the years of the Republic of China. Sadly, only a fraction of the original 4,000 or so Buddha statues remains intact. Loo played a role in contributing to the tragic fate of the Xiangtangshan Grottoes by dispatching individuals to remove numerous exquisite statues and subsequently selling them overseas. However, during this time, Chinese stone statues did not capture widespread attention in the West, and as a result, these statues struggled to find buyers in Paris, France. Consequently, Loo opted to gift these artworks to various museums as a means of building connections. George Byron Gordon (1870–1927), the discerning director of the Museum of Archaeology and Anthropology at the University of Pennsylvania, displayed remarkable foresight. Recognizing the value of the sculptures from South Xiangtangshan, he approached Loo and acquired the complete set for 5,000 US dollars each, including a Pratyeka-Buddha and two Bodhisattvas, esteemed as rare and exquisite works

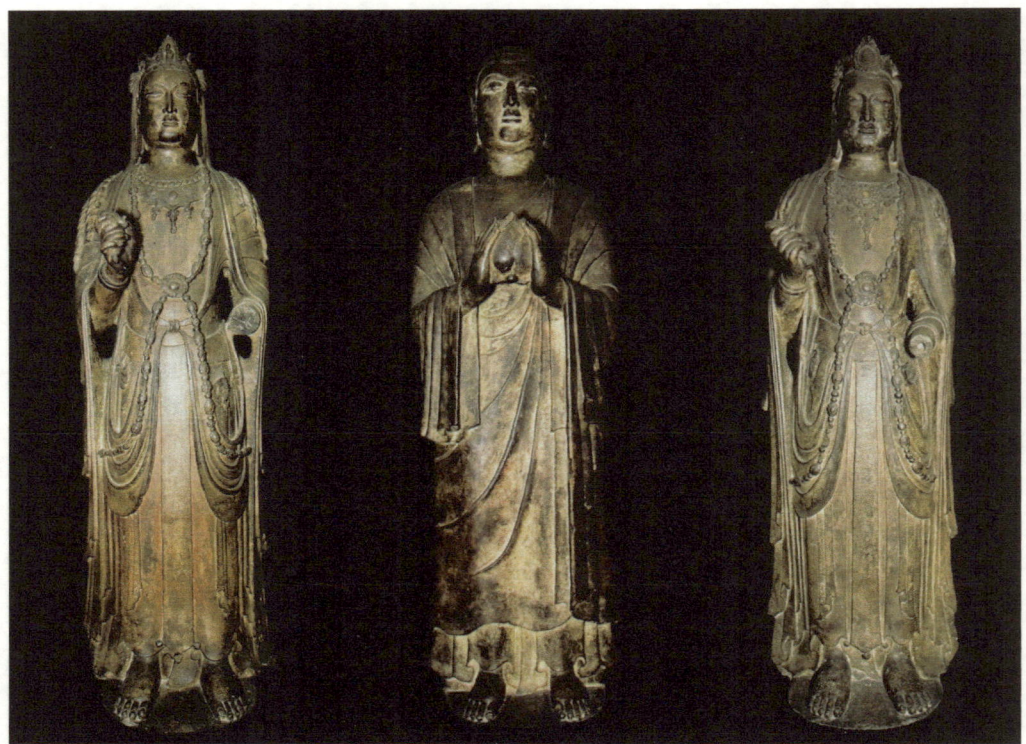

Figure 9-5 Northern Qi stone statues of Pratyeka-Buddha and two Bodhisattvas from the South Xiangtangshan Caves in Handan, Hebei Province (now in the Museum of Archaeology and Anthropology at the University of Pennsylvania, numbered from left: C113, C151, C150)

among the Xiangtangshan Grottoes statues collected overseas. While the price of 5,000 US dollars per piece may be one zero less than the 50,000 US dollars for a Qianlong period calligraphy and painting, the profit margin is substantial.

Driven by his passion for Chinese art, Gordon showcased these Chinese exhibits in the museum's most distinctive circular dome hall. The Pratyeka-Buddha and two Bodhisattvas statues now grace this space (Figure 9-5). The centerpiece, Pratyeka-Buddha, is the most complete statue. Adorned with a spiral-shaped bun atop his head, a right-sided monk's branch inside, and an outer lapel-style coat, he delicately places his hands on his chest while holding a budding lotus. Reflecting the typical tube-shaped simplicity of the late Northern Qi Dynasty, it is complemented by the intricate carvings and elaborate attire of Avalokitesvara and Mahasthamaprapta. Wearing complex crowns, necklaces, armlets, and bracelets, they exude grace and opulence. These three statues showcase the exceptional cave carving skills of the Northern Qi Dynasty. Due to the multitude of ancient Chinese artworks on display within, this hall has earned the moniker Chinese Rotunda.

Loo's dealings with the University of Pennsylvania Museum extended to the sale of two Bodhisattva heads and a Buddha head from the Xiangtangshan Grottoes. These exquisite works of Xiangtang stone carving art showcased natural and realistic techniques, portraying faces with gentle and serene expressions, evoking a sense of compassion. This marked the maturity of sculpture during the Northern Qi Dynasty. However, this museum's generous acquisitions inadvertently triggered heightened poaching of the Xiangtangshan Grottoes and other cave temples in China. Statistics reveal that, aside from the University of Pennsylvania Museum, the Metropolitan Museum of Art houses four Xiangtangshan statues (Figure 9-6). The Victoria and Albert Museum in London possesses Xiangtangshan Grottoes statues with fully preserved halo-ornaments on their backs. The Freer Gallery of Arts boasts a substantial collection of Xiangtangshan statues, notably the monumental Western Pure Land relief from South Xiangtangshan, a masterpiece of the Xiangtangshan Grottoes. Additionally, plenty of Xiangtangshan Grottoes statues are housed in institutions such as the Asian Art Museum in San Francisco, Columbia University Libraries in New York, Harvard Art Museums, San Diego Museum of Art, Osaka City Museum of Art in Japan, and some became the possession of private collectors. In pursuit of increased sales profits, Loo once divided a Buddha statue into multiple pieces, resulting in the rare historical occurrence of a dismembered Buddha statue. The Buddha's head stands now in the Victoria and Albert Museum in London, its right hand is in the Metropolitan Museum of Art in New York, and its left hand, holding a ribbon, is housed in the Asian Art Museum in San Francisco. Such dismemberment of a Buddha statue is a rare occurrence in history.

As an astute businessman, Loo recognized the ambition of major Western museums to establish unparalleled collections and outshine others. Rather than selling the entire collection he acquired in China at once, he adopted a strategic approach, requesting prices individually and navigating the market trends. His exceptional discernment of Chinese cultural relics, genius business vision, and extensive high-quality Chinese cultural relics gradually earned him acclaim within European and American collecting circles. His fame and connections soon positioned him as a supplier and cultural relic appraisal consultant for numerous museums. Visitors to his antique shop were predominantly business tycoons or experts actively engaged in the cultural relics and art realms (Figure 9-7), attesting to the invaluable Chinese cultural relics involved in his transactions, ranging from exquisite sculptures and murals to bronzes and jades.

Loo, with his distinctive aesthetic appreciation of Chinese art, systematically sent dozens of Avalokitesvara statues from various Chinese dynasties to the United States, predominantly featuring the renowned Water-Moon Avalokitesvara (Figure 9-8). Originating in the Tang Dynasty, this Avalokitesvara image gained popularity during the Song Dynasty, embodying a native representation not seen in India, specifically found in locations like the Dunhuang Mogao Grottoes, Yulin Caves, and various temples. The serene and tranquil demeanor of the Water-Moon Avalokitesvara resonates with Western aesthetics. Among the Water-Moon Avalokitesvara statues sold overseas by Loo, the one housed in the Nelson-Atkins Museum of Art in Kansas City stands out as the most complete and beautiful. This 2-meter-high wooden statue from the Liao Dynasty (AD 907–1125) impeccably preserves

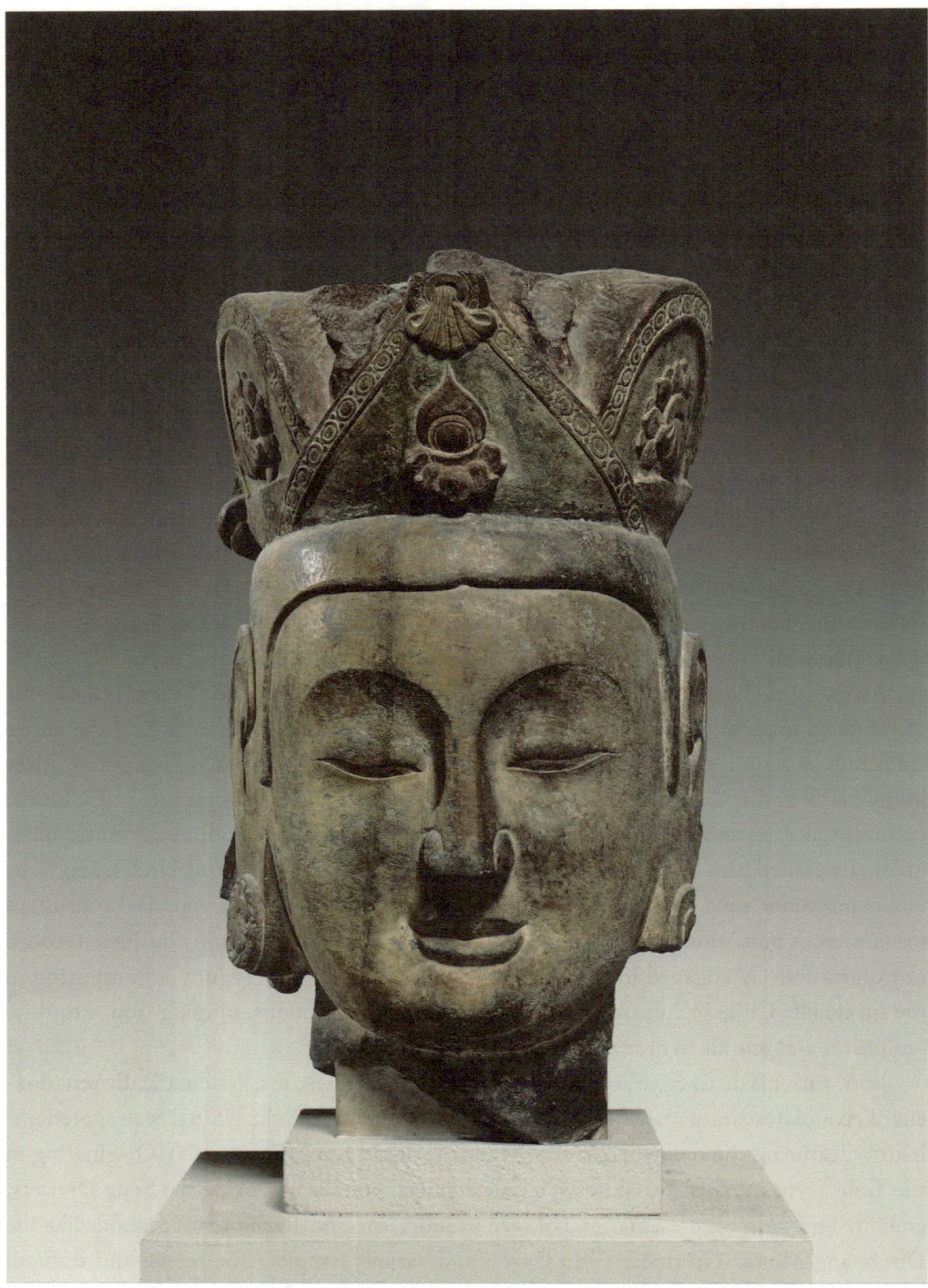

Figure 9-6 Northern Qi stone Bodhisattva head from the middle cave of North Xiangtangshan Grottoes in Handan, Hebei Province (81.3 cm high, 44.5 cm wide, 30.5 cm thick, now in the Metropolitan Museum of Art, No. 51.52)

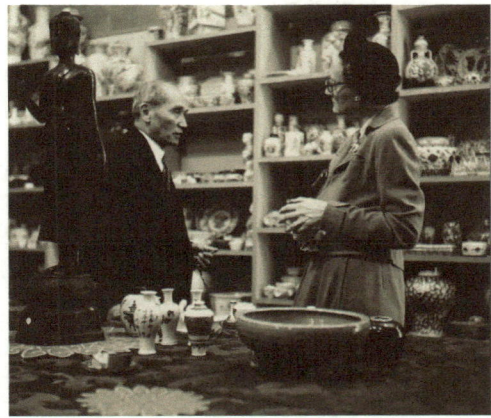

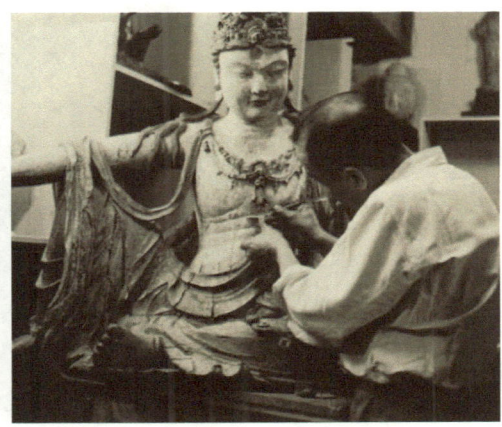

Figure 9-7 Loo receiving important customers in his antique shop (first half of the 20th century)

Figure 9-8 The technician hired by Loo repairing the wooden statue of Water-Moon Avalokitesvara from the Song Dynasty that he acquired (first half of the 20th century)

vibrant colors such as red, green, and yellow on its surface, along with traces of gold foil. The upper body is exposed, adorned in a long skirt with a flowing ribbon and jewelry. With a casually elegant sitting posture—his right leg bent and supported, and the left leg stretched down—the statue captivates viewers, marveling at the artist's exceptional skills in bringing life to seemingly inanimate wood.

During those days, Loo was known for his integrity in the antique business, making Chinese antiques he sold highly credible among collectors. Every year upon Loo's return to the United States or France from China, collectors or museum curators eagerly sought a glimpse and promptly acquired their favored antiques. For instance, in 1928, Luoyang Jincun unexpectedly unearthed the tombs of Eastern Zhou (770–256 BC) royals and nobles, with eight large tombs subsequently being looted (Figure 9-9), revealing thousands of cultural relics, including numerous exquisite jades and bronzes. Many of these cultural relics found their way to the United States through Loo, with a significant portion entering the collection of the Fogg Museum at Harvard University, while others were acquired by the Freer Gallery of Art. Between 1912 and 1950, numerous Western museums, thanks to Loo, gradually established dedicated exhibition areas for their Asian collections.

In summary, since 1915, the Loo-Wu Company has been actively exporting cultural relics to the West for 30 years, resulting in a continuous outflux of countless national treasures to the United States and Europe (Figure 9-10). Even a small shareholder in the company could rake in hundreds of thousands of silver dollars annually. During this period, the annual turnover of an antique shop in Liulichang paled in comparison. Loo's peak in the antique business coincided with China's tumultuous era. The collapse of the Qing government led to the bankruptcy of many Qing Dynasty people, compelling the prodigal sons of former aristocratic families to sell their ancestral treasures for survival. The chaos ensuing from the

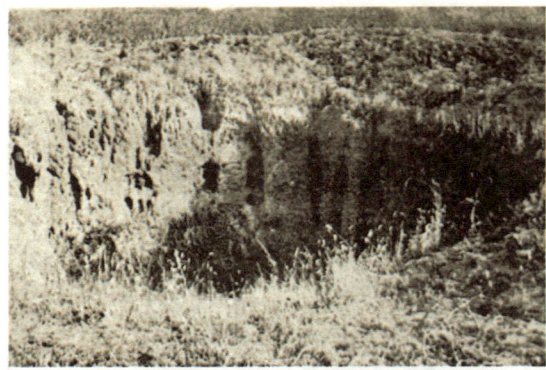

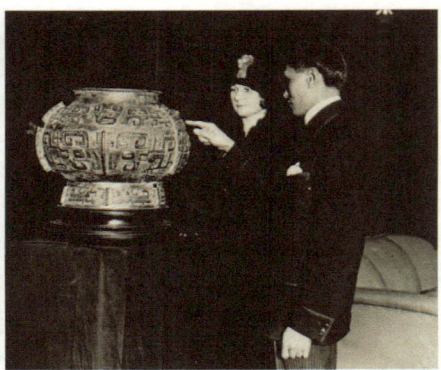

Figure 9-9 The looting of the Eastern Zhou tombs in Jincun, Luoyang, in 1928 (first half of the 20th century)

Figure 9-10 Loo introducing bronze wares to a client (1930s)

clashes between the Beiyang warlords and the Japanese invasion left the Chinese government with little capacity to protect historical relics. These circumstances presented Loo with the "greatest opportunity" to acquire treasures at bargain prices.

Post-1930, the international market for Asian art and antiques underwent significant transformations. In the West, the study of Asia and Asian art evolved into a professional domain within the museums. This evolution necessitated curators to possess an in-depth understanding of the Asian cultural relics in their collections, facilitating comprehensive and profound research. Concurrently, Asian culture and art began to feature prominently in the curriculum of universities and research institutes worldwide. In China, the Nationalist Government also began to emphasize ancient art exhibitions as a means to promote and enhance China's image in the West. This unique convergence of interests between China and the West propelled Loo's antique business to its zenith, with Loo-Wu Company dominating a significant share of the international Chinese antique market. During this period, his international art network flourished and extended to affluent locations such as the United Kingdom, France, Germany, and the United States.

9.3 The Tragedy of *Six Steeds of Zhao Mausoleum*

A significant number of national-treasure-level cultural relics found their way to the United States through the hands of Loo. Among the most renowned are "Saluzi" and "Quanmaogua" reliefs depicting two of *Six Steeds of Zhao Mausoleum*, associated with Emperor Taizong, Li Shimin of the Tang Dynasty (r. AD 626–649) (Figure 9-11). Zhao Mausoleum serves as the joint burial mausoleum for Emperor Taizong of the Tang Dynasty and Empress Wende, Zhangsun (AD 601–636). Constructed over 13 years, it stands as the largest imperial mausoleum in China, covering several times the area of a Pharaoh's pyramid in Egypt. Wen Tao, the military governor of Chongzhou (present-day Tongchuan, Shaanxi

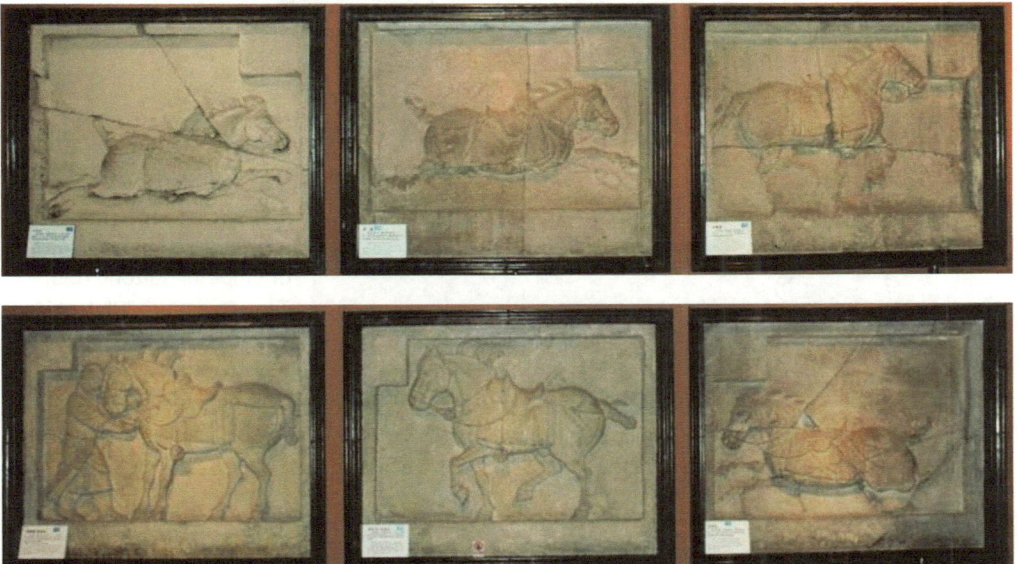

Figure 9-11 The reliefs of *Six Steeds of Zhao Mausoleum* of Emperor Taizong of the Tang Dynasty on display at the Forest of Stone Steles Museum in Xi'an—from top left: "Shifachi," "Qingzhui," and "Telebiao"; from bottom left: "Saluzi" (replica), "Quanmaogua" (replica), and "Baitiwu"

Province) during the Five Dynasties and Ten Kingdoms period, once pillaged the Zhao Mausoleum, describing it as "a majestic palace, with no difference from the human world. There is a central bedroom with stone beds in the east and west compartments, as well as an iron box in the stone box on the bed, housing ancient collections, including the handwriting of Zhong Yao and Wang Xizhi, with the paper and ink appearing as new."

In the tenth year of his reign in AD 636, Emperor Taizong of the Tang Dynasty, self-proclaimed as the Khan of Heaven, commissioned the creation of reliefs depicting six war horses that had accompanied him on the battlefield and achieved military feats. These became the renowned *Six Steeds of Zhao Mausoleum*. The reliefs, consisting of three in a standing posture and three in a galloping posture, were crafted by the brothers Yan Lide (AD 596–656) and Yan Liben (AD 601–673), both high-ranking officials and artists of the imperial court. Originally displayed in the corridors on both sides of the tribute hall adjacent to the Zhao Mausoleum holy path, these reliefs, three on the right and three on the left, in symmetry, stood toward the direction of the tomb. Each of the six steeds stands nearly 1.7 meters high, approximately 2 meters wide, and weighs 4 tons. French sinologist Édouard Chavannes visited Zhao Mausoleum in 1907, during which the Six Steeds were still there. The photos he captured became the only historical record of the Six Steeds before their removal (Figure 9-12).

Many antique dealers sought to acquire the sculptures, and numerous theories emerged about their theft. In 1921, Paris antique dealer Paul Mallon (1884–1975) recounted his failed

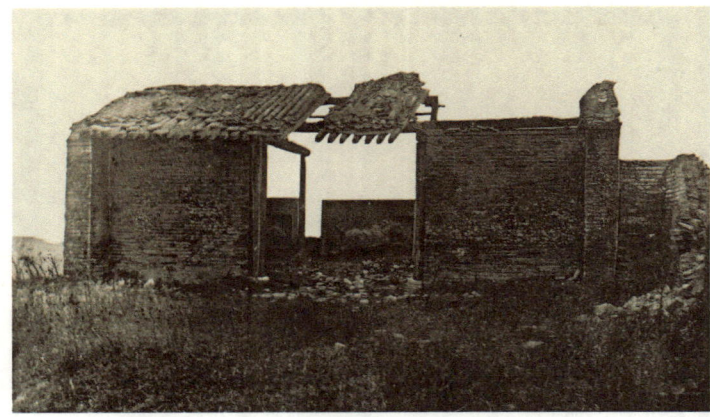

Figure 9-12 Three of the *Six Steeds of Zhao Mausoleum* at the original site of Zhao Mausoleum of Emperor Taizong of the Tang Dynasty—"Shifachi," "Qingzhui," and "Telebiao" (photographed by Chavannes in 1907)

attempt in 1913 to transport the reliefs in a letter to the Museum of Archaeology and Anthropology at the University of Pennsylvania. Mallon had employed an intermediary in Beijing to plan the removal of the Six Steeds, "In May 1913, the reliefs of the *Six Steeds of Zhao Mausoleum* were being transported from Zhao Mausoleum. Regrettably, the carriers fell victim to an attack by local farmers, resulting in the precious cultural relics being cast off a cliff." As the plan failed, the government confiscated all Six Steeds in Xi'an. Mallon also mentioned losing a substantial amount of money paid upfront to purchase the reliefs. However, this marked only the beginning of the story, not its conclusion. Records indicate that two of the Six Steeds were intercepted by the Shaanxi warlord Lu Jianzhang (1862–1918) during transportation to Xi'an. Yuan Shikai's (1859–1916) second son, Yuan Kewen (1890–1931), instructed Lu Jianzhang to transport the two steeds to Beijing as a congratulatory gift for Yuan Shikai, who was about to ascend the throne. Consequently, the transportation document for the preserved cultural relics bore the Yuan family's seal, authorizing the Six Steeds reliefs to leave Xi'an for Beijing. As a result, the two steeds, "Saluzi" and "Quanmaogua," were shipped out of Xi'an in 1915. However, they vanished before reaching Beijing.

In 1918, "Saluzi" and "Quanmaogua," whose whereabouts had long remained a mystery, inexplicably surfaced at the Metropolitan Museum of Art in New York, a development linked to Loo. Loo purportedly claimed to have acquired it from a highly significant individual of the time. Speculation arose as to whether this individual could have been Yuan Kewen. In his correspondence with George Gordon, the director of the Museum of Archaeology and Anthropology at the University of Pennsylvania, Loo adopted an air of mystery, hinting to Gordon: "If you desire to acquire the two steeds, your path leads to the Metropolitan Museum." How Loo obtained these two steeds remains shrouded in mystery. He asserted that he procured them by establishing a connection with Yuan Kewen via Beijing antique dealer Zhao Hefang (1881–1936). Another theory posits that Loo might have deceived Yuan Kewen into issuing the "gift" order, with the intention of transporting the two steeds to the United States. According to Loo's accounts, while traveling by train from Northeast China to Beijing, he received a telegram warning of his imminent arrest by the authorities. "The Beijing government at that time sought to apprehend me for my involvement with Emperor Taizong's steed reliefs, prompting me to alter my travel plans at a transfer station a few kilometers away and hastily board a passing train."

In summary, between 1916 and 1917, Loo acquired "Saluzi" and "Quanmaogua," two of the six steeds, through various connections and channels, smuggling them to the United States. At the time, both reliefs were disassembled and fragmented to facilitate transportation. Loo's correspondence records indicate his initial intent to relocate all six steeds from Zhao Mausoleum, but he encountered opposition from local villagers during the smuggling attempt. This suggests his involvement in the theft of the Six Steeds from the outset. The four preserved steeds are now housed in the Forest of Stone Steles Museum in Xi'an. The original set of six steeds was artificially divided in this manner. On March 9, 1918, George Gordon encountered the two reliefs, "Saluzi" and "Quanmaogua," at the Metropolitan Museum of Art's warehouse. Following negotiations, Loo lent them to the University of Pennsylvania Museum, offering to "waive the rental fee." On May 8, "Saluzi" and "Quanmaogua" arrived at the University of Pennsylvania. Finally, in 1920, Loo sold them to the Museum of Archaeology and Anthropology at the University of Pennsylvania for 125,000 US dollars.

The "Saluzi" preserved in the United States is the only relief among the six steeds that depicts a human figure. It portrays the scene of Qiu Xinggong, the general who accompanied Li Shimin on the frontier expeditions before Li Shimin became emperor, drawing an arrow for the war horse (Figure 9-13). In AD 621, during a battle with the warlord Wang Shichong in Henan, Li Shimin, then-prince of Qin, encountered a dire situation when his mount, Saluzi, was shot in the chest. Qiu Xinggong gave his own mount to the prince, held the wounded Saluzi with one hand, and valiantly fought with a sword to break

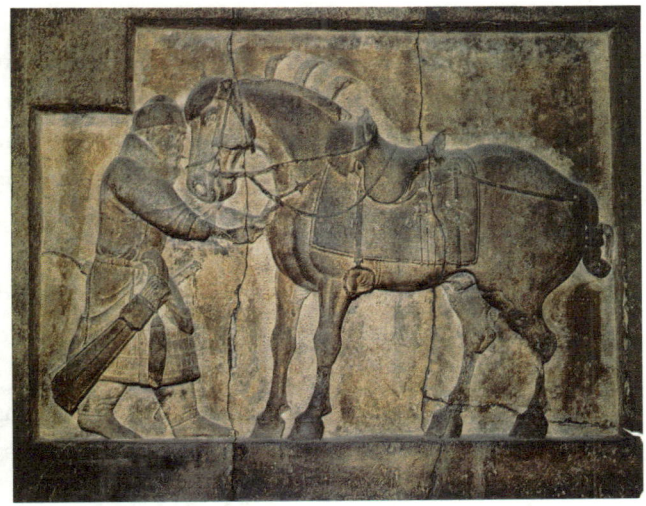

Figure 9-13 Qiu Xinggong and the "Saluzi" relief (Museum of Archaeology and Anthropology, University of Pennsylvania)

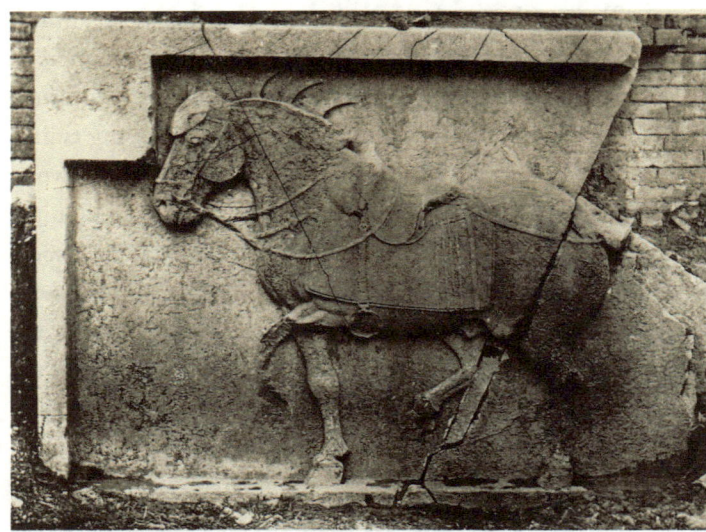

Figure 9-14 "Quanmaogua" at the original site of Zhao Mausoleum of Emperor Taizong of the Tang Dynasty (Photographed by Chavannes in 1907)

through, saving Li Shimin's life. Upon Qiu Xinggong's passing at the age of 80, he was interred in Zhao Mausoleum, commemorated as part of the reliefs of the Six Steeds. This serves as a testament to his posthumous honor and Emperor Taizong's respect. Another relief, "Quanmaogua," depicts a galloping horse struck by six arrows in front and three arrows in its back during battle, ultimately succumbing amid the clash between opposing forces (Figure 9-14).

Loo did not harbor any sense of guilt regarding the transaction, as evidenced by the two paragraphs of text he left behind.

> The transaction was entirely legal, and the individual who sold me the two steed reliefs held the highest authority in the country at that time. If purchasing something from the president is deemed illegal, then who holds the right to sell it? If the transaction was lawful then and is deemed illegal now, how many antique dealers and collectors would find themselves in similar circumstances? It has been 12 years since these two artifacts were acquired, and no one has ever questioned the legality of this transaction with me. I have visited China on numerous occasions during this period, and no government department has ever raised concerns regarding this matter.
>
> At that time, the nation was engulfed in war and chaos. Might was right, and there existed no rule of law. Hence, I had to exercise caution.

In essence, he perceives no wrongdoing in procuring national treasures. However, in Loo's letter to Gordon in 1926, he offered a different perspective:

Three gentlemen, Yang, Jin, and Ma, will receive 33% of the proceeds from the two steed reliefs ... They dedicated four or five years to acquiring these two cultural relics, enduring various hardships and dangers, risking imprisonment, and even their lives. Acquiring antiques in China nowadays is exceedingly challenging. Rare cultural relics such as these are nearly impossible to obtain. First, the risks are too high, and second, almost all fine cultural relics have been unearthed.

These contradictory statements add to the mystery surrounding the acquisition of "Saluzi" and "Quanmaogua." It remains challenging to ascertain through which "highest authority in the country" they were sold to Loo, how he smuggled them out of the country, and why they mysteriously surfaced in the Metropolitan Museum of Art a few years later. However, it is undeniable that Loo, who supported the 1911 Revolution alongside Zhang Jingjiang, enjoyed an inexplicably close relationship with the National Government. This act of smuggling national treasures serves as compelling evidence of his intimate ties with government officials at the time.

9.4 Personal Brand

Loo ascended to the forefront of the international antiques trade due to a confluence of factors: a rare, epochal opportunity, astute business prowess, reliable sources of antiques, and an unparalleled capacity for learning coupled with a distinctive aesthetic perspective. Possessing a photographic memory of the artifacts he dealt with, he could vividly recall every detail of his transactions decades later. Diligent and scholarly, he seamlessly integrated Chinese art into the framework of European art history, employing familiar ancient Greek and Roman concepts to elucidate Buddhist sculptures. In his 1937 publication *An Index of the History of Chinese Arts: An Aide-Memoire for Beginners*, Loo aptly employed terms like Baroque to delineate the Chinese sculptures of the late Tang Dynasty, facilitating Western comprehension and mitigating Eurocentrism.

Furthermore, he nurtured intellectual discourse within his establishment by sponsoring prominent Chinese art historians, cultivating an atmosphere where esteemed scholars convened, free from casual onlookers. Notable sinologists such as French Pelliot and New York University professor Alfred Salmony (1890–1958) contributed to the Chinese cultural relics atlas under his stewardship. Transitioning from an antique dealer to a custodian of Chinese culture, Loo achieved his most triumphant branding endeavor (Figure 9-15).

With the burgeoning recognition of his personal brand, Loo gradually gained acceptance from museums worldwide. In 1935, the Chinese Art World Expo held at the Royal Academy of Arts in London captivated a staggering 420,000 attendees. Among the impressive exhibits was a towering 5-meter-high white stone standing Buddha statue

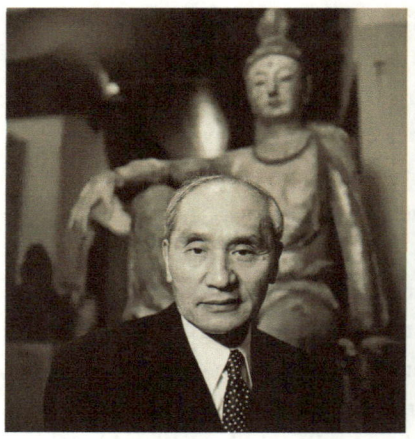

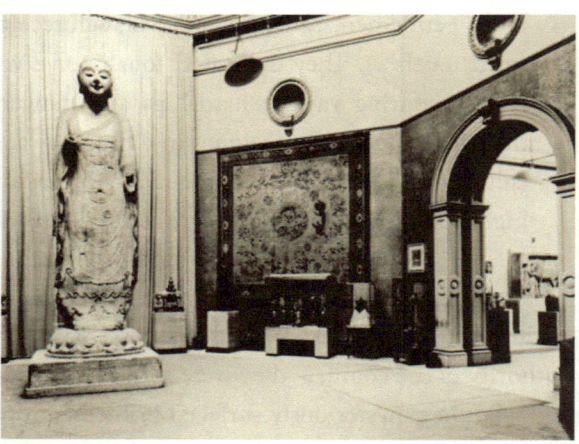

Figure 9-15 Loo and the Water-Moon Avalokitesvara wooden statue (first half of the 20th century)

Figure 9-16 The white-stone statue of Amitabha dating from the fifth year of Kaihuang in the Sui Dynasty (AD 585), exhibited at the Royal Academy of Arts in London (1935–1936)

(Figure 9-16) from the Sui Dynasty, curated by Loo, which captivated audiences with its remarkable size, form, and material composition. This monumental Buddha statue had been under Loo's custodianship for an extended period. To facilitate its transportation, he meticulously disassembled it into multiple pieces, albeit with the hands of the Buddha missing. Nonetheless, transporting a 20-ton stone statue posed considerable logistical challenges. Previously, Loo had suggested this magnificent artifact to prominent clients in New York, yet both the Metropolitan Museum of Art and Rockefeller Jr. deemed its size unwieldy, lacking a suitable exhibition space. Seizing an opportunity at the inaugural art fair where China made its debut, Loo astutely and generously donated the stone Buddha statue to the Chinese government, which then presented it to the British Museum as a gesture of friendship. In a letter to Guo Taiqi (1888–1952), the Chinese Minister in London, Loo articulated his intentions, "The donation of this precious stone Buddha aims to bolster China's image while enhancing the visibility of my company." His motive was clear: to have his company's name featured in the collection introduction, gaining endorsement from the British government. However, this commercial promotion did not align with the museum's ethos at the time. After protracted negotiations, the British Museum opted to acknowledge the statue's provenance with the following inscription, "Presented to the Chinese government by Mr. Loo, and subsequently donated to the British Museum by the Chinese Minister to the United Kingdom, commemorating the Chinese Art World Expo in London from 1935 to 1936. Mr. Loo, a Paris art dealer, provided this exhibit through his New York branch for the 1935–1936 World Expo."

Even within the esteemed halls of the British Museum, renowned for its vast collections, finding a suitable location for this colossal and weighty Buddha statue posed a challenge. Today, it occupies a prominent position on the museum's first-floor steps, inviting visitors to ascend and immerse themselves in the ambiance reminiscent of ancient Buddhist pilgrimages. As they ascend, they can marvel at the intricate carvings adorning the statue from its feet to its head (Figure 9-17). According to the inscription on its base, this towering Amitabha Buddha statue was enshrined at Chongguang Temple in Hancui Village, Hebei Province, during the fifth year of Kaihuang (AD 585). Sadly, the temple's exact location has been lost to time. Based on the white marble utilized in its construction, scholars speculate it was situated near Baoding, Hebei. Emperors of the Sui Dynasty were devout Buddhists, elevating Buddhism to the status of the state religion. Consequently, monumental single statues like this one became prevalent. While the Buddhist statues of the Sui Dynasty retained elements of the Indian Gupta style, they gradually evolved toward localized expressions and early naturalism. Despite the Sui Dynasty's short-lived existence, spanning a little over 30 years, it bequeathed a rich legacy of Buddhist cultural relics, including numerous inscribed statues. Nevertheless, this Buddha statue stands out for its exceptional craftsmanship, towering stature, and employment of precious materials. Its significance in the annals of Chinese Buddhist art cannot be overstated. Upon close examination, traces of mottled gold foil and remnants of colorful paintings on its white stone surface evoke visions of its former grandeur and opulence, offering a glimpse into its illustrious past.

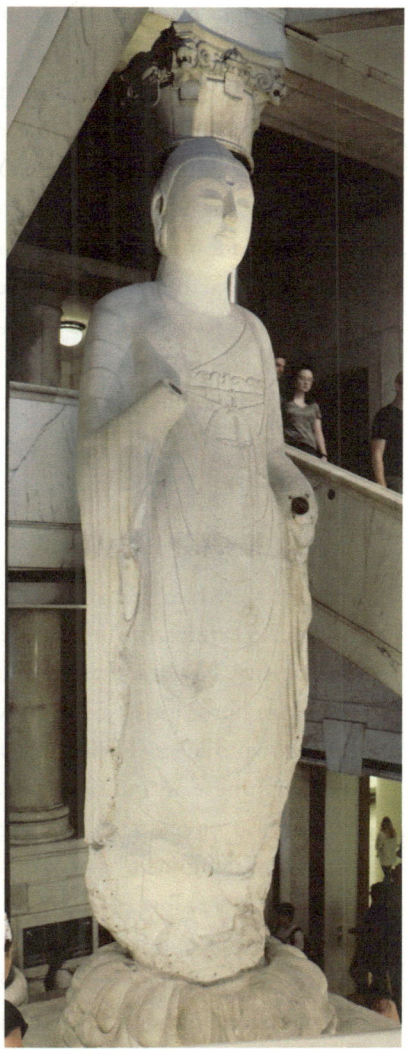

Figure 9-17 The white stone statue of Amitabha in the fifth year of Emperor Kaihuang's reign (585) on display in the British Museum (5.78 meters high, serial number: Asia 1938.0715.1, photographed by Chang Qing on June 28, 2019)

Beyond his role as a cultural relic dealer, Loo placed great emphasis on fostering close relationships with scholars. He frequently extended invitations to renowned academics to study his collection of cultural relics. For instance, he collaborated with Pelliot on the publication of the *Jades Archaïques De Chine Appartenant À M. C. T. Loo* and enlisted the expertise of Pelliot and the seal engraver and archaeologist Chu Deyi (1871–1942) to compile the *Illustrated Catalog of Bronze Ware*. These collaborative efforts significantly enhanced the value and appeal of Chinese cultural relics and artworks in the Western world. In 1944,

Chen Mengjia (1911–1966), a prominent modern Chinese paleographer, archaeologist, and poet, along with his wife Zhao Luorui (1912–1998), was warmly welcomed by Loo during their studies at the University of Chicago (Figure 9-18). Chen Mengjia, who was planning to write a monograph on Chinese bronzes scattered abroad, found invaluable support from Loo. He diligently facilitated Chen's research endeavors, arranging visits to private and public museums worldwide and providing access to his photography studio. In total, 850 photographs of cultural relics were captured for Chen's study. In 1948, Chen expressed his gratitude for Loo's help:

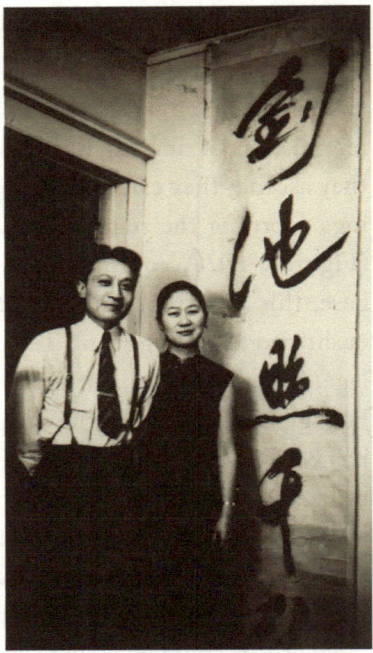

Figure 9-18 Chen Mengjia and his wife Zhao Luorui (first half of the 20th century)

> Mr. Loo, hailing from Wuxing, Zhejiang Province, is well into his sixties. Despite his slender frame, he exudes vitality and moves with remarkable agility. His command of Northern Mandarin is lacking, prompting us to converse in our shared hometown dialect. Reflecting on his four decades in the Chinese antiquities trade, Mr. Loo reminisces about the frequent visits from British, European, and Japanese scholars seeking materials. However, this time, he finds rare delight in hosting his fellow countrymen, expressing eagerness to assist in any way possible.
>
> For the past four years, I've been abroad, dedicated to procuring Chinese bronzes scattered across the United States, Canada, and Europe. Financial support from the Rockefeller Foundation's Humanities Group, the Harvard-Yenching Society, and the University of Chicago has sustained my endeavors. Yet, amid my pursuits, Mr. Loo's contributions stand out. Indeed, my journey into this field began at Loo-Wu Company. His correspondence cards provided the addresses of private collectors and details of their bronze collections; his sales records unveiled museum holdings; and his photographic plates yielded over a thousand images of bronzes. With the assistance of his aide, Frank Caro, we documented every bronzeware we could access and meticulously examined hundreds of bronzes in his warehouse. Additionally, we made two trips to the New York warehouse to photograph the Chinese bronzes owned by French magnate Michel David-Weill. Leveraging Loo-Wu Company's Paris roots, I later traveled to Europe with remarkable ease. Mr. Loo's New York establishment served as a hub for scholars and collectors alike, where I frequently found myself during my visits to the city to inspect bronzes.

The *Catalog of Chinese Bronze Wares Overseas*, compiled by Chen Mengjia and published by The Commercial Press in 1946, owes much to the assistance of Loo. Remarkably, in 1962, Science Press republished the book under the title *A Collection of Chinese Yin and Zhou Bronze Wares Looted by US Imperialism*, marking China's first monograph on bronze wares after 1949. Ironically, it was American cultural institutions that funded Chen's investigation and acquisition of these overseas bronze materials.

Furthermore, in 1948, at the urging of Chen Mengjia, Loo generously donated the Warring States (476–221 BC) bronze Linghu Sizi kettle (Figure 9-19), unearthed in Jincun, Luoyang, Henan in 1928, to the exhibition hall of cultural relics of Tsinghua University. Reflecting on the return of this kettle to China, Chen recounted:

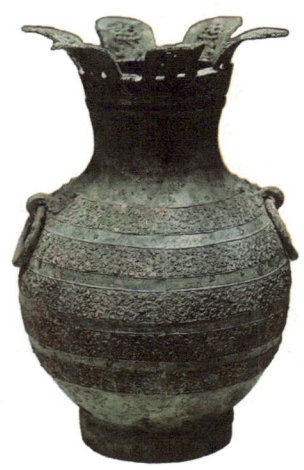

Figure 9-19 The Warring States bronze Linghu Sizi kettle donated by Loo and unearthed in Jincun, Luoyang, Henan in 1928 (46.5 cm high, now in the National Museum of China)

> In early August of the 36th year of the Republic of China (1947), I flew from New York to Europe. During the trip, I bid farewell to Mr. Loo and expressed my hope that he would assist me in returning to Tsinghua to prepare a museum, to which he readily agreed. He also pledged his willingness to repatriate any significant bronze vessels with inscriptions to his homeland. Specifically requesting the Sizi kettle, he assured me that he would dispatch it by mail once our museum had formulated plans … Due to logistical arrangements, this kettle was shipped by New York Air in early August (1948) and arrived in Peking at the end of August. Customs held it for three months. Mr. Loo valued it at five thousand US dollars on the shipping list … With this bronze now securely housed in the showroom, I am personally relieved. Not only have we added an important piece to our collection, but we have also fulfilled a longstanding personal aspiration, thanks in large part to Mr. Loo. He has helped me realize my dreams of university museums relying on public and private exchanges and donations, and of preserving antiquities with historical significance within the country and repatriating those that have been exported.

Indeed, Mr. Chen's dreams align with the aspirations of many Chinese today. In 1959, the Sizi kettle was transferred to the Chinese History Museum, now the National Museum of China. Additionally, Loo contributed funds to the renowned writer and translator Lin Yutang (1895–1976) for the invention of the Mingkuai Chinese typewriter, further advancing Chinese cultural endeavors.

9.5 Pagoda Paris

In 1925, Loo acquired a modest building at No. 8, Rue du Cource, situated in the less fashionable 17th district on the Rive Droite of Paris. With grand ambitions, he undertook its transformation into the renowned Pagoda Paris (Figure 9-20). Loo held lofty expectations and exacting standards for this project, enlisting the services of French architect Fernand Bloch (1864–1945) with a budget of 8 million francs. Amid the neoclassical Haussmann-style edifices of the Parisian neighborhood, the emergence of a Chinese-style pagoda made of red bricks, adorned with a green glazed roof, intricately carved and painted beams, and a crimson entrance, seemed incongruous even in a city celebrated for its avant-garde painters like Monet, Matisse, and Picasso. Local residents, municipal authorities, and the press all vocally opposed and criticized the endeavor. Nevertheless, Loo remained steadfast in his determination to see it through. Undeniably, the media frenzy generated by this venture elevated the status of the Pagoda Paris, attracting celebrities and sophisticates and leaving an indelible impression on a 20th-century Paris characterized by rebellion.

Bolstered by supporters, Pagoda Paris, as he dubbed it, became a hub of Chinese cultural immersion through its extensive collection and exhibition of Chinese and Asian artifacts, while also serving as a coveted salon for luminaries and socialites (Figure 9-21). Each year, luminaries from diverse spheres crossed oceans to attend events hosted by Loo at the Pagoda Paris. Following his demise, the building fell into neglect and disrepair. Yet, owing to its erstwhile renown, former opponents among the neighbors protested against the government's plans to demolish it. Presently, it enjoys cultural heritage status bestowed by the Paris City Government, ensuring its perpetual preservation. In 2010, a French investment entrepreneur acquired the Pagoda Paris, restoring it as a venue for artistic

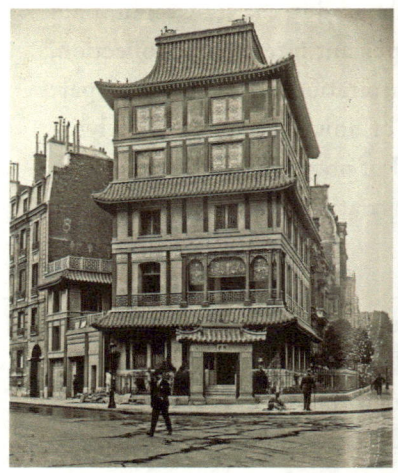

Figure 9-20 Pagoda Paris in the 1920s or early 1930s

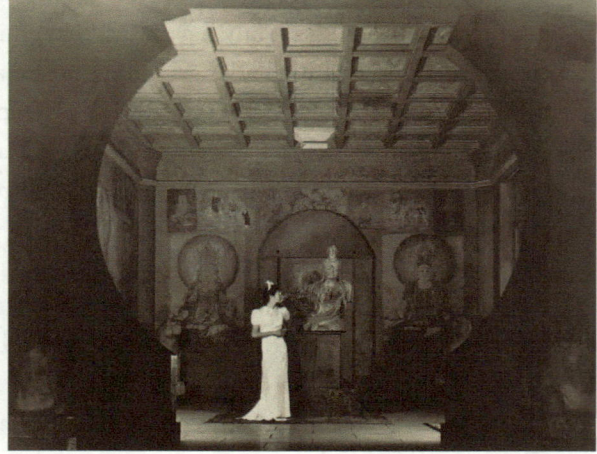

Figure 9-21 Loo's youngest daughter Jenny's wedding photos in Pagoda Paris when she was 17 years old (1937)

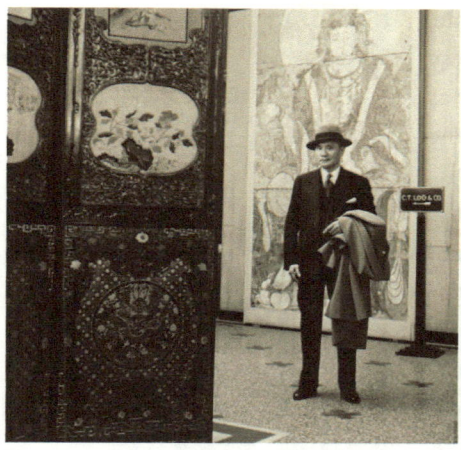

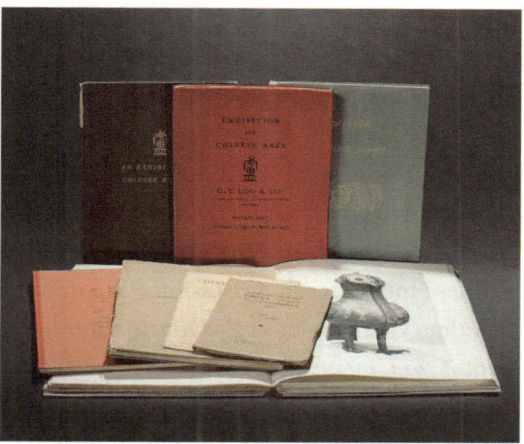

Figure 9-22 Loo posing with the Bodhisattva mural in Pagoda Paris (photographed in the first half of the 20th century)

Figure 9-23 Catalogs of cultural relics published by Loo from 1924 to 1950

pursuits. The library within the Pagoda Paris, once curated by Loo, remains accessible to scholars, continuing to contribute to the study of Chinese art history.

Among the photographs capturing Loo within the confines of Pagoda Paris, none is as striking as his portrait alongside the Bodhisattva mural (Figure 9-22). These exquisite Bodhisattva murals, standing several meters tall, originated from the Five Dynasties to the Northern Song Dynasty and have been meticulously preserved on the walls of the Pagoda Paris. Serving as integral adornments within Pagoda Paris, they constitute a cherished part of Loo's collection, never intended for sale. According to Loo's own recollection, in 1923, he became aware of a temple ruin near the Henan-Shanxi border. Following consultations with authorities, he arranged for the retrieval of the murals from the temple remnants and had them transported to Paris. It wasn't until 1948 that Loo transported them to the United States, presenting a thematic exhibition titled Chinese Frescos of Northern Sung at the Fifth Avenue Gallery in New York. Conducting such thematic exhibitions aimed at sales was a hallmark of Loo's expertise. Leveraging his extensive collection and art historical insights, Loo meticulously curated and extensively expounded on Chinese art through these exhibitions, while simultaneously publishing catalogs for sale (Figure 9-23). Distinguished from previous thematic exhibitions, this collection of murals represents decades of dedicated curation by Loo.

Perhaps sensing the urgency of time or desiring to entrust his most treasured collection to a caring custodian, in 1950, Loo proactively approached Laurence Sickman, curator of the Nelson-Atkins Art Museum, to select gifts from his collection. Delighted, Sickman penned in a letter, "We have just received a Chinese Buddhist art mural donated by Mr. Loo. Measuring 1.8 meters in length and 0.9 meters in width, this masterpiece had been housed at Mr. Loo's Paris residence for many years. Among the oldest Buddhist murals in China, it stands as the most exceptional discovery to date, dating back to the 11th to 12th centuries AD. Courtesy of Mr. Loo's generosity, we were allowed to choose as we wished, and we acquired this masterpiece for the modest price of 16,000 US dollars."

Sickman refers to merely one piece. However, the Nelson-Atkins Museum of Art boasts a collection of Chinese murals, each possessing extraordinary artistic value. Works such as *Bodhisattva Burning Incense*, *Part of the Cintāmaṇicakra*, and *Avalokitesvara Holding Lotus* grace its halls. Scholars have traced these murals to the Cisheng Temple in Dawu Village, situated northwest of Wen County, Jiaozuo City, Henan Province. Dating from the Later Zhou of the Five Dynasties (AD 951–960) (Figure 9-24), these murals represent rare remnants from a tumultuous era marked by warfare. Remarkably, the craftsmanship exhibited in the murals from Cisheng Temple is unparalleled, rendering them unique masterpieces. In the catalog of the themed exhibition, Loo wrote:

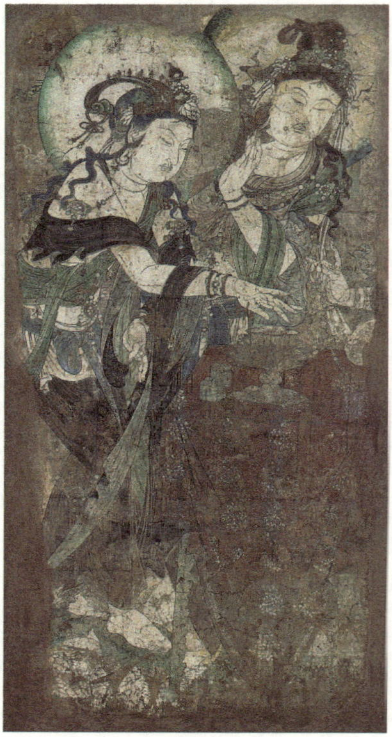

Figure 9-24 The Five Dynasties *Bodhisattva Burning Incense* mural donated by Loo (175.26 cm × 90.17 cm × 3.81 cm, now in the Nelson-Atkins Museum of Art, No. 50-64 A)

If there are some of my compatriots who should feel that the removal of these frescos out of China, is a loss to our Country, I trust that they also should feel satisfied that those frescoes will be safely and permanently preserved in a friendly Country. Art should have no frontiers and should, on the contrary, be a source of enjoyment for people the world over.

As he mentioned, prior to closing his business in 1951, Loo generously donated his collection of murals to seven art museums in the United States. Upon consulting relevant information, it was revealed that the murals owned by these museums did not encompass the entirety of the exhibited murals. It appears that a significant portion of the exhibits were sold by Loo to private collectors and have since disappeared from public view.

A series of exhibition catalogs published by Loo underscore his expertise in antiques and his extensive experience in trading cultural relics. Scholars can still trace the whereabouts of past cultural relics through the photographs preserved in Pagoda Paris. From 1933 to 1941, Loo hosted at least one exhibition annually, showcasing and selling cultural relics. His exhibition catalogs reveal stone statues from various renowned sites, including the Longmen Grottoes in Luoyang, Henan, the Yungang Grottoes in Datong, Shanxi,

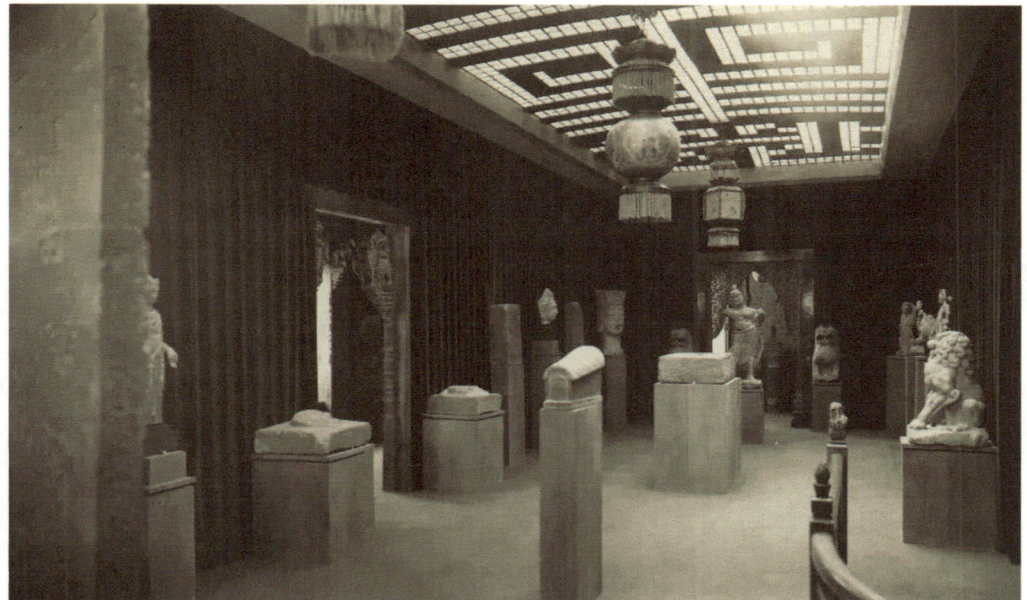

Figure 9-25 Chinese stone carvings exhibition hall in Pagoda Paris (first half of the 20th century)

Tianlongshan Grottoes in Taiyuan, Xiangtangshan Grottoes in Handan, Hebei Province. Additionally, there is a significant collection of individual stone statues and statue steles from Chinese Buddhist temples (Figure 9-25). These exquisite Buddhist sculptures have since found homes in many esteemed American museums, such as the Metropolitan Museum of Art and the Freer Gallery of Art, as well as in private collections. While it may be an exaggeration to claim that half of the antiques shipped overseas from China passed through Loo's hands, it nonetheless underscores his significant role in the Western antique world during the early 20th century.

Pagoda Paris also left a lasting imprint on Loo's personal life. In 1908, shortly after Loo established Laiyuan & Co., he crossed paths with Olga Hortense Libmond (1876–1960), a millinery shop owner near his company. Olga's father hailed from Poland, while her mother was of Italian descent. Working as a housekeeper in Paris from a young age, Olga was raped by the house owner and gave birth to a girl named Marie Rose (1895–1971) when she was 19. Later, she opened a successful millinery shop with her lover's support.

Olga had just celebrated her 30th birthday when she met Loo. Loo, four years her junior, quickly fell in love with her. The two became inseparable. With her strong will and passionate nature, Olga found herself torn between not wanting to lose her wealthy lover, who financed her millinery shop, and her desire to remain with Loo. So, she decided to marry her 15-year-old daughter Marie Rose to Loo, in order to continue her relationship with him. On December 29, 1910, Loo and Rose held a brief wedding.

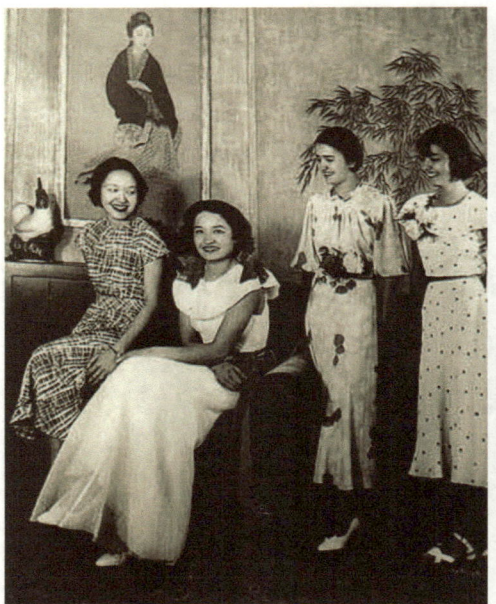

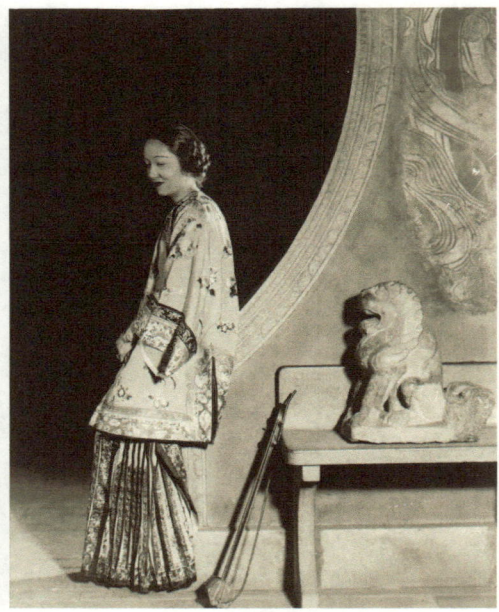

Figure 9-26 Loo's four daughters in Pagoda Paris

Figure 9-27 Loo's eldest daughter Monica, 24 years old, wearing a Qing Dynasty garment, was photographed in the foyer of Pagoda Paris (on the right is a Tang Dynasty stone lion, 1937)

After their marriage, Rose assumed the role of a housewife and bore four daughters for Loo (Figure 9-26). Rose, who married at a young age, was accustomed to obeying her mother and knew no other life. Loo was highly content with this wife, who never imposed restrictions on him. Rose, with her simple demeanor, consistently offered unconditional support to her husband. Whether it was regarding his career, finances, or personal interests, she always deferred to his preferences. In the accounts of many, she was depicted as an elegant and gentle French woman with a distinct fondness for Chinese cultural relics.

The only aspect of this marriage that disappointed Loo, deeply influenced by traditional Chinese beliefs, was the absence of sons among his offspring; he had four daughters but no sons. In his perspective, there were three forms of unfilial conduct, the gravest being the lack of heirs. To him, having only daughters meant having no heirs. He further believed that since his daughters were French, they would marry and transmit the family lineage to other families in the future, unrelated to him or China. Consequently, he never taught his daughters Chinese nor shared Chinese stories with them. Consequently, until the youngest daughter's passing in 2013, none of the four daughters had ever revisited Loo's hometown, nor expressed any desire to connect with the Loo family from their father's birthplace of Huzhou. However, Loo, passionate about antiques, effectively utilized his daughters' resources. These four naturally charming young ladies of mixed Chinese and French heritage frequently featured in promotional photographs for Loo's cultural relics, becoming unpaid models who enhanced the appeal of the mundane antiques. They were beautiful scenery in the otherwise dull Pagoda Paris, brimming with antiquities. (Figures 9-26, 9-27).

9.6 Merits and Demerits

Faced with such a figure who facilitated the trade of Chinese cultural relics, evaluations from both Chinese and Western perspectives were drastically different. In the eyes of Westerners, Loo was an eminent Chinese art antique dealer in the first half of the 20th century. He played a pivotal role in introducing early Chinese art to Europe and the United States, earning praise as an enlightener who fostered Western understanding of Chinese antiques. His profound expertise and unique vision of cultural relics enabled people to learn the art of appreciating various Chinese tomb artifacts, such as tomb carvings, bronzes, ancient jade, pottery figurines, and Buddhist statues. Without his Loo-Wu Company, many major American museums

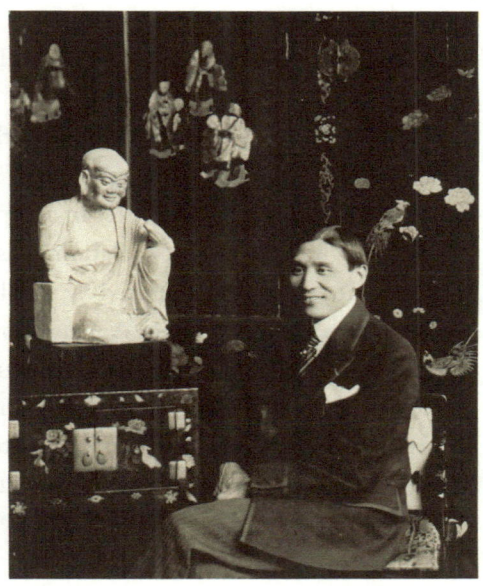

Figure 9-28 30-year-old Loo and his antiques

would lack the foundation for their Chinese art collections. Moreover, he cultivated a group of distinguished Western collectors (Figure 9-28).

Jeannine Auboyer, curator of the Guimet Museum in Paris, France, wrote in a tribute to Loo:

> Loo's affection for cultural relics transcends mere business acumen. He sought to safeguard historical treasures, ensuring their preservation for future generations and widespread accessibility. This is why European and American museums acquired significantly more objects than individual clients; museums are best equipped to further them noble objectives ... Loo dedicated his life to the admiration of Chinese cultural relics, finding solace in entrusting his artworks to responsible custodians who would safeguard them from harm.

Auboyer's commendation stems from the numerous collections donated by Loo to the Guimet Museum between 1929 and 1950. However, another reason for her admiration might lie in her rumored romantic involvement with Loo. Through this lens, it became natural for her to defend him.

Chinese evaluations tend to be more critical, focusing on the adverse impact of Loo's antique company on ancient Chinese cultural relics. While he denied direct involvement in the destruction of Chinese historical and cultural relics, including the theft of Buddhist statues from caves, these artworks nonetheless ended up overseas through his transactions. Many Chinese view Loo as a mercenary businessman who amassed great wealth at the expense of the nation, attributing to him the primary blame for the dispersion of Chinese cultural heritage.

In his later years, Loo reflected on his life with a tinge of remorse:

I feel so ashamed to have been one of the sources by which these National treasures have been dispersed. Our only excuse is that none have ever been taken by us but all bought in the open market in competition with other buyers. China has lost its treasures but our only consolation is, as Art has no frontiers, these sculptures going forth into the world, admired by scholars as well as the public, may do more good for China than any living Ambassador. Through the Arts, China is probably best known to the outside world. Our monuments may be preserved even better in other countries than in China, because of constant changes and upheavals and so our lost treasures will be the real messengers to make the world realize out ancient civilization, and culture thus serving to create a love and better understanding of China and the Chinese people

Loo further remarked:

I take comfort in knowing that the artworks I exported are safely preserved for posterity, as I believe many would have been destroyed had they remained in China.

Loo used to defend his actions by asserting that the cultural relics passing through his hands originated from the open market, legitimate channels, rather than from illegal excavations. He cited instances such as a Western Zhou (1046–771 BC) bronze vessel discovered by a friend while digging a well in his new home. He believed that the responsibility for the outflow of cultural relics rested on the plunderers and buyers, absolving himself as a mere middleman. However, he acknowledged his pivotal role in facilitating transactions, likening himself to a vital link between buyers and sellers. Without his mediation, many transactions would not have occurred, and cultural relic theft would not have been as widespread. His role is comparable to that of a drug trafficker who orchestrates transactions without directly engaging in drug cultivation or consumption. Despite not directly participating in relic excavation, Loo had created a network of interests spanning from traffickers and robbers to buyers. His actions were akin to weaving a complex web, enabling the trade of cultural relics. Furthermore, the potential destruction of relics in China could not justify his transporting them out of the country as it is a post hoc rationalization rather than a genuine effort to preserve cultural heritage.

For instance, in a letter Loo wrote, he attached a photo of the collection owned by the Belgian banker and renowned collector Adolphe and Suzanne Stoclet, instructing Chinese antiquities dealers to seek Buddha heads resembling those depicted. This serves as evidence that he orchestrated the deliberate search for cultural relics remotely. As for the methods employed by his domestic informants to acquire the desired artifacts, they were beyond his direct control. Loo regularly returned to China each summer to entertain antique dealers and tomb raiders from various parts of China. Whenever an opportunity arose, he seized it promptly, often bypassing intermediary profits as his company, Loo-Wu Company, was affluent and frequently purchased antiques worth tens of thousands of silver dollars. During this time, Europe was undergoing a period of fervent fascination with Eastern culture, with collecting Chinese antiques symbolizing status and erudition. Consequently, the intentional trading of antiques proved highly lucrative for his company (Figure 9-29).

Nevertheless, individuals are seldom purely good or bad. While Loo engaged in large-scale exportation of cultural relics abroad, he was also actively involved in patriotic endeavors such as donations for the War of Resistance against Japanese Aggression. From

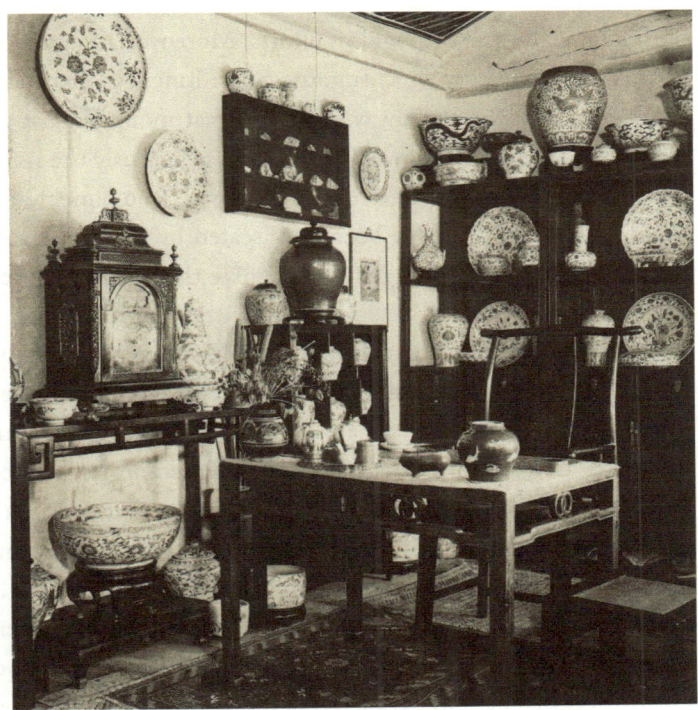

Figure 9-29 A corner of Pagoda Paris filled with antiques (first half of the 20th century)

the Revolution of 1911 to the July 7 Incident, Loo was at the forefront of patriotic actions, contributing not only financially but also rallying donations from various quarters in Paris and New York to support China's resistance against Japan. His wife, Marie Rose, served as the financial director of the War Orphans Relief Society, extending aid to Chinese refugees and the wounded. Their efforts were instrumental in these initiatives. Collaborating closely with him were diplomat Gu Weijun and his wife, as well as writer Lin Yutang and his wife. Loo was also a member of the Association for Friendship with China and actively supported the Communist cause. In October 1937, Loo traveled to Geneva to attend a charity sale organized by the local Chinese Women's Federation, offering nine auction items. All proceeds were donated to the Red Cross Society of China to assist war victims. In addition to his personal contributions, Loo actively rallied support from his affluent clientele by writing letters urging collective donations to aid China.

In January 1938, Loo sponsored an exhibition of Chinese cultural relics in London with the aim of soliciting donations from collectors. All proceeds from the exhibition were donated to American Medical Aid China. In 1942, Soong Meiling received an invitation from US President Franklin Roosevelt to address the US Congress. Following this, US First Lady Anna Eleanor Roosevelt extended an invitation for Soong Meiling to stay at the White House and organized a press conference in her honor. Loo was among the many inspired listeners who took immediate action to support the anti-Japanese war effort. During this period, the Ambassador of the Republic of China to the United States organized various activities to promote Sino-US relations, and Loo actively contributed both financially and through his efforts. Moreover, in 1938 alone, Loo and his wife adopted 40 orphans, reflecting their ongoing commitment to charitable activities until his passing. Loo remarked, "I have always believed that money is just a tool for people to exchange what they have. If I have wealth, I should generously use it to benefit those in need."

In a poignant open letter in March 1950, Loo lamented, "A large number of cultural relics I had acquired have been confiscated by Shanghai authorities, including my most prized collection. This led me to recognize the impending demise of my antique business, prompting my regretful decision to withdraw from the industry." This letter caused a stir in the Western collecting community, with many mistakenly attributing the termination of Loo's cultural relics business to the founding of the People's Republic of China in 1949. While it's true that the escalating difficulty in acquiring cultural relics from China significantly affected him, this wasn't the sole reason for his decision to withdraw from the antique industry. The main catalyst was a significant batch of counterfeit antiques and paintings he purchased in 1948 for millions of francs. These meticulously crafted forgeries, sourced from the esteemed Chinese calligraphy and painting collector Tan Jing (1911–1991), ensnared Loo due to his lack of expertise in the field. In order to safeguard his reputation, Loo opted to silently absorb the losses and liquidate the goods to settle his debts. Subsequently, his business was transferred to his longtime associate, Frank Caro.

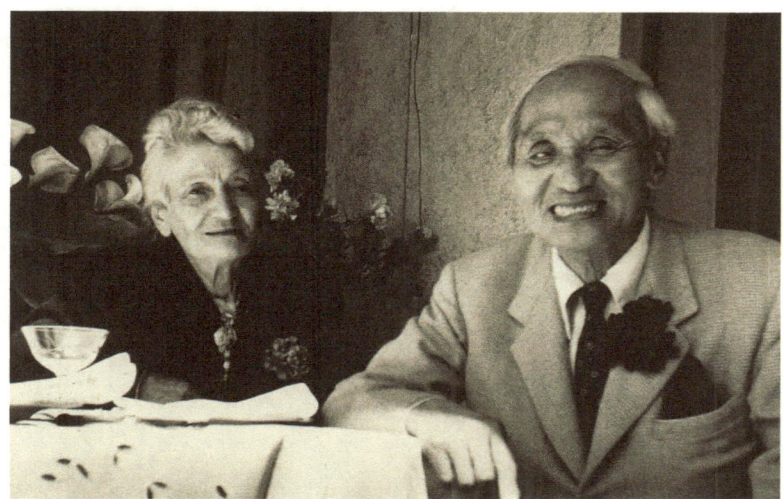

Figure 9-30 Loo and Olga (1950s)

Following his bankruptcy, Loo (Figure 9-30) fell into dire financial straits, compounded by declining health. He suffered from muscle atrophy, leading to his inability to care for himself. His deteriorating health culminated in neurosclerosis, commonly known as ALS, a condition that remains a medical challenge today. Loo watched helplessly as his muscular functions gradually deteriorated, eventually succumbing to respiratory failure in 1957 at the age of 78 in Nyon, Switzerland. His body was laid to rest in the family cemetery of his wife in Hobevoie, Paris, marking the end of a controversial life for this legendary figure in the world of cultural relic trading.

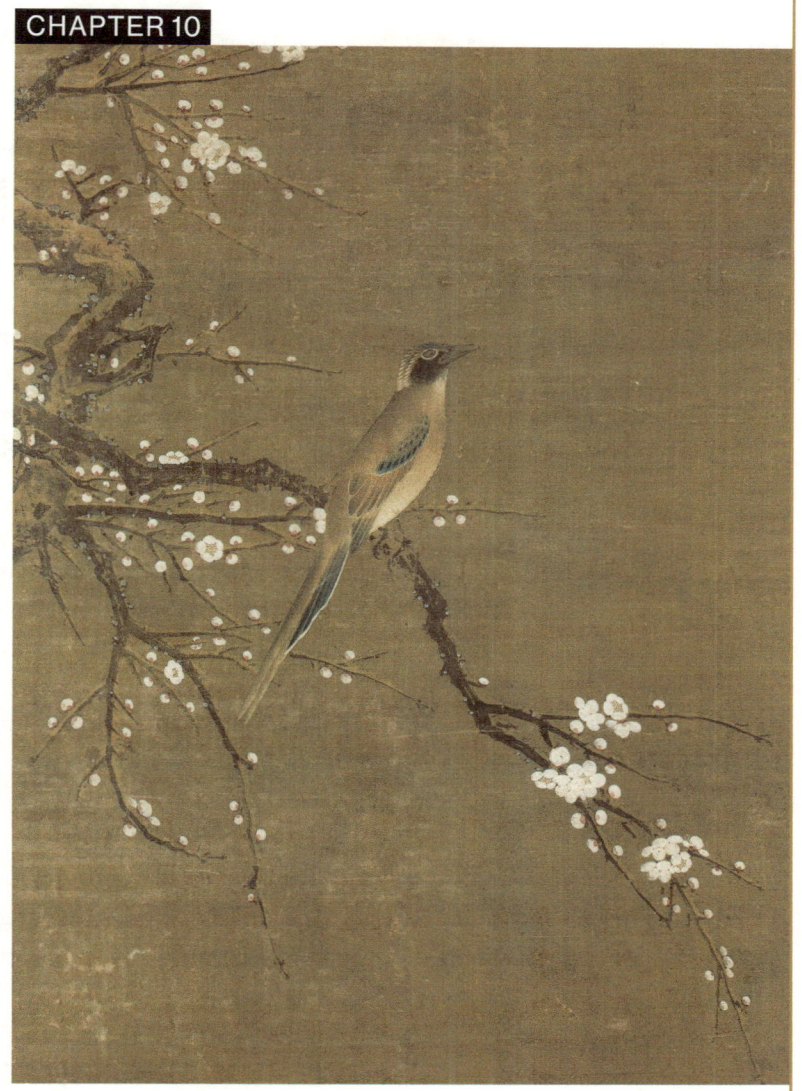

CHAPTER 10

Yamanaka Sadajirō and Yamanaka & Co.

1912

Yamanaka & Co. purchased the collection of bronzes, ceramics, jades, jade, and other artifacts in Prince Gong Mansion for 340,000 silver dollars, except for most of the paintings and calligraphy.

1915

On the 22nd day of the second lunar month, the Prince Chun Mansion sold six ancient calligraphy and painting works recorded in *Midian Zhulin* (Forest of Treasures in the Imperial Palace) and *Shiqu Baoji* (Collected Treasures of the Stony Moat) compiled during the Qianlong period to Yamanaka & Co.

1916

Yamanaka & Co. held 11 Chinese antiques and art auctions in New York, establishing itself as the world's largest Chinese art dealer.

1917

Yamanaka Sadajirō purchased the courtyard house of Prince Su in Beijing as the branch of Yamanaka & Co. in Beijing.

1924–1927

Yamanaka Sadajirō successively went to Tianlongshan Grottoes, Longmen Grottoes in Luoyang, and Yungang Grottoes in Datong to investigate, and began to steal a considerable number of statues from Tianlongshan Grottoes.

1932

In November, Yamanaka & Co. held the World Ancient Art Exhibition at the Tokyo Art Association, Japan, and put the stone sculptures of Tianlongshan Grottoes up for public auction.

10.1 From Osaka to the World

Yamanaka & Co. had humble beginnings as a modest family antique store nestled in Osaka Prefecture, Japan. However, its trajectory was forever altered by one child hailing from a lineage of antiquarians—Yamanaka Sadajirō, who not only propelled the establishment from obscurity to international acclaim but also catalyzed its evolution into a sprawling multinational chain. In the annals of Chinese cultural dissemination, the saga of Yamanaka Sadajirō stands as a pivotal chapter.

Born in 1866 and christened Adachi Sadajirō, Yamanaka Sadajirō (Figure 10-1) emerged as the eldest scion of Andashi Shingoro, heir to a legacy of antiquarian pursuits in Osaka. Raised amid the trappings of his family's antique emporium, he imbibed the intricacies of antiquities from tender years, apprenticing under his father's tutelage. His academic journey commenced in 1873 when he enrolled in the Sakai City Primary School. Upon graduation, at the age of thirteen, Sadajirō embarked on a formative odyssey, joining the esteemed Yamanaka Kichibei's antique emporium in Osaka as an apprentice, thereby inaugurating his career in the realm of antiquities. In the crucible of Yamanaka Kichibei's

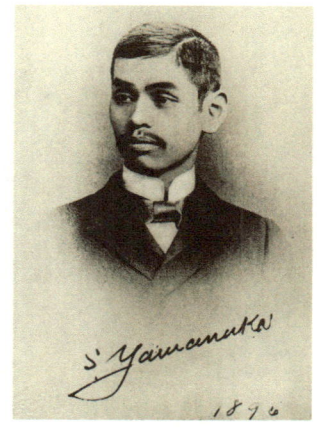

Figure 10-1 31-year-old Yamanaka Sadajirō (1896)

establishment, Sadajirō's mettle shone brightly. Renowned for his indefatigable work ethic and unwavering integrity, he navigated the labyrinthine world of antiquities with aplomb. Through assiduous study and relentless inquiry, he amassed a formidable reservoir of expertise in business operation and appraising cultural artifacts. Moreover, his interactions with luminaries and collectors from across Europe and the United States unveiled vistas of opportunity in the Western antiquarian sphere, igniting his entrepreneurial zeal. The years spanning 1883 to 1886 witnessed Sadajirō's relentless pursuit of knowledge, as he concurrently pursued studies at a commercial night school and an English private institution in Osaka City, laying the groundwork for his envisioned foray into international markets.

Adachi Sadajirō swiftly garnered the favor and personalized mentorship of Yamanaka Kichibei, marking a pivotal juncture in his career at the tender age of 23. Yamanaka Kichibei, recognizing Sadajirō's burgeoning potential, extended an unprecedented offer: adoption into the esteemed Yamanaka lineage and betrothal to his eldest daughter. With this momentous union, Sadajirō assumed the mantle of the Yamanaka name, ushering in a new chapter as an integral member of the Yamanaka family. Assiduously assuming the reins of the Yamanaka Antique Shop, he embarked on a fervent quest to export its antique legacy to the distant shores of Europe and America (Figure 10-2).

In 1894, at the age of 29, Yamanaka Sadajirō discerned the burgeoning allure of Eastern cultural treasures in Western markets, recognizing therein a golden opportunity. Brimming with ambition, he promptly embarked on a transcontinental odyssey, accompanied by his spouse, to establish a foothold in the United States. Setting anchor at No. 4, West 27th Street, New York City, the inaugural Yamanaka & Co. (Figures 10-3 and 10-4) outpost materialized. In less than six months, the couple set up the New York branch of Yamanaka & Co. and orchestrated art exhibitions and auctions, catalyzing its ascent from provincial obscurity to transatlantic prominence.

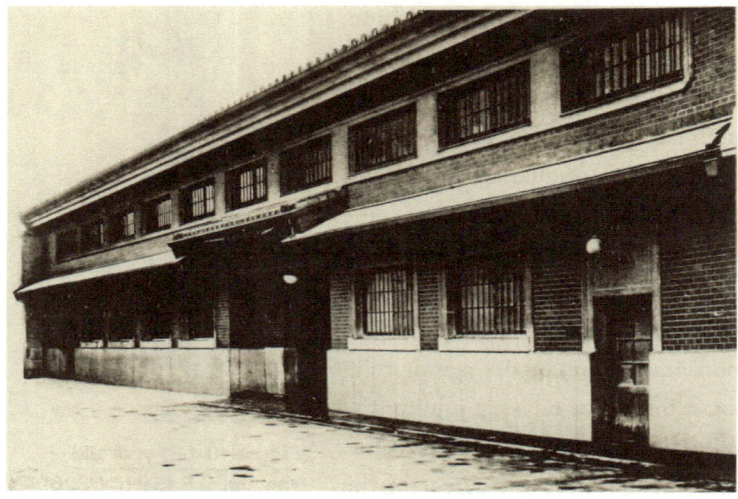

Figure 10-2 Yamanaka & Co. headquarters at Koryobashi 1-chome, Osaka, Japan (early 20th century)

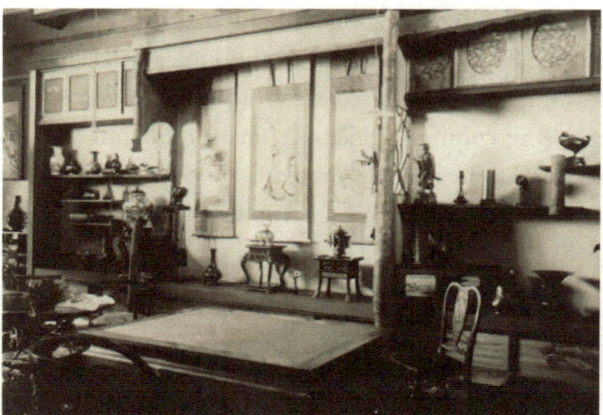

Figure 10-3 Interior view of the New York branch of Yamanaka & Co.

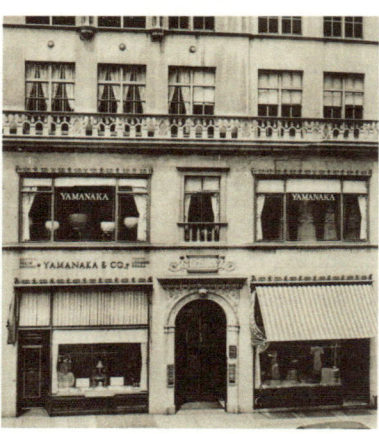

Figure 10-4 New York branch of Yamanaka & Co. (early 20th century)

The transmutation of Yamanaka & Co. from Osaka to New York is a testament not only to Yamanaka Sadajirō's intrepid spirit but also to his astute business acumen. Recognizing the elite echelons of antique aficionados as his primary clientele, he brazenly relocated the gallery to the opulent environs of Fifth Avenue, heedless of exorbitant rents. Departing from prevailing European aesthetics, Yamanaka infused the establishment with a distinctly Japanese ambiance, drawing inspiration from the serenity of temple architecture. Adorned with tatami-style flooring and bathed in ethereal shafts of light, the gallery exuded an aura of timeless elegance, punctuated by whimsical displays of commonplace Japanese artifacts. This ingenious design ethos not only captivated the denizens of New York but also reverberated across the American landscape, casting Yamanaka & Co. into the limelight of American consciousness.

In 1899, propelled by his vision for expansion, Yamanaka Sadajirō replicated his successful business model by establishing branches in strategic locales such as Boston and Chicago (Figure 10-5). Shimotsuma Toyoyoshi, entrusted with the stewardship of Yamanaka & Co. in Chicago, eloquently articulated Sadajirō's strategic ethos, "Our selection of this locale mirrors the sophistication of Fifth Avenue in New York City. Situated amid the city's premier hotels, upscale residences, and burgeoning fashion districts, it is destined to emerge as a bastion of high-end commerce."

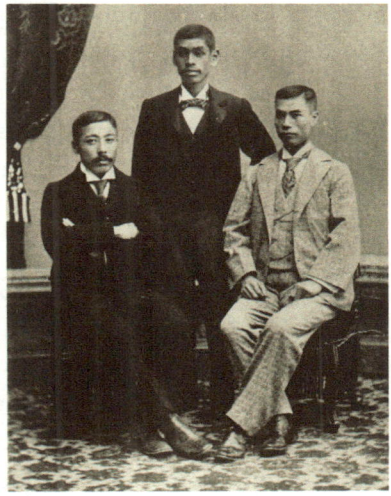

Figure 10-5 New York Branch Manager Yamanaka Sadajirō (middle), London Branch Manager Yamanaka Rokuzaburo, and Boston Branch Manager Yamanaka Shigejiro (early 20th century)

A discerning analysis reveals that Yamanaka Sadajirō's market strategy mirrors the playbook of European luxury brands venturing into China, characterized by a resplendent allure designed to captivate the discerning eye. This innovative approach reverberated across continents, influencing contemporaries such as Ching Tsai Loo, who, a decade later, meticulously replicated Sadajirō's blueprint in New York, fashioning an opulent emporium reminiscent of exotic splendor. In a watershed moment in 1928, Ching Tsai Loo transposed this paradigm to the heart of Paris, erecting the flagship establishment—Pagoda Paris.

Buoyed by the resounding success of his pioneering strategy, Sadajirō expediently propagated it to distant shores. By 1900, emissaries were dispatched to London (Figure 10-6), and by 1905, Paris became the latest epicenter of Yamanaka & Co.'s burgeoning empire. Consolidating these ventures under the aegis of the Yamanaka & Co. Group, Yamanaka Sadajirō assumed a hands-on role as its chief executive. Subsequent expansions saw the emergence of branches in key metropolises such as Beijing, Shanghai, Kyoto, and Tokyo, culminating in the ascendance of a formidable global entity. In 1917, the president of

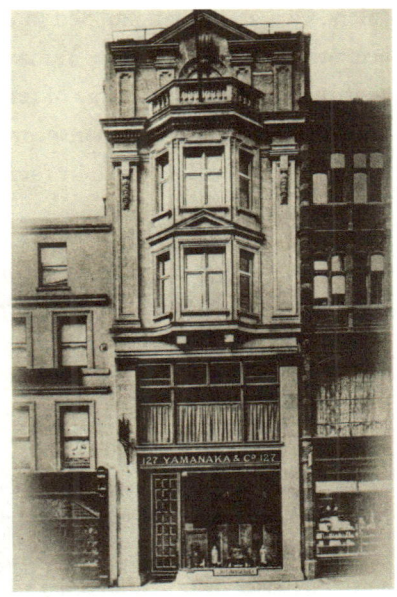

Figure 10-6 London Branch of Yamanaka & Co. (early 20th century)

Yamanaka & Co., Yamanaka Kichibei, departed this world. In the ensuing year of 1918, Yamanaka Sadajirō orchestrated a transformative reorganization into Yamanaka & Co. Ltd., with himself at the helm as president. In a milestone of validation, Yamanaka Sadajirō garnered royal recognition in 1919, as King George V and Queen Mary of the United Kingdom bestowed upon him coveted Royal Warrants. This august honor, reserved for purveyors of unparalleled excellence, served as a testament to Yamanaka & Co.'s eminence in providing superlative antiquities to discerning clientele. Since 1923, Yamanaka & Co. has continued to showcase its treasures through grandiose exhibitions in Japan.

10.2 Expansion in Beijing

After establishing a formidable presence in Europe and the United States, Yamanaka Sadajirō cast his gaze upon China, a reservoir of profound cultural heritage. China, with its venerable history and abundant troves of relics and artworks, stood as a beacon of opportunity, boasting the most vibrant antique market on the globe. Recognizing the potential for acquiring Oriental treasures and leveraging the burgeoning demand in overseas markets, Yamanaka Sadajirō embarked on the establishment of a Yamanaka & Co. branch in Beijing, thus heralding a new epoch in the illustrious saga of Yamanaka & Co. In 1901, the inaugural office of the Yamanaka & Co. materialized at No. 3 Maxian Hutong, Dongcheng, Beijing, amid the tumultuous backdrop of the Boxer Rebellion and the subsequent incursion of the Eight-Power Allied Forces (Figure 10-7). In the wake of the upheaval, as the Qing Dynasty rulers, Cixi and Guangxu, fled in disarray, a deluge of cultural relics cascaded from the palace, primed for acquisition. Yamanaka & Co. seized upon this unprecedented opportunity, swiftly amassing a vast array of relics.

Recognizing the immense promise of the Chinese market, Yamanaka Sadajirō embarked on a decisive move in 1917, acquiring a 300-square-meter courtyard nestled within

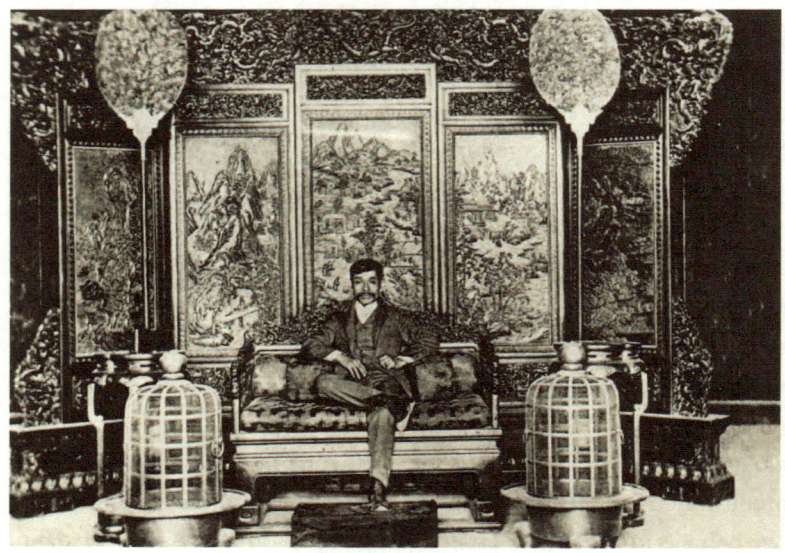

Figure 10-7
Yamanaka Sadajirō sitting on a chair in the Forbidden City (early 20th century)

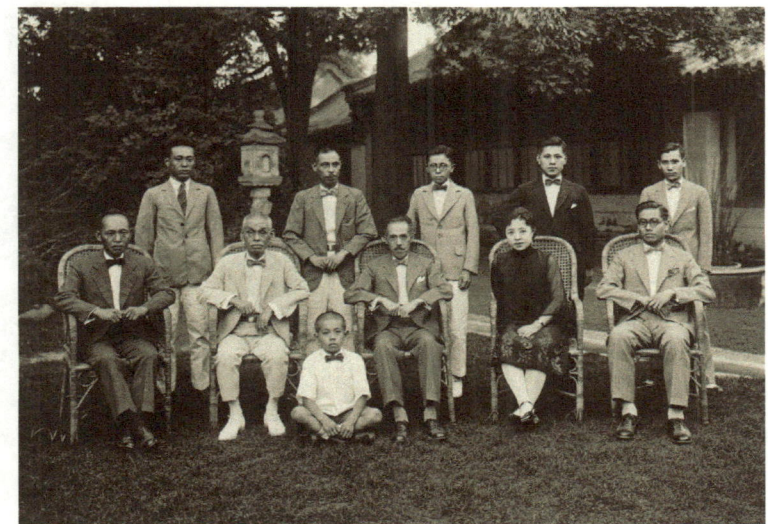

Figure 10-8 Yamanaka Sadajirō (front row, second from left) with the clerk of the Beijing branch of Yamanaka & Co. in Prince Su Mansion (early 20th century)

the esteemed confines of Prince Su's residence to serve as the Beijing branch of Yamanaka & Co. Under the stewardship of branch manager Takada Matajiro, leading a team comprising four Japanese clerks and fifteen Chinese staff members (Figure 10-8). Notably, during the Beijing operation, branch manager Takada cultivated robust ties with antique dealers in Beijing's Liulichang, remaining abreast of market trends and procuring rare and exquisite artifacts at premium prices. The branch's procurement practices extended beyond private collections to include treasures once ensconced within the royal precincts, sourced from various locales and erstwhile nobility. Yamanaka Sadajirō's unwavering commitment to product quality was matched only by his dedication to securing a steady supply of goods. Every spring and autumn, he embarked on a two-week procurement expedition from Osaka to Beijing. In meticulous preparation, the Beijing branch proactively liaised with antique industry operators, vendors, and dealers spanning the expanse of Beijing. Invitations were extended for them to converge upon the courtyard of Yamanaka & Co., where they erected stalls to showcase their prized antique collections atop 2-meter-long tables. Guided by the discerning eye of Yamanaka Sadajirō, his purchasing staff stationed in Europe and the United States made purchases in accordance with prevailing demand. Subsequently, the dedicated personnel at the Beijing branch assumed the mantle of responsibility for sorting, transporting, and facilitating transactions. During the multi-day procurement proceedings, an impressive procession of approximately 200 antique dealers traversed the country, navigating bustling thoroughfares via rickshaws, bearing their treasures and cultural relics to the hallowed grounds of Yamanaka & Co.'s Beijing branch for its selection. Over the course of more than three decades of operations in China, Yamanaka & Co. amassed a prodigious collection of ancient artworks, leading to the lamentable consequence of numerous Chinese national treasures finding their way overseas (Figure 10-9).

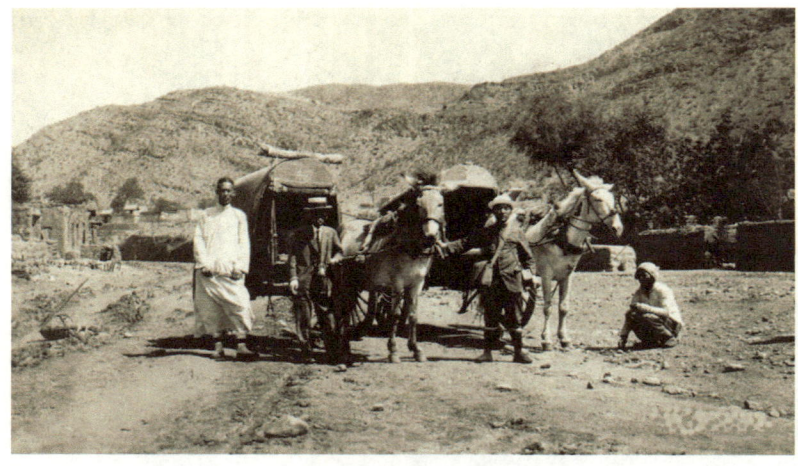

Figure 10-9
Yamanaka Sadajirō
(second from left)
traveling in China
(early 20th century)

Among the acquisitions secured by Yamanaka & Co. in Beijing are four exquisitely rare large Buddha statues crafted with ramie dry lacquer, dating back to the era of the Sui Dynasty (Figure 10-10). China has a long tradition of lacquerware craftsmanship. Lacquerware is an everyday utensil and handicraft made by coating the surface of various utensils with lacquer. Initially conceived as utilitarian objects, lacquerware gradually evolved into cherished artifacts, revered for their lightweight composition, resistance to corrosion, and imperviousness to insects. With the burgeoning popularity of Buddhism since the Wei and Jin dynasties, lacquerware found favor within temple precincts, emerging as a quintessential medium for the production of Buddhist statues. The Buddha statues crafted with ramie dry lacquer epitomize a pinnacle of artisanal mastery, characterized by a labor-intensive process fraught with intricacies. First, the Buddha statue undergoes a meticulous sculpting process, crafted delicately from clay. Next, a delicate layer of ramie cloth is gently draped over the clay structure, meticulously secured in place using natural lacquer. As the lacquer gradually sets and solidifies, subsequent layers of ramie cloth are carefully applied, each one meticulously fixed with lacquer, creating a composite shell of ramie and lacquer around the original clay core. This painstaking process is repeated numerous times, until a sturdy and refined exterior encapsulates the statue's essence. Allowing ample time for the lacquer to dry thoroughly, the skilled artisan proceeds to remove the inner clay structure meticulously, leaving behind only the exquisitely thin shell. With the foundation set, the artisan proceeds to adorn the statue with intricate lacquer decorations, meticulously refining details and contours to accentuate the statue's inherent beauty. Finally, hues of vibrant colors are carefully applied, and the surface is delicately adorned with shimmering gold foil.

Creating a 1-meter-high Buddha statue from dried lacquer is a labor of love that spans dozens of months, a testament to the pinnacle of lacquerware craftsmanship. Such masterpieces are never mass-produced; instead, they are cherished as rare treasures, with

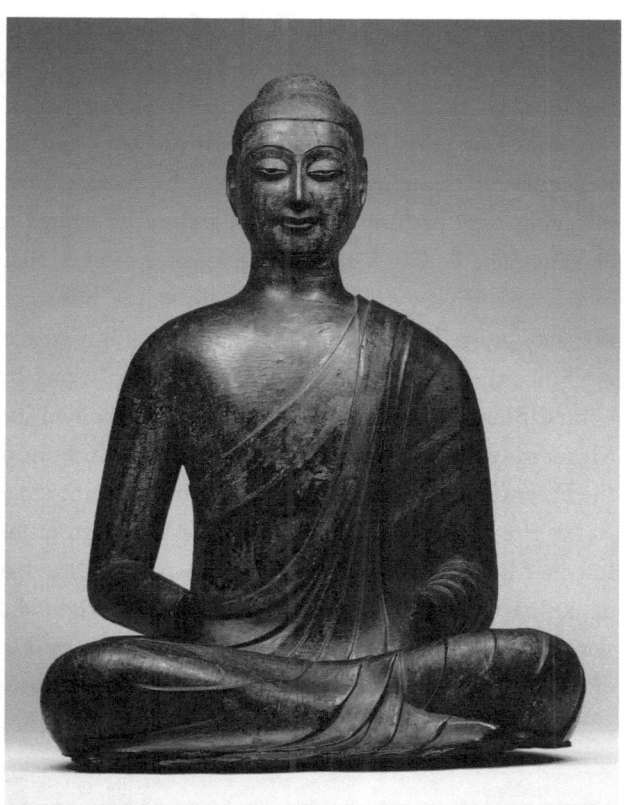

Figure 10-10 Sui Dynasty ramie lacquered seated Buddha statue purchased from Yamanaka & Co. (105.1 cm × 73.1 cm × 55.1 cm, now in the Walters Art Museum, Baltimore, Maryland, USA, No. 25.9)

only one or two carefully crafted by each temple for the sacred "walking the statue" ritual, where the Buddha statues are gently placed upon ornate floats and paraded through the streets, inviting awe and reverence from all who behold them. The esteemed monk Zanning (919–1001) of the Northern Song Dynasty documented in the book *History of Song Monks*: Since the divine passing of Sakyamuni Buddha into Nirvana, the yearning to behold the true countenance of the Buddha compelled the royals and nobles to create these divine images, symbolizing the scene of Prince Sakyamuni's vigilance over the city after his birth. Traditionally held on the auspicious occasion of Sakyamuni's birthday (the eighth of the lunar April), the ritual may also grace other significant days. In this way, the Buddha statue does not have to be Sakyamuni, but a regular Buddha statue will do, such as the four dry lacquer statues procured by Yamanaka & Co. Dry lacquer statues possess a unique advantage: their lightweight construction facilitates easy mobility. Crafting a Buddha statue from materials such as stone, wood, or copper presents significant challenges when it comes to their practical use in such a ritual. Yet, despite their practicality, dry lacquer Buddha statues are vulnerable to the ravages of time. Consequently, the rarity of preserved dry lacquer Buddha statues underscores the significance of those held by Yamanaka & Co., elevating their status to that of invaluable relics.

While inspecting goods sent by antique dealers at his Beijing headquarters, Yamanaka Sadajirō stumbled upon these dusty, dilapidated Buddha statues. Despite their missing details, such as hands, halo ornament on their backs, and hair bun intricacies, his keen eye, honed by years of familiarity with lacquer craftsmanship, discerned their true worth. Recognizing them as rare treasures, he swiftly made the decision to purchase them, reserving one for himself and dispatching the remaining three to the New York branch of Yamanaka & Co. Little did he know, however, that what he had encountered was not merely an ordinary dry lacquer Buddha statue, but a peerless treasure dating back to the Sui Dynasty, crafted 1,400 years ago and exceedingly scarce in the world.

Since then, these three precious Buddha statues have found a permanent home in the United States, gracing the collections of esteemed institutions such as the Metropolitan Museum of Art in New York, the Walters Museum of Art in Baltimore, Maryland, and the Freer Gallery of Art in Washington. From 2017 to 2018, the National Museum of Asian Art at the Smithsonian Institution in Washington hosted the enlightening Secrets of the Lacquer Buddha exhibition (Figure 10-11). Smaller than real person sizes, these statues, all depicting Padmasana, adorned in a coat with right shoulder exposed, captivate with their slender form. Their clothing patterns exhibit a striking realism, embellished with traces of color and delicate gold foil. Glass beads are embedded in their eyes, while the hollow bodies, intended to house scriptures and sacred relics, now stand empty, their treasures

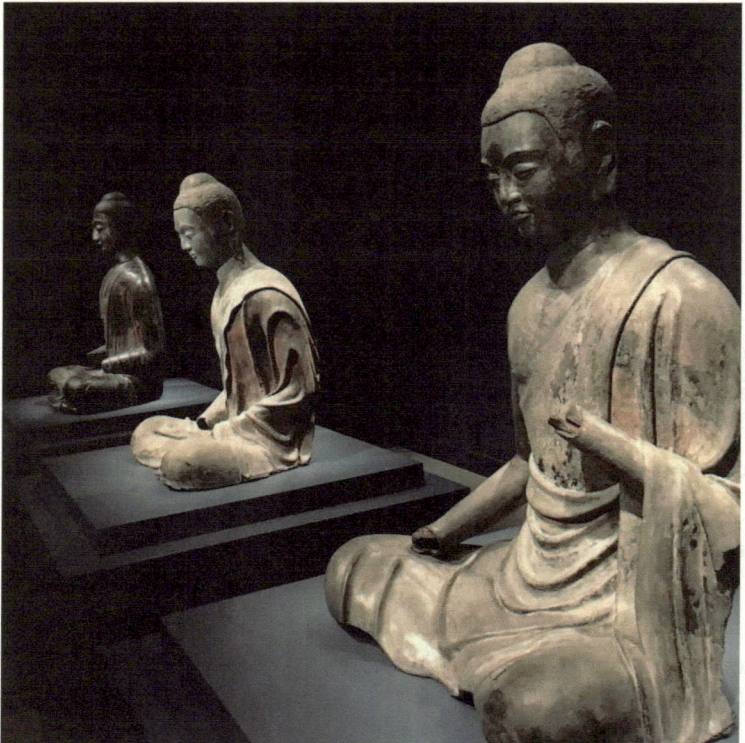

Figure 10-11 Three Sui Dynasty seated Buddha statues with ramie lacquer on display at the Secrets of the Lacquer Buddha exhibition in 2017–2018 (from right to left are currently in the collections of the Freer Gallery of Art, the Metropolitan Museum of Art, and Walters Museum of Art)

lost to time. Through cutting-edge scanning technologies such as X-ray and MRI, their origins and ages have been meticulously traced, confirming their heritage from the Great Buddhist Temple of the Sui Dynasty in Zhengding, Hebei. Meanwhile, the dry lacquer Buddha statue in the private collection of Yamanaka Sadajirō, once featured in the seminal work *Chinese Sculpture from the 5th to 14th Centuries* by Swedish art historian Osvald Siren (1879–1966), sadly vanished from Japan after World War II, a loss deeply felt and mourned.

10.3 Treasures in Prince Gong Mansion

The crowning achievement of Yamanaka & Co. since its inception was undoubtedly the acquisition of ancient cultural relics from the Prince Gong Mansion. Amid the tumultuous Revolution of 1911, Prince Gong Puwei (1880–1936) (Figure 10-12) and other Qing imperial relatives staunchly opposed the tide of change, forming the Royalist Party to rally forces against the revolutionary fervor and adamantly refusing to acquiesce to the abdication decree of the Qing emperor. However, with Emperor Xuantong's proclamation of abdication on February 12, 1912, Puwei and his fellow Royalist Party members pivoted to support the restoration efforts of the Qing Dynasty. In a bold move to bolster military coffers and aid the restoration cause of the last emperor, Puyi, Puwei resolved to liquidate his extensive collections housed within Prince Gong Mansion. Upon learning of this decision, Yamanaka Sadajirō swiftly initiated negotiations with Prince Gong to secure the acquisition of these prized artifacts (Figure 10-13).

Yamanaka Sadajirō recounted his entry into Prince Gong Mansion in 1912:

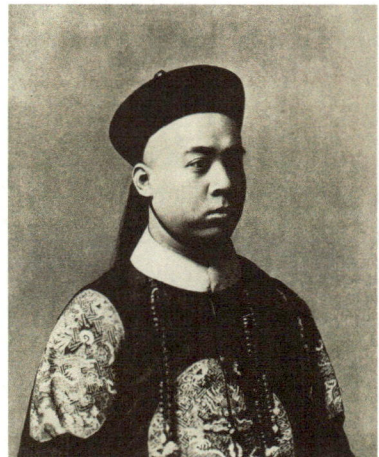

Figure 10-12 Prince Gong Puwei (before 1911)

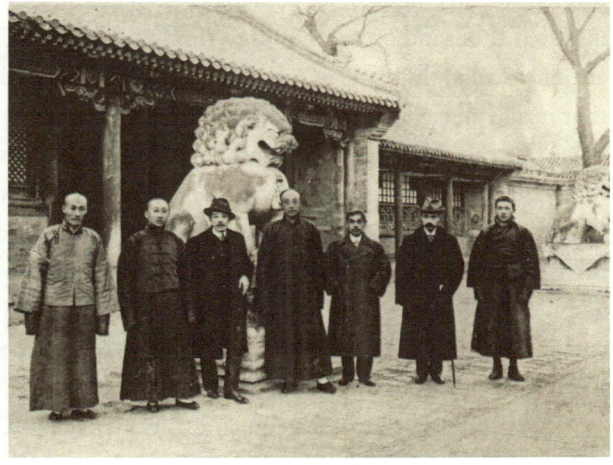

Figure 10-13 Yamanaka Sadajirō (third from right), Yamanaka Rokusaburo, and others in front of the main hall of Prince Gong Mansion (March 1912)

Beyond the gates of Prince Gong Mansion lie meticulously arranged structures, housing a retinue of three to four hundred individuals, including Prince Gong's esteemed family, dedicated attendants, and vigilant palace guards. Within the compound, nestled amid serene courtyards and lush gardens, stands a grand edifice housing a vast study adorned with an impressive array of literary treasures flanked by splendid displays of bronze and jade artifacts. Adjacent to this scholarly enclave, a stately two-story structure, akin to an imposing L shape, serves as an unparalleled repository of artistry, housing an opulent collection of priceless treasures.

As one traverses through this veritable treasure trove, crossing thresholds adorned with stone archways, there is a picturesque garden adorned with exotic blooms, a tranquil teahouse, a tranquil lake pavilion, and a celestial moon viewing platform. In this harmonious fusion of natural splendor and artistic opulence, visitors are ensnared by the allure of beauty.

Upon his initial entry into Prince Gong Mansion, Yamanaka Sadajirō was struck with awe at its opulence. Diligently, he embarked on a meticulous inspection of the treasure troves housed within, from the Ruyi Warehouse to the Painting and Calligraphy Warehouse and from the Jade Warehouse to the Bronze Warehouse, each chamber overflowed with priceless relics gathering dust, waiting to be rediscovered. In the Jade Warehouse, he witnessed a breathtaking array of jade jewelry, so many that he lost count. The butler of Prince Gong Mansion presented a plethora of these exquisite treasures and asked, "How much do you offer to pay?" Yamanaka's surprise was palpable, recognizing the enormity of the transaction unfolding before him. The Biography of Yamanaka Sadajirō, published in 1939, encapsulates the intricacies of his endeavor to procure the cultural relics of Prince Gong Mansion. Its account paints a picture of a transaction whose magnitude transcends mere monetary figures; as Yamanaka Sadajirō muses, "The amount is different from one hundred thousand or two hundred thousand." Indeed, to him, and perhaps to any seasoned antique dealer, this was an unparalleled lifetime experience—an opportunity of such rarity that it may never present itself again.

After careful deliberation and negotiations, Yamanaka Sadajirō made the bold decision to acquire the extensive collection of bronzes, ceramics, furniture, jades, clocks, and other artifacts from Prince Gong Mansion, with the exception of most paintings and calligraphy, for the substantial sum of 340,000 silver dollars. This move, though perceived as a risky gamble at the time as in the Western antique world of that era, the market for Chinese antiques had yet to fully emerge and flourish, proved to be an astute investment, catapulting Yamanaka & Co. to unprecedented heights of success.

In the aftermath of the acquisition, Yamanaka & Co. exercised patience, opting to ship the treasures to the United States rather than rush to sell them. A year later, they meticulously cataloged each piece, held auctions, and gradually solidified their dominance in the field. In 1913, Yamanaka & Co. hosted a landmark auction titled Heavenly Art Treasures at

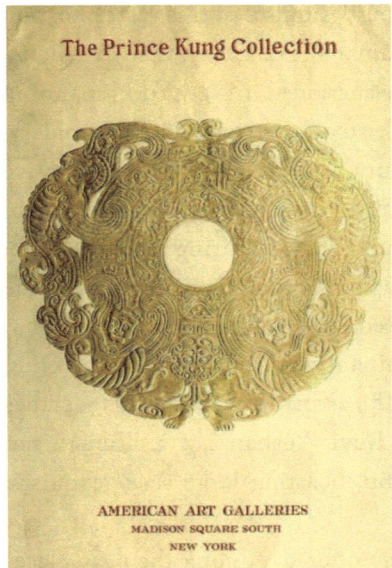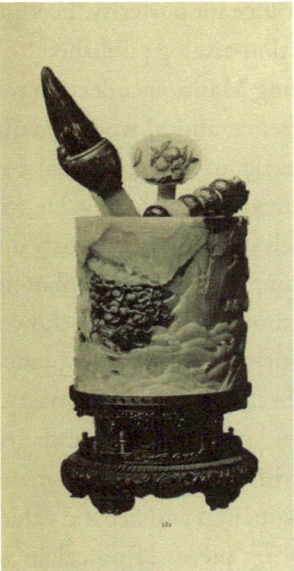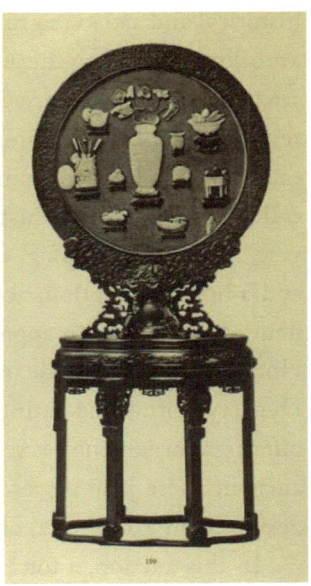

Figure 10-14 The jade pen holder and the jade-inlaid round light seat screen on the rosewood lacquer base made for Emperor Qianlong of the Qing Dynasty on the cover and catalog of the Prince Gong Mansion Photo Catalog held by Yamanaka & Co. at the American Art Galleries in New York in 1913

the prestigious American Art Galleries in New York, accompanied by a lavish gilded catalog (Figure 10-14). This event reverberated throughout the American collecting community, hailed as the epitome of Chinese art collections. The auction's impact was monumental, with a staggering total transaction volume exceeding 276,000 US dollars. Speculations abound that in the year between the purchase and the auction, Yamanaka & Co. may have sold a significant portion of the artifacts through in-store and individual sales. This unprecedented success, culminating in a record-breaking sum of 270,000 US dollars, underscored the monumental triumph of the auction, marking it as a pivotal moment in the annals of art history.

In 1914, Yamanaka & Co. once again orchestrated a special auction titled Private Collections of Chinese Nobles in Tianjin and Cultural Relics Purchased by Yamanaka & Co. in Beijing at the esteemed American Art Galleries in New York. This auction, too, proved to be a resounding success, boasting sales totaling nearly 200,000 US dollars. These twin triumphs catapulted Yamanaka & Co. into a veritable golden age, solidifying its position as a powerhouse in the world of art dealing. Buoyed by the momentum of their previous successes, Yamanaka & Co. embarked on a prolific spree in 1916, hosting a remarkable total of 11 Chinese antiques and art auctions in New York. This remarkable feat firmly established Yamanaka & Co. as the preeminent dealer of Chinese art on a global scale.

The cultural relics acquired from Prince Gong Mansion by Yamanaka & Co. remain shrouded in mystery, leaving future generations to wonder at their splendor. One can only imagine the magnificence of a museum showcasing these treasures in situ, preserving their historical and artistic significance for posterity. Fortunately, glimpses of this vast collection are afforded through the auction catalog published by Yamanaka & Co. In that year alone, 536 items from the Prince Gong Mansion collection were auctioned in New York, spanning seven categories: jade, bronze, ceramics, wood, enamel, stone carvings, and embroidery, each representing the pinnacle of Qing Dynasty court artwork. This comprehensive collection boasts high historical and artistic value, rivaling even the royal collections of yore. Within the catalog, each item is meticulously documented, featuring its name, date, and a brief description, accompanied by vivid photographs. Among these treasures, jade items dominate, with approximately 244 pieces showcased. The jade materials range from Hotan white jade to jade, jasper, and black jade, predominantly originating from the Qing Dynasty, with some dating back to the Han Dynasty. The assortment of utensils includes offerings, ornaments, screens, pen holders, pendants, Ruyi, Yushanzi, etc. Though not ancient, these jade pieces exhibit superior craftsmanship, boasting large sizes, exquisite designs, and exceptional ornamental and artistic value.

In this auction, a total of 133 pieces of porcelain were offered. Among them, 35 pieces were characterized by their elegant white glaze, comprising water bowls from the Ding kiln system in the Song Dynasty, white bowls from the Yongle official kiln in the early Ming Dynasty, and white-glazed study supplies from the renowned kilns of Jingdezhen during the Yongzheng period of the Qing Dynasty. Another 35 pieces showcased exquisite blue and white multicolored porcelain, predominantly featuring Avalokitesvara statues and mallet bottles hailing from the esteemed kilns of Jingdezhen during the late Ming and early Qing dynasties. Furthermore, the auction boasted 63 pieces of single-color glaze porcelain, meticulously crafted by the official kilns of Kangxi and Yongzheng. These pieces encompassed a rich spectrum of hues, including black gold, blue glaze, blue and gold, red glaze, cowpea red, Lang kiln red, yellow glaze, sky blue glaze, malachite green glaze, gold glaze, coral red, Lang kiln green, apple green, tea leaf color, and more. Notably, the porcelains in the old collection of Prince Gong Mansion spanned from the Northern Song Dynasty to the Qing Dynasty, with predominant representation from the renowned kilns of Jingdezhen in the Ming and Qing dynasties. Other famous kilns, such as Jun kiln, Ding kiln, and Ge kiln from the Song Dynasty, were also represented, alongside a smattering of local kilns like Dehua kiln and Fahua porcelain. Each porcelain piece exuded elegance and finesse in its shape and craftsmanship, accentuated by its original hardwood base. These exquisite items likely graced the daily surroundings of Prince Gong Mansion. Yet, these porcelains represent just a fraction of the opulent treasures originally curated by Prince Gong Mansion, testifying to the magnificence and discerning taste of its illustrious proprietor.

Within the aforementioned auction catalog, a noteworthy inclusion comprises 99 bronzes, ranging from conventional utensils like *zun, jue, hu, gui,* and *ding* to more intriguing specimens such as animal-shaped wine *zun*s, wine *hu*s, and wine *gong*s (Figure 10-15). Among these artifacts are pieces dating back to the Shang (c. 1600–1046 BC) and Zhou (1046–256 BC) dynasties, as well as the Spring and Autumn and the Warring States periods

(770–221 BC). Others hail from later periods, particularly the Song and the Qing dynasties. During the Qianjia period of the Qing Dynasty, a surge in textual research precipitated a societal fascination with antiquity, prompting literati and officials to embrace the display of antique bronzes as a fashionable statement. This trend extended to the Qing palace offices, with collections likely sourced from establishments like the Qing Palace Workshop, strategically positioned within Prince Gong Mansion to evoke a sense of ancient elegance. In addition to the bronzes, the auction also features 11 items crafted from ivory and rhino horn, alongside other ritual vessels, fabrics, paintings, etc.

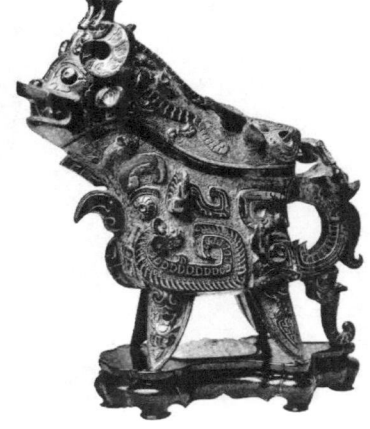

Figure 10-15 Shang Dynasty bronze *gong* in *Prince Gong Mansion Photo Catalog*

In fact, many of the cultural relics procured by Yamanaka & Co. from Prince Gong Mansion never made it to the auction block. Instead, these invaluable treasures from the old Qing palace collections found their way into the hands of private collectors through discreet private transactions. One such prominent buyer was Francis Lee Higginson (1877–1969), a renowned American banker and esteemed patron of Harvard University, which later honored him with the namesake Higginson College. Among the remarkable acquisitions from Prince Gong Mansion purchased by Higginson through Yamanaka & Co. was a distinctive four-pronged halberd vessel embellished with phoenix patterns (Figure 10-16). This ancient bronze wine vessel, known as *you*, represents a rare and sizable specimen dating from the late Shang Dynasty to the early Western Zhou Dynasty. Adorned with intricate geometric motifs, delicate cloud and thunder patterns typical of the Shang and Zhou dynasties, as well as elaborate phoenix reliefs, this *you* stands as a testament to the exquisite craftsmanship of its time. Notably, its three-dimensional phoenix sculptures adorning the lid and handle exhibit unparalleled artistry. This particular piece, more intact than its counterpart housed in the Shanghai Museum, holds significant value for artistic research. In 1934, Higginson facilitated the sale of this bronze to the Museum of Fine Arts, Boston, through Yamanaka & Co.

Additionally, Higginson acquired another notable bronze *you* adorned with animal face patterns from the early Western Zhou Dynasty (Figure 10-17). Detailed information about this vessel can be found in Volume 15 of *Xiqing Gujian* (Xiqing Catalog of Ancient Treasures), compiled by the Imperial Household Department during the Qianlong period of the Qing Dynasty. *Xiqing Gujian* meticulously documents the images, sizes, and weights of all the bronze Yi vessels housed within the collection of the Qing Imperial Household Department during that era. It meticulously outlines their titles and offers detailed annotations. The entry pertaining to this animal-faced *you* vividly documents an eight-character inscription found on both the body and cover of the vessel: "Zi Cheng Zha Wen

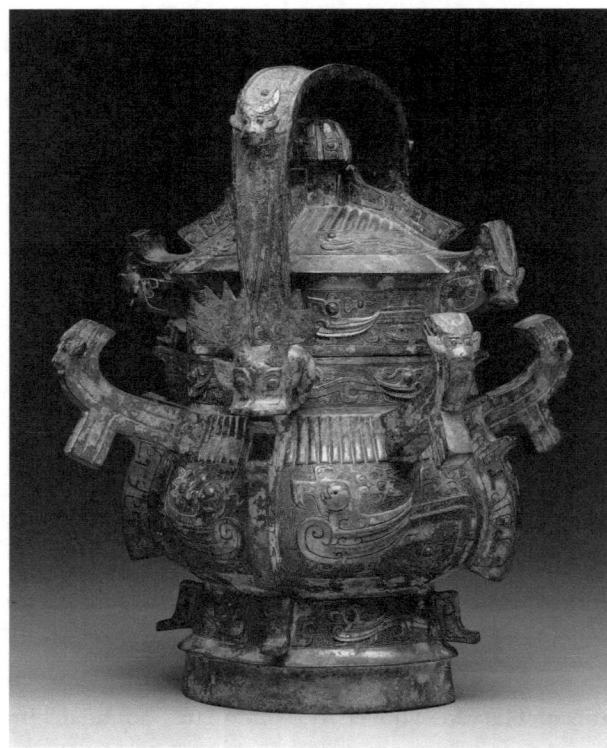

Figure 10-16 The four-pronged halberd vessel embellished with phoenix patterns in the late Shang Dynasty or early Western Zhou Dynasty (35.5 cm high, 22.8 cm wide, now in the Museum of Fine Arts, Boston, No. 34.66, purchased from Yamanaka & Co. in 1934)

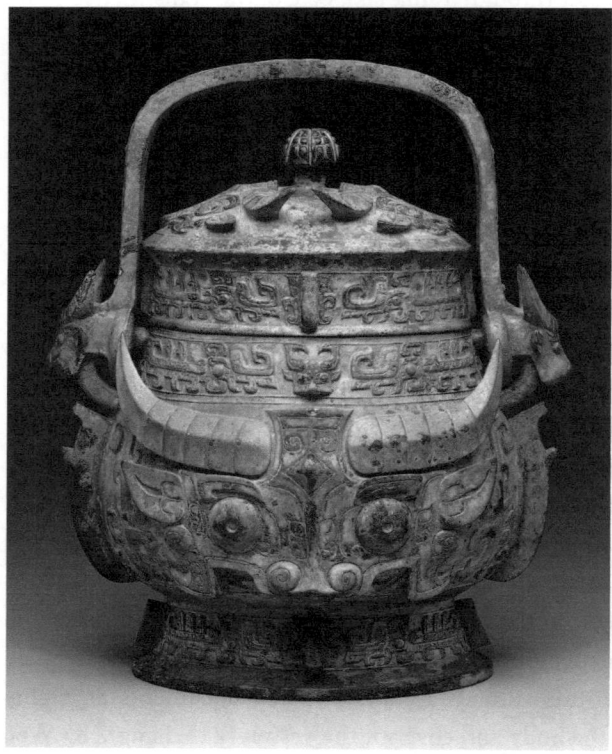

Figure 10-17 Bronze *you* with animal face patterns from the early Western Zhou Dynasty (25 cm high, now in the collection of the Museum of Fine Arts, Boston, No. 34.63a-b, purchased from Yamanaka & Co. in 1934)

Fu Ding Zun Yi," denoting its function as a ritual vessel utilized by Fu Ding for sacrificial ceremonies. Diverging from the conventional bas-relief ritual vessels adorned with cloud and thunder motifs, this particular vessel accentuates the imagery of the mythical beast with distinctive horns and ears. Moreover, intricate relief ox-head-shaped animal faces adorn the lid and the end of the handle, enhancing its ornate appearance. Due to its earlier discovery and longstanding heritage, the overall shape of the vessel remains remarkably intact, devoid of extensive rust. Its graceful demeanor and exceptional preservation contribute to its heightened allure and significant research value.

Previously owned by Liu Tizhi (1879–1963), an esteemed official and bibliophile in the Republic of China, this animal-faced *you* was documented in his publication *Shan Zhai Ji Jin Lu* (The Collected Bronze Works in Shan Zhai), published in 1934. Following its dispersal overseas, the *you*, alongside the four-pronged phoenix halberd vessel, found a new home at the Museum of Fine Arts, Boston, on February 1, 1934, facilitated by Higginson's collaboration with Yamanaka & Co., with funding provided by the Anna Mitchell Richards Fund.

10.4 Western Clocks in the Qing Palaces

To this day, Yamanaka & Co. has maintained secrecy regarding a comprehensive inventory of the artifacts acquired from Prince Gong Mansion. Besides the Museum of Fine Arts, Boston, and the Fujita Museum, the Nezu Museum, established by Japanese private collector Nezu Kaiichiro (1860–1940), also procured a substantial number of cultural relics from Yamanaka & Co. Nezu's passion for collecting extended from tea sets and Buddhist artifacts to calligraphy, painting, bronzes, ceramics, lacquerware, sculptures, and textiles. Among the renowned pieces in the Nezu Museum's collection are Mu Xi's *Fishing Village Sunset* from the Southern Song Dynasty (AD 1127–1279), a celadon vase dating back to the Southern Song Dynasty, *Eighty-One Large Mandalas of the Diamond Realm*, as well as various Buddha statues acquired from Yamanaka & Co. Notable among these are Buddha statues originating from the Tianlongshan Grottoes in Taiyuan, Shanxi, large

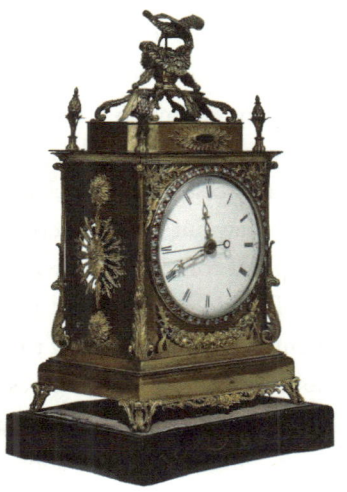

Figure 10-18 A treasure-embedded clock from the royal collection made during the Qianlong period of the Qing Dynasty (44 cm high, formerly housed in Prince Gong Mansion, now in the Nezu Museum, purchased from Yamanaka & Co.)

bronze square wine vessels from the tombs of Shang kings, and bronze double sheep statues from Henan. However, perhaps the most intriguing piece remains the clock from Prince Gong Mansion, which Nezu Kaichiro has chosen to keep shrouded in secrecy, a Western-style clock originally housed in the imperial palace of the Qing Dynasty (Figure 10-18).

European mechanical clocks made their debut in the 14th century, and even by the 18th century, they remained objects of luxury across Europe. It was during the mid-16th century that Western missionaries, aiming to curry favor with the Ming court and establish a foothold for the church in China, presented clocks as tribute. Thus, Western clocks found their way to China through these diplomatic channels. In the 29th year of the Wanli period in the Ming Dynasty (1601), the Italian missionary Matteo Ricci (1552–1610) astounded the court by gifting two self-ringing clocks to Emperor Shenzong (r. 1573–1620). It caused quite a sensation at the time. Subsequently, during the Qing Dynasty, successive emperors lauded clock art, sparking a nationwide craze for clocks. By the 10th year of the Yongzheng reign (1732), the Workshop of the Imperial Household Department of the Qing Palace established the Clock Making Workshop, dedicated to the storage, repair, and making of clocks. This department primarily crafted various types of clocks for the royal family, including watches, self-ringing clocks, and musical clocks. The production process involved coordination among workshops specializing in lacquer, wood, gold, jade, ivory, foundry work, and gunsmithing. To maintain quality standards, components such as springs and dials were occasionally sourced from Western countries via Guangdong Customs. Crafting a large clock could take several years. Notably, the emperors of the Qing Dynasty not only favored chiming clocks but also amassed collections of clocks and penned imperial poems praising their allure. According to estimates by Jesuit priest Valentin Chalier (1697–1747), during the early Qianlong period, the Qing court boasted over 4,000 self-ringing clocks, their chimes resonating throughout the Forbidden City day in and day out. This underscores the integral role clocks played in palace life, serving as the temporal cornerstone for various ceremonial events.

The clocks bestowed upon the Chinese emperor by foreign dignitaries and governments boasted secondary time-telling functions, with an increasing number incorporating novel entertainment features such as automatic mechanisms and music boxes. Among the 15 clocks housed in the Nezu Museum's collection, 13 possess musical capabilities, and 12 are automatic, each adorned with stunningly unique cases and lavish gilding and inlays featuring an array of vibrant gemstones—a sight to behold. Utilizing cutting-edge production techniques of the time, including musical movements and intricate automatic mechanisms, these clocks boasted an impressive array of moving parts.

Within the Nezu Museum, eight chiming clocks crafted in Guangzhou during the late Qianlong period are on display. Guangzhou, being an early window to the West, was instrumental in introducing various types of clocks to China. The Imperial Workshop established a dedicated institution in Guangzhou for the development of clocks, and local craftsmen had ample exposure to European clockmaking techniques. Their craftsmanship incorporated finely painted enamel clock faces, vibrant artificial gemstones, and other European decorative elements, which earned favor from the royal family and nobility. Concurrently, China actively imported clockmaking technology from Europe, resulting in timepieces that combined Western Industrial Revolution advancements with opulent palace aesthetics, becoming coveted luxury items during the Qianlong period.

Most mechanical chiming clocks crafted in the Guangzhou Workshop fused Chinese and Western decorative elements. Craftsmen adorned these clocks with precious gemstones like rubies, sapphires, and jade, incorporating auspicious motifs such as dragons, phoenixes, and symbols of longevity—distinct from their Western counterparts. One clock in the Nezu Museum's collection features a scholar figurine that emerges hourly, unveiling a scroll bearing the inscription "Long Live." Such prized clocks were often bestowed upon favored royal relatives and ministers by the emperor, comprising a significant portion of the clocks found in Prince Gong Mansion and thus holding exceptional collection value.

In 2008, the Nezu Museum embarked on an ambitious project to construct an exhibition hall in Tokyo's upscale Omotesando district. To raise funds for the endeavor, the museum auctioned off 15 antique clocks from the Qing Palace collection at Christie's auction house. This event shed light on the abundance of overlooked cultural relics from Prince Gong Mansion. At the heart of this auction stands a true marvel: a three-layer "bonsai" inlaid enamel chiming

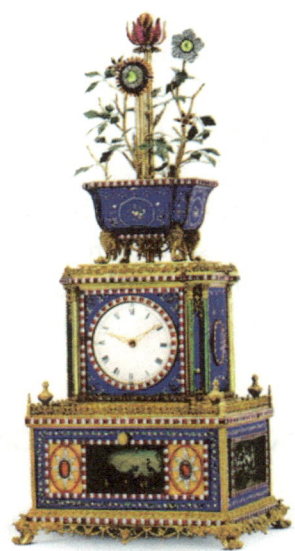

Figure 10-19 A musical clock with gilt-copper inlaid with an enamel flower pot made during the Qianlong period of the Qing Dynasty (formerly housed in Prince Gong Mansion, now in the Nezu Museum, purchased from Yamanaka & Co.)

clock crafted by the artisans of the Guangzhou Workshop. This extraordinary timepiece transcends the ordinary, boasting not only the use of Phoebe zhennan—a material of tribute—but also a captivating array of floral motifs. The top of this clock is also adorned with tulips, peonies, sunflowers, and orchids meticulously inlaid with precious stones. Upon winding, the delicate flowers gracefully sway in harmony with the melodious chimes (Figure 10-19). This auction garnered an astounding 36 million US dollars for the 15 clocks, ten times their estimated value, underscoring the exquisite rarity of the cultural treasures procured by Yamanaka & Co.

Yamanaka's clientele extended to illustrious figures such as the Rockefeller family from New York, renowned art collector Charles Lang Freer of Detroit, Ernest Francisco Fenollosa (1853–1908), and Isabel Stewart Gardner (1840–1924) of Boston, among others. Freer, a preeminent Oriental art collector and Yamanaka & Co.'s foremost patron, acquired 1,598 items from their New York and Boston chapters. Following Freer's passing, these acquisitions formed the cornerstone of the East Asian collection at the Freer Gallery of Art. In his correspondence, Freer lauded Yamanaka & Co. as "the largest Japanese art dealer in existence … a strong influence among American antique dealers … almost all dealers in New York purchase from there."

Yamanaka Sadajirō, known for his business acumen and pursuit of maximum profits, sought to diversify procurement channels, even venturing to remote Japanese temples in the mountains. In 1905, he corresponded with Freer about his exploits in search of treasures at the ancient temples of Mount Koya—a sacred Buddhist site in Japan. Despite the challenges posed by the harsh climate and unappealing food, Yamanaka's efforts yielded treasures such as a 13th-century Bodhisattva portrait from the Kamakura period (1185–1333) and various Buddhist scriptures and scrolls. Touched by Yamanaka's account, Freer purchased these exquisite Japanese Buddhist scroll paintings for 6,000 US dollars, which remain on display at the Freer Gallery of Art to this day.

10.5 Mysterious Calligraphy and Paintings

When it comes to the triumph of Yamanaka & Co. in the United States, one cannot overlook the pivotal role played by Ernest Fenollosa (Figure 10-20). A distinguished American scholar of Japanese art, Fenollosa immersed himself in Eastern culture during his extended stay and teaching tenure in Japan, becoming one of the earliest Americans to embrace and study Eastern artistic traditions. As a renowned Orientalist, his profound appreciation and collection of Asian cultural artifacts left an indelible mark on prominent figures such as collector Freer and painter James Abbott McNeill Whistler (1834–1903). His discerning eye and refined taste in Oriental art set a standard for American collectors in the 19th century. In his capacity as the director of the Department of Japanese and Chinese Art at the Museum of Fine

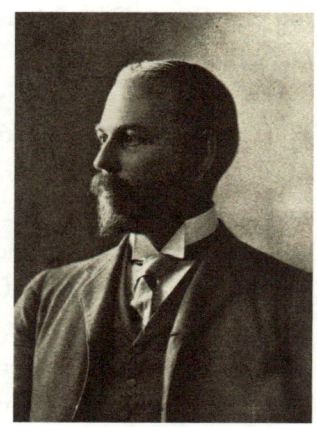

Figure 10-20 Ernest Fenollosa

Arts, Boston, Fenollosa made significant acquisitions of various Asian artifacts from Yamanaka & Co. in 1890. Notably, his pursuit led to the eventual acquisition of two bronze *you*s, initially purchased by Higginson, through Yamanaka & Co., cementing their place as prized possessions in the Museum of Fine Arts, Boston.

Beyond bronzes, Fenollosa amassed a notable collection of calligraphy and paintings through Yamanaka & Co. Among these acquisitions, the most esteemed is *Nine Dragons* (Figure 10-21) by Southern Song Dynasty painter Chen Rong. Chen Rong (c. 1200–1266), known by his courtesy names Gongchu and Suoweng, hailed from Changle, Fujian (now part of Fuzhou). Renowned as a Jinshi, an imperial examination title, he held esteemed positions as the director of the Imperial College and the governor of Putian. Notably multifaceted, Chen Rong's talents extended beyond his administrative roles to encompass poetry, prose, and the mastery of ink dragon paintings. Renowned for his adeptness with ink, Chen Rong possessed a unique ability to conjure intricate layers of ink clouds on paper

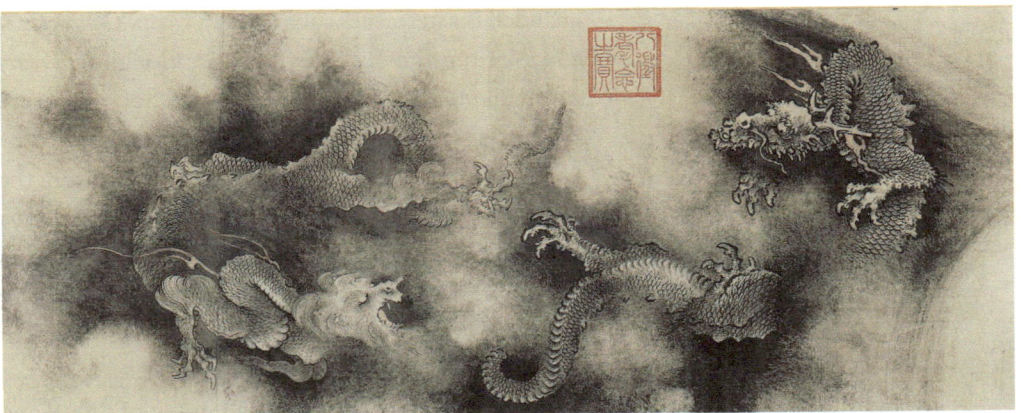

Figure 10-21 Part of *Nine Dragons* by Chen Rong of the Southern Song Dynasty in 1244 (painted in 1244, color on paper, 46.2 cm × 958.4 cm, now in the Museum of Fine Arts, Boston, USA, No. 17.1697, purchased from Yamanaka & Co.)

by deftly controlling the dry and wet shades of ink. His ink dragons captivated audiences in the Song Dynasty, garnering widespread acclaim and popularity. Among his surviving works, *Nine Dragons* stands as a pinnacle of his artistic prowess. In *Nine Dragons*, ethereal clouds envelop the scene, concealing nine ink dragons amid the swirling rain and mist. Each dragon exudes a sense of imminent flight and dynamic energy. This masterpiece, characterized by its technical finesse, conceptual depth, and emotive resonance, is hailed as the epitome of dragon painting. Chen Rong's dragons exerted a profound influence on Eastern painting traditions, shaping depictions of dragons for centuries to come. Esteemed Japanese artists such as Katsushika Hokusai (1760–1849) and Koizumi Junsaku (1924–2012) were notably inspired by his evocative renderings. Originally housed in the Qing Dynasty court's collection, *Nine Dragons* found its way to Prince Gong Mansion during the late Qing Dynasty. Subsequently, it was acquired by Yamanaka & Co. along with the rest of Prince Gong Mansion's collection. Fenollosa's astute acquisitions eventually led to the painting's permanent residence in the Museum of Fine Arts, Boston.

Many of the ancient Chinese paintings procured by Yamanaka & Co. in Beijing originated from the esteemed lineage of Prince Chun. The inaugural Prince Chun, Yihuan (1840–1891), was the seventh son of Emperor Daoguang and the father of Emperor Guangxu. His successor, Zaifeng (1883–1951), the second-generation Prince Chun, was the fifth son of Yihuan and the father of the last emperor, Puyi. Notably, Zaifeng assumed the role of regent during the Qing Dynasty. Transaction records of Yamanaka & Co. reveal that Prince Chun Zaifeng undertook the sale of his collection to bolster military funds for national restoration efforts. Personally intervening, Zaifeng orchestrated the sale of six precious calligraphy and painting pieces on February 22, in the fourth year of the Republic of China (1915). These artworks, chronicled in the *Midian Zhulin* (Forest of Treasures in the Imperial Palace) and *Shiqu Baoji* (Collected Treasures of the Stony Moat) compiled during the Qianlong period,

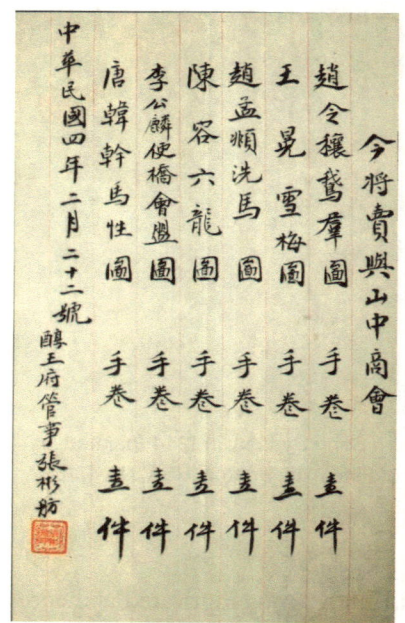

included masterpieces such as Han Gan's *Character of a Horse* from the Tang Dynasty, Li Gonglin's *Treaty at the Bian Bridge* from the Northern Song Dynasty, Zhao Lingrang's *Willows and Geese* from the Northern Song Dynasty, Chen Rong's *Six Dragons* from the Southern Song Dynasty, Wang Mian's *Snow Plum Blossoms* from the Yuan Dynasty, and Zhao Mengfu's *Bathing Horses* from the Yuan Dynasty. Supervising the transaction was Zhang Binfang, the steward of Prince Chun Mansion (Figure 10-22).

Renowned as a luminary painter of the Tang Dynasty, Han Gan's artistry diverged from traditional horse-painting conventions, focusing instead on capturing the essence of real horses. His meticulous depictions not only exude lifelikeness but also convey the distinct temperament of each equine subject. Han Gan's oeuvre was revered by successive dynastic palaces, with later generations of renowned equine painters emulating his style. *Character of a Horse* held a place of honor in Emperor Qianlong's study (Figure 10-23). *Night-Shining White* showcases a Central Asian steed with fiery eyes, flaring nostrils, and animated hooves. The profusion of seals and inscriptions adorning the painting attest to its esteemed status among past collectors.

Figure 10-22 The receipt for the sale of six paintings to Yamanaka & Co. issued by Zhang Binfang, steward of Prince Chun Mansion, on February 22, the fourth year of the Republic of China (1915)

Every cultural relic from the Qing palace has its own intricate story, but what perplexes me most are the six ancient paintings sold by Prince Chun. According to records from Yamanaka & Co., the receipts for them bear Prince Chun's signature and seal. However, the four calligraphy and paintings by Zhao Lingrang, Wang Mian, Li Gonglin, and Chen Rong all feature the Prince Gong's seal. Combining historical data from the Qing Dynasty, it becomes apparent that these four scrolls were bestowed upon Prince Gong by the emperor, yet they were sold by Prince Chun. What sort of transfer occurred in between, and how were they sold to Yamanaka & Co.? Perhaps only by bringing Puwei and Zaifeng back to life from their graves can these questions be answered. Nonetheless, these mysteries underscore a larger issue. In the early 20th century, royal relatives, eunuchs, maids, and even ordinary citizens participated in a fervent exodus of national treasures. Even the last emperor, Puyi, joined in. During his residency in Tianjin, Puyi sold the imitation of Guo Zhongshu's *Traveling on the River in Snow* by Song painters to the Nelson-Atkins Museum of Art in Kansas City. *The Rise and Fall of National Treasures* by Professor Yang Renkai (1915–2008) traces the vast array of calligraphy and painting treasures that Puyi took with him upon leaving the palace and their lamentable fates.

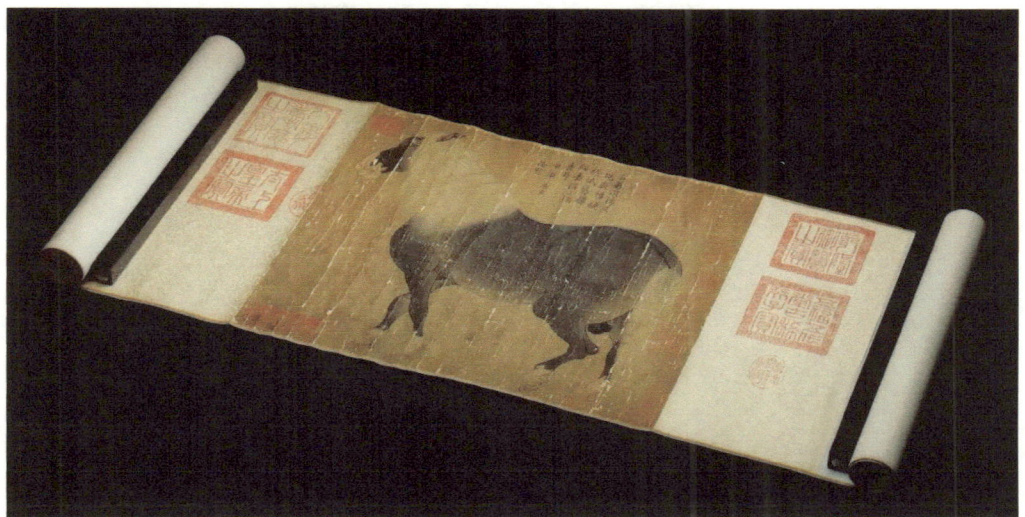

Figure 10-23 *Character of a Horse* by Han Gan in the Tang Dynasty (formerly collected by the Fujita Museum in Osaka, Japan)

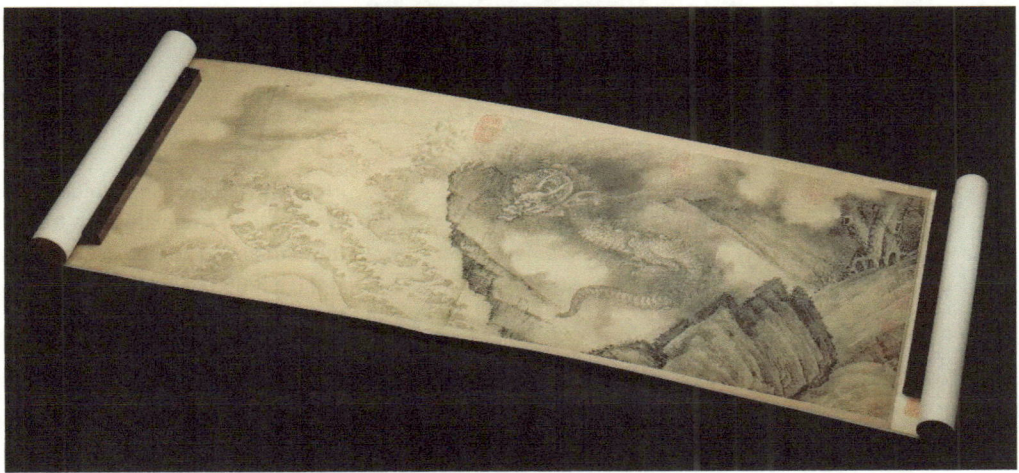

Figure 10-24 *Six Dragons* by Chen Rong of the Southern Song Dynasty (formerly collected by the Fujita Museum in Osaka, Japan)

The six ancient paintings belonging to Prince Chun, along with various collections of bronzes, gold and silverware, and clocks, were sold by Yamanaka & Co. to the Fujita Museum, owned by Fujita Denzaburō (1841–1912). Due to poor museum management and financial challenges, the Fujita Museum auctioned off six paintings, including *Character of a Horse* and *Six Dragons*, and some bronzeware at Christie's spring auction in New York in 2017. Among these works, *Six Dragons* (Figure 10-24) alone fetched a staggering price of 48.9675 million US dollars (equivalent to over 300 million RMB).

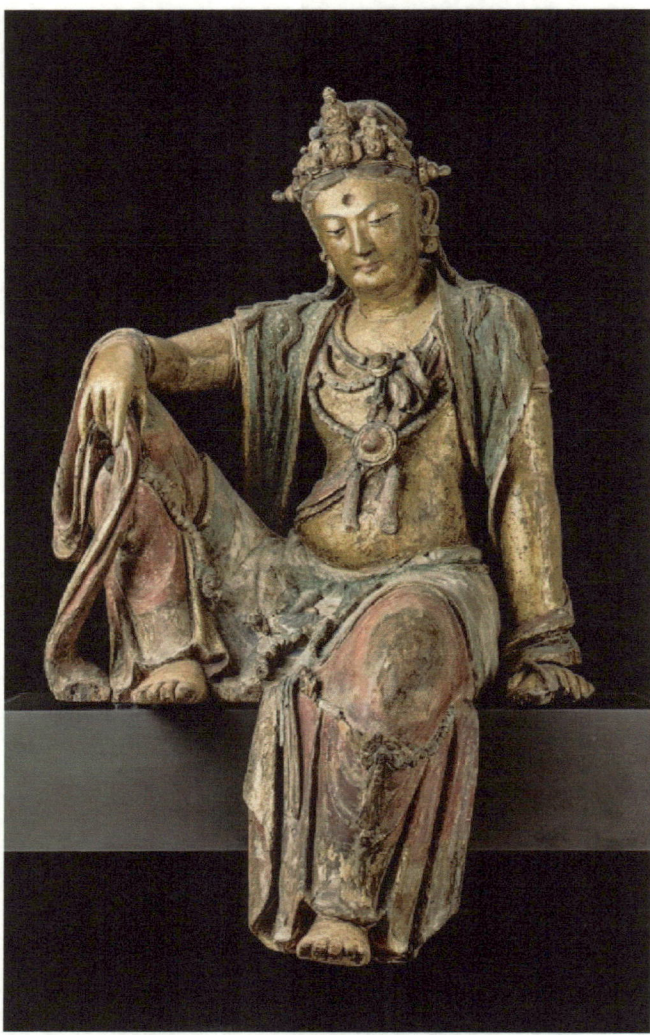

Figure 10-25 Wooden statue of Water-Moon Avalokitesvara from the 12th century in the Jin Dynasty (141 cm × 88 cm × 88 cm, now in the Museum of Fine Arts, Boston, No. 20.590, purchased from Yamanaka & Co. in 1920)

In addition to paintings and calligraphy, the Museum of Fine Arts, Boston, also boasts numerous pieces that have left an indelible mark on the history of Japanese art. In 1920, the Museum of Fine Arts, Boston, acquired a Jin Dynasty Water-Moon Avalokitesvara statue (Figure 10-25) from Yamanaka & Co. Ambiguous inscriptions on the statue suggest it originated from Jishan, Shanxi. The statue features a small Amitabha statue atop Avalokitesvara's crown, signifying his identity. With a slightly lowered head, widened cheeks, and a gentle smile, he appears as if admiring moonlight on water. The statue's rich form and languid expression reflect the aesthetic sensibilities of Avalokitesvara among northern nomads. It encapsulates the essence of Water-Moon Avalokitesvara—indicating the transient nature of all things, akin to the moon's reflection in water or flowers in a mirror, destined to fade into oblivion.

10.6 The Demise of Tianlongshan Grottoes

The history of the Tianlongshan Grottoes in Taiyuan, Shanxi Province, dates back to the Eastern Wei Dynasty. Situated approximately 40 kilometers southwest of Taiyuan, these grottoes were excavated over several dynasties, including the Eastern Wei, Northern Qi, Sui, and Tang Dynasties, reaching completion during the reign of Emperor Xuanzong of the Tang Dynasty (AD 713–756). Comprising 25 caves and over 1,500 Buddhist sculptures, the grottoes may not be vast in size but possess a distinct and captivating style. Historical research indicates that Tianlongshan Mountain, where the grottoes are situated, was near the summer palace of Gao Huan, a prominent official in the Eastern Wei Dynasty. Gao Huan, originally of Han ethnicity but assimilated from the Xianbei, wielded significant influence as the de facto ruler and prime minister of the Eastern Wei Dynasty. While the dynasty's capital was Yecheng (now Linzhang, Hebei Province), Jinyang (now Taiyuan, Shanxi Province) served as its summer capital. Gao Huan, residing mostly in Jinyang, established it as his political hub to govern the Eastern Wei Dynasty. It was during this era that the history of the Tianlongshan Grottoes commenced.

The 25 caves on Tianlongshan Mountain are nestled along the steep mountainside of the southern slopes, arranged in an east-to-west sequence (Figure 10-26). The east peak houses 12 caves, while the west peak accommodates 13. Notable among these are Cave 2 and Cave 3 on the east peak, a group of adjacent smaller caves excavated during the Eastern

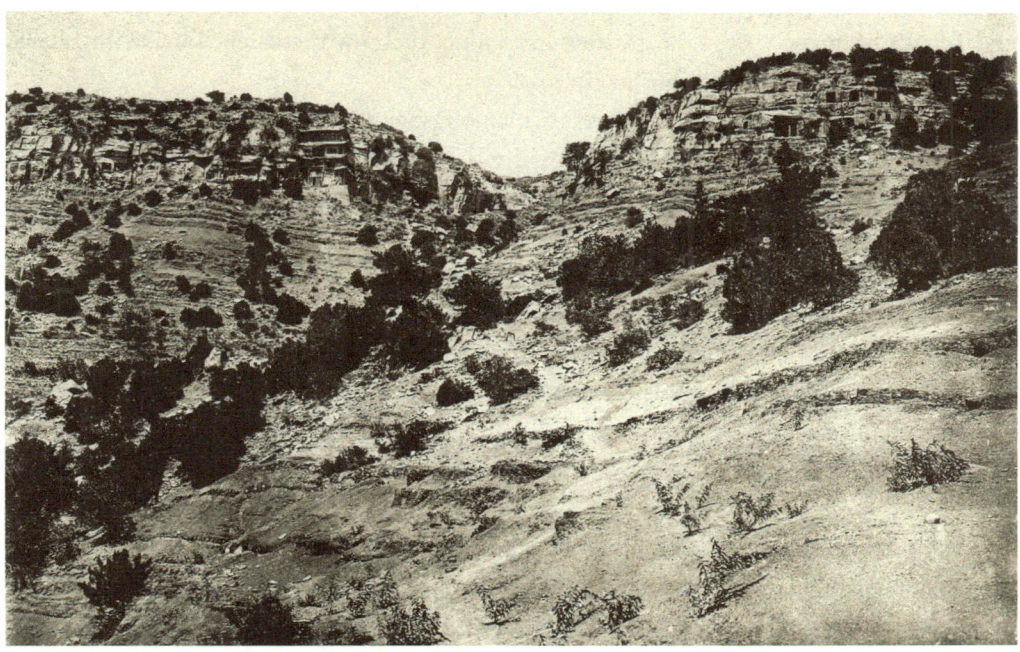

Figure 10-26 The exterior view of the Tianlongshan Grottoes in Taiyuan, Shanxi, in the 1920s (from Plate VIII-1 of *China Cultural and Historical Sites* by Sekino Tadashi and Tokiwa Daijō)

Wei Dynasty, and Cave 1, 10, and 16 from the Northern Qi Dynasty, slightly bigger than Eastern Wei caves. Additionally, Cave 8 was constructed during the Sui Dynasty, with 19 caves added during the Tang Dynasty. The sculptures within the grottoes represent significant works of northern stone statuary from the late 6th to the mid-8th century AD. Of particular value are the caves dating to the reign of Emperor Xuanzong of the Tang Dynasty. Due to the emperor's lack of belief in Buddhism, the activity of carving statues in the northern part of the Central Plains significantly declined. Works from the Xuanzong period are rare finds in renowned grottoes like the Yungang Grottoes in Datong, Shanxi, the Longmen Grottoes in Luoyang, Henan, and the Gongxian Grottoes in Zhengzhou, Henan. Consequently, the caves of Emperor Xuanzong in Tianlongshan have become prized possessions, showcasing the style of the prosperous Tang Dynasty. Particularly noteworthy are the Bodhisattva statues, characterized by exaggerated body postures such as slim waists, broad hips, and twisting forms. The closely-fitted clothing accentuates the beauty of the characters' voluptuous skin, exemplifying the Tang Dynasty's emphasis on physical fitness. This blend of exaggeration and realism represents the pinnacle of Buddhist carving art during the Tang Dynasty.

In 1918, Japanese scholar Sekino Tadashi rediscovered the Tianlongshan Grottoes, which had fallen into neglect and obscurity, based on local historical records. Conducting a thorough investigation, Sekino published his findings in the 375th issue of Japan's journal *Kokka* in 1921 under the title "Tianlongshan Grottoes." This publication brought global attention to the Buddhist statues of the Tianlongshan Grottoes. Following Sekino's work, scholars such as Swedish researcher Osvald Siren and Japanese academics Tokiwa Daijō and Tanaka Shunitsu visited the grottoes to conduct their own research. Tanaka Shun'itsu's findings were subsequently published in 1922.

The scholarly interest in the statues of Tianlongshan Grottoes caught the attention of Yamanaka Sadajirō. In 1924, after his initial visit to Tianlongshan Mountain, Yamanaka Sadajirō expressed his excitement in his diary:

> The opportunity to explore the Buddhist sanctuary of Tianlongshan has long been a dream of mine. Here lies the magnificence of Chinese Buddhist art during its zenith from the Northern Qi to the Sui and Tang Dynasties. Upon entering the grottoes, the sight of Buddhist alcoves, statues, and carvings left me speechless with wonder and delight. Armed with a flashlight, I meticulously examined every corner, reluctant to depart.

Upon returning to Japan, Yamanaka Sadajirō found himself unable to quell his longing for the statues of Tianlongshan Grottoes. In October 1926, at the age of 61, he embarked on another journey to Tianlongshan (Figure 10-27). During this expedition, his team extensively documented their findings through photography and subsequently published the book *Tianlongshan Stone Buddha Collection* in 1928. This publication objectively preserved a

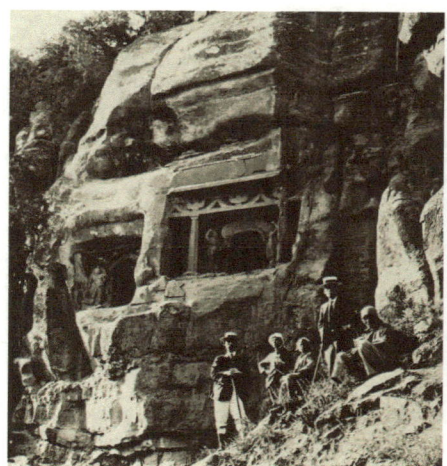

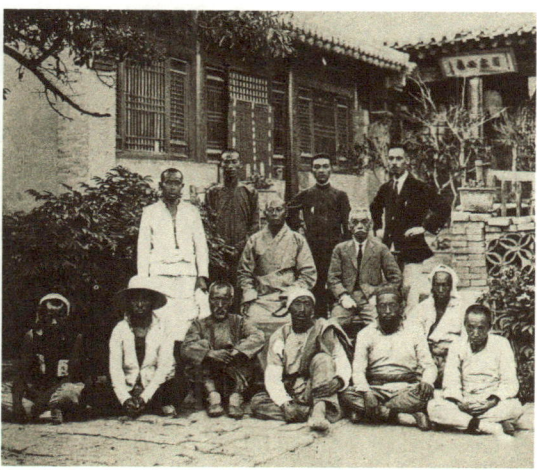

Figure 10-27 Yamanaka Sadajirō's team inspecting the Tianlongshan Grottoes (1926)

Figure 10-28 In 1927, the team of Yamanaka Sadajirō (first from right in the middle row) with the abbot of Shengshou Temple in Tianlongshan Mountain, Monk Jinliang, and others

wealth of historical information about the Tianlongshan Grottoes. However, by the time the book was published, the Tianlongshan Grottoes had been utterly destroyed by Yamanaka Sadajirō himself. Regrettably, his album was intended to showcase the statues he had extracted from the caves for auction.

In 1927, Yamanaka Sadajirō visited the abbot Jinliang, who oversaw the Tianlongshan Grottoes and the Shengshou Temple nestled at the mountain's base. Through bribery, he secured the abbot's cooperation and effectively granted him permission to engage in theft (Figure 10-28). Furthermore, he actively liaised with the local government and obtained tacit approval for his actions. Evidently, to Jingliang and the local authorities, the statues of the Tianlongshan Grottoes were mere remnants of ancient times, deemed worthless and disposable. Consequently, they were all too eager to assist their Japanese acquaintance. Thus began the tragic demise of the Tianlongshan Grottoes.

Through the despicable acts of theft and vandalism perpetrated by Yamanaka's team, numerous statues from Tianlongshan suffered grievous damage, with many losing their heads or having their entire bodies chiseled off. Across 25 caves, they callously extracted 45 Buddha heads, inflicting severe harm, particularly to the exquisite Cave 18 and Cave 21 from the Tang Dynasty, which were left in a state of ruin (Figures 10-29, 10-30). Yamanaka Sadajirō callously remarked, "Every time I find a Buddha head, the joy is more than ten thousand taels of gold." Only large Buddha and Bodhisattva statues remained relatively intact in Cave No. 9 due to their massive size, making them impractical to transport and, consequently, unsellable after being severed from their original context (Figure 10-31). While it cannot be definitively asserted that all these desecrated carvings were orchestrated

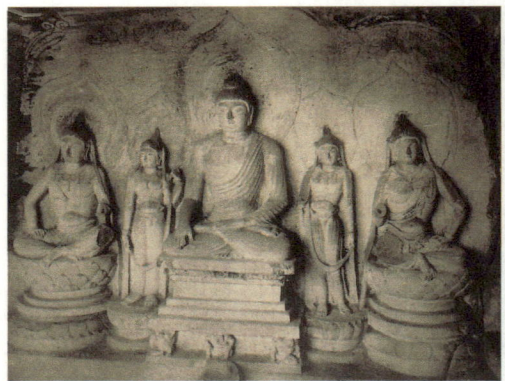

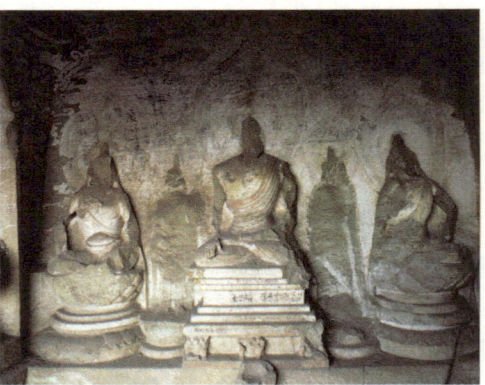

Figure 10-29 Statue on the back wall of Cave 18 of Tianlongshan Grottoes (1922)

Figure 10-30 Current status of the back wall of Cave 18 of Tianlongshan Grottoes

by Yamanaka & Co., it is evident that a substantial portion found their way abroad through their nefarious dealings.

Initially shipped to Japan, where they were displayed in the Tianlongshan Buddhist Sculpture Art Exhibition, many Tianlongshan sculptures were subsequently resold to museums or private collectors in Europe and the United States, yielding substantial profits. Tragically, more than 150 Tianlongshan statues have since been lost overseas. In November 1932, Yamanaka & Co. brazenly held the World Ancient Art Exhibition at the Tokyo Art Association, auctioning off these stolen treasures to the public (Figure 10-32). Consequently, the sculptures of Tianlongshan Mountain were scattered across the globe, forever sundered from their rightful place. Adding to the tragedy, several Buddha heads donated by Yamanaka Sadajirō to the Museum of Asian Art in Berlin were

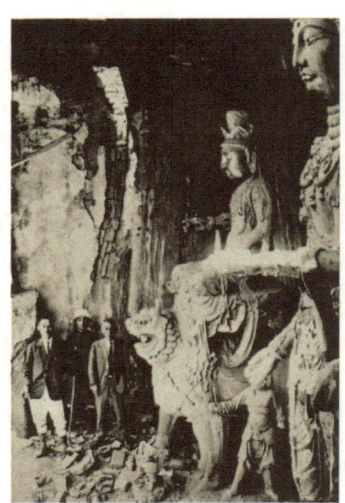

Figure 10-31 Yamanaka Sadajirō investigating Cave 9 at Tianlongshan (1926)

destroyed during the chaos of World War II in 1937, robbing future generations of the opportunity to behold their true magnificence. The sole silver lining is that once a Tianlongshan statue is identified within a collection, its original location in the grottoes can be traced with relative ease, thanks to the historical data meticulously documented by previous investigators.

Some Tianlongshan sculptures have found their way into the esteemed collections of American museums. Notably, the Harvard Art Museums boasts the largest assortment of Tianlongshan Grotto statues, comprising 25 relief fragments primarily sourced from Caves 2 and 3 excavated during the Eastern Wei Dynasty. These artifacts, including disciples, Manjushri, flying apsaras, and donors, were acquired by the museum in 1943 and serve as

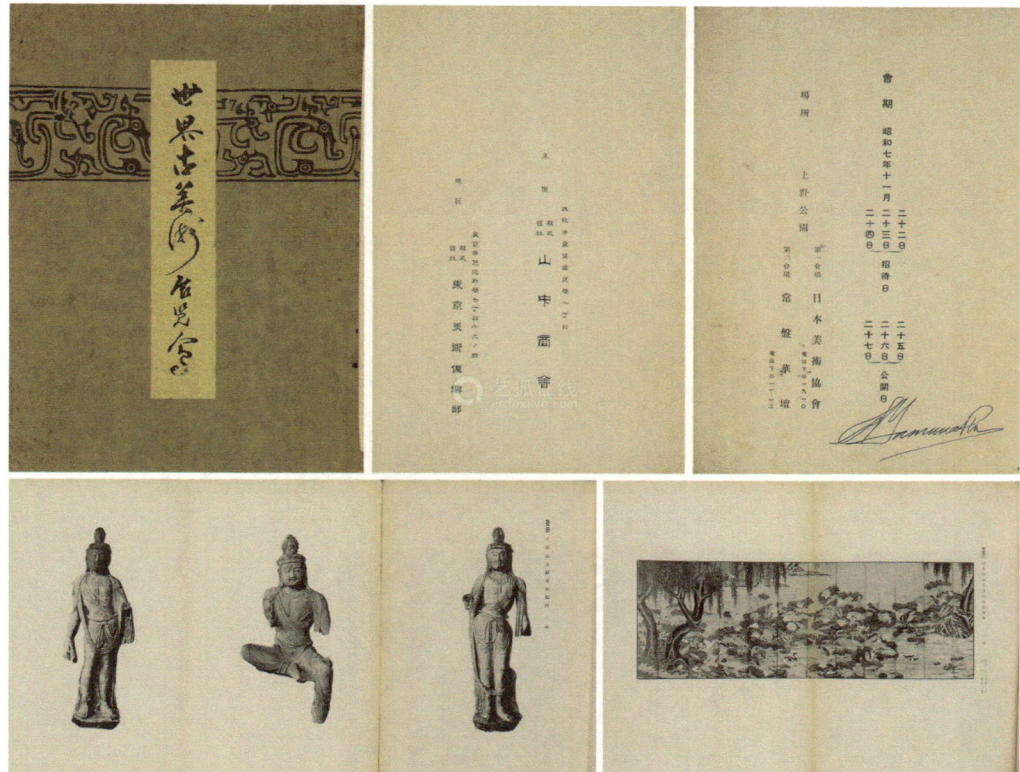

Figure 10-32 Auction catalog of the World Ancient Art Exhibition in November 1932

crucial reference points for the ongoing restoration efforts of these caves. Among these treasures is the principal seated Buddha statue from the north wall of Cave 21 (Figure 10-33). Remarkably, an invoice from Yamanaka & Co. in 1943 documents the purchase of this Tang Dynasty seated Buddha, totaling 25,000 US dollars. These Tianlongshan statues are prominently displayed in the Chinese Gallery of the Harvard Art Museums. Notably, the seated Buddha from the Tang Dynasty (Figure 10-33) hails from Cave 21, standing as one of the few relatively intact statues from the Tianlongshan Grottoes, where others sadly suffer the loss of their heads. Through this Tang Dynasty statue, viewers can glean insights into the aesthetic and artistic sensibilities of the era, as well as the Buddhist art style forged through multicultural interactions.

Another significant artifact is a Bodhisattva head housed in the collection of the Metropolitan Museum of Art, originating from Cave 21 of the Tianlongshan Grottoes (Figure 10-34). When Yamanaka & Co. auctioned Tianlongshan statues in the United States, the Rockefeller family acquired this Bodhisattva head. In 1942, Abby Greene Aldrich (1874–1948), wife of John Davison Rockefeller Jr. (1874–1960), generously donated this cherished piece to the Metropolitan Museum of Art. Originally part of a group of a sitting Buddha and two standing Bodhisattva statues on the north wall of Cave 21, this Bodhisattva head

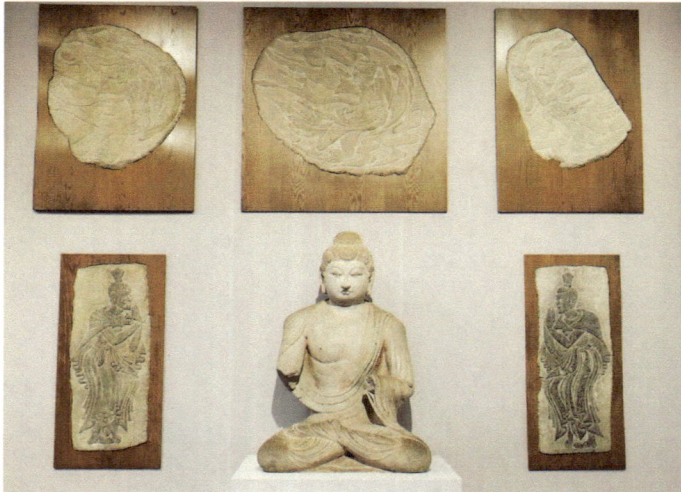

Figure 10-33 Sculptures from the Tianlongshan Grottoes on display at the Harvard Art Museums (the middle statue in the lower row is the seated Buddha from the north wall of Cave 21, and the rest are reliefs from the Eastern Wei Dynasty caves)

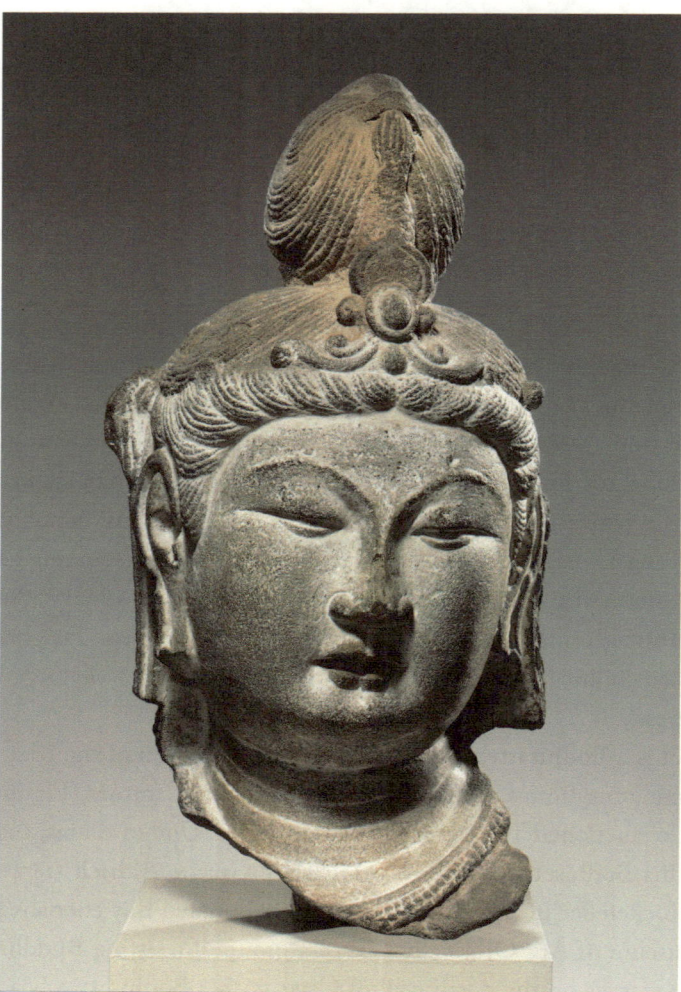

Figure 10-34 The head of the Bodhisattva statue on the west side of the north wall of Cave 21 of the Tianlongshan Grottoes in the prosperous Tang Dynasty (sandstone, 40 cm high, now in the collection of the Metropolitan Museum of Art, donated by Mrs. Rockefeller Jr. in 1942, No. 42.25.12)

represents the western side of the group. Remarkably, the body of the Bodhisattva now resides in the collection of the Idemitsu Museum in Japan, while the head of the eastern Bodhisattva is housed in the Nezu Museum, also in Japan, and the seated Buddha rests in the Harvard Art Museums. Thus, because of Yamanaka & Co., statues from the same cave now grace four museums across two countries.

Additionally, the Nelson-Atkins Museum of Art in Kansas City is also a proud custodian of Tianlongshan statues. The museum's collection includes a Buddha head statue from Cave 8 of the Sui Dynasty, a seated Maitreya Buddha, and two Bodhisattva statues from Cave 4 of the Tang Dynasty, as well as a splendid seated Bodhisattva and Nio statues from Cave 17 of the Tang Dynasty.

Furthermore, in 1925, Yamanaka Sadajirō ventured to the Longmen Grottoes in Luoyang and the Yungang Grottoes in Datong for investigation. Subsequent trading records indicate the involvement of Yamanaka & Co. in the looting of these grottoes as well. Freer acquired stone carvings from Dalishan, Longmen, and Xiangtangshan Grottoes through Yamanaka & Co. Additionally, it facilitated the purchase and sale of numerous Chinese individual statues and statue steles, many of which ended up in Freer's collection, albeit including several fakes. The exhibition catalog published by Yamanaka & Co. that year meticulously chronicled the journey of these national treasures as they transitioned from their possession into the hands of museums and private collectors worldwide.

10.7 A Tragic Ending

Despite having esteemed cultural relics consultants like Fenollosa and Okakura Kakuzō, Yamanaka Sadajirō, the head of Yamanaka & Co. (Figure 10-35), also possesses some experience in antiques. However, due to the inherent uncertainty of antiques and the prevalence of imitations, Yamanaka & Co. used to fall victim to deception by antique dealers and inadvertently purchase counterfeit goods. One notable instance is the Qianlong-style vase of bottle shape with "garlic" mouth sold by Yamanaka & Co. in 1927 and later resold to the Freer Gallery of Art by Loo in 1954, which has been met with skepticism. This garlic-shaped vase, featuring a vivid depiction of a beautiful woman in pastel cloisonné, even graced the cover of the 1943 auction catalog of Yamanaka & Co. However, many scholars doubt

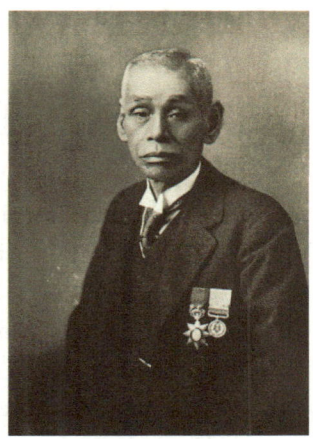

Figure 10-35 Yamanaka Sadajirō in 1928

its authenticity, believing it to be a 19th-century imitation rather than a genuine artifact from the old collection of Prince Gong Mansion (Figure 10-36). Their skepticism is largely fueled by the fact that its purported origin was altered from its true source to the old

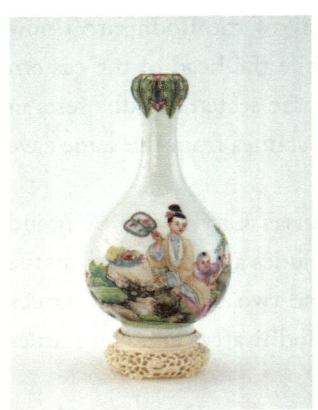

Figure 10-36 Qing Dynasty Qianlong-style vase of bottle shape with "garlic" mouth (17.2 cm high, now in the Freer Gallery of Art, number: F1954.127a-e)

collection of Prince Gong Mansion by Yamanaka & Co. after it arrived in the United States for exhibition.

This practice of altering the origins of artifacts is not uncommon in the company's sales strategy. To cater to customers' preferences for items from the old collection of Prince Gong Mansion, Yamanaka & Co. often falsely attributed items to Prince Gong Mansion. Consequently, contemporary collectors must exercise caution when selecting relics purportedly originating from the old collection of Prince Gong Mansion or Yamanaka & Co. Presently, the garlic-shaped vase displayed at the Freer Gallery of Art and on its website is labeled with a warning stating "may be a modern imitation." Moreover, the Freer Gallery of Art has also acquired fake Buddhist statues from Yamanaka & Co. Correspondence between Yamanaka & Co. and major museums and art galleries, such as the Victoria and Albert Museum and the British Museum in London, reveals doubts expressed by curators and scholars regarding items from Yamanaka & Co. Regardless, Yamanaka & Co. failed to provide any evidence or explanations, opting instead to swiftly repackage the items and move on to the next market. Such behavior only serves to exacerbate suspicions surrounding the authenticity of their offerings. This rapid circulation of cultural relics through multi-level and multi-regional sales channels may partly explain why Yamanaka & Co. persisted in paying high rents and expanding its branches worldwide.

In 1932, Japan backed the establishment of the puppet state of Manchukuo in Northeast China, with Puyi serving as its puppet emperor. This move raised tensions with the United States, leading to a gradual deterioration of political ties between the two nations. It was also during this period that Yamanaka Sadajirō ceased his travels to the United States and passed away in 1936 (Figure 10-37). Before his death, he expressed his hope for the continued expansion of Yamanaka & Co. Subsequently, Yamanaka & Co. capitalized on Japan's military expansion into China, exploiting the war to acquire various cultural relics from China, North Korea, and Southeast Asia at reduced prices. Under the protection of the Japanese army, these items were openly transported to Japan and the West. However, as World War II deepened, especially with the United States' entry into the war, Yamanaka & Co. was seized and liquidated by the United States.

On December 7, 1941, the Japanese military launched a surprise attack on the US Naval Base Pearl Harbor, prompting the United States to declare war on Japan the following day. As part of this declaration of war, the United States classified all Japanese nationals as enemies of the state. In 1917, during World War I, the United States passed the Trading with the Enemy Act, allowing for the seizure, use, management, and liquidation

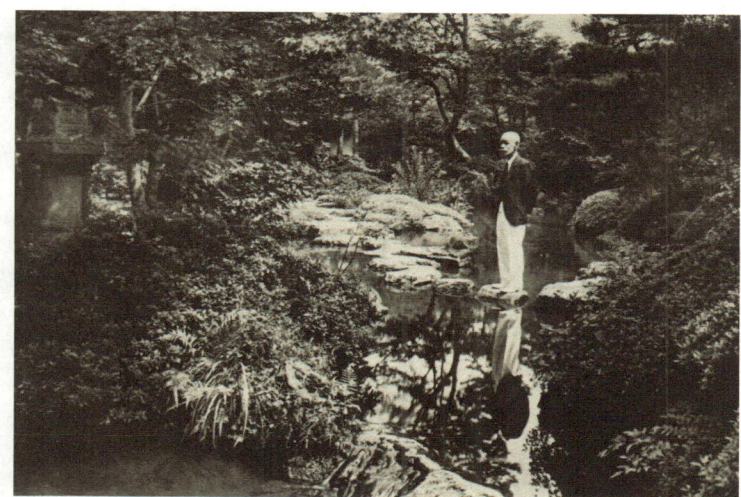

Figure 10-37 The old Yamanaka Sadajirō in his Kyoto residence garden

of property owned by "foreign enemies" within the United States. Consequently, all properties of Yamanaka & Co. in the United States, including art, stocks, and real estate, were confiscated by the US government. Due to the vast number of confiscated items, the US Foreign Assets Administration and the FBI hired Japanese staff from Yamanaka & Co. to run inventory and sell the items.

Under the weight of exorbitant rental costs, Yamanaka & Co. found itself struggling to stay afloat under the management of the US Foreign Assets Administration. In 1943, facing financial hardship, it was compelled to organize a grand auction across its three branches in New York, Boston, and Chicago, titled Treasures of Chinese and Far Eastern Art. This extraordinary event showcased a total of 1,683 items, comprising metal and bone artifacts, jades, statues, murals, embroidery, paintings, furniture, ceramics, and more, spanning all dynasties of China. The auction drew the attention of numerous antique dealers, museums, and private collectors, including notable figures like Loo, Rockefeller, Freer, and Fenollosa. Harvard's Fogg Museum, among others, acquired a significant number of Tianlongshan carvings during this event, with the archives meticulously documenting the collection date as 1943. Lasting until the conclusion of June 1944, this expansive auction amassed a total of 500,000 US dollars (Figure 10-38), with proceeds from the three-year endeavor flowing into the coffers of the US government. The abrupt liquidation of Yamanaka & Co., a venerable institution with a legacy spanning two centuries, came as an unexpected blow to many. Its entire fifty years of presence and accumulation in the United States were absorbed into the pockets of the US government.

Despite being hit by seizures and liquidations, Yamanaka & Co.'s headquarters in Japan persisted in operation. Even after the war ended in 1952, they resumed business in New York. However, their source of cultural relics shifted to antique merchants outside China.

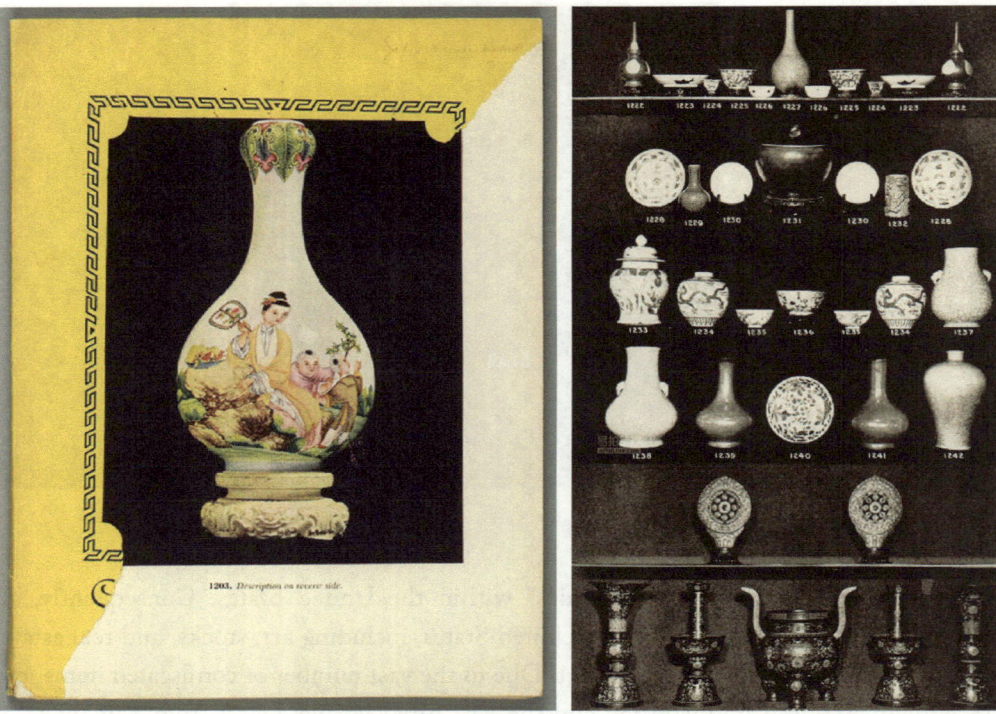

Figure 10-38 Cover and one page of the 1943 American first edition of the *Yamanaka & Co. American Exhibition Catalog* (28.1 cm × 21.1 cm)

Over time, former heads of each branch passed away, and Yamanaka & Co. gradually lost its former dominance in the Western antique world. Nonetheless, it remains operational to this day, boasting a history spanning three centuries. Many major museums in Europe and the United States still showcase cultural relics sold by Yamanaka & Co., preserving the legacy of this antique store. For instance, the Freer Gallery of Art alone houses over 700 items attributed to Yamanaka & Co., serving as a testament to its erstwhile glory.

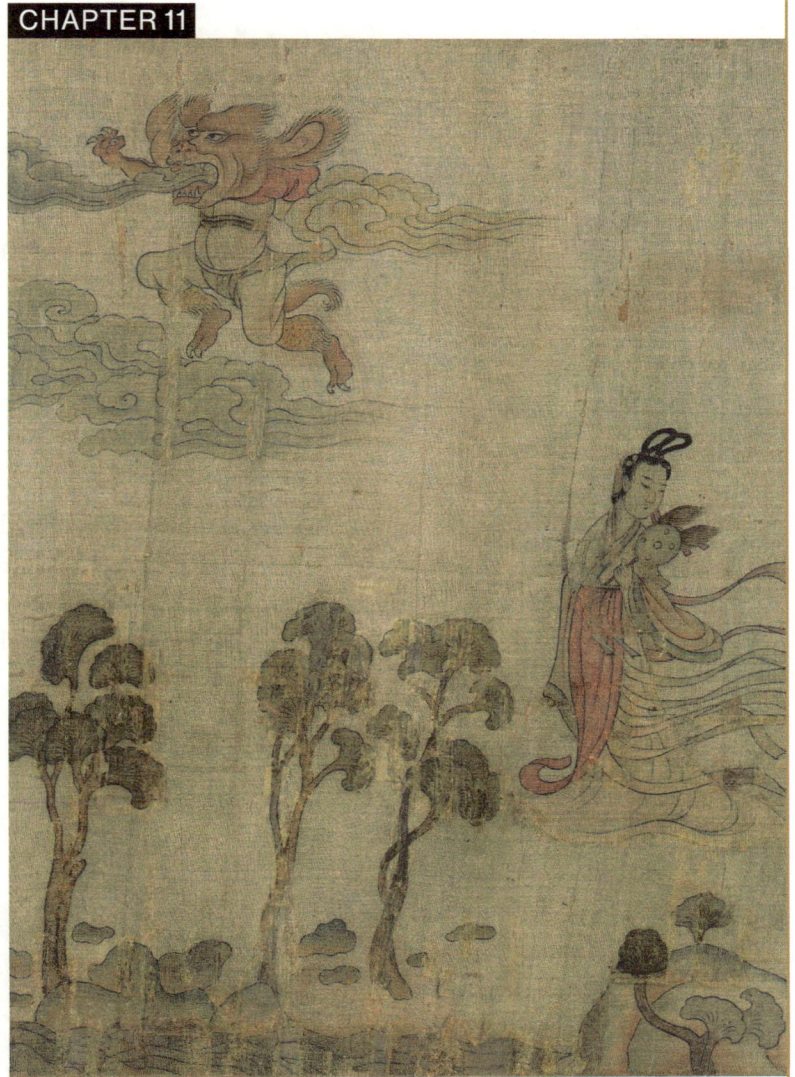

CHAPTER 11

Freer: An American Industrialist Who Loves Chinese Culture

— 1895

First time, the United States–Hong Kong–Shanghai–Japan

— 1907

Second time, the United States–Hong Kong–Guangzhou–Hong Kong–
Shanghai–Japan

— 1909

Third time, the United States–Hong Kong–Shanghai–Qingdao–Tianjin–Beijing

— 1910–1911

Fourth time, the United States–Nagasaki, Japan–Shanghai–Qingdao–Beijing–
Tianjin–Beijing–Anyang–Kaifeng–Zhengzhou–Gongxian (Gongxian Grottoes,
Imperial Tombs of the Northern Song Dynasty)–Luoyang (Longmen Grottoes)–
Beijing–Shenyang–Dalian–Lüshun–Shanghai–Hangzhou–Shanghai–Nagasaki,
Japan

11.1 A Self-Taught Collector

The Freer Gallery of Art, graciously bestowed upon the public by the esteemed American art aficionado Charles Lang Freer (Figure 11-1), is nestled on the southern expanse of the illustrious National Mall, at the heart of Washington, D.C., the capital of the United States.

Freer himself, renowned both as an American industrialist and an astute collector of fine art, curated a collection of unparalleled distinction, renowned globally for its assemblage of Asian treasures and American 19th-century artworks. In a momentous decision in 1906, Freer resolved to bequeath his life's work to the Smithsonian Institution, the preeminent bastion of scientific inquiry within the

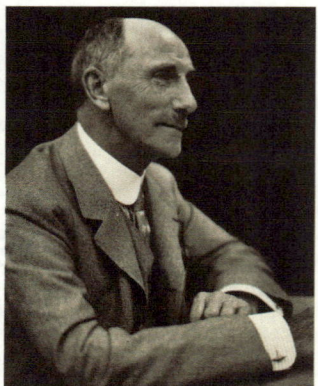

Figure 11-1 Charles Lang Freer

United States federal purview and an institution of eminence located within the same august city. The Smithsonian, the largest museum complex on the planet, overseeing 19 museums, galleries, the national zoo, and nine research institutions (Figure 11-2), welcomed Freer's magnanimous offering with open arms. Upon the formalization of his pact with the Smithsonian, Freer, in an act of enduring munificence, undertook the funding of the

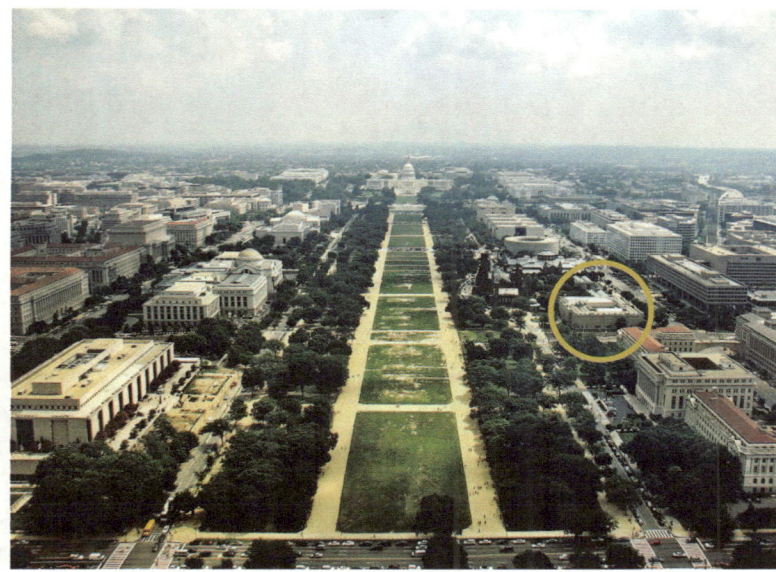

Figure 11-2 Aerial view of the Capitol Building and the Smithsonian Institution on the National Mall in Washington D.C. (the Freer Gallery of Art is marked in the circle)

eponymous Freer Gallery of Art. With unwavering dedication, he continued to amass treasures from the realms of China, Japan, and the United States, each acquisition an augmentation to his opulent endowment. Over time, the Freer Gallery of Art burgeoned into a repository boasting tens of thousands of artistic marvels (including contributions from other benefactors).

In 1923, the doors of the Freer Gallery of Art swung open to the eager public. Among its prized possessions, the gallery's collection of Chinese cultural artifacts stands as indispensable touchstones in the annals of Chinese art history research. Today, the Freer Gallery of Art, standing in harmonious adjacency to the Arthur M. Sackler Gallery, operates as two independent entities under unified administrative oversight. While the Freer Gallery of Art steadfastly maintains a policy of non-lending, the Arthur M. Sackler Gallery operates under different auspices. Together, these sister institutions constitute the National Museum of Asian Art, proudly affiliated with the venerable Smithsonian Institution.

Freer was born on February 25, 1856, in the quaint town of Kingston, New York. Descended from French Huguenots who sought refuge from religious persecution in 17th-century France, Freer's ancestral roots intertwined with the fertile soil of New Paltz, New York, where his forebears were among the original proprietors of the land grant. Following the footsteps of his familial legacy, young Freer embarked on the path of industry after completing his education in the halls of public schooling. At the tender age of 14, he toiled amid the churning gears of a neighbor's cement factory. By 16, he found himself ensconced within the confines of John C. Brodhead's general grocery store in Kingston, where fate would intertwine his destiny with the corridors of the New York, Kingston & Syracuse Railroad Company. Within the bustling precincts of the railroad company's offices, young

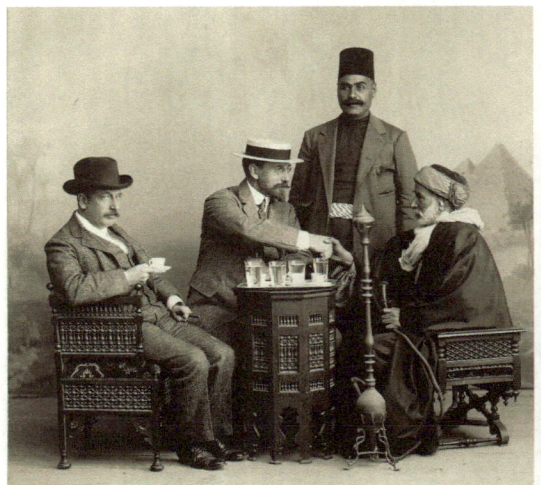

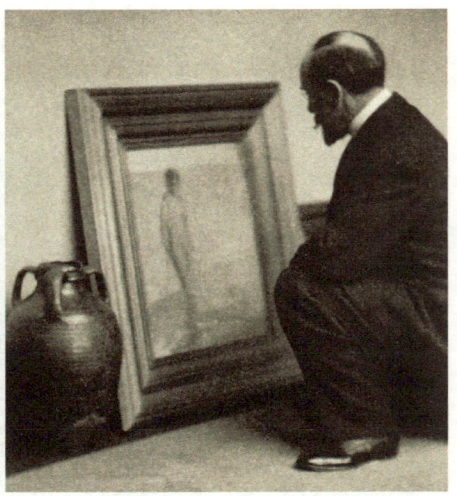

Figure 11-3 Freer (second from left) and his friends in a photo studio in Cairo, Egypt (1909)

Figure 11-4 Freer and his collection of American painter Whistler's work *Venus* (photographed by Alvin Langdon Coburn in 1909)

Freer's mettle caught the discerning eye of Colonel Frank J. Hecker, a luminary in his own right. In 1873, Freer was ushered into the folds of the railroad fraternity, marking the auspicious inception of his storied career in rail transport. Accompanying Hecker to the bustling city of Detroit, Freer played a pivotal role in the establishment of the Peninsular Car Works, assuming the mantle of financial stewardship with diligence and acumen. For two decades, from 1880 to 1900, Freer's indomitable spirit fueled the engine of progress within the corridors of industry. In the year 1900, upon the successful completion of a merger resulting in the establishment of the new American Car & Foundry Co., Freer made the decision to gracefully retire from his bustling business ventures at the tender age of 44. (Figure 11-3).

In the 19 years that followed, Freer's passion for the arts blossomed into a fervent pursuit of knowledge and collection. Casting his gaze upon the vast expanse of artistic expression, he began his foray into the world of art acquisition in the early 1880s. Etchings and lithographs formed the initial tapestry of his collection, with the acquisition of a set of etchings by the illustrious American Impressionist Whistler—*Venice, Second Series*—marking a seminal moment in his artistic voyage in 1887. In 1888, he met Whistler in person during a sojourn to England (Figure 11-4). Yet, Freer's interests meandered, flowing inexorably toward the captivating allure of Japanese art. From a brief interest in ukiyo-e prints to greater enthusiasm for ancient Japanese paintings and ceramic art, his gaze traversed the cultural tapestry of the Far East, eventually converging upon the rich heritage of Chinese classical art.

Freer embarked on a series of journeys to East Asia, spanning four distinct expeditions in the years 1895, 1907, 1909, and 1910–1911. Throughout these odysseys, Freer engaged in rigorous research, immersed himself in the exploration of public and private art collections, engaged in discussions with esteemed local scholars and collectors, and eagerly procured significant quantities of art that captivated his discerning eye, meticulously chronicling his experiences in diaries and letters.

In the autumn of 1895, at the age of 39, Freer's inaugural voyage to China unfolded unexpectedly as a fortuitous detour en route to Japan. His brief sojourn commenced with a fleeting visit to Hong Kong, where he lingered for three days before traversing the bustling streets of Shanghai for a week. From there, he set sail for a four-month sojourn across Japan. It was during this serendipitous journey that Freer's fascination with China was first kindled, sparked by the fleeting glimpses of its rich cultural tapestry. Upon his arrival in Japan in April 1895, fate intervened once more as Freer serendipitously crossed paths with Hara Tomitaro (1868–1939), a luminary in the realm of silk exportation and a connoisseur of the fine arts. Freer's frequent visits to Tomitaro's opulent mansion nestled in the Yokohama suburbs afforded him unparalleled access to the magnificence of Tomitaro's illustrious art collection. Through these encounters, Freer found himself enveloped in the erudite company of Masuda Takashi (1848–1938), the esteemed president of Sumitomo Mitsui Banking Corporation and an internationally renowned collector in his own right. Under the tutelage of these esteemed luminaries, Freer's passion for Far Eastern art flourished, as he delved deeper into the intricacies of its heritage and embarked on the journey to cultivate his own distinguished collection of Asian art.

In the year 1907, twelve years following his initial foray into China, Freer, now renowned as a distinguished collector, embarked on another brief yet impactful journey to the enigmatic land of China. Arriving in Hong Kong on March 31, Easter Sunday, Freer wasted no time indulging his passion for art acquisition, promptly securing a selection of exquisite Chinese ceramics (Figure 11-5) before venturing onward to Guangdong on

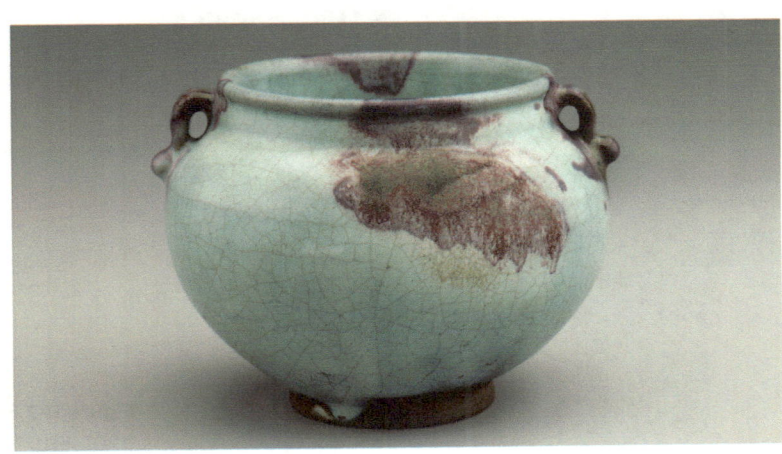

Figure 11-5 Jun kiln porcelain jar from the Yuan Dynasty (12 cm × 16.1 cm, now in the Freer Gallery of Art, No. F1907.64)

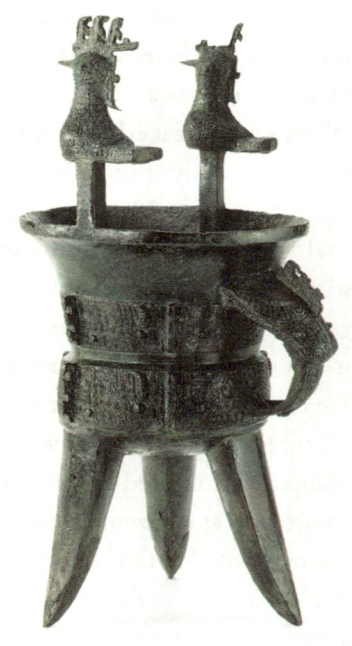

Figure 11-6 Bronze *dou* from Shang Dynasty (41.8 cm × 21.5 cm × 22.3 cm, now in the Freer Gallery of Art, No. F1907.37)

April 2 in pursuit of further treasures. The stark contrast between the Western modernity of Hong Kong and the ancient allure of Guangzhou, enclosed within its formidable city walls, left an indelible mark upon Freer's impressionable mind. Returning once more to Hong Kong, Freer expanded his acquisitions, acquiring pottery and bronzes (Figure 11-6) before setting sail for Shanghai. During his brief three-day sojourn there, Freer focused his efforts on procuring cultural relics, before continuing his journey to Japan. Upon his arrival in Japan, Freer was greeted with warm enthusiasm by Japanese collectors, eager to showcase their own collections and extend invitations for Freer's perusal. Freer availed himself of the opportunity to explore early Chinese paintings housed within Japanese museums and private collections (Figure 11-7).

In the subsequent year of 1909, Freer's returned to Hong Kong. Nestled within the verdant embrace of the mountains, Freer found respite in the villa of the German Consul General, where panoramic views of

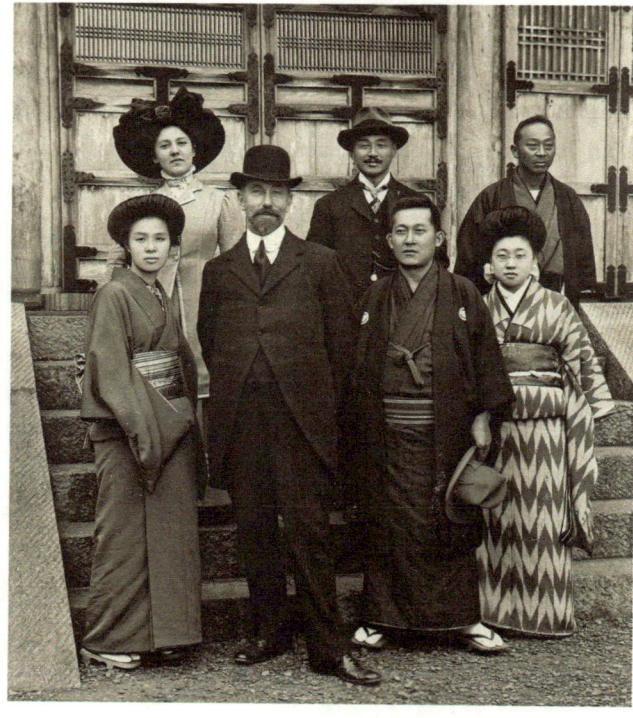

Figure 11-7 Freer visiting Japan (1907–1911)

Hong Kong Bay unfolded before him. Embraced by the consul's shared passion for ancient Chinese art, Freer was introduced to a plethora of antique experts, collectors, and dealers from Guangdong and Hong Kong. From there, Freer's travels led him to Shanghai for a brief interlude before journeying onward to Qingdao in Shandong Province and then to the historic city of Beijing via Tianjin. In Tianjin, Freer had the privilege of visiting the private collection of Duanfang (1861–1911), a distinguished Manchu nobleman, epigrapher, and collector. Enthralled by the splendor of Duan's collection, Freer found himself in awe of the nobleman's passion and discerning eye.

In Beijing, Freer visited several iconic historical landmarks, such as the Temple of Heaven, the Xiannong Altar, and the resounding Drum Tower. To facilitate his endeavors, Freer took the pragmatic step of renting several houses within the city—a decision that inadvertently led many Chinese antique dealers to misconstrue his intentions, assuming him to be a businessman procuring Chinese cultural relics for American auction houses. The vibrant tapestry of Beijing's bustling streets and ancient architecture captivated Freer's imagination, prompting him to draw comparisons with other renowned historical and cultural cities such as Cairo, Egypt, and Constantinople, Turkey. During his immersive four-and-a-half-week sojourn in Beijing, Freer seized the opportunity to explore further afield, venturing to iconic sites like the Summer Palace, the Great Wall, and the Ming Tombs. Yet, perhaps most significantly, he augmented his burgeoning collection with a vast array of treasures, including bronzes, ceramics, and paintings. Before bidding adieu to the ancient capital, Freer meticulously packed his acquisitions into eight shipping crates, destined for his home in Detroit (Figure 11-8). With a sense of pride and accomplishment, he wrote: This latest acquisition had elevated my Chinese collection above and beyond my existing holdings of Japanese and Persian artifacts.

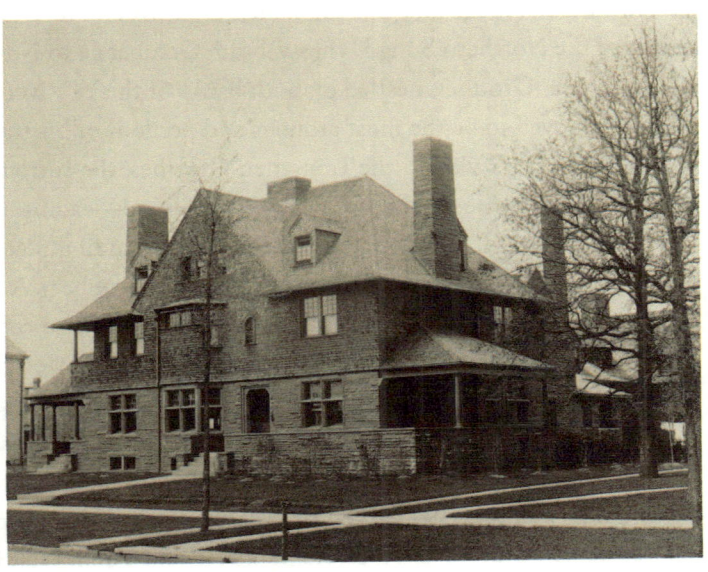

Figure 11-8 Freer's former
home in Detroit (c. 1906)

11.2 Investigate Chinese Historical Sites

Freer's final journey to China in 1910–1911 left an indelible impression upon him. His meticulously kept diaries and correspondence bear witness to his interactions with a plethora of antique dealers, collectors, and connoisseurs, including notable personalities such as the German-American sinologist Friedrich Hirth (1845–1927), the American Chinese art historian and collector John Calvin Ferguson (1866–1945), the American archaeologist and East Asian art historian Warner, and the American art critic and collector A. W. Bahr (1877–1959). Arriving in Shanghai on September 11, 1910, from Nagasaki, Japan, Freer wasted no time in embarking on a whirlwind tour of Chinese ceramics and paintings. Within three days, he embarked on a voyage to Qingdao, only to return to Beijing before the 21st of the same month. During his stay in the capital, he had the rare privilege of attending a dinner hosted by the US Secretary of Defense and his wife, who happened to be visiting the city, thus affording him the opportunity to explore the Forbidden City and partake in its storied history. Subsequently, Freer journeyed to Tianjin once more to visit Duanfang, beholding collections of unprecedented magnificence.

The primary objective of Freer's final expedition was to explore mainland China, with plans to visit the ancient capitals of Kaifeng, Luoyang, and Xi'an. On October 19, he embarked on a train journey to Zhangde Prefecture (now Anyang, Henan Province), arriving in Kaifeng the following day. The ancient cities, temples, and palace ruins of Kaifeng captivated his imagination, drawing comparisons to the allure of the Hōryū-ji Temple in Nara, Japan. In Kaifeng, Freer embarked on an extensive exploration, visiting cultural relics and scenic spots such as Wolong Palace, Daxiangguo Temple, Erzeng Temple, Dragon Pavilion, Youguo Temple, Iron Pagoda, Tianqing Temple, Fan Pagoda, and King Yu Terrace. From October 26 to 27, his journey continued to Gongxian County, where he visited Baisha Village and saw the famed Dali Mountain Grotto Temple and the imperial tombs of the Northern Song Dynasty. From October 29 to November 12, Freer journeyed to the Longmen Grottoes, nestled on both banks of the Yi River in Luoyang. This expedition, however, proved to be the most arduous and perilous of his travels in China.

During Freer's visit to the Longmen Grottoes, the surrounding area presented significant challenges due to the presence of busy roads leading to Longmen Dongshan and Xishan Grottoes. These mountain caves served as hiding places for local bandits who frequently obstructed the roads and engaged in acts of robbery. Aware of the potential dangers, Feer's Chinese acquaintances cautioned him to prioritize safety. In preparation for their expedition, Freer sought counsel from the local governor of Henan Province, who, recognizing the importance of safeguarding their journey, allocated a dedicated contingent of six soldiers to provide protection throughout their entire endeavor. Freer's expedition team was further bolstered by the inclusion of Mr. Zong, dispatched by Henan Prefecture to create rubbings, as well as a chef named Jia, a servant named Cai from Beijing, a local assistant, a laborer named Shitou, and a photographer Zhou Yutai. Guiding the expedition was Nan

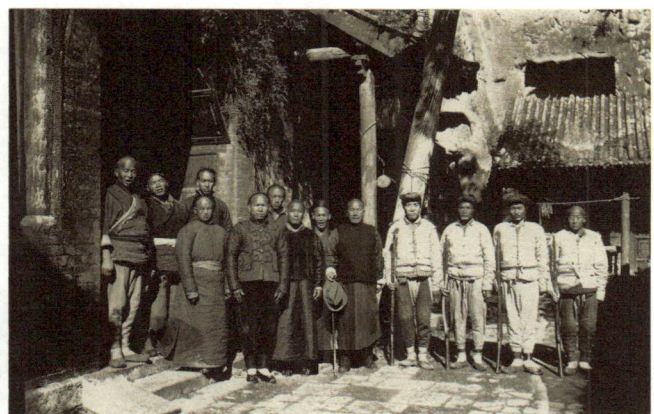

Figure 11-9 Freer's entourage, four soldiers from Henan Prefecture, and monks from the temple in front of Binyang Cave of Longmen Grottoes (photographed by Zhou Yutai on November 9, 1910)

Mingyuan, who not only served as a guide and translator but also assumed the role of director of the Freer expedition team (Figure 11-9). Thanks to the vigilant care provided by the government, Freer and his team were always closely guarded by a minimum of four soldiers wherever they ventured. Additionally, local officials in Luoyang dispatched guards to patrol the Longmen area, periodically firing shots into the sky to deter potential bandit activity. The reassuring sound of gunfire served to alleviate the tension and fear among expedition members, ensuring their safety throughout their explorations. Each day, Freer and his team dedicated themselves to the meticulous documentation of the Longmen Grottoes. They captured numerous photographs of the intricate caves and sculptures adorning the cliffs of Longmen Mountain on both banks of the Yishui River. Additionally, they diligently made relief rubbings. These photographs and rubbings now reside in the Archives Department of the Freer Gallery of Art, serving as invaluable resources for scholars studying Chinese Buddhist sculpture.

Following their exploration of the Longmen Grottoes (Figure 11-10), the Henan prefectural governor graciously hosted a lavish banquet for Freer and his esteemed team members within the confines of the *yamen*. The banquet was conducted with the utmost standards, a testament to the hospitality extended by their hosts. In Luoyang, Freer took the opportunity to visit the Guanlin Temple and capture photographs. Originally intending to continue their journey to inspect the Yungang Grottoes in Datong, Shanxi, Freer and his team encountered a setback as the team members felt they had garnered sufficient money and unanimously declined to proceed to Shanxi. Additionally, the onset of floods further thwarted Freer's desire to venture westward. Consequently, Freer and his disheartened team members returned to Beijing, their spirits tempered by the setbacks encountered during their ambitious expedition.

Upon his return to Beijing, Freer immersed himself in the acquisition of ceramics, bronzes, and paintings (Figure 11-11). However, on December 21, Freer embarked on yet another expedition, this time to Shenyang, to inspect the collection of palace cultural

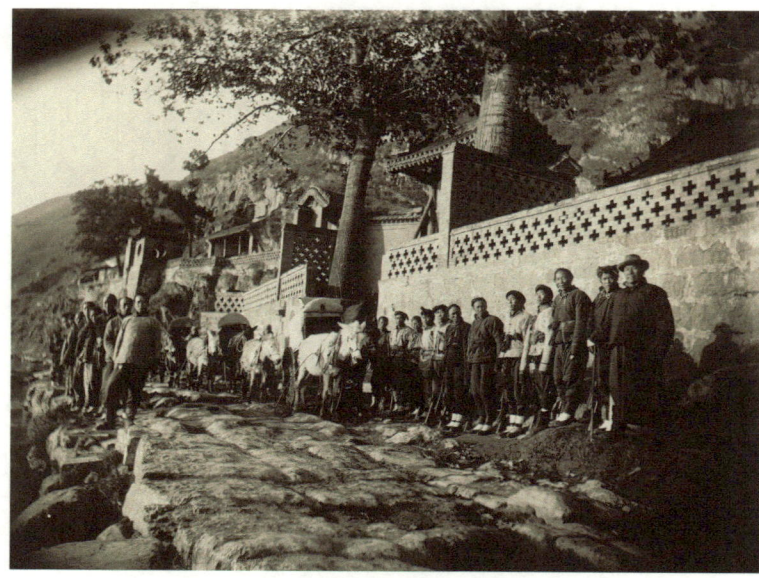

Figure 11-10 In front of Qianxi Temple of Longmen Grottoes, Freer and his team preparing to leave (photographed by Zhou Yutai on November 12, 1910)

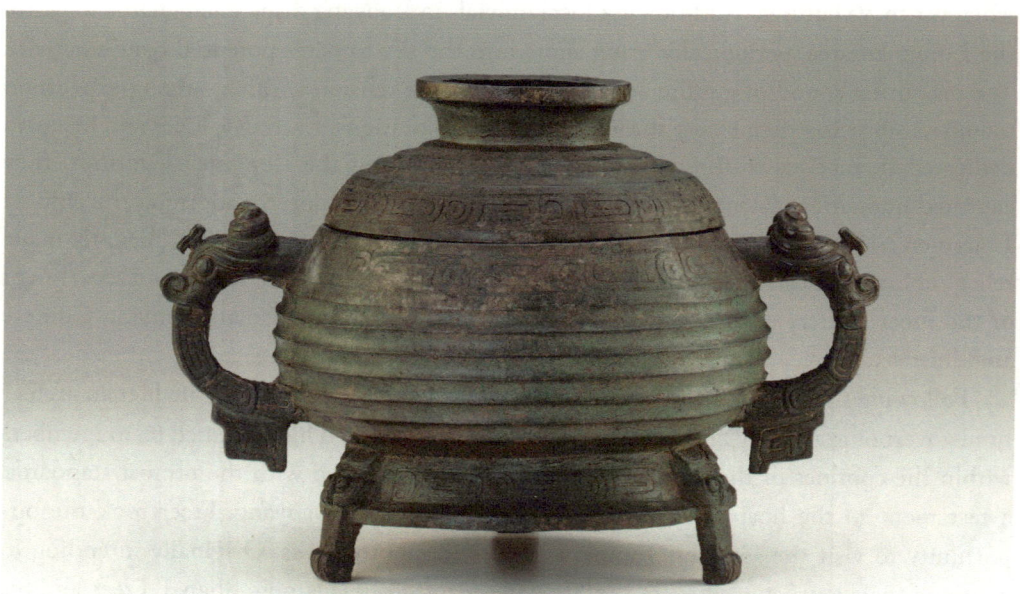

Figure 11-11 Bronze *gui* from the Western Zhou Dynasty (24.8 cm × 35.6 cm, now in the Freer Gallery of Art, No. F1909.259a-b)

relics housed there. Despite enduring a chilly Christmas in this northeastern city, Freer continued his journey to Dalian and Lüshun, before boarding a ship bound for Shanghai in January 1911. In Shanghai, Freer had the privilege of beholding the exquisite collection of cultural relics amassed by the renowned collector Pang Yuanji (1864–1949). Pang Yuanji, hailing from Nanxun, Zhejiang Province, was revered as "the most renowned collector of Chinese calligraphy and painting in the world." Commencing from the 21st year of Emperor Guangxu's reign in 1895, Pang embarked on a remarkable entrepreneurial journey, co-establishing enterprises such as the Shijing and Dalun Silk Reeling Factories, along with the Tongyi Public Yarn Factory in Gongchen Bridge, Hangzhou, and Tangqi, Deqing (now known as Tangqi, Yuhang). Later, he played a pivotal role in the founding of the Longzhang Machinery and Papermaking Co., Ltd. in Shanghai, assuming the position of general manager. In addition to these industrial ventures, Pang ventured into diverse sectors, including rice shops, soy sauce factories, wineries, traditional Chinese medicine stores, pawn shops, and banks, establishing a significant presence in Nanxun, Shaoxing, Suzhou, Hangzhou, and beyond. He also owned plenty of farming land and real estate there. His astute business acumen not only afforded him substantial financial resources but also endowed him with a keen eye for art appreciation. Pang Yuanji's passion for cultural relics, particularly in the realms of bronzes, porcelain, calligraphy, paintings, and jades, positioned him as one of the preeminent collectors of calligraphy and painting in the country. Among his prized possessions was a Yuan-Ming Dynasty copy of the *Chen Yuanda Advising Liu Cong*, a renowned masterpiece attributed to the esteemed Tang Dynasty painter Yan Liben. This remarkable artwork depicts Chen Yuanda, the minister of justice of the Former Zhao Kingdom (AD 304–329) of the Sixteen Kingdoms, bravely advising Emperor Liu Cong (r. 310–318), risking his life to convey his message. The painting evokes a palpable sense of tension, with the characters' expressions rendered in vivid detail, making it a standout among Chinese figure paintings housed in the esteemed collection of the Freer Gallery of Art (Figure 11-12).

After an extensive period of travel, Freer made the decision to indulge in a well-deserved vacation, opting for the serene beauty of Hangzhou alongside a few companions, seeking solace and relaxation. On February 9, they chartered two spacious boats resembling houses, christened Annie and Lois, which were navigated by trackers as they embarked on a leisurely journey from Shanghai to Hangzhou by waterway (Figure 11-13). In Hangzhou, Freer and his companions meandered along the picturesque West Lake, marveling at its tranquil allure, and visited various cultural landmarks including Lingyin Temple, Feilaifeng Grottoes, Leifeng Pagoda, Baochu Pagoda, Jingci Temple, Yuewang Temple, Su Xiaoxiao Tomb, and Zhusu Garden, capturing countless precious historical moments through the lens of his camera (Figures 11-14). In Freer's diaries and letters, Hangzhou left an indelible imprint on his heart, its beauty stirring his soul. On February 20, 1911, Freer bid farewell to Hangzhou and returned to Shanghai by train, subsequently embarking on a boat journey from Shanghai to Nagasaki, Japan, marking the conclusion of his final voyage to China. Upon his return to the United States, Freer's arduous task of documenting his vast collection and a series of illnesses precluded any further travels to East Asia. However, the profound impact of his four journeys to East Asia enriched his understanding and appreciation of collections (Figures 11-15, 11-16).

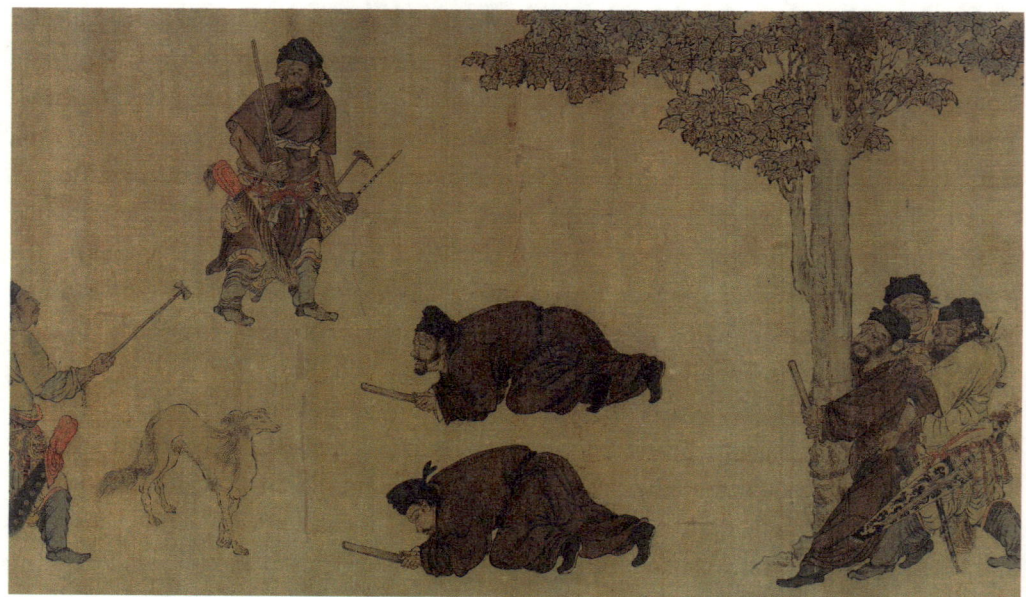

Figure 11-12 Part of a Yuan and Ming Dynasty copy of *Chen Yuanda Advising Liu Cong* painted by Yan Liben of the Tang Dynasty (color on silk, 36.9 cm × 207.9 cm, now in the Freer Gallery of Art, No. F1911.235, photographed by Chang Qing)

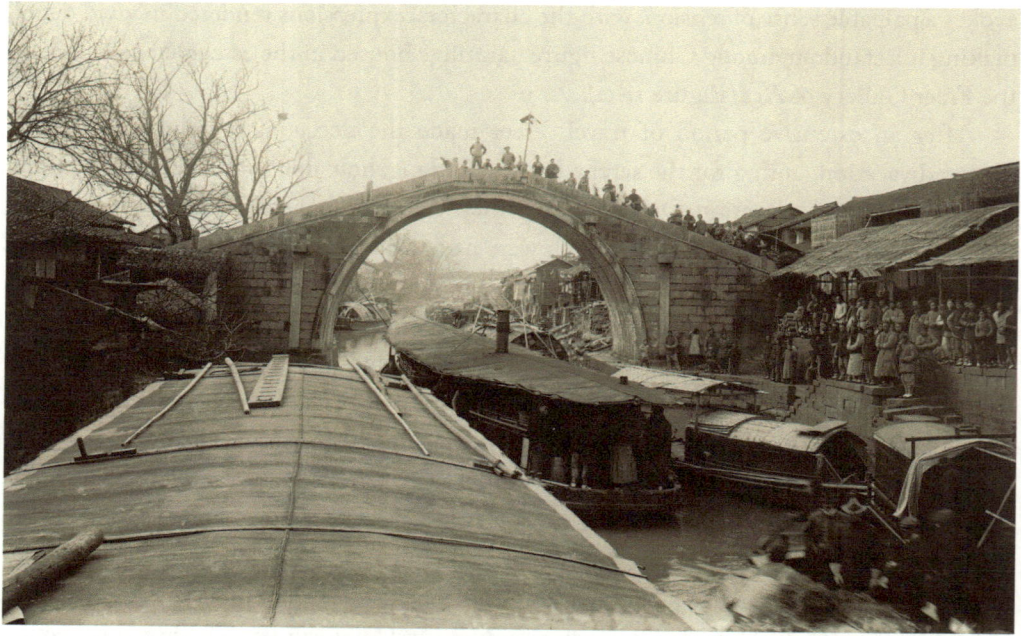

Figure 11-13 Hangzhou's canal, arch bridge, and ships with foreigners (photographed by Freer in 1911)

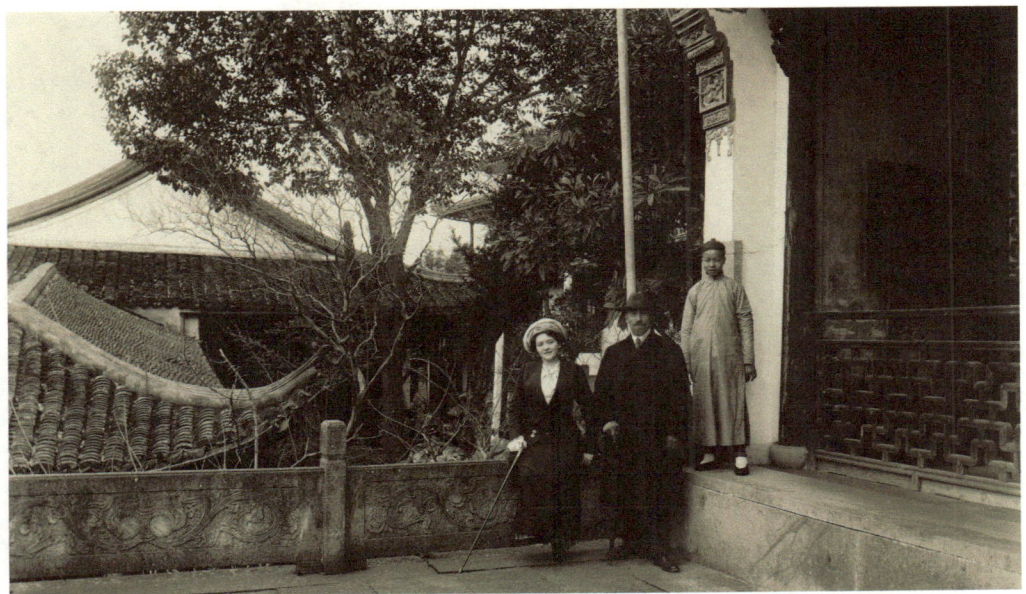

Figure 11-14 Freer and Claire Dallam in Hangzhou Zhusu Garden (1911)

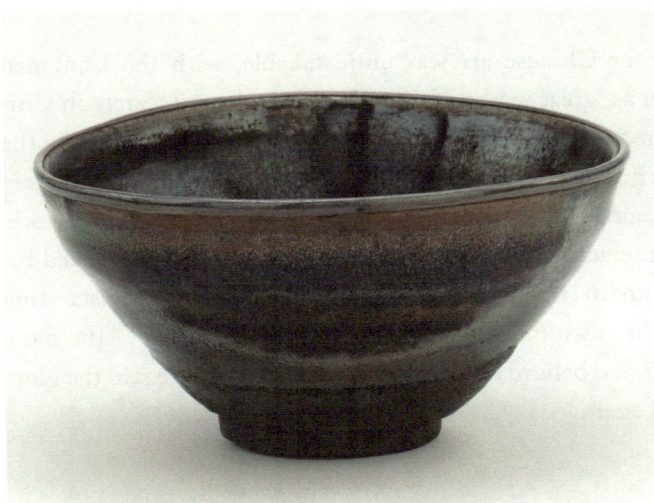

Figure 11-15 Black porcelain cup from Jian kiln, Southern Song Dynasty (6.7 cm × 12.9 cm, now in the Freer Gallery of Art, No. F1911.355)

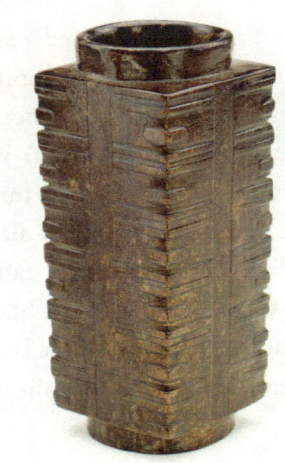

Figure 11-16 Liangzhu culture jade *cong* (18.8 cm × 7.7 cm × 7.8 cm, now in the Freer Gallery of Art, No. F1916.157)

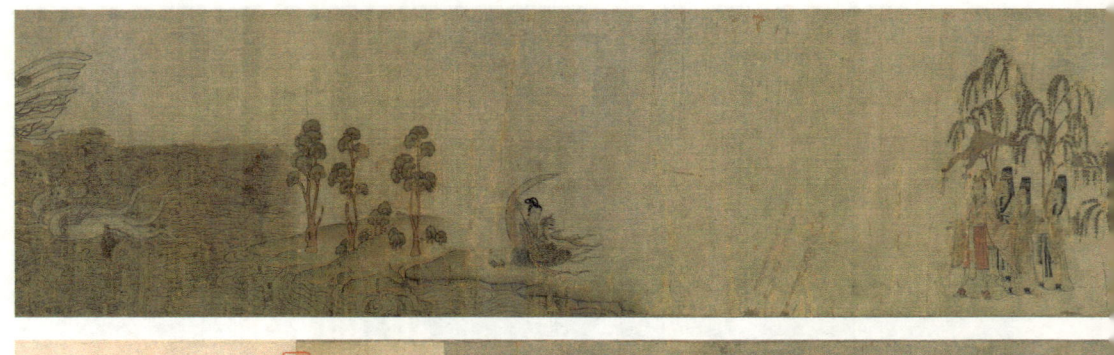

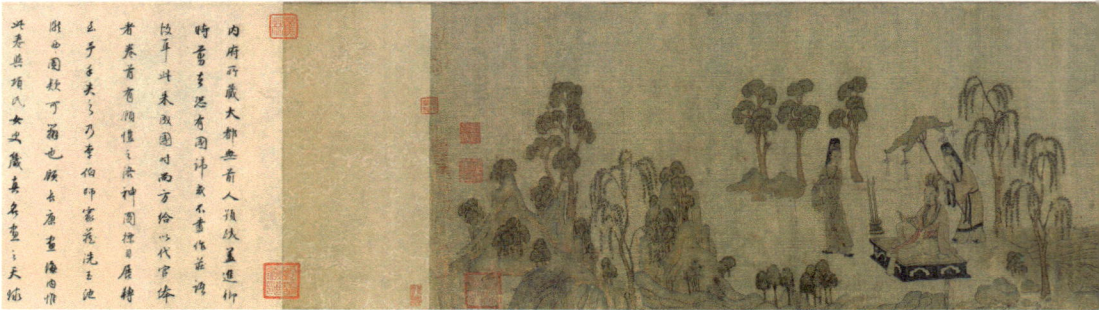

Figure 11-17 Part of the Southern Song Dynasty copy of *Nymph of the Luo River* (color on silk, screen size 24.2 cm × 310.9 cm, now in the Freer Gallery of Art, No. F1914.53)

Freer's deep-seated passion for Chinese art was unmistakable, with the Longmen Grottoes earning his admiration as "great works of art." His meticulous research on Chinese cultural relics, as documented in his travel diaries, showcased his keen interest in the characteristics of China's renowned porcelain kilns and their wares. Additionally, Freer endeavored to grasp the fundamentals of spoken Chinese, which is evident from his notes on pronunciation in his diary. Interacting with the people of China further deepened his affinity for the country, leading him to lament, "There is such an inadequate understanding of China in the United States. So much for Americans to learn for Chinese." "The more Chinese I met, the more I respect and believe in them. Some day, they will regain the glory centuries ago and lead the world again."

11.3 Precious Collection

Freer's comprehensive collection of Chinese artworks spans the breadth of Chinese history, encompassing pieces from the Neolithic Age to modern and contemporary art. This diverse collection includes ceramics, jades, bronzes, paintings, sculptures, lacquerware, musical instruments, and more, offering invaluable resources for academic research and scholarly exploration.

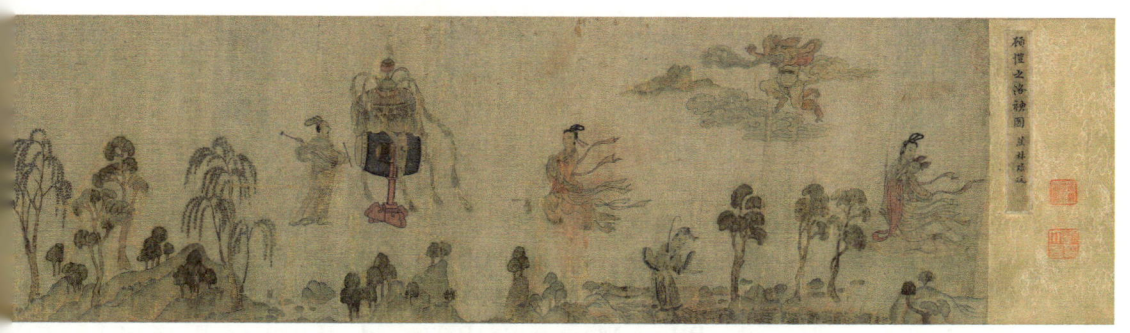

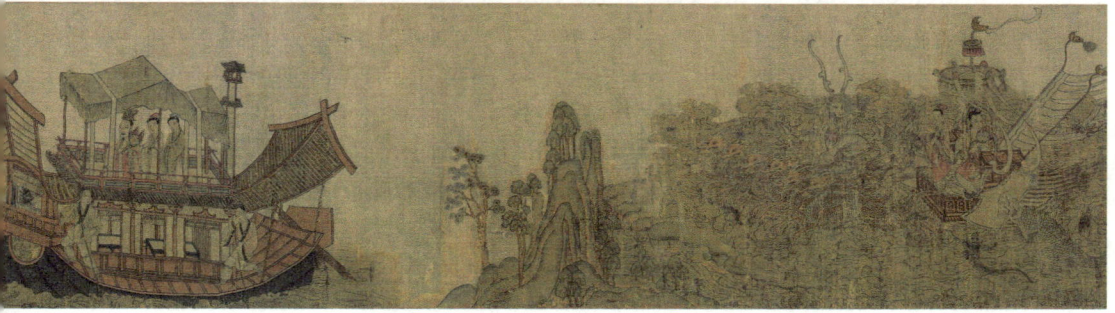

Among Freer's notable acquisitions in the realm of Chinese paintings are masterpieces dating back to the Northern Song Dynasty, such as Guo Xi's *Clearing Autumn Skies over Mountains and Valleys*, Fan Kuan's *Fishing Alone in a Mountain Stream* and *Clearing Skies over Mount Hua*, as well as Mi Fu's *Pavilion of Rising Clouds*. Additionally, Southern Song Dynasty contributions include Yan Ciyu's *Hostelry in the Mountains* and Xia Gui's *Autumn Moonlight on Dongting Lake*. Noteworthy Yuan Dynasty pieces include Sheng Mao's *Landscape Painting in the Shape of a Fan*, Wang Meng's *Dwelling in Seclusion in the Summer Mountains*, and Qian Xuan's *Consort Yang Mounting a Horse*. Furthermore, Freer's collection boasts numerous masterpieces from the Ming and Qing Dynasties. The imitation copy of *Nymph of the Luo River*, a remarkable piece from the Southern Song Dynasty (Figure 11-17), holds a place of great significance within Freer's esteemed collection. Originally part of Duanfang's collection, this painting's journey to Freer's possession is a tale marked by historical upheaval and fortuitous acquisition. During the tumultuous events of the Wuchang Uprising in 1911, Duanfang was beheaded. His family, confronted with uncertain circumstances, made the difficult decision to sell his entire collection. It was during this period of uncertainty that the painting found its way into the hands of John Calvin Ferguson, who was then serving as a consultant to the Palace Museum in Beijing. Ferguson, recognizing the exceptional value of the copy, endeavored to secure a buyer for the painting, approaching the Metropolitan Museum of Art with an asking price of 100,000 US dollars, but was declined. However, fortune smiled upon the painting when Freer, upon learning of its availability, eagerly acquired it at a significant price.

Nymph of the Luo River is attributed to Gu Kaizhi, a renowned painter from the Eastern Jin Dynasty, drawing inspiration from Cao Zhi's poetic masterpiece of the same name. Regrettably, Gu Kaizhi's original work has been lost to time, leaving behind only a handful of surviving copies. Cao Zhi's texts, infused with themes of unrequited love, unfold a narrative of romantic pursuit between mortals and celestial beings within a dreamlike realm. Presently, seven copies of *Nymph of the Luo River* are known to exist, housed in esteemed institutions such as the Palace Museum in Beijing, the Liaoning Provincial Museum, the Palace Museum in Taipei, the Freer Gallery of Art in the United States, and the British Museum in London. Each rendition adheres to the stylistic conventions of the Six Dynasties period, delineating the storyline into five acts and twelve scenes. Noteworthy editions include the Beijing edition and the British edition, with the Liaoning version believed to date back approximately 1,162 years to the reign of Emperor Gaozong of the Southern Song Dynasty. The Beijing edition bears no poem verses as notes but includes imperial inscriptions and the seal of Qianlong, along with transcribed text by Zhao Mengfu of the Yuan Dynasty, accompanied by inscriptions and postscripts from successive emperors. Also, the Freer version lacks such poem notes, resembling the Beijing edition closely in its imagery; both are believed to be copies from the Song Dynasty era. Contemporary scholars often refer to the version housed in the British Museum for study, despite ongoing debates among calligraphy and painting appraisers regarding its authenticity. However, the consensus remains steadfast in attributing the original composition to Gu Kaizhi, suggesting that extant copies are reproductions based on his original manuscript. Opinions vary regarding the period of reproduction, with some suggesting Tang Dynasty origins and others positing Song Dynasty provenance, reflecting the diverse perspectives within the scholarly community.

The *Nymph of the Luo River* preserved within Freer's collection is a distinguished facsimile from the Southern Song Dynasty. Scholars have noted that its landscape composition bears a resemblance to the style of Ma Yuan and Xia Gui from the 13th century AD, particularly evident in its corner composition. However, what truly sets this painting apart is its depiction of figures larger than the mountains, a characteristic emblematic of landscape paintings from the Six Dynasties period. As such, this artwork serves as a significant resource for studying both the landscape paintings of the Six Dynasties and the distinctive style of Gu Kaizhi, the original artist.

In addition to this masterpiece, Freer amassed a remarkable collection of over 330 Chinese Buddhist sculptures. Spanning from the Southern and Northern Dynasties to the Qing Dynasty, these sculptures encompass a diverse array of materials, including gilt copper, stone, wood, ramie dry paint, iron castings, and porcelain sculptures. They offer a comprehensive chronicle of Chinese Buddhist sculpture throughout history. Among the treasures in Freer's collection are exquisite stone carvings from renowned sites such as the Longmen

Grottoes, Gongxian Grottoes, and Xiangtangshan Grottoes. Notable additions include two stone Avalokitesvara statues originating from the Qibao Terrace of Guangzhai Temple in Chang'an City, endowed by Wu Zetian, as well as a rare early Southern Dynasty statue—a gold and bronze seated Maitreya statue crafted by Liu Guozhi in the 28th year of Yuanjia during the Liu Song Dynasty (AD 451) (Figure 11-18).

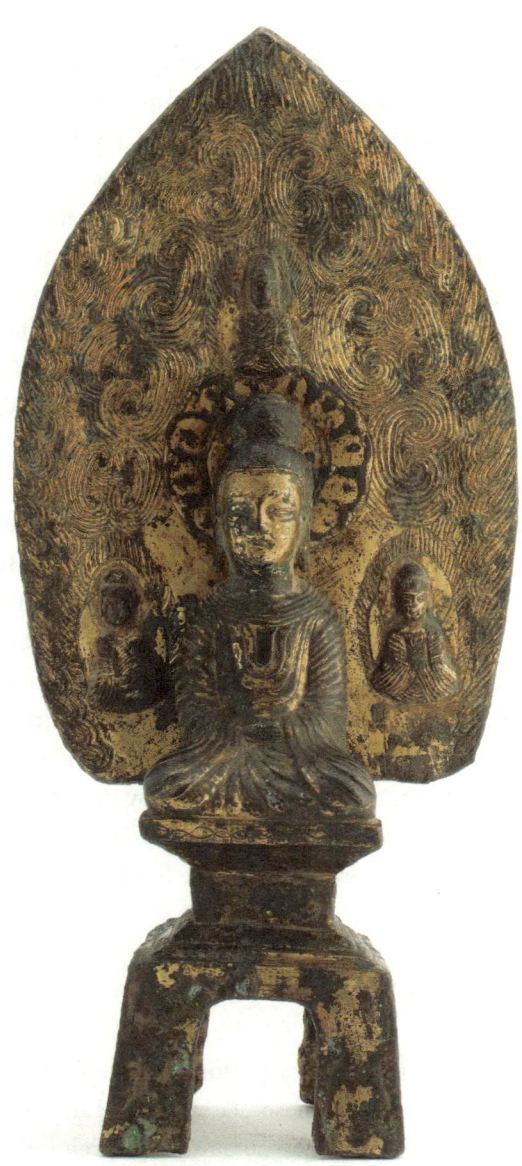

Figure 11-18 The gold and bronze seated Maitreya statue Liu Guozhi made in the 28th year of Yuanjia of the Liu Song Dynasty (451) (29.3 cm high, now in the Freer Gallery of Art, No. F1911.121)

Throughout the history of Chinese Buddhist art, significant reforms have left enduring marks, none more pivotal than the transformation in the attire of Buddhist statues. During the reign of Emperor Xiaowen of the Northern Wei Dynasty (r. AD 471–499), a profound sinicization reform took place, enabling the Xianbei people to adopt Han customs. This cultural shift found expression in Buddhist art, as the attire of Buddha statues transitioned from the traditional Indian bare right shoulder or shoulder-length styles to the Chinese style, characterized by the donning of a voluminous coat and a long belt. Notably, the primary Buddha statue within the Binyang Middle Cave of the Longmen Grottoes exemplifies this Han-style Buddhist attire, carved during the early 6th century of the Northern Wei Dynasty. The emergence of this new style of Buddha statues in the Southern Dynasties raises intriguing questions about its origin and rationale for the adoption of Chinese-style clothing over traditional Indian attire. A deeper exploration of statues from the Southern Dynasties promises significant insights into this theoretical inquiry. Examining extant statues from both the Northern Wei and Southern Dynasties reveals common characteristics among Buddha statues adorned in Han-style attire. These figures, often referred to as "slender-bone pretty face," typically exhibit delicate facial features and slender physiques. A notable example is the gilt-bronze seated Buddha statue from the Liu Song Dynasty (AD 420–479), housed within the esteemed collection of the Freer Gallery of Art. While this statue retains Indian-style clothing rather than the later Chinese attire, its pretty facial expression and slender form epitomize the morbid aesthetic preferences prevalent during the Southern and Northern Dynasties—a fascination with a delicately refined beauty. Through the study of such statues, it becomes evident that the evolution of Han-style Buddhist statues during the Southern Dynasties was a gradual process. Initially maintaining Indian-style attire, these statues gradually adopted Chinese-style facial features and body proportions before incorporating Chinese clothing. The seated Buddha statue from the Southern Dynasty, represented by this exemplary artifact, stands as a rare testament to this transitional period in Buddhist statue art. It serves as a cornerstone in the scholarly discourse surrounding the development of Chinese Buddhist statues, as evidenced by its frequent mention in literature discussing this rich history. Truly, this statue is a treasure of immense value, offering profound insights into the cultural and artistic evolution of the Southern Dynasties.

11.4 An Educational Art Gallery

As a discerning collector, Freer possessed a profound perception and insight into beauty, deeply enriching his exploration of Chinese classical art. His stipulations regarding the expansion of the gallery's collection and the pursuit of research hold immense significance in delving into the academic and artistic value of the artworks under its care (Figure 11-19).

Freer's philanthropic gestures extended far beyond the mere donation of his lifetime collection to the Smithsonian Institution and the provision of funds for the gallery's

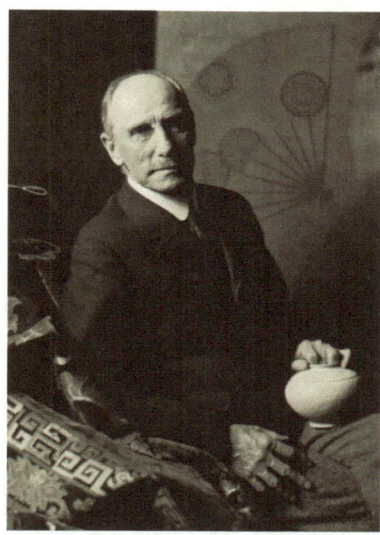

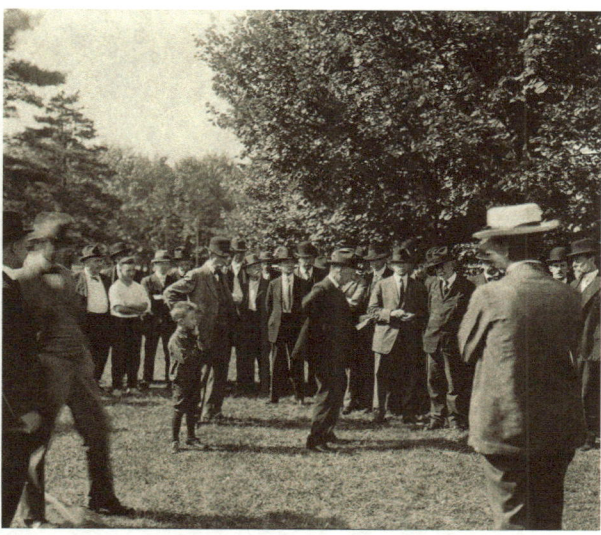

Figure 11-19 Freer (photographed by Edward Steichen in 1915)

Figure 11-20 The groundbreaking ceremony of the Freer Gallery of Art in 1916

construction. He established a dedicated fund, fueled by his personal resources, to continually acquire Oriental art for the museum while also financing research endeavors focused on Eastern civilizations. Moreover, his testamentary provisions granted access to the gallery's warehouse for any scholar or student studying Oriental art, facilitating countless research endeavors. The inscription on the donation seal encapsulates his enduring legacy, "For the enhancement and dissemination of human knowledge."

In 1916, the Freer Gallery of Art (Figure 11-20) commenced construction. Tragically, Freer succumbed to illness in New York on September 25, 1919, before witnessing the completion of his gallery. Delays due to World War I further postponed the gallery's inauguration until 1921. It must be a regret that he did not get to see its completion. Despite that, on May 2, 1923, the art gallery he founded officially opened its doors to the public. While not a scholar himself, Freer's profound understanding of artworks and his philanthropic contributions left an indelible impact, significantly advancing the Western world's comprehension and scholarly exploration of Eastern art (Figure 11-21).

In accordance with Freer's testamentary wishes, the gallery staff embarked on a continuous journey to augment the collection of Eastern art from its inception. Over the years, their fascination with and expertise in Eastern art deepened, coinciding with the escalating market prices for Far and Near Eastern art. By the mid-to-late 20th century, the Freer Gallery of Art's collection not only burgeoned in quantity but also attained unprecedented levels of quality. Today, its collection stands as a beacon, serving as a paradigm for both public and private collections of Asian art, whether for acquisition or scholarly inquiry.

Despite constraints posed by exhibition hall space and the imperative to maintain the refined ambiance of regular displays, only a fraction of the collection can be showcased

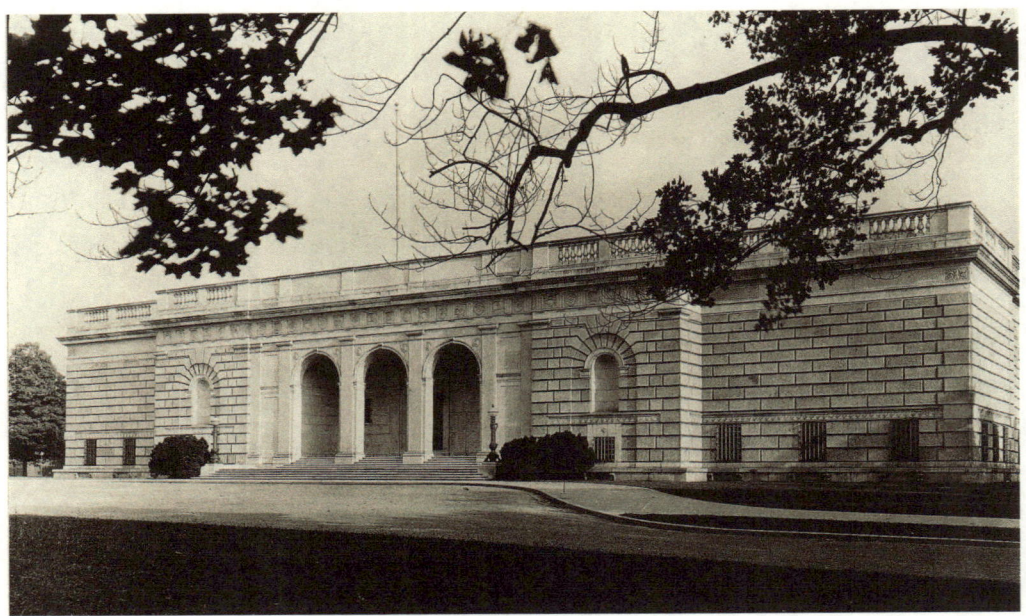

Figure 11-21 Freer Gallery of Art in Washington, USA, 1927

at any given time (Figure 11-22). Nonetheless, the rotating exhibitions ensure a dynamic viewing experience. For those artifacts residing in the warehouse, individuals with a vested interest can arrange pre-scheduled visits to scrutinize and photograph them meticulously (Figure 11-23). Freer underscored this accessibility in the opening lines of his *Deed of Gift*, "The School of Museums will allocate resources from the bequest to construct and furnish the gallery, with a specific focus on facilitating the continuous study of the collection by students and other interested individuals." The gallery organizes special exhibitions to highlight specific aspects of Oriental art. The *Deed of Gift* explicitly forbids the loan of the museum's collections for display elsewhere and also prohibits art collected from other sources from being exhibited at the Freer Gallery of Art.

In 1951, the establishment of a Conservation Science Laboratory marked a significant milestone for the Freer Gallery of Art. Research projects focused on the production techniques and materials of Eastern dynasty artworks serve a dual purpose: to deepen understanding of Asian art-making traditions and to bolster the gallery's conservation efforts, ensuring the preservation of entrusted artworks.

Today, the Freer Gallery of Art, gracing the National Mall in Washington, remains faithful to Freer's legacy. The Oriental art collection continues to expand, not only in breadth but also in depth. Concurrently, the gallery's scholarly pursuits yield fresh insights into the religious, historical, and material underpinnings of artworks. Past and present directors of the gallery remain steadfast in upholding Freer's vision, striving to uphold its offerings at the zenith of excellence while keeping a watchful eye on future development prospects.

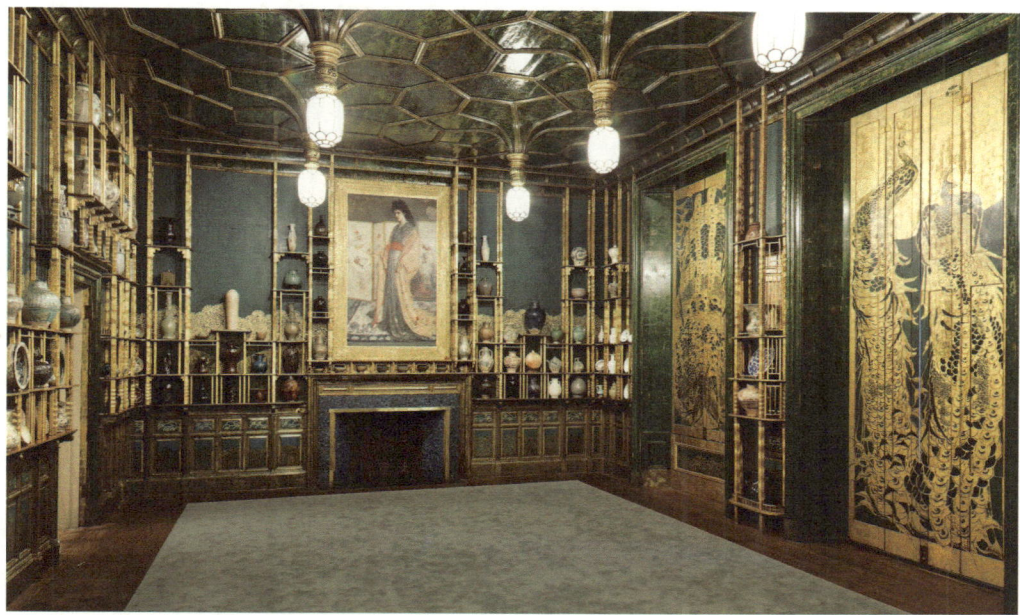

Figure 11-22 Chinese porcelain displayed in the Peacock Hall of the Freer Gallery of Art

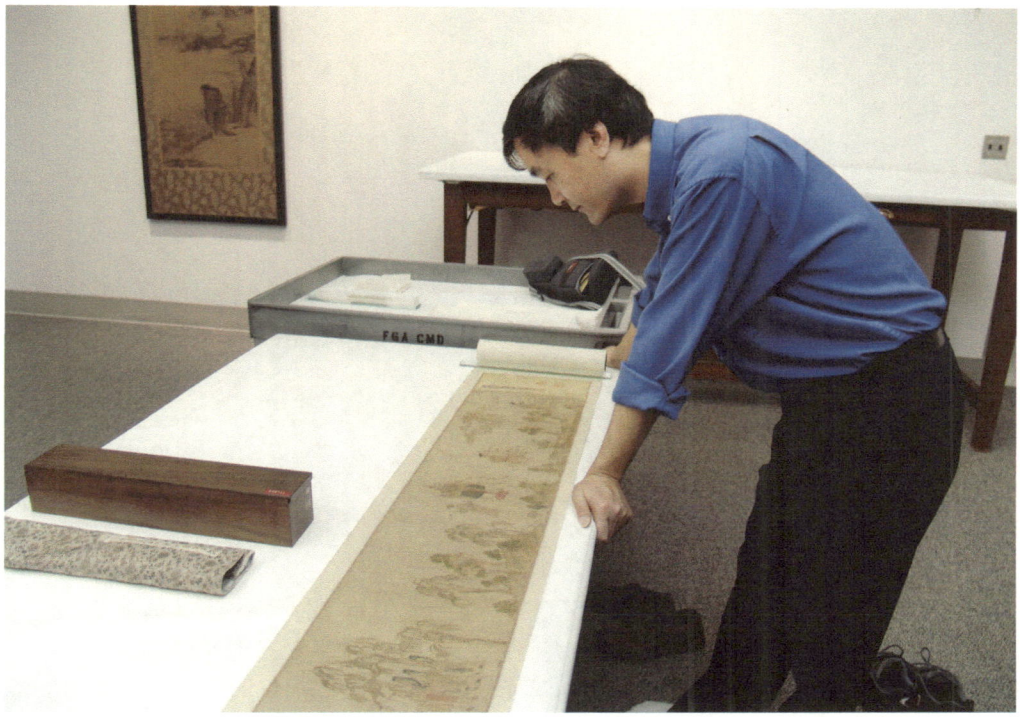

Figure 11-23 The author of this book, Chang Qing, observing the Southern Song Dynasty copy of *Nymph of the Luo River* in the warehouse of the Freer Gallery of Art (May 22, 2006)

Bibliography

I. CHINESE LITERATURE

Anonymous. "A Brief List of the Northern Wei Dynasty Statues from Gongxian Grotto Temple Scattered Abroad." In *Chinese Grottoes: Gongxian Grotto Temple*, edited by Henan Provincial Institute of Cultural Relics. Beijing: Cultural Relics Publishing House; Tokyo: Heibonsha, 1989.

———. "Sculptor Liu Kaiqu and Ten Others Wrote a Letter to the *People's Daily* to Expose the Serious Crimes of Profiteer Yue Bin in Stealing from Longmen Grottoes." *Cultural Relics*, no. 12 (1953).

Bhattacharya, Chhaya. "Study on the Style of Wooden Buddha Statues Unearthed in Kizil in the Turpan Collection of Museum of Indian Art, Berlin." Translated by Yang Fuxue. *Dunhuang Studies*, no. 1 (1994).

Chang, Qing. *Compassionate Beings in Stone and Metal: Chinese Buddhist Sculptures in the Freer Gallery of Art (2 Volumes)*. Beijing: Cultural Relics Publishing House, 2016.

———. "Chinese Buddhist Art Collection in the United States and its Research Value." *Arts*, no. 1 (2018).

———. "Exploration and Research: Tracing the Origin of the Longmen Statues in the Freer Gallery of Art." *Orientations*, no. 18 (July 2017): 52–69.

———. "The Metropolitan Museum of Art in New York and its Chinese Art Collection." *Chinese Art*, no. 1 (2019).

———. *Old Photographs of Splendid Treasures: Freer's View of the Chinese Cultural Heritage in 1910–1911*. Beijing: Cultural Relics Publishing House, 2019.

———. "Re-study of the Longmen Statues in the Collection of the Metropolitan Museum of Art." *Orientations*, no. 18 (July 2017): 70–81.

———. "Research and Problems on Shanxi Temple Murals Housed in North America." In *Art History Research (Thirteenth Edition)*, edited by the Art History Research Center of Sun Yat-sen University, 333–367. Guangzhou: Sun Yat-sen University Press, 2011.

Chao, Huashan. "German Investigation of the Kizil Caves in the Early 20th Century and Subsequent Research." In *Chinese Caves: Kizil Caves*, edited by Xinjiang Uygur Autonomous Region Cultural Relics Management Committee et al. Vol. 3. Beijing: Cultural Relics Publishing House, Tokyo: Heibonsha, 1997.

Chen, Mengjia. *Catalog of Chinese Bronze Wares Overseas*. Shanghai: The Commercial Press, 1946; in 1962, Science Press republished the book and changed the title to *A Collection of Chinese Yin and Zhou Bronze Wares Looted by US Imperialism*.

Flandrin, Philippe. *The Biography of Pelliot*. Translated by Yiwu. Guilin: Guangxi Normal University Press, 2017.

Freer, Charles Lang. *The Endless Light of Buddha–Journey to Longmen in 1910*. Translated by Li Wen et al. Shanghai: Shanghai Painting and Calligraphy Publishing House, 2014.

Fudge, Lloyd. "Cultural Relics Collected by Pelliot in Dunhuang." Translated and reviewed by Yang Hanzhang and Yang Aicheng. *Dunhuang Studies*, no. 4 (1990).

Hedin, Sven. *History of the Expedition in Asia, 1927–1935*. Translated by Xu Shizhou et al. Urumqi: Xinjiang People's Publishing House, 1992.

———. *My Life as an Explorer*. Translated by Li Wanrong. Taipei: Marco Polo Cultural Publishing House, 2010.

———. *Through Asia*. Translated by Zhang Ming, Zhao Shuxuan, and Wang Bei. Urumqi: Xinjiang People's Publishing House, 2013.

———. *The Wandering Lake*. Translated by Jiang Hong. Urumqi: Xinjiang People's Publishing House, 2000.

Higashiyama, Kengo. "Longmen Grottoes Statues Distributed in Europe, America, and Japan." In *Chinese Caves: Longmen Grottoes*. Vol. 2, Beijing: Cultural Relics Publishing House; Tokyo: Heibonsha, 1992.

Hopkirk, Peter. *Foreign Devils on the Silk Road: The Search for the Lost Cities and Treasures of Chinese Central Asia*. Translated and proofread by Yang Hanzhang and Song Ziming. Lanzhou: Gansu People's Publishing House, 1983.

Institute of Oriental Studies. Russian Academy of Sciences. *Russian Dunhuang Documents (17 Volumes)*. Shanghai: Shanghai Ancient Books Publishing House, 1992–2001.

Jiang, Hongyuan. "The Ins and Outs of Warner's Stripping of Dunhuang Murals." *Shanghai Archives*, no. 5 (2000).

Jin, Ronghua. "Stein–S Key Figure in the Outflow of Dunhuang Cultural Relics." *Dunhuang Studies*, no. 2 (1989).

Le Coq, Albert von. "The Origin, Itinerary, and Gains of the First Royal Prussian (i.e., German Second) Turpan Expedition." Translated by Chen Haitao. *Dunhuang Studies*, no. 3 (1999).

Lenain, Géraldine. *The Biography of C. T. Loo*. Translated by Bian Wanyu. Beijing: China Federation of Literary and Art Circles Press, 2015.

Liu, Jinbao. "Pelliot and His Dunhuang Posthumous Letters." *Journal of Northwest Normal University* (Social Science Edition), no. 4 (1989).

Longmen Grottoes Research Institute. *Collection of Scattered Longmen Statues*. Shanghai: Shanghai People's Art Publishing House, 1993.

Menshikov, Lev. "The Ignored Dunhuang Treasure Robber—Samuel Matilovich Dudin." Translated by Liao Xia. *Dunhuang Academic Journal*, no. 2 (2000).

Mirsky, Jeannette. *Sir Aurel Stein: Archaeological Explorer*. Translated by Tian Weijiang et al. Urumqi: Xinjiang Fine Arts Photography Press, 1992.

Nakano, Teruo. "The German Expedition Team's Investigation of the Kumtura Caves in the Early 20th Century and Subsequent Research." In *Chinese Caves: Kumtura Caves*, edited by Xinjiang Uygur Autonomous Region Cultural Relics Management Committee et al. Beijing: Cultural Relics Publishing House; Tokyo: Heibonsha, 1992.

Oldenburg, Sergey. "Excerpts from the Diary of Edenburg's Expedition in China." Translated by Yang Zifu. *Dunhuang Academic Journal*, no. 1 (1994).

Pelliot. *Pelliot's Beijing Diary.* Translated by Xiao Jing. Guilin: Guangxi Normal University Press, 2017.

Pelliot et al. *Pelliot's Adventures in the Western Regions.* Translated by Geng Sheng. Kunming: Yunnan People's Publishing House, 2001.

Rong, Xinjiang. "Taoist Wang—Discoverer of the Dunhuang Library Cave." *Dunhuang Studies*, no. 2 (2000).

Russian State Hermitage Museum and Shanghai Ancient Books Publishing House, eds. *Dunhuang Artworks Collection of the Russian State Hermitage Museum (6 Volumes).* Shanghai: Shanghai Ancient Books Publishing House, 1997–2000.

Shi, Pingting. "Questions and Answers about the Ōtani Expedition." *Dunhuang Studies*, no. 4 (1994).

Stein, Aurel M. *Sand-Buried Ruins of Khotan: Personal Narrative of a Journey of Archaeological and Geographical Exploration in Chinese Turkestan.* Translated by Xiang Da. Beijing: Zhonghua Book Company, 1936; reprinted in 1946. Urumqi: Xinjiang People's Publishing House, 2010.

Taipei National Palace Museum Editorial Committee. *Overseas Treasures · Buddha Statues.* Taipei: Taipei National Palace Museum, 1986.

———. *Overseas Treasures · Buddha Statues (Continued).* Taipei: Taipei National Palace Museum, 1990.

Tucci, Giuseppe. "Tibetan Art (Part 1 and 2)." Translated by Zhang Yasha and Li Jianxiong. *Tibetan Art Research*, no. 2 (1993), no. 2 (1994).

Vanderstappen, Harry, and Marilyn M. Rhie. "Sculpture of T'ien Lung Shan: Reconstruction and Dating." Translated by Li Chongfeng and Li Yuqun. *Dunhuang Studies*, no. 1 (1995).

Wang, Jiqing. "Aurel Stein's Fourth Expedition to Central Asia." *Dunhuang Academic Journal*, no. 1 (1993).

Wang, Kexiao. "Overview of the Dunhuang Cultural Relics Collection of the Russian State Hermitage Museum." *Dunhuang Studies*, no. 4 (1996).

Wang, Shixiang. "Recording the Seven Centers Where America Collected Chinese Cultural Relics." *Cultural Relics*, no. 7 (1955).

Whitfield, Roderick, eds. *Art of the Western Regions: The Stein Collection of the British Museum (Volumes 1 and 2).* Translated and compiled by Lin Baoyao. Taipei: Artist Publishing House, 2014.

Xinjiang Kucha Research Institute. *Collection of Overseas Kizil Caves Murals and Cave Restoration Images.* Lanzhou: Gansu Education Press, 2018.

Xu, Yang. *The Lost Kingdom on the Silk Road: Buddhist Art in Khara-Khoto, Western Xia.* Taipei: History Museum, 1996.

Yan, Sheng. "The Bankruptcy of Warner's Second Conspiracy to Strip Dunhuang Murals from the Diary of Chen Wanli's Journey to the West." *Archives*, no. 4 (2000).

Zhang, Huiming. "Russian Exploration of the Silk Road in China from 1896 to 1915 and the Loss of Chinese Buddhist Art—A Review of the Investigation of Buddhist Art Collections from Dunhuang, Xinjiang and Khara-Khoto in St. Petersburg." *Dunhuang Studies*, no. 1 (1993).

Zhang, Lintang, and Sun Di. *Xiantangshan Caves—Research on Lost Overseas Stone Carvings.* Beijing: Foreign Languages Press, 2004.

Zhao, Li. *Research on the Restoration of Kizil Caves Murals.* Shanghai: Shanghai Painting and Calligraphy Publishing House, 2020.

———, ed. *Collection of Restoration Images of Overseas Kizil Caves Murals*. Shanghai: Shanghai Painting and Calligraphy Publishing House, 2018.

II. JAPANESE LITERATURE

Akiyama, Terukazu. "Archaeological Achievement of Pelliot's Expedition Team in Central Asia (Part 1 and 2)." *Buddhist Art*, no. 19 (1953): 82–96; *Buddhist Art*, no. 20 (1953): 56–70.

British Museum. *Art of the Western Regions (3 Volumes)*. Tokyo: Kodansha, 1982.

Compilation Association of the Biography of Yamanaka Sadajirō. *The Biography of Yamanaka Sadajirō*. Osaka, 1939.

Giès, Jacques, ed. *Western Art—Pelliot Collection I at Guimet Museum*. Tokyo: Kodansha, 1994.

Nagasawa, Kazutoshi, ed. *Silk Road Exploration: Otani Expedition Team*. Tokyo: Hakusuisha, 1998.

Nakamine, Masanobu. "Restoration of Longmen Grottoes: The Center of the Head of the Kasyapa Statue in the Old Lotus Cave of Longmen Grottoes at the Paris Guimet Museum." *Art Studies*, no. 6 (March 1983): 23–41.

Tokyo National Museum. *Future Products of the Otani Exploration Team*. Tokyo: Tokyo National Museum, 1971.

———. *The Silk Road Grand Art Exhibition*. Tokyo: Yomiuri Shimbunsha, 1996.

Uehara, Yashitaro, ed. *New Record of the Western Regions (Otani Edition) Part 1 and 2*. Tokyo: Arikosha, 1937; Tokyo: Ikusa Publishing, 1984.

Yamanaka, Sadajirō. *Collection of Tianlongshan Stone Sculptures*. Osaka: Yamanaka & Co., 1928.

III. WESTERN LITERATURE

Baumer, Christoph. *Southern Silk Road: In the Footsteps of Sir Aurel Stein and Sven Hedin*. Bangkok: White Orchid Books, 2000.

C.T. Loo & Co. *An Exhibition of Ancient Chinese Ritual Bronzes*. Detroit, Mich.: Detroit Institute of Art, 1940.

Chang, Qing. "Genuine or Forged: Methods of Identifying Forgeries of Chinese Buddhist Sculptures." *Ars Orientalis* 36 (2009): 78–109.

———. "Revisiting the Longmen Sculptures in the Collection of The Metropolitan Museum of Art." *Orientations* 38, no. 1 (January/February 2007): 81–89.

———. "Search and Research: The Provenance of Longmen Images in the Freer Collection." *Orientations* 34 (May 2003): 16–25.

Chavannes, Édouard. *Mission Archéologique La Chine Septentrionale*. Paris, 1909.

Dabbs, Jack A. *History of the Discovery and Exploration of Chinese Turkestan*. Mouton: The Hague, 1963.

Farjenal, Fernand. "Les Manuscrits de la mission Pelliot." Paris, *La Revue Indigene*, December 1910.

Galambos, Imre, and Kitsudo Koichi. "Japanese exploration of Central Asia: The Ōtani expeditions and their British connections." *Bulletin of the School of Oriental and African Studies* 75 (2012): 113–134.

Galambos, Imre. "Japanese 'spies' along the Silk Road: British suspicions regarding the second Otani expedition (1908–09)." *Japanese Religions* 35, no. 1 & 2 (2010): 33–61.

Giles, Lionel. *Six Centuries at Tunhuang: A Short Account of the Stein Collection of Chinese Mss. in the British Museum.* London: China Society, 1944.

Grünwedel, Albert. *Alt-Buddhistische Kultstattenin Chinesisch-Turkistan.* Berlin, 1912.

———. *Alt-Kutscha, Tafelwerk.* Berlin, 1920.

Hadl, Richard. "Langdon Warner's: Buddhist Wall-Paintings." *Artibus Asiae* 9, no. 1/3 (1946): 160–164.

Hartel, Herbert. *Along the Ancient Silk Routes: Central Asian Art from the West Berlin State. Museums: an Exhibition Lent by the Museum fur Indishe Kunst. Staatliche Museen Preussischer Kulturbesitz. Berlin, Federal Republic of Germany.* New York: Metropolitan Museum of Art, 1982.

Hedin, Sven. *Central Asia and Tibet.* 2 Vols. Hurst and Blackett, 1903.

———. *History of the Expedition in Asia, 1927–1935.* Parts 1–3. Stockholm, 1943–1944.

———. *Through Asia.* 2 Vols. Methuen, 1898.

Hoernle, A. R. "A Collection of Antiquities from Central Asia." *Journal of the Asiatic Society of Bengal*, Part 1, 1899; Part 2, 1901.

Hopkirk, Peter. *Foreign Devils on the Silk Road: The Search for the Lost Cities and Treasures of Chinese Central Asia.* Amherst: The University of Massachusetts Press, 1980.

Klementz, Dimitri. *Turfan und seine Altertumer in Nachrichten uber die von der Kaiserlichen Akademie der Wissenschaften zu St. Petersburg im Jahre 1898 ausgerustete Expedition nach Turfan.* St. Petersburg, 1899.

Kozlov, Pyotr Kuzmich. *Mongolia and Amdo and the Dead City of Khara-Khoto.* Moscow, 1923.

Le Coq, Albert von. *Buried Treasures of Chinese Turkestan.* London: George Allen & Unwin Ltd., 1928.

———. *Chotscho: Koniglich Turfan-Expedition.* Berlin: Dietrich Reimer, 1913.

———. *Die Buddhistische Sprtantik in Mittelasien.* Berlin, 1922–1924.

———. *Kokturkisches aus Turfan.* Leipzig, 1909.

———. *Sprichworter und Lieder aus Turfan.* Leipzig, 1911.

———. *Von Land und Leuten in Ostturkistan.* Leipzig: White Lotus Press, 1928.

Loo, C. T. *An Exhibition of Chinese Stone Sculpture.* New York: C. L. Loo & Co., 1940.

Mirsky, Jeannette. *Sir Aurel Stein: Archaeological Explorer.* Chicago: University of Chicago Press, 1977.

Morgan, E. Delmar. "Dr. Regel's Expedition from Kuldja to Turfan in 1879-80." *Proceedings of the RGS* (June 1881).

Musee Guimet. *Catalogue Raisonne des Objets en bois Provenant de Dunhuang et Conserves au Musee Guimet.* Paris: Editions des Musees Nationaux, 1976.

Nyman, Lars-Erik. *Great Britain and Chinese, Russian and Japanese Interests in Sinkiang, 1918–1934.* Stockholm: Esselte Studium, 1977.

Pelliot, Paul. *Grottes de Touen-houang : Carnet de Notes de Paul Pelliot.* Paris, 1981.
1922–1924.

———. *Les Grottes de Touen-houang.* 6 Vols. Paris: Librarie Paul Geuthner,

———. *Paul Pelliot.* Paris: Societe Asiatique, 1946.

———. *Toumchouq.* 2 Vols. Paris, 1961, 1964.

Piotrovsky, Mikhail, ed. *Lost Empire of the Silk Road: Buddhist Art from Khara Khoto (X–XIIIth Century)*. Milano: Electa; Lugano: Thyssen- Bornemisza Foundation, 1993.

Prejevalsky, Col. N. "From Kulja, across the Tian Shan, to Lob-Nor." Translated by E. Delmar Morgan. *Nature* 20, no. 4 (1879).

Priest, Alan. *Chinese Sculpture in the Metropolitan Museum of Art*. New York: Metropolitan Museum of Art, 1944.

———. "A Stone Fragment from Lung Men." *Metropolitan Museum of Art Bulletin* 36, no. 5 (May 1941): 114–116.

Segalen, Victor. *Mission Archuoorgique en Chine (1914 et1917) Atalas*. Paris, 1923–1924.

Shih, Hsio-yen. *Chinese Art in the Royal Ontario Museum*. Toronto: The Royal Ontario Museum, 1972.

Siren, Osvald. *Chinese Sculpture from the Fifth to the Fourteenth Century*. London: Ernest Benn Ltd.1925; Reprinted by Hacker Art Books, New York, 1970.

Stappen, Harry Vander, and Marilyn M. Rhie. "Sculpture of T'ien Lung Shan: Reconstruction and Dating." *Artibus Asiae* 27 (1965): 189–237.

Stein, Aurel M. *Ancient Khotan: Detailed Report of Archaeological Explorations in Chinese Turkestan*. Oxford: Clarendon Press, 1907.

———. *Innermost Asia: Detailed Reported of Explorations in Central Asia, Kan-su, and Eastern Iran*. Oxford: Clarendon Press, 1928.

———. *On Ancient Asian Tracks: Brief Narrative of Three Expeditions in Innermost Asia and North-West China*. London: Macmillan, 1933.

———. *Ruins of Desert Cathy: Personal Narrative of Explorations in Central Asia and Westernmost China*. London: Macmillan, 1912.

———. *Sand-Buried Ruins of Khotan: Personal Narrative of a Journey of Archaeological and Gorgraphical Exploration in Chinese Turkestan*. London: T. F. Uniwn, 1903.

———. *Serindia: Detailed Report of Explorations in Central Asia and Westernmost China*. Oxford: Clarendon Press, 1921.

Stein, Aurel M., and L. Binyon. *Ancient Buddhist Painting from the Cave-Temples of Tun-Huang on the Western Frontier of China*. Oxford, 1921.

Stuart, Jan, and Chang Qing. "Chinese Buddhist Sculpture in a New Light at the Freer Gallery of Art." *Orientations* 33, no. 4 (April 2002): 32–35.

Tsiang, Katherine R., ed. *Echoes of the Past: The Buddhist Cave Temples of Xiangtangshan*. Chicago and Washington DC: Smart Museum of Art, Arthur M. Sackler Gallery, 2010.

Walravens, Hartmut. *Paul Pelliot (1878–1945): His Life and Works—a Bibliography*. Bloomington, Ind.: Indiana University, Research Institute for Inner Asian Studies, 2002.

Warner, Langdon. *Buddhist Wall-Painting: A Study of a Ninth-Century Grotto at Wan-Fo-Hsia near Tun-huang*. Cambridge: Harvard University Press, 1938.

———. "The Freer Gift of Eastern Art to America." *Asia* 23, no. 8 (August 1923): 590–594.

———. *The Long Old Road in China*. New York: Doubleday, Page & Company, 1926.

Yamanaka & Company, Inc. *Collection of Chinese and Other Far Eastern Art*. New York, 1943.

———. *Exhibition of Early Chinese Bronzes, Stone Sculptures, and Potteries*. New York, 1926.

Expedition Routes of Western Explorers

▶ **Hedin's Expedition Routes**

1886
A brief stay in Iran

1888
First time in China with only a brief stay in Xinjiang

1890
Iran–Mashhad–Ashgabat–Bukhara–Samarkand–Tashkent–Kashgar

1893–1897
First exploration, Stockholm–St. Petersburg–Tashkent–Pamir Mountains–Kashgar–the northern edge of the Tarim Basin–the southern edge of the Taklimakan Desert–Hotan Prefecture Dandan Oilik–Lake Kalajun–Bosten Lake–Hotan Prefecture–northern Xizang–Beijing–Mongolia–Russia–Stockholm

1899–1902
Second exploration, Kashmir–Kolkata–Yarkant River, Tarim River, Kaidu River–Lop Nur–ruins of the ancient city of Loulan–northern Xizang–near Lhasa (prohibited to enter)–Leh–Lahore–Delhi–Agra–Lucknow–Varanasi–Kolkata

1905–1909
Third exploration, Xizang

1927–1933

Fourth expedition, most of Mongolia, Xinjiang, and northern Xizang. Beijing–Baotou–
Mongolia–Urumqi–the northern and eastern areas of the Tarim Basin, etc.

▶ The German Turpan Expedition Routes

December 1902–April 1903

First expedition

Captain: Grünwedel; members: Le Coq, Huth, Bartus

Route: Ghulja (now Yining, Xinjiang)–Urumqi–Turpan (Ancient City of Gaochang,
    Bezeklik Caves, Shengjinkou Caves, Toyuk Caves)–Toksun–Karasahr–Kuqa (Kumtura
    Caves, Kizil Caves)–Aksu–Tumxuk–Maralbexi–Kashgar

November 1904–December 1905

Second expedition

Captain: Le Coq; member: Bartus

Route: Urumqi–Turpan (Ancient City of Gaochang, Jiaohe ruins)–Hami–Turpan–
    northern edge of Tarim Basin–Kashgar

1905–June 1906

Third expedition

Captain: Grünwedel; members: Le Coq, Pohrt, Bartus

Route: Kashgar–Tumushuk–Kucha (Kumtura Caves, Kizil Caves, Kerixi Caves)–Korla
    (temples and Shorchuk Caves)–Turpan–Urumqi–Hami–Toyuk Caves–Shorchuk
    Caves–Turpan–Urumqi–return

June 1913–February 1914

Fourth expedition

Captain: Le Coq; member: Bartus

Route: Kashgar–Kuqa (Kizil Caves, Kerixi Caves, Senmusaimu Caves, Kumtura Caves)–
    Tumushuk–Kashgar

▶ Stein's Expedition Routes

1900–1901

First expedition, the southern edge of the Tarim Basin–Hotan–Niya ruins–Miran ruins–
    Loulan ruins

1906–1908

Second expedition, the southern edge of the Tarim Basin–Rawak ruins of Hotan–Niya ruins–Miran ruins–Dunhuang–northern edge of the Tarim Basin–Turpan–Taklimakan Desert–Hotan–Kunlun Mountains

1913–1916

Third expedition, the southern edge of the Tarim Basin–Miran ruins–Dunhuang–Khara-Khoto ruins on the Ejin River in Inner Mongolia–Turpan (Astana, Bezeklik Caves)–Kuqa (Kizil Caves)–Kashgar–Pamir Plateau (Afghanistan border)–Sistan region in western Iran

1930–1931

Fourth expedition, the southern edge of the Tarim Basin–Dunhuang and the east area–Turpan (Astana, Bezeklik Caves)–Kashgar

▶ Pelliot's Expedition Route

1906–1909

Paris–Moscow–Tashkent–Kashgar–Tumxuk–Kuqa (Kumtura Caves, Subashi Buddhist Temple ruins)–Urumqi–Turpan–Hami–Dunhuang–Xi'an–Beijing

▶ Ōtani Kōzui's Expedition Routes

1902–1904

First expedition

Members: Watanabe Tesshin, Hori Kenyu, Honda Eryu, Inoue Koen

Route: London–Russia–Kashgar–Hotan–Kuqa, Baicheng (Kizil Caves)–Xi'an–Japan

1908–1909

Second expedition

Members: Tachibana Zuicho, Nomura Eizaburo

Tachibana Zuicho and Nomura Eizaburo's route: Beijing–Mongolia–Junggar Basin–Turpan (Bezeklik Caves)–Korla

Tachibana Zuicho's route: Korla–Loulan ruins–Ruoqiang–Hotan–Kashgar–Over the Karakoram Pass–Leh City

Eizaburo Nomura's route: Korla–Kuqa (Kizil Grottoes)–Aksu–Kashgar–Over the Karakoram Pass–Leh

1910–1912, 1911–1914

Third expedition

Members: Tachibana Zuicho, Yoshikawa Koichiro

Tachibana Zuicho's route (1910–1912): London–Russia–Tacheng–Urumqi–Turpan–Loulan
ruins–Qiemo–Across the Taklamakan Desert–Kuqa–Kashgar–Hotan–northern
Xizang–Qiemo–Ruoqiang–Dunhuang–Anxi–Hami–Turpan–Urumqi–Siberia–Japan

Yoshikawa Koichiro's route (1911–1914): Japan–Shanghai–Wuhan–Lanzhou–Dunhuang–
Hami–Urumqi–Turpan–Yanqi–Kuqa (Kumtura Caves, Subashi Buddhist Temple
ruins, Kizil Caves)–Kashgar–Hotan–Ili–Urumqi–Turpan–Hami–Dunhuang–Jiuquan–
Beijing–Japan

► Kozlov's Expedition Routes

1884

First expedition, Kyakhta–Gobi Desert–Origin of the Yellow River–Tanggula Mountain–
northern Xizang–Xinjiang (Lop Nur, Tarim River)–Karakul

1889–1890

Second expedition, Karakul–Issyk-Kul–Tian Shan–Southern Xinjiang–Yarkant–Kashgar–
Niya Ancient City–Lop Nur–Lake Zaysan–Russia

1893–1895

Third expedition, Karakul–Tian Shan–Turpan–Hami–Dunhuang–Qilian Mountains–
Amne Machin–Qinghai–Origin of the Yellow River–Turpan–Lake Zaysan–Russia

1899–1901

Fourth expedition, Kyakhta–Khovd–Altai Mountains–Central Gobi–Tengger Desert–
Hexi Corridor–Xi'ning–Qinghai Lake–Qaidam Basin–Chamdo–Source of the
Yangtze and Yellow Rivers–Lanzhou–Küriye (today's Ulaanbaatar, Mongolia)–
Kyakhta–Russia

1904

Fifth expedition, Russia–Küriye (visiting the Dalai Lama Thubten Gyatso)

1907–1909

Sixth expedition, Moscow–Irkutsk–Kyakhta–Küriye–Tüshiyetu Khan Aimag, Sain Noyon
Khan Aimag–Khara-Khoto ruins–Northern edge of Ala Shan Desert–Dingyuan
Camp, the capital of Ala Shan Banner–Amdo Tibetan area–Qinghai Lake–Lanzhou–
Khara-Khoto ruins–Khalkha Mongolia–Küriye–Russia

1923–1926
Seventh expedition, Küriye–Noin-Ula Mountain (excavation of Xiongnu tombs)–Khentii Mountains–Khara-Khoto

▶ Oldenburg's Expedition Routes

1909–1910
First expedition, St. Petersburg–Omsk–Tacheng–Urumqi–Yanqi (Shorchuk Temple)–Turpan (Jiaohe Ancient City, Turpan Ancient City, Gaochang Ancient City, Astana, Shengjinkou Caves, Bezeklik Caves, Mutougou, Tuyugou Caves), Kuqa (Subash Temple ruins, Senmusaimu Grottoes, Kerixi Grottoes, Kizil Caves, Kumtura Caves)

1914–1915
Second expedition, St. Petersburg–Tacheng–Urumqi–Turpan–Hami–Dunhuang

▶ Warner's Expedition Routes

1923–1924
First expedition, Beijing–Luoyang (Longmen Grottoes)–Xi'an–Ejin Banner Khara-Khoto ruins–Dunhuang–Lanzhou–Beijing

1925
Second expedition, Beijing–Dunhuang–Yulin Caves in Anxi–Xiangdong Caves in Jingchuan County–Beijing

▶ Freer's Routes to See and Purchase Cultural Relics in China

1895
First time, the United States–Hong Kong–Shanghai–Japan

1907
Second time, the United States–Hong Kong–Guangzhou–Hong Kong – Shanghai–Japan

1909
Third time, the United States–Hong Kong–Shanghai–Qingdao–Tianjin–Beijing

1910–1911

Fourth time, the United States–Nagasaki, Japan–Shanghai–Qingdao–Beijing–Tianjin–
Beijing–Anyang–Kaifeng–Zhengzhou–Gongxian (Gongxian Grottoes, Imperial
Tombs of the Northern Song Dynasty)–Luoyang (Longmen Grottoes)–Beijing–
Shenyang–Dalian–Lüshun–Shanghai–Hangzhou–Shanghai–Nagasaki, Japan

Important Records Pertaining to This Book

1840–1842 (20th to 22nd year of Daoguang's reign in the Qing Dynasty)
The first Opium War.

1851 (1st year of Xianfeng's reign in the Qing Dynasty)
On the momentous January 11, amid the rustic tranquility of Jintian Village in Guiping County, Guangxi, Hong Xiuquan solemnly pledged his allegiance and ignited the flames of rebellion against the Qing Dynasty. Thus, he inaugurated the grand saga of the Taiping Heavenly Kingdom. With the rallying cry echoing through the ages, the insurgent forces took shape as the formidable Taiping Army. As the years unfolded, by the dawn of 1864, a tragic toll was exacted upon the revered Buddhist relics scattered across the southern landscape. Notably, the venerable Ming Dynasty Great Bao'en Temple Porcelain Tower in Nanjing stood among the relics ravaged by the unforgiving tides of conflict.

1854 (4th year of Xianfeng's reign in the Qing Dynasty)
Charles Lang Freer, an American industrialist and art collector, was born in Kingston, New York, on February 25.

1856 (6th year of Xianfeng's reign in the Qing Dynasty)
On July 31, German archaeologist Albert Grünwedel was born in Munich.

1860 (10th year of Xianfeng's reign in the Qing Dynasty)
On September 8, German archaeologist Albert von Le Coq was born in Berlin.

In the fateful month of October, the forces of Britain and France descended upon Beijing. Among the grievous losses was the wanton destruction of the Old Summer Palace, its once-grand halls consumed by flames. Within its storied gardens, an irreplaceable trove of cultural heritage fell prey to looting, with priceless artifacts pillaged and scattered to the winds. Among the plundered treasures were ancient bronze ritual vessels hailing from the pre-Qin era, alongside relics spanning the illustrious epochs of the Tang, Song, Yuan, Ming, and Qing dynasties.

1862 (1st year of Tongzhi's reign in the Qing Dynasty)

On November 26, British archaeologist Marc Aurel Stein was born in Budapest, Hungary.

1863 (2nd year of Tongzhi's reign in the Qing Dynasty)

On September 26, Russian Orientalist Sergey Fyodorovich Oldenburg was born in Byankino, Russia.

On October 3, Russian archaeologist Pyotr Kuzmich Kozlov was born in Dukhovshchina, Smolensk Oblast, Russia.

1865 (4th year of Tongzhi's reign in the Qing Dynasty)

On February 19, Swedish geographer Sven Hedin was born in Stockholm.

1866 (5th year of Tongzhi's reign in the Qing Dynasty)

On August 20, Japanese antique dealer Yamanaka Sadajirō was born in Sakai City, Osaka.

1874 (13th year of Tongzhi's reign in the Qing Dynasty)

On September 12, Japanese explorer Watanabe Tesshin was born in Mihara, Hiroshima Prefecture.

1876 (2nd year of Guangxu's reign in the Qing Dynasty)

On December 27, Ōtani Kōzui, the 22nd abbot of Nishi Hongan-ji of Jodo Shinshu in Kyoto, Japan, was born.

1878 (4th year of Guangxu's reign in the Qing Dynasty)

Russian officer explorer Nikolay Przhevalsky inspected Lop Nur in Xinjiang and found that the location of Lop Nur on the Chinese map was wrong.

On May 28, French sinologist Paul Eugène Pelliot was born in Paris.

1879 (5th year of Guangxu's reign in the Qing Dynasty)

The president of the Hungarian Geographical Society, Lajos Lóczy, went to Gansu in northwest China to inspect the geology and geography, and visited the Dunhuang Mogao Grottoes.

Przhevalsky entered Dunhuang on his third expedition to Central Asia.

From 1879 to 1880, Johann Albert von Regel, a Russian doctor, botanist, Central Asian researcher and archaeologist, visited Turpan when he was investigating plants in Central Asia and reported on the ruins of abandoned Buddhist temples and relics in the Turpan area.

1880 (6th year of Guangxu's reign in the Qing Dynasty)

On February 1, antique dealer Ching Tsai Loo was born in Lujiadu, Huzhou, Zhejiang.

1881 (7th year of Guangxu's reign in the Qing Dynasty)

On August 1, American Asian art historian Langdon Warner was born in Massachusetts.

1884 (10th year of Guangxu's reign in the Qing Dynasty)
Russian archaeologist Kozlov began to explore Xinjiang, Xizang, and Mongolia with Przhevalsky.

1885 (11th year of Guangxu's reign in the Qing Dynasty)
On May 23, Japanese explorer Yoshikawa Koichiro was born in Shimogyō-ku, Kyoto.

1888 (14th year of Guangxu's reign in the Qing Dynasty)
Swedish geographer Sven Hedin visited Xinjiang for the first time for a brief investigation.

1890 (16th year of Guangxu's reign in the Qing Dynasty)
On January 7, Japanese explorer Tachibana Zuicho was born in Nagoya City, Aichi Prefecture.

In December, Sven Hedin once again entered Xinjiang and stayed in Kashgar before leaving the following year.

1894 (20th year of Guangxu's reign in the Qing Dynasty)
On May 1, Sven Hedin arrived in Kashgar, Xinjiang again.

That year, Japanese antique dealer Yamanaka Sadajirō opened the Yamanaka & Co. branch in New York, USA.

1895 (21st year of Guangxu's reign in the Qing Dynasty)
Russian archaeologist Kozlov began to lead an independent team and continued exploration in Central Asia.

On April 10, Sven Hedin's camel caravan left Rajlik Village in Makit, Xinjiang, and began its death journey in the Taklimakan Desert.

That year, Freer paid a short three-day visit to Hong Kong on his way to Japan. After that, he visited Shanghai for a week, and then took a boat to Japan for a four-month trip, where he began to build his own Asian art collection system.

1896 (22nd year of Guangxu's reign in the Qing Dynasty)
On January 23, Sven Hedin discovered the ruins of the Dandan Oilik Buddhist Temple in the ancient Khotan Kingdom.

1898 (24th year of Guangxu's reign in the Qing Dynasty)
The Russian Academy of Sciences sent D. A. Klementz to lead a team to inspect Turpan. They inspected the ancient city of Gaochang, excavated the Astana Cemetery, surveyed and mapped the Bezeklik Caves, and brought back several printed Buddhist scriptures in Sanskrit and Uighur.

1899 (25th year of Guangxu's reign in the Qing Dynasty)
On November 25, Russian Orientalist, geographer, and explorer Gombojab Tsybikov was dispatched by the Russian Geographical Society to Xizang. Arriving in Lhasa in August 1900,

he traveled to many places in Xizang and Qinghai. On April 4, 1902, he returned home from his expedition and brought back about 300 volumes of Tibetan classics from Xizang.

That year, Japanese antique dealer Yamanaka Sadajirō opened Yamanaka & Co. branches in Boston, Chicago, and other places in the United States.

1900 (26th year of Guangxu's reign in the Qing Dynasty)

In March, Sven Hedin discovered the ruins of the ancient city of Loulan in Xinjiang.

In March, Stein began his first expedition to Central Asia.

On June 26, Dunhuang Taoist Wang Yuanlu discovered the Library Cave (Cave 17) on the corridor wall of Cave 16 of Mogao Grottoes.

In August, the Eight-Power Allied Forces captured Beijing, and Empress Dowager Cixi and Emperor Guangxu fled to Xi'an.

On November 25, Stein began excavating the village of Yurturgan, the site of the former capital of Khotan, and obtained nearly a hundred cultural relics.

From December 19 to January 3, 1901, Stein excavated the Dandan Oilik site in Khotan and discovered a total of 15 temple houses and obtained about 180 cultural relics.

In that year, the French sinologist Pelliot was selected as a sponsored student of the École Française d'Extrême-Orient (French School of the Far East) in Hanoi. He was sent to China three times for inspections and collected a large number of antiquities and ancient books.

That year, the Japanese antique dealer Yamanaka Sadajirō opened a branch of the Yamanaka & Co. in London, England.

That year, the American collector Freer retired from his business and devoted himself to to the research and development of art collections.

1901 (27th year of Guangxu's reign in the Qing Dynasty)

From January 28 to February 13, Stein discovered urban ruins buried in sand in Niya, located in Minfeng County, Hotan today, and conducted archaeological excavations. He found a large number of wooden slips in Chinese and Arabic script, various paintings, and engravings. The wooden chairs, wooden tables, and door frames with the characteristic carvings of the Kushan Empire were brought back to the British Museum.

In March, Sven Hedin excavated the ruins of the ancient city of Loulan.

From April 11 to 18, Stein excavated the ruins of the Rawak Stupa on the other side of the Yulong Kashgar River, about 40 kilometers northeast of Hotan County. He discovered the temple centered on the pagoda and the tall statues on the wall of the pagoda, excavated more than 90 standing Buddha relief statues, and took away smaller ones.

From May to December, Sven Hedin inspected and mapped the territory of Xizang.

On July 2, Stein returned to London with about 1,500 excavated cultural relics, concluding his first expedition to Central Asia. The cultural relics are now mainly housed in the Department of Oriental Antiquities of the British Museum and the Oriental Department of the British Library.

That year, Pelliot, professor of Sinology at the École Française d'Extrême-Orient in Hanoi, visited China for the second time and brought back a large number of Chinese, Mongolian, and Tibetan books and works of art to the school.

1902 (28th year of Guangxu's reign in the Qing Dynasty)
In August, the first Central Asian expedition organized by Ōtani Kōzui set off with explorers Watanabe Tesshin, Hori Kenyu, Honda Eryu, and Inoue Koen.

In that year, researchers such as Grünwedel and Le Coq from the Museum of Ethnology in Berlin formed the first German Central Asian expedition to the Turpan area to inspect the ancient city of Gaochang, among other ruins.

That year, Pelliot visited China for the third time and collected a great number of books and sculptures for École Française d'Extrême-Orient.

That year, Ching Tsai Loo followed Zhang Jingjiang to Paris, France.

1903 (29th year of Guangxu's reign in the Qing Dynasty)
In April, Watanabe Tesshin and Hori Kenyu of the Ōtani Kōzui expedition team arrived in Baicheng, Xinjiang, to investigate the Kizil Caves. They took pictures of the murals and cave exteriors, and cut murals in some caves, becoming the first expedition team to cut the Kizil Caves murals; cleaned up the caves and found many remaining documents and wooden slips, and obtained the famous *Kongmusi Documents in the Fifth Year of Jianzhong of the Tang Dynasty*; excavated some tombs and found some documents.

In May, Watanabe Tesshin and Hori Kenyu concluded the first Central Asian expedition of the Ōtani expedition and returned home via Xi'an with a great number of looted Chinese cultural relics.

1904 (30th year of Guangxu's reign in the Qing Dynasty)
In September, the Royal Prussian expedition led by Le Coq set out from Berlin for the second time to the Turpan region.

On November 18, Le Coq's team arrived in Turpan, and commenced exploration and archaeology of Gaochang Ancient City and Bezeklik Caves, cutting out a great number of murals. Afterward, they investigated the Tuyugou Caves and discovered many precious murals.

1905 (31st year of Guangxu's reign in the Qing Dynasty)
The American Huntington Expedition investigated the ruins of the ancient city of Loulan in Xinjiang.

That year, Russian archaeologist Kozlov met with the 13th Dalai Lama Thubten Gyatso in Küriye (now Ulaanbaatar, Mongolia).

That year, the Japanese antique dealer Yamanaka Sadajirō opened an agency in Paris, France, and reorganized his company into the Yamanaka & Co. Group, with himself responsible for business execution.

1906 (32nd year of Guangxu's reign in the Qing Dynasty)

On February 26, the third German Central Asian expedition arrived at the Kizil Caves. The expedition leader was Grünwedel, and the team members included Le Coq, Bartus, and Pohrt. They cut away a great number of murals.

On June 15, Pelliot, geographer Louis Vaillant, and natural historian and photographer Charles Nouette formed a three-person expedition team that set out from Paris for China. The three entered Xinjiang by train via Moscow and Tashkent.

At the end of August, the Pelliot expedition arrived in Kashgar and inspected and excavated three pre-Islamic civilization monuments in the Kashgar oasis. They also inspected several Buddhist sites in the Kashgar area for more than a month.

On October 8, the British Stein Expedition conducted its second Central Asia expedition and conducted a second excavation at the Hotan Rawak Stupa.

In late October, Stein returned to repeat the excavation near the Niya site.

On October 29, Pelliot's archaeological expedition arrived at Tumushuk Village, located between Kashgar and Kuqa, and stayed in the area until December 15 of the same year, excavating Buddhist ruins and obtaining Buddhist clay statues, murals, pottery and sundries, engravings, prints, etc. Pelliot cut up and moved three of the large-scale painted statues, which are now in the Guimet Museum in Paris, France.

In November, Stein headed to the Loulan ruins in Lop Nur, excavated the Ruoqiang Miran ruins south of Lop Nur, and discovered Buddhist temples, pagodas, and winged angel murals. In Lop Nur, Stein excavated 14 ruins, including the famous Tibetan Fort, and successively obtained more than 500 precious cultural relics, and took away murals from the Miran temple ruins.

That year, Freer decided to donate his lifelong collection of art to the Smithsonian Institution, the highest scientific research institution in the United States managed by the US federal government.

Between 1906 and 1907, A. I. Kokhanovsky headed an expedition to revisit Turpan. The team acquired 20 documents, including one Sanskrit manuscript, nine Chinese manuscripts, two Tibetan manuscripts and prints, one Mongolian print, three Uighur manuscripts, two bilingual Uighur and Chinese documents, and numerous Manichaean documents in Sogdian. These materials were initially handed over to the Royal Geographical Society of Russia and later transferred to the Asiatic Museum.

1907 (33rd year of Guangxu's reign in the Qing Dynasty)

Pelliot's expedition reached Kuqa, where they conducted surveys and excavations for eight months. He excavated the remains of Buddhist temples in Duldur and Subashi near Kuqa, unearthing numerous invaluable cultural artifacts. They also discovered ancient documents in Tocharian.

On February 11, Stein completed the excavation at the Miran site and packed the cultural relics for transport to Kashgar.

In March, Stein arrived in Dunhuang.

On March 31, Freer arrived in Hong Kong and purchased some Chinese ceramics.

In April, Freer purchased large quantities of cultural relics in Guangdong, Hong Kong, and Shanghai before sailing to Japan.

At the end of May, Stein went to Mogao Grottoes for the fourth time and obtained the Library Cave more than 7,000 manuscripts, over 200 pieces of Buddhist paintings and embroidery from Taoist Wang, which filled up 29 boxes, at a cost of only 40 pieces of horseshoe silver, equivalent to 500 rupees, and all were shipped to the British Museum in London.

In October, Pelliot's expedition team arrived in Urumqi, met Duke Zailan, and was presented with a volume of the *Lotus Sutra* discovered in the Dunhuang Library Cave.

That year, French sinologist Émmanuel-Édouard Chavannes inspected historical sites and cultural relics in northern China, took a great number of photos, and published the Archaeological Atlas of Northern China in 1909.

From 1907 to 1909, Sven Hedin visited Xizang.

From 1907 to 1909, leading the sixth Russian expedition team, Kozlov uncovered the ancient Western Xia city's ruins on the edge of the Badain Jaran Desert on the east bank of the Nalin River in Ejin Banner of Ala Shan League, Mongolia. Over 300 Buddhist paintings, over 20 woodblock prints, over 70 wood carvings, clay statues, copper and gilded casts, silk and linen fabrics, coins, and banknotes, as well as many Western Xia, Han, Tibetan, Uighur, Turkic, Jurchen, Mongolian books and documents were discovered, totaling 3,500 pieces of cultural relics.

1908 (34th year of Guangxu's reign in the Qing Dynasty)

In February, Pelliot's expedition arrived at the Mogao Grottoes in Dunhuang.

On March 3, Pelliot entered the Library Cave to browse documents for more than three weeks, totaling more than 20,000 documents. Using a silver ingot weighing about 50 taels for the price of a bundle of manuscripts, he purchased more than 6,000 volumes of documents, as well as more than 100 Tang and Song Dynasty scrolls and banners, fabrics, wood products, wooden movable type printing stencils, and other Buddhist devices. The documents are all owned by the National Library of France. The paintings, wood carvings, silk banners, sutras, and various silk fabrics were first collected in the Louvre and then in the Guimet Museum in 1947. Pelliot and others also investigated various caves in the Mogao Grottoes, took photos of the statues and murals in the caves, numbered the caves, and took detailed notes, especially the many Inscriptions in the caves that are now unreadable. The results of the inspection were later edited and published as *Les grottes de Touen-houang* (*The Dunhuang Caves*) and *Grottes de Touen-houang : Carnet de Notes de Paul Pelliot* (*Pelliot's Notes on Dunhuang Caves*).

In June, the second expedition organized by Ōtani Kōzui set off. The team members included Tachibana Zuicho and Nomura Eizaburo. They mainly excavated ancient ruins in Turpan, Loulan, Kucha, etc., cutting off seven pieces of murals at the Bezeklik Caves in Turpan and obtaining seven clay Buddha statues.

That year, an exhibition on the cultural relics and materials obtained by Russia's archaeological expedition in Xinjiang, China, was held at the Russian Imperial Palace.

That year, Ching Tsai Loo officially opened Laiyuan & Co. in Paris and later opened branches in Beijing and Shanghai to start his own antique business.

1909 (1st year of Xuantong's reign in the Qing Dynasty)

In February, Nomura Eizaburo of the Ōtani Expedition conducted excavations and surveys around Kuqa, and then reached Kashgar via Aksu.

From March 18 to 20, Eizaburo Nomura excavated 13 caves in the Kizil Caves, cutting away portions of the rhombus Jataka and Karma Story murals on the side wall of Cave 206, and the mural of Brahmin Drona, the presiding officer of the division of sarira among the eight kings, within the *Picture of the Eight Kings Dividing the Sarira* on the inner wall of the left corridor of Cave 224. Zuicho entered the Lop Nur Desert to explore Loulan and obtained the famous Li Bo Documents from the Former Liang period. After that, he arrived in Kashgar along the South Desert Road via Ruoqiang and Hotan. After the two reunited, they ended their second 18-month expedition to Central Asia.

In June 1909, Kozlov successfully excavated the ruins of a pagoda known as the Glorious Sarira Pagoda in Khara-Khoto and discovered more than 20 Buddha statues and books in the underground palace, numerous scripture manuscripts in Chinese, Mongolian, Tibetan, and Western Xia languages, as well as more than 300 Han-style Buddhist paintings and Tibetan-style thangkas.

In June, the Russian Oldenburg formed his first Russian expedition to Xinjiang based on the Klementz expedition. They began to excavate and inspect ancient ruins in Kashgar, Turpan, Kuqa, and other places, and it ended in 1910 with a great number of cultural relics obtained.

On September 29, the Russian Oldenburg expedition team arrived in Turpan.

From October 3 to November 12, the Russian Oldenburg team inspected dozens of cave temple sites in the Ancient City of Jiaohe, the Ancient City of Turpan, the Ancient City of Gaochang, the vicinity of Astana Village, the northern Turpan Canyon, Shengjinkou, Bezeklik, the vincinity of Mutugou Village and Tuyugou, and carried out archaeological numbering, mapping, photography, and recording. Afterward, they went to the Kuqa area, taking the Kizil Caves as the main object of investigation, and harvested a great number of murals. Oldenburg's first inspection brought back more than 30 boxes of murals, wood carvings, and other artworks, nearly a hundred manuscript fragments, and more than 1,500 inspection photos. The manuscript fragments contain secular documents in various languages, including Chinese, Uighur, Sogdian, and Sanskrit manuscripts. These artifacts are preserved in the State Hermitage Museum.

In October, Pelliot returned to Paris, concluding his expedition.

In the autumn of that year, the cultural relics of Khara-Khoto acquired by Kozlov arrived in St. Petersburg and were stored in the newly built building of the Royal Geographical Society of Russia. They were publicly displayed for the first time in early 1910. Subsequently, the art and archaeological artifacts were sent to the Ethnology Department of the Museum of His Imperial Majesty Alexander III in Russia. The books and manuscripts were transported to the Russian Academy of Sciences, now the St. Petersburg branch of the Institute of Oriental Studies, for preservation. In 1933, the artifacts in the museum's collection were transferred to the Oriental Department of the State Hermitage Museum.

That year, Freer came to Hong Kong again. Next, he went to Shanghai, Qingdao, Tianjin and Beijing. During this trip, Freer accumulated numerous collections including bronzes, ceramics, and paintings, and eventually shipped eight boxes full of Chinese artifacts to his home in Detroit.

1910 (2nd year of Xuantong's reign in the Qing Dynasty)

In August, the third expedition organized by Ōtani Kōzui began. Tachibana Zuicho entered China from Russia to Tacheng, Xinjiang, then passed through Urumqi and Turpan and entered the Loulan area again for inspection. Then, he went north from Qiemo and crossed the Taklimakan Desert to Kucha in northern Xinjiang. He then went west from Kucha to Kashgar, then southward from Hotan into northern Xizang, and returned to the Qiemo and Ruoqiang areas for inspection. He did some excavations in Turpan, Loulan, Hotan, and other places.

On September 11, Freer arrived in Shanghai from Nagasaki, Japan.

From October 19 to November 14, Freer visited historical sites in Kaifeng, Gongxian, and Luoyang, focusing on the Longmen Grottoes. After that, he returned to Beijing and focused on buying ceramics, bronzes, and paintings.

That year, the Qing government's Ministry of Education officially allocated 6,000 taels of silver and ordered Mao Qingfan, the governor of Shaanxi and Gansu, and Chen Ze, the county magistrate of Dunhuang, to transport all the remaining documents from the Mogao Grottoes to Beijing. Taoist priest Wang, foreseeing the situation, pre-packed two wooden barrels with what he considered valuable scriptures, labeled "scripture transfer barrels." Before the more than 8,600 fragments collected from the Library Cave were handed over to the academic department, Li Shengduo took all the ancient manuscripts of some significance to himself, and then tore the longer ones into two or three volumes to make up the original number of more than 8,600 volumes. These documents are now in the National Library. Based on them, historian Chen Yuan compiled *Records of the Remaining Dunhuang Manuscripts*. Most of those stolen by Li Shengduo later went to Japan.

1911 (3rd year of Xuantong's reign in the Qing Dynasty)

In January, Freer went to Shanghai, visited the famous collector Pang Yuanji, and purchased from him a Yuan and Ming Dynasty copy of *Chen Yuanda Advising Liu Cong* painted by Yan Liben, a famous painter of the Tang Dynasty.

That year, Ōtani Kōzui sent Yoshikawa Koichiro to China to find Tachibana Zuicho, and Yoshikawa arrived in Dunhuang on May 5, inspected and photographed some caves.

On October 10, the Wuchang Uprising broke out.

That year, Duanfang's great collection of bronzes, calligraphy and paintings were sold by his family to the Metropolitan Museum of Art and the Freer Gallery of Art.

1912

On January 26, Tachibana Zuicho arrived in Dunhuang and met Yoshikawa.

In February, Tachibana Zuicho and Yoshikawa Koichiro left Dunhuang, where Yoshikawa used special chemical tape to tape away 26 square meters of the exquisite murals in the Mogao Grottoes, bought two Buddha statues, obtained some rubbings of the inscriptions, took a lot of photos of the cave, and also spent 11 taels of silver to fraudulently purchased more than 100 Tang Dynasty scriptures from Taoist Wang. Zuicho obtained 260 volumes of written scriptures from Taoist Wang. They hired more than 100 camels, loaded with 86 pieces of "luggage items" with a total weight of more than 6,000 kilograms, to transport these treasures out of Dunhuang.

On February 12, Emperor Xuantong of the Qing Dynasty issued an edict to abdicate.

In November, Ōtani Kōzui held an exhibition of his collection at Nirakusō in Kyoto.

That year, Yamanaka & Co. purchased a collection of bronzes, ceramics, jades, and other artifacts in Prince Gong Mansion for 340,000 silver dollars, except for most of the paintings and calligraphy.

1913

That year, Yoshikawa Koichiro of the Ōtani expedition excavated near Turpan. In February, he left Turpan and passed through Yanqi to Kuqa. After investigating the Kumtura Caves, Subashi Temple, and other places, he stayed at the Kizil Caves for several days, cut out some murals, and photographed and copied some of the murals. Then, he went west to Kashgar, south to Hotan, and north to Aksu, Yining and other places to investigate Buddhist relics.

In May, Paris antique dealer Paul Mallon moved the six-steed relief sculpture from the Zhao Mausoleum of Emperor Taizong of the Tang Dynasty from its original location. However, it was attacked by local farmers and all six steeds were confiscated by the government in Xi'an.

On July 1, Germany's fourth Turpan Expedition arrived at the Kizil Caves, led by Le Coq and including Bartus, and cut away a great number of murals.

That year, at the American Art Galleries in New York, Yamanaka & Co. held the Heavenly Art Treasures auction, auctioning treasures purchased from Prince Gong Mansion. The total transaction volume of this auction reached over 276,000 US dollars.

1914

At the beginning of the year, the British Stein Expedition began its third expedition to Central Asia. Stein and his party arrived in Miran, Ruoqiang, Xinjiang, and peeled off all the exquisite murals that could not be taken away during the second inspection. A total of 11 pieces of murals were peeled off and put into six large boxes for transportation.

In March, Stein came to the Mogao Grottoes in Dunhuang again and obtained hundreds of documents from the Library Cave from Wang Yuanlu. He paid a total of 500 taels of silver and also stripped a batch of murals from the Mogao Grottoes.

In April, the last batch of wooden boxes of cultural relics from the fourth German expedition arrived in Berlin.

In May, Stein headed north along the Ejin River to inspect the ruins of Khara-Khoto in Inner Mongolia.

In the first half of the year, Yoshikawa Koichiro of the Ōtani expedition visited Urumqi, Turpan, Hami, Dunhuang, Jiuquan, and other places. In May, he returned to Japan via Beijing. He completed three expeditions to northwest China sent by Ōtani and collected cultural relics packed into nearly a hundred pieces of luggage.

In May, the second Russian Oldenburg expedition set out from St. Petersburg. The team consisted of photographer and painter Dudin, painter Binkenberg, mining engineer and topographic surveyor Smirnov, ethnologist Romberg, and translators and support staff.

In June, Stein discovered a great number of documents written in Han, Western Xia, Turpan, and Uighur languages in the garbage dumps and ruined towers of Khara-Khoto, as well as a well-preserved document in Persian.

World War I broke out on July 28 that year and ended on November 11, 1918.

That year, the second Russian Oldenburg expedition passed through Tacheng, Urumqi, Turpan, and Hami in Xinjiang. After an 80-day journey, it arrived at Dunhuang Mogao Grottoes on August 20. They made quite detailed research records on the Mogao Grottoes, surveyed and mapped the floor plans and sections of the caves, and made written records of the shape and content of the caves. Dudin and Romberg took thousands of photos inside and outside the south and north caves. They also did some archaeological cleaning of the caves in the northern area of Mogao Grottoes. The Oldenburg team surveyed and mapped a total of 443 caves, cleaned the caves, and obtained many cultural relics remaining in the caves, including 130 pieces of Uighur wooden movable type in Cave D464. In total, they unearthed more than 10,000 manuscript fragments in the cave.

In October, Stein came to Turpan, Xinjiang, and began to strip away the murals from the Bezeklik Caves. He obtained about 90 boxes of murals in total. By February of the following year, Stein had acquired 141 boxes of cultural relics around Turpan.

That year, Ōtani Kōzui resigned from the title of abbot and duke, and the cultural relics obtained from his three expeditions began to be scattered throughout the world.

That year, Ching Tsai Loo held a grand antique exhibition in Paris, including six complete round-shaped Buddha statues carved from the Xiangtangshan Grottoes.

That year, Yamanaka & Co. once again held the special auction of Private Collections of Chinese Nobles in Tianjin and Cultural Relics Purchased by Yamanaka & Co. in Beijing at the American Art Galleries in New York. It auctioned treasures from Prince Gong Mansion, with a turnover of nearly 200,000 US dollars.

1915

On January 26, the second Russian Oldenburg expedition team set out to return home. He left six written records about the Mogao Grottoes (a total of 177 caves were recorded), about 2,000 black and white photos, as well as actual measurements and plans, copy drawings and line drawings of murals, two diaries of Oldenburg and other investigators, and Dudin's notes on Dunhuang murals, etc. The cultural relics they harvested from the Dunhuang grottoes include 66 banner paintings, 137 silk paintings, 43 paper paintings, 58 fabrics, 14 cut murals, 28 large and small painted statues, and a huge number of various cultural relics. There are as many as

11,014 documents, 364 of which are relatively complete manuscripts. Oldenburg deposited the manuscripts in the Asiatic Museum, today the St. Petersburg branch of the Institute of Oriental Studies of the Russian Academy of Sciences. The artworks, surveying and mapping materials, expedition diaries, and so on that he acquired were stored in various categories in the Russian Ethnology Museum, among other places, and were later all collected in the Eastern Department of the State Hermitage Museum.

On the 22nd day of the second lunar month, Prince Chun Mansion sold six ancient paintings and calligraphy works recorded in *Midian Zhulin* and *Shiqu Baoji* compiled during the Qianlong period to Yamanaka & Co., namely Han Gan's *Character of a Horse* from the Tang Dynasty, Li Gonglin's *Treaty at the Bian Bridge* from the Northern Song Dynasty, Zhao Lingrang's *Willows and Geese* from the Northern Song Dynasty, Chen Rong's *Six Dragons* from the Southern Song Dynasty, Wang Mian's *Snow Plum Blossoms* from the Yuan Dynasty, and Zhao Mengfu's *Bathing Horses* from the Yuan Dynasty. Supervising the transaction was Zhang Binfang, the steward of Prince Chun Mansion.

In May, Stein went to Kuqa to inspect the Kizil Caves and took some photos of the murals. After that, Stein returned to Kashgar, and packed 182 boxes of cultural relics and materials acquired during his third expedition to Central Asia, as well as eight boxes of films, negatives and other items. At this point, Stein's third Central Asia inspection tour officially ended, spanning 2 years and 8 months.

That year, Ching Tsai Loo and Wu Qizhou, a Shanghainese, opened the Loo-Wu Company at the intersection between Madison Avenue and 57th Street in New York, the largest antique store in the United States, specializing in selling Chinese cultural relics to Americans.

That year, *Saluzi* and *Quanmaogua*, among the *Six Steeds in the Zhao Mausoleum* of Emperor Taizong of the Tang Dynasty, were smuggled out of Xi'an and later transported to the United States by Ching Tsai Loo.

1916

Warner, an American historian of Asian art, came to China to collect Chinese cultural relics for the newly established Cleveland Museum of Art in Ohio.

That year, Yamanaka & Co. held 11 Chinese antiques and art auctions in New York, establishing its reputation as the world's largest Chinese art dealer.

1917

Yamanaka Sadajirō purchased a 300-square-meter courtyard house from Prince Su in Beijing.

It is the branch of Yamanaka & Co. in Beijing. The branch manager is Takada Matajiro and includes four Japanese clerks and 15 Chinese employees.

1918

On March 9, George Gordon, director of the Museum of Archaeology and Anthropology at the University of Pennsylvania, saw the two reliefs of *Saluzi* and *Quanmaogua* among the *Six Steeds of Zhao Mausoleum* of Emperor Taizong of the Tang Dynasty in the warehouse of the

Metropolitan Museum of Art. After negotiation, Ching Tsai Loo loaned them to the University of Pennsylvania Museum of Archaeology and Anthropology and charged no rental fee. On May 8, the two steeds arrived at the University of Pennsylvania.

That year, Yamanaka Sadajirō reorganized the company into Yamanaka & Co., Ltd. and took office as president.

1919

On September 25, American collector Freer passed away in New York at the age of 65.

1920

In November, more than 900 soldiers from the remnants of the Russian Imperial Army, led by Major Annenkov, were deported to Dunhuang by the Xinjiang government and were arranged to live in the Mogao Grottoes. They cooked in the caves, and the smoke blackened the murals beyond recognition. Some also carved random scrawls on the murals, cut off the hands and gouged out the eyes of a great number of painted Buddha statues, and even dug into their hearts to see if there were treasures hidden inside. In August 1921, they were deported from Dunhuang and sent to Shanghai, Tianjin, and other places.

That year, Ching Tsai Loo sold two steeds from Zhao Mausoleum to the University of Pennsylvania Museum of Archaeology and Anthropology for 125,000 US dollars.

1923

On May 2, the Freer Gallery of Art officially opened to the public.

In July, Warner, a professor at Harvard University and curator of Oriental art at the Fogg Museum, arrived in Beijing with his first archaeological team to China, including Horace Jayne. After that, they visited the Longmen Grottoes and visited the Khara-Khoto ruins in Inner Mongolia for about two weeks.

That year, Ching Tsai Loo learned that there was a destroyed temple near the border between Henan and Shanxi. After consultation with the authorities, he removed the murals from the temple ruins and transferred them to Paris.

1924

In January, the Warner archaeological team arrived at the Mogao Grottoes in Dunhuang. Warner used glue to peel off 26 square meters of exquisite Tang Dynasty murals from Caves 320, 321, 323, 328, 329, 331, 335, and 372 of Mogao Grottoes, totaling 32,006 square centimeters. At the price of 70 taels of silver, he obtained from Taoist Wang a 120-centimeter-high, exquisitely painted sculpture of the Bodhisattva from the Tang Dynasty in Cave 328. In Dunhuang, he also bought a fragment of the *Lotus Sutra* manuscript.

In April, Warner and his party returned to Lanzhou and went home via Beijing. They put pieces of murals between flat plates, wrapped them tightly in blankets, and tied them with leather strips. After being transported by carriage, train, and ship for 18 weeks, they were sent to the Fogg Museum of Harvard University.

From 1924 to 1925, Kozlov discovered a great number of Xiongnu tombs from the Han Dynasty in the Noin-Ula Mountains in Mongolia. He excavated six large tombs and four small tombs, and obtained a great number of Han Dynasty and Xiongnu cultural relics.

That year, Japanese antique dealer Yamanaka Sadajirō visited the Tianlongshan Grottoes and took plenty of photos.

1925

On February 16, the second American Warner expedition team left Beijing and began inspection activities.

On May 19, Warner arrived in Dunhuang. Due to the close surveillance of locals, they were unable to obtain cultural relics from the Mogao Grottoes. Warner and others only purchased a Dunhuang manuscript, the *Mahaprajna Sutra*, and took some photos of the caves before hastily ending their inspection.

On May 23, Warner left Dunhuang. After that, they went to Anxi Yulin Caves and took some photos. Warner and his team also visited and photographed the Xiangdong Caves (the Queen Mother Palace Caves) in Jingchuan County in the Longdong region of Gansu Province.

In that year, Ching Tsai Loo bought a modest building at No. 8, Rue du Cource, situated in the less fashionable 17th district on the Rive Droite of Paris and transformed it into a Chinese pagoda-like building, which became the famous Pagoda Paris.

That year, Yamanaka Sadajirō went to investigate Luoyang Longmen Grottoes and Datong Yungang Grottoes.

1926

On July 9, the National Revolutionary Army swore to start the Northern Expedition in Guangzhou.

1927

From 1927 to 1933, Sven Hedin organized a scientific expedition to northwest China, conducting inspections in various scientific fields such as archaeology, botany, geology and geography, and meteorology in Mongolia, Xinjiang, and other places.

From 1927 to 1928, Bergman led a Swedish expedition to investigate Khara-Khoto.

That year, Yamanaka Sadajirō visited the abbot Monk Jingliang, who managed the Tianlongshan Grottoes and the temple at the foot of the mountain, and began to steal statues from the Tianlongshan Grottoes. More than 150 exquisite carvings were stolen from 25 caves.

1928

On December 29, Zhang Xueliang announced the Northeast Flag Replacement in the three eastern provinces, and the National Revolutionary Army would formally unify China and establish Nanjing as its capital.

That year, the tombs of the Eastern Zhou Dynasty kings and noble cemeteries were discovered in Jincun, Luoyang, Henan. In the following years, eight large tombs were robbed, and thousands of cultural relics were unearthed, including many exquisite jades and bronzes. Many of the cultural relics were sold to the United States by Ching Tsai Loo, and most of them entered the collection of the Fogg Museum of Harvard University, while others entered the Freer Gallery of Art and so on.

1930

On April 21, Le Coq died in Berlin, Germany, at the age of 70.

That year, Stein organized the fourth expedition to Central Asia. The expedition was unsuccessful, and all the cultural relics obtained were not taken away.

1931

On September 18, the Japanese army launched the Mukden Incident.

1932

In November, Yamanaka & Co. held the World Ancient Art Exhibition at the Tokyo Art Association, Japan, and put the stone sculptures cut from Tianlongshan at a public auction.

That year, Pelliot investigated the development of Chinese literature and history at that time and purchased general application books for China Institute of University of Paris and came to China again, passing through Hong Kong and Shanghai to Beijing.

That year, the Northern Wei Dynasty's *Empress Wenzhao Attending Buddhist Rituals with Her Court* relief in the Binyang Middle Cave of the Longmen Grottoes in Luoyang, Henan was chiseled and the fragments found their way into the antique market.

1933

Sven Hedin returned to Lop Nur, Xinjiang.

1934

On February 28, Oldenburg died in St. Petersburg, Russia, at the age of 71.

On October 21, Alan Priest, curator of Oriental art at the Metropolitan Museum of Art, and Yue Bin, an antique dealer from Liulichang, Beijing, signed a contract to purchase the Northern Wei Dynasty *Emperor Xiaowen and His Entourage Worshiping the Buddha* relief from the Binyang Middle Cave of the Longmen Grottoes in Luoyang, Henan. The price is 14,000 silver dollars.

1935

Kozlov died in Peterhof, St. Petersburg, Russia, on September 26 at the age of 72.

On October 28, Grunwedel passed away in Lenggries, Germany, at the age of 79.

That year, Yue Bin, an antique dealer in Liulichang, Beijing, with the cooperation of bandits, security chiefs, and stonemasons in the Luoyang area, plundered the Northern Wei Dynasty *Emperor Xiaowen and His Entourage Worshiping the Buddha* relief from Binyang Middle Cave. The relief was collected by the Metropolitan Museum of Art in the same year.

That year, London held the Chinese Art World Expo, and Ching Tsai Loo donated a 5.78-meter-high white stone standing Buddha statue from the Sui Dynasty to the British Museum.

1936

On October 30, Japanese antique dealer Yamanaka Sadajirō passed away in Kyoto, Japan at the age of 70 years old.

1937

On July 7, the Japanese invaders launched an incident at Lugou Bridge in Wanping County, Hebei Province, and the War of Resistance against Japanese Aggression broke out.

In October, Ching Tsai Loo went to Geneva to participate in a charity sale organized by the local Chinese Women's Federation, offering a total of nine auction items. All proceeds from the charity sale were donated to the Red Cross Society of China to aid war victims.

That year, Yamanaka & Co. donated several Tianlongshan Buddha heads to the Asian Art Museum in Berlin.

1938

In January, Ching Tsai Loo sponsored an exhibition of Chinese cultural relics in London to solicit donations from collectors. All proceeds are donated to American Medical Aid China.

1939

From 1939 to 1940, Sickman, the curator of the Eastern Department of the Nelson-Atkins Art Museum, acquired the relief fragments of *Empress Wenzhao Attending Buddhist Rituals with Her Court* in the Binyang Middle Cave of Longmen Grottoes from various antique markets, and spliced them together based on the photos and rubbings in previous publications. It is then on display in the museum.

1943

On October 26, Stein died at the age of 81 while on an archaeological expedition in Afghanistan. His body was buried in the British military camp in Kabul.

That year, Yamanaka & Co. planned and auctioned items from stores across the United States, and 1,683 items were auctioned for the first time. The Fogg Museum at Harvard University acquired numerous Tianlongshan sculptures in this sale. This grand auction lasted until the end of June 1944. The total amount of the auction was as high as 500,000 US dollars, and the proceeds from the auction went to the US government.

1944

Chen Mengjia, a famous modern Chinese paleographer, archaeologist, and poet, and his wife Zhao Luorui were studying at the University of Chicago when they investigated Chinese bronzes scattered overseas and received help from Ching Tsai Loo with taking a total of 850 pictures of cultural relics.

1945

In the first half of the year, the British and American coalition forces carried out indiscriminate strategic bombing of Germany, and the Museum of Ethnology in Berlin was destroyed.

On August 15, Emperor Showa of Japan issued the End of War Edict via radio, announcing Japan's unconditional surrender. China won the Anti-Japanese War.

On October 26, Pelliot died of cancer in Paris at the age of 67.

That year, Lin Yutang completed the invention of the Mingkuai typewriter with the funding of Ching Tsai Loo.

1948

On October 5, Ōtani Kōzui died of illness in Beppu City, Oita Prefecture, Japan, at the age of 72.

That year, at the instigation of Chen Mengjia, Ching Tsai Loo donated to the Tsinghua University Cultural Relics Exhibition Hall the Warring States bronze ware Linghu Sizi kettle unearthed in Jincun, Luoyang, Henan, in 1928.

That year, Ching Tsai Loo spent millions of francs to acquire a batch of fake antiques and paintings from Tan Jing, a famous Chinese calligraphy and painting collector. After that, he was bankrupt and forced to sell out his company's stocks, conduct liquidation sales, so as to pay off debts, and transferred the business to his long-term colleague Frank Caro.

1949

On October 1, the People's Republic of China was founded.

1951

Ching Tsai Loo donated his collection of Chinese Buddhist temple murals to seven art museums in the United States.

1952

On November 26, Sven Hedin passed away in Stockholm, Sweden, at the age of 88.

That year, Yamanaka & Co. returned to New York and continued its business.

1954

Over 600 Dunhuang manuscripts obtained from Ōtani Kōzui's three expeditions were transferred from the Lüshun Museum to the Beijing Library for preservation.

That year, antiques dealer Yue Bin died in prison in Beijing.

1957

On March 17, Japanese explorer Watanabe Tesshin passed away at the age of 83.

On August 15, antique dealer Ching Tsai Loo passed away in Nyon, Switzerland, at the age of 78. His body was brought back to Paris and buried in his wife's family cemetery in Hobevoie.

1968
On November 4, Japanese explorer Tachibana Zuicho passed away at the age of 78.

1978
On September 5, Japanese explorer Yoshikawa Koichiro passed away at the age of 93 years old in Saikyo District, Kyoto City.

Index

Page numbers in *italics* refer to figures.

Chang Qing has bachelor's and master's degrees from the Department of Archaeology at Peking University and a PhD in Chinese Art History from the University of Kansas, specializing in Chinese grotto temple art. He has worked at the Longmen Grottoes Research Institute, the Institute of Archaeology of the Chinese Academy of Social Sciences, and the Institute of Buddhist Culture of China. After 2000, he served as a postdoctoral lecturer and visiting professor at the University of Missouri-St. Louis, where he taught Asian and Chinese art history and worked as a research curator at the Dallas Museum of Art in Texas. Since 2018, he has been a professor and doctoral supervisor at the School of Art, Sichuan University. He has published 12 monographs and over 100 research papers in Chinese and English.

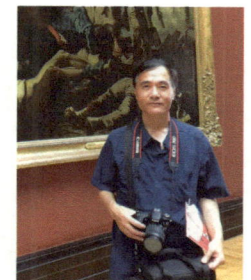

Huang Shan has a passion for art, history, and ancient languages. She graduated from Central Saint Martins, University of the Arts London, with a master's degree in 2021. Due to her interest in ancient artifacts and geopolitics, she is pursuing a PhD in history at the School of Oriental and African Studies, University of London. Her main research focuses on the dissemination and circulation of artifacts in ancient Central Asian cultures.

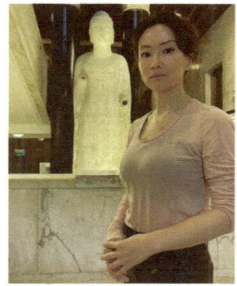